Martial R
Tel: 0196

WITHDRAWN FROM
THE LIBRARY

UNIVERSITY OF
WINCHESTER

D1357728

KA 0394421 2

On the State

Lectures at the Collège de France, 1989–1992

Pierre Bourdieu

Edited by
Patrick Champagne, Remi Lenoir, Franck Poupeau
and Marie-Christine Rivière

Translated by
David Fernbach

polity

UNIVERSITY OF WINCHESTER
LIBRARY

First published as *Sur l'État* © Éditions Raisons d'Agir/Éditions du Seuil, 2012

This English edition © Polity Press, 2014

ROYAUME-UNI

This book is supported by the Institut Français (Royaume-Uni) as part of the Burgess programme.

Polity Press
65 Bridge Street
Cambridge CB2 1UR, UK

Polity Press
350 Main Street
Malden, MA 02148, USA

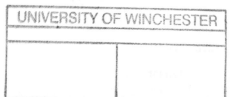

UNIVERSITY OF WINCHESTER

All rights reserved. Except for the quotation of short passages for the purpose of criticism and review, no part of this publication may be reproduced, stored in a retrieval system, or transmitted, in any form or by any means, electronic, mechanical, photocopying, recording or otherwise, without the prior permission of the publisher.

ISBN-13: 978-0-7456-6329-6

A catalogue record for this book is available from the British Library.

Typeset in 10 on 11 pt Times New Roman MT by
Servis Filmsetting Ltd, Stockport, Cheshire
Printed and bound in Great Britain by Clays Ltd, St Ives plc

The publisher has used its best endeavours to ensure that the URLs for external websites referred to in this book are correct and active at the time of going to press. However, the publisher has no responsibility for the websites and can make no guarantee that a site will remain live or that the content is or will remain appropriate.

Every effort has been made to trace all copyright holders, but if any have been inadvertently overlooked the publisher will be pleased to include any necessary credits in any subsequent reprint or edition.

For further information on Polity, visit our website: www.politybooks.com

Contents

The editors would like to thank Gabrielle Balazs, Jérôme Bourdieu, Pascale Casanova, Christophe Charle, Olivier Christin, Yvette Delsaut, Paul Lagneau-Ymonet, Gilles L'Hôte, Pierre Rimbert and Gisèle Sapiro for their valuable comments which have made it possible to clarify certain passages in the lectures, and in particular Loïc Wacquant for his close reading of the text.

Editors' note

Establishing the text of Pierre Bourdieu's lectures given at the Collège de France required a number of editorial choices. These lectures form a lattice of written texts, oral commentaries and more or less improvised reflections on his own approach and on the conditions that led him to present this. The material for the lectures was a mixture of manuscript notes, extracts from special presentations and marginal notes on books and photocopies. Bourdieu's remarks on the conditions in which his teaching was received, by a large and very varied audience in the big amphitheatre of the Collège de France,[1] show how his lectures cannot simply be reduced to the written versions of them that he left, given that they could take unexpected turns as they proceeded, depending on his perception of audience reactions.

One solution, which would have had the apparent merit of neutrality and formal fidelity to the author, would have been to publish a literal raw transcription of the whole lecture course. But reproducing the spoken word would not have been enough to preserve its properties, i.e. the whole pedagogic work conducted during each lecture. Nor was the text pronounced that of the 'published' version, as we have been able to verify in the case of a number of lectures whose retranscriptions had been substantially reworked, sometimes even completely reshaped, for conversion into articles published in scholarly journals. In fact, the form explicitly chosen in the lectures is closer to the logic of scientific discovery than to that of a perfectly arranged written exposition of research results.

If the editors clearly cannot substitute for the author after his demise, and write in his place the book that he would have made on the basis of his lecture course, they can try to ensure that the properties bound up with the spoken character of the exposition are preserved as far as possible – which presupposes that they should be detectable and perceived, and conversely, that the effects specific to the transcription should be reduced as far as possible. The editors have also had to bear in mind that this publication, without replacing that which the author would have conceived, has to give the work that it continues its full force and necessity. The transcription accordingly seeks to avoid two reefs, literalness and literariness. And if

Bourdieu always recommended people to refer to his writings to understand what he was saying,[2] he also took advantage of oral delivery and the
freedom of expression this afforded, vis-à-vis an audience that he knew
were already familiar with his work, to raise implications and go over his
line of argument and presentation.

There is a paragraph in *The Weight of the World*, headed 'The risks of
writing', in which Bourdieu analyses the transition from oral discourse to
written text as 'a genuine translation or even an interpretation'.[3] And he
reminds his reader that 'mere punctuation, the placing of a comma' can
'govern the whole meaning of a sentence'. The publication of these lectures thus seeks to reconcile two contrary but not contradictory demands:
fidelity and readability. The inevitable 'infidelities' that are inherent to
any transcription (and, more generally, to any change of medium) are
undoubtedly here, as in the interviews that Bourdieu analysed in *The
Weight of the World*, the 'condition for true fidelity', in his own expression.

The transcription of these lecture courses at the Collège de France
respects procedures that Bourdieu himself applied when he revised those
of his lectures or seminars that he went on to publish: minor stylistic corrections, tidying of awkward passages in spoken discourse (interjections,
repetitions, etc.). Some obscurities and inexact constructions have been
corrected. Where digressions remained within the theme being developed
they have been noted by dashes; where they involved a break in the line
of argument they have been placed in parentheses; and where they were
too long, they have been made into a separate section. The division into
sections and paragraphs, as well as subtitles, punctuation and notes giving
references and cross-references, are those of the editors, likewise the
subject index. The bibliographic references given in footnotes are those of
Bourdieu himself, and have been completed when they gave insufficient
information. Some have been added to facilitate understanding of the
discourse: explanations, cross-references, implicit or explicit reference to
texts that continue the reflection. The reader can also consult the list of
books, articles and working documents that Bourdieu drew on throughout
the course, and that has been reconstituted on the basis of his working
notes and his many reading files.

Part of the material in these lectures was subsequently reworked and
published by Bourdieu himself in the form of articles or chapters of books.
These have in all cases been indicated. As an appendix to the lectures we
reproduce the course summaries published each year in the *Annuaire* of the
Collège de France.

These three years of lectures on the state have been selected to com-
mence the publication of Bourdieu's Collège de France courses because,
as can be seen from the 'position of the lectures' at the end of the present
volume,[4] they make up an essential piece in the construction of Bourdieu's
sociology, but one rarely seen. The following volumes will complete the
full publication of his lectures over the next few years, in the form of books
on autonomous problematics.

Year 1989–1990

Lecture of 18 January 1990

An unthinkable object – The state as neutral site – The Marxist tradition – The calendar and the structure of temporality – State categories – Acts of state – The private-home market and the state – The Barre commission on housing

An unthinkable object

When we study the state, we must be on guard more than ever against 'prenotions' in the Durkheimian sense, against received ideas and spontaneous sociology. To sum up the analyses I gave in previous years' lecture courses, and particularly the historical analysis of the relationship between sociology and the state, I noted that we risked applying to the state a 'state thinking', and I insisted on the fact that our thinking, the very structures of consciousness by which we construct the social world and the particular object that is the state, are very likely the product of the state itself. By a procedural reflex, a professional effect, each time I have tackled a new object what I was doing appeared to me to be perfectly justified, and I would say that the further I advance in my work on the state, the more convinced I am that, if we have a particular difficulty in thinking this object, it is because it is – and I weigh my words – almost unthinkable. If it is so easy to say easy things about this object, that is precisely because we are in a certain sense penetrated by the very thing we have to study. I have previously tried to analyse the public space, the world of public office, as a site where the values of disinterestedness are officially recognized, and where, to a certain extent, agents have an interest in disinterestedness.[1]

These two themes [public space and disinterestedness] are extremely important, since I believe that they bring to light how before arriving at a correct conception – if this is indeed possible – we must break through a series of screens and representations, the state being – in so far as it has an existence – a principle of production, of legitimate representation of the social world. If I had to give a provisional definition of what is called 'the state', I would say that the sector of the field of power, which may be called 'administrative field' or 'field of public office', this sector that we particularly have in mind when we speak of 'state' without further precision, is defined by possession of the monopoly of legitimate physical and symbolic violence. Already several years ago,[2] I made an addition to the famous definition of Max Weber, who defined the state [as the] 'monopoly of legitimate violence',[3] which I corrected by adding 'monopoly of legitimate physical *and symbolic* violence', inasmuch as the monopoly of symbolic violence is the condition for possession of the exercise of the monopoly of physical violence itself. In other words, my definition, as I see it, underlies Weber's definition. But it still remains abstract, above all if you do not have the context in which I elaborated it. These are provisional definitions in order to try to reach at least a kind of provisional agreement as to what I am speaking about, since it is very hard to speak about something without at least spelling out what one is speaking about. They are provisional definitions designed to be improved and corrected.

The state as a neutral site

The state may be defined as a principle of orthodoxy, that is, a hidden principle that can be grasped only in the manifestations of public order, understood simultaneously as physical order, the opposite of disorder, anarchy and civil war, for example. A hidden principle that can be grasped in the manifestations of public order understood in both the physical and the symbolic sense. Durkheim, in *The Elementary Forms of the Religious Life*, makes a distinction between logical conformity and moral conformity.[4] The state, as it is commonly understood, is the foundation of both the logical and the moral conformity of the social world. Logical conformity, in Durkheim's sense, consists in the fact that the agents of the social world have the same logical perceptions – the immediate agreement established between people who have the same categories of thought, of perception, of construction of reality. Moral conformity is agreement on a certain number of values. Readings of Durkheim have always stressed moral conformity, forgetting the logical conformity that, in my view, is its foundation.

This provisional definition would consist in saying that the state is that which founds the logical conformity and moral conformity of the social world, and in this way, the fundamental consensus on the meaning of the social world that is the very precondition of conflict over the social world. In other words, for conflict over the social world to be possible, a kind of agreement is needed on the grounds of disagreement and on their modes of expression. In the political field, for example, the genesis of that subuniverse of the social world that is the field of high public office may be seen as the gradual development of a kind of orthodoxy, a set of rules of the game that are broadly laid down, on the basis of which a communication is established within the social world that may be a communication in and through conflict. To extend this definition, we can say that the state is the principle of the organization of consent as adhesion to the social order, to the fundamental principles of the social order, that it is the foundation, not necessarily of a consensus, but of the very existence of exchanges that lead to a dissension.

This procedure is a little dangerous, in that it may appear to go back to what is the initial definition of the state, the definition that states give themselves and that was repeated in certain classical theories such as those of Hobbes and Locke, the state in this initial belief being an institution designed to serve the common good, the government serving the good of the people. To a certain extent, the state would be a neutral site or, more exactly – to use Leibniz's analogy according to which God is the geometral of all antagonistic perspectives – the point of view overlooking all points of view, which is no longer a point of view since it is in relation to it that all points of view are organized. This view of the state as a quasi-God under-lies the tradition of classical theory, and is the basis of the spontaneous sociology of the state that is expressed in what is sometimes called adminis-trative science, that is, the discourse that agents of the state produce about the state, a veritable ideology of public service and public good.

The Marxist tradition

This ordinary representation that my definition would appear to repeat – though you will see it is very different in reality – is opposed in a whole series of traditions, particularly the Marxist tradition, by an antagonistic representation that is a kind of reversal of the primary definition: the state is not an apparatus oriented to the common good, it is an apparatus of constraint, of maintenance of public order but to the benefit of the domi-nant. In other words, the Marxist tradition does not pose the problem of the existence of the state, resolving it right from the start by defining the functions it fulfils; from Marx to Gramsci, to Althusser and beyond, it always insists on characterizing the state by what it does, and by the people for whom it does what it does, but without investigating the actual structure of the mechanisms deemed to produce its foundation. Clearly, it is possible to emphasize more strongly the economic functions of the state or its ideological functions: to speak of 'hegemony' (Gramsci)[5] or 'ideo-logical state apparatus' (Althusser);[6] but the accent is always placed on the functions, and the question of the being and acting of this thing designated as the state is sidestepped.

It is at this point that the difficult questions arise. This critical view of the state is often accepted without discussion. If it is easy to say easy things about the state, it is because, both by position and by tradition (I have in mind, for example, Alain's famous book *Le Citoyen contre les pou-voirs*),[7] the producers and receivers of discourse on the state like to have a somewhat anarchistic disposition, a disposition of socially established rebellion against authority. I have in mind, for example, certain types of theories that denounce discipline and constraint, and enjoy great success, even being destined for eternal success because they fall in with adolescent rebellion against constraints and disciplines, and flatter an initial disposition towards institutions, what I call an anti-institutional mood,[8] which is particularly strong at certain historic moments and in certain social groups. Owing to this fact, they are unconditionally accepted, whereas in reality, I would say, they are only the pure and simple reversal of the ordinary definition, having in common with this definition that they reduce the question of the state to the question of function, substituting for the divine state a diabolical state, substituting for 'optimistic functionalism' – the state as instrument of consensus, as a neutral site on which conflicts are managed – a diabolical state, *diabolus in machina*, a state that always operates by what I call a 'pessimistic functionalism'[9] in the service of the dominant, in a manner that is more or less direct or sophisticated.

In the logic of hegemony, the agents of the state are conceived as being in the service not of the universal and the public good, as they claim, but of the economically dominant and the symbolically dominant, and at the same time in their own service, that is, the agents of the state serve the economically and symbolically dominant, and serve themselves by serving. That comes down to explaining what the state does, what it is, on the basis of its functions. I believe that this mistake, which we can call functionalist and which is even found with structural-functionalists such as the Althusserians, who were in fact very close to the optimistic structural-functionalists – Parsons and his successors – was there already in the Marxist theory of religion, which amounts to describing an authority such as religion by its function, without asking what structure is needed to fulfil these functions. In other words, nothing is learned about the mechanism by simply investigating its functions.

(One of my difficulties, in seeking to understand what we call the state, is that I am obliged to say in traditional language something that goes against the meta-language, and provisionally make use of this old language in order to destroy what it conveys. But if I were to substitute each time the vocabulary I am trying to construct – field of power, etc. – this would no longer be intelligible. I constantly ask myself, especially before I teach, if I will ever be able to say what I mean, if it is reasonable to believe this . . . That is a very particular difficulty, which I believe is characteristic of scientific discourse on the social world.)

By way of a provisional synthesis, I would say that it is inasmuch as the state is a principle of orthodoxy, of consensus on the meaning of the world, of very conscious consent on the meaning of the world, that it fulfils, as I see it, certain of the functions that the Marxist tradition ascribes to it. In other words, it is as orthodoxy, as collective fiction, as a well-founded illusion – and I take up here the definition that Durkheim applies to religion,[10] the analogies between the state and religion being considerable – that the state is able to fulfil its functions of social preservation, preservation of the conditions of capital accumulation – as certain contemporary Marxists put it.

The calendar and the structure of temporality

In other words, to sum up in advance what I am going to tell you, I would say that the state is the name that we give to the hidden, invisible principles – indicating a kind of *deus absconditus* – of the social order, and at the same time of both physical and symbolic domination, likewise of physical and symbolic violence. In order to make this logical function of moral conformity understandable, I need only develop an example that I see as suited to making what I have said up to now apparent. There is nothing more ordinary than the calendar. The republican calendar with its civic festivals and public holidays is something completely trivial, to which we do not [pay] attention. We accept it as a matter of course. Our perception of temporality is organized as a function of the structures of this public time. In *Les Cadres sociaux de la mémoire*,[11] Maurice Halbwachs recalls that the foundations of every evocation of memory are to be sought in the direction of what he calls the social contexts of memory, that is, those specifically social reference points in relation to which we organize our private life. Here is a fine example of the public at the very heart of the private: at the very heart of our memory we find the state, the civic festivals, secular or religious, and we find different categories of specific calendar, the school calendar or the religious calendar. We thus discover a whole set of structures of social temporality marked by social reference points and collective activities. We find it at the very heart of our personal consciousness.

It would be possible to repeat here the analyses of storytelling behaviour, old but still valid, that Pierre Janet proposed:[12] it is clear that when we tell a tale that implies a time dimension, when we do history, we take our bearings from divisions that are themselves the product of history, and which have become the very principles of evocation of history. Halbwachs [noted that] two individuals will say: 'In such-and-such a year I was in the *sixième* class, I was at such-and-such a place, we were at school together . . .' If two social subjects are able to communicate to one another the time they have experienced, that is, a time that in Bergsonian logic is said to be incommensurable and incommunicable, it is on the basis of this agreement over the temporal reference points which find objective inscription in the form of the calendar of public holidays, of 'solemnizations', anniversary ceremonies and in consciousness, and are also inscribed in the memory of individual agents. All this is completely bound up with the state. Revolutions revise the official calendars – 'official' meaning universal within the limits of a definite society, as opposed to private. We can have private calendars, but these are themselves situated in relation to the universal calendars; they are notches in the intervals marked by the universal calendar, within the limits of a society. You can do the following amusing exercise: take the public holidays of all the European countries, and the defeats of some are the victories of others . . . calendars are not completely superimposable, Catholic religious festivals have less weight in Protestant countries . . .

There is a whole structure of temporality, and I believe that, if one day the Brussels technocrats want to do something serious, they will inevitably work on calendars. At that moment, we shall discover that extremely deep mental habits are attached to festivals, habits on which people put much store. We shall perceive that these calendars, that seem a matter of course, mark social conquests: 1 May is a date that many people will not so easily give up, while for others the Feast of the Assumption is a key date. Remember the debate that was triggered by the intention of cancelling the 8 May celebration. We buy a calendar each year, we buy something that is a matter of course, we buy a completely fundamental principle of structuration that is one of the foundations of social existence, and makes it possible for example to make appointments. The same can be done for the hours of the day. There is consensus about these, and I don't know any anarchist who does not change his clock when we go over to summer time, who does not accept as a matter of course a whole set of things that relate, in the last analysis, to state power, as is clear, moreover, when different states are at odds over something apparently anodyne.

This is one of the things I had in mind when I said that the state is one of the principles of public order; and public order is not simply the police and the army, as the Weberian definition suggests – monopoly of physical violence. Public order rests on consent: the fact that people get up on time presupposes that clock time is accepted. Sartre's very fine analysis, a completely intellectual one, about 'I am free, I can decide not to go to work, I have the freedom not to get out of bed', is wrong despite being quite seductive. Apart from the fact that this analysis implies that everyone is free not to accept the idea of clock time, what it tells us more profoundly is that the fact of accepting the idea of clock time is already something quite extraordinary. Not all societies, in all countries, at all times, have had a public time. One of the first acts of civil bureaucracies, of the clerks,[13] historically, when a number of towns federated together or when several tribes combined, was the establishment of a public time; the founders of states, if it is allowable to construct such remote genealogies by anthropological comparison, were faced with this problem. (In working on societies without the state, without that thing which we call the state, for example segmentary societies in which there are clans or groups of clans, but no central organ holding the monopoly of physical violence, no prisons, there is among other problems that of violence: how is violence to be controlled when there is no authority above families engaged in a vendetta?)

Collecting calendars is an anthropological tradition: the agrarian calendar of peasants, but also the calendars of women, of young people, of children, etc. These calendars are not necessarily attuned in the same sense as our calendars. They are approximately in tune: the calendar of children's games, the calendars of young boys, young girls, adolescents, young shepherds, adult men, adult women – cooking or women's work – all these calendars are approximately in tune. But no one took a sheet of paper – the state is bound up with writing – so as to put all these calendars side by side and say: 'Look, there's a little discrepancy here, the summer solstice with . . .' There is not yet a synchronization of all activities. Now this synchronization is a tacit condition for the proper functioning of the social world; it would be useful to calculate all the people who live by maintaining the order of time, who are partly involved in maintaining the order of time, charged with governing temporality.

If you think back on some very well-known texts such as Lucien Febvre's book on Rabelais,[14] you will see that the period when what we are going to call the state was established reveals some interesting things about the social usage of temporality, the collective regulation of time, which we consider a matter of course, with clocks striking more or less at the same time, and everyone having a watch. All this is not so old. A world in which this public time is not established, institutionalized, guaranteed not only by objective structures – calendars, watches – but also by mental structures, people wanting to have a watch and being in the habit of consulting it, making appointments and arriving on time. This kind of accounting of time, which presupposes both public time and a public relationship to time, is a relatively recent invention that stands in relation with the construction of state structures.

This is very far from the Gramscian topoi on the state and hegemony; which does not rule out that those who govern the clocks or who are governed by them are not privileged in relation to those who are less governed. We must start by analysing these anthropologically fundamental things in order to understand the true functioning of the state. This detour, which may seem to break with the critical violence of the Marxist tradition, seems to me to be absolutely indispensable.

State categories

The same thing can be done for public space, but giving the term a different sense from the somewhat trivial one that Habermas gives it, and that everyone repeats.[15] A quite fundamental analysis would have to be made as to what is the structure of a space in which the public and the private confront one another, in which the public square is opposed not just to the private home but also to the palace. There are studies of this differentiation of urban space. In other words, what we call the state, what we point to confusedly when we think of the state, is a kind of principle of public order, understood not only in its evident physical forms but also in its unconscious symbolic forms, which apparently are deeply self-evident. One of the most general functions of the state is the production and canonization of social classifications.

It is no accident that there is a link between the state and statistics. Historians say that the state begins with the appearances of censuses, investigations of property with a view to taxation, since, in order to impose taxes, it is necessary to know what people possess. They start from the relationship between the *census* and the *censor* who lays down legitimate principles of division, principles so self-evident that they do not come into discussion. It is possible to discuss about how social classes are divided, but not the idea that there are divisions at all. The occupational categories defined by the INSEE,[16] for example, are a typical product of the state. This is not just an instrument to make measuring possible, enabling those who govern to know the governed. The categories are also legitimate ones, a *nomos*, a principle of division that is universally recognized within the limits of a society, about which no discussion is needed; it is printed on one's identity card, or on the payslip which says 'third grade, such-and-such a point on the scale'. People are quantified and coded by the state; they have a state identity. The functions of the state clearly include the production of legitimate social identity; in other words, even if we do not agree with these identities, we have to put up with them. Certain social behaviours, such as rebellion, may be determined by the very categories that are rebelled against by those who rebel. That is one of the major explanatory principles in sociology: individuals who have difficulties with the educational system are often determined by their very difficulties, and certain intellectual careers are entirely determined by an unfortunate relationship with the educational system, that is, by an effort to give the lie, without knowing it, to a legitimate identity imposed by the state.

The state is this well-founded illusion, this place that exists essentially because people believe that it exists. This illusory reality, collectively validated by consensus, is the site that you are headed towards when you go back from a certain number of phenomena – educational qualifications, professional qualifications or calendar. Proceeding step by step, you arrive at a site that is the foundation of all this. This mysterious reality exists through its effects and through the collective belief in its existence, which lies at the origin of these effects. It is something that you cannot lay your hands on, or tackle in the way that people from the Marxist tradition do when they say 'the state does this', 'the state does that'. I could cite you kilometres of texts with the word state as the subject of actions and proposals. That is a very dangerous fiction, which prevents us from properly understanding the state. By way of preamble, therefore, what I want to say is: be careful, all sentences that have the state as subject are theological sentences – which does not mean that they are false, inasmuch as the state is a theological entity, that is, an entity that exists by way of belief.

Acts of state

To escape theology, to be able to offer a radical critique of this adhesion to the being of the state that is inscribed in our mental structures, we can substitute for the state the acts that can be called acts of 'state' – putting 'state' in quotes – in other words political acts intended to have effects in the social world. There is a politics recognized as legitimate, if only because no one questions the possibility of acting otherwise, because it is unquestioned. These legitimate political acts owe their effectiveness to their legitimacy, and to the belief in the existence of the principle that underlies them.

I will give a single example, that of a primary school inspector who goes to visit a school. He has to perform an act of a quite particular type: he goes to inspect. He represents the central authority. In the great preindustrial empires, you see the appearance of bodies of inspectors. The problem that is raised right away is that of knowing who will inspect the inspectors? Who will guard the guardians? This is a fundamental problem of all states. Some people are charged with going to look in the name of authority; they have a mandate. But who gives them this mandate? The state. The inspector who goes to visit a school has an authority that inhabits his person. [As the sociologists Philip Corrigan and Derek Sayer have written:] 'States state.'[17] They make 'statements', they lay down 'statutes', and a statement is what the inspector will deliver.

I have analysed previously the difference between a private insult and an insulting judgement made by an authorized person.[18] In school exercise books, teachers who forget the limits of their responsibility deliver insulting judgements; there is something criminal about these authorized and legitimate insults.[19] If you say to your son, your brother or your boyfriend: 'You're an idiot!', that is a singular judgement delivered on a single individual by a single individual, and therefore reversible. Whereas if a teacher says, in a euphemistic way, 'Your son is an idiot', this becomes a judgement that has to be reckoned with. An authorized judgement has the whole force of the social order behind it, the force of the state. One of the modern functions of the teaching system is to award certificates of social identity, certificates of the quality that most contributes to defining social identity today, in other words intelligence – in the social sense of the term.[20]

Here then we have examples of acts of state: these are authorized acts, endowed with an authority that, by a series of delegations, goes back step by step to an ultimate site, like Aristotle's god: the state. Who guarantees the teacher? What guarantees the teacher's judgement? A similar regression can also be traced in quite other domains. If you take the judgements of justice, it is still more evident; similarly, if you take the investigating report of a policeman, the regulations drawn up by a commission or laid down by a minister. In all these cases, we are faced with acts of categorization; the etymology of the word 'category' – from *categorein* – means publicly accusing, even insulting; state *categorein* publicly accuses with public authority: 'I publicly accuse you of being guilty'; 'I publicly certify that you are a university *agrégé*'; 'I categorize you' (the accusation may be positive or negative); 'I sanction you', with an authority that authorizes both the judgement and, evidently, the categories according to which the judgement is made. Because what is concealed here is the opposition 'intelligent/not intelligent'; the question of the pertinence of this opposition is not raised. Here we have the kind of sleight of hand that the social world constantly produces, and that makes life very hard for the sociologist.

To escape from theology is therefore very difficult. But let us return to things on which we certainly agree. You will grant me that the examples I gave are indeed acts of state. They have in common the fact of being actions performed by agents endowed with a symbolic authority, and followed by effects. This symbolic authority refers, step by step, to a kind of illusory community, a kind of ultimate consensus. If these acts obtain consent, if people accept them – even if they rebel, their rebellion presupposes a consent – it is because, at bottom, they consciously or unconsciously participate in a kind of 'illusory community' – that is an expression of Marx's about the state[21] – which is the community of belonging to a community that we shall call a nation or a state, in the sense of a set of people recognizing the same universal principles.

Reflection would also be needed on the different dimensions that characterize these acts of state: the ideas of official, public and universal. I have just made a contrast between insult, on the one hand, and authorized and universal judgement, on the other – authorized and universal within the limits of a constituency, a legally defined competence, a nation, certain state frontiers. This judgement may be pronounced openly, as opposed to the judgement of insult, which not only has something unofficial about it, but also something rather shameful, if only because it might be returned. Authorized judgement is thus framed both by its foundation and its form. Among the constraints imposed on those who wield the capacity of official judgement is the necessity to respect the forms that make official judgement genuinely official. There are things to be said about this bureaucratic formalism that Weber opposed to magical formalism, the formalism expressed in a ritual test by uttering a magic formula ('Open sesame!'). For Weber, bureaucratic formalism has nothing in common with magical formalism: it is not mechanical and arbitrary respect, whose strictness is arbitrary, but rather respect for a form that authorizes because it conforms to norms collectively approved, either tacitly or explicitly.[22] In this sense, the state also falls on the side of magic (I said just now that, for Durkheim, religion was a well-founded illusion), but it is a magic quite different from how this is generally conceived. I now want to try and extend this inquiry in two directions.

(As soon as you work on an object from the social world, you always come up against the state and state effects, without necessarily looking for it. Marc Bloch, one of the founders of comparative history, says that in order to raise the problems of comparative history it is necessary to start from the present. In his famous book comparing the French *seigneurie* and the English manor,[23] he starts from the shape of fields in England and in France, and from statistics on the proportion of peasants in France and in England; this is the starting point from which he raises a certain number of questions.)

I am therefore going to try and describe how I encountered the state in my own work; I shall then try to give a description of the historical genesis of this mysterious reality. Better description of the genesis gives a better understanding of the mystery, you see things taking shape by starting from the Middle Ages, by taking the English, French and Japanese examples. I shall have to justify myself about the type of historical work I shall propose to you, work that raises formidable problems that I do not want to tackle naively: methodological preambles will take a great deal of time in relation to substance. And you will say: 'He's raised a lot of questions for us but given little in the way of answers . . .'

The examples I have taken fall into a whole tradition of socio-linguistic or linguistic reflection on the notion of the performative, but at the same time, they risk stopping short at preconstructed representations of what lies behind the state effects.[24] So as to try to give an idea of the mechanisms that produce state effects, and to which we attach the idea of state, I shall summarize a study I made several years ago of the single-home market, the production and circulation of that economic good with a symbolic dimension that a house is.[25] I want to show, on the basis of this very concrete example, the form under which the state manifests itself. I hesitated a good deal before giving you this example, since I could spend the whole year's lecture course on this study alone. To a certain extent, the meta-discourse I am going to offer on this work is somewhat absurd, since it assumes that all the detailed meanderings of the work are known. Such are the contradictions of teaching . . . I do not know how to articulate research, with its rhythm, its demands, and the teaching that I seek to orient in the direction of research.

The single-home market and the state

I undertook this inquiry into the market in single homes with rather ordinary and trivial questions in mind, such as are regularly raised by researchers: Why do people buy rather than rent? Why at a certain point in time do they seek to buy rather than rent? Why do social categories who used not to buy now seek to buy, and what social categories are these? It is said that the total number of owners is rising, but how the rate of increase is differentiated in social space according to classes is not examined. The first thing needed is to observe and measure: that's what statistics are for. A whole series of questions is raised: who buys, who rents? Who buys what? How do they buy? With what kind of loans? Then you come on to ask: but who produces? How do they produce? How should the sector constructing single homes be described? Are there small craftsmen building one home a year, on the one hand, side by side with big companies linked with enormous banking powers, building three thousand homes a year? Is this the same world? Is there a genuine competition between them? What is the balance of forces? Questions that are classical ones, therefore. The research methods were very varied: interviews with buyers – why buy

rather than rent? – observations, the recording of acts of sale and negotiations, contracts between buyer and seller, study of sellers and their strategies, through to listening to the representations that the buyers came up
with [vis-à-vis] the sellers.

What is interesting is that gradually, by a kind of regression imposed
by the logic of the inquiry itself, the centre of research shifted: what was
initially a study of transactions, the constraints weighing on these transactions, the economic and cultural conditions determining the choice,
the study of a system of factors explaining the choice between becoming
a renter or a buyer, and a buyer of this rather than that, a renter of this
rather than that – this investigation gradually dwindled to the point that
in the final text it makes up only 5 per cent, that is, scarcely a dozen pages.
The centre of research interest shifted to the institutional conditions of
production, both of the supply of homes and of their demand. It became
very quickly apparent that, in order to understand what happens in the
transaction between a single seller and a single buyer – a meeting that ultimately is apparently random – you have to go back step by step, and at the
end of this regression you find the state.

At the Salon de la Maison Individuelle in Paris, a buyer arrives, a little
embarrassed, accompanied by his wife and two kids; he asks about a house.
He is spoken to politely because he has a wife and two kids, he's a serious
customer . . . If it was a woman by herself, we know what she would say:
'I'll come and look at it with my husband' – so the salesman does not make
a great effort. He says to the couple: 'Come and sit down.' We have to spell
things out in concrete detail in order to see how the state is involved. At the
beginning, I didn't start with the idea of studying the state: it forced itself
on me. In order to understand what happens in this single encounter, you
have to do everything that I shall mention very quickly, whereas you would
ultimately have to study the French state back to the Middle Ages . . .

Two people are talking to one another: a salesman who is in a bit of a
hurry, who first has to gauge if the man opposite him is a serious customer
or not. On the basis of a spontaneous sociology, but a very good one, he
knows that the most common buyer is a family with two children. He has
to lose as little time as possible, so he has to anticipate. Whether it's worth
the effort, and having determined that it is worth the effort, he also has to
accelerate the process. The communication, the structure of the exchange,
is very standardized, very stereotyped; it always takes the following form.
For a few minutes, the buyer, going by what his friends have said or his
mother-in-law on lending him money, asks the salesman a few questions,
to try and make him compete with other possible sellers, to try and get
information and see if there are any hidden defects. The situation turns
round fairly quickly; sometimes, by the third question, the buyer is already
hooked. It's then the salesman's turn to ask questions; he makes the potential buyer pass a regular examination as to his payment capacities.

It is clear enough that the potential buyer becomes the object of a kind
of social assessment; it is his identity as a customer of the bank that is

at issue. The salesman often has his arguments ready prepared; that is a characteristic of the bureaucratic situation which is always forgotten, especially if you don't do empirical research: if you start from the state, as [Nicos] Poulantzas did, you never get to this. The salesman is in a completely asymmetrical relationship to the buyer. For the salesman, the buyer is simply one more in the series, he has seen others and will see others again; he has generic anticipations that are sociologically well-founded, and accordingly he has generic strategies for all sorts, which have been validated by experience. Opposite him, the buyer is experiencing a unique situation, which is unlikely to be repeated. On the one hand the repetitive and on the other the unique; the person on the repetitive side has the advantage both of his accumulated experience and of an experience accumulated by others as well. Sometime he also has at his elbow a vicarious experience of the bureaucratic type, protocols fully prepared, forms, that is, a rational, informational bureaucratic capital that is already considerable. But if we stopped there, we would be forgetting the essential, which is that behind him he also has a considerable force: the power given him by the fact of being the representative of an organization acting in the name of a bank; he is the delegate of a credit institution. What he appears to be doing is selling houses, but in fact he is selling the credit that makes it possible to buy a house.

Discourse analysis, which studies discourse without studying the social conditions of production of this discourse, does not understand anything. (I was particularly attentive to the implicit conditions of production of discourse.) There is the apparent definition of the situation: the customer comes to buy a home from someone selling homes, who is competing with other sellers of homes. The real definition becomes clear very rapidly: the buyer comes to buy credit in order to be able to buy a home. He will have the home that corresponds to his credit, that is, his social value as measured by the standards of the bank. 'How much are you worth?' – that is the question posed by the salesman, who is equipped for assessing the customer's social value in as economical a manner as possible, in the least time possible. Behind him he has the authority of the bank that delegates him; in this sense, he is a bureaucrat. The second characteristic of the bureaucrat is to be general as opposed to singular, and a delegate by virtue of his delegation. He can say 'that's ok', 'that's not ok', 'you'll get there with a bit of a stretch, if you make an effort'. That enables him to transform himself into the role of protector, an expert who gives advice and assesses capacities. Behind this structure of an exchange relationship there is an economic and symbolic balance of forces.

That said, it is clear from listening to the salesman that there is a third level involved in his strength; he is not simply a private agent of a private bank, he is also an agent of the state, in the sense that he says: 'You have the right to . . .', 'No, you can't do that . . .' He is an agent who wields legal and financial powers; he has a pocket calculator and never stops calculating, it's a way of reminding people of his authority . . . These situations are clearly very painful for the customer, who discovers that what is being measured is his own social value: he arrives with his dreams, and leaves with a reality. The fourth function of the salesman is to make the customer let down his defences. The customer arrives, he needs so many square metres, he wants light from the left side, etc. The salesman tells him: 'This is your market value, what you're worth; given what you're worth, this is the home you can have. If you want 200 square metres, that will be 200 kilometres from the city centre; if you want 100 square metres it will be 100 kilometres away.' The two main parameters of the negotiation are distance and surface area. The salesman constantly says: 'You're entitled to . . ., you're not entitled to . . . Given what you've got, there's the APL [*aide personalisée au logement*] which is a kind of bonus designed to help first-time buyers.'

You can see that it's very complicated, and it is impossible to draw a sharp line and say either that 'the bank is in the service of the state' or that 'the state is in the service of the bank'. The salesman (for Phénix homes he is generally a former worker) has neither an explicit mandate from the state nor any official mandate; he has not been appointed as legitimate seller of legitimate homes by the legitimate state, but he acts as agent of the state in saying: 'I know the rates, I tell you what you're entitled to; you've got two children, so you're entitled to such-and-such an alloca-tion.' You then have to go back to the origin of this housing support. How was it produced? By whom? Under what conditions? In what field? You also have to go back to the origin of the rules governing the management of credit. In the 1960s, for example, with the invention of personalized credit, you find the problem of the assessment of the buyer by the seller. Personalized credit is granted not as a function of the possession of visible goods, but as a function of what economists call steady income: what is assessed is what you are worth on a lifetime scale. That is easy to calculate, especially if you're a civil servant. If you have a career, it is possible to cal-culate what you are worth, that is, the total sum of money you will earn in the course of your life. Behind this assessment lies a whole legal structure, the rules that govern credit and the institutional rules that govern credit support.

This negotiation concludes, if successful, with a contract that I have called a 'contract under constraint', since the game is artificial and people believe they are negotiating whereas in reality the dice are already cast, and the size of home they will have can be predicted. In order to under-stand the seemingly free game that is played out in negotiations, therefore, we have to go back to the whole legal structure that supports what we can call the production of demand. If people who have no visible property, not much money for their down payment (which is the case with skilled or semi-skilled workers, all those whose over-indebtedness is discussed today), if they are able to fulfil the dream of home ownership, it is because a whole series of facilities have been produced by people who can be referred to under the category of state, in certain conditions.

The Barre commission on housing

I found the same problem on the supply side. In the 1970s there was a kind of boom; companies produced a lot of identical homes by industrial methods, drawing very heavily on the banks both to guarantee their business and to provide themselves with means of production. It is possible to ask how they came to enter the market and succeed there, given that, for historical reasons, the dominant expectations in terms of housing were for 'hand-made' homes built one by one . . . The question was referred to the higher authorities. A reform movement in the years 1970–3 led to commissions and committees being set up, the most important of which was the Barre commission.[26] The regulations that used to govern 'bricks and mortar' support – which essentially helped builders – were changed to support for the individual – which essentially helped buyers.

I was led to study the world of those people who had a say in this series of decisions. I did not ask the traditional questions of the type: what is the state? Do the big banks use the state to impose a policy favourable to the development of a certain kind of property that makes it possible to sell on credit, by asking for the development of credit? Who makes use of whom? I rather asked who were the agents acting, in order to understand the origin of these regulations that have their effect right through to the ordinary seller. I established the field of acting agents on the basis of objective data about their characteristics (which individuals are effective here, the director of construction at the Ministry of Finance, or the director of social affairs who makes it possible for people to obtain loans through the state?) And also on the basis of statutory information (Is it the function of this or that agent of the state to intervene? Is he mandated to decide whether loans will be granted or not, in the way that an inspector is mandated to inspect?) For example, the Ministry of Equipment and its departmental counterparts can obviously not be left out: I took people whose official definition was such that they could be considered a priori as involved, contrasting this with what might be said by informants according to the reputational method (was such-and-such a person important?) The problem then arises as to where the boundary lies. The famous articulation between the state and the banks or major industries is often effected by way of these individuals, but in forms that are not at all those described by a theory in terms of functions. I discovered therefore senior officials in the Ministries of Finance, Highways and Equipment, mayors of large cities, as well as representatives of voluntary associations and HLMs,[27] social workers who dealt with these questions, for whom there was an issue involved that was worth fighting for, people who were ready to die for the principle of 'bricks and mortar' support.

The question then was to know what were the principles according to which this world operated: were we going to see the state on the one hand and the local authorities on the other? This is the way people think. In the spontaneous sociology that is in the minds of all high officials, there is the

UNIVERSITY OF WINCHESTER
LIBRARY

central and the local. We discover here one of the key questions of a whole sociology: central/peripheral, central/local . . . the answer comes automatically, in the form of taxonomies. The central is the state. That is the vision they have of themselves: they have more general interests, as opposed to people who are local, particular, always suspected of being the expression of lobbies – like that of the HLMs for example. They were individuals who had histories, trajectories, who had circulated in the space that I was in the process of establishing, they had successively occupied various functions, they carried their whole former itinerary in their habitus, and therefore in their strategy. I assumed that this space had a structure, it was not just made up any old how. By way of statistical analysis, I tried to reveal the structure as it appeared, taking the set of pertinent agents and the set of pertinent properties.

You will say to me, what are the criteria? The first of these is to take the pertinent agents, since they have something to do with this problem and can do something about this problem; they have the specific power enabling them to be effective, to produce effects. Secondly, it is to consider the pertinent properties, that is, the properties that are needed to be effective in this field. We are in what the Germans, in scholarly fashion, call the 'hermeneutic circle': how do we determine this? This is done by trial and error, by successive attempts, because it is the very object of research. We determine the properties that make for someone being effective. For example, the fact of being an inspector of finances is very important, or the fact of being an engineer with the Corps des Mines or the Ponts et Chaussées.[28] On the basis of these properties of effectiveness, I constructed the objective space, the structure of this space, which could be called the relation of forces or the division into camps. This was thus therefore a complex space with divisions.

Finally, I made a chronicle of these reforms, a diary of events; I interviewed informants, evidently selected among people who had played a prominent role in this enterprise – good informants, at all events, are those who are informed, and to be informed, they have to be insiders – people who sat on commissions, who were able to tell how the members of the commissions were selected, which is quite decisive . . . It is possible to determine what will come out of a commission on the basis of its composition. I reconstituted the series of events, as a historian would do, from what happened in the process that led to the elaboration of the regulation whose effects I could see with the property sellers. I related the ensemble of pertinent events and only those, that is, the ones that need to be known in order to understand. In other words, it is not a formal account of proceedings, but an account of the events capable of explaining.

(This does not necessarily mean that a historian, giving a good account of the events that make explanation possible, is always completely aware of the principles on which he selects events. Marc Bloch spoke of the historian's craft:[29] this is a habitus on the basis of which it is possible to make methodical selections, without building these up into an explicit method.

The recourse to history is very useful: presenting myself as a historian made it possible to get information that would have been refused me point blank as a sociologist.)

I put forward the hypothesis that, since structures are relatively invariant, by studying the structures of twenty years previous I was studying structures that were still in place. So I first gave the account, and then I presented the structure of the space in which what I related happened, with proper names and the characteristics of the individuals who had these names. Here is the structure of the space of those agents who produced this history.[30] Did this structure make it intelligible? I was surprised to see how far the structure of the field of forces, the distribution of camps, explained the oppositions I am speaking about. We see by and large that the site where this regulation was generated – 'regulation' being a state word – was a structured space in which there were representatives of the administrative field, senior officials and representatives of the local economic and political fields, mayors . . . A first opposition, therefore.

The second opposition was that, within the administrative field, there was an opposition between those who were on the side of the Ministry of Finance and those on the side of the Ministry of Equipment, the technical side. This opposition is very interesting. The issue in this opposition was between those in favour of support for bricks and mortar, that is, a rather statist form of support for housing, a collective, collectivist form (support for the HLMs, for collective construction), and those in favour of a more liberal, personal, personalized, personalistic, Giscardian support. On the side of the administrative sector you find an opposition between those on the side of the statist approach and those on the side of the liberal approach. The state is opposed here to freedom, the state to the market, but if you find the market within the state, that complicates matters . . . One may well ask why the engineers of the Ponts et Chaussées were on the side of the state, the collective and collectivism. They were *polytechniciens*,[31] not suspect at all . . . Yet they were on the side of the social, the collective, the side of the past, of preservation, against the liberals seeking to make a liberal turn, anticipating the subsequent political direction.

Among the neo-Marxist theories of the state, one developed by a German, Hirsch, stresses the fact that the state is the site of class struggle, the state is not the dumb instrument of the dominant class's hegemony.[32] There are people within the state who are more on the liberal side or [more on] the statist side. This is a major issue of struggle. If this were translated back into terms of political division, you would more or less have socialists on one side, liberals on the other. I think however that in order to understand this opposition, it is necessary to refer to the history of the bodies under consideration, and the interest that the respective bodies (technical engineers and inspectors of finance) have in one political line or another. To understand the interest of the technical bodies in an attitude that can be called 'progressive', it is necessary to assume that they have a professional interest bound up with progressive positions. It is not because they are progressive that they have a progressive position, but because they belong to a body that is partly bound up with a form of progressive regulation. Once a 'social conquest' has been inscribed in a state institution, once a body has been established whose existence is partly bound up with the perpetuation of this thing (the Ministry of Social Affairs), it is certain that there will be within this state body a defence of this social conquest, even if the beneficiaries have disappeared and are no longer there to protest. I am pressing the paradox here, but I think it is very important.

The state, in other words, is not a bloc, it is a field. The administrative field, as a particular sector of the field of power, is a field, that is, a space structured according to oppositions linked to specific forms of capital with differing interests. These antagonisms, whose site is this space, have to do with the division of organizational functions associated with the different respective bodies. The opposition between financial ministries and spending or social ministries is part of the spontaneous sociology of the senior civil service; as long as there are social ministries, there will be a certain form of defence of the social. As long as there is a Ministry of National Education, there will be a defence of education that has very wide autonomy in relation to the characteristics of those who occupy these positions.

Third opposition: in my chronicle, by way of objective indications and informants, I saw the appearance of protagonists, individuals who were said to be the authors of this bureaucratic revolution. I asked myself, what am I studying here? I am studying a specific revolution, a bureaucratic revolution, the transition from one bureaucratic regime to another. I am dealing with specific revolutionaries. By studying who these people are I could perhaps answer the question, what has to be done in order to make a bureaucratic revolution? It turns out, then, that the third factor miraculously singled out these people, practically all individuals designated as revolutionaries by objective indicators and indicators of reputation, and only these. What characteristics did these people have? They were very dispersed, in all corners of the space. They had some very surprising characteristics in common: a major bureaucratic inheritance – they were often the sons of senior officials, they were part of the high state nobility, with several quarters of bureaucratic nobility. I tend to believe that, in order to make a bureaucratic revolution, you have to be thoroughly familiar with the bureaucratic apparatus.

Why was Raymond Barre appointed president of the commission that played a decisive role? It is possible to do a sociology of individuals (sociologically constructed) and of what they do in very particular situations.[33] These revolutionary protagonists, these innovators who formed this bureaucratic avant-garde, had very surprising characteristics: they had a sum of characteristics that are very improbable in this world. They were people who had been in the technical sector, *polytechniciens*, but who then did econometrics and followed Sciences-Po. They combined their regular bureaucratic capital with a technical, theoretical capital; they could make an impression on men of politics by calculating the costs and benefits of different political forces. Or else they were those inspectors of finance who transgressed a taboo by going on to chair HLM commissions. Robert Lion, current president of the Caisse des Depôts, committed an act of derogation that was viewed in his milieu as quite barbaric: he went from high to low in the state and bureaucratic space; he is an individual in a mixed and unstable position.[34]

This explanatory history, this sociogenesis, was indispensable for understanding what went on in the interview between a salesman and a buyer, for understanding the trend in ownership statistics, the fact that owners always have in mind the social spaces elaborated in *Distinction* – the right side of the social space is made up by those wielding more economic capital than cultural capital.[35] Now the big push forward in access to property was effected on the left side of the social space, among people who had more cultural capital than economic capital. It is here that the rates of increase were strongest. I can find, at the political level, the political formula, both cunning and naive, that managed to inspire those responsible for this policy: 'We are going to associate the people with the established order by the tie that is property.' That is explicitly said in the writings of Valéry Giscard d'Estaing, and by everyone in the milieu of these kinds of reforms. In the series of events, there was a whole prophetic work of conversion, people who wrote articles, who made mathematical models, who made use of all the instruments of persuasion. In modern societies, mathematics has become a great instrument of political persuasion. These people had a political intention based on a philosophy: attachment to the social order follows from adhesion to property, and to make the left side of the social space adhere to the established order meant carrying through a considerable change. To understand certain changes in the French political universe, it was as important to follow housing politics as to follow the writings of Jean Daniel (in the *Nouvel Observateur*) or the discourse of the Communist Party, which might on the contrary have been determined by these changes.

We can understand how, on the basis of a political programme borne by certain individuals, an effective regulation was generated that governed demand and supply, the market, and constructed the market from scratch. It is one of the functions of the state to construct markets. How then was this regulation applied? How did the social agents on the ground put it into practice, at the level of the *département* and the town? We find the acts, the *statements* that I discussed above: the building permit, the granting of dispensations, derogations, authorizations. Certain regulations specified that roofs must overlap by 20 centimetres and no more. That is completely arbitrary. Architects all said: 'It's ridiculous, why not 25 centimetres, why not 23?' This arbitrariness generates a specific form of bureaucratic profit: either apply the regulation very strictly and later relax it, or grant a derogation. A dialectic that I call the dialectic of *droit et passe-droit* [law and dispensation][36] ends up with bribes and scandals. We discover here the regular management of the state by the depositories of power.

I conducted only a very minimal historical regression here, to the immediate historical cause. To understand this historical section, which explains
another historical section, you have to regress. What does telling this
history mean? Is the history of the administrative field – that of the state
as a whole remains to be told – simply a series of sections of the kind that
I made for each of these regulations decreed by the state? (It is intimidat-
ing to keep saying 'the state . . .'. I can't continue saying sentences starting
with 'the state . . .'.) I took the example of support for housing. The same
should be done for social security. Each moment, to be completely intelligible, calls for knowledge of all the preceding sections. To understand the
complexity of a body of technicians, you have to know that these bodies
were created in France in such-and-such a year, that they were established
at the local level, then at the national level . . . Unfortunately, in the
social sciences we are faced with the problem of drawing up impossible
programmes. Perhaps the greatest merit of what I am going to do will be
precisely to make an impossible research programme.

Lecture of 25 January 1990

The theoretical and the empirical – State commissions and stagings – The social construction of public problems – The state as viewpoint on viewpoints – Official marriage – Theory and theory effects – The two meanings of the word 'state' – Transforming the particular into the universal – The *obsequium* – Institutions as 'organized fiduciary' – Genesis of the state. Difficulties of the undertaking – Parenthesis on the teaching of research in sociology – The state and the sociologist

The theoretical and the empirical

I want rapidly to refer to the last lecture in order to stress the contrast you may have observed between its two parts. In the first part, my aim was to present a number of general propositions about the state, and in the second part I presented a kind of schematic and hasty description of a study I recently made of a certain aspect of state action. Among the indexes that I have of your selective attention and reception, there is one that is particularly important: the level of note-taking. I observed that in the second part there was a considerable decline in the taking of notes. I might put this down to the quality of my performance, but I think that it actually bears on the fact that I was speaking of things that seemed to you less worthy of being noted. This is a problem, since to my mind the second part was the more important, the more worthy of being noted. The very fact that I was explaining things at an accelerated pace was already an anticipated reaction to your reception, since I might well in fact have devoted the whole of this year's lecture course to this work, and to the detailed analysis and methods that I used.

If I return to this now, it is because it raises a quite fundamental question, one that is also raised for me. It is extremely hard to combine mentally, to keep together, the description and analysis of a state of the state as it can be observed today, and general propositions about the state. I think that if the theory of the state, in the ramshackle state it is in today – at least to my mind – can keep going, this is because it floats in a world that is independent from reality. Theorists can discuss ad infinitum, whether they are from Marxist or neo-functionalist traditions, precisely because the connection with the things of the real world, of everyday life, is not made, and there is a kind of *epoche*, as phenomenologists would say, a suspension of any reference to what is happening, which makes so-called 'theoretical' discussions possible. Unfortunately, this status of theory is reinforced by social expectations. In every discipline, the theoretical is placed above the empirical, above experience. The more famous scientists become, the more 'theoretical' they become. In old age, all scientists become philosophers, especially if they win a Nobel Prize . . . These very general considerations are important, as they are among the obstacles to progress in social science and, among other things, to communicating the results of scientific work in the social sciences.

I shall return to this dualism. I am so much aware of the difficulty of conveying what I want to convey that I am constantly wedged between strategies of communication (how should I say what I have to say?) and the imperatives of coherence in what there is to communicate. The contradiction between the two can sometimes give what I am saying a very strange appearance, which is probably as painful for me as it is for you. In this particular case, I am raising the question of the link between these two levels, and I am not sure I am able to answer it fully. But I think that by inviting you to be attentive to this difficulty, I can indicate a difficulty that also arises for you, if you take an interest in the state, or if you are working on something that has a connection with the state.

State commissions and stagings

So as to try and link the two levels a bit, I shall return to a point that I touched on very quickly in passing: the idea of commission. I told you that commission is something very odd, it is a form of social organization that raises several questions. First of all, it is a historical invention, an English invention whose genealogy we can trace. It was originally known as a 'royal commission': a body of people mandated by the king, commissioned to perform an important and socially recognized mission, generally to do with a problem that was also considered important. Two underlying acts were involved in the constitution – the word is important and should be taken in the strong sense – of a commission. First of all, the nomination and appointment – if it was a state act, this was indeed appointment – of a body of people recognized as capable, socially nominated to deal with public problems. A public problem is a problem that deserves to be dealt with publicly, officially. This notion of 'public' deserves reflection, in others words, what things deserve to be presented openly to all? Clearly, social critique always tends to look for what lies behind this public. There is a spontaneous view on the part of social agents, very often made into a sociological posture, which can be called 'theatrical'; we find this with

Goffman,[1] who [elaborated] this spontaneous view that we have about interactions between persons. They play out a scene; one is the actor and the other the audience, a good audience or a bad one. This theatrical view of interactions may be applied to the world of theatre par excellence, that of state theatre, the world of officialdom, official ceremony – the ceremony of the law, for example. A major English historian has studied in detail the ceremony of English law, and the fundamentally effective role of this ceremonial, which is not simply an end in itself but acts, as a ceremonial, by having itself recognized as legitimate.[2]

These public commissions, then, are stagings, operations that consist in staging a set of people who have to play out a kind of public drama, the drama of reflection on public problems. The commissions of wise men that are constantly proposed deserve to be studied. If we adopt this reductive, theatrical view, it leads to saying: 'So there is the stage, there is the backstage, and for my part, as a clever sociologist, I shall show you behind the scenes.' I often tell you, and this is important for those of you who are sociologists, that one of the unconscious motivations that lead people to become sociologists is the pleasure of discovering what goes on behind the scenes. With Goffman this is quite patent: it is the view of someone who is behind a grocery counter and watches the strategies of the grocer and the customer. See the magnificent description he gives of what goes on in a restaurant. When the waiters come out through the swing door they change their posture completely, and when they go back inside they make a racket . . . This description of the social world as theatre is ironic by definition. What it involves, in the rigorous sense of the term, is saying: 'The world is not what you think it to be, don't be taken in . . .' And when you're young, when you rather like to appear clever, and especially to feel clever, it's most agreeable to demystify appearances.

This view could be the spontaneous sociology of the semi-wise sociologist, to use Pascal's expression. This semi-wise person says: the world is a theatre, and this applies very well to the state. (I'm rather afraid that you might have understood my analysis in this way.) I said: the state is a legal fiction, so it doesn't exist. The theatrical view of the social world does see something important: a commission is a trick; the [typical] view of a commission that *Le Canard enchaîné* gives is true at a certain level. It is the task of the sociologist to know how a commission was made up: who chose it and why? Why was such-and-such a person asked to chair it? What were his or her properties? How does cooption take place? Isn't everything already settled by the mere fact of defining the members? This is all very well, and is part of the work. But it is often very hard to do it in such a way that it is publishable, and thus publicly refutable by the participants. [. . .]

This approach, however, despite its completely legitimate aspect, risks missing something important. Commission is an organizational invention – we can give the date when it was invented. It is like a technological invention, but of a quite particular kind. The state is itself one of those inventions, an invention that consists in putting people together in such a way that, being organized in this manner, they do things that they would not do if they were not organized like that. Spontaneously, we forget the existence of this kind of technology. There are lots of publications on the effects of the introduction of computers in offices, but people overlook the way in which the invention of the circular changed the world of bureaucracy; or at a much earlier stage, how the transition from oral custom to written law changed the whole bureaucratic world. There are often words for such organizational techniques, inventions, but rarely a person's name: the names of scientific inventors are rembered, but not those of bureaucratic inventors. Personal credit, for example, is a very complex organizational invention.

The commission is a historical invention that functions, and if it is still used today – I call this 'minimal functionalism' – that is because there are functions for it to perform. The word functionalism is one of those concepts that is used as an insult, and so is not much use scientifically. I simply say – this is something sociologists can agree on – that an institution that is constantly used over a long period merits the hypothesis that it has some function, it does something. The organizational invention that is the commission produces a considerable effect, which leads people to forget the theatrical view of the institution: it generates the symbolic effects produced by the staging of the official, of official conformity with the official representation. I shall explain what I mean. What was the Barre commission doing, which I spoke about last time? It was elaborating a new definition of a problem constituted as public, in this case the right to housing, which itself would merit a historical analysis. Clearly, one of the elementary precepts of sociology as I conceive it consists in never taking a problem at face value, but seeing that problems are a problem, and so there is a historic genesis of problems. As regards the right to housing, we should ask when it arose and how, who were the philanthropists who established it, what were their interests, what space did they inhabit, etc.

We admit, therefore, that the problem exists, and we say: this commission deals publicly with this public problem, and takes as its mission to come up with a solution that can be made public. There will be an offical report that is officially submitted, with a quasi-official authority. A report is not ordinary discourse but performative discourse, addressed to whoever it was who asked for it, and who, by asking for it, gave it an authority in advance. The writer of the report is the person who writes a discourse of authority because authorized to do so, a discourse of authority on behalf of whoever authorized him by asking for it and giving him a mandate in advance. This report is a historically determined report that has to be analysed in each particular case, depending on the state of the balance of forces between the principal and the representative, depending on the abilities of the two sides to make use of the report. Do those commissioned have sufficient strategic strength to make use of the commission, and everything that was implicit in the mission they were given, to have the conclusions of their commission accepted? Do they have the intention and capacity for this? There is a whole empirical work to be done each time, which does not mean that the model does not hold good. The model is there as an invitation to study the variations in parameters.

The social construction of public problems

These people thus elaborate a new legitimate definition of a public problem, they propose a new way of providing citizens with the means of satisfying what is granted them as a right, that is, the need for housing. The problem would be raised in the same way if it concerned drugs or the problem of nationality. Who is entitled to vote in municipal elections? Who should rightfully be punished? Joseph Gusfield made a study of the debates on the link between drunkenness and car accidents.[3] His problematic is what in the United States is called 'constructivist'; he is among those who emphasize, in the tradition of Alfred Schütz[4] and certain American psycho-sociologists such as Mead,[5] that social agents do not take the social world as a given but construct it. To give a very simple idea of this thesis, we have to reconstitute the operations of construction that social agents conduct in constructing their partly formatted interactions or relations, such as the relation of students to teacher or the relation of customer to bureaucratic staff. In his book, Gusfield emphasizes the origin of a public problem, and shows among other things how work with a scientific appearance, statistics, whether state or private, is itself a social rhetoric by way of which statisticians participate in the construction of a social problem. It is they, for example, who establish as self-evident the connection between the fact of drinking and having road accidents; they provide the ratification that discourse perceived as scientific, that is, universal, can bring to a social representation which is morally based, something that is very unevenly distributed in the social world. Gusfield showed that official agents, legislators who elaborate new norms, as well as lawyers, men of the law who apply these, bring a symbolic reinforcement – which may be authorized by scientific arguments – to moral dispositions that are unevenly distributed in what is called 'public opinion'.

If a poll is taken, for example, it is noticeable that not everyone is in favour of suppressing drink driving, that not everyone is in favour of abolishing the death penalty, and a majority probably do not favour it. If a poll were conducted on the reception given to immigrants from the Maghreb, it is likely that it would not validate what is the norm for the practice of teachers in schools or lycées, that is, an official definition of anti-racist discourse. What do the social agents of the official do in such cases, teachers who make anti-racist speeches, judges who condemn people who drive while intoxicated? Even if their discourse is flouted, even if there is an extraordinary contradiction in this theatrical performance – in the English sense of the word – of official truth, this official truth is not

without effect for all that. The intention of Gusfield's book is to say that
the symbolic has a real effect, and that even if all these symbolic expressions are no more than pious or hypocritical wishes, they operate none the
less. It would be naive – and this is the same naivety that is already found
with the clever little demystifier – not to take seriously these acts of theatricalization of the official that have a real effect, even if the official is never
more than the official, something that in all societies is established only to
be transgressed.

The state as viewpoint on viewpoints

I do not want to express reservations about Gusfield's book, but I think
it is possible to go further on the basis of what he says. He reminds us of
one important thing, that a social fiction is not fictitious. Hegel already
said that illusion is not illusory. Despite the official being never more than
official, despite the commission not being what it would like to have people
believe it is, it produces an effect none the less, because despite everything
it succeeds in having people believe that it is what it wants to have believed.
It is important that the official, despite not being what it presents itself as,
is effective all the same. How and why is it effective? What reinforcement
does it bring, for example, to those who, supporting the maintenance of
order, want marijuana smokers to be heavily punished, and how is this
reinforcement exerted? It is by way of this analysis that we can grasp one
of the forms of effectiveness specific to the state.

To put things in a very simplistic way, before we go on to express them
in a more complicated fashion, if we follow Gusfield we could say that the
state, in the case that he studied but also more generally (the commissions
of wise men on racism, on nationality, etc.), strengthens one point of view
among others on the social world, which is the place of struggle between
points of view. He says of this point of view that it is the right point of
view, the viewpoint on viewpoints, the 'geometral of all perspectives'. This
is a divinization effect. And this means that it must make believe that it
is not itself a viewpoint. It is necessary therefore for the commission to
appear as a commission of wise men, that is, above contingencies, interests, conflicts, ultimately outside the social space, because as soon as you
are in the social space, you are a point, and therefore a viewpoint, that can
be relativized.

In order to obtain this effect of de-particularization, this set of institutions that we call 'the state' must theatricalize the official and the universal, it must put on the spectacle of public respect for public truths, public
respect for the official truths in which the totality of society is supposed
to recognize itself. It must present the spectacle of universality, on which
everyone is ultimately in agreement, on which there cannot be disagreement because it is inscribed in the social order at a certain moment in
time.

Official marriage

An in-depth analysis of what lies behind this effect, however, is extremely difficult. In a publication of mine several years ago on Berber marriage,[6] I already encountered this problem. You will see that the analogy between state situations and this seemingly quite different reality is very strong. Anthropologists often speak of preferential marriage, an expression that is a euphemism for official marriage (sociologists and anthropologists often take up indigenous concepts and neutralize them in order to create a scientific effect, which means that they lose the problem I am raising here). They say that preferential marriage is marriage with a parallel cousin: a man tends to marry his son to the daughter of his father's brother. They examine the reality as ethnologists, who normally do not do statistics. As a somewhat deviant ethnologist, I did do statistics, and I observed that so-called preferential marriage, legitimate, official marriage, was practised by between 3 and 6 per cent [of cases] in the most official families, *marabout* families, those who conform most to the official definition of what is official – also those who remind people of the official when things turn out wrong. You are then led to raise questions. You can say: this is all false, it's of no interest, the informants are mystifiers or mystified. Or else you can say that they are deceived or deceive themselves, or that they are obeying unconscious rules, their statements are only rationalizations – and in this way you get rid of the problem. In fact, by analysing matters more closely I observed that a certain number of marriages existed that did correspond to the official definition, and that these were especially celebrated, recognized as ensuring fertility in the mythico-religious logic of prosperity and bringing blessings on those who conform to them, as well as on the whole group. Looking still more closely, I observed that these marriages could be in apparent conformity with the official rule despite being determined by motives that were completely contrary to this. In other words, even the 3 per cent that were pure and conformed to the rule could be a result of interests that were quite antagonistic to the rule. To take an example: that of a family in which there is a girl who is a bit deformed and hard to marry; it turns out that one of her cousins sacrifices himself to protect the family from 'shames', as they say, and in this case the marriage is especially celebrated – exactly as a successful commission is celebrated – since it has done something extremely important, made it possible to realize the official norm in an extreme case, one that is extremely dangerous for the official norm. In other words, it saved face, not only for an individual but also for the whole group. It rescued the possibility of believing in the official truth despite everything.

There are heroes of the official. The bureaucratic hero is the person whose major function is to enable the group to continue to believe in the official, that is, in the idea that there is a group consensus on a certain number of values that are indispensable in dramatic situations in which the social order is deeply challenged. There is thus a prophetic role in periods of crisis, when no one knows any more what to do. The ordinary official discourse is what priests say in everyday routine when there is no problem – priests are people who resolve public religious problems outside situations of crisis. But in a situation of great crisis, whether moral or political, one that challenges the very foundations of the symbolic order that religion guarantees, the prophet is the person who manages to restore the official norm. In the societies that we call precapitalist, without state or writing, where there are no official guarantors of the official, no agents who are officially mandated to pronounce the official in difficult moments, no civil servants because there is no state, there are individuals who are poets. Mouloud Mammeri has given a very fine analysis of the character of the *amusnaw* in *Actes de la Recherche en Sciences Sociales*,[7] the person who says what has to be done when no one knows what to think . . . These are people who bring the group back into line with its order, who tell it what has to be done in tragic situations where there are antinomies. These sages can be naively described as conciliators who arrange things. But this is not the case. They actually arrange things that cannot be arranged, in tragic situations where both antagonists are in the right. The adversaries each have right on their side in the name of values that the group cannot fail to recognize – the right to existence, the right to autonomy – without destroying itself as a group. When these values are in conflict, the prophetic spokesperson or the poet is the person able to reconcile the group with its professions of faith, with its official truth.

Theory and theory effects

I started out, in this presentation, from the notion of commission, to show you how at a certain level of elaboration the most trivial things of the ordinary bureaucratic order are those that I have the most difficulty accepting as an object of thought, because if there is something that seems trivial when you are sociologically constituted as an intellectual, it is reflecting on the meaning of a circular or a commission; this really demands a very special effort when you have been prepared to reflect on Being or *Dasein*, whereas it is in fact extremely difficult: the problem of the state is as complex as the problem of Being . . . I have expanded on this a bit to make you understand something that I want to communicate, the effort that has to be made in order to reject the dichotomy between theoretical propositions and empirical propositions if you really want to advance reflection on these problems, which need to be looked at theoretically because they exist by way of theory effects.[8] The state is to a large extent the product of theorists. When they take the writings of Naudé on the coup d'état or Loyseau on the state,[9] or the writings of all those jurists in the sixteenth and seventeenth centuries who produced theories of the state, some philosophers treat them like colleagues whose theories they are discussing, forgetting that these colleagues produced the very object they are reflecting on.

Loyseau and Naudé, all those jurists, produced the French state, and they produced the thinking of the individuals thinking them. There is a form of history of ideas that has a very ambiguous status, and is not usable without precaution from the viewpoint at which I place myself. The same holds for the jurists who say that the state is a legal fiction. They are right, and at the same time they do not concretely conceive the social conditions that make this fiction not fictitious but operative – which is what the sociologist has to do. That was the pedagogic intention of this excursus on commissions.

To recapitulate very briefly. Something that is apparently very anodyne, in this case the fact that President Valéry Giscard d'Estaing set up a commission chaired by Raymond Barre to report on support for housing, which in due course drew up a report advising the government – the notion of advice is very important – to adopt a policy of support for individuals instead of support for bricks and mortar, is in fact an extremely complex operation of officialization, which consists in theatricalizing a political action involving the creation of imperative rules of action imposed on the whole of society, theatricalizing the production of this type of order capable of confirming and producing the social order in such a way that it appears backed by the official discourse of the society in question, thus by the universal on which all agents are obliged to fall into agreement – and to do so successfully. This is an operation that can succeed or fail. The conditions of its success can be sociologically analysed: the operation will have a greater chance of success, the more that the theatricalization of the official is conducted in such a way that it actually reinforces official representations that are actually internalized by agents on the basis of the primary education of the nineteenth century, the action of the republican schoolteacher, on the basis of all kinds of things . . . Otherwise, it would be no more than a pious wish. This makes the question of the distinction between state and civil society completely vanish.

The two meanings of the word 'state'

French dictionaries give two adjacent definitions of the state: (1) the state in the sense of the bureaucratic apparatus that manages collective interests, and (2) the state in the sense of the territory on which the authority of this apparatus is exercised. When people say 'the French state', they think of the government, the armed forces, the state bureaucracy, and on the other hand they think of France. A symbolic operation of officialization such as is effected in a commission is a work in and through which state 1 (in the sense of the government, etc.) manages to be perceived as the expression, the manifestation, of state 2, of what state 2 recognizes and grants state 1. In other words, the function of the commission is to produce an official view that imposes itself as the legitimate view; it is to have the official version accepted, even if there are grimaces, even if there are articles in *Le Canard Enchaîné* on the underside of the commission's operations, etc. This is the intention of the analysis I gave you of the relationship between the salesman for the Phénix housing corporation, who is not a state employee, and the customer. The salesman may set himself up as a statutorily mandated embodiment of the official, and say: 'With three children, you are entitled to this', and be immediately understood and accepted by his interlocutor as bearer of a legitimate definition of the situation. That is by no means automatic. It is clear that on a question such as housing there are antagonistic perspectives, conflicting interests on the part of a whole series of agents – think of the law on rents.[10] The stakes are enormous, and so there are a large number of private viewpoints endowed with very unequal strengths in the symbolic struggle to construct the legitimate social view of the world and impose this as universal.

To continue the analysis of the opposition between state and civil society, which goes back to a duality that is simply the transposition into concepts of the ordinary dictionary definition, we could say, in a Spinozist perspective, that there is the state as *natura naturans* and the state as *natura naturata*. The state as subject, as *natura naturans*, is – according to the Robert dictionary – 'the sovereign authority exercised over the whole body of a definite people or territory: for example, all the general services of a nation. Synonyms: public authorities, administration, central government.' The second definition is 'a human grouping settled on a definite territory, subject to an authority and capable of being considered as a legal entity. Synonyms: nation, country, power.' Lalande's dictionary of classical philosophy gives the two definitions in the following order: (1) 'An organized society having an autonomous government and playing the role of a distinct legal entity in relation to other similar societies with which it is in relation.' And (2): 'The sum of the general services of a nation, the government and the whole administration.' In other words, the two definitions are given in the reverse order. The hierarchy in which these two definitions are placed expresses a philosophy of the state that we all have in mind, and this is, I believe, the implicit philosophy that underlies the distinction between state and public service. The view of the state as a set of organized individuals who mandate the state is the tacitly democratic definition of a civil society from which the state, in bad times, cuts itself off (when people speak of civil society, it is to say that the state should remember the existence of civil society). Implicit in this ordering is the assumption that what exists first of all is the organized society with an autonomous government, etc., and that this society is expressed, manifested, perfected, in the government to which it delegates organizing power.

This democratic view is completely false, and what I should like to demonstrate – this was implicit in what I said in the previous lecture – is that it is the state in the sense of the 'sum of the services of a nation' that makes the state in the sense of the 'whole body of citizens with a frontier'. There is an unconscious reversal of cause and effect that is typical of the logic of fetishism, a fetishizing of the state that consists in acting as if the nation-state, the state as organized population, were first, whereas the thesis I would like to propose, and will test in relation to a kind of history of the genesis of the state in two or three different traditions, is the very opposite: that is, that there are a certain number of social agents – including jurists – who played an eminent role, in particular those possessing that capital in terms of organizational resources that was Roman law. These agents gradually built up this thing that we call the state, that is, a set of specific resources that authorizes its possessors to say what is good for the social world as a whole, to proclaim the official and to pronounce words that are in fact orders, because they are backed by the force of the official. The constitution of this instance was accompanied by the construction of the state in the sense of a population contained within frontiers. In other words, it was by constructing this unprecedented kind of organization, this extraordinary kind of thing that is a state, constructing this set of organizational resources, both material and symbolic, with which we associate the notion of the state, that the social agents responsible for this work constructed the state in the sense of a unified population speaking the same language, which we generally see today as the initial cause.

Transforming the particular into the universal

There is a kind of process of fetishization that is inscribed in the logic of the commission, a real sleight of hand (to use again the reductive language of 'behind the scenes'). The members of the commission, as I regarded them in this particular context, are in effect particular agents who are the bearers of particular interests with very uneven degrees of universalization: promoters who want to obtain legislation favourable to the sale of certain kinds of products, bankers, senior civil servants who want to defend the interests associated with a particular department or a bureaucratic tradition, etc. The logic within which these particular interests work is such that they are able to achieve a kind of alchemy that transforms the particular into the universal. Basically, each time the commission meets, the alchemy of which the state is the product is reproduced, and moreover, using the resources of the state. To be a sucessful commission chair you need to have state resources, to understand what a commission is, the proper behaviour associated with it, the laws of cooption that are not written down anywhere, unwritten laws that govern the selection of the spokespeople who play a determining role in preparing the authoritative discourse that will emerge from the commission's work, etc. A whole capital of resources is deployed, functioning as an alchemist's retort for the person able to operate them, and the universal is reproduced in this way. There are cases in which the logic of the commission gives itself away, when it is patently obvious ('This Mr Clean that they've foisted on us, who can credit him?'). The commission's message may be immediately buried. There are defeats, but both defeat and success implement the same logic of officialization.

To sum up what I have been trying to say about the notion of

commission, I would say that a commission (or a ceremony of inaugura-
tion or appointment) is a typical act of state, a collective act that can only
be performed by people who maintain a sufficiently recognized relationship to the official to be in a position to use the universal symbolic resource
involved in mobilizing what the whole group is supposed to agree about.
Not to mobilize consensus, but to mobilize the *doxa* and transform what
is tacitly accepted as self-evident, what everyone grants to this order: to
mobilize in such a way that the statements pronounced by this group
can operate as watchwords and effect the extraordinary operation that
consists in transforming an observation into a norm, moving from the
descriptive to the normative.

I once spent a long time exploring Kantorowicz's analysis of the state
as mystery.[11] He took up the play on words of the twelfth-century English
canon lawyers who played on the similarity between *ministerium* and *mysterium*, speaking of the 'mystery of the ministry'. In the ministry there is
delegation. What I have tried to describe in the case of the commission is
the empirical form of the mystery of the ministry.[12] What takes place when
M. Raymond Barre, who is a man just like anyone else, on becoming chair
of a commission finds himself invested in a quite mysterious way with the
delegation of the state, that is, of the entire social world? He proposes
things that are universally recognized. This work is difficult because it has
to hold together both Raymond Barre and the theoretical . . .

[Break in the lecture]

The *obsequium*

I am tempted to go over again what I said previously with a view to cor-
recting, completing, qualifying, appeasing my remorse and regrets, but I
shall try and go forward despite everything. I would just like you to keep
in mind, for further development, the analogy I suggested very briefly
between the work of the official commission producing discourse whose
authority is founded on reference to the official, and the behaviour of the
Kabyle peasant who in a sense brings himself into line by conducting a
marriage in accordance with the rules, and in this way obtains the benefits
of the official, the benefits that in all societies, as I see it, come from actions
that appear to conform with what the society universally tends to view as
right. For this idea, there is a concept in Spinoza that has been the subject
of very little philosophical comment, and has always struck me forcefully
because it touches on personal things. Spinoza speaks of what he calls the
obsequium,[13] a respect that is not for individuals, forms or people; it is
something very fundamental, a respect that, by way of all this, is paid to
the state or the social order. These 'obsequious' acts display a pure respect
for the symbolic order, which the social agents of a society, even the most
critical, the most anarchistic, the most subversive, pay to the established

order, all the more so as they do this without knowing it. As an example of this *obsequium*, I always propose the formulas of politeness or rules of conduct that are seemingly insignificant, that bear on trivia and yet are all the more strictly demanded because they have a pure and Kantian side. By respecting them, homage is paid not to the individual who is the apparent object of respect, but to the social order that makes this person respectable. This is the most fundamental tacit demand of the social order. It is the reason why sociologists, if they do their work well, often find themselves in difficulty, because they are inevitably led to bring to light, thus to appear to denounce, things of this order that touch on the sacred – a sacred that finds its way into the smallest things.

In appointing the members of a commission, the choice of individuals is extremely important. This choice must focus on respectable people, respectful of the forms, knowing how to impose the forms, to do things in the proper form, to respect the rules, the rules of the game, to play the game; knowing therefore how to have right on their side – and this is a magnificent formula that does not simply mean 'respect the law'. The bureaucratic alchemy that has been working for ten centuries, and still continues today, is embodied in the Garde Républicain and the red carpet, in words (for example a 'summit meeting' assumes that there is a summit and a base), in ready-made turns of phrase, in insignificant gestures . . . On this terrain, sociology is extremely hard, as it has to analyse in detail things that are perceived as insignificant about a subject that is the noble subject par excellence, and accordingly on which very general things must be said (as for example Raymond Aron's book *Peace and War*),[14] great universal reflections. This is a case where the gap between theory and empirical work is greatest. Hence the malaise that I feel.

It is also necessary to explore further what is meant by official: what is an official newspaper?[15] What is published in it? What does the publication of marriage bans mean? What is official truth? Not exactly the equivalent of universal truth. French town halls have inscribed over their doors the words 'Liberté, Égalité, Fraternité': this is a programme, the reality is far from the legal fiction. That said, this fiction has its effects and can always be referred to, if only to say that there is a gap between the official and the reality; one of the weapons of criticism is to confront a regime with its official truth in order to show that it does not conform to what it says.

This official truth is not universal and recognized by everyone or at all times. And above all, it is not the constant generative principle of all actions of all agents in a particular society, which does not mean that it does not have its effects and that it does not exist by the very fact that it is unanimously recognized as official, that it is unanimously not disavowed. It exists both in a certain type of structure – in the social ministries, for example, there are objective principles of equalization, a claim to equalize – but also in people's minds, as the representation of something that one might well say does not exist, but that people agree would be better if it did. It is on this little lever of fundamental *obsequium* that one can lean in order to produce the effect of the official, of alchemy, by 'paying homage to the official', as the English put it. Following the logic of hypocrisy that is a homage vice pays to virtue, an official effect is produced far greater than one would believe. I would much like to analyse the negotiations between employers and trade unions that are arbitrated by civil servants; I am certain, having seen snippets of these, that the effects of *obsequium*, of the official, the effects of 'Mr Chairman', play a considerable role, because they act on the official as inscribed in people's minds. For example, the school system is a tremendous institution for getting the official incorporated, establishing wellsprings that can be mobilized later on, what is known as 'civic spirit'.

The distinction between state 1 as government, public service, public powers, and state 2 as the entire people that this state has as its base, should be challenged and replaced by a distinction in terms of degree. Maurice Halbwachs spoke of the 'focus of cultural values' from which people are more or less removed;[16] it would be possible to speak of a 'focus of state values' and establish a fairly simple index of a linear hierarchy of distance from the focus of state values by taking, for example, the capacity to make interventions, to proclaim amnesties, etc. A cumulative index could be arrived at, more or less rigorous, of the differential proximity of different social agents to this centre of state-type resources: one could also produce an index of proximity in mental structures. I would tend to substitute, for the simple opposition of state and civil society, the idea of a continuum which is a continuous distribution of access to the collective, public, material or symbolic resources with which the name 'state' is associated. This distribution, like all distributions in all social worlds, is the basis of constant struggles and the stake in them, political struggles (majority/opposition) being the most typical form of struggle to change this distribution.

Institutions as 'organized fiduciary'

So there we are. All this is very simple and very provisional. In order to try to condense things in a rather pedagogic way, I shall quote you a sentence from Valéry, taken from the chapter of his *Cahiers* devoted to teaching. He has a very nice sentence that has the virtue of summing up in a mnemonic and synoptic fashion the essentials of what I have just said. Poets have the good fortune of not having to argue in a coherent manner, they have the advantage of being able to put things in a formula. The phrase I shall cite you here seems to me richer and more subtle than Weber's on the monopoly of violence. Valéry said of Napoleon: 'This great man, truly great as he had the sense of institutions, of the organized fiduciary, endowed with automatism and independence from individuals – and if personal, seeking to reduce the role of personality, the irregularities of which he was well aware – accomplished everything too quickly.'[17] What is meant by institutions? They are an organized fiduciary, organized trust, organized belief, a collective fiction recognized as real by belief and thereby becoming real. Clearly, to say of a reality that it is a collective fiction is a manner of saying that it has a tremendous existence, but not as people believe it exists. There are lots of realities that the sociologist is led to say do not exist in the way people believe they exist, in order to show that they do exist but quite differently – which means that people always retain one half of my analysis and make me say the opposite of what I meant.

Institutions are an organized fiduciary endowed with automatism. The fiduciary, once organized, operates as a mechanism. From the pen of the sociologist, this often becomes: the mechanism that makes cultural capital goes to those with cultural capital. It is observed that there is a correlation between the father's occupation and that of the son, between the father's level of education and that of the son. People speak of mechanisms to mean that these are regular and repetitive processes, constant and automatic, which react in the manner of an automaton. This fiduciary exists independently of the people who inhabit the institutions in question. Weber laid great store on the fact that bureaucracy appears when you have individuals who are separate from their function. In the historical genesis that I am going to present in a very summary way, you will see a most interesting period in which the venality of offices [produced] a very ambiguous situation. An English historian has shown how until the nineteenth century in England this dissociation between functionary and function had not yet been completely effected, that the functionary still performed a function with the (accepted) idea of enriching himself on the back of his function.[18] These mechanisms are independent of individuals. Napoleon, paradoxically, who was so personal, so little bureaucratic (the very type of the charismatic character), so extra-ordinary, tried to reduce the role of personality so that it was abolished in the function, in the automatisms, in the autonomous logic of the bureaucratic function. That is Weberian or Kantian: you cannot base an order on the affective dispositions of the individual, a rational morality or policy on dispositions that are basically fluctuating. In order to have regularity, repetition, you have to establish automatisms, bureaucratic functions.

Genesis of the state. Difficulties of the undertaking

Having said, about the two meanings of the word state, that in my view the state as the set of social agents unified and subject to the same sovereignty is the product of the set of agents commissioned to exercise sovereignty, and not the other way round, I would like to try and verify the proposition that it is the constitution of bureaucratic instances that are autonomous in relation to family, religion and economy that is the condition for the appearance of what is called the nation-state, starting from the process by which this constitution is gradually effected. How is such a legal fiction constructed, consisting essentially of words, modes of organization, etc.?

A certain number of agents who have made the state, and have made themselves into state agents by making the state, have had to make the state in order to make themselves into holders of a state power. There are people who have been partly connected with the state from the start. How do we go about describing this genesis? On this point, I am to some degree a victim of my culture. Because I know that this is a rather crazy project, which has been attempted a number of times in the course of history and often failed, it is quite frightening to embark on it, and I hesitated a good deal before presenting it to you. So that you will make allowances for me, I will show you how dangerous it is by demonstrating how previous attempts have, in my view, run aground. I shall give you weapons against me; but at the same time, by showing how difficult it is, I shall make you far more indulgent than you would be if you did not know this.

How do you give a historical genealogy of the thing that we call the state? What method should be used? If you turn towards what is called comparative history or comparative sociology, you are immediately faced with terrible problems: what is there in common between the military state in Peru, the Aztec state, the Egyptian empire, the Chinese Han empire and the Japanese state after the Meiji restoration? You are already faced with a monstrous undertaking, disproportionate and discouraging. Yet there are many people who have tackled it. I shall mention some important efforts, partly just to set myself at ease with my conscience . . .

Parenthesis on the teaching of research in sociology

The official definition of my role here authorizes and forces me to present my own intellectual productions, [. . .] to be original, even prophetic, whereas the ordinary definition of the professorial function is very different: it requires the professor to be the agent of the institution and convey established knowledge, canonical knowledge, to explain work already done instead of relating work that is both personal and still under way, that is, uncertain. This ambiguity is particularly pronounced in a discipline such as sociology. According to the position of the science in question in the hierarchy of their degree of officialness, of recognized universality – with mathematics at the top and sociology at the bottom – the situation I am now describing takes on a completely different meaning. By giving you the elements to analyse it, I am also giving you elements to objectify what I am doing, but also to understand better the difficulties that I feel, and thus to share them with you. What I say here challenges the very status of scientific-type discourse on the social world. If officialness, universality in the limits of a social universe, is only granted so grudgingly to sociology, this is also because it makes a demonic claim quite analogous to that of the state, that of constructing the true view of the social world, more true than the official one. It is in competition with the official construction of the state, even if it says what the state says, even if it says that the state speaks the official truth and thereby finds itself in the position of meta-state, something that is not envisaged by the state. The sociologist does something analogous to the *coup de force* that creates the state by appropriating the monopoly of the construction of legitimate representation of the social world, that is, by tacitly dispossessing each of the social agents of [. . . their] claim to construct a personal representation of the state, by claiming to speak the truth about the social world. The state says, on the question of housing, 'here is the truth', and relegates partial views to the status of interests that are particular, conflict-bound and local.

A very fine text of Durkheim identifies the sociologist with the state.[19] He says that fundamentally the sociologist does something that Spinoza calls 'knowledge of the second kind': he produces a truth freed from the lack bound up with particularity. Each agent has a particular truth (according to Spinoza, error is a lack), and social agents have private truths, that is, errors. The sociologist, Durkheim says, is the person able to place himself at the point from which particular truths appear as particular, and he is therefore able to utter the truth of particular truths, which is truth pure and simple. By doing this, the sociologist is close to the state; and it is not by chance that Durkheim's view was that the sociologist is spontaneously an agent of the state. He is the person who places this de-particularized knowledge at the service of the state, whose function is to produce official, that is, de-particularized, truths.

The state and the sociologist

How then does the sociologist obtain the concrete means to escape relativization? How can he produce a non-relativizable point of view on the genesis of a point of view that lays claims to non-relativization? How can the sociologist arrive at a scientific theory, claiming universal recognition, of the process by which an instance is constituted that claims to have a universal view and generally distributes degrees of legitimacy in the claim to speak the universal? The state also establishes the professorial chairs at the Collège de France; the state distributes degrees of claim . . . The problem of the degree of scientificity of the various sciences – the social sciences and the natural sciences – is [often] presented in a very naive manner. I shall now try and formulate it along the lines of what I have just been saying.

A conventional way of tackling the problem of the state is to give a definition of the state in terms of function – a definition that may be Marxist. Another conventional approach is to say: 'As a historian of the Middle Ages, I say that in the twelfth century wars played a pre-eminent role in the construction of the state by introducing Roman law, etc . . .' These ambitions are socially recognized as legitimate. The sociologist, for social and historical reasons, is faced with a very difficult situation. If he takes his role seriously, he cannot be content with either one or the other, that is, he can neither propose grand definitions, universal but almost empty, of the type: 'The function of the state is to reproduce the conditions of reproduction of economic capital or profit', nor can he, without abdicating his specific role, be content with simply recording propositions about the state that are partial and circumscribed. He is condemned therefore to rather crazy attempts of two kinds: either he can try to construct contemporary empirical objects in such a way as to try to find the state under his scalpel, that is, construct observable historical objects in such a way that, in the particular case in question, he can hope to find universal mechanisms to which the notion of state is attached (that is perhaps the example of Gusfield, who studies something that looks trivial, but in which something very fundamental is involved; that may be what I tried to do in my analysis of the Barre commission that I explained to you); or he can embark on a rather crazy undertaking, which a certain number of [thinkers] have attempted, which is to produce a general theory of the state based on comparing a large number of historical trajectories of the state.

The danger, as has been said of Perry Anderson, an English Francophile and Althusserian, who undertook a grand history of the genesis of the modern state, is to end up proposing no more than a pretentious redefinition of what historians have already said, on the basis of historical propositions taken second-hand.[20] One can also criticize the position taken by a very great sociologist, Reinhard Bendix,[21] who gave the most radical formulation of scepticism [towards] all universal propositions about the state, in particular all tendential laws of the kind of 'Elias's law' on the civilizing process,[22] 'Weber's law' on the process of rationalization,[23] etc. He systematically challenged the possibility of generalizing on the basis of a historical sociology that was very popular in the 1970s in the United States. There was then a whole group of young sociologists who defined themselves against the dominant 'establishment' of the time and insisted on the use of quantification. They worked for the most part on the present time, in pure synchrony, with statistical methods. In reaction against this, there were young sociologists among whom Theda Skocpol was particularly prominent; her book *States and Social Revolutions*[24] was important in drawing attention to new ways of doing sociology.

I embarked on the question of the position of the sociologist because I wanted to escape from the prophetic role of the sociologist and move towards the priestly role, which is more restful for the *auctor* in question, and so that you do not feel I am imposing on you the monopoly of symbolic violence that has been conferred on me. In the same way as the state usurps the power of constructing social reality that belongs to every citizen, a professor is invested with a kind of provisional monopoly that lasts for two hours each week, the monopoly of social construction of reality. This is a difficult psychological situation. In explaining Gusfield's book I was satisfying myself, but I would not want to give you the impression of only hearing some Bourdieu, even if in principle that is what I am here for. Skocpol's book was very important because it showed the possibility of doing sociology by drawing on other kinds of facts, facts that are not quantified but constructed differently. Her second intention was to show that it was possible – in the native language – to do empirical macrosociology.

The opposition between macrosociology and microsociology, borrowed from economics, is a fictional opposition, but it has a considerable social force, existing both in minds and in reality, and is in my view one of the great obstacles to scientific work. People generally say: 'Yes, macrosociology is all very well, but it's speculation, theory, it doesn't have any empirical foundation . . .' The researchers I mentioned showed that it is possible to do macrosociology based on data of a new type, those given by the historical tradition when comparative method is applied to it. The limitations of this current are due to the fact that it partly originated from false problems generated by the social divisions of the American scientific field, which were converted into mental divisions and false problems. Which does not mean that what they have done is not interesting.

For Bendix, there was no question of establishing general tendential laws, which are often projections of the researcher's unconscious, the problem of the state being one of the major areas of this projective temptation; one of the places where the function of certain subjects as projective tests is most clearly visible. This is very clear in the Marxist tradition. It is a terrain on which it is hard to establish the constraints of empirical validation, and on which the most blatant naiveties of the authors' social unconscious can find expression. Bendix took it as his task to explain the divergent responses to similar problems in different historical circumstances, while rescuing the sense of historical particularity. This remained in an American context, as is very clear with structural-functionalists such as [Shmuel] Eisenstadt, who believe societies confront universal problems that can be listed. That is typical of Parsons, for whom there are a certain number of questions that all societies face, with the role of comparative history being to list the responses that different societies, at different historical moments, have given to this universal problem, with a sense of historical particularity, that is, avoiding wild generalizations.[25] More generally, attempts at comparative history have also been criticized for juxtaposing two forms of uninteresting propositions: on the one hand, general laws that are completely empty, empty macrosociological laws, universal because empty, of the kind: 'Everywhere there are dominant and dominated', laws that are one of the sources of certain ideological debates; and on the other hand, propositions that bear on historical singularities, without the linkage between the two ever being made. What the majority of books I shall be speaking to you about have been criticized for is stripping these tendential laws of particular historical references.

They are criticized for what a great historian of science, Holton, called 'adhoc-ism':[26] inventing explanatory propositions as a function of what there is to explain, finding ad hoc explanations, which is all the more tempting and easy as far as historical comparison is concerned, since the outcome of this history is known. What is very likely the cause of the subsequent situation is isolated in the antecedent situation. Some authors, in particular Barrington Moore,[27] have tried to combat this danger of assuming causes on the basis of known effects by using the comparative method as an antidote to the temptation of drawing a general law from a particular case. He says for example that with a knowledge of American history, one is tempted to say that a situation in which a country has two parts, one based on a big agrarian nobility with a slave base and the other on a modern industrial bourgeoisie whose power is based on free labour, will lead to civil war. One need only think of Germany in the late nineteenth century, its Junkers whose power relied on the use of a quasi-servile labour being confronted by a bourgeoisie, to see that the structure here was different. Against this temptation of 'adhoc-ism' and ex post lucidity, comparative history – and this is one of its virtues – provides counterpropositions and forces a real consideration of the particular case in its individuality, which is one of the imperatives of the scientific method.

Another important argument developed by researchers is the idea that each historical series is unique. If you want to compare the English state, the Japanese state and the French state (as I shall try to do within the limits of my knowledge), you are tempted to say that, because the founding agents of these three states were literati, clerks, you are dealing with a state bureaucracy whose capital has a cultural component. This objection is hard to overcome. It consists in saying that since history is linear, the point of departure in a certain sense governs the whole succession. This is something that historians have an intuition of, and in the name of which they refuse to offer generalities in the manner of sociologists, whom they criticize for making use of the laborious, serious and erudite work of historians in order to put forward general and empty propositions. Historians may well use this argument, but I believe that it would make life difficult in their own work. That is why they have never formulated it explicitly.

I shall use an analogy to help you understand. There is an analogy between the history of a state, in both senses of the word, and that of an individual. [Concerning the] genesis of a habitus, initial experiences cannot be placed on the same level as later experiences, inasmuch as they have a structuring effect and are the basis from which all other experiences are thought, constituted, conceived, legitimized. The logic of precedence is used not only in law, but also in politics. To have the official on your side, to have right on your side, is often to say, for example: 'I am only doing what De Gaulle did in 1940 . . .' Certain historical bifurcations can be treated as relatively irreversible. By the same token, you may think that there is a kind of accumulation in the course of history, which means that, if you compare today the mental structures of a French professor with those of an English or a German one, it is likely that you would find the whole history of the educational system, and through this, of the French state from the twelfth century on. Think of what Durkheim did in his famous book *L'Évolution pedagogique en France*.[28] In order to understand the educational system today, he was obliged to go back to the twelfth century, back to the hierarchy of faculties. In my book *Homo Academicus*, I showed that the mental faculties of professors in different faculties are structured following the division of faculties as institutions, a division that has been established over the centuries. In other words, the principles of division and vision of the world associated with different disciplines are themselves associated with the history – in large part contingent – of the teaching institution, itself associated with the history of the process of state formation.

This is more or less the argument I wanted to give by way of warning before going on to speak to you of the attempts of three authors: Barrington Moore in *The Social Origins of Dictatorship and Democracy*, Eisenstadt in *The Political Systems of Empires* and Perry Anderson in his two books *Passages from Antiquity to Feudalism* and *Lineages of the Absolutist State*.[29] I shall try to give you the broad outlines of these books, which are enormous volumes, with two objectives. On the one hand, to try and see what they each contribute as instruments in providing a historical genesis of the state, and on the other hand, what lessons may be drawn from their errors, and from their failings from the methodological point of view.

Lecture of 1 February 1990

The rhetoric of the official – The public and the official – The universal other and censorship – The 'legislator as artist' – The genesis of public discourse – Public discourse and the imposition of form – Public opinion

The rhetoric of the official

I want to go over again here, in a deeper and more systematic way, what I sketched out in the last lecture. The title for what I am going to propose to you could be 'the rhetoric of the official'. I shall try to bring together, if not in a systematic form then at least as coherently as possible, a series of reflections that I have been offering you for several years now, starting from law, proceeding by way of analysis of the pious hypocrisy of law, then by way of analysis of disinterestedness, etc., and I ended up last time with a series of reflections that must have appeared to you disjointed – which indeed they were both objectively and subjectively. I want to take up again the analysis of the official that I sketched out in the last lecture, around the notion of commission, the idea of the mandated agent, in which a commission of this kind, by its very existence, raises the question of those who appoint it. In its original use, in English, the word 'commission' meant a mandate: to have a commission meant being mandated to do a certain thing. The question, therefore, is to know who commissions the members of a commission. Whose mandataries are they? And isn't it part of their action to theatricalize the origin of their mandate, to make people believe in the existence of a mandate that is not just self-proclaimed? One of the problems of members of commissions, whoever they are, is to convince themselves that they are speaking not just for themselves, but in the name of a higher instance that has to be defined and brought into existence. The question I should like to raise today is: whose spokesperson is the mandatory? If we are talking about a commission charged with reforming support for housing, people will say: this commission is mandated by the state, and the regression back to the principals stops there. Basically, all the work I am doing with you here consists in going back beyond the state. What is this reality in the name of which those who speak *ex officio* officiate? What is the reality in the name of which those who have an *officium* speak in the name of the state? And what therefore is this reality that those who speak *ex officio*, that is, officially, bring into existence by the fact of speaking, or that they must bring into existence for their speech to be official?

You might think this is just playing with words, but I justify this manner of proceeding by the fact that a certain analysis of language is essential inasmuch as language is the depositary of a whole social philosophy that has to be recovered. I always cite as example, to justify this way of pro-ceeding, Benveniste's magnificent work *Le Vocabulaire des institutions indo-européennes*,[1] in which he reveals, from analysis of the original forms of Indo-European languages, the political philosophy of the language that is inscribed in them. I think that Benveniste wrote on the one hand, as a linguist, an explicit theory of the performative, while on the other hand he presented an entire reflection on the implicit philosophy of the discourse of authority that is contained in Indo-European legal language. I think that the theory he revealed from what is implicit in the Indo-European vocabu-lary is far stronger and more interesting than that which he revealed simply as a linguist (albeit a very competent one, and basing himself on the whole linguistic tradition of Austin).[2] I think that this work has nothing in common with traditional philosophical word play in the manner of Alain or Heidegger, which consists in making words do things, and I believe that what I am going to do is not of this type.

I shall try and reflect, therefore, on those social agents who speak in the name of the social whole, whom Max Weber somewhere calls 'ethical prophets' or 'law prophets',[3] that is, the founders of a discourse designed to be unanimously recognized as the unanimous expression of the unani-mous group. Among these legal prophets, the Kabyle sage, the *amusnaw*, is the person who speaks in difficult situations. He is often a poet, and expresses himself in a language that we would call poetic. He is mandated, either tacitly or explicitly, to tell the group what the group thinks, and to do so in difficult situations when the group no longer knows what to think; he is the person who thinks even when the group no longer knows what to think. The work of the poet, who is the man of extreme situations, situations of conflict, tragic situations in which everyone is both right and wrong, is to reconcile the group with its official image, especially when the group is obliged to transgress this official image. In the case of a moral antinomy, moral conflicts over ultimate values, the sage or poet refers to authorities, and one of the rhetorical procedures he employs – exactly as politicians do – is prosopopoeia, a rhetorical figure that consists in speaking in the place of an absent person or an object, and in the name of something that can be a person, ancestors, the lineage, the people, public opinion. He speaks then in the name of an ensemble that is made to exist by the fact of speaking in its name. Prosopopoeia can be institutionalized when the spokesperson is mandated to voice this trans-personal speech.

Think for example of De Gaulle saying 'France believes' to mean 'I believe
...' Someone who took himself for De Gaulle and said 'France believes'
would obviously be seen as mad, whereas someone who speaks *ex officio*
in the name of France is seen as normal, even if people find it a little bit
excessive. The ethical prophets are interesting because they bring about a
reappearance of what is taken for granted in the case of the routine legitimate spokesperson. The president of the republic constantly speaks as
an institution embodying a collectivity that is reconciled in him. He may
sometimes say: 'I am president of all the French people', but normally
he does not have to say this. When he receives congratulations from the
constitutional bodies, it is France and not he who receives the congratulations of these bodies that are constitutive of France; even the opposition
is there to acknowledge the transcendence of this biological person who is
in reality an institution.

Why do we need to go back to original situations, that of the Kabyle
amusnaw, that of the juridical creator or, that of the beginnings of the
state, with the canon lawyers of the twelfth century who invented the
modern state, all these things that have become self-evident and commonplace in our minds? Because it is in these circumstances that the questions 'who is speaking?', 'what is he speaking about?', 'in whose name
is he speaking?' are posed, while the rhetoric that is also present in the
congratulations of the constitutional bodies is far more obvious: the functions it fulfils are visible and declared. One of the virtues of beginnings
– Lévi-Strauss speaks in *Tristes tropiques*[4] of the 'grandeur inseparable
from beginnings' – is that they are theoretically interesting because what
will become taken-for-granted, and will therefore be destroyed in the
invisibility of this taken-for-granted, is still conscious, still visible – often
dramatically visible. The *amusnaw*, or the ethical prophet, is the person
who, in Mallarmé's verse (quoted in dissertations to the point of having
become completely trite), 'gives a purer sense to the words of the tribe',
that is, the person who will speak to the tribe using the words in which
the tribe ordinarily utters its highest values, but effecting a poetic work on
these words. This work on form is necessary in order for these words to
regain their original meaning – often the role of the *amusnaw* is to return to
the sources, to what is pure, as opposed to the routinized, the corrupted –
or to reveal an unheeded meaning, obscured by ordinary language, which
makes it possible to conceive an extraordinary situation. In analysing, for
example, the great pre-Socratics, people like Enpedocles – I have in mind
Jean Bollack's book[5] – or the poets of pre-literate societies, it is often
noticeable how poets are people who invent within certain limits; they take
up a well-known proverb and make it undergo a minuscule alteration that
changes its meaning completely, which means that they [combine] the benefits of conformity to the official with those of transgression. There is the
famous case cited by Bollack of a verse of Homer's that contains the word
phos, which generally means 'light', but which has a very rare secondary
meaning in which *phos* means 'man'. So the verse that everyone knows

is cited, in its ordinary form, but giving it a little alteration – which may be a difference of accent or pronunciation – and the commonplace and routinized ordinary expression is 'debanalized' and reactivated, though the ordinary meaning remains present. You have, at the level of form, the exact equivalent of what is required at the level of function: a conforming transgression, a transgression within the proper forms. This requires a mastery of language. Jurists are masters of language.

I do not want to go too fast, as afterwards I criticize myself for such telescoping – I think things are clearer in my head than in what I say – but I want to turn to something that is important, a remark by Kantorowicz in a very fine text, 'The sovereignty of the artist'.[6] Kantorowicz sees the legislator as close to the poet, though he does not make too much of this. He carries out a similar work on history to that which Benveniste does on language, discovering a deep philosophical truth in the juridical act, but without exploiting this completely. I think that to understand fully what Kantorowicz tells us, it is necessary to do the work, slowly and carefully, of deepening what is implicit in the notion of official. I shall return to this later, so as not to jump too quickly from one theme to another.

The prophet catches the group in its own trap. He invokes the collective ideal that tells the group the best of what the group thinks of itself: basically he expresses the collective morality. We have again here the notion of the pious hypocrisy of the supreme juridical bodies of the state, such as the Conseil d'État. The logic of pious hypocrisy consists in taking people at their word, at their grand words. The ethical mandatories act as persons to whom the group delegates the utterance of the 'must-be' that the group is obliged to recognize because it recognizes itself in this official truth. The Kabyle *amusnaw* is the person who embodies the values of honour, which are the official values, to the highest degree. Making fun of bourgeois idealism, Marx speaks in his 'Contribution to the critique of Hegel's Philosophy of Right' [1843] of the 'spiritualist point of honour'. The point of honour is typically what is involved when people recognize the official: it is the disposition to recognize what has to be recognized when one is before other people, facing other people. This is why 'losing face' is such an important notion in this logic – viz. the logic, in many civilizations, of 'in front of' and 'behind', 'what one shows when facing people' and 'what one hides'. The *amusnaw*, as embodiment of honour, is the person who recalls that the values of honour are indispensable, and [at the same time] that in certain tragic situations they can be superseded in the name of honour itself – I refer you to a dialogue I had with Mammeri, published in *Actes de la Recherche en Sciences Sociales*;[7] he enables the group to transgress its official ideals without denying them, saving what is essential, the *obsequium*, that is, the recognition of ultimate values. He requires the group to bring itself to order, to save the rules precisely in the case of their transgression. We find here one of the foundations of the notion of legitimacy. People very often confuse legitimacy with legality. Weber made the point that the thief recognizes legitimacy by concealing himself in order to steal. This opposition between public and private is found again here; in concealed transgression there is a recognition of public values. This is basically the key idea.

The official, therefore, is the public. It is the idea that the group has of itself, and the idea that it wants to give of itself, the representation (in the sense of mental image but also of theatrical performance) that it wants to give of itself when it presents itself as a group. One might say 'before other groups', but not necessarily: before itself as a group. All the mirror effects have to be taken into account here. In other words, the idea that it wants to give of itself in public representation: you see here the link between the official and the theatre, theatricalization, with the official being the visible, the public, the theatrical – the *theatrum*, that which is seen, which is given as a spectacle. It is therefore the idea that the group wants to have and give of itself before itself as other. This has the air of metaphysical speculation, but you will see that an entire analysis is needed of the mirror and the role of the spectacle in the mirror as realization of the official.

The public and the official

We need to deepen here the opposition between public and private. The word 'public' has many meanings. I stumbled on these themes when commenting on a text of d'Aguesseau,[8] who was one of the great founders of the modern juridical and state order in France, in which, in a completely unconscious way, he played with three or four different meanings of the word 'public'. I shall focus on two of these for the purpose of my demonstration. The public is first of all that which is opposed to the particular, the singular, the *idios* of the Greeks, that which is unique in the sense of 'idiot', 'lacking common sense', 'special', 'particular', 'personal'; a private opinion is a singular opinion. The private is also what is independent of the collective, and public actions, in the original sense, are attributed to agents who 'speak for'; they are actions or thoughts that are attributed to representative representatives of the group, the collectivity, those who are called 'official personalities', who act officially. For example, when an official wants to make the point that he is no longer being official, he says he is speaking 'in a private capacity'. The property that is key to all the acts of an official personage is then put in parentheses, the property that he always commits more than just himself. So much so that when he wants to commit only himself, he is obliged to suspend this particular property. A consideration of political scandal would be needed here, but I don't want to go off on a tangent and lose your attention; political scandal owes its dramatic aspect to the fact that it plays on this property of the official person who has to act officially, and when he publicly shows himself or is revealed to have made a private appropriation of his public personage, that is patrimonialism, nepotism, one or other form of misappropriation of the collective symbolic capital to the benefit of the private individual.

It is clear that the imperative division between public and private, official and unofficial, public and hidden or secret, is imposed on public men to the greatest degree. 'Waffle' goes with the territory; it is what makes it possible for public men to field questions on private life. Is it possible to make confidences in public?

The public is thus opposed to the particular, to the singular. Secondly, it is opposed to the concealed, the invisible. To speak in public, to do something in public, means to do so in a visible manner, ostensibly, even ostentatiously, without hiding anything, without leaving anything behind the scenes. Once again, the theatrical analogy is apt: the public is what takes place on stage. Hence the essential link between the public, the official, and the theatrical. Private acts are invisible, they take place behind the scenes, backstage; the public, on the contrary, is conducted in view of everyone, before a universal audience, in which it is not possible to select, or to make an aside and say: 'I'm talking to you in confidence' – it is immediately heard by everyone. An effect of radio and television is that confidences are made before millions of people. You can't select people in the audience, and this universal audience means that official statements are *omnibus* statements, intended for everyone, and for no one in particular. I believe that the anxiety theatrical situations create (stage fright) is due to this confrontation with a universal public to whom it is impossible to say anything concealed or inadmissible. It is clear here that you can never be quite sure of not saying what must not be said in public, hence the constant danger of a lapsus, a gaffe, a lack of proper behaviour, a Dostoyevskian fault. People who give public lectures suffer from stage fright. It is impossible to exclude witnesses, and basically the official situation is the opposite of the situation of the invisible man.

Thought experiment is an important instrument of understanding and knowledge, for breaking with what is self-evident and is taken for granted. There is a splendid thought experiment on the problem I am dealing with here in Plato's *Republic*, with the myth of Gyges' ring, the story of a shepherd who finds a ring by chance, puts it on his finger, turns the signet and becomes invisible, seduces the queen and becomes king. The philosophy of this myth raises the question of private morality. Can there be a non-public morality, not subject to publicity, to actual or potential publication, that is, to public revelation, to denunciation, to bringing to light what is hidden? Gyges' ring is to morality what the evil demon is to the theory of knowledge. Official announcement would be to morality what the evil demon is to knowledge . . .[9] Could there be a morality for an invisible man, that is, a man protected from publication, from becoming public, from being revealed to all, before the tribunal of public opinion? In other words, is there not an essential link between visibility and morality? The problem comes up again in the especially demanding morality imposed on people whose job it is to be visible embodiments of the morality and officialness of the group.[10] We feel that the politician who transgresses the values of disinterestedness betrays a kind of tacit contract, that of the official: I am official, and so I must conform to the official. Political delegation involves a kind of tacit contract that lies at the root of the sense of scandal provoked by the publication of private interests – interests of a bureaucracy, of a party, of currents of thought – dissimulated beneath the professions of faith, universal and disinterested, that are constitutive of the role. If politicians make professions of disinterested faith, this is not from faith, but because they are constitutive of the role, constitutive of the official; they cannot do otherwise, it is constitutive of the fact of their being mandated.

If the distinction between private and public is of this kind, if the private is both that which is singular and that which is concealed or capable of being concealed, then the official effect necessarily involves an effect of universalization, moralization, and here we can take up all the analyses that Goffman makes of the presentation of self and the behaviour of social agents in public.[11] I mentioned to you last time the magnificent example that Goffman gives of waiters in a restaurant who, when they pass through the swing door, change their posture, adjust their jacket, hold themselves straight and put their napkin correctly over their arm. As the saying goes, 'it's no longer the same person'. They change, and this kind of change, which corresponds to the boundary between the public and the private, is the entrance onto the stage. These things may be insignificant, but at the root of them is the correctness that self-presentation in public demands. A whole analysis could be done on confidentiality or confession, and official or public discourse. There are magazines, often designed for women, that specialize in this: confidence is typically a private language for a private person, intimate and rather feminine (the division of labour between the sexes is closely bound up with the opposition between public and private). Women are on the side of the intimate, the private, confession, it is they who are entitled to confidences. Confidence is therefore on the side of the private, in contrast with official discourse, that is, acts performed in the name of the group and in the eyes of the group. There is in fact a word to denote the person who makes confidences in public: he is an 'exhibitionist'. He shows publicly what is supposed to be concealed. The scandal of Rousseau's *Confessions* was that this role was not established, hence the sense of transgression. (Today, the right to narcissism is one of the professional properties of all artists. On [the radio channel] France-Culture you hear legitimate narcissistic professions of faith; if you don't talk about your mum and dad, you haven't done your job as a writer . . .)

This opposition between confidence and official discourse is bound up with a whole series of oppositions that lie at the heart of the mental structures of most societies, Kabyle society in particular: inside/outside, private/public, house (female)/marketplace, assembly or *agora* (male); female/male; the biological or natural that is reserved for the home (where children are made, cooking done, etc.)/culture; facing people, holding your ground with a certain stance – there is a very fine article by Goffman on stance, 'knowing how to carry yourself'[12] – the front/the back – this great opposition lies at the root of the deepest representations we can have about the sexual division and homosexuality; between economics and honour, which is a very important opposition, as it is by way of this that you get the identification of the official with disinterestedness.[13] The case of Kabylia is interesting, because things are said there in a more explicit fashion: economics in the strict sense, that is, the sense in which we understand it, contracts, repayments, etc., is only proper between women. A man of honour does not say: 'I'll lend you an ox until autumn'; he says: 'I'll lend you an ox', whereas women are reputedly [thrifty], clearly in the view of men, who have the official Kabyle philosophy in which the good side is always the public, male side, the other side being wretched and shameful. The male view of the female economy, that is, our economy, is one of disgust – it's alright for women, as they call a spade a spade. The woman says: 'I'm lending you, so you give it back', whereas the man of honour says: 'I'm lending you something, I know that you are a man of honour and so you will give it back, and as I only lend to a man of honour, I am sure that you'll give it back.' So that goes without saying. You may think this is something very archaic, but if you reflect on it, you will see that in our own society – think of the division of labour between the sexes in your own household – in awkward situations, the man gets his wife to say what he cannot say himself, discreetly reminding his friends of the repayment date: 'My wife is getting impatient . . .'

[Break in the lecture]

Women are on the side of the contract economy, of an economy that does not deny its nature. Men also do economic transactions, of course, make gifts for example, but these are denied in the Freudian sense: I make exchanges as if I was not making them. The exchange of gifts is advantageous to both parties, but this is concealed, disguised as an act of generous exchange; mutual advantage is to the exchange of gifts what the real economy is to the ideal official economy. I believe that one of the universal properties of all societies is that the economic economy is never really acknowledged. Even today, the most capitalist capitalists always have a collection of paintings (this is simplistic, but I could develop it), or else they set up a foundation and are patrons . . . Historically, societies (it is ridiculous put like that, but this is in order to proceed quickly) have found it very hard to admit that they had an economy, because this is one of the shameful things. The discovery of the economy as economy was difficult to make. 'In business, feelings don't come into it.' 'Business is business.' These tautologies were extremely difficult discoveries, since they run counter to the official image of disinterestedness, generosity and gratuitousness that societies, and the dominant within these societies, that is, men, wanted to have. Within these universes of opposition, you can see outlined the link between the official and the disinterested. What I said last year on disinterestedness will be more coherent in the analysis I am giving now.[14]

This series of oppositions defines a fundamental opposition, between

UNIVERSITY OF WINCHESTER
LIBRARY

the private universe, that of impulses, nature, spontaneity, and the universe of the public, of manners, bearing, morality, asceticism. In Durkheim's *Elementary Forms of Religious Life* there is an astonishing passage – God knows that he cannot be suspected of a naive or naively relativist universalism – in which he says that if there is one thing that is universal, it is the fact that culture is always associated with the idea of asceticism.[15] As Durkheim was a professor under the Third Republic, with his little beard and his intention of honouring a secular morality, you may think this is a nice ethical anachronism. I believe that he was right. This opposition between nature and culture, between spontaneity and proper form, is fundamentally the Freudian opposition between the id and the superego; and in fact the public, this kind of anonymous character within which one cannot arbitrarily decide who has the right to hear and who does not, is a universal public, that is, a public before whom a whole lot of things are censored. In the nineteenth century, people said: 'not in front of women and children'. The official excludes barrack-room jokes, that is, jokes intended for a group made up solely of men, for example soldiers released from naive moral censorship. The opposition between the id and the superego is in full vigour here, that is, the basis of the Freudian theory of the superego and censorship. The point I intended to reach here is of course that the official is censorship.[16]

The universal other and censorship

Censorship is something that is at the same time imposed from outside (by way of sanctions) and internalized in the form of the superego. There is a famous expression of George Herbert Mead, an American psychosociologist and a major thinker, who talks of a 'generalized other'.[17] In certain situations we are dealing with a kind of generalized other, a universal other. This is what I shall now try to develop.

Censorship of the moral kind, which Gyges' invisibility makes it possible to escape, is not only fear of the policeman, it is something far deeper, the kind of universal eye constituted by the world of all social agents, which brings to bear on an action the judgement implied by recognition of the most universal values in which the group recognizes itself. The kind of terror that public appearance arouses, on television for example, is bound up with confrontation not with a universal other, but with a kind of universal alter ego that is a kind of generalized superego, a universal alter ego formed by everyone who acknowledges the same universal values, that is, values that cannot be denied without denying oneself, since one identifies oneself with the universal by affirming oneself as a member of this community that acknowledges the universal, the community of men who are really men. This is a point that I shall naturally come back to.

There is always something implicit in these invocations of the universal: the Kabyles are thinking of men of honour when they say 'universal';

the Kanaks think of men who are really men, as opposed to non-men, who begin with the neighbouring tribe, or women.[18] This universal is always particular. I will quote to you [later on] a splendid sentence from Mackinnon, an English nineteenth-century writer on public opinion, who gives in a naive manner – no one would dare to speak like this nowadays, but everyone feels like this when they are confronted with the universal public – the content of this universal audience that exerts a function of censorship on the speaker who speaks publicly in the name of the official.[19]

(All this is by way of reminder. I have analysed hypocrisy at length as a homage that vice pays to virtue. I am afraid of always going both too fast and too slow . . . I have a problem with tempo, not because I think that what I am saying is very important, and thus deserves to be spoken slowly in the manner of philosophers who are thinking. I think that one always proceeds too quickly. And so it is not because of the importance I ascribe to what I am saying that I think I should go more slowly, it is rather because I believe I am still going too quickly for the importance of what I am trying to say. And by going too quickly there is a risk of passing too quickly over important things, of missing a bifurcation, implications. I am constantly repeating the same thing, but if there is one thing that I want to communicate, it is this kind of respect in conceiving the social. If the social is conceived so poorly, it is because the weighty and pedestrian modes of thought normally associated with the philosophical, the uttermost depth, are not applied to it. This is to justify that although I'm going slowly, I still think I'm going too fast.)

This analysis of the universal other needs further development. What exactly is this universal alter ego, an instance that I cannot revoke without denying my human quality (with the limitations I have stated), a court whose verdict I tacitly accept by the fact of addressing myself publicly, with an official function, to these people? This superego is a kind of practical embodiment of the constraining reminder of what 'must-be', something experienced in the mode of feeling, stage fright experienced in the mode of panic, timidity, intimidation, the bodily fear that is often associated with the earliest learning experiences of socialization. The relationship to the father and to this universal audience might make it possible to show the link between sociology and psychoanalysis . . . This universal other is a kind of ungraspable transcendence, the weakened form of which manifests itself to us as 'what will people say?', what Kabyles call the word of men. The man of honour is always obsessed by the word of men, what men might say. We are close here to public opinion, to 'what will people say?', to gossip, all those statements that are doubly transcendent. They have the transcendence that Sartre called the serial, an indefinite regression as practical infinity; and there is also the fact that this purely additive set of people have something in common which is that officially they always recognize the official values in the name of which they judge what I am doing.

This universal other is a kind of fantasy – we are getting close here to the state and law – that can be materialized by a public, by an audience, but it is a fantasy in which is embodied the idea of self that each singular individual seeks to give to others, for others and before others. It is not a simple, commonplace being-for-other, the gaze in Sartre's analysis, which contains a bit of truth but does not go very far. It is a *super ego*[20] constituted by the ensemble of alter egos that have the same *super ego* in common. This kind of collective *super ego*, at once transcendent and immanent, transcendent because immanent in thousands of agents, is censorship in the strong sense of the term – Freud did not develop his notion of censorship in much detail. It is clear here that there is no antimony between sociology and psychoanalysis.

The 'legislator as artist'

I shall return now to the legal prophets, and those people who perform original acts of uttering the 'must-be' that a society recognizes. Their pious hypocrisy is the recognition of everything I have just been saying. They are people who speak in the name of this generalized *super ego*, of the official, and who, by this token, can even rule on an official transgression of the official rules, since they are masters. They succeed in releasing the group from the fatality that the group is for the group, because groups are caught up in their own game. Groups constantly say that a man of honour is a truly masculine man. How can groups be released from the traps that they set for themselves, and that are constitutive of their group existence? Jurists are people who assert the official even in those extreme cases when the official must be officially transgressed. The extreme case is particularly interesting.

The sociologist finds himself in a difficult position in this game. What is he doing? Is he not himself in an official position? Is he not speaking officially about the official? Is he not exposed to tacitly accepting the implications of the official? He places himself somewhat outside the game; he is not the Kabyle *amusnaw*, or the wise man on the commission of wise men, that is, someone explicitly mandated by a bureaucratic society. He is self-mandated by his specific competence, known and acknowledged, in saying things that are hard to think. The sociologist does something that is both disappointing and disturbing. Instead of doing this work with the official, he states what is involved in doing the official work – he is '*meta-meta*'. If it is true that the state is *meta*, then the sociologist is always a step beyond. This means that he is very irritating, and people always want to say to him, 'and what about you . . .?' He is 'beyond the beyond', as Achille Talon puts it;[21] he doesn't act the wise man, he says what those who do act the wise man are doing. Which is perhaps a kind of wisdom.

To come back now to Kantorowicz. In his article 'The sovereignty of the artist', Kantorowicz speaks of the legislator as an artist able to make something out of nothing. Drawing on Renaissance texts, he says that the poet and the jurist have a comparable function in that they both seek to imitate nature thanks to their specific genius and inspiration. The difference between them is that the legislator draws his strength from divine inspiration and creates judgements and legal techniques from nothing; but in order to do so, he acts *ex officio* and not simply *ex ingenio*. The jurist is a professional officially mandated to create official fictions *ex officio*. This is a work on language that is not just playing with words. One line of research in social science consists in awakening dead meanings, killed off by what Weber calls routinization, banalization. In order to create the official, it is necessary to create the *officium*, the function on the basis of which one has the right to create the official. The state, in other words, is the place from which the official is spoken. Its word is *ex officio*, it is therefore official, public, with the right to be recognized; it cannot be disavowed by a tribunal. If it is true that the generative principle of the official is the *ex officio*, how then is the *officium* created? The description of the official, in fact, refers to the genesis of the official, of the state that has made the official. Kantorowicz worked on the jurists who stood at the origin of the official. I am simplifying, as you cannot say that it was the jurists and canon lawyers who made the state, but they did make a great contribution to it. I believe that it is impossible to give a genealogy of Western society without bringing in the determining role of jurists brought up on Roman law, capable of producing this *fictio juris*, this legal fiction. The state is a legal fiction produced by lawyers who produced themselves as lawyers by producing the state.[22]

[Break in the lecture.]

The genesis of public discourse

To pick up the threads. I received a question: 'You located the secret of the state on the side of the public. How do you explain that?' I will not answer this [separately], as the answer will be contained in what I am about to say. I tried to analyse the opposition between the public and the private, and I will return to the problem of the genesis of a public discourse, of the social conditions in which a public discourse can be produced. But I think that in order to deal in a systematic and coherent way with the problem of the genesis and history of the state, preliminary reflections of this kind are needed, or else a very major part of the historical material is overlooked. Perhaps you think that what I am telling you is abstract and speculative. In fact, it is the precondition for concrete operations of reading documents. There are texts that I might have read without really reading them, and that today I believe I am capable of reading and will find something in them. Historical documents, like all documents, an interview, a statistical table, etc. – this is an epistemological commonplace, but it needs to be repeated here – only speak if you have questions [to put to them]. In relation to this particular object which I said was particularly difficult because it is inscribed in our heads, you have to make explicit these categories that it instils in us, simply to succeed in seeing, to be amazed by things that pass unperceived because they blind our eyes, because with mental structures that are adjusted to the structures from which the materials in question are constructed we do not even see these materials. We read them distractedly . . . Sociology is difficult because you have to have the eye. It is very hard to teach this. You can only say: 'In your position, I would have said that.' It is a trade with a very long apprenticeship. What I am trying to convey is a manner of constructing reality that makes it possible to see facts that are normally not seen. This has nothing to do with intuition, it is very slow. So much for the justification of my impatient harpings, which are as much for myself as for you.

Proceeding from this analysis, it is possible to distinguish three situations. The first is that of the law prophet, the sage, the *amusnaw* who has to win his mandate afresh each time – he has to succeed on every occasion. The prophet, as Weber says, has no guarantor beyond himself; he is not *ex officio*. If he is not up to the mark, his prophetic status collapses, whereas if the philosophy professor is not up the mark, his status sustains him, likewise the priest who does a daily miracle *ex officio*, who cannot fail to succeed. A part of the work that the prophet does, particularly poetic work on form, is designed to assert his 'commission' and have it recognized; and if he is not up to the mark, he loses his mandate. He is therefore extraordinary. He cannot do miracles every day. The law prophet is a kind of continuous creation of his own mandate.[23] He exists in Cartesian time, the time of a miracle repeated each moment. If the prophet stops creating himself as creator, he falls; he becomes just another person, even a madman, since, given that what he says is extreme, there is only a step between the discredit that destroys the madman and the respect, the aura, that surrounds the recognized prophet.

The second situation is that of jurists, legislator-poets in a position of legal prophecy, of creation. These are the English canon lawyers of the twelfth century whom Kantorowicz discusses, who were the first to put forward the theory of the state. One of Kantorowicz's historic merits is to have reconstructed the philosophy of the state that was explicit for the founders of the state, following the principle that at the beginning obscure things are visible – things that later no longer need to be said because they are taken for granted. Hence the interest of anthropology and comparative methods, Durkheim's subjects. I believe that the main interest of this research on the genesis of the state is the clarity of beginnings. At the beginning, you are still forced to say things that later go without saying because the question is no longer raised, precisely because the state has the effect of resolving the problem of the state. The state has the effect of making people believe that there is no problem of the state. Basically, that is what I have been saying all along. I'm pleased with this formula. It is what I wanted to say when I said that the state poses a particular problem for us because we have state ideas that we apply to the state.

The third situation: jurists who are still close to the *amusnaw*. You still see what they are doing, and they are themselves obliged to know this to some extent in order to do it. They are obliged to invent the notion of *fictio juris*, to theorize their own work and ask themselves: 'In whose name are we speaking? Is it God or public opinion . . .?' Jurists in a normal state situation, on the other hand, who are mandated, institutionalized, are reproducers and no longer legal creators, at most charged in certain circumstances with judging the judges, dealing with the most thorny cases, those that Alain Bancaud[24] discusses, those that raise the question of the justice of justice, those that are the site of infinite regression: there is a judgement, an appeal, then an appeal against the appeal, but there has to be an end-point . . . Either you say 'It's God', or else you say: 'There is a human court of justice that judges the legitimacy of judges.' It's with them that you find the concept of pious hypocrisy. These jurists in a normal situation, even if they ask themselves problems about justice, do not raise the actual problem of their existence as justiciaries. A whole work could be done on 'justiciaries and judges': the justiciary is the self-mandated legal prophet who imposes a new form of prophetic justice. A fine work could be carried out on the enforcer in Western movies and the official representation of justice. This character is a juridical creator of a certain type who opposes a personal and private justice to juridical common sense, and he naturally has problems with justice.

What happens in any juridical act, or any act of state foundation, is clearer in the first and second cases, that is, the case of the legal prophet and the case of jurists in a situation of legal prophecy, than it is in the third case where nothing is visible any more. Yet there are common features none the less, and if it is interesting to study the original prophetic situations, this is because they reveal things that continue to operate in the routinized cases without this being visible. If there were a difference in kind, it would no longer be interesting to study the origins because they reveal things that continue to operate but that pass unnoticed. What the legal prophets teach is that in order for legal prophecy to function it has to be self-legitimizing, and they reveal that the state is the *fictio juris* that founds all the acts of juridical creation. This is what leads to the ordinary *fictio juris* being forgotten as such. And so it is this that makes for what Max Weber called the 'routinization of (juridical) charisma',[25] making this commonplace and everyday.

We can now ask how the original or routinized jurist has to act in order to carry out this juridical creation, for his act not to be just an ordinary act among others. We see that there is a link between juridical creation and the imposition of form. I will not repeat here an analysis I have already made in another context. (Very often, in my reflections, I go back over the same points but from a higher perspective, seeing differently something different in what I had previously been able to see from a certain point of view.) I elaborated in my work on Heidegger, where I was working on the notion of censorship in a field,[26] [the idea of] the imposition of form that a scientific or philosophical field exerts; I emphasized the relationship between this censorship that a field exerts and the imposition of form that those who wish to be recognized as full members of the field carry out. If you want to be recognized as a philosopher, you must assume philosophical forms simply in order to say things – all the more so if what you say is hostile to the tacit presuppositions of the philosopher's trade. I particularly focused on Heidegger, as what he had to say was fundamentally hostile to the implicit philosophy of philosophers. In this way I established a link between censorship exerted on the scientific or philosophical field, and two operations: the imposition of form and observing the forms. I emphasized the fact that the imposition of form always involves observing the forms: the social world demands that you bring yourself into line with the official, by extending to the world under consideration the fundamental recognition of the official that consists in observing the forms, that is, not saying things bluntly, putting them into a poetic form, expressing them in a euphemistic way, as against the cacophony of the barbarian or blasphemer. Philosophical euphemism, of no matter what kind, is the result of an operation that consists in the imposition of form and, by the same token, manifesting that you respect the forms. Huizinga, in *Homo Ludens*,[27] emphasized that the cheat, like Max Weber's thief, transgresses the rule of the game while concealing himself. But there is also the spoiler who refuses to be polite, who rejects the game of the *obsequium*: it is he whom the social world completely expels. If you remember what I was saying about the sociologist, who is *meta-meta*, stating the rule of the game that consists in observing the forms, you will understand why he is often perceived as a spoiler.

Public discourse and the imposition of form

The person who expresses himself politely is the person who respects himself and who respects in himself the generalized ego that I discussed above, which translates into form by the fact that these Kabyle poets write like Mallarmé: they play on words in as complicated a way as he did, they have forms of versification that are as complicated as Mallarmé. One might ask how, in the absence of writing, it is possible to invent such complex and refined verbal forms; this presupposes a tremendous training. There are schools of poets who are often, as in Homer, smiths, *demiurgoi*. They are professionals of dodgy verbal improvisation and, contrary to accepted ideas, 'oral' and 'popular' does not mean 'simple'. These poets use complex verbal forms, archaisms, things that ordinary people no longer understand, and this enables them to speak above people's heads, to address themselves to certain individuals, as the pre-Socratics did. When Empedocles is translated by French academics who aim to translate him into Voltairean terms, not a great deal remains . . . You have the Heideggerian reading that adds meaning, and the rather positivist reading that subtracts meaning . . . Between the two, these poets are professionals of a highly regulated formalization, all the more so in that what is to be said touches on fundamental questions. The classical tragedies, those of Aeschylus or Sophocles, for example, are extremely complex discourses that theatricalize extreme situations, in which ultimate things are said in a form that everyone may hear, but that only the elect understand. One of the solutions for these public men is a double discourse on two levels: esoteric for the initiates, and exoteric for the others. The Kabyle *amusnaw*, or Empedocles, or the great pre-Socratics, were able to speak on two levels. There is an inherent polysemy – I am not speaking of postmodern polysemy – that is bound up with the contradiction of speaking publicly: how to speak before all, in the face of all, while being understood only by a few initiates?

Imposition of form is a very important property of this discourse, since it is in this way that the inexpressible, the ineffable, things that are sometimes unnameable, become nameable; it is the price to be paid in order to bring what could not be named into the realm of the potentially official. To put it another way, poetry in the strong sense, juridico-poetic creation, makes something ineffable, unsayable or implicit exist in a universally recognized form. Either something is collectively repressed, something that the group does not want to know, or something cannot be said because the group lacks the instruments to say it. Here we see the role of the prophet, which is to reveal to the group something in which the group deeply recognizes itself. It's 'you wouldn't look for me if you hadn't found me', the paradox of prophecy that at the same time can only succeed because it says what people knew, but which however succeeds because people could not say it. All the rather inflated discourses about creative poetry are not mistaken, but they bear on a quite different context. (The dissertation routine has a terrible effect, because often it manages to say true things, but in such a manner that no one can believe it any more. A very fine analysis could be made of what scholarly belief is. Is it effective? How do people believe something scholarly?)

Mallarmé developed this theme of the poet who brings something into existence by the words he pronounces. The person making such creative nominations can make things exist that should not exist, that are unnameable. For example, he can have homosexuality recognized in a society that despises it, he can make it legal, nameable, by replacing the insult 'queer' by 'homosexual'; that is a juridical work. He can make the unnameable nameable, which means that people can talk about it publicly, even on television, and individuals who were previously unnameable can be given voice. If it is possible to speak of it, this is because there are the words to say it; if there are the words to say it, this is because these individuals have been given them; if the only word was 'queer' they would be frustrated. What is involved is therefore the unnameable or the implicit, that is, things – this is an analogy I often use – that are experienced in the mode of unease, and end up being transformed into symptoms. Political work is of this kind: a group feels uneasy somewhere, for example with the social security, with its middle-ranking officials, with its petty state nobility. No one knows how to name this. Then someone succeeds in doing so, thereby carrying out an act of constitution, making exist as a symptom what previously existed simply as unease. You know what you have, and that is an enormous change, you are already half cured, you know what has to be done . . . This is what the originating poet does: he makes the group speak better than the group can do itself, and yet he does no more than say what the group would say if it were able to speak. He is involved in a very subtle game, he cannot allow himself to say 'Queers forever!'; if he is not ready to be followed, he might be lynched or treated as mad. His discourse is avant-garde, and so rather solitary, but ready to be followed because he provokes an effect of revelation; he reveals to the group things that the group did not know or did not want to know – in the sense that people say: 'I know this, but I don't want to know it.' The censored, the denied, is what I do not want to know. He says something that no one wants to know, yet without provoking scandal in everyone's face. Someone who respects himself cannot say things that would make him lose his self-respect in the company of people who respect him and who respect in him what should be respected. For example, you don't go to see a porn film with your son . . . This reflects on the official . . . The work of euphemizing consists in transgressing a fundamental taboo, that of saying publicly, and saying without arousing scandal, something that was previously inexpressible in both senses of the term.

The prophet is the person who says in the place of the group what the group cannot or will not say, and who mandates himself while not arousing scandal by the fact of saying things that the group previously did not or could not say. By the same token, the prophetic word is the archetype of correct speech, conforming in its forms to the requirements of the group, formally respecting the group's formal demands. A common-sense proverb, something consensual, is given a slight alteration, which is in no way heretical, it's not a black mass, mass upside down, this being the absolute opposite of regulated transgression. The *amusnaw* is a transgressor respectful of those he respects, and the imposition of form shows that he respects himself to the point of still respecting the rules in the inevitable transgression of the rules that the harshness of life, the necessities of existence, the wretchedness of women's condition, human weakness, etc. impose on him. He is therefore the spokesperson of the group, who gives the group what the group asks of him, and in exchange the group gives him what he asks: the permission, the mandate, to speak, and this mandate is negotiated. People forget that these archaic poets were always face to face with their audience; they did not write in the security given by a sheet of paper . . . In the 1960s, everyone transgressed, that was the fashion, but in the solitude of their study. This was comic: imagine what would have happened if that *homo academicus* had to say such things publicly. Whereas the Homeric poet or the *amusnaw* were people who had to carry out things *in presentia*.

In order to produce this catalysing effect on the group's values, they use rhetorical procedures such as euphemism. The most mysterious of these is prosopopoeia, in which speech invokes someone absent, dead or departed, or even a thing in the personal mode: 'The Republic calls you . . . The Republic demands . . .' Prosopopoeia is a rhetorical figure inherent to official discourse, since it is what transforms the *idios logos*, in the contrast that Heraclitus made between *idios logos* and *koinon kai theion*: between singular, idiotic, personal discourse and universal man, between the common and the divine. What transforms singular discourse into common and sacred discourse, into common sense, into discourse capable of receiving the consent of the totality of individuals and thus generating consensus, is rhetorical alchemy, the alchemy of the oracle. The delegate is someone who speaks not as an individual but in the name of what is right: 'You have raised a question, and it is not the singular Pythia, the *idios*, that is answering you, it is the Pythia as mouthpiece of something other of which she is the spokesperson.' Official man is a ventriloquist who speaks in the name of the state. He takes an official stand (the staging of the official should be described), he speaks in favour and in place of the group that he is addressing, he speaks for and in place of all, he speaks as representative of the universal.

Public opinion

We come now to the modern notion of public opinion. What is this public opinion that the lawgivers of modern societies invoke, those of societies in which law exists? Tacitly it is the opinion of all, of the majority, or of those who count, those who deserve to have an opinion.[28] I think that the ostensible definition in a society with a claim to democracy, that is, that official opinion is the opinion of all, conceals a latent meaning, that public opinion is the opinion of those who deserve to have an opinion. There is a kind of qualified definition of public opinion as enlightened opinion, as opinion that deserves the name. The logic of commissions is to create a group constituted in such a way that it gives all the outward signs, socially recognized and recognizable, official, of the capacity to express the opinion that deserves to be expressed, and in the forms of conformity. One of the most important tacit criteria in the selection of members of a commission, particularly its chair, is the intuition of the people in charge of the composition of the commission that the person in question knows and recognizes the tacit rules of the bureaucratic world. In other words, someone who knows how to play the game of the commission in the legitimate fashion, which goes beyond the rules and the game, which legitimizes the game. You are never so much in the game as when you are beyond the game. In any game there are rules and fair play. In relation to the Kabyles, as well as to the intellectual world, I have used the formula that excellence, in most societies, is the art of playing with the rules of the game, using this playing with the rules of the game to render a supreme homage to the game. The controlled transgressor is the complete opposite of the heretic.

The dominant group coopts members on minimal indexes of behaviour that are the art of respecting the rules of the game in the regulated transgressions of these rules: correct behaviour, bearing. In Chamfort's famous phrase, 'the priest must believe, the canon may have doubts, the cardinal can be an atheist'.[29] The higher you rise in the hierarchy of dignitaries, the more you can play with the rules of the game, but *ex officio*, on the basis of a position that is beyond any doubt. The cardinal's anti-clerical humour is supremely clerical. Public opinion is always a kind of double reality. It is what must always be invoked when you want to legislate on ground that is not yet established. When people say that 'there is a legal vacuum' (an extraordinary expression) in relation to euthanasia or test-tube babies, individuals are convened who work with their full authority. Dominique Memmi[30] describes an ethics committee [on assisted reproduction], its composition in terms of disparate individuals – psychologists, sociologists, women, feminists, archbishops, rabbis, scientists, etc. – with the aim of transforming a sum of ethical idiolects into a universal discourse that will fill a legal vacuum, that is, provide an official solution to a difficult problem that is shaking society – by legalizing surrogate motherhood, for example.

If you are working in this kind of situation, you have to invoke a public opinion. The function attributed to opinion polls is readily understandable in this context. Saying that 'the polls are with us' is the equivalent of 'God is with us' in another context. But the polls are awkward, as sometimes enlightened opinion is against the death penalty, for example, whereas the polls are rather for. What is to be done? A commission is set up. The commission constitutes an enlightened public opinion that will establish enlightened opinion as legitimate opinion in the name of public opinion – no matter that this says the opposite or has no opinion at all (which is the case with many subjects). One of the characteristics of opinion polls is that they present people with questions that they do not ask themselves, that they slip in answers to questions that people have not asked, and in this way impose these answers. It is not a question of bias in the samples taken, but the fact of imposing all these questions that are asked by enlightened opinion, and thereby producing answers from everyone on problems that only certain people pose, thus giving enlightened responses since these have been produced by the question itself. Questions have been brought into existence for people that did not exist before for them, whereas the real question is what questions did exist for them.

I shall translate for you here a text by Mackinnon from 1828, taken from Peel's book on Herbert Spencer.[31] Mackinnon defined public opinion, giving a definition that would be official if it were not inadmissible in a democratic society. What I mean is that, when you talk about public opinion, you always play a double game between the admissible definition (the opinion of all) and the authorized and effective opinion that is obtained as a restricted sub-set of this democratically defined public opinion: 'that sentiment on any subject which is entertained by the best informed, most intelligent and most moral persons in the community, which is gradually spread and adopted by nearly all persons of any education or proper feeling in a civilized state'. The truth of the dominant becomes the truth of all.

In the National Assembly in the 1880s, what sociology has since had to rediscover was openly stated, that is, that the education system was supposed to eliminate children from the lower social classes. At the beginning, a question was raised that was subsequently completely repressed, since the education system turned out to achieve what was expected of it, without having to be asked. No need therefore to talk about it. The interest in going back to the genesis is very important, because there are debates at the beginning in which all kinds of things are said which later appear as the provocative revelations of sociologists. The reproducer of the official is able to produce (in the etymological sense of the word: *producere* means 'bringing to light'), by theatricalizing it, something that does not exist (in the sense of palpable, visible), and in the name of which he speaks. He has to produce what it is that gives him the right to produce. He cannot avoid theatricalizing, imposing proper form, doing miracles. The most ordinary miracle, for a verbal creator, is the verbal miracle, rhetorical success. He has to produce the staging of what authorizes his speaking, in other words the authority in whose name he is authorized to speak.

I have found the definition of prosopopoeia that I was looking for a while back: 'A figure of rhetoric by which a person who is evoked is made to speak and act: someone absent, a dead person, an animal, a personified thing.' And in the dictionary, which is always a tremendous instrument, you find this phrase of Baudelaire's, speaking of poetry: 'Skilfully manipulating language amounts to practising a kind of evocatory magic.' Intellectuals, who like jurists and poets manipulate a scholarly language, have to produce the imaginary referent in the name of which they speak, producing it by speaking in the proper form; they have to bring into existence that which they express, and in the name of which they express themselves. They must at the same time produce a discourse, and produce belief in the universality of their discourse by palpable production in the sense of evocation of spirits, phantoms – the state is a phantom . . . – of the thing that will guarantee what they are doing: 'the nation', 'the workers', 'the people', 'the state secret', 'national security', 'social demand', etc. Schramm has shown how ritual ceremonies are the transfer of religious ceremonies into the political order.[32] If religious ceremonial can be transferred so easily into political ceremonies, by way of ceremonial ritual, this is because what is involved in both cases is making believe that there is a foundation to the discourse, which only appears as self-founding, legitimate, universal because there is theatricalization – in the sense of magical evocation, sorcery – of the united group consenting to the discourse that unites it. Hence we have juridical ceremonial. The English historian

E. P. Thompson emphasized the role of juridical theatricalization in eighteenth-century England – wigs, etc. – which cannot be fully understood unless you see that what is added here is not simply what Pascal calls apparatus, but rather something constitutive of the juridical act.[33] To speak the truth in a lounge suit is risky, you risk losing the pomp of the discourse. People always talk of reforming legal language, but they never actually do so, because this is the last item of clothing: naked kings are no longer charismatic.

One very important dimension of theatricalization is the theatricalization of interest in the general interest; the theatricalization of the conviction of interest in the universal, of the disinterestedness of the politician – theatricalization of the priest's belief, the politician's conviction, his faith in what he is doing. If the theatricalization of conviction is one of the tacit conditions for exercising the profession of intellectual, if a philosophy professor must seem to believe in philosophy, it is because this is the essential homage of 'official man' to the official, it is what has to be paid to the official in order to be an official. Disinterestedness has to be accorded, faith in the official, in order to be a genuine official. Disinterestedness is not a secondary virtue, it is *the* political virtue of everyone with a mandate. Political scandals, or the escapades of priests, involve a collapse of this kind of political belief in which everyone displays bad faith, belief being a kind of collective bad faith in the Sartrean sense: a game in which everyone lies to themselves and lies to others, while knowing that they are lying. And that's what the official is . . .

Lecture of 8 February 1990

The concentration of symbolic resources – Sociological reading of Franz Kafka – An untenable research programme – History and sociology – Shmuel Eisenstadt's *The Political Systems of Empires* – Perry Anderson's two books – The problem of the three routes according to Barrington Moore

I offered you last week an analysis of what I call the logic or rhetoric of the official, an analysis presented as a general anthropology that could serve as a basis for empirical analyses, in particular genetic ones. I tried in this way to show how the state presents itself, either in a nascent state or in an institutionalized one, as a kind of reserve of symbolic resources, of symbolic capital, which is both an instrument for agents of a certain type, and the stake in struggles between these agents. This analysis of what the state does, and what it has to be to do what it does, is a preliminary for any analysis of a historical kind. It is in fact only if one knows what the state consists of, what it is (not simply, as in the Marxist tradition, the functions it is held to fulfil), and if one is able to note the specific operations and specific conditions of these operations, that it is possible to investigate the history, and in particular to describe the process of concentration, of a particular form of resources with which one can identify the genesis of the state. Even if it was repetitive and emphatic, this analysis was indispensable in order to actually introduce you to the question of genesis that I wanted to raise, and that unfortunately I did no more than raise.

The concentration of symbolic resources

One of the historical questions that are raised, if you accept the analyses I gave in the last sessions, is that of knowing why and how this concentration of symbolic resources could come into being, that is, the concentration of the official and of the specific power that access to the official gives. To a certain extent, in fact, every individual agent stakes a claim to the monopoly of the naming operation that official discourse constitutes. I want to look now at injury or insult, which has been the object of work by linguists. Insult belongs to the same series as official declarations, official acts of naming, the most fundamental institutional acts that we traditionally associate with the state. Insult is an individual act of naming, with a claim to universality, but incapable of giving any other guarantees of its universal ambition than that of the person pronouncing it. Because of this, the extreme situation of insult would be something like a state of absolute anarchy from the symbolic point of view, that is, a state in which each person could say of himself or of anyone else what they are; each person could say, for example: 'I am the greatest living philosopher', or 'the best street-sweeper in France and Navarre', while others could say: 'You're nothing but a . . .'[1]

(For purposes of comprehension, this kind of imaginary variation is highly useful. Situations of political crisis, revolutionary situations, are close to these symbolic struggles of all against all, in which everyone can claim the monopoly of legitimate symbolic violence, of naming, with an equal chance of success. The question of origins may appear naive, and has to be dismissed by science, but it has nonetheless the virtue of posing in a radical manner questions that ordinary functioning tends to obscure. If you imagine this state of symbolic struggle of all against all, in which each person claims for himself, and himself alone, the power of naming, it is easy to see how the question arises of knowing how this kind of progressive abdication of these individual claims comes about, in favour of a central instance that has steadily concentrated the power of naming.)

By way of a simple image, it is possible to imagine a great number of agents, each struggling against each other for the power of naming, the power to be named and to name others, and gradually, through these very struggles, the different agents delegating, or abandoning, or resigning themselves to abandon this power, in favour of an instance that will tell each person what he is. A mythical genesis of the state could be described in this way, a Platonic myth invented. Keeping this question in mind makes it possible first of all to be amazed: how could we have got to this point? For someone with a rather anarchistic temperament, it is amazing that people have abdicated this right to judge and be judged. In this way, you can become attentive to historical processes that often pass unnoticed. What I am trying to sketch out for you here is a story of this process of concentration that has nothing in common with what is sometimes said. Those historians who come closest to this kind of investigation emphasize the fact that the birth of the state is accompanied by a process of concentration of instruments of legitimation, as well as the development of a symbolic apparatus and symbolic rituals surrounding the royal power.

There is a more fundamental question, the one that I raised; and to give you an idea of this symbolic struggle of all against all, I shall quote you a text by Leo Spitzer on what he calls polyonomasy in *Don Quixote*.[2] Spitzer remarks that Cervantes' characters often bear a number of names;

depending on the scene or the situation, they are called 'the knight of the doleful countenance', etc. This plurality of names raises a question. Spitzer interprets this as a kind of empirical realization of a practical perspectivism in which every agent has a right to his own point of view. This strikes me as an excellent realization of the myth I introduced: each person names each other as he sees fit. Clearly, this power of naming is particularly exercised in emotional, amorous relationships. One of the privileges of the lover or the beloved is to name and be named, to accept a new convention, a re-naming in which the autonomy of a certain emotional relationship is asserted in relation to previous namings – a de-christening and re-christening. This is not just anecdotal. It is no accident that this happens in a very general and universal way. You can imagine a situation in which this privilege of naming is randomly distributed and each agent has the right to his own perspective. There would no longer be – to use Leibniz's metaphor about God – a 'geometral of all perspectives', a central place from which authentic names are given, the names of the civil register. Nicknames, pet names, are swept away in favour of the official name, a publicly recognized name.

Spitzer's article is about proper names, but the utopia can be pursued further by imagining a polyonomasy for nouns in general, a situation in which there would only be idiolects, in which each person would seek to impose his own naming, and put in question what is precisely the specific characteristic of an official language, that is, that all social agents in the same group associate the same sound with the same meaning and the same meaning with the same sound.[3] One effect of the construction of an official language, imposed on a certain territory, is to establish a linguistic contract, a code in both senses of the word, both legislative and communicative, between all the agents of a community, a code that each person must respect on pain of being unintelligible, being dismissed as barbarian or talking gibberish. The state has concentrated linguistic capital by establishing an official language, in other words it has got individual agents to renounce the privilege of free linguistic creation and abandon this to a few individuals – linguistic legislators, poets, etc. You can see how, on the basis of a generalization of Spitzer's image, the establishment of an official language, which is the product of a historic action of imposition, normalization, both of language and of the social subjects who have to use it, is accompanied by these agents renouncing a radical perspectivism, the equivalence of all points of view, the universal interchangeability of points of view.

Sociological reading of Franz Kafka

This utopia of radical anarchy can be generalized, if we imagine a world in which each person fully exercises his right to judge and be judged, without renouncing or abdicating this in any way. This theme is present in Kafka's *The Trial*.[4] Novelists are useful because they construct utopias that are the equivalent of Platonic myths. The mysterious, unreachable lawyer, whom the hero, K., solicits and who claims to be a great lawyer, says: 'But who will judge the quality of a great lawyer?' This is quite a regular theme in Kafka. There is a tendency to make a theological reading of Kafka's work. But a sociological reading can also be made, not that the two are in any way contradictory. This search for the place where the true identity of social agents is defined can be presented as a search for God as the convergence point of all perspectives, the ultimate instance of that instance that is the court, an instance where the question of the just judge is raised; or as a theological search for the absolute as opposed to perspectivism, or again as a sociological search for a central place where the resources of legitimate authority are concentrated, and which is accordingly the point where regression stops. As with Aristotle, there is a moment at which you have to stop,[5] and this place where you stop is the state. In the Durkheimian tradition, Halbwachs speaks of the 'central focus of cultural values';[6] he posits the existence of a central place where the cultural resources specific to a society are capitalized and concentrated, and on the basis of which distances are defined (as with the Greenwich meridian), so that one can say: 'This man is cultivated or uncultivated. He speaks French or does not speak French, etc.' This central place is the point from which all perspectives are taken.

There is therefore a central perspective. On the one hand, perspectivism; on the other hand, an absolutism, a point of view on which there is no point of view, and in relation to which all points of view can themselves be measured. This central perspective cannot be established without all partial perspectives being disqualified, discredited or subordinated, no matter what their claims may be: the point of view of the king in relation to that of the feudal magnates; or, in the seventeenth and eighteenth centuries, of the Sorbonne professors as opposed to the surgeons.[7]

There is a dominant place from which a point of view is taken that is not a point of view like the others, and which, by establishing itself, establishes a fundamental asymmetry such that nothing will afterwards be the same. From now on, all other points of view than this will be deprived of something, they will be partial or mutilated. Gurvitch, starting from the phenomenological tradition, speaks of the 'reciprocity of perspectives':[8] a world in which every agent is to another agent what the other is to himself. There is thus an absolute reversibility of relations, which is established for example in the insult. I say 'you're just a . . .', and you can say the same to me. But there is now a third term in relationship to which perspectives can be judged; between two perspectives, one is better than the other because it is less far from the focus of central values, from the convergence point of all perspectives.

The coup d'état from which the state was born (even if this was an imperceptible process) attests to an extraordinary symbolic act of force, which consisted in getting universally accepted, within the limits of a certain territorial jurisdiction that is constructed by way of the construction of this dominant point of view, the idea that all points of view are not equally valid, that there is one point of view that is the measure of all points of view, one that is dominant and legitimate. This third-party agency is a limit to free agency. On the one hand, there is the free agency of individuals who claim to know what they truly are, and on the other hand, a supreme arbiter of all the judgements of free arbiters – free and arbitrary – on truths and values, a supreme arbiter that is collectively recognized, within certain limits, as having the last word on matters of truth and value. Am I guilty or not guilty? I claim that I am not guilty, others claim that I am: there is now a legitimate instance able to say, in the last resort, 'he is guilty', or 'he is not guilty', who can deliver a judgement both of truth and of value, without discussion or appeal.

An untenable research programme

This kind of analysis may seem almost metaphysical; metaphysics is often nothing but transfigured sociology, as I have tried to show in relation to Heidegger.[9] Better to know this and to really do sociology. But it is on the condition that these questions are kept in mind that one can see what is astounding in the most commonplace history of the constitution of state instances, parliaments, etc. The work programme I shall elaborate is practically untenable, at all events for one person. The positivist representation of science that almost requires scientists never to propose anything that they cannot immediately demonstrate exercises a terrifying effect of castration and mutilation on the mind. One of the functions of science is also to conduct research programmes perceived as almost unrealizable; programmes of this kind have the effect of showing how research programmes viewed as scientific because realizable are not necessarily scientific. In positivist resignation, instead of seeking the truth where it lies, people look for it under the street lamp where they can see it . . .

My programme – which I hope I shall be able to convince you of – immediately has effects. It makes it possible to see, in historical documents or in contemporary empirical observations, things that other programmes completely ignore. It has a critical effect, showing the extent to which programmes taken as realistic are in fact mutilated. It goes without saying, then, that one cannot be satisfied with certain scientific programmes that amount to reducing the history of the state to the history of taxation. A very good historian is able to say: 'What the modern state does is fundamentally to establish a state fiscality', and, five pages further on: 'In order for taxes to be established, the legitimacy of the instance establishing taxation had to be recognized.' In other words, everything was needed that I said was needed, that is, instances capable of having their monopoly of legitimate constitution of the social world recognized.[10] Simple programmes are dangerous, they succumb very easily to a certain form of economism. There is a whole Marxist tradition that reduces the accumulation process to its economic dimension, and accumulation to an accumulation of material resources. For example, people say that the state begins with the concentration of resources that makes redistribution possible, but all they have in mind are economic resources. Now, everything I have said suggests that there is another form of accumulation, just as important if not more so, that makes the accumulation of economic resources possible.

There are some very fine anthropological works on the accumulation that religious capital makes possible. In North Africa, the founders of very prestigious confraternities, holy men, can accumulate tremendous economic resources on the basis of a purely symbolic capital, an accumulation that subsequently leads to a bureaucratization, a rational management of this capital, and a decline in symbolic capital in proportion to the accumulation of economic capital. In certain cases, economic accumulation may be subordinate and secondary in relation to symbolic capital. One of the dangers of partial research programmes is to mutilate reality, either on the economic or political side. Certain historians, who have transposed the logic of fashion onto the terrain of history and act as if paradigms changed like hemlines, say: 'It's the end of the Marxist, materialist paradigm.' Once everything was economics, now everything is politics. This inversion of signs, with Pareto in opposition to Marx, was done more elegantly by Raymond Aron,[11] if elegance has any scientific value . . . Economism describes the genesis of the state in the logic of the steady accumulation of economic capital. And if you say that the opposite is true, that is, that what counts is the accumulation of political capital, you then have a history reduced to politics.

These perversions arise because people are not sufficiently amazed at what is extraordinary in the problem of initial accumulation – to use the Marxist vocabulary – that Marx constantly raised.[12] What comes closest to the analyses I have sketched is Hegel's famous analysis of the master/slave relationship, a philosopher's analysis that places a social contract at the origin.[13] Giving a historical anthropology of the state, a structural history of the genesis of the state, means raising the question of the conditions in which this initial accumulation was effected. A certain number of people abandon the power of judging in the last instance, and receive from other people an abdication in relation to certain very important things – the right to make peace and war, to say who is guilty or not guilty, who is a real advocate or a real builder . . . We find ourselves today in a state of the state where these things are taken for granted. But they need only be placed in the logic of their genesis for the question to arise: how did each individual builder, for example, abandon to a kind of 'trans-builder' the right to say who is really a builder?

After this preliminary critique of the attempts of general sociology or social history of the state that are found in the tradition of comparative history, I come to my own programme. I have cited three authors who stand in the tradition of the great founders of sociology: Marx with his analysis of primitive accumulation, Durkheim with the social division of

labour, and Weber with his description of the genesis of modern societies as a process of rationalization. These authors have in common their
attempt to describe a very general process, to offer a global history of the
state. Their respective visions of the state and this process are organized on
the basis of very different assessments of the final state. We can mention
here Marc Bloch's *Seigneurie française et manoir anglais*, which can be
treated as a comparative study of the genesis of the English and the French
states. A very important author, Karl Polanyi, to whom I have referred
indirectly in relation to the processes of unification of the market (which
are correlative with the processes of constitution of the state and are precisely, like the process of unification of the linguistic market, the effect of
state action), in *The Great Transformation*[14] and *Trade and Market in the
Early Empires*,[15] studied the way that the market was gradually established
independent from constraints exerted by the family and communities.
Two other authors are Karl Wittfogel in *Oriental Despotism*,[16] who developed a general theory on the basis of the Asiatic mode of production, and
Rushton Coulborn, whose *Feudalism in History*[17] would not satisfy contemporary historians but assembled work by a number of historians on
Japanese feudalism as well as feudalism in France, England, etc. For my
synthesis on the genealogy of the modern state, I shall take up just some of
the results of these books, having decided not to deal with them in detail.

History and sociology

One of the functions of teaching – if it has one – is to give bearings, to
display the map of an intellectual universe, and what I am going to do
now is located in a universe whose map you may be unacquainted with; it
is the product of tacit or explicit references to this space. One of the ways
of checking an idea that is proposed to you consists in checking, not its
sources in the naive sense of the term, but rather the theoretical space in
relation to which this discourse is produced. Scientific communication
should always spell out, not the 'state of the question', which is stupid,
bureaucratic, like a CNRS research project, but rather what the state of
the scientific space is that you have actively mobilized to construct your
problematic. Very often, lay people do not have the problematic in relation to which the professional produces his discourse. They have their
ideas: for or against the *grandes écoles*, for [or against] direct democracy,
self-management, etc. Every science historically develops complex structures of problematics, by a process of accumulation that is not simply
additive. In the same way, being a painter today, if you want to avoid
being naive, means being up to date with the whole history of painting and mastering its problematic. The naive visitor to an art gallery,
unaware of these problematics, might say of certain paintings: 'My son
could have done the same . . .' The sociologist is like a non-naive painter
who is the unfortunate victim of naive judges . . . A rational pedagogic

communication should at least seek to show the problem space. I shall give you a few indicators. You will see that the three authors I am going to talk to you about played a very small role in the construction of what I shall propose. But they are none the less important, because they represent the spontaneous manner of doing what I am doing today. These books, with which I disagree completely, at least deserve to be read with respect; they represent an enormous work, and systematic attempts aiming to construct coherent, explicit and conscious approaches. Historians, masters of their little monopoly, may well grimace at attempts of this kind; they can naturally say that it is bad sociology applied to bad history. But their merit is that, instead of being satisfied with combining histories, they have tried to construct systematic models, to bring together a collection of connected features by way of relationships that are controlled and capable of being validated or falsified by confrontation with reality. I am well aware that these models are rather summary and arbitrary.

Historians are social agents, and their works are the product of an encounter between social habituses that are formed partly by the historical field, as a system of demands and censorships. They are what they are because the historical field is what it is. Part of the things they do not do, as well as of the things that they do, is explained by what the field asks them to do or not to do. They rightly criticize sociologists for being in a field that demands certain things of them that may seem presumptuous, arrogant, exhibitionist, while on the other hand it does not ask them to do other things that appear to historians as indispensable and necessary. In other words, the relationships between disciplines, like the relationships between high officials or artists, are relationships between fields that have different histories, in which people endowed with different habituses respond without knowing it to different programmes produced by different histories. The same would be true of the relationship between philosophers and sociologists, etc. I am not in any logic of accusation here; there is nothing to condemn. One of the virtues of sociology, when applied to itself, is to make everything understandable. One of the normative intentions that I keep in mind – if there are historians among you – is to say: 'Put in question the programme in whose name you are going to reject the programme implied in the works that I shall expound to you, and ask yourself whether this positivist certainty is not the product of an incorporated censorship, thus of a mutilation, and whether it would not be good to reintroduce this ambitious programme, without abandoning anything of the traditional requirements of historians . . .' This was my implicit message, so I may as well make it explicit . . .

Shmuel Eisenstadt's *The Political Systems of Empires*

I will start with Eisenstadt's *The Political Systems of Empires*. The project he set himself – which was bound to startle historians – was to study twenty states that he viewed as belonging to the type of historical bureaucratic empires, that is, 'preindustrial regimes characterized by a high degree of centralized power, acting through a vast impersonal administration'. The key words here are 'preindustrial', 'centralized power', and 'impersonal administration', that is, independent of individuals in its operation and transmission. This set includes the absolutist states of the premodern era (France and England), the Arab caliphates of the Abbasids, the Ottoman empire, the successive dynasties of the Chinese empire, the Aztec and Inca states, the Moghul empire and its Hindu predecessors, Sassanid Persia, the Hellenistic empires, the Roman empire, the Byzantine empire, the empires of ancient Egypt and the colonial empires (the Spanish in Latin America, the British in the Indian subcontinent). This is a listing in the Prévert style . . . but you can see that the attempt was an interesting one, and presupposed a certain culture.

First of all the question of method. This stands in a tradition that sociologists call structural-functionalist, embodied by Parsons and his notion of 'profession',[18] a tradition that seeks to discover the fundamental characteristics of all political systems. His postulate involves revealing structural properties, since every state has to fulfil a certain number of universal functions. The conditions for accomplishing these functions are that the state has to be legitimate, to concentrate resources, etc. These functional requirements are accompanied by structural properties. In actual fact, however, and contrary to appearances, structural-functionalists, who are rather conservative on the political spectrum, are very close to Marxists in terms of these fundamental postulates. (This point may seem arbitrary and simplistic, and I should develop it and argue it in detail, as I can understand that the idea that Marx and Parsons are not very different might upset certain people. But I don't have the time to do so, or a great desire . . .)

In a structural-functionalist philosophy, there are fundamental features of all possible political systems and their relationship with the other constitutive systems of a society. These fundamental features are used as variables that make it possible to characterize all societies. Hence the idea of developing a model. Other approaches view society as a system of systems (political, economic, cultural, etc.). On the basis of a listing of these invariants one can investigate the variations, and thus define the variables that divide different states as different realizations of these combinations of systems. This has the merit of being coherent and explicit . . . People such as Eisenstadt, with their pedestrian heaviness, have a certain virtue in my eyes. They tried to think with the whole conceptual arsenal of the world's sociology in the 1960s (status, role, etc.). The first operation is one of classification. The types of state are classified, in a typology based on the listing of a certain number of characteristics or combinations of features common to different societies, while maintaining that these configurations have systemic properties. (This comes to us from Germany through the neo-functionalist theory of Niklas Luhmann, a very general theory that swallows everything. This parenthesis is a way of inoculating you in advance when the thing arrives . . .)

The idea is that it is possible to isolate characteristics within a political regime, and that regimes that have the same characteristics can be put in the same class. At the same time, it is not forgotten that these characteristics will enter into different combinations, and will thus make for different systems. Behind this lies the analogy with biology. We have therefore, at one and the same time, an analytical thinking, which isolates elements in complex ensembles, and a synthetic thinking, which remembers that these elements enter into singular historical configurations, that the Japanese state is not the French state or the Abbasid state. That is what is attempted. Having defined these classifications based on comparative research, by grasping common characteristics, the next thing is to try to reveal common properties, a kind of historical essence. The common characteristics of all the empires classified in the type that is the object of this study, that is, centralized historical-bureaucratic empires, are listed as constitutive of this political order.

The first characteristic is the limited autonomy of the political sphere:[19] these are worlds in which the political sphere has to some extent freed itself from immersion in relations of kinship or economic relations. A relatively autonomous political order has appeared. This contribution is important, as every theory of the genesis of the state has to agree. This limited and relative autonomy of the political sphere is manifest in the appearance of autonomous political goals among the ruling milieus. They begin to have a political reason that is not only family reason – the beginnings of what will come to be known as raison d'état. The second major property is the differentiation of political roles in relation to other activities, for example the appearance of a specific role of official, as distinct from warrior, scribe or priest. Correlative with the appearance of this division of political roles, or a division of political labour to put it into Marxist language, we see the appearance of a struggle within the political world; this acquires autonomy, differentiates, and because it differentiates becomes the site of a struggle. The third characteristic is that leaders seek to centralize the political sphere; in other words, there is a work of concentrating power. The fourth characteristic (it is not very clear how this is distinguished from the second): there is on the one hand the appearance of specific administrative instances, bureaucracies, and on the other hand of instances of legitimate political struggle, the paradigm of which is a parliament, that is, institutionalized sites where the political struggle is concentrated and circumscribed. This is bound up with the process of centralization and concentration. The struggle of all against all, which can be waged anywhere, is replaced (in Marx's metaphor) by a place where political struggle can be waged in legitimate forms, parliament being this theatre of the political.

I am combining Eisenstadt with Marx. Eisenstadt says that the state appears with the concentration of 'freely floating' resources, resources in silver, gold, techniques; we could add symbolic resources, as the state is bound up to an extent with these floating symbolic resources. The process that Eisenstadt describes may be analysed as a process of differentiation, autonomization, centralization. He emphasizes – this is another important idea – the fact that this process of centralization and concentration of floating resources is limited by the fact that it has to reckon with the traditional ties against which it has been constructed. I shall return to this very important point. It is clear that what all these people have in mind is the question of feudalism, and – in Marxist terms – the transition from feudalism to absolutism. Marx imposed his problematic on a series of people, who have themselves posed this kind of problem, and perhaps still more so on those who thought contrary to him. Thus the structural-functionalists, despite being completely opposed to Marx politically, stress the idea of the contradiction involved in this concentration of resources, which was effected against the feudal lords but at the same time for them. We find the same theme with Perry Anderson.

After defining these common characteristics, Eisenstadt describes what he sees as the set of factors that determine or are favourable to the appearance of this historical configuration. In order for this kind of empire or state to appear, the first thing needed is for the society to have reached a certain level of differentiation. The Parsons tradition, continuing the traditions of Durkheim and Weber, emphasizes the idea that the historic process is a process of differentiation of the world into spheres, an idea that I completely agree with, although I do not define these spheres in the same way as they do. We thus have the necessity of a certain degree of differentiation, in particular of the administration in relationship to the religious sphere.

Secondly, a certain number of people must have escaped the rigid status of traditional agrarian relations. We can base ourselves here on a remark by Max Weber, who noted that in order for the notable to appear, this elementary form of politician, the man who agrees to devote himself to the common interests and spend his time settling conflicts in the village (which is not something to be done with a light heart in so-called archaic society), there must already be a bit of surplus, *skhole*, leisure, distance – a reserve of free time.[20] The process of differentiation is supported by a process of initial accumulation of resources that is translated into free time, time that can be devoted to the specifically political. I am developing Eisenstadt by using Weber, as he located himself in Weber's line.

Thirdly, it is necessary that certain resources – religious, cultural, economic – are no longer dependent on the family, religion, etc. They are 'disembedded'. Polanyi uses this notion in relation to the market that exists in traditional, precapitalist societies. In his jointly authored work on trade in the early empires, there is a very fine chapter on the Kabyle market by an English anthropologist,[21] which is exactly as this could still be observed until quite recently. There is a market where people bring their cattle or buy grain for seed, but this market is immersed in family relationships. For example, it is forbidden to conduct transactions outside of a limited social space, people act under the security of guarantors, all kinds of controls are applied, which means that purely economic relations, such as are described by economic theory, cannot acquire autonomy. In order for the state to exist, according to Eisenstadt, there must be floating resources that are 'disengaged', resources that may be incomes, symbols, workers, which are not appropriated and pre-empted in advance by an 'ascriptive' primary group, hereditary and particularist, as they say in Parsonian language. The example par excellence is Max Weber's free labourer – see his very famous article on the replacement of the domestic servant by the agricultural worker in eastern Germany.[22] To understand what Eisenstadt means, we must have in mind [this] agricultural [worker] who is typically trapped in domestic relationships. His labour is not constituted as such; he invests in his master's children, whom he treats as his own children, he is thus involved in emotional relationships. Because of this, paradoxically, it is impossible to establish the notion of free labour. In order for the worker to be exploitable, he has to be free (Marx brought out this paradox very well), he has to be freed from his relationships of personal dependence on the employer in order to become a free worker, thrown onto the market, to be subject there to another form of domination, impersonal and anonymous, that is exercised on interchangeable individuals.

These freely circulating resources are clearly both an instrument of power for the initial accumulators of capital, the instrument of their domination, and at the same time the stake in their struggle. The rulers are engaged in the accumulation of resources, in the struggle to accumulate resources and to appropriate accumulated resources. This struggle, which is the product of the beginning of accumulation, is also the product of its acceleration. There is a dialectic here between the freely floating resources and the conflicts generated for and by these resources. Eisenstadt's intuition is correct, even if it needs to be integrated into a more complex system that also includes symbolic resources; initial accumulation is possible because of the existence of these resources, which themselves generate, by the conflicts they arouse, the development of new resources designed to control the use of these resources and their redistribution. There is a snowball effect, and the state is born in this dialectic.

Eisenstadt points to the existence of a contradiction; he remarks, as also does Perry Anderson, that these empires arise out of a contradiction. Their rulers, in fact, emerge from the traditional feudal order, from a system of power based on kinship that is hereditary and transmittable in a more or less charismatic fashion; yet they have to construct the state against the very spirit of their spirit of origin. They find themselves in a 'double bind',[23] constantly torn between submission to the feudal values they embody and the demolition of these same values. Their state-making enterprise presupposes the dissolution of the very order from which they emerged. These people have to attack the aristocracies from which they emerged; they have to attack the privileges of the aristocracy in order to defend it, to defend the interests of these aristocracies. More broadly, they have to undermine the very foundations of the former feudal order, its values, privileges, implicit representations and beliefs, in order to reach new realities and representations that are totally anti-feudal, that is, bureaucratic, impersonal and anonymous. Many of these empires give power to individuals who are pariahs: eunuchs, slaves, foreigners, stateless, etc. The reason for this is clear. Inasmuch as the object is to establish an independent political order, obeying laws of operation and transmission that are contrary to the traditional laws of family transmission, one of the ways to radically break the mechanism is to appeal to people outside the game. The extreme case is the eunuch, or priestly celibacy. These strategies are found everywhere, from the Ottoman empire through to China. Paradoxically, the most important positions are held by people outside the game. An opposite effect is that in the Ottoman empire the ruler's brothers were very often executed, as a way of preventing feudal palace wars arising from inheritance claims under the logic of heredity. Bureaucracy establishes a political order which is its own beginning.

Eisenstadt offers typologies, he breaks down historical systems into properties, he observes variations, but without losing sight of the idea of the systematic and coherent character of each historical combination. Another of his merits is that he describes a phenomenon that may be called the 'phenomenon of emergence'. The notion of emergence is bound up with an epistemological tradition according to which one system gives rise to another not in a simple additive way, but by qualitative leaps that correspond to changes in the structure of its elements.[24] People talk of the emergence of a political order when what they have in mind is not simply the result of the additive aggregation of pre-existing elements, but each step in this process is accompanied by changes in the whole structure. Another metaphor very often employed is the idea of crystallization. At a certain moment, disparate elements take shape and effect a combination (a notion that Althusser juggled with . . .). The emerging ensembles have systemic properties that involve the existence of patterns, self-reinforcing overall structures.

I am being very unfair to Eisenstadt, but given the laws of transmission in our French universe, you might well never have heard his name. What I have told you here will perhaps prepare you to read him in a positive and constructive way . . .

Perry Anderson's two books

I shall now present to you briefly two books by Perry Anderson, *Passages from Antiquity to Feudalism* and *Lineages of the Absolutist State*. Like Eisenstadt, Anderson stands in the tradition of a totalizing history that aims to grasp a historical movement as a whole, rather than being satisfied with writing a history of the state, the army, religion, etc. He aims to grasp the totality, with the intention – as explicitly asserted by Marc Bloch – of understanding the present. Anderson's question is completely naive: how is it that France has a revolutionary tradition whereas England never had a revolution? That France has critical thinkers like the Althusserians while England has conformist thinkers? This is more or less how he puts the problem, I am hardly caricaturing it . . . To put the question in a more elevated way: what are the factors favouring the socialist forces in England? Anderson seeks to draw from a comparative global history of the great Western states, to which he adds Japan for the purpose of comparison, instruments for understanding the particularities that he approves or disapproves of in France and in England. He is critical of Marxist evolutionism. His project is completely Weberian, even though he situates himself in the Marxist tradition. He aims to grasp the specificity of the history of Western Europe by comparing firstly the history of Europe, from Greece to France under the Bourbons or tsarist Russia, with the history of the Near East, from Byzantium to Turkey, or that of China, in order to see what are the particularities of European history from the standpoint of state construction. Secondly, by comparing within Western history the development of the east and the west of Europe. You will understand right away how he is actually seeking to find out why socialism in Russia is what it is: is it not tied to the previous history of the state in Eastern and Western Europe? And you will see that Barrington Moore, the third author I shall speak to you about, spells things out in a completely clear fashion, saying that his problem is to understand the 'three routes': that leading to Western democracy, that leading to fascism, and that leading to communism. He tries to do this by a comparative history of China and Russia on the one hand, Japan and Germany on the other, and finally the European countries. He tries to discover the explanatory factors in the history of these three major traditions.

In current discussions about events in the East [the fall of the Berlin Wall in 1989] people tackle things in a rather confused way, without taking the trouble to make their models explicit, and particularly without being capable of this, since it presupposes a considerable historical elaboration. The merit of constructing models is that it forces you to make the system of investigation obvious. That is why we see far better the politically naive or naively political questions that these historians of comparative history pose. Historians of straightforward history raise the same type of questions – about the French Revolution – but this is more hidden because the models are less obvious. An obvious model, however, is easier to oppose than a concealed one, trickily hidden under supposedly neutral material. It would be too easy to be clever about these kinds of research, all the more so in that I am not making clear to you here the immense historical work that the construction of these models presupposes; I am only giving you its general patterns. But although this historical work is second-hand – and I have tried for years myself to adopt this second-hand culture – it is no small thing to master this world of knowledge. I say this as it's the least one can do when talking of people who have done this kind of work.

These authors have ulterior motives, problematics bound up with the present and with the intellectual tradition in which they are situated. Their two major types of question are the Marxist question that I was just referring to, and that of the historical culmination of differing trajectories. They answer these in different ways. Anderson aims to rehabilitate the European absolutisms, to overcome Marx's ambivalence about the absolute monarchies of modern Europe. He transposes to the absolute monarchies Marx's classical analysis of capitalism. Just as Marx and Engels characterized modern Europe as 'an executive committee for managing the common affairs of the bourgeoisie as a whole', so Anderson sees the absolute monarchies, such as France under Louis XIV, as executive committees for the final defence of the common interests of the feudal nobility. The absolutist state was the last rampart of the feudal nobility, swept away by the Revolution; it was 'an apparatus of government redeployed for and by the feudal nobility', a regime that served the feudal nobility. But just as the capitalist democratic state, according to Marx, has to discipline and even destroy certain individual capitalists in order to ensure the triumph of the capitalist order, likewise – and this is the contradiction of the absolutist order, according to Anderson – the absolutist order has to discipline and even destroy certain lords, or certain sectors of the feudal caste, in order to save a feudal system of exploitation, that is, serfdom. What was a major objection to the thesis of the functionality of the absolutist state for the feudalists, that is, feudal revolts, is not so for Anderson. In order to rescue the interests of the class, absolutism has to sacrifice a part of the class. It is the sacrificed part of the class that revolts, which does not refute the claim that this absolutist state serves the class's overall interests. In other words, the resistance of the feudal nobility is not an argument against the feudal nature of the regime.

Absolutism gave the feudal lords of the West a compensation for the loss of serfdom in the form of properties, court privileges, sinecures. The accumulation made possible by taxation, and the redistribution that accumulation made possible, meant that the nobles could receive compensatory subsidies to make up for the shortfall in feudal revenues. For the lords of the East, however, absolutism – which was moreover a borrowing – was not just designed to compensate for the loss of feudalism, it made possible its perpetuation. An important remark that you will also find in Barrington Moore: the Eastern states were induced states, constructed after the model of the English and French states, as if the state was an import. Marxist historians, not very happy with the fate of Marxist regimes, raise the question as to why Marxism in Russia took the form that it did. Does a state that was self-generated from the start have different properties from a state generated on the basis of a borrowing, an imported model?

A book by another very famous historian, Alexander Gerschenkron, on the economic backwardness of Russian capitalism,[25] follows the same line. It is impossible to understand the fate of capitalism in Russia without understanding that this capitalism made a late start, when French and

English capitalisms were already very developed. Its backwardness was bound up with the fact that it started later. Marc Bloch wrote, against the common opinion of spontaneous sociology in the English-speaking world, that the English state was established well before the French.[26] Does a state that develops according to its own inherent logic, by spontaneous invention, not owe part of its particularities to this particularity, and in particular the feature that always strikes observers, that is, that this state has been able to perpetuate extremely archaic institutions, starting with royalty, beyond the industrial revolution? This leads to another false problem that Marx bequeathed to historiographical tradition, that of the bourgeois revolution: why did England not have a bourgeois revolution? This causes a great deal of trouble to English Marxists. And Japanese Marxists have developed large quantities of literature in response to the question of the Japanese road as a deviation from the only road that leads to the only true revolution, the bourgeois revolution . . . This reconverted feudalism takes completely different forms from one country to another. There are sometimes terrible naiveties. Thus Perry Anderson explains the unusual Scandinavian road as follows: the fundamental determinant of the Scandinavian specificity lies in the particular nature of the Viking social structure – here you are in a perfect circle. (That said, I would at least like to teach you today to read charitably, to read on the basis of enlightened self-interest. I do not understand why people read books that they despise; you either read or you don't . . . Charitable reading on the basis of enlightened self-interest consists in reading things in such a way that they have an interest.)

To return to Scandinavia. If you make a comprehensive reading, the history of a country becomes a one-way street, like that of an individual. One of the functions of the notion of habitus is to remind us that first experiences orient second ones, which orient third ones: we perceive what happens to us by way of structures that have been put into our minds by what has happened to us – this is commonplace but it needs to be borne in mind all the same. We do not recommence our history at each moment, and neither does a country. To have had a Viking social structure is indeed important. But it remains to be studied what this 'Viking road' means, in what way it has governed institutions, in what way later institutions were preconstructed by minds themselves constructed by these early institutions. I am already sketching out a bit the scientific perspective I am going to develop. I shall try to show how a genuinely genetic history, a historical sociology, seeks to grasp the processes of permanent creation that aim at transforming structures on the basis of constraints objectively inscribed in the structure and in people's minds, processes that change the structure and that are fashioned in part by the previous state of the structure. The philosophy of history I shall apply in my further analysis is that at each moment the whole of history is present in the objectivity of the social world and in the subjectivity of the social agents that make further history. This does not mean that we are in a system with a fatalism such that on the basis of the initial moment it is possible to deduce the following moments, but rather that at each point in time the space of the possible is not unlimited. One may even ask whether the space of the possible does not steadily contract . . .

Anderson develops the contradiction indicated by Eisenstadt between the absolutist state and feudalism. This thesis is present already in Marx and Engels. Engels says, for example: 'The political order remained feudal, while society became more and more bourgeois.'[27] This is the old contradiction that has been pointed out time and again. Anderson develops it a bit, and describes the conflicts that Eisenstadt already mentioned: the absolutist state, as a redeployed feudal apparatus, is led to conduct repressive actions against the very people whose interests it serves. Absolutist states act as a repressive machine of the feudal class that has just abolished the traditional foundations of the community, and at the same time they attack the essential foundations of the feudal order by practising a direct fiscal control that replaces the practice of feudal fiscality. In order to serve the interests of the feudal class, absolutism has to go against feudalism. One remark in passing: Anderson ascribes a very great importance to the role of Roman law, because the West had this inheritance from antiquity, because there is a distinct Western way. The jurists who were at the origin of the modern state were able to draw on the capital of accumulated juridical resources, used as technique.

I had intended to compare Eisenstadt and Perry Anderson in order to show you how, beneath the apparent opposition between a structural-functionalist tradition and a Marxist tradition, there are many resemblances. To sum up very quickly: Eisenstadt is functionalism for everyone, whereas Anderson is functionalism for certain people. Eisenstadt asks what the functions of the state are for the totality of the social order, all classes together, whereas Anderson examines the class functions for the dominant of that time, that is, the feudalists. But the essential thing is that they are both functionalists. Instead of asking what the state does, and the conditions that have to be met for it to do what it does, they deduce what it does from the functions they posit almost a priori, such as the function of maintaining unity, serving, etc.

The problem of the 'three routes' according to Barrington Moore

The third historian I am going to speak to you about, Barrington Moore, in *The Social Origins of Dictatorship and Democracy*, says quite clearly that his question is to understand the role of the landed upper classes and the peasants in the revolutions leading to capitalist democracy, fascism and communism. This is the problem of the 'three routes', and in order to answer this question, he goes on to compare England, France and the United States as examples of bourgeois revolution leading to democracy,

Japan and Germany as examples of conservative revolution leading to
fascism, and China and Russia as examples of peasant revolution leading
to communism. It is Moore who is the most consistent comparativist: he
seeks to isolate one variable viewed as the principal variable, and see how
what happens varies as this variable varies. Clearly, this presupposes a
tremendous mutilation, and any historian who is at all aware will say that
it is impossible to do this. But I repeat that an obvious fault is better than
a hidden error. It is better to construct a system of explanatory factors that
are restricted but explicit than to change the explanatory system from one
page to the next. Moore writes, for example, that the state is born with
taxation and that everything lies in this, but three pages later he spells out
that, if the legitimacy of the state is not recognized, there is no taxation . . .
(I see in this manner of thinking an analogy with the opposition between
mythical thinking and rational thinking. One of the conditions for mythical systems to operate with partial coherence is that they are never tested
simultaneously. If at a certain moment you say: 'Man is to woman as the
sun is to the moon', and later: 'Man is to woman as the toad is to the frog',
you are not comparing these two statements, you are just applying the
same practical schemas – the 'historian's trade'. This kind of construction
is not subject to the brutal test to which people expose themselves when
they say: 'I am taking three explanatory factors and I am going to see how
they vary.' This is therefore an advance.)

For Barrington Moore, it is necessary to consider, in the period when
modern states were being established, a relationship between three terms:
large landed property, the peasants, and the urban bourgeoisie. He tries to
account for the characteristics of his three end-points as a function of the
combinations that these three factors enter into. Democracy appears in the
traditions where there is an approximate balance between the three, where
there is not an alliance between the aristocracy and the bourgeoisie made
on the back of the peasants and workers, where there is a commercial,
urban, bourgeois tendency strong enough to counterbalance the feudal
traditions. When the three types are viewed simultaneously, each one characterizes the others negatively. Japan and Germany are characterized by
an imbalance in favour of the landed aristocracies, by a survival of feudal
traditions that continue to dominate the state bureaucracies. The Junkers
were the first to enter the great state apparatus: 'The pressures of capitalist
groups able to act as a counterweight were not sufficient to compensate for
the political consequences of a form of agriculture that exerted an oppression over the peasants and relied on very strong political controls.'[28] To
distinguish Japan from Germany, he adds that in the Japanese case the
feudal tie had a particular character and accentuated loyalty of a military
type, discipline, to the detriment of a loyalty that was more contractual,
more freely chosen. The model becomes more complicated if you take
into account the relative weight of the three forces. In the case of the
route leading to communism, the tendencies to commercialization, the
urban and bourgeois capitalist development with its associated values, are

weak, the forms of repressive agriculture very strong (serfdom, etc.), the absolutist forces arouse rebellion in the peasant base, which reverses in a mechanical way the old forms of domination. You thus have the renewal of a primitive absolutism.

I apologize to these authors whom, despite everything, I respect. I would have liked to go on to tell you about the schema that I intended to propose to you, and that is not made up of fragments taken from various others. I want to give you the means to criticize models by making these connections visible. I shall try next time to show you that it is necessary to change one's philosophy of history in order to account for the same things more systematically, and to discover in passing certain things that have been seen by these authors, whom I exhort you to read . . .

Lecture of 15 February 1990

The official and the private – Sociology and history: genetic structuralism – Genetic history of the state – Game and field – Anachronism and the illusion of the nominal – The two faces of the state

The official and the private

I have received a number of questions, but I won't answer these directly, as I would usually. They are extremely complex and bear on the foundations of what I am trying to do. One of them was about the control of violence, and another on the logical role of the state as instance of rationalization. These two problems will be dealt with in the continuation of these lectures next year.

To return to the thread of my argument, I focused last time on the question of the official and the establishment of the monopoly of the official, which was another way of posing the question of the establishment of the monopoly of legitimate symbolic violence. I recalled that the agents of the state are characterized by the fact that they are invested with functions that are called official, that is, with official access to official speech, the speech that is current for official instances and the state. You could say that the state is ultimately the place where official speech, regulations, rules, order, mandate and appointment is current. In this logic, the state is characterized by being the site of a universally recognized power, recognized even when challenged, which is a paradox I shall tackle later on. The state is the site of a recognized power that has behind it social consensus, a consensus granted to an instance charged with defining the public good, that is, that which is good for the public, in public, for the set of people who define the public. You could say that one of the paradoxes of the state lies in the fact that those who have a monopoly of the public good are also those with a monopoly of access to public goods. In a previous lecture, I contrasted, in a logic that was more sociological than traditionally philosophical, the Marxist and the Hegelian views of the state, suggesting that these represented two opposite poles of a state anthropology. I think that these two seemingly antithetical views of the state are as it were two sides of the same coin: you cannot have the Hegelian state without having the Marxist state. (Formulas of this kind, in the form of slogans, are mnemonic techniques, and somewhat dangerous. They are things I would not express in writing, but teaching is designed to say things you do not write down, and to communicate the things that you do write by expressing them in the simplest, most elementary, strongest terms, which writing cannot carry or tolerate.) Basically, the key argument I want to develop here is this kind of fundamental ambiguity of the state. Those who embody the public good are, by the same token, subject to a number of obligations – one characteristic of men in public life, for example, is that they do not have a private sphere, but are always on public display even when their private life is involved.

According to an analysis by Monique de Saint Martin,[1] nobles are people who are on display even in their domestic life, people whose private space is official. Noble education constantly teaches future nobles, right from childhood, to be subject even in domestic life to rules that are imposed on ordinary people only when they are in public, on stage. Men in political life, especially members of the state nobility, those who have access to the political field as a site of legitimate, official politics, likewise high officials as nobles of the state, are subject to all kinds of constraints that also bear on their private world. In the extreme case, they have no private life, as their private life is always liable to publication, a form of denunciation that consists in making the private public. Discussion is needed of the role of satirical papers such as *Le Canard enchaîné*. Their obvious political function consists in transgressing a boundary that official or semi-official papers, such as *Le Monde*, cannot transgress. These papers denounce scandals, but under certain conditions, within certain limits, and as a relatively extraordinary matter. There are organs that are officially mandated, at least by themselves, to cross this boundary between official and private, to officialize the private in the sense of making it public, which may be in contradiction with the official definition of the private individual concerned. This also deserves discussion, and I will dwell a bit more on it here.

Here is a titbit to show how, on the basis of an analysis that may be abstract, it is possible to conduct very concrete operations. I am currently working on the legal protection of private life; these are matters that you hear people talking about vaguely all the time, but that you don't examine closely. If a star is photographed in a swimsuit, or *Le Canard enchaîné* publishes a photograph of a meeting between two politicians, Chirac and Le Pen, is there the same infringement of private life in the second case that there is in the first? Is the law the same for a star and a politician? Are the sanctions the same? What is the official definition of the official and the private in each case? How would judges rule, as holders of the official right to state the official? The invention of photography gave rise to a host of unprecedented problems. Painters were always official painters. They painted nudes, but in conformity with official definitions, whereas the photographer who photographs nudes where he finds them, without the agreement of the individuals photographed, runs foul of jurisprudence relating to scandals. There is a trail here for a whole series of analyses.

(The 'big problems' require a certain cunning. To speak of the state with great emphasis, with a philosophical resonance, may confer a certain form of success, but I believe it is not a good strategy, as these problems are too difficult. My own strategy is always to catch hold of these 'big problems' by an accessible side, where they reveal the essential thing that is hidden beneath insignificant appearances.)

My previous analyses led to certain questions that I shall try to raise in a historical context. I have already developed the idea that the state can be characterized as the constitution of official resources, of legitimate symbolic violence. I shall now investigate the history of the genesis of the state on the basis of this definition of the state as a site made by agents commissioned to state the public good, to be the public good and to appropriate public goods. In the so-called socialist countries, dignitaries appropriated public goods and had a relatively unprecedented privilege in the name of the socialization of the means of production (which indicates the strangeness of these regimes), the privilege of appropriating, in the name of the abolition of privileges, such public goods as official residences, official platforms, official radio stations, etc. With us, the form is less marked, but we also have official cars, official personalities, official platforms, official bodyguards. This legitimate appropriation of public goods is associated with what is both a duty and a privilege, that is, the duty of doing what privilege requires, and so not having a private life. Officials only have access to certain privileges on condition that they deserve them, by paying homage, at least officially, to the values that legitimize these privileges.

After reminding you of all this, I hope now to stick to the two themes I want to stress, otherwise my lecture will be an unfinished symphony . . . Firstly, I shall say what it means to give a history of the genesis of the state, and secondly, in what way this manner of doing history is different from certain ordinary ways of doing history. Before going on, however, I shall mention a problem of method, then present the broad lines of what this description of genesis involves. This will in fact be a summary of the course I shall give next year on the historical genesis of the state institution.

Sociology and history: genetic structuralism

My first subject is the specificity of the method. What is involved in historically describing the genesis of the state? Is the comparative method, as applied by the three authors I discussed last time, the only way? Does putting forward a universal proposition on the genesis of the state force you to make a universal comparison of forms of state from the Inca empires through to the Soviet type? My answer is no. It is possible to study a particular case – or a small number of particular cases – in such a way that your project is to grasp the universal forms of state in it, the logic of the genesis of a logic. Demonstrating this would be long and hard. I have suggested something of it in the reservations I particularly expressed in relation to Eisenstadt and Perry Anderson. It seems to me doubly justified to take as the central object the cases of France and England, treated explicitly as particular cases of a universe of possible cases, as privileged particular cases, because historically, what was invented here served as a model for all other forms of the modern state. Doing historical sociology or social history means tackling a particular case, but constituting this, in Bachelard's expression, as a particular case of those possible, grasping its particularity as such, a particularity that can be compared with possible cases. I shall often refer to the comparison between England and Japan. Many justifications for this way of proceeding can be given, not only for reasons of method, treating them as particular cases, but also because, historically, they each have the particularity of having been a general model, as singular cases on the basis of which the models that were later generalized were shaped.

In order to justify these particular cases, you could find several justifications in history. In *Capital*, for example, Marx says more or less that the historian acts a bit like the physicist who observes physical phenomena where they appear in their most typical form, most free from disturbing influences. Each time it is possible, Marx tries to conduct experiments in conditions of normality, that is, assuming that the phenomenon is taking its normal form, undisturbed by anything else. Marx says, on the question of examining the capitalist mode of production and the conditions of its production, that he will make use of the classical case of England, because England is not simply a privileged illustration, but above all a pure and exemplary case. You can find similar formulations in Marc Bloch, in his study of feudalism, in which he likewise treats France and England as examples, pointing out that these two cases contain between them the complete form of the historical archetype he is seeking to reveal, variations that themselves make it possible to grasp the invariant more completely.[2]

The essential point of my argument, however, is to justify this undertaking of historical analysis in relation to sociology. The classic opposition can be brought up that the sociologist studies invariant general laws whereas the historian studies particular times and places. This opposition between Durkheim and Seignobos, which was originally about history, has become an opposition structuring the cultivated unconscious.[3] This, however, strikes me as absurd. It is impossible to do sociology on a contemporary phenomenon without giving a genetic history and a genetic sociology of this phenomenon. Sociology as I conceive it is a genetic structuralism or a structural genesis. The sociologist is someone who does comparative history on the particular case of the present; the sociologist is a historian who takes the present as object, with the ulterior motive of constituting the present as a particular case and locating it in the universe of possible cases. We need to avoid the major error – which historians as well as sociologists can easily fall into – of unconsciously universalizing the particular case, drawing universal conclusions from a particular case that is not constituted in its particularity. When I say, 'I am a French teacher', I forget to constitute myself as a particular case of the possible. I may draw universal conclusions, for example on the functions of reproduction, which are an unfounded generalization of the particular properties of the particular case.

The idea of a boundary between sociology and history has no meaning. It has only a historical justification inasmuch as it is bound up with a traditional division of labour. If it is perpetuated, this is because there are social interests attached to the existence of disciplines: investments of time and apprenticeship, as well as psychological investments. The same holds for the boundary between sociology and anthropology. This has a social existence, and corresponds to the requirements of the CNRS, which is an institution with directors, presidents, positions and mental structures. This opposition between sociology and history is a historical artefact, constructed historically, and it can be deconstructed historically. The function of historicization is to release these historical constraints inserted into the unconscious by history. I repeat Durkheim's formulation, 'The unconscious is history.' To explore the history of a discipline or a state, therefore, means exploring the unconscious of each of us, which, in its agreement with the unconscious of others, acquires a reality every bit as objective as that of a head of state. The strength of the social world lies in this orchestration of unconscious mental structures. And there is nothing more difficult to revolutionize than mental structures. That is why revolutions very often fail in their project of making a new man (a new *homo economicus* or a new *homo bureaucraticus*). In the same way, the division between geography and history is the product of history; the grounds for the existence of these disciplines mobilize fantastic social forces, with the result that it may be easier to reform the social security system than to abandon the academic division of disciplines.

This genetic structuralism, which I see as constitutive of social science in general, and which consists in saying that one of the ways of understanding the social functioning of an institution is to analyse its genesis, is scientifically justified. If I feel obliged to make rather more explicit something that basically can be taken for granted and is even trivial, this is because things do have to be spelled out, and each of you need only be in a situation to apply in practice what I am in the process of saying, to see that the old disciplinary reflexes still manifest themselves, leading to practical consequences. To exorcise this, one of the ways of understanding what I have just said would be Durkheimian. It was Durkheim's conviction that, in order to understand social structures, you had to go back to the elementary, which is what led him to privilege anthropology – see his book *The Elementary Forms of the Religious Life*, or his article with Marcel Mauss, 'On some primitive forms of classification'.[4] Durkheim sought the elementary in the primitive. The main instrument of his genetic thinking was anthropology. For him, primitive forms lead to the elementary. This is a metaphor from chemistry: the elementary is that from which the complex is created by combination.

This fantasy of the elementary was reactivated, at a certain point in time, by the linguistic model. People dreamed of having a system of phonemes from which it would be possible to reconstitute languages. I do not have this kind of intention. I do not believe that the quest for the original – in the case of our own tradition, the medieval state – should be confused with a quest for the elementary. For me, the original is the place where a certain number of things are formed, things that, once formed, pass unnoticed. The original is the site of the essential, the site where struggles are visible, since resistances to the constitution of the state were very important. The best historians, for reasons that are understandable, forget marginal groups, dominated people. Revolts against taxation are certainly studied, but resistances to linguistic unification or the unification of weights and measures are not studied. If beginnings are interesting, this is not as the site of the elementary, but as the site where you can see the fundamental ambiguity of the state, which is that those who theorize the public good are also those who profit from it. The two-sidedness of the state can be seen far better at its beginnings, because the state exists in our thinking and we are constantly applying a state thinking to the state. As our thinking is to a large extent the product of its object, it no longer perceives the essential, in particular this relationship of a subject belonging to the object.

Genetic structuralism has to establish the specific logic of the genesis of bureaucratic logic, and simultaneously to describe the specific nature of this logic. This is the problem of practical logics as opposed to logical logics.[5] Specialists in the social sciences, historians and sociologists, are often challenged by specialists in the more advanced sciences, who increasingly tend to intervene in the social sciences and exercise a jurisprudence in the name of their status as more advanced sciences. A very fine article calls the hard sciences 'masculine' and the soft sciences 'feminine'.[6] Quantitative/qualitative: oppositions of this kind are neither socially nor sexually neutral, and have effects that are quite disastrous. Apart from the fact that specialists in the soft sciences may mimic the outward signs of the hard sciences and obtain easy symbolic profits from doing so, a more serious danger lies in the fact that specialists in the hard sciences, with the complicity of a fraction of the specialists in the soft sciences, can impose a conception of the logic of historical things that does not conform to reality. In my work on Kabyle ritual, or on the categories of French professors as revealed by analysing obituaries of former pupils of the École Normale, or the judgements that professors make of their students,[7] I came to the conclusion that the logics according to which social agents and social institutions operate are logics that can be called soft, fuzzy; there is a logic of history that is not the logic of logic. If the results of specialists in the social sciences are measured by the yardstick of logical logics, social science is mutilated in its most specific characteristic. One of the most important tasks for specialists in the social sciences is to bring out the specific logic of their object, and the specific logic of their work on the object, so as to have their specific rigour recognized, a rigour that has nothing to do with the logical logic that is met with in theory in some scientific spheres. The terrorism of logical logic is also exerted on other human sciences that are supposedly more 'advanced', such as biology, for example.

Practical logics – those of institutions, of human practices – must be constituted in their specificity. It is a major scientific error in the historical sciences to be more rigorous than the object, to put more rigour into discourse on the object than there is in the object itself, in order to meet demands of rigour that are prevalent not in the object, but in the field of production of discourse on the object. Falsifications of this kind, even if sincere and spontaneous, are serious, above all because they prevent the logic of the discourse being matched to the logic of the object, and by the same token prevent the specificity of these logics being grasped, logics that are not 50 per cent logics, but are simply different. If you want a more thorough argument, *The Logic of Practice* deals with this subject. Despite dealing chiefly with problems of ritual practices and mythical systems, it applies to the problem of the state, where you also have practical logics that logical logic destroys.[8] One of the paradoxes of the social sciences is that in order to describe practical logics we only have logical logics that were constructed in opposition to practical logics by a very difficult and protracted historical effort. Probability theory was constructed against spontaneous probability. All the fundamental principles of probability theory amount to saying: 'Do not do what you do spontaneously.'

In the same way, games theory was constructed against the spontaneous strategies of players. This means that the instruments of knowledge that we have are destructive of their object. Understanding the instruments of knowledge is important; epistemology is not an optional extra for the scientist, but an integral part of scientific work. It is a question of understanding our instruments of knowledge in order to know the effect that these instruments produce on our objects; and we have to know our object in order to know in what way it obeys a specific logic, opposed to that of the instruments of knowledge that we apply to it. This double effort is very important. Historians, and a fortiori geographers, are victims of a form of symbolic domination that consists in simultaneously rebelling and being crushed. To give an example, the first issue of the radical geography magazine *Hérodote* published an interview with Michel Foucault. This was a significant slip – the lowest requesting a guarantee from the highest . . .

Historians are extremely irritated by theorization, sometimes even by any kind of theorization, inasmuch as the vocation of historian very often demands an entrance fee of abandoning the ambition to generalize, leaving this to sociologists with a somewhat ambivalent contempt. The dominant historians humbly pay their homage to the philosophers. A certain form of reflection that is traditionally called 'philosophical' (and should rather be called epistemological) is a constitutive part of the craft of the historian, the sociologist, and any specialist in the social world, not an optional extra, and it should be taught as an element of specific competence in the historical sciences. This competence, which is not very widespread among philosophers and historians, would be an instrument of liberation for historians in relation to the forms of domination that philosophers exert over them; it would also be an element of progress towards the unification of the social sciences and the abolition of the boundary between sociology and history.

Genetic history of the state

Sociology as I conceive it emerges from the limits traditionally imparted to the discipline and implies a genesis of the objective structures that it takes as its object. The task of this genetic sociology – as Piaget talks of genetic psychology – is to study the genesis of individual structures and social structures, in our particular case that of the field of high public office, the bureaucratic field, the state field. How should this genetic history of collective structures be conducted? In what way does it differ from history as this is ordinarily practised? What else does it demand? There are a number of collective works on the genesis of the state that I much admire, and which I shall draw on here. The bibliographic references are as follows: Françoise Autrand, *Prosopographie et genèse de l'État moderne*; Jean-Philippe Genet and Bernard Vincent, *État et Église dans la genèse de l'État moderne*; Jean-Philippe Genet and Michel Le Mené, *Genèse de l'État moderne*; *Culture et idéologie dans la genèse de l'État moderne*.[9] I could naturally cite several other works, which I shall mention later in this course. But I believe that these ones are important, as they will enable you to see the best of what historians can do.

The object of the remarks I have just made is to encourage historians, to try and free them – making use of the sociology of science that brings to light forms of domination that can be objectified and thus controlled – from the various forms of censorship they accept because these are immanent in the very structure of the field of history. It is a matter of saying to them: 'You would do what you are doing still better if you pursued it thoroughly, if you did not let yourselves be confined within the rather castrating limits of the historical discipline, which is not designed to press concepts to their conclusion, to construct models and systems of variables.' Not all historians are in agreement, and it is impossible to cite more than fifteen coherent works of history that are falsifiable in the Popperian sense. It is characteristic of the field that it produces constraints, objective and embodied censorships, and people do not even notice the censorships they subject themselves to by entering the field . . .

Having said this, not in order to shock, to blame or give a lesson, but to try and make a small contribution to freeing the social sciences both from the dictatorship of the hard sciences and, what is worse, from the incorporated forms of domination, I shall extend my explanation of the presuppositions of this kind of genetic history a bit, in order to say in what way, methodologically, it is different from what historians do. One of the major differences is that historians would not do what I am doing here because they would think it superfluous, pretentious. I have in mind Saussure's formula, which I much like to cite, and which says that you have to know what the linguist is doing. I want to show what is involved in what the historians I have mentioned are doing, as without these historians I could not try to do what I shall try to do in relation to the genesis of the state. If you know what you are doing, you do it better – it's the transition from a practice to a method. Marc Bloch entitled his book *The Historian's Craft*; a craft is something that exists in a practical state, you can do wonderful things without having any meta-discourse on its practice. I prefer a historian or a sociologist who knows his craft without the accompaniment of epistemological discourse to a sociologist who gives speeches on his methodology but does not know his craft. A methodology has never protected anyone from technical error; only a craft protects. Yet the craft is a necessary condition but not a sufficient one. You can practise your craft all the better if you master it at a conscious level, if you are able to explain the practical principles that you apply in your practice, if you have transformed schemas into rules, if you have posited rules that can become collective rules and be utilized even by opponents as a call to order. Codifying has a considerable importance.[10] Epistemology is the codifying of a craft, which makes it undergo a transmutation; you move to a different order when you do what you are doing with awareness.

In my project of a genetic history of the state, I shall introduce right away the idea that there is a logic of the genesis of logics. In other words, doing history is quite different from telling a story: history is not an account, but a selection of pertinent facts (Saussure). You have to know what is historically constituted. First property: this logic of the genesis of logics is neither in the order of logical necessity, nor in that of chance or pure contingency. There is a specific logic of the genesis of these strange objects that are historical social objects, they have a specific logic that is not that of logic. In order to spare you a great philosophical development in the classical vein, I refer you to Ernst Cassirer's last article, published in *Word*.[11] Cassirer is not just a useful philosopher, he is necessary for correctly understanding the craft of the historian or the sociologist. At the end of his life he spoke of structuralism and tried to give a philosophical foundation to this notion of structure, a strange reality that escapes the Leibnizian alternative between 'truth of fact' and 'truth of reason'. According to Cassirer, it is a kind of de facto reason, a contingent reason, both in its operation and in its genesis. If you see it in terms of the logic that opposes pure contingency to necessity, you don't understand it at all. In this magnificent article, he develops this ambiguity of historical reason in the sense of process, and of historical reasons in the sense of the logic immanent to historical orders grasped at a given moment. As I see it, being a historian or a sociologist means realizing that you are dealing with logics that escape this alternative, both in their existing state and in their genesis. By the same token, what has to be understood is a form of necessity in contingency, or contingency in necessity, of social acts performed under structural necessities, under the constraint of the products of previous history, under structural necessities that are embodied in the form of permanent dispositions, what I call habitus.

The sociologist or historian who approaches the social world would do what he does more completely if he knew that what he had as his object was a provisional state, neither random nor necessary, of a relationship between a structure that is the product of history, a field, and an embodied structure that is also the product of history. When the historian studies a statement of Guizot in the Chamber of Deputies, he is dealing with something conjunctural, accidental, a 'happening' that is basically devoid of interest. The same goes for the sociologist who studies a declaration by Cohn-Bendit from 1968, or the attitude of a certain professor at that time, or of Flaubert at the time of the case brought against his novel *Madame Bovary*. When he studies a 'happening', what he is actually studying is the encounter between the habitus – product of an ontogenesis, of the embodiment under certain conditions of the state of a certain structure, the structure of a global social space and a field within this space – and an objectified structure – that of a social space as a whole, or more often that of a sub-world, the field of history, the literary field, the state field. The sociologist does comparative history when he takes the present as his object. When I study the reform of housing policy in 1975, I do exactly the same thing as someone studying a debate in the English Parliament in 1215; I am dealing with the encounter between two histories, at a moment that is itself history on the side of both individuals and structures.[12]

Game and field

I want to continue this for a couple of minutes. In what way does it change in practice our view of the craft of the analyst of social or historical facts? In order to understand this, I shall move very quickly to a comparison between field and game. This genetic structuralism is distinguished from the ordinary way of doing history, firstly in that it seeks to make explicit what is involved in doing what it is doing. Secondly, in that it makes explicit what is the specific logic of historical change and historical realities, of fields in particular. Thirdly, when dealing with differentiated societies in which the state is constituted as a differentiated region among other differentiated regions, the sociologist knows that what he is taking as object are sub-worlds, fields. When he does literary history, the history of art, of the state, of constitutional law, he studies the genesis of social games, of what I call fields. Everything I have said can be summed up as follows: in my view, the historical project I set myself is to study the genesis of a particular field, which I can compare to a game for purposes of communication, while noting the difference I have just mentioned. Let us take the game of chess, the most intellectual of games. Those who belong to the pole that Kant dogmatically called human sciences, those who try to formalize at all costs, all support the chess metaphor; they constantly make an ontological leap, moving from things of logic to the logic of things, or from logical logic to practical logic, abolishing practical logic. By making the distinction between a game of chess and a field, I am trying to bring to your attention a concrete way of grasping what I see as the real philosophy of social fields and their genesis.

In the game of chess there are explicit and conscious rules, formulated and listed, which are outside the game, pre-exist it and outlive it. They are stable unless they are revised, and they are explicitly acknowledged by the players, who accept the rules of the game. A very important property is that the rules that organize this game are outside the game; there is no question of negotiating them with the opponent while the game is under way. In a field, the rules are implicit regularities, only a very small part of which are made explicit: this is the same difference as that between craft and method that I just mentioned. Part of these regularities governs the sanctions to be applied to practices. These sanctions are immanent to the game, implicit in it; the rules are within the game and are always being challenged; one of the properties of fields is precisely that people struggle here to triumph according to the immanent rules of the game. Weber said the same thing: the person who does not bend to the rules of the capitalist cosmos goes bankrupt if he is an employer, and is dismissed if he is a worker.[13] The immanent rules are recalled by way of sanctions, but they can remain implicit. Secondly, the regular order of the economic or bureaucratic cosmos is such that there is no struggle over the rules of the game. But there can be a struggle to change the rules of the game (by revolution or a policy of reform), which consists in cheating on the game and establishing a tacit regularity that will become the rule. Something that started off as cheating or casuistry or evasion . . .

In other words, the rules are implicit regularities that the players ignore most of the time, rules that are mastered in a practical state without the players being able to formulate them explicitly. They are not stable, as distinct from rules of a game; they are not outside the game. The constraints according to which the game is played are themselves the product of the game. A structural analysis of the game therefore implies an analysis of the history of the game, of the becoming that led to this stage of the game, of the process by way of which the game generates and maintains the constraints and regularities according to which it is played. The game does not contain its whole truth within itself. A field is a game that is played according to regularities that are its rules, but in which play can also involve transforming these rules or regularities.

To describe the genesis of a field in no way means describing the genesis of a game. If you are trying to show the genesis of a game, you have to find a lawgiver and know who invented it. The game of basketball, for example, appeared in 1890, invented by someone who wanted to create a less violent game that could also be played by women. For the field, it involves following a process. In relation to the concentration of law, the transition from feudal law to royal law, the process by which the king, as instance of last appeal, gradually concentrated juridical power, Marc Bloch said that there was a process of concentration of law that was done without an overall plan, without a legislative text, and, one could say, by makeshift.[14] Does this mean by chance and any which way? No. Here we have a very strange necessity, with neither a rational calculating lawgiver, nor an inventor, nor a madman who does no matter what ('sound and fury'). We have someone who does things by makeshift, combining elements that are borrowed from previous states and constructing jigsaw puzzles. This seemingly incoherent construction generates semi-coherent things that are the object of study for specialists in the social sciences. Whether you want to or not, when you do history you have a philosophy of history, and so it is best to know what this is. The philosophy of history that Marc Bloch had in mind, what I was trying to show on the basis of the comparison between game and field, was to apply a philosophy of logic by which fuzzy logics are generated, with not only a principle of pertinence of what is important to retain, but also a principle of meta-pertinence. I am trying to constitute at least as a problem what great historians do very well. I would like to show in what way this philosophy changes the manner of reading historical facts, and the manner of reading what historians are doing. If I was cynical, I would say: 'Let historians carry on working in this way, and provide ready-made material for sociologists.' But my work is completely respectful of their work and, even if I shock, my discourse is an exhortation for historical work to be pursued thoroughly, for historians to have their specific work taken away if they do not do it thoroughly.

The sociology of history avoids two constant temptations, two current forms of finalism: a collective finalism, which consists in seeking in the immanence of the historical world a reason oriented towards goals, and a finalism of individuals, which is periodically reborn in the social sciences. Rational action theory views social agents as rational calculators who maximize this or that form of material or symbolic profit. I believe that the paradox of the social world is that you can discover an immanent order without being forced to put forward the hypothesis that this order is the product of conscious intention on the part of individuals, or of a function inscribed in collectives that transcends individuals. The state has been a great protector of ignorance, in the sense that it can serve as repository for everything that people are unable to explain in the social world, and it has been endowed with every possible function: the state maintains, etc. You will see, in books with a 'theoretical' pretension, that a fantastic number of sentences have the state as subject. This kind of hypostatizing of the word 'state' is everyday theology. In fact, there is practically no sense in making the state the subject of statements. That is why I always rephrase my sentences when speaking of it . . .

There is order and a certain form of logic. But this does not mean it is correct to suppose that this logic has a subject; it is a logic without subject, but – in the social sciences, one mistake is often avoided only to fall into another – this does not mean that social agents are mere *Träger* of the structure, as the Althusserians used to say in the name of Marx (*Träger* can be translated as 'bearers', though this is not a good translation). Social agents are acting, active, but it is history that acts through them, the history whose product they are. This does not mean that they are totally dependent.

Another important thing that follows from this way of conceiving the logic of history is that the logic of the process is not the logic of progress. The process is not necessarily continuous, though it is more so than is commonly believed, and it does present discontinuities. When philosophers intervene in these kinds of problems, they re-create sharp dichotomies and dismiss all those who, thanks to their craft, go beyond such dichotomies in practice. This is why the social sciences have to be liberated from philosophers, at least from those who do not respect the specificity of the social sciences, those who do not take the work of the social sciences as it is, and descend with a whip, as Nietzsche called on men to do among women, to establish an epistemological reign of terror. I respect wholeheartedly the philosophers who do respect the specificity of the social sciences, as they can help the social sciences to clear up problems such as those I mentioned in two words, rule and regularity. I can tell you that I have made much use of good philosophers, who have tremendous things to say on these subjects.

Tracing the genesis of the state means selecting a principle of pertinence, for example the distinction between premodern, modern and postmodern that implicitly conveys a philosophy of history. If you believe that the state is the universal, and that the constitution of the state is the constitution of a world in which a few agents monopolize universal speech, it is clear that the constitution of the state has something in common with the process of universalization: a movement from the local to the universal. Can such a movement towards universalization be viewed as progress? We are dealing here with inventions constrained by the structure against which they are made. The alternative between individual and structure, a subject for fine dissertations, is useless here, since the structure exists within the individual as well as in the objective realm. Moreover, the social order may have a constraining effect on invention. (The world of science, for example, constrains scientific invention.) Sociology has to explain the constitution of social worlds in which the stakes of power are historical. The logic of these worlds means that transhistorical things are generated such as science, law, the universal, that is, things that, though socially produced, are not reducible to their social conditions of production. If certain agents have a social interest in appropriating this universal, that does not mean it is not universal . . .[15]

Anachronism and the illusion of the nominal

One latent error, when you leave the philosophy of the history of the state in an implicit state, is anachronism. Paradoxically, historians are more given to anachronism than any other scholars, largely because they are victims of the illusion of the constancy of the nominal, an illusion according to which an institution that has kept the same name today as in the Middle Ages is thereby the same. Historians warn us, but the fact remains that the objects they construct include the collection of self-interests bound up with present questions about the past. In order to produce a linguistic effect, or to seem modern, they make unjustified analogies, saying for example, on the question of medieval institutions, that 'Josquin des Prez was the Bernard Pivot of the sixteenth century'.[16] This anachronism, and the retrospective illusion, are often bound up with an error in philosophy of history arising from the fact that, when you give the genesis of a structure, you have at each moment a state of the structure in which the same element is enmeshed in different states of the structure and is therefore changed. Levenson, a great historian of China, said that a canonical text of Confucius changed because it did not change in a changing world.[17]

All this follows from the metaphor of games that are in fact fields, where the rules of the game are in play in the game, where the overall structure of the balance of forces changes. We can no longer assume that what is nominally the same really is the same, but must always make the hypothesis that nominal identity is hiding real difference. Historians make longitudinal series, and since 1830 there have been censuses in France that classify people into socio-occupational categories. But a 'doctor' in the 1830s was very different from the 'doctor' of the 1980s, even if the professional body remained the same. These longitudinal studies of institutions often fail to have an object. Biographies, when they are sociologically constructed, actually give the history of the field in which a biography is situated. The historian who says: 'I am working on the history of the Conseil d'État' should rather say: 'I am working on the history of the bureaucratic field . . .' If you accept the idea that you are dealing with the genesis of structures, and that each state of the structure defines each of its elements, it follows that you can only compare structure with structure, a state of the structure with a state of the structure, since all atomistic longitudinal series contain the pitfall of nominal constancy.

The two faces of the state

The question is whether all these preliminaries are justified in terms of a substantial scientific gain. Is it possible, in other words, on the basis of all this, to add something to the historical works that have been cited? What is revealed by all the readings and reflections I have made on the basis of the principle I put forward is the fundamental ambiguity of the state, and of the process from which the state arose. The state is a Janus about which it is impossible to state a positive property without simultaneously stating a negative property, a Hegelian property without a Marxist property, a progressive property without a regressive and oppressive property. This is troubling for those people who like to think that everything will turn out rosy . . . What I believe I can do, instead of giving a preliminary methodological orientation of a rather incantatory kind – you remember: Hegel and Marx, Spinoza, etc. – is to base this dualism on a genetic analysis. To describe the genesis of the state is to describe the genesis of a social field, a relatively autonomous social microcosm inside the surrounding social world, within which a particular game is played, the game of legitimate politics. Take for instance the invention of parliament, a place where there is public debate, in forms and rules that are laid down, on questions and conflicts involving opposed interest groups. Marx only saw the 'behind the scenes' side. Recourse to the theatrical metaphor, the theatricalization of consensus, masks the fact that there are people who pull the strings, and that the real stakes, the true powers, lie elsewhere. To give the genesis of the state is to give the genesis of a field in which politics is played out, symbolized, dramatized in prescribed forms, and by the same token the people with the privilege of entering this game have the privilege of appropriating for themselves a particular resource that we can call the 'universal' resource.

Entering this game of compliant, legitimate politics means having access to the gradually accumulated resource that is the 'universal', entering universal speech, universal positions on the basis of which it is possible to speak in the name of all, of the *universum*, the totality of a group. One can speak in the name of the public good, of what is good for the public, and at the same time appropriate it. This is what lies at the root of the 'Janus effect': there are people who have the privilege of the universal, but you cannot have the universal without at the same time having a monopoly over the universal. There is a universal capital. The process by which this managing instance of the universal is constituted is inseparable from the process of constitution of a category of agents who have the property of appropriating the universal. To take an example from the realm of culture, the genesis of the state is a process in the course of which a whole series of concentrations of different forms of resources is effected: the concentration of information resources (statistics, by way of investigations and reports), linguistic capital (making one particular dialect the official one, which is established as the dominant tongue, with the result that all other tongues become errant and delinquent, inferior forms of this). This process of concentration goes hand in hand with a process of dispossession. To establish one city as the capital, as the place where all these forms of capital[18] are concentrated, means dispossessing the provinces of capital; establishing the legitimate language means relegating all other tongues to patois.[19] Legitimate culture is the culture guaranteed by the state, guaranteed by this institution that guarantees the qualifications of culture, that delivers diplomas that guarantee possession of a guaranteed culture. The school syllabus is a concern of the state; changing the syllabus means changing the structure of the distribution of capital, devaluing certain forms of capital. Removing Latin and Greek, for example, means relegating a whole category of small owners of linguistic capital to an outmoded cultural petite bourgeoisie. In my own earlier work on the school, I completely overlooked the fact that legitimate culture is the culture of the state . . .

This concentration is at the same time a unification and a form of universalization. Where there was diversity, dispersion, localism, there is now uniformity. Germaine Tillion and I compared units of measure in different Kabyle villages over a 30-kilometre distance, and found as many different units as there were villages. The creation of a national, state standard of weights and measures is an advance in the direction of universalization: the metric system is a universal standard that presupposes consensus, agreement on meanings. This process of concentration, unification and integration is accompanied by a process of dispossession, since all the skills and knowledge that were associated with these local measures are disqualified. In other words, the very process that brings about a gain in universality is accompanied by a concentration of universality. There are those who want the metric system (mathematicians) and those who are relegated to the local. The very process of establishing common resources is inseparable from the establishment of these common resources as a capital monopolized by those who have the monopoly of struggle for the monopoly of the universal. This whole process – constitution of a field; autonomization of this field in relation to other necessities; constitution of a specific necessity in relation to economic and household necessity; constitution of a specific reproduction of the bureaucratic type, which is specific in relation to domestic, family reproduction; constitution of a specific necessity in relation to religious necessity – is inseparable from a process of concentration and constitution of a new form of resources that turn out to be universal, or in any case to have a degree of universalization that is higher than those that existed previously. You move from the small local market to the national market, whether at the economic or the symbolic level. The genesis of the state is basically inseparable from the constitution of a monopoly of the universal, with culture being the example par excellence.

All my earlier work on this subject could be summed up as follows: this culture is legitimate because it presents itself as universal and open to all, because it is possible in the name of this universality to eliminate without fear those who do not possess it. This culture, which appears to unite but in reality divides, is one of the great instruments of domination, since there are those who have the monopoly of this culture, a terrible monopoly since this culture cannot be criticized as being particular. Even scientific culture simply presses this paradox to its extreme. The conditions of constitution and accumulation of this universal are inseparable from the conditions of constitution of a caste, a state nobility, the 'monopolizers' of the universal. On the basis of this analysis, it is possible to undertake the project of universalizing the conditions of access to the universal. But you still have to know how this can be done: do you have to dispossess these 'monopolizers'? Clearly the answer does not lie in this direction.

I shall end with a parable designed to illustrate what I have said about method and content. Some thirty years ago, one Christmas night, I went to a small village deep in the Béarn to see a country dance.[20] Some people danced, others didn't. A number of men, rather older than the others and dressed in peasant style, just talked among themselves, with an expression meant to justify that they were there without dancing, to justify their unexpected presence. They might have been married, as once you're married you don't dance any more. The dance is a place for matrimonial exchange, the market for symbolic matrimonial goods. There was a very high level of bachelors, 50 per cent of the men between twenty-five and thirty-five. I tried to find a system to explain this phenomenon, in that there was a protected local market, not unified. When what we call the state was formed, there was a unification of the economic market, which the state contributed to by its policy, and a unification of the market for symbolic exchanges, that is, the market in bodily stance, manners, clothing, personality, identity, presentation. These people had a protected market with a local basis, over which they had control, which made possible a kind of endogamy organized by families. The products of the peasant mode of reproduction had their opportunities on this market: they were still sellable and found girls. In the logic of the model I mentioned, what happened at this dance was the result of the unification of the market for symbolic exchanges, which meant that a soldier from the small town nearby who came swaggering in had a disqualifying effect, taking value away from the peasant competitor. In other words, the unification of the market that can be presented as an advance, at least for those people who leave, that is, women and all the dominated, can have a liberating effect. The school imparts a different bodily stance, different ways of dress, etc., and the student has a matrimonial value on this new unified market whereas peasants are disqualified. The whole ambiguity of this process of universalization lies in this. From the standpoint of the country girls who leave for the town and marry a postman or the like, this is an access to the universal.

But this degree of higher universalization is inseparable from the domination effect. I recently published an article, a kind of re-reading of my analysis of the Béarn bachelors, of what I said at that time, which I entitled, for amusement, 'Reproduction forbidden'.[21] I showed that this unification of the market has the effect of forbidding de facto the biological and social reproduction of a whole category of people. At the same time, I had been working on material that I found by chance, the records of communal debates in a small village of two hundred inhabitants during the French Revolution. In this region, men would vote unanimously. Decrees then arrived that they had to vote by majority. They discussed and there was opposition, one side and another. Bit by bit, the majority won out: it had the universal behind it. There has been much discussion around this question raised by Tocqueville about the continuity or discontinuity of the Revolution. It remains a real historical problem: what is the specific strength of the universal? The political procedures of these peasants with very coherent age-old traditions were swept away by the strength of the universal, as if they bowed to something that was logically stronger: coming from the city, put into explicit discourse, methodical and not just practical. They became provincials, locals. The records of their debates become: 'The prefect having decided . . .', 'The municipal council met . . .' The other side of universalization was a dispossession and monopolization. The genesis of the state is the genesis of a site for the management of the universal, and at the same time for a monopoly of the universal, and that of a group of agents who participate in the de facto monopoly of that thing which is, by definition, the universal.

UNIVERSITY OF WINCHESTER
LIBRARY

Year 1990–1991

Lecture of 10 January 1991

Historical approach and genetic approach – Research strategy – Housing policy – Interactions and structural relations – Self-evidence as an effect of institutionalization – The effect of 'that's the way it is . . .' and the closing of possibilities – The space of possibilities – The example of spelling

Historical approach and genetic approach

This year's course will continue to deal with the question of the state. I shall tackle two main points. The first of these bears on the genesis of the state, or rather its sociogenesis, to use an expression favoured by Norbert Elias, the sociogenesis of the state – that is, the history of the birth of the state in the West, conducted accoding to particular logics. The second point will bear on the structure and functioning of the state, this second part being a kind of balance sheet in which I shall seek to sum up the findings that may have been gained over these years on the question of the state.

I should say right away, as you have surely noticed, that the question of the state is a supremely difficult question. I do not think there is any more difficult question for a sociologist. One of my colleagues, the French sociologist Michel Crozier, entitled a book of his *État modeste*.[1] I often think that the state is something that necessarily makes you modest, that the state is a problem that condemns the sociologist to modesty, especially when he undertakes to do what I shall try and do, something rather crazy, which is to try and 'totalize' – I use the word in apostrophes – both the findings of theoretical research on the state – few subjects have caused theorists both good and bad to say so much – and the findings of historical research on all countries at all times. Merely stating this project already implies that it is unrealizable. I think however that the attempt deserves to be made. I think that the social sciences are often faced with this antinomy and this dilemma of a totalization both necessary and impossible.

The solution I am going to propose to you implies a very acute awareness of what is involved in my undertaking. I do not want to proliferate preliminaries about the state and the theory of the state, theoretical or methodological preliminaries that are rather boring, but it strikes me that a certain number of precautions are indispensable. First of all, I shall distinguish between the approach I call genetic and the common historical approach. This could by itself provide the object for a whole year's teaching, but I shall only say a few words on this subject to suggest to you a path for reflection. I essentially want to show what the ambition of the sociologist is as distinct from that of the historian. The sociologist's ambition is distinguished from that which the majority of historians apply in their work; the sociologist seeks to construct a theoretical model of a process, that is, a set of statements that are systematically connected and capable of systematic verification, able to account for as large a set of historical facts as possible. This is a simple definition of the model. This ambition, I repeat, is out of proportion given the immense amount of data that has to be integrated and the complexity of the theoretical schemas that have to be developed. That said, [it should be the ambition] of everyone who utters the word 'state'. If, as I just said, we have despite everything to attempt the impossible, this is because those who do not make this explicit do so surreptitiously, and because every discourse that bears on the state has the same ambitions, but they are not matched by an analysis of the conditions of possibility, which may be conditions of impossibility.

The first point, then, is to distinguish the genetic approach from the ordinary historical approach; and secondly, to try and show in what way the genetic approach is particularly indispensable. Why, faced with a phenomenon such as the state, is the sociologist forced to turn historian, at the evident risk of committing one of the acts most strongly tabooed in scientific work, the sacrilege of transgressing a sacred boundary between disciplines? The sociologist exposes himself to being rapped on the knuckles by every specialist, and, as I have indicated, there are very many of these. That said, if the genetic approach is forced on us in this particular case, I believe this is because it is, let us say, not the only instrument of rupture, but a major one. Taking up the well-known indications of Gaston Bachelard, for whom a scientific fact is necessarily 'conquered' and then 'constructed',[2] I think that the phase of conquering facts against accepted ideas and common sense, in the context of an institution such as the state, necessarily implies recourse to historical analysis.

One analysis that I conducted at considerable length concerned the tradition, from Hegel to Durkheim, of developing a theory of the state that, in my opinion, is simply a projection of the representation that the theorist has of his role in the social world. Durkheim is characteristic of this fallacy to which sociologists are very often prone, and which consists in projecting onto the object, into the object, one's own thinking about the object which is precisely the product of the object itself. In order to avoid thinking the state with state thinking, the sociologist has to avoid thinking about society with a thought produced by society. And unless we believe in the a priori, in transcendent ideas that escape history, we can posit that all we have for conceiving the social world is a thought that is the product of the social world in a very broad sense, that is, common sense from the lay to the scholarly. In the case of the state, this antinomy of research in social science, and perhaps of research in general, is particularly felt, an antinomy arising from the fact that if you know nothing then you see nothing, and if you do know, you risk seeing only what you know.

The researcher totally lacking in instruments of thought, who knows nothing of current debates, scientific discussions and findings, who does not know who Norbert Elias is, etc., risks either being naive, or reinventing what is already known, but if he is familiar with all this, then he risks being the prisoner of his knowledge. One of the problems that faces every researcher, and especially in the social sciences, is to know how to free yourself from the things you know. This is easy to say, and in epistemological discourses on the art of invention you can read things of this kind, but in practice it is terribly difficult. One of the major resources of the researcher's trade consists in finding ruses, ruses of scientific reason if I may say so, that make it possible precisely to get round, to put in parentheses, all these presuppositions that are involved in the fact that our thought is the product of what we are studying, and has all kinds of adherences. 'Adherence' is better than 'attachment' [*adhésion*], as if it were just this, things would be too easy. One always says: 'It's difficult because people have political biases', yet everyone knows there is an epistemological danger in leaning either to the right or to the left. Attachments are actually easy to bracket out; what are hard to bracket out are adherences, that is, implications of thought so deep that they remain unknown.

If it is true that the only thought we have for conceiving the social world is the product of the social world itself, if it is true – and you can take Pascal's famous phrase but give it a quite different meaning – that 'the world comprehends me but I comprehend the world', and I would add that I comprehend it in an immediate way because it comprehends me,[3] if it is true that we are the product of the world in which we are, and which we try to understand, it is clear that this initial comprehension that we owe to our immersion in the world we are trying to comprehend is particularly dangerous, and that we have to escape this initial, immediate comprehension, which I call doxic (from the Greek word *doxa* that the phenomenological tradition has adopted). This doxic comprehension is a possession possessed or, you could say, an alienated appropriation. We possess a knowledge of the state, and every thinker who has conceived the state before me has appropriated the state with a thought that the state has imposed on him, an appropriation that is only so easy, so self-evident, so immediate, because it is alienated. It is a comprehension that does not comprehend itself, that does not comprehend the social conditions of its own possibility.

We have in fact an immediate mastery of state things. For example, we know how to fill in a form. When I fill in an administrative form – name, forename, date of birth – I understand the state; the state gives me orders for which I am prepared. I know what a registry office is, a progressive historical invention. I know that I have a legal identity, since I have an identity card. I know that on the identity card there are a certain number of characteristics. In short, I know a lot of things. When I fill in a bureaucratic form, which is a great state invention, when I fill in a request or sign a certificate, if I am authorized to do so, whether it is an identity document, a sickness certificate, a birth certificate, etc. – when I do operations of this kind, I understand the state perfectly; I am, in a sense, a man of the state, the state-made man, and by the same token I understand nothing about it. That is why the work of the sociologist, in this particular case, consists in trying to reappropriate those categories of state thought that the state has produced and inculcated in each one of us, that were produced at the same time as the state was produced, and that we apply to everything, particularly to the state in order to conceive the state, with the result that the state remains the unthought, the unthought principle of the greater part of our thoughts, including those on the state.

Research strategy

This may strike you as somewhat abstract and verbal, but I shall try to give you examples to show you that we have before our eyes 'coups d'état' that we cannot see. An example of this is spelling, which can become a real matter of state, especially in the present conjuncture, and which I shall go on to analyse right away. It is a magnificent illustration of everything I have just been saying. In order to try to emerge from state thought, I carried out in recent years a series of critical analyses. I did what you could call – transposing the expression 'negative theology' – a kind of 'negative sociology', but this led to very disappointing results. At the end of each year, I have to admit to you (if I did not say this, I thought it very strongly) that I was aware of not having made much headway, of having often replaced the theses, theories, what is given in lectures on the state, with theoretical rubble or little titbits like analyses of certificates, forms, disinterestedness, public service, the gradual invention of the notion of the public in the eighteenth century, etc.

I am telling you this so as to explain my way of proceeding, because it may not be understood, which is quite understandable. I am proceeding in a completely conscious way, this is a research strategy. Generally in sociology, and particularly when the state is concerned, you have no other strategies than those of Horace before the Curiatii, or David before Goliath, that is, to make yourselves as small as possible, because otherwise it's too difficult. Now, it's a law of society that the bigger people feel, the more they deal with 'big problems'. There is a social hierarchy of problems, and elevated people will think, for example, about international relations or the state, and look down from a great height on those who concern themselves with certificates . . . The strategy that has worked for me in much of my research, at least in my own eyes, consists in accepting a bias towards ancillary status, towards gathering up remnants, those little questions that big theorists abandon, because I believe it is at this level that you are most protected from 'coups d'état', from the imposition of the state.

The difficulty does not just come from common sense, from the fact that we know how to fill in a form and accept phrases of the type 'the state decides that . . .' without reflection, that we accept that the state is a reality on which an adjective can be pinned: it is modest, it is ambitious, it is glorious, it is centralist, etc. We accept a great many things without explanation. The worst, however, for a scientist, is scientific common sense, that is, the set of obligatory questions that are constitutive of the profession and hence of professionalism: the questions that you have to raise in order to be recognized as a legitimate scientist. It is very hard to break with this kind of common sense, and the younger you are, the more you are just setting out, giving yourself an air of freedom, the more in fact you are subject to the great questions of the day, you have a duty to pay homage to these great questions . . . It should not be thought that this is a cynical homage. People who defend established spelling tooth and nail are not cynical, that would be too easy. This homage is sincere and obligatory. A big question calls for great reverence, and therefore weighty theses, major works and big concepts.

We can take for example the way that the problem of the state, which had more or less disappeared (there are fashions also in science, as everywhere else unfortunately), made a strong comeback in the intellectual world around the 1960s, in the wake of the social movements that shook that decade on both sides of the Atlantic. In the United States, the resurgence of so-called conflict theories and Marxism, including Marxism of structuralist inspiration (represented by Göran Therborn, Claus Offe, Nicos Poulantzas), had a major effect, and this resurgence was expressed right away in the form of a debate around the autonomy or heteronomy of the state. Was the state dependent, as Marxists say, even if this was a relative dependence, as Poulantzas said? Was there a correspondence between the state and one or other class? And what class would this be: was it the Junkers, the industrial bourgeoisie, the gentry? There were several works on this subject. Clearly, however, a relationship was being examined without examining its terms. What was meant by the gentry, by a class, by the state, was taken as given, and what was investigated was the dependence or independence between these terms . . .

There was subsequently a reaction against this current, which made a great deal of noise and whose most well-known representative was the American sociologist Theda Skocpol. Skocpol opposed the thesis of dependence – which was subversive at that time in the United States, in the logic of the student movement – with the thesis of autonomy, developed in her book *States and Social Revolutions*, which was a corrected amplification of Barrington Moore's thesis – he had been her teacher at Harvard. She subsequently co-edited a collective work entitled *Bringing the State Back In*.[4] She demonstrated in this book that it is impossible to

do sociology, to understand the social world, without bringing in the role
of the state, a role that is independent of that of the social forces within
which the state operates. There are all kinds of works in this tradition. You
have here an example of one of those screen problems that thousands of
researchers bump into. I read a very fine article, for example, with a magnificent bibliography, that lists all the champions of the state dependence
theory in the United States.[5] It is very professional, and the same should
be done in France, but on condition that something more than that is
done. The author lists all the champions of dependence, all the champions
of independence, he explains the two theories and, taking one empirical
case, that of Germany in the first half of the eighteenth century, tries to see
whether the state really was dependent or independent, using the historical
indications of dependence and independence. There is much writing of this
kind. [But] this type of work strikes me as an obstacle to knowledge, since
working empirically may also be a way of escaping theoretical reflection.

Housing policy

For my part, I tried to tackle the problem of the state in a very modest and
very empirical way by studying housing policy in France in the 1970s.[6]
As soon as there exists what is called a 'policy', involving a certain type
of legislation and regulation of support for housing, it is possible to say
that perhaps one does not know what the state is, but there is in any case
something in the region of what is called 'the state'. Yet it is impossible to
say any more on the subject than that, following the work of commissions,
a certain number of laws, decrees and regulations were passed that aimed
to replace what was called at the time 'support for bricks and mortar' with
what was called 'support for individuals'. I am a Wittgensteinian. I say:
'Here is a state action', and I ask myself: 'What does a state action consist
in? How does it happen and how is it determined or decided?' Once you
have questions of this kind in mind, the problem of the dependence or
autonomy of the state crumbles away, since what you observe is a space of
agents, a very complicated space.

Commissions are typical in this respect. They are sites at which you
find, and I'll say this in a very few words as I said a bit about it last year,
agents whom you can call state agents – ten years later they will have gone
over to the other side, through the 'revolving door', and be working for
the banks – agents of local authorities, representatives of housing associations, agents of banks that have major interests in this kind of business,
since if the mode of financing house-building changes, then all kinds of
investment strategy change. I will not develop the full analysis here, as it
would take me too far afield. You discover a space of competing agents
who maintain an extremely complex balance of forces with very complex
and very different weapons: some have knowledge of the regulations and
precedents; others have scientific authority and have mathematical models

that played a major role in this struggle; others again have prestige. M. de Fouchier, for example, combined a whole series of prestigious character-istics: his noble name, the fact of having been an inspector of finances, and being the director of the largest French bank. [7] All these agents enter into an extremely complex balance of forces, both material and symbolic, which for many of them is by way of discourse, and from this very complex balance of forces, which has to be analysed in a very subtle way, a decision results that contributes to strengthening or undermining a certain state of the balance of forces. I am giving only a very small idea of the empirico-theoretical complexity (given that there is neither pure theory nor pure empirical data here) that has to be manipulated in order to escape the simple alternative between a dependent or an independent state. What is the result of an analysis of this kind? The result is that the word 'state' is a kind of shorthand designation, but by this token a very dangerous one, for a set of extremely complex structures and processes. It would take me hours to develop what I mean by the state when I say that 'the state has decided to replace support for bricks and mortar by support for indi-viduals'. There are thousands of people in these fields, in articulated and opposing sub-fields, etc., in complex relationships.

Interactions and structural relations

There is a very fashionable technique in the United States known as 'network analysis'. This consists in analysing, by relatively elaborate sta-tistical methods, the networks of interactions between individuals. One of the promoters of this method is Edward Laumann. He is a Chicago sociologist who first used this method to investigate networks of power in a small town in Germany, subsequently venturing to apply this to larger networks, such as White House policies on certain questions, and he arrived at some very interesting results.[8] I do not agree with everything he says, and he would certainly be most surprised by my agreeing with him, but even if I do not share his theories, his philosophy or his politi-cal positions, he is on the path that eventually leads out of the Skocpol/ Poulantzas rut. This is why I feel rather close to him. In a couple of words, the difference between his view and my own is that he describes the spaces of public policy ('policy domains') as spaces of interaction far more than as relationships between structures. This is one of the major divisions in social science, the division between those who, faced with a social space to study – and I have already chosen my camp by saying 'social space' – focus on interactions between individuals: do they know one another or not? Does So-and-so have So-and-so's name in his address book? Do they speak on the phone? Do they communicate before deciding at the White House, etc.? In brief, there are those who focus on interactions, that is, on real social exchanges that are actually conducted. And then there are those, among whom I count myself, who believe that interactions are very important, that they are often the only way in which we are able to grasp things, and that it is only by way of interactions that structures reveal themselves. But structures are not reducible to interactions between two people talking. There is far more going on than what meets the eye. The example I often take to have this point understood is that of strategies of condescension. Interaction between two people may be the actualization of structural relations irreducible to interaction, with interaction being both its expression and its dissimulation. An intelligent interaction analysis is not far from a structural analysis, but there is a difference all the same in the way of explaining this, in the way of speaking of it, which means that the difference remains important. At all events, when studies of this kind are conducted – and here I agree with Laumann – instead of asking whether the state is dependent or independent, you examine the historical genesis of a policy, how this happened, how a regulation, a decision or a measure was arrived at, etc. You then discover right away that the academic *Streit* [dispute] between dependence and independence has no meaning, that it is impossible to give a response that is valid for all circumstances. Naturally this seems like a capitulation. Theorists are horrified when you say to them that you shouldn't give a once-and-for-all answer; they find that 'positivist'. You cannot give a once-and-for-all answer to this question, which does not mean that you cannot give very general answers, but it assumes that you start by throwing out this kind of badly posed question. It is impossible to give a once-and-for-all answer. For each particular case, in other words at every moment, in every country and even for every problem, you have to ask what the structure of the space is within which the policy in question is generated.

To help you understand this, if I set out to study a reform of the teaching system, I am going to find a certain space; if I set out to study a certain international crisis, I will find a different space with different agents, and the question is to know what is particular about them, especially those involved in both: are they more 'state' than the others? This is a key question: what are the properties of those agents who stand at the intersection of all the fields within which policies are constructed? If I study armaments policy, this is a quite different space from national education policy, which does not mean I will not investigate the invariants of what the state is, those things that happen each time that a state policy is decided. I believe that there is a specific logic of the bureaucratic field, this being a space within which contentious issues and quite specific interests are generated. In the case of the policy I studied, for example, there were two state bodies, two bodies that were historical products of the state, bodies that were produced in the production of the state, that the state had to produce as part of its own production, that is, the Corps des Ponts and the Inspecteurs des Finances. These two bodies had completely differing interests, bureaucratic interests bound up with their history, with their position in the social space, maintaining differing alliances with other agents, such as bankers . . . And so there are specific issues at stake, specific interests that are in part the effect of the position of agents in the social space, or in the bureaucratic sub-space constituted by the policy in question. There are also specific constraints and regularities that are irreducible to the constraints and regularities that weigh on all those involved.

There is a specific logic of the state, and these constraints, regularities, interests, this logic of operation of the bureaucratic field, may be the origin of a dependence or independence in relation to external interests; or rather, of unintended correspondences in relation to external interests. One might be able to say ex post, for example, that the engineers of the Corps des Ponts, for very complex historical reasons, had a rather more 'left' position towards public housing, and the Inspecteurs des Finances a more 'right' position. But this might well be a coincidence (I exaggerate a little). In the extreme case, these agents, by serving themselves, have additionally, without intending to, served the interests of one group rather than another. You can even say a bit more: 'all things considered', 'all in all', 'globally', all these state games serve some people more than others, and serve the dominant more than the dominated. But is it necessary to raise great ahistorical questions in order to reach this conclusion?

That is a first point. I meant, therefore, that when you are faced with a problem such as this, vigilance means having an attitude of great suspicion towards the state, to the point that I only began to use the word 'state' in my writing just two or three years ago. Up until then I never wrote 'state', as I did not know what it was, but I did know enough to distrust the use of the concept, even as shorthand. Bachelard talks of 'epistemological vigilance'; this should also apply to words.

(The only privilege of oral communication, which is always less good than written communication, because you do not have time to check it, is that it makes it possible to communicate things that are almost improper, that you cannot write down, because you are read by hostile or malicious colleagues.)

It is necessary, in other words, to break with grand theories, just as it is necessary to break with the ideas of common sense and to distrust immediate comprehension, since the more I understand the less I understand. That has a radical air, and is why I speak of 'negative sociology'. The more I understand, the more I need to distrust. I particularly need to distrust school questions – it is very vexing to say this within a school – but it is an antinomy of the teaching of research, quite especially in the social sciences. It is true that the teaching of research has to be a kind of permanent double bind:[9] 'I tell you what I am telling you, but you know that it's wrong, you know that it may be wrong.'

(On the subject of this last pedagogic advice, I would say that one of the problems of teaching here, which makes it terrifying for the person doing it, is the extreme diversity of the audience [I am addressing]. This can be analysed sociologically: the homogenization of educational audiences is an effect of the school system. Here we again have the historical unconscious. This was formed over centuries: pupils were put into a certain class at more or less the same age, with the same syllabus, etc. This was not invented overnight, there were times when you had side by side students of eighteen and boys of six. The more teachers lecture to a homogeneous audience, the more formally homogeneous the discourse can be. One of the problems raised by teaching at the Collège de France is that, for better or worse, it juxtaposes listeners with extremely diverse specialisms, backgrounds, ages, etc., and the weight of this diversity is extremely heavy, especially when you are aware of it. It is better not to be aware of it, but from a professional point of view I am not unaware of the problems of pedagogy; and when you are aware of it, it is quite crushing, since you have it in mind all the time. When I analyse the interaction/structure pair, for example, there are those among you who have heard me do this forty times, and it bothers me a bit to repeat it, and others for whom it would be worth two hours' development. So I try to make a 'historic compromise' . . .)

Self-evidence as an effect of institutionalization

In order to escape state thought about the state, I have adopted several modes of operation: empirical analysis, critique of the theoretical presuppositions of current theories, questioning of the dominant problems. But the most powerful weapon against state thought is genetic thought. Why is this privileged? Durkheim wrote a magnificent book called *The Evolution of Educational Thought*, which is the equivalent for education of what I am trying to do for the state. He tried to give, not an anecdotal history of education, but a genetic sociology revealing the properties that were pertinent to understanding what is the case today. Why is genetic analysis privileged in this way? One thing I sought to demonstrate in earlier lectures is that the state exercises an effect of symbolic imposition that is absolutely without any equivalent, an effect of symbolic imposition that tends to protect it from scientific questioning. What can be called the established state, the prevailing state, the current state, has been established by way of the very symbolic order it establishes, that is, both objectively, in things – for example, the division into disciplines, the division into age groups, and subjectively – in mental structures in the form of principles of division, principles of viewing things, systems of classifications. By way of this double imposition of symbolic order, the state tends to make a large number of practices and institutions appear self-evident and needing no explanation. One result, for example, is that we do not investigate the notion of national borders, the fact that in France we speak French rather than another language, the absurdity of spelling, in brief, lots of questions that could be raised and yet are not raised but bracketed out, a whole series of questions that could have been at the origin of institutions. As soon as you conduct historical research, you discover in fact that at the origin of institutions things were discussed that nowadays have to be discovered in an extremely laborious way.

One thing that struck me when I was working on education is that the idea that the school system could have a function of reproduction was put forward in the 1880s, when the possibility of establishing a compulsory school system was discussed. At the beginning, it turned out that the functions, the functioning, many things that subsequently went into the routine of the established order, were questioned and discussed. There is another situation in which questions are asked, that is in periods of decomposition. Movements of involution, as some biologists call them, periods of dissolution, 'pathological' situations, moments of state crisis, as for example the time of Algerian independence, are very interesting, since questions that, even if not repressed, were rejected because already resolved before even being raised, came forward again. Where do the borders lie? Do you need to speak French to be French? And if you don't speak French are you still French? Is it enough to speak French in order to be French?

One effect of the symbolic power associated with the state institution, in other words, is precisely the naturalization, in the form of *doxa*, of certain more or less arbitrary presuppositions that lay at the very origin of the state. And so only genetic research can remind us that the state, and everything that follows from it, is a historic invention, a historical artefact, and that we ourselves are inventions of the state, our minds are inventions of the state. To give a genetic history of the state, rather than a 'genealogy' in Foucault's sense,[10] is the only genuine antidote to what I call the 'amnesia of genesis' that is inherent to every successful institutionalization, since the successful imposition of any institution implies that its genesis is forgotten. An institution is successful when it has succeeded in imposing itself [as a matter of course]. I remind you of the definition of an institution as I use it:[11] an institution exists twice, both in objectivity and in subjectivity, in things and in minds. An institution that has been successful, that is therefore capable of existing both in the objectivity of regulations and in the subjectivity of mental structures in tune with these regulations, disappears as an institution. People no longer conceive it as being *ex instituto*. (Leibniz, in order to say that language was arbitrary, used the term *ex instituto*, that is, on the basis of an institutional act.) A successful institution is forgotten, and makes people forget the fact of its having had a birth or a beginning.

Genetic thought, as I define it, seeks in a sense to make the arbitrariness of beginnings resurface; it is [therefore] opposed to the most ordinary usages of ordinary history. The ordinary usages of ordinary historical thinking tend to fulfil, even unbeknown to those practising them, a function of legitimation, which is one of the most common usages of history. For example, in my lectures about the state I have introduced French parliamentarians from the eighteenth century such as d'Aguesseau, etc. These people spontaneously began to write the history of the Parlements. They were literati, they needed to legitimize their existence, they wrote a history which had the aim of showing what they wanted to demonstrate, that is, that the Parlements were very ancient, were the successors of the

États Généraux and therefore represented the people: a way of asserting and founding a power that was independent in relation to the king,
showing that they had a different legitimacy. History is very often given to
this discourse of legitimation, partly because it knows what has happened
since; there is a kind of constitutional anachronism in historians' works. I
read many historians, and with my nasty mind I see many anachronisms.
No one is more anachronistic than historians. To speak, for example, of
'France in the year 1000' strikes me as monstrous; it took ten centuries for
France to be constituted . . .

The return to the uncertainty attaching to origins, to the opening of
possibilities that is characteristic of beginnings, is extremely important
in order to overcome common sense. I am simply giving a real content
to the notion of rupture, which precisely means: stop viewing something
as not being problematic when it should be problematic. To de-banalize
and overcome the amnesia of beginnings that is inherent to institutionalization, it is important to return to the initial debates, which show us
that where only one possible outcome remained for us, there were in fact
several, with camps supporting each of these. This has very serious consequences from the standpoint of the philosophy of history that you apply
when you relate a history. As soon as you relate a linear history, you have
a philosophy of history, which has very important consequences from the
standpoint of what you have to look for when you are a historian, what
should be viewed as a fact from the standpoint of the construction of the
object. History is linear, that is, a one-way street. Where there were several
possible trajectories, at each moment – I am sometimes hesitant at putting
things like this, it's so much the *pons asinorum* of regular philosophical
discourse – there is a space of possibilities, several possible futures. What
was a principality could develop into feudalism or empire; what became
the Habsburg empire could have become something else . . . When I take
dynastic examples (you will see later on that this is important), this is
readily apparent. But when possibilities of a rather theoretical kind are
involved, it is far harder to discern.

The effect of 'that's the way it is . . .' and the closing of possibilities

I shall take a very concrete example, to show how at every moment
history contains a spectrum of possibilities. We might have not developed
nuclear power, but we did develop nuclear power; we might have not had
a housing policy based on individual investment and support for individuals, etc. There is an irreversibility that is correlative with the unilinear
nature of processes. History destroys possibilities: at every moment the
space of possibilities constantly closes, and if you relate this fact to what
I was saying just now, you see that the history of a successful institution
implies amnesia about its genesis, that history eliminates possibilities
and makes them forgotten as possibilities, that it even makes possibili-

ties unthinkable. There are possibilities that are abolished once and for all, more seriously than if they were simply forbidden, as they are made unthinkable. What we are familiar with as historical reality, things such as nuclear power stations, spelling, the division between history and geography, the existence of geology, etc. – all this seems such that the contrary is not even ruled out, but is actually unthinkable. This is what I was referring to above as a 'coup d'état'.

The major coup that the state carries out on us is what we could call the 'that's the way it is' effect. It's worse than if someone said: 'It can't be otherwise.' 'That's the way it is', there's nothing else to say – like Hegel when he saw the mountains. It amounts to making social agents accept thousands of things without their even knowing it (without asking them to swear an oath), it's making them accept without condition thousands of presuppositions that are more radical than any contract or convention, than any attachment.

(I am well aware of making digressions in my talk. It's a pedagogic choice. I have often said that the difficulty of sociology is that it has to destroy common sense, remove everything that bears on proto-belief, that is more than a belief: a belief that is unaware of itself as such. Sociology has to destroy a *doxa*. There is very often an authority effect in the pedagogic relationship, the effect of 'I've not thought too much about it', the effect of 'he tells me this, so I agree with him'. The sociologist's discourse is granted a support that is not a genuine adhesion, since it can coexist with the continuation of a kind of proto-*doxa*. In order to break this manner of benevolent adhesion, something must be done that may seem like provocation, that is, to take burning issues that will shock and divide. This is the only way to reconduct the operation that the sociologist conducts in order to arrive at saying what he says: he plays with fire. I am not saying this to sacrifice to the myth of science, but it is a dangerous game all the same to challenge the *doxa*, the basic certainties. Otherwise, what is too easy, you will say: 'He gave us a *topos*.'[12] *Topoi* have a particular status: they are neither true nor false. But science, sociology, is not made up of *topoi*.

The space of possibilities

I'll continue my analysis with another example. There is now in the National Assembly a bill that the advocates' lobby is championing. I have already shown how the process of constituting a profession of the Anglo-Saxon type is extremely interesting, because it shows how a certain capital could be historically constituted.[13] I showed that there was a strange anomaly in the fact that those professions that are called 'liberal' in France, that are supposed to be practised freely, are in fact completely dependent on the state; I showed that, if there are activities that depend on the state, these are well and truly the liberal professions. They owe their scarcity, and hence their monopoly, entirely to state protection, which defines the right of entry to these professions, and they struggle in a phenomenally vigilant way to maintain this boundary, the boundary of their monopoly. I also told you how in the course of the 1970s there was a renewal of legal sociology in the United States, in the same context as the renewal of work on the state that I mentioned just now. A number of sociologists began to interest themselves in the genesis of law, raising questions that were not generally raised, and they did so in association with the rise in leftist movements of alternative lawyers, that is, people who, outside the established body, outside the legal profession, sold or freely provided legal services, such as associations of legal help for women in a feminist context, or for Puerto Ricans by way of protection for disadvantaged minorities. There was also a tradition of this kind in France, that of the legal offices of consumers' associations, political parties and trade unions; these legal services were very often run by people who did not have a formal legal qualification. Today, a certain number of parliamentarians on all sides, with the common particularity of being connected with the law (they have legal qualifications, which makes them forget their party differences), are attempting to prevent anyone from providing legal services if they do not have a legal qualification. The reform envisages the compulsory holding of a legal degree or equivalent diploma for anyone providing legal consultations on a regular and remunerated basis. It's the restoration of a monopoly.

How does this relate to the space of possibilities? Because the measure is still in an embryonic state, there is a discussion going on. I can quote a [Socialist] minister of justice, who none the less had the right reflex. 'If the text is applied,' he said, 'this means that a trade-union activist who has twenty or twenty-five years' experience on an industrial tribunal but does not have a qualification would be unable to perform a legal act for which he might ask a small remuneration.' And, pillorying the corporation of certified lawyers: '(According to him), a land expert from the chamber of agriculture, a trade-union expert on the right to work, a specialist in land consolidation with the FNSEA,[14] would all be disqualified.' In other words, these associations will either have to disappear, or appoint a professional advocate. What is the connection with my question? It is that there are still people struggling, there is still hope. Consumers and trade unions will mobilize, otherwise these legal offices will have to disappear in four years' time. I am not making any prognosis. Let us suppose that they disappear in ten years: unless you are historians, you will have forgotten the alternative possibility, that is, that there could be legal offices run by non-professionals. It is likely, moreover, that the structure will have changed, that the unions will give scholarships for people to study law, that the members of industrial tribunals will no longer be the same, will not defend people in the same way, will not understand problems in the same way . . . What is certain is that mental structures will have changed. The manner of addressing an industrial tribunal will be different, you won't be able to use coarse expressions. People who have little except coarse expressions will not be able to speak at all, as is already the case in most legal situations. The legal situation will be brought into conformity, and the genesis will be forgotten. The same holds for housing policy. The alternative between collective housing estates and small privately owned bungalows is a false alternative; there is a third possibility, that of small rented bungalows, which does not currently exist. This is something that no sociologist speaks about . . . In other words, the alternative, the opposition between collective and individual housing, is swept away by a historical process that has constituted the problem in a form whose genealogy we can investigate. And there are thousands of questions of this type.

The example of spelling

Spelling is another magnificent illustration.[15] Can you believe that this debate supposedly took up more space in the newspapers, at least in *Le Figaro*, than the Gulf War? How is that possible? Is it enough simply to smile, to say that this is silly nonsense, an illustration of French futility? In the United States, at least, people would say that it was a laughing matter, ridiculous. No, I believe that if the problem takes such proportions, it is because it is very serious for the people that it mobilizes. The whole of my sociological work has consisted in making problems of this kind intelligible, making people understand that there are issues of life or death in the suppression of geography [in the school curriculum], in the suppression of fifteen minutes of gymnastics, in the replacement of fifteen minutes of music by fifteen minutes of mathematics, that their direct interests are involved just as in the case of the advocates, or their indirect interests, and here it is even worse, since interests of identity are at stake. Why? Their salary doesn't depend on it. In order to understand problems of this kind, to understand that these problems are very serious, that civil wars can be triggered by statements that are seemingly a matter for ridicule, you need an extremely complex and rigorous explanatory system, in which the state has a fundamental role. What is in question here is one of the most important things from a sociological point of view, that is, social passions, very violent emotional feelings of love and hate, which ordinary sociology tends to exclude as belonging to the order of the irrational, the incomprehensible. Some language wars take the form of wars of religion, some educational wars are wars of religion, which have nothing in common with the opposition between public and private – that would be too easy.

To give you the basis of my analysis, orthography is *ortho graphia*, proper writing, the manner of writing that is conforming, correct, corrected – as is language. Spelling is clearly the product of a historical process. The French language is an artefact, but spelling is a fourth-order artefact, produced by a series of historical decisions that were more or less arbitrary, from the monks of the Middle Ages through to the interventions of all those commissions and committees, which are always commissions

and committees of the state. As soon as the question of spelling reform
arises, the people who rally in defence are often men with state credentials,
members of the Académie Française. If they fall into this trap, it is because
answering this kind of question is a function of their position. They were
faced with a double bind. The first response was to say: 'The state asks us
to ratify a state measure concerning state spelling.' There is a series of state
decisions, but these state decisions have become mental structures through
the mediation of the educational institution that has inculcated respect for
proper spelling.

Among the most interesting arguments, which make journalists laugh,
are aesthetic arguments. A *nénuphar* [water lily] with 'ph' is more beautiful
than one with an 'f'. This raises a laugh, but it is true; it is true that it is
more beautiful for someone who is a product of the state, adjusted to state
spelling. This raises the problem of aesthetics, but I won't say any more,
I'll let you reflect on this . . . Here, the state is communicating with itself,
and if spelling can become an affair of state, it is because it is the state
unthought that is thought in the minds of the writers concerned. We conducted an investigation, some years back, on the defenders of Latin. It was
very similar: the most bitter defenders of Latin were to be found among
people who had done a little Latin, who taught in the technical [stream],
because for them it was the site of ultimate difference, the ultimate *diacri-
sis* [distinction], whereas people who had done a great deal of Latin did
not face that dilemma. If spelling is currently an extremely sensitive site
of difference, this is, among other things, because there are generational
problems. There is a photograph in my book *Distinction* in which you see a
young man with long hair and an old gentleman with a small moustache.[16]
This is a very common situation in the bureaucracy, the old gentleman
with a small moustache has learned proper spelling, I would say that this is
all he does know, whereas the young man with long hair reads *Libération*
and understands computers . . . but he doesn't know proper spelling, he
makes lots of mistakes. This is one of the sites of ultimate difference, and
there clearly are people for whom their whole cultural capital, which exists
in a relational fashion, is bound up with this ultimate difference.

I said 'cultural capital', but I need to spell out the connection this has
with the state. The whole of my course this year will be on this subject.
Spelling is a very good example, and the French language is another one.
The genesis of the state, as I see it, is the genesis of spaces within which,
for example, a mode of symbolic expression is imposed in a monopolistic
fashion; you have to speak in the correct manner, and in this manner
alone. This unification of the linguistic market, the unification of the
market in writing that is coextensive with the state, is made by the state as
it makes itself. One of the ways in which the state makes itself is by making
a standardized spelling, making normalized weights and measures, normalized law, replacing feudal rights by a unified legal code . . . This process
of unification, centralization, standardization, homogenization, which is
the act of making of the state, is accompanied by a process that reproduces

itself: the phylogenesis reproduced in ontogenesis with each generation by way of the educational system, a process which also involves the making of normalized individuals, who are homogenized in terms of writing, spelling, their way of speaking . . . This twofold process becomes completely unconscious (amnesia of genesis), with the result that something which is quite arbitrary is forgotten. If you take the Robert dictionary, you will find ten quotations on the absurdity of French spelling, including one from Valéry.

Things that are quite arbitrary thus become in this way very necessary – more than necessary, natural. So natural that to change them is like pumping away the atmosphere, making life impossible for a lot of people. In order to understand what happens in cases such as this, you have to conduct a differential sociology of positions taken: who takes a position for or against . . . This is a magnificent experimental situation. People say that sociology does not do experiments, but that is completely wrong, you have here an experimental situation that need only be observed. Naturally, far more needs to be done in order to explain it, but the basic principle of what is happening is this kind of encounter of the state with itself, the state that, as institution, has the properties of every institution: it exists objectively in the form of grammar, the form of the dictionary, the form of the rules of spelling, government recommendations, the form of teachers of grammar, textbooks of spelling, etc., and it exists in mental structures in the form of dispositions to write in the correct, that is, corrected manner (those who defend proper spelling also include some who make spelling mistakes). What is important is doxic adherence to the necessity of orthography. The state can simultaneously ensure that there are teachers of spelling, and that there are people ready to die for correct spelling.

Lecture of 17 January 1991

Reminder of the course's approach – The two meanings of the word 'state': state as administration, state as territory – The disciplinary division of historical work as epistemological obstacle – Models of state genesis, 1: Norbert Elias – Models of state genesis, 2: Charles Tilly

Reminder of the course's procedure

Last week I gave you a rather too long preamble, with the intention of explaining to you the particular difficulties you encounter when you attempt to conceive the state, and I took the example of spelling. This is in no way a trivial example, since there is as much danger of being thought by the state when dealing with spelling wars as when dealing with wars that could be called more real, or more exciting. In both cases I believe there is a state effect exerted on the person trying to think, and it is this state effect that I tried to analyse, to focus on it more exactly, having already tackled this question in the past. Before undertaking a genetic analysis of the birth of the state, which seems to me one of the ways that makes it possible to escape at least a bit from the state effect, I want to indicate to you today the main lines of the approach I am going to follow this year, so that you can follow me in the meanders and detours of the trajectory I shall take. It is important to know where I want to end up, in order to understand, and sometimes to accept, the seemingly discontinuous and somewhat erratic details I shall go into on the way.

What I want to try to show is how a great fetish like the state was constituted, or, to use a metaphor that I shall go on to explain, this 'central bank of symbolic capital', this kind of site where all the fiduciary currency circulating in the social world is produced and guaranteed, as well as all the realities we can designate as fetishes, whether an educational qualification, a legitimate culture, the nation, the notion of state border, or spelling. The question for me is to study the creation of this creator and guarantor of fetishes, for which a whole nation, or a section of it, is prepared to die. I think we must always bear in mind the fact that the state is a symbolic power that can obtain what is called the supreme sacrifice over things that may be as derisory as spelling, or seem more serious, such as borders. I refer you to the very fine article by Kantorowicz, '*Pro patria mori*'.[1] It is this tradition of thought that we must enter in order to understand the state. I am convinced that genetic analysis is one of the only ways of breaking with the illusion inherent to specifically synchronic perception, that is, breaking with the doxic adhesion resulting from the fact that the state and all its creations – language, law, spelling, etc. – are inscribed both in reality and in people's minds; as well as all the effects that can be called psychological, and that I prefer to call symbolic so as to be more rigorous, all the effects that lead us to think the state with a state thought.

The two meanings of the word 'state': state as administration, state as territory

So as to make this general line more clear, I shall remind you of a distinction I made, and that you will find in every dictionary. Whether you take up Robert, Lalande or Larousse, they traditionally distinguish between two meanings of the word 'state', which in my view are basically linked. On the one hand, the restricted meaning that comes second in the dictionaries: the state is the administration, a set of ministerial directorates, a form of government. On the other hand, the wider sense: the state is the national territory and the whole of its citizens. Historians debate as to whether the nation makes the state or the state makes the nation, a debate that is very important politically, but scientifically insignificant. And, as often happens, debates that are socially important act as a screen and an obstacle to those that are scientifically important. The alternatives may divide national traditions, political traditions, and be a very important issue, since according to whether you give priority to the state or the nation, you have very different instruments of legitimation at your command. This is why it is such a burning political issue.

To my mind, this distinction is useful but artificial, and the model of the genesis of the state I want to propose is based on a simple formula. The state in the restricted sense, state 1 (administration, form of government, set of bureaucratic institutions, etc.) is made by making the state in the broad sense, state 2 (national territory, citizens united by relations of recognition, who speak the same language, who fall under the notion of nation). State 1, then, is made by the making of state 2. So much for the simplified formula. In a more rigorous manner, the construction of the state as a relatively autonomous field exerting a power of centralization of physical force and symbolic force, and constituted accordingly as a stake of struggle, is inseparably accompanied by the construction of the unified social space that is its foundation. To put it another way, using the classical philosophical distinction, the relationship between state 1 and state 2 is that of *natura naturans* to *natura naturata*. Perhaps you will say that this amounts to explaining the *obscurum* by the *obscuro* . . .

(There is always someone in the hall for whom obscure things are clear, and who suddenly says to himself: 'That's what he meant!' This is why I deliberately use several different languages. I often say, so as to make clear my way of thinking and talking, that by changing the manner in which you say things, you free yourself from being trapped in the ordinary manner; it's a way of finding paths, tracks. Things that have been useful to me as paths may be of use to others. This is why I share them with you, whereas in a book only one path remains. From the standpoint of communication, books are more rigorous than live discourse, but they are also much poorer, less effective . . . Many people say to me: 'When we listen to you we understand everything, when we read you we don't understand anything', and the same applies to me. The difference is precisely this semantic openness that can be maintained orally, but that I feel obliged to remove from writing.)

The genesis of the state as *natura naturans*, as principle of construction, is thus accompanied by the genesis of the state as *natura naturata*. Why is it necessary to recall this? Because naive perception leads to the form of fetishism that consists in acting as if the state as territory, set of agents, etc., was the foundation of the state as government. In other words, you could say that in the extreme case fetishization reverses the real process. I said that the state is made by making itself, but it is true that genetically you are constantly led to see how the invention of procedures, legal techniques, techniques of assembling resources, of concentrating knowledge (writing) – how these inventions on the part of the centre were accompanied by deep changes in the more or less long term on the part of territory and populations. When you follow the genetic order you are tempted to give a certain priority to the construction of the central state over the construction of the state as territory, whereas the spontaneous perception is exactly the opposite: nationalism, in particular, always arms itself with such facts as linguistic unity, for example, in order to conclude the need for governmental unity, or to legitimize demands for governmental unity in relation to territorial unity. In the reality of genesis, what the fetishism of spontaneous perception constitutes as the motive force, the origin, is in reality often second. That is another reason to conduct a genetic analysis.

The state as sovereign authority exercised over a definite people and territory, as the set of general services of a nation, what are known as public services (central government, administration, etc.), seems to be the expression of the state as a 'human group settled on a definite territory, subject to the same authority and capable of being viewed as a legal person', or as an 'organized society having an autonomous government and playing the role of a legal person in relation to other similar societies with which it is in relation'.[2] By first of all presenting organized society, and then general services, Lalande tacitly accepts, since philosophers too have an unconscious, the common representation according to which these general services are an expression of the society.

One of the functions of the genetic analysis I shall undertake slowly and at length is to break with this illusion inherent to synchronic perception, and show how a whole series of social agents, who can be indicated in the social space (the king, jurists, members of the king's council, etc.) have made the state, and have made themselves the embodiment of the state by making the state. Recalling this leads to raising a question that I raised in a rather obsessional way in previous lectures. You could put this in quite simple, even somewhat simplistic terms: Who has an interest in the state? Are there state interests? Are there public interests, interests in public service? Are there interests in the universal, and who are their bearers? As soon as you pose the question as I have just done, you are led to describe both the process of state construction and those responsible for this process of production. And thus to ask the question – if you accept the expanded Weberian definition of the state that I proposed as a mnemonic technique, that is, the state as possessing the monopoly of both legitimate physical and legitimate symbolic violence – as to who has the monopoly of this monopoly. A question that is raised neither by the Weberian definition nor by all those who adopt this themselves, in particular Norbert Elias.

The disciplinary division of historical work as an epistemological obstacle

Having defined the broad lines of my thesis, I shall embark on the genetic analysis of the state. On this path I come across two categories of facts: on the one hand, historical works that are immense, countless, inexhaustible and terrifying because hard to master; on the other hand, in the throng of general theories of the state, certain that are close to what I want to develop. So as to give a very quick idea of the immensity of the facts and the hubris of my undertaking, I shall simply cite an expression of the English historian Richard Bonney, taken from his article 'Guerre, fiscalité et activité d'État en France, 1500–1600. Quelques remarques préliminaires sur les possibilités de recherche',[3] which, I remind you, only refers to a small zone of history: 'The zones of history that are most neglected are border zones, for example, borders between specialisms. The study of government accordingly demands familiarity with the theory of government, that is, the history of political thought.' One of the fields of learning I have sought to penetrate, a field that is quite exciting and has been developed especially in the English-speaking countries, is not the history of political theories (in the narrow sense of the term: those put forward by theorists viewed as worthy of being treated as such – Bodin, Montesquieu, always the same), but the history of all the discourses on the state from the Middle Ages that accompanied the creation of the state (I deliberately use a word that does not imply any causal action), that were the work of those who manufactured the state, and were inspired initially by Aristotle, and subsequently by Machiavelli.

These theories were [quite different] from what is generally done when you give a history of ideas and treat them as interesting theories on which to take a position today: asking whether Bodin was right as against some other theorist, teaching these theories rather like the teaching at Sciences-Po . . . To my mind, they have a completely different status. They are structures structured by the social conditions of production of their producers, who themselves were located in a certain state space, in certain positions, and structures structuring the perception of those agents who contributed to bringing about real organizational structures. For example, it was on the basis of the Aristotelian idea of *phronesis* that the first legislators began to define the 'prudence' of the man of state as opposed to the *virtù* of the knight – somewhat impetuous, not very much master of his senses in every sense of the term. On this point you may refer to some very fine pages of Georges Duby.[4] It was no longer then a matter of reading Aristotle with a view to dissertation, but reading Aristotle to know what the state is.

This is a little field of learning that one must try to master, but you need to get up early just to be a specialist on these questions. I will cite you one of the few statements by Michel Serres that I agree with: he says that one of the great phenomena of censorship in the sciences bears on the divisions between the sciences.[5] Censorship is exercised by the fact of dividing knowledge and making certain things unthinkable on either side of the border. [To repeat the quote from] this English historian [Richard J. Bonney]: 'The zones of history that are most neglected are border zones, for example, borders between specialisms. The study of government accordingly demands familiarity with the theory of government, that is, the history of political thought.' These legislators produced discourses whose relationship with their practice is unknown to us. All those who write on the subject of 'too much state, not enough state', produce discourses that need to be examined as to the relationship they maintain with what they are actually doing; this is a quite problematic relationship, variable in each case. To continue:

> knowledge of the practice of government, that is, of the history of institutions [which is a speciality distinct from history]; finally, a knowledge of the government personnel [institutions, the royal council and its members; there are people who do prosopography, people like Mme Autrand[6] who work on the genealogy of lawyers and legislators] . . . and therefore a knowledge of social history. [This is a historian's short cut: social history cannot be reduced to the history of people who make history.] Now, few historians are capable of acting in these different specialisms with the same assurance. On the scale of a period [he has in mind 1250–70], there are other border zones that would demand study, for example, the techniques of war at the start of the modern age. [War is one of the factors that contributed to the constitution of states: taxes were needed to make war.] Without a

better knowledge of these problems, it is hard to measure the importance of a logistic effort undertaken by a certain government in a particular campaign; but these technical problems must not be studied simply from the standpoint of the military historian in the traditional sense of the term; the military historian must also be a historian of government. Many unknowns also remain in the history of public finances and taxation; here again, the specialist must be more than a narrow historian of finances in the traditional sense of the term; he has also to be a historian of government, as well as something of an economist. Unfortunately, the fragmentation of history into subsections, each the monopoly of specialists, and the sense that certain aspects of history are fashionable while others are out of date, has hardly helped this cause.

For thirty years, for example, historians would not speak of the state, whereas now everyone in France is talking about it, whereas in the United States it is hardly being talked about any more.

The difficulty, when you try to tackle the social history of the process of state constitution, is the immensity of historical sources, their dispersion and their diversity: a disciplinary diversity at the level of a single era, the diversity of eras, the diversity of national traditions. I have tried to master what I saw as pertinent in this 'monstrous' literature. I am of course constantly prone to error, misunderstanding, and above all at risk of repeating in a more pretentious and abstract form what historians have already said. This is more or less the historians' defence system, and unfortunately they are very often right. It is therefore necessary on the one hand to be familiar with this immense, dispersed, disjointed history, in which the most important theoretical intuitions are often concealed in a footnote, and on the other hand to master the major theories of the state, and among these especially those of the category of theorists who have tried to give models of its genesis, and who radically distinguish themselves in my view from the theoretical production I mentioned above, as well as from the theorists of the genesis of the feudal state that I presented last year.

Models of state genesis, 1: Norbert Elias

The first theory I shall mention today is represented by Norbert Elias; this is a development of Weberian theory. I say this in a rather blunt and reductive manner, but strangely enough, historians always have a kind of tense irritation towards sociologists, and Elias was one of those mediating heroes who made sociology acceptable, albeit in a watered-down form. And since historians don't want to know much about Max Weber, especially in France for complicated reasons, Elias provided them with a way into Weber without knowing it, and they could therefore ascribe to Elias, who was a very original thinker, what actually comes from Weber. I believe it is important to know that Elias's theory was not born from thin air. He tried to apply on the genetic terrain a certain number of basic ideas of Max Weber concerning the state; he offered a genetic theory of the state of Weberian inspiration. His main text on the question is *The Civilizing Process*, in which he sought to show how the state was constituted, that is, in Weber's formulation, the organization that successfully claims the exercise of power over a territory, thanks to its monopoly of the legitimate use of violence.[7] The violence that Weber had in mind was physical violence, either military or police. The word 'legitimate', if you take it quite seriously, is enough to evoke the symbolic dimension of this violence, since the idea of legitimacy includes the idea of recognition. Despite everything, however, Weber did not develop this aspect of the state in his theory very strongly; with Elias, this aspect – which I see as very important, perhaps the most important aspect – disappears almost completely. That is the main criticism I make of his model. Elias, in fact, lets the symbolic dimension of state power disappear, and essentially retains the constitution of a double monopoly, that of physical violence and that of taxation. He sets out to describe the process of monopolization that went hand in hand with the process of transformation of a private monopoly (that of the king) into a public monopoly. Where I do see Elias as truly innovative, and I will draw on this to develop the genetic theory of the state, is in the elements of the analysis he makes of the transition from a private monopoly (what I call the dynastic state) to the public monopoly of the state. He was aware of the importance of this problem, and described a certain number of important mechanisms. I shall try to be completely honest, and tell you what I see as the origin of Elias's model, its limitations and its strong point.

First of all, according to Elias, you have two processes that are closely connected: the gradual concentration of instruments of violence, which Charles Tilly calls instruments of coercion – he is very close to Elias, but with different emphases – and the concentration of tax-raising in the hands of a single ruler or administration in each country. You could sum up the genesis of the state with the words 'concentration', 'unification' or 'monopolization', but 'monopoly' is best. This process went hand in hand with the extension of territory by way of competition between the ruler of one state and the rulers of adjacent states, a competition that led to the elimination of the defeated. Elias says – and I believe he is right – that one can compare the processes of monopolization that led to the constitution of the state with processes of monopolization in a market. He sees an analogy between the process of state monopolization and the process of monopolization resulting from the competition of firms in the market – the famous law of monopoly that says that the bigger fish have a good chance of swallowing the smaller and growing at their expense.[8] (I may be a bit reductive here, but you will read the book. It goes without saying that, when I give references, it is in the hope that you will use these, and will be able to defend yourselves against what I am saying.) The two monopolies are connected, that of taxation and the army, and that of territory. It is the monopoly of resources arising from taxation that made it possible to ensure the monopoly of military force that made it possible to maintain the monopoly of taxation.

There is a debate on this subject: was it that taxation was necessary for war, or was it war that gave rise to taxation? For Elias, these two monopolies are two sides of the same coin. He gives a very good example of this: a protection racket organized by gangsters, such as you have in Chicago, is not so very different from the state.[9] The sociologist must be capable of constructing a particular case in order to show convergences, to locate the particular case in a series of cases where it displays both its full particularity and its full generality. There is no difference in kind, in fact, between rackets and taxation. The state says to people: 'I will protect you, but you will pay taxes.' But a protection racket organized by gangsters infringes on the state monopolies: those of both legitimate violence and taxation. At one and the same time, Elias makes three points: (1) the state is a racket, but not just a racket; (2) it is a legitimate racket; (3) it is a legitimate racket in the symbolic sense. Here I will introduce the problem as to how a racket becomes legitimate, that is, no longer perceived as a racket. No historian would ever make a comparison between taxation and a racket, even though I believe this is correct. One of the differences with historians is that sociologists have nasty minds: they raise disturbing questions, but questions that are also scientific. Elias raises the question: isn't the state a particular case of a racket? Which raises the question of the particularity of this legitimate racket. In my view, this first point is far more interesting than the law of monopoly. But historians do not see it. What they reject most in the sociological approach is this kind of impertinence. In this respect, one should do a comparative sociology of the genesis of sociologists and historians: how does one become a sociologist or a historian? How do historians and sociologists write? How is a structure reproduced that could be described as psychological, which characterizes both historians (who themselves form a field) and sociologists (who form another field)?

Second point. The process of monopolization takes the form – still the analogy with a racket – of a series of eliminatory jousts at the end of which one of the competitors disappears. After a while there is just one state, and an internal pacification at the end of a series of wars that leads to an internal peace. Elias was well aware of the ambiguity of the state. The state establishes domination, but the other side of this domination is a form of peace. The fact of belonging to a state offers a benefit of order – unequally distributed, but positive even for the most disadvantaged. The concentration of means of violence in a very small number of hands has the consequence that the number of men of war able to acquire territory by using the military resources at their command steadily declines. Their military capacities and activities are gradually subordinated to those of the central ruler. The absolutist state is thus established by a process of concentration that leads to a balance of forces between the ruler (the king) and the subjects. This is Elias's most original point, to my mind. He develops a kind of antinomy of the central power: the more the king extends his power, the more he extends his dependence on those who depend on his power. That is a more intelligent way of saying that the extension of the state raises more and more problems – what is simple at the level of a district is more complicated at the level of a county . . . What is conventionally ascribed to an effect of space, of spatial distance, Elias describes in terms of social space. Elias has the principle of sociological construction as a reflex; he never accepts that anything is not constructed sociologically. He says that concentration is not simply a spatial extension that raises problems.

There is a good deal of work on problems of communication and distance, which is very far from useless. A Roman soldier fully equipped, for example, marches so many kilometres per day; how much time did a messenger take to get from one end of the empire to the other? These are real problems, but they acquire their full meaning in the context of a theory of government. The greater the accumulated power, the less easy it is for its holder to supervise it, and the more he comes to depend on his dependants; and this arises from the very fact of his monopoly. There are contradictions in the very genesis of the state, which are important in order to understand what the state is. The holder of power becomes increasingly dependent on his dependants, who become increasingly numerous.

To the extent that the dependence of the king or central ruler towards his dependants grows, his degrees of freedom grow in parallel: he can also play on rivalries between his dependants. His margin of manoeuvre – that is a good way of speaking of his freedom – increases; the leader can play on the multiplicity of antagonistic interests of the groups or classes on which the central power can count. Elias describes one particular case of this, which it is possible to generalize. This is a particular case of a very general proposition that I call the 'office effect'. In a group of fifteen people, one is designated, or designates himself, as the office, the central place; the others are atomized and dispersed, and only communicate with one another through the intermediary of the one who occupies this central position. This central position generates its own development and the decay of other relationships by the very fact of its being central. I believe this is very important in order to understand, for example, why one particular prince among others is recognized as king. That is a question that historians put very well, particularly Le Goff: the fact that the prince of Île-de-France was recognized as king gave him a symbolic advantage over his competitors.[10] But the symbolic advantage given by the title of king is not sufficient to understand the specific advantages of the king in competition with other principalities. The structural advantage of being at the centre is extremely important, as Elias indeed indicates: 'Every individual, every group, every order or class is in some way dependent on one another; they are friends, allies and potential partners; they are at the same time opponents, competitors, potential enemies.'[11] In other words, the king is in a meta-social position, it is in relation to him that others have to measure and situate themselves, these others all being themselves situated in relation to one another in relations of alliance or competition on which he can play. So what Elias puts forward is not just the principle of concentration, which is rather simple.

In parallel with this, Elias describes another process – this is the most interesting point – at the end of which 'the centralized and monopolized resources tend gradually to pass from the hands of a few individuals to the hands of an increasing number of individuals, and eventually become a function of a whole human network that is interdependent'. In other words – and this is the culmination of his analysis, this is what I mean when I speak of the state or bureaucratic field – Elias has the idea that, to the extent that power is concentrated, instead of having a central subject of power there is a network of interdependence among the powerful. I would add: a network of interdependence of the powerful holders of different principles of power – religious, bureaucratic, legal, economic. With the result that the structure of this space, in its complexity, becomes the generating principle of state decisions. You move – and this is the essential point of his analysis – from a relatively private monopoly (Elias is always cautious: a monopoly is never completely private, being shared with a family, a lineage) to a public monopoly (I would say 'relatively public', as monopolies are never completely public). I always cite the following passage of Elias: 'The depersonalization and institutionalization of the exercise of power leads to ever longer chains, to ever denser networks of interdependence between the members of society.' Here you have the idea of the lengthening of chains of dependence, what I call chains of legitimization: A legitimizes B, who legitimizes C, etc., who legitimizes A. This lengthening is one of the fundamental processes when you are looking for major laws in the long timeframe of history. The only general tendential law that I see is this process of differentiation that is inseparable from a process of lengthening of chains of dependence and interdependence. For Elias, who is a very controlled author, interdependence does not mean interdependence between equals; he does not forget that there can be structures of interdependence with a dominant. You could understand what Elias is saying as a kind of dissolution of power: 'everyone equal'. In the 1970s there were vexing debates in France as to whether power came from above or below. I am forced to say this, so that you understand that we are light-years beyond such things that are perceived as the alpha and omega of French thought . . .

There is a sentence of Elias in *The Court Society*, a magnificent and exciting book that changes our view of the classical French world: 'The complex and immense apparatus at the summit of which stood Louis XIV remained private in many respects, it remained an extension of the king's house, and you can refer to it [here I believe Elias quotes Weber] as a patrimonial bureaucracy';[12] bureaucracy in the service of grandeur, of the illustration of an inheritance both material (crown, territory) and symbolic (the name of the king). Elias remarks (in Weberian vein) that there was not yet a clear distinction between public expenditure and the king's private expenses; it was only after the Revolution, he writes, that private monopolies genuinely did become public monopolies. On this point I believe he is mistaken (I find it very hard to explain someone else's theory without saying something of this kind). It is only when a complex apparatus took over the running of the state monopoly that one can really speak of a state: 'From this time on, conflicts no longer had the object of challenging the existence of the state monopoly (they were no longer conflicts between prince and king to overturn this monopoly), but conflicts to appropriate this monopoly, to control it and distribute its offices and benefices.'[13] Elias, as I am presenting him to you, is not a one-sided Elias, but refined, remodelled, sifted through my own brain, if you like. And so you will have to read him in the original, if you are interested.

Models of state genesis, 2: Charles Tilly

The second author I want to present to you is Charles Tilly. His book *Coercion, Capital and European States* is the culmination of a whole series of books and articles. I discovered to my great surprise a proximity between Tilly and Elias. Strangely, I had viewed Elias in the German context, in relation to things I had read twenty years ago, and he appealed to me as a weapon of defence and struggle against the sociological thought dominant at that time, that is, American sociology. I did not think about Elias in relation to Tilly, whom I had read as something completely new. And it was by trying to present a working model of Tilly's contribution that I realized how very close he was to Elias. This was at least the perception I had. At the same time, he is original, otherwise I would not present him to you.

Tilly tries to describe the genesis of the European state while paying great attention to the diversity of types of state. He warns that while the English and French models are most prominent, there are also the Russian, Dutch and Swedish models. His ambition is to escape the effect of the imposition of what I call one of the most classic fallacies, the 'universalization of the particular case' without understanding its particularity. Keeping within the scope of preliminary reservations, Tilly seems to me an advance in relation to Elias in that he seeks to construct a model with more parameters, taking account of both the common features of the European states and the differences among them. He tries to validate his model empirically, having in mind the multivariable analysis that all American sociologists have instilled into them. He aims to manipulate these variables, and that is all well and good. But he is completely silent on the symbolic dimension of state domination; this does not touch him at all, there is not a single line about it, or only by accident (perhaps I am mistaken). Elias is not free from economism any more than Weber was, but Tilly is trapped still more

in an economic logic: he is quite insensitive to the specific process of constitution of a state logic (how the shift from the private to the public takes
place, how chains of dependence are created). He ignores, as I see it, the
symbolic dimension and the specific logic of the accumulation process of
symbolic capital. At the heart of his problematic lies the dialectic between
towns and the state, and this is certainly interesting. It is true that this is
what underlies many state histories. Physical constraint is the work of the
state, and capital accumulation is more the work of towns. For Tilly, the
problem of state genesis is the combination of the two.

The merit of Tilly's achievement is to demonstrate the particularity of
the French and English cases, which are often taken as the basis of general
theories of the state. This particularity of the particular French and
English cases lies in the fact that cities with capital were the capital cities:
London resolved the antinomy of state coercion and capital. How should
we explain the problem raised by Tilly? It is always interesting to know
where a researcher set out from, what he had in mind when he started. You
can then understand much better what he is trying to do.

First question. When you look at a map of Europe, why do you
observe a concentric structure, with vast and weakly controlled states
on the periphery (what other theorists would call empires), where social
integration and social control are weak? Some village communities are
scarcely affected by the existence of a central state, as was the case with the
Ottoman empire or Russia. In the intermediate zone, central Europe, we
find city-states, principalities, federations, that is, units with a fragmented
sovereignty, and in the West, units that are strictly governed and centralized such as France.

Second question, and we see that Tilly is working on a broad canvas,
like the authors I cited last year, but he is working differently – he is not
Barrington Moore: Why are there such differences in the integration of oli-
garchies and urban institutions into the state? Why do different states treat
urban units so differently? At one extreme, the Dutch republic, which was
scarcely more than a collection of cities, a network of municipal govern-
ments, and at the other extreme, the Polish state, almost devoid of urban
institutions. Tilly sees continuums here.

Third question – why do economic and commercial powers vary
from city-states (such as Venice) or city empires on the Mediterranean
coast, through to cities subordinate to powerful states on the shores of
the Atlantic? The answer is that modern states are the product of two
relatively independent processes of concentration: the concentration of
the physical capital of armed force, bound up with the state; and the concentration of economic capital, bound up with the city. The towns as site
of accumulation of economic capital, and those who govern them, tend
to dominate the state by their control of capital, credit and commercial
networks (people often talk of a 'state within the state'). They have connections of power that are transnational and trans-state. The states, for
their part, concentrate the instruments of coercion.

Tilly describes three phases in the process of concentration of economic capital. He goes on to describe three phases in the process of concentration of coercive capital, showing, correctly I believe, that these correspond to those of the concentration of economic capital. In the first phase, to sum up very quickly, 'monarchs generally extracted what capital they needed as tribute or rent from lands and populations that lay under their immediate control'.[14] Here we are still in a logic of the feudal type, where the state concentrates capital on the basis of pre-state relations. One historian remarks, for example, that at the start of the Middle Ages tribute payments were known as *dona*.[15] We are still in the logic of gift and counter-gift, of homage, as if the idea of taxation was not yet established in its objective truth. The second, intermediary phase, between 1500 and 1700: states draw support from independent capitalists who make loans to them, or from enterprises that generate profit, or again from enterprises that raise taxes for them, tax-farmers. There is therefore an autonomous, mercenary financial structure that is not yet integrated into the state. And the third phase, from the seventeenth century on: many sovereigns incorporate the fiscal apparatus into the state.

A parallel process takes place with coercion (the instrument of force). In the first phase, monarchs raise armed forces composed of servants or vassals; the latter owe the king a personal service, but always within contractual limits. In the second phase, between 1500 and 1700, they chiefly rely on mercenaries provided by professionals, suppliers, the equivalent of tax-farmers. In the third phase, they absorb the army and navy into the structure of the state, abandoning foreign mercenaries and relying on troops raised by conscription among the citizens. In the nineteenth century, the two processes of incorporation were complete: European states had incorporated both armies and fiscal mechanisms, abolishing tax-farmers, military entrepreneurs and other intermediaries. States continue to negotiate, as in the feudal era or the intermediary phase, but with different interlocutors and, in an interesting shift, they negotiate over pensions, subsidies, public education, town planning, etc.

If you combine the aspect of coercion and the aspect of capital, you can distinguish three phases, which may be characterized as follows. First of all, a phase of patrimonialism based on feudal forces and tributes; then a phase of brokerage, with intermediaries, mercenaries and lenders; and finally a phase of nationalization: mass army and integrated fiscal apparatus. This final phase is marked by the appearance of specialization in the army and a separation between army and police. All this happens gradually. Now, the answer to the question that Tilly raised at the start: the different intersections between the two processes make it possible to explain the differences in the evolution of European states, because these processes, which I have presented as homogeneous and unified, actually took place differently in the different countries, and because the relative weight of coercion can vary. The Dutch state, for example, avoided massive resort to mercenaries by privileging naval combat and establishing state finances at a very early date, but it remained very dependent on the capitalists of Amsterdam and other commercial cities. In this respect, the Dutch state – a city with very little state – contrasts with the Polish state – a state with no cities. At the opposite extreme, in Castile, land forces were dominant: the monarchy supported itself on credit from merchants, who were thereby converted into rentiers, and on colonial revenue for their repayment. Here you had a structure that was favourable to state concentration.

To schematize, we can thus distinguish three major paths in the process that led to the state: the coercive trajectory, which gave primacy to state concentration of armed forces (Russia); the capitalist trajectory, which gave primacy to concentration of capital (Venice); and the mixed trajectory (England), where the state, formed very early on, had from the start to coexist with and adjust to a large commercial metropolis, and accordingly represents the synthesis of the two forms of accumulation. England and even France are typical of the third possible trajectory: a strong national state that finds economic resources for maintaining powerful armed forces. One of the major results of Tilly's analysis is to show why England and France are particular cases that I can essentially use for my analysis; but certain particular cases are particularly favourable to a genetic analysis of concepts. One of the secrets of scientific work in the social sciences is to find a particular case whose particularity one does not know but in which one can best see the model – on condition that its particularity is not forgotten. Next week we shall look at the third model, that of Philip Corrigan and Derek Sayer.[16]

Lecture of 24 January 1991

Reply to a question: the notion of invention under structural constraint – Models of state genesis, 3: Philip Corrigan and Derek Sayer – The exemplary particularity of England: economic modernization and cultural archaisms

Reply to a question: the notion of invention under structural constraint

I am grateful to those who sent in questions, particularly the person who gave me a stimulating file on the subject of spelling. There is one question to which I shall briefly reply. It is a difficult question and would require a very long response, but I shall just give an outline of this, elements that may serve as a basis for a possible answer:

> At the start, to clarify the definition of the word 'state' or its related concept, you announced that your work would bear on the genesis of the state; you went on to indicate that the state is a solution to certain questions but that there could have been other solutions, and that study of its genesis can clarify this fact. If we want to pursue the idea of an analogy with similar studies of genesis in other disciplines (phylogenesis, ontogenesis, psychogenesis, etc.), the same question always arises: is the choice of the path actually taken the result of chance or necessity? If we are to believe Darwin, the choice in biology, as we know, results from the environment, and in particular, it is the best choice because most adapted to the environment. Is man's choice of the state solution the most adapted one, or if not, is there choice or necessity in sociology? Besides, the word 'adaptation' corresponds to a value judgement, and one generally rejected by non-scientists; is it possible in the human sciences, particularly in sociology, to make such judgements about the state, or must we be satisfied with objective judgements of fact?

This is an important question and well put, but difficult because it goes beyond the limits of what a sociologist can say on the question without turning into a philosopher of history. I shall however try to give something of a reply, as it is a question that you all ask yourselves in a more or less confused fashion.

First point, on the question of chance or necessity, I gave elements of a reply last year. I indicated that in order to understand social phenomena, and the state in particular, one can make use of an analogy employed by Husserl among others: that of the genesis of a city. At each moment in history, new arrivals have to reckon with products of history that are inscribed in the objective world in the form of buildings, constructions and institutions, and which, I would add, are also inscribed subjectively in the form of mental structures. By the same token, inventions, innovations, advances and adaptations are inventions under structural constraint; at each moment, in other words, the world of those possibilities that really are possible is extraordinarily confined by the existence of choices already made in the past, which exist in the form of both objectivized constraints and internalized, incorporated ones. We are not faced with the alternative between chance and necessity, freedom and necessity, but with something more complicated, which I sum up in the formula: 'invention under structural constraint'. I also indicated that as history moves forward, this space of possibilities closes in, among other reasons because the alternatives from which the historically established choice emerged have been forgotten. And one of the forces of historical necessity that is exerted by way of objectivation and incorporation bears on the fact that the co-possible possibilities, what Ruyer in his book on utopia calls 'lateral' possibilities,[1] those possibilities that surround the possibility actually realized, are not only discarded, but discarded as possibilities. The realized possibility has a kind of destiny effect. One of the virtues of historical sociology or social history is precisely to reawaken these dead possibilities, the lateral possibilities, and offer a certain freedom. To say that sociology is an instrument for imposing necessity demonstrates a sad naivety. Sociology is on the contrary an instrument of freedom, since it reawakens buried possibilities, at least for the thinking subject. This does not mean that it makes them really exist as historical possibilities, because, in the minds of the majority of social agents, they are indeed dead and buried. One of the effects of the state is to make people believe that there is no other path but the state. This question thus arises quite particularly about the state.

The space of possibilities closes in, and in place of dead possibilities 'history' – here again, we need to be careful and not make entities such as history into active agents; this is just for ease of expression – puts interests, agents who have an interest in certain possibilities not being reawakened. By the same token, history is a kind of funnel that always tends to contract. You could say that historians are free by definition in relation to this necessity. In fact, they are perhaps less free than other people, because they are subject to the effects of what Bergson called the 'retrospective illusion':[2] they know how history continues. This is something that has often been said, but has not really been the subject of proper reflection, except by Weber: what does the fact of knowing how history continues imply? In actual fact, historians are rather poorly placed to bring back these dead possibilities, because they always tend to accept, like everyone does, that what happened had to happen. We have an implicit philosophy of history that is inscribed in the fact of accepting what follows as what had to come, to postulate its necessity. Consider all the sorry and often ridiculous debates on the French Revolution, and you will see that what I am saying is particularly true here, especially on the part of those who claim to introduce freedom into history . . .

The second point is the question of finalism. There is the question of the logic of history (chance versus necessity) and then there is the question of the end of history, in the double sense. It is a big step forward not to pose it. It is often said of Saussure that he brought about an extraordinary advance in the sciences of language – this is a commonplace, but I believe it can be useful to recall it – by refusing to pose the question of the origin of language, the beginning of language. We can equally bring about certain advances in the social sciences by rejecting not only the question of origin but also the question of ends, which is more of a theological, eschatological question. That said, the question remains. Science must dismiss certain questions in order to think, but it can keep them in mind for its fifteen minutes of metaphysics. (I have nothing against this. I simply say it with a bit of irony, because there are people for whom these fifteen minutes of metaphysics last their whole life. It is very hard to say things of this kind on these questions, because you always have the air of being sectarian. I have nothing against them, but on condition that they do not obstruct those who are doing something different.) When you want to bring about scientific progress, you have to provisionally suspend these metaphysical questions, no matter how exciting you may find them, or even believe they are the most important ones. One of the prices to pay for doing science is that you expose yourself to being treated as a philistine, a positivist.

A number of sociologists, accordingly, have asked themselves whether the state as it exists is the best because, having survived, it may be viewed as the most adapted to its environment, according to the Darwinian postulate. What is an institution – marriage, family, prayer, state – adapted to? How can its degree of adaptation be measured? For the social world, the environment is the social world itself. Hegel said this, and since then people repeat that it is characteristic of societies to produce their own environment and to be transformed by the transformations of the environment that they transform. Sociologists are poorly placed to reply to this question, since it is as if society were in dialogue with itself. You can then go on to ask the question as to its functions. It is in these terms that sociologists have raised the question: what are the functions of the state? There are people known as 'functionalists' – I am speaking as if they were just one single category – who investigate the functions of institutions and try to interpret these in terms of the functions they fulfil. But there is a question that the functionalists do not ask. They assume that institutions have a global, undifferentiated function; for the state, this would be the maintenance of order in the streets. One of the major questions that the state poses, however, is whether it fulfils functions for everyone, or only for some. Corrigan and Sayer ask whether the state does not perhaps fulfil so well the functions that it fulfils for some because it fulfils them for all. Isn't it because it fulfils the function of maintaining order for all that it fulfils functions for those who particularly profit from this order? Here again, we are not faced with simple alternatives, as in the Marxist tradition with its dichotomies: the state serves the ruling class, and the state serves it so well because it also serves everyone else sufficiently for them to feel obliged to submit to the injunctions and imperatives by which the state serves them too. These are complicated questions that biologists do not have (they have enough of these, but of a different kind).

The state fulfils functions, but for whom? It is adapted, but to what? To whose interests? We can agree that what the sociologist has to reckon with is the fact that he is dealing with institutions that have certain qualities by virtue of having survived. For anthropologists dealing with relatively undifferentiated societies, it is not immediately visible that institutions in them serve some people rather than others. In this case, you can be a 'minimal' functionalist without being accused of serving the higher interests of the ruling class. They can say: 'This functions, so I must account for it.' The work of science is to dismantle the mechanism so as to understand why it functions. And so I must postulate that there is reason even if it is not rational, even if this reason serves unwelcome ends. Whether I am studying the Kabyle house, the system of the *grandes écoles*, social security or housing policy, I tacitly accept the idea that there is a rationale here, that there is some reason because these things have survived, have stayed the course, and that I have to explain this reason, to make it intelligible: why something exists, how it exists, how it manages to perpetuate itself, how it is reproduced.

This kind of 'postulate of intelligibility' – it needs a name – is constitutive of the scientific approach in the social sciences. But sometimes this is a dangerous postulate, since it leads you to forget that there are human acts that may not have any reason; in this case, the scientific bias that always inclines you to seek reasons may lead to mistakes: it is impossible to understand certain forms of violence perceived as 'gratuitous', even if their causes are discovered. (I am as always moving from one correction to another. Sometimes this is complicated, but I believe that things are complicated, and even so I censor a lot so as to remain within the bounds of intelligibility. To speak of the social world, discourses like musical scores are needed, with fifteen levels that you can correct as you go along. Hence the problem of communication . . .)

Institutions function, they have a reason, but in the sense of the reason of a series of events, and when you have understood, this is no longer random, it is no longer just any which way. For example, once you have understood that in the Kabyle house there is a dry part and a wet part, that here you do this, there you do that, you understand in the sense of being aware of a necessity, where previously there was a perception of chance, of no matter what. And sometimes, explanation has virtues that are not just scientific but also political. It removes the absurdity of things; in the case of rituals, for example, showing that rituals are not absurd means removing a whole segment of human behaviour from racist hatred. But this is not the goal, it's an induced effect. To accept that an institution that has survived has a reason, given that it functions, accordingly means taking on the mission of seeking a logic. This would need developing at length. The word 'reason' is very dangerous, because you may think this means a rational reason, that is, that at the origin of this institution someone had a project or a plan, that the action in question is the product of a rational calculation, with conscious subjects. That is in no way my philosophy of history. It is the paradox of the social world that in certain ways it has quasi-biological, almost natural aspects: there are heaps of things that have a reason without having had this reason at their origin, which have a raison d'être, a reason in the sense of a series of events, without rational calculation having been at their origin.

This is one of the problems of relationships between scientists and those on the humanities side. Scientists, even biologists, when they have to judge the work of historians or sociologists, do not always have the right criteria of judgement, since they apply to sciences that deal with quite particular reasons a single principle of evaluation: mathematical reason, logical reason, formal reason. If we find institutions or actions that have a reason without having reason at their origin, this is because they were established under an everyday kind of logic; they are inventions under structural constraint, under a constraint that is internalized and objectivized, which means that what is done is not done any which way. This is a series like a sequence of moves in a game, like an old house that has been inhabited for thirty-six generations and has a strange kind of charm that can be justified aesthetically because it is the product of a large number of infinitesimal choices, the result being quite different from a house conceived by the most skilled and talented architect, who thinks of every detail. These social objects often have an aesthetic aspect, since they are, like old houses, the product of a large number of intentions that were not conscious either of their external constraints or of their internal ones, and yet were in no way random.

Structural-genetic analysis of the state, just like synchronic structural analysis, has the aim of grasping these logics that are not of a logical order, and that moreover formal logic very often destroys. One of the major problems in the human sciences is that the different logics that they use as tools (games theory, probability calculus) were constructed against everyday practical reason. To apply them to things that they were constructed against has very nice formal effects in books, but it is very destructive for the progress of science. In the social sciences, you have to be able to resist the effect of ostentatious scientificity obtained by applying products of reasoning reason to historical reasons.

Models of state genesis, 3: Philip Corrigan and Derek Sayer

I come now to the third book, Corrigan and Sayer's *The Great Arch* – a formula taken from the great English historian E. P. Thompson. This book makes a complete break with the previous two, both that of Elias and that of Tilly. The two present authors say clearly in their introduction that they oppose the theory of the state as an organ of coercion. For them, Marxism and those theories that can be classified as economism, that of Tilly and partially that of Elias, reduce the state to an organ of coercion and make it a reflection of economic power. They point out that Gramsci seems to have distanced himself somewhat from this view. (Much could be said about Gramsci as the Ptolemy of the Marxist system, who gave the appearance of a path of rescue from the system while hemming people even more into this blind alley.) Gramsci ascribed to the state not only the function of constraint and maintaining order, but also that of establishing and reproducing consensus, which is by no means nothing. For Corrigan and Sayer, Marxist theories forget 'the meaning of state activities, forms, routines and rituals – for the constitution and regulation of social identities, ultimately of our subjectivities'.[3] This is a key sentence, which sums up their thesis quite well. For them, the role of the state is to regulate not only the objective order but also the mental order, the subjective order, and to orchestrate this kind of constant regulation of subjectivities. If they had to give a definition of the state, it would be something like this: 'The state is a set of cultural forms.' They are not very clear on this subject, they are sociologists doing history, they go in what I believe is the right direction, but with a theoretical confusion that underlies the richness of their book. They lack the theoretical instruments to measure up to their ambitions; their theoretical instruments are foggy and confused. They say one interesting thing that is untranslatable, playing on the word 'state': 'States state.'[4] This is the kind of thing that Heidegger would say: 'The state establishes', 'The state makes statements', 'theses', 'statutes'; 'the state statutes'. They give examples of these 'statements': the rituals of a court of justice, the formulas of royal assent to an Act of Parliament, the visit of inspectors to a school, etc. All these are state 'statements', acts of state. Their book is entirely devoted to examining the genesis of these institutions that enable the state to assert its political judgements and actions.

One example, which is very close to things I have said myself, will enable us to understand this: the state defines all the codified and legitimate forms of social life. The state codifies, and these codes include classifications. It has become a *pons asinorum* to say that the state begins with statistics, that the word 'statistics' contains the word 'state', but Corrigan and Sayer say more than this: the reason why statistics is a typical state act is that it imposes a legitimate view on the social world. I remind you here that there is a difference between the state statistician and the sociologist. The former imposes categories without examining them, he only begins to examine them when he is contaminated by sociologists; the state statistician is a *censor* in the Roman sense of the term, he conducts *census*, that is, censuses with a view to raising taxes, assessing the rights and duties of citizens. His thought (*censeo*) is typically a state thought: his categories of thought are categories of state thought, categories of order and the maintenance of order. State statisticians do not raise questions at random: they are recruited and trained in such a fashion that they only raise the questions that their statistical operations raise. The state effects a unification of codes. The example par excellence is language, but so are the names of professions, all the terms that denote social identities, all the taxonomies used to classify men and women . . . In this way, it imposes a legitimate view against other views, against other moralities, you could say, that express the view of the dominated. Corrigan and Sayer strongly emphasize the fact that the state has imposed its view against the dominated in a systematic way; this is at the same time a kind of history both of the genesis of the state and of what the state has eliminated against other possibilities bound up with the interests of the dominated.

To continue this summary in a rather more general way, Corrigan and Sayer leave aside everything that bears on the accumulation of instruments of physical violence and economic capital, as analysed by Tilly and Elias; what interests them is the cultural revolution that underlies the development of the modern state. They say that the formation of the state is a cultural revolution. They situate themselves in a Durkheimian perspective. They are interesting because they juggle between Marx, Durkheim and Weber – as I believe you have to in order to understand state questions – but in a confused fashion; they have not clarified the linkage between the theoretical contributions of these different authors to the understanding of what symbolic power is, and this I believe is key to understanding what the state is as the site of accumulation of symbolic and legitimate power.[5] They privilege in an explicitly Durkheimian perspective what they call the 'moral dimension of state activity'; they describe the construction of the state as the construction and massive imposition of a set of common representations and values. Here they link up with Gramsci: they see the genesis of the state, from its origin but especially in the nineteenth century, as a kind of enterprise of domesticating the dominated. Where Elias speaks of a 'civilizing process' (with all the political unreality this view implies), they reintroduce the function of domesticating the dominated. This is the ambiguity of all those state structures involved in the 'welfare state',[6] about which you never know whether they are institutions of control or of service; in fact, they are both at the same time, they control all the better by serving. That is also true of institutions such as parliaments. Parliaments are quite typical of the state invention: they are the site of legitimate politics, the site where a legitimate manner of formulating and settling conflicts between groups and interests is institutionalized. The institutionalization of this site of legitimate politics is tacitly accompanied by the institutionalization of non-legitimate politics as whatever is excluded from these places, intrinsically excluded; certain forms of non-verbal violence are excluded by the fact that a [different] form of violence has been established as legitimate.

[Corrigan and Sayer] associate the construction of the state with the construction and massive imposition of a set of common ethical and logical representations. If they were theoretically consistent, they would say with Durkheim, as I already cited him, that the state simultaneously imposes a logical conformity and a moral conformity. Durkheim made this distinction in *The Elementary Forms of the Religious Life*: what he calls logical conformity is the agreement of minds made possible by the possession of common logical categories, while moral conformity is the same thing in the ethical order, participation in a common world of shared values.[7] For Durkheim, therefore, logical categories are social categories – groups or clans – that have become mental categories. Logical conformity is this basic agreement with the world and among agents that makes it possible for them to participate in a common world of logical categories. [For Corrigan and Sayer] the birth of the state is associated with a work that aims to encourage people to 'identify themselves predominantly in terms of nationality, rather than either more locally (e.g. subjects of a particular lord) or more widely (as e.g. in the medieval concept of Christendom)'.[8] The birth of the state is associated therefore with the imposition on the entire body of individuals of a nation of a privileged viewpoint on their own identity, this privileged viewpoint being that of the nation. They identify as French, and not as belonging to the Holy Roman Empire or as Basques or Bretons. A level of privileged identification is defined and, at this level of identification which is introduced by way of the fetishism of the state and the nation, a series of secondary properties are associated that are imposed on whoever accepts this identification. There is [in *The Great Arch*] a fine presentation of Englishness, that is, a series of traits associated with the English national character: 'the supposed reasonableness, moderation, pragmatism, hostility to ideology, "muddling through", quirkiness, eccentricity, and so on of the "English"'.[9] There are dozens of books on the English by English writers, writers being major contributors to the construction of this kind of national ideal, which is acceptable to intellectuals because each particular class has its nationalism. (In my travels abroad, what always strikes me is the strength of nationalism in intellectual circles. That is surprising, but it is a very subtle nationalism linked with reading, something masked.) Englishness is eccentricity, or a whole series of properties that are constitutive of what was called in the nineteenth century the 'national character'. [. . .] Read the very fine article by E. P. Thompson, 'The peculiarities of the English', in which he notes this singularity in terms of table manners, ways of speaking and bodily stance. For example, linguists have studied the distance from which individuals speak to one another, which shows considerable variation; people speak more or less closely according to their ethnic group or nation, so that certain categories of people strike you as invasive because their national traditions require you to speak to someone more closely, which [others] find an intolerable penetration into their circle of intimacy.[10] All those boundaries of inside and outside that are linked with the national character are largely products of the state, by way of the educational system, literature and all kinds of paths for the transmission and inculcation of these deep and unconscious dispositions bound up with the state.

[*The Great Arch*] is not a very clear [book], as I said. Which is why I find it very hard to relate it. If I did so in my own fashion, I would annex it completely – it would then be coherent, but it would no longer be their book. I have difficulty relating it because it is at the same time very close to what I want to say to you and very distant. You will have to read it yourselves . . . One of the mediations by which 'Englishness' is transmitted – religion, faith, belief in the state – and likewise 'Frenchness', is the school system, education, geography, etc. It is very remarkable that defenders of established spelling almost always associate [their cause] with the defence of geography: this is one of the basic, primary disciplines. Geography is the map of France, it is part of the national or nationalist libido. This kind of relationship to one's identity as nationally constituted is the product of institutions, but also of all state rituals. [The intuition from which Corrigan and Sayer set out, I believe,] is that the state is a collection of rituals. These authors are undoubtedly well placed to [make this point]: why is the society that made the industrial revolution the one that has preserved most in the way of archaic state rituals? This is the very interesting question that they raise, and I shall try and generalize it rather further by taking the example of Japan.

England and Japan are two ultra-conservative countries in terms of state rituals – wigs, etc. – while they were at the same time revolutionary, in their time, in economic terms. E. P. Thompson's very fine writings on the judicial system analyse what I will call the symbolic violence of justice as exercised through the apparatus (apparatus in Pascal's sense, rather than Althusser's), that is, by display.[11] Their reference would be Pascal: state rhetoric, state discourse. They give examples. For example, when you say 'rule of law' you have said it all; today, people talk of a 'state of law'.[12] Likewise, England as the 'mother of Parliaments'. . .[13] [. . .]

The idea of Corrigan and Sayer is that, far from being antithetic to the perpetuation of archaic traditions, the English miracle of the nineteenth century was made possible by this kind of cultural unity, displayed in rituals and embodied in visceral beliefs, in 'Englishness'. This common culture – culture taken in the anthropological sense of the term – maintained, orchestrated, rehearsed by the state by way of state rituals, coronation ceremonies (nowadays television has become central to this state ceremonial, this culture), has functioned as an instrument of legitimation that has protected the traditional forms of authority and domination from radical critique and challenge. Basically it's Durkheim in the service of Weber. They are right: it is because the state is an instrument that establishes the foundations of both a logical and a moral conformity that it fulfils at the same time the mysterious function of legitimation that Weber was forced to introduce in order to understand the state effect, to understand that the state is not just what Marx said about it, it is also something that succeeds in gaining recognition, to which very many of things are granted, obedience among others. How does the state get people to obey it? That is really the underlying problem.

The state, accordingly, is the instance of legitimation par excellence, which consecrates, solemnizes, ratifies, records. There is a very good presentation in *The Great Arch* of the impalpable process by which the state gradually involves itself in all public manifestations, in publication, in making public.[14] I have analysed at length what the publication of marriage banns means. Why does a marriage become a marriage by being made public?[15] Making public is the state act par excellence; by the same token you can understand that the state is involved in everything.

(I want to make a very political excursus on this point. The difficulty of sociological analysis lies in the fact that it is often confused with social criticism. People say: 'Censorship isn't good, etc.', whereas the point is to explain, and explaining means understanding that the state has an integral connection with censorship: *censor, census*. The state is integrally connected with any public expression, especially when the public sphere is involved. By its very definition, the state does not like satirical papers, caricature. Today, the state deals with all this very cleverly, but if censorship is invisible that does not mean it does not exist; it is perhaps still stronger than when it was exercised by the police. When the editorials of certain eminent journalists amount to advertising, that is an extreme form of particularly invisible censorship. The symbolic violence is perfect, a violence exercised with complete unawareness on the part of those on whom is it exercised, and hence with their complicity.)

The state is the legitimizing instance par excellence, which ratifies, solemnizes and records acts or individuals, making the divisions or classifications it establishes appear self-evident. The state is not just an instrument of coercion. Corrigan and Sayer repeatedly cite, in order to disparage it, Lenin's phrase about the state being 'special bodies of armed men, prisons, etc.', and show how simplistic that is.[16] The state is not just an instrument of coercion, but an instrument for the production and reproduction of consensus, charged with moral regulation. Here they take up Durkheim's definition: the state is an organ of moral discipline.[17] If I agree with them completely on this, it is because they use Durkheim to give meaning to a question of Weber, and at the same time do not forget Marx, they do not forget that this organ of moral discipline is not in the service of just anyone, but rather serves the dominant. None the less, their demonstration is rather confused.

The exemplary particularity of England: economic modernization and cultural archaisms

I shall deal now with two questions that their book raises. First of all, the particularity of England: in what way does the particular case of England, when taken seriously, enable us to pose the general question of the state particularly well? The French case is very privileged in many aspects: it is a centralized state, but on the other hand it is an unfavourable case given that the French Revolution was a revolution made in the name of universalism; it is a particular case that presents itself as universal. By the same token, the effects of symbolic domination of the kind that we can see in the English state risk escaping us, since they are especially well dissimulated. Universalization is the rhetorical strategy of dissimulation par excellence. Think of the Marxist analysis of ideology as the universalization of particular interests. The French state has the most powerful rhetoric of universalization: compare its colonization with English colonization . . . It is interesting here to return to 'Englishness' in order to grasp the effects of symbolic domination in their pure state, that is, in a truly singular form. The French state is also singular, but it is able to present itself as universal. This is all very much bound up with contemporary concerns: viz. the positions taken up on the question of the so-called Islamic veil, with this very French fashion of making use of the universal in order to do the particular, which is one of the pinnacles of political hypocrisy . . .

The first question, then, is the particularity of both England and Japan, as an opportunity to challenge the myth of generalized modernity: is industrial modernization necessarily accompanied by the modernization of state ritual? Is an 'archaic' state ritual hostile to economic modernization, or on the contrary, can it not be a formidable instrument of modernization, to the extent that it enables the production of consensus, and, in a certain sense, of material gain?

The second set of theoretical questions is the construction of legitimacy. I shall try and show that if Corrigan and Sayer rather flounder here, this is because they lack the concept of symbolic capital, symbolic violence, and because of this lack they cannot explain what they really want to, that is, the voluntary submission, voluntary dependence, that the state obtains, this kind of submission that escapes the alternative between coercion and freely chosen submission. To say that the state is legitimate is to say that it can obtain submission without constraint, or rather with a form of constraint that I call symbolic power, and which is quite particular. In order to understand this kind of constraint, you need to integrate into your theory, in a non-scholarly way, Kant by way of Durkheim, Marx and Weber.

What I intend to develop today is the first question: the particularity of the English, but also referring to the example of Japan. First of all, why is it the English themselves who raise this question of English particularity? Curiously, this question arises for these English writers because they are English Marxists. These authors – Thompson and those who follow him –

have been subject, like Marxists the world over, to the question posed by the French path of revolution. The theory of revolution that Marx proposed took as its focal point the French Revolution, and so Marxists in every country were all led to ask why they had not had a French Revolution. I discovered that there was also a great debate among Japanese Marxists, between those for whom there had been a French Revolution in their country and those who maintained there had not been – and this on the basis of the same historical materials. But neither one group nor the other asked if there was any sense in asking whether there had been a French Revolution in Japan, or if there really had been a French Revolution at all. The English very seriously asked the question whether this revolution was a real revolution, and what was needed for there to be a revolution. The imposition of the Marxist paradigm of revolution generated in particular a bevy of writings that are absolutely without interest to my mind. That is one of the reasons that makes the hold of Marxism over certain sectors of the social sciences rather worrying, and the book we are discussing, which is also a reaction against the domination of Marxism in England, amounts to saying that the reason that the English are 'paleo' is not because they did not have a French Revolution. And that there is no contradiction between the fact that the English did not have a French Revolution and the fact that they did have an industrial revolution. The advent of an industrial revolution does not imply a break with feudal remains. And the fact that they did not experience a symbolic revolution corresponding to the political revolution – something that people like to see as inevitable – perhaps explains why they were able to have an industrial revolution that presupposed a working class that was dominated and domesticated. That is the thesis. In the same way, the case of Japan becomes very interesting . . .

Corrigan and Sayer's book is complicated because it deals simultaneously with both questions. The paradox is as follows: 'The "archaic", non-bureaucratized, flexible forms of the English state were in practice far more favourable to capitalist transformation than no matter what form of absolutism favourable to enterprise and private initiative.'[18] Not only do they question the traditional problematic of Marxism in relation to the French Revolution, they actually reverse it. They insist that English civilization is marked by an extraordinary continuity, by the persistence of a number of 'unmodernized' features, anachronisms, that are without equivalent in other societies: 'We have suggested that exactly the supposed "anachronisms" of English polity and culture lie at the heart of the security of the bourgeois state in England.'[19] In other words, what is perceived as an anachronism is not an obstacle, a survival, an archaism (when people want to explain something, they do not talk of 'survivals'), but is constitutive and lies at the very heart of the bourgeois revolution and its success.

Those agencies and institutions which ultimately came to be identifiable as 'the' state in many cases had . . . an extremely long – precapitalist pedigree . . . [T]he organisation of these agencies into the kind of polity Weber describes as 'rational-bureaucratic' or Marx contrasts with feudal forms of rule was protracted, and indeed in many instances remains – in terms of the model's expectations – no more than partial.[20]

[Corrigan and Sayer] challenge the equation 'industrial revolution = break with the feudal state'. They give examples such as the uncodified common law (in contrast to rational Roman law) being the basis for a capitalist economy, or the fact that there was no professional state bureaucracy before the nineteenth century. An English historian has shown how until that time high officials drew payment from the functions they performed, as they had done in France in the seventeenth and eighteenth centuries.[21] Another feature, which they call a 'patrimonial pre-bourgeois heritage' (pre-revolutionary in Marxist language): appointments were very often made in a logic of patronage, of a patron–client relationship. A further pertinent trait is that monarchical forms remain central, not only to legitimization, but to the whole machinery of central power. This machinery is not a kind of wedding cake to decorate the English state, it is constitutive of it: Her Majesty's Government, the monarchy, lies at the heart of a legitimizing corpus, based on antiquity, tradition, continuity, self-conscious 'Englishness'.

Another analysis that [Corrigan and Sayer] develop at length is that of national security interests. They show in great detail how this notion is a very ancient historical invention, by way of which it is possible to arouse fears, impulses, phobias, ostracism, racism, etc. And a final example is the House of Lords, which still has a legislative role. On the basis of these archaic examples, they then ask whether one should not challenge the myth of the bourgeois revolution described by Marx as the measure of all revolutions. Paradoxically, the Marxist redefinition of the bourgeois revolution makes all modern histories into exceptions, from Japan to England to the United States. The cases of England and Japan thus become incomplete bourgeois revolutions burdened with survivals – politics has not caught up ... The thesis I shall put forward, going rather further than them, is that a wrong model of the French Revolution, which is a false revolution even in the perspective of state construction (there was a strong continuity via the *noblesse de robe*),[22] but which was used for all countries as a yardstick of revolutionary break – whether they had a revolution or not – generated a host of false questions all over the world. One of the functions of genetic history is to free historians from the terrible model of the French Revolution. And Corrigan and Sayers's book has the merit of inciting a rebellion against this model.

In *The Poverty of Theory* (1978), which has a great chapter on the Althusserians, E. P. Thompson includes his 1965 article I already cited on English particularity. As a very heterodox Marxist, he makes fun of what he calls the 'urban bias' of Marxist-type theories of revolution that seek at any cost a classic bourgeoisie living in the towns and struggling against the feudal state. He showed how in England it was the embourgeoisement of the rural gentry that lay at the origin of the industrial revolution. The Japanese case is even clearer, with the role played by the class of declassed samurai in the industrial revolution.

In the next lecture I shall talk very briefly about Japan, before going on to sum up the theoretical foundations of the state as power, in particular of symbolic power. My article 'On symbolic power' will give you the outline of this. I shall try to show how, in order to understand symbolic power, you have to integrate Kant – the neo-Kantians such as Panofsky and Cassirer – and the Durkheimians, as well as Marx on domination and Weber on legitimacy and the spaces in which instruments of legitimization are produced: the bureaucratic field and the field of power, etc. I cannot avoid speaking of all this in the logic of my argument.

Lecture of 31 January 1991

Reply to questions – Cultural archaisms and economic transformations – Culture and national unity: the case of Japan – Bureaucracy and cultural integration – National unification and cultural domination

Reply to questions

Your questions first of all. One of these bears on the problem of the state in African societies; this is a complicated problem, which I cannot answer in a few sentences. Then a group of questions that the author believes I shall not be able to reply to publicly . . . so much for that. Finally, a question on problems of definition in sociology: are preliminary definitions legitimate in sociology? There are differing positions on this problem. Durkheim made preliminary definition an indispensable moment of what I call the construction of the object. I do not share this position. Durkheim's preliminary definitions are often weak, and what he says [in his analyses] is far better than what he puts forwards in his definitions. In this epistemological debate, I place myself in the camp of defending vague and provisional concepts, since in sociology as in all other sciences, the advance of science may be blocked by false formal rigour at the preliminary stage, which can have what an American epistemologist calls an effect of closure.[1] It is important to know what one is speaking about, and try to give rigour to the language used, but it very often happens that this apparent rigour conceals a lack of genuine rigour, and that the formal rigour of the discourse goes far beyond the rigour of the realities denoted by the discourse. In the sciences, and not just the social sciences, an overly formal apparatus is often scientifically counter-productive.

This question continues with the idea of coercion: doesn't defining the state by coercion involve a value judgement? Secondly, doesn't characterizing the state by coercion amount to characterizing a pathological form of state? To speak of coercion, even in its most elementary form, does indeed involve an implicit value judgement, and there is also an assumption as to the functions of the state. I would like to show today that a well-constituted state should be able, in the extreme case, to dispense with coercion. The constraint that the state exercises on our most intimate thoughts, the fact that our thinking can be possessed by the state, constitutes an exemplary case of the 'invisible' coercions that are exercised with the complicity of those subject to them. That is what I call symbolic violence or symbolic domination, that is, forms of constraint that rely on unconscious harmony between objective structures and mental structures.

Cultural archaisms and economic transformations

Discussing Corrigan and Sayer's book [in the previous lecture] I raised two sets of questions: the first of these concerned the particularity of the English path towards the state, to which I added the case of Japan; the second set of questions bears on the theoretical foundations of state thinking as a form of power, as symbolic power. Corrigan and Sayer's merit is to have seen that the state is something other than the army and the police: the state intervenes with forms of domination that are quite particular and could be characterized as soft. They set a direction of analysis more than they follow it, partly for want of rigorous concepts making it possible to conceive the complexity of symbolic domination. I shall therefore take up these two points today. In the cases of England and Japan, what I say will be laborious and superficial. I am not a specialist on Japan; I have done my best to acquire a certain knowledge, but I am venturing onto terrain that I am constantly aware is inhabited by professionals. Not that I live in terror of making mistakes, but I respect a competence that I shall never completely possess. And so I shall be rather hesitant, even nonsensical, but it is out of respect for my subject matter . . .

The idea developed by Corrigan and Sayer is that there is no antinomy between certain cultural traits in the English tradition that may be viewed as archaic and the fact that England saw the miracle of the industrial revolution. One could say, by way of generalization, that neither is there an antinomy between the cultural archaism of Japan and the Japanese miracle. It is commonplace in the literature on Japan to ask how it is that you have on the one hand a technological miracle and on the other hand this folkloric state, a cultural ensemble that fascinates both tourists and scholars alike. How is it that on Japan you have on the one hand Orientalists – a dreadful word – and on the other hand economists specializing in Japan, without either side being familiar with or acknowledging the other? This schism is a contributing factor to the 'culture effect'. In fact, the dualism that the technique/culture division imposes is one of the invisible ways by which a symbolic domination is exercised, ways by which a social order defends itself against those who try to think it. Disciplinary divisions, or divisions of intellectual tradition, are often places where censorship is exercised. Orientalists are not economic specialists on Japan, and vice versa; by the same token, the problem I have just formulated

cannot be raised either by one side or by the other, despite the fact that
both sides always talk about it.

The English 'economic miracle' of the nineteenth century, or the
Japanese miracle today, are in no way antithetical to the existence of
all kinds of archaisms. This paradoxical thesis breaks with academic
doxa and goes right against the Weberian theory of rationalization.[2]
This theory, which is extremely widespread and accepted as self-evident,
has resurfaced in modernized forms (in the United States, people spent
fifteen years talking of 'modernization theory').[3] It assumes, without
overtly saying so, that there is a unified historical process leading up
to the present, a process tacitly oriented towards a *telos*, towards what
Nietzsche called 'English happiness'[4] (today one would say 'American
happiness'). There is therefore a *telos*, and on the other hand a unity, an
advance towards an end that has a certain coherence. I shall not repeat
here the whole Weberian theory of rationalization, but for those familiar with it, one of Weber's key ideas is that what he calls a 'rational'
legal system is one in harmony with a rational economy; and a rational
economy cannot function without a rational legal system able to ensure
for this economy what it requires above all else, that is, calculability and
predictability as the two criteria of rationality. Weber is aware of this:
he distinguishes between formal rationality and material rationality (a
law that is formally just may be unjust, but at least it is coherent).[5] A
rational legal system, Weber says, ensures calculability for the economy,
so that American corporate lawyers can foresee the sanctions a firm will
incur when it breaks the law. A rational legal system is one that makes
possible calculation and rational economic management. Weber says the
same about a rational or rationalized religion, that it either underlies or is
compatible with a rational economy. The same holds for science. Weber
thus has the idea of a unified process of rationalization in which different domains of human activity accompany the rationalization process of
a rationalizing economy. What I say about rationalization in Weber is
highly simplistic, but I want to do rather more than just give a reference.[6]
For in order to understand that what Corrigan and Sayer are saying is
a paradox, you have to have the idea of rationalization in mind. It is
to Corrigan and Sayer's credit that they break with this kind of doxic
philosophy that sociologists confusedly have in mind: that the modern
world is rationalizing in a unitary way. They stress that there are lags, dis-
cordances, intelligible gaps – which are not necessarily contradictions –
between the autonomous development of cultural processes (the tea
ceremony, kabuki, Elizabethan theatre) and economic development. It
is not necessary for every sector of society to march at the same pace in
order for the economy to move forward.

To recall here our authors' conclusions: England's examples of
backwardness and cultural oddity were not obstacles to capitalism,
to the upsurge of the industrial revolution; it was on the contrary the
cultural integration ensured by these practices, seemingly scattered and

disparate – from the political tradition to that of the royal family – that contributed to forging the unity of the population that constitutes the nation, a unit capable of surviving the conflicts and contradictions bound up with the development of industrial society. Durkheim, in his introduction to *The Division of Labour in Society*, says that the price of economic development is anomie, the absence of *nomos*, of agreement on what is basically right and on everything that follows from this; among the indicators of anomie he counts the rates of suicide and divorce, industrial conflict and the rise of socialist demands.[7] This antinomy between the development of industrial society (and the division of labour that is a correlate of it) and social integration around a *nomos* is what Corrigan and Sayer challenge. For them, the antinomy is merely apparent; in reality, the social order is far more integrated than is generally believed: it is integrated around culture. Culture is an instrument of cohesion, of social unity, and the industrial revolution was possible largely because there were forces of cohesion able to counteract the forces of dispersion. These forces of cohesion were on the side of culture, understood not only in the restricted sense of legitimate culture, cultivated culture – Corneille, Racine – but also in the anthropological sense, that is, ways of living, of serving tea, of sitting at table, [what in the British intellectual tradition comes under the heading] of 'civilization'. Here there is a clear break with Elias, who remains very close to Weber in this respect. For him, the civilizing process is completely dissociated from any political component, as if the process of civilization did not have any counterpart or functions . . .

Culture and national unity: the case of Japan

Corrigan and Sayer's book accordingly raises a very important question, that of the link between national unity, social integration and culture, or correlatively that between culture and nation, culture and nationalism. It is particularly hard for French people to think in these terms. For example, the idea that the school may be a place where the nation or nationalism is established is astonishing for a French person. This is the problem I shall now confront, taking the most favourable cases, England and Japan, where this contrast leaps to the eye for even the most superficial observer. For Japan, I ask your indulgence, without false modesty, because it's not easy for me, all the more so as I have to master the empirical material and construct it differently from how it is generally constructed. (If it was only a matter of relating the history of Japan, I would take the time needed and succeed, but I have to use material that I do not have expert mastery of, and make of it something quite different from what is made by the experts [on Japan]. And right away, I am particularly exposed to those experts who will say: he can't do any of that because he's not an expert . . . which I don't believe. I think that people often call themselves experts so as to

avoid raising a certain number of problems; they are Orientalists to avoid
raising these problems about Japan . . . I shouldn't say things like this, but
as I deeply believe them, they come out despite everything.)

Japanese Marxists battled over the question as to whether there was
a Japanese way, and why the poor Japanese had not had a French
Revolution.[8] They were struck by a certain number of constant features that leapt to the eye; they noted with despair that they would be
deprived of a revolution – there was no 'great day' to await – since they
did not have all the signs by which the probability of a revolution could
be recognized. They noted that the Meiji regime had not led either to
the abolition of feudal relations of production in agriculture or to the
overthrow of the absolute monarchy, since Japan still had the imperial
regime – two fundamental elements by which one could recognize that
a revolution had not been accomplished. They noted that the system
of accumulation on which the Japanese economic and social order was
based relied on a system of tax on land that had not made a genuine
break with the feudal tradition, and remained associated with ties of a
feudal type even in the modern world. And finally, a third feature that
disturbed them greatly, the political leadership of the Meiji restoration
was not assured, as it should have been in theory, by urban bourgeois as
in the French Revolution, but by the class of samurai, warriors who converted themselves into literati, minor nobles. Japanese Marxists accordingly wondered whether this revolution was not in fact a rebellion of the
nobility, as is said of certain revolutions that took place in the West. The
revolution was not a revolution, since it did not have as its subject those
people who are normal subjects of a revolution, that is, revolutionary
petty bourgeois, but rather impoverished warriors who sought by revolution to convert their capital of nobility into bureaucratic capital. The
analogy is striking . . .

(I am in a difficult position here. I know too much on the subject to be
comfortable in the manner of philosophers talking about such problems,
while not enough to be comfortable in the manner of historians . . . I am
unfortunate in both directions. I hope that I don't say anything mistaken;
after all, you will correct me. Those who don't know are warned.)

I believe that the Meiji revolution may be described as a 'conservative
revolution'.[9] Certain Nazi groups, or precursors of the Nazis, were conservative revolutionaries, that is, people who make a revolution aiming
to restore certain aspects of an old order. The Meiji revolution offers
many analogies with certain forms of noble reforms; on this point, I refer
you to the very fine book by Arlette Jouanna, *Le Devoir de révolte*.[10] She
studies here the rebellions of the petty nobility threatened in the sixteenth
century by the rise of the bourgeoisie; they sought liberties for themselves,
but liberties that could be perceived as liberties for everyone. This class
demanded civil rights and liberties that could accordingly have a 'modern-
ist' air, but were in fact rights and liberties defined from the standpoint of
the privileged, with all the ambiguity this implies. The Ligue Catholique,

for example, was a very ambiguous movement, with petty nobles and certain fractions of the bourgeoisie in greater or lesser difficulty side by side ...[11] The Meiji reform was of the same type: petty samurai who claimed civil rights and liberties, but who, to the extent that they universalized their particular interests, demanded the expansion of the power of the samurai in the guise of demanding universal rights.

Why was the initial paradox greatest in the case of Japan? A new history of the nobility would have to be written, from the feudal era through to contemporary Todai;[12] the court nobility perpetuated itself continuously from the eighth century to the present day, while undertaking constant reconversions in the sense of the acquisition of culture, and the culture associated with bureaucracy. You could say of traditional Japan, feudal Japan, what Needham, the great historian of science, said about China,[13] that it was a 'bureaucratized feudalism'. From the eighth century on, Japan was endowed with a very strongly bureaucratized state, with all the indications of bureaucratization in Weber's sense: the use of writing, the bureaucratic division of labour, the delegation of state acts to functionaries, the division between the household and the office, the separation of the royal house from the state, etc. In association with this bureaucratization, you find very early on people who combine properties of warrior nobles and noble literati. But it is particularly in the seventeenth century that the connection between the nobility and culture is very clearly effective: the cult of the samurai with his sword is enshrined precisely at the time that these figures were disappearing, rather as today you have museums of popular arts and traditions at the time that peasants are disappearing. The myth of the samurai, the martial arts, the whole cult of Japanese civilization, begins to develop at the time when the samurai are converting themselves into bureaucrats and literati. In the 1600s, the great majority of samurai were illiterate, and their leader, who held central authority, founded large numbers of schools, so that by the 1700s we know that the great majority of former soldiers were educated. Most of them were integrated into the bureaucracy, but this left a surplus who were redundant. Supernumeraries of this kind are always very interesting. One of the major factors in historical change is the gap between the output of the educational system and the positions available.[14] This is why I am against any *numerus clausus* in education, as supernumeraries of this kind are a major factor of change. People who are superfluous, in too great supply, either seize positions they are not supposed to occupy, or else transform positions so that they can occupy them. In this sense, they carry out a whole work of historical change. These supernumeraries, these educated samurai without a bureaucratic position, launched themselves in business (you find major dynasties of former samurai at the head of big contemporary corporations), they struggled for liberty and civil rights, exactly like the petty nobles studied by Arlette Jouanna; they particularly launched into journalism, becoming marginal, 'free' intellectuals, with all that this involves.[15]

Bureaucracy and cultural integration

In order to understand the Japanese 'miracle', you must take into account the fact that Japan was bureaucratized at a very early date, as was England (Marc Bloch said that England had a state very early on, long before France). There is no incompatibility between cultural originality and bureaucratization, quite the contrary. Bureaucratization goes hand in hand with the interest in culture as an instrument of access to the bureaucracy. Weber noted this, but it goes well beyond what he said about it. In France, the accumulation of cultural capital became a path of access to power very early on, from the moment that bureaucratic institutions were established, demanding, if not genuine competence, at least competence as guaranteed by the school system. There is a connection here that you see becoming established in France from the twelfth century. People are thus bound up with the state, and by the same token with the school and its culture, the 'berobed' [*robins*] of the French tradition. The samurai come into this category. This bureaucratic feudalism, which became ever more bureaucratic, has ever increasing links with educational qualification. There are few countries where the tyranny of qualifications is as strong as in Japan; the school system is perverted to the point that the rate of suicide following educational failure is astronomical. Japan is a society in which educational qualification is an instrument of social advance and consecration of the first magnitude. When people speak of the 'Japanese miracle', they forget a determining factor, which is the role of cultural capital accumulated with a particular intensity in a society in which the whole tradition is geared to this accumulation. This is something that is not mentioned very much, especially in the writings of economists.

This work of cultural accumulation, both individual and collective, is accompanied by an immense work of cultural construction. And you can say that the Japanese state, like the English and the French states, was constructed by constructing an artefact of the kind that is Japanese culture, an artefact that puts on airs of being natural and original, which is relatively easy to the extent that it mimics traditional Japanese features. There is a whole work of naturalization of culture, a naturalization that is effected by the evocation of antiquity, what the old common lawyers called 'time-honoured'. This culture is actually a historical artefact that can be associated with particular authors and inventions [. . .]. This culture is an artefact completely invented by literati; and what I had never realized before working on the problem of the state is that this culture is not only legitimate but national. This political dimension of culture had escaped me, and basically everything I am going to say consists in taking up a number of my old analyses – the role of legitimate culture, of the school – but situating these in their context – a completely historical one – and connecting this culture with its functions of national integration, and not just social integration, as Durkheim had it.

English culture was thus constructed against the French model.

'Englishness' was defined against France; each of the adjectives that are constitutive of 'Englishness' can be set against an adjective characterizing 'Frenchness'. Japanese culture is a cultural artefact constructed against the foreign with the intention of rehabilitation. Japan was a nation dominated but not colonized. It experienced subjection to European domination without for all that being directly subject to this domination as was China. Because of this, Japanese culture was inspired by the intention of rehabilitation, of 'dignification' in the face of the contempt of Westerners. I refer you to the book by Philippe Pons, *Le Monde*'s Japanese correspondent, *D'Edo à Tokyo: Mémoire et modernité*.[16] This book falls into the same trap of Orientalist mysticism that the Japanese themselves are caught in – an example of symbolic domination – but it gives a good presentation of this kind of cultural arsenal. Another book, *Tokugawa Ideology*, by the sociologist and historian Herman Ooms, one of the rare few to break with the Orientalist tradition, describes the historical genesis of the idea of Japanese-ness drawing on texts and authors of the time.[17]

A typical example of cultural invention with a clear intention of rehabilitation is the nineteenth-century ban on public baths, which were part of the Japanese tradition. Since the Western model saw these as bizarre, they were banned, and a traditional cultural practice was excluded from legitimate culture, while practices were introduced that had existed only for small fractions of court society, and were now constituted into elements of general culture. The early twentieth century saw a reinvention of traditional arts – martial arts, calligraphy, etc. The example of these par excellence was the art of tea: *sadô* was the product of a kind of scholarly codification pushed to the point of parody, the constitution of an everyday practice into a work of art – in this connection, Japan is interesting as an extreme case of 'Englishness'. Codification, canonization and constitution of something 'authentic': a dangerous word, think of Heidegger . . . Japan is [the place where] an 'authentic' Japanese culture was constituted, into which was integrated the martial tradition and an extraordinarily violent division between the sexes – few traditions contrast masculine and feminine so strongly.

In the Japanese case, the state was constructed by constructing the legitimate definition of culture, and imposing this definition in a systematic fashion by way of two instruments: the school and the army. People often think of the army as an instrument of coercion (as we have seen with Elias and Tilly), but the army is also an instrument for inculcating cultural models, an instrument of training. In the case of Japan, school and army were charged with diffusing and inculcating a tradition of discipline, sacrifice, loyalty. You thus have a kind of artificial state culture, cut off from popular traditions. The performances of Japanese theatre, for example, are totally inaccessible; spectators have to read summaries before they can follow them. The artefact becomes totally artificial – which does not mean that spectators do not have a genuine pleasure, but simply that these so-called popular arts are in fact de-popularized arts, which can only be perpetuated with the support of the school system. There could be a similar case with classical theatre in France. If the school system stopped teaching Corneille and Racine, a whole part of the repertoire would completely disappear, and the need, the pleasure, the desire to consume them would likewise disappear . . . The Japanese scholarization of culture has its effects on the content of culture, and is at the same time what makes possible the consumption of this transformed culture. René Sieffert calls kabuki a 'museum theatre',[18] accessible to an audience of initiates who often consume these products at one or two removes, with accompanying notes, commentaries, etc.

National unification and cultural domination

In this example the connection between culture, school and nation appears very clearly, and perhaps because it is a foreign example, you can see that there is a school nationalism, that the teaching system is an instrument of nationalism. But I believe this is true everywhere. The school system that sees itself as universal, the French school in particular – quite apart from the desire, consciousness and responsibility of the teachers – is a great instrument for the constitution of national emotions, those things 'that only we can feel', or 'that you have to be born in the country in order to feel', things for which people are prepared to die, like spelling.

To finish with this point, I would say that in both the English and the Japanese cases you can clearly discern the role of school culture, legitimate culture, as both constructive and unifying, and you also see that this school culture is a national culture, in other words that school and culture have a function of internal integration – what Durkheim called social integration: all French kids have a minimum adhesion to the legitimate culture, and if they are not familiar with the culture, they at least recognize it. Everyone is supposed to know what proper culture is, which basically means what is taught at school. When we do interviews on cultural questions, it is very rare to find people who reject culture; the most uncultured people seek to conform to a cultural legitimacy that they are absolutely incapable of satisfying. If familiarity with culture is very unevenly distributed, recognition of culture is very widespread, and through it recognition of everything that culture guarantees: the superiority of cultured people over those who are not cultured; the fact that graduates from the École Nationale de l'Administration [ENA] occupy positions of power, etc. – all these things are indirectly guaranteed by cultural capital. One thing I had always overlooked in my analyses is that school also has a function of national integration against the outside, the external: the cultural institution is one of the sites of nationalism. I shall now simply mention a number of very delicate questions.

Nation-states are constituted by processes of a similar type, a kind of artificial construction of an artificial culture. For certain nation-states, the initial culture, which they can draw on to construct this artefact, is religious: that is the case with Israel and the Arab states. How is a national culture established, a culture in the official sense of the term, when the material which has to be worked with is essentially religious? How can a culture with a universal claim be made from the particularity of a historical or religious tradition? All these antinomies inherent to the question need detailed development. I mentioned the very singular case of France, which in this respect is at the opposite extreme to Israel or the Arab countries: it is a nation-state established in the illusion of universality, this universality and rationality being in fact its particularity. The particularity of the French is reason; that is their subjective image, but it is not without objective foundation. Already before 1789, revolutionary work was being performed under the sign of reason, that is, the sign of universality. It is a tradition constituted by its claim to the universal, with a particular relationship to the universal, which explains the inability of French thinkers to conceive the particularity of French thinking and to free themselves from the nationalism of this supposed internationalism, as well as explaining France's traditional position in conflicts.

This national tradition of the rights of man, of reason and the universal, to which we can add the tradition of the intellectual from Zola to Sartre – a national speciality, even if there are intellectuals elsewhere – this national speciality of the universal, of the 'would-be' universal, is one of the particularities of the French situation, with this idea that its national culture is an international culture, immediately exportable and needing to be exported. It is no bad thing to export French culture; there's nothing better than going off to teach French in Greece – I deliberately take the Greeks as example, the Bantu might be a different case . . . Until the Second World War, this claim to universality was based on certain facts. There was a domination of French literary culture across the globe. Paris was a nationalist myth, but one with a real foundation: it was in Paris that artists made their careers; the revolutions in German art were made with reference to Paris. This sort of supposed, assumed universality was accompanied by signs of a practical form of universality, a domination unaware of itself as such. This is very deeply anchored in the French unconscious. If we have reactions of quasi-fascist ultra-nationalism, this is because we are great universalist dominators in decline . . .

The French were able to do what the Japanese did with the art of tea, that is, make an artificial culture with a likely chance of success. This was not a national mania: there was a market for it. You didn't get hauled over the coals for speaking French in Ankara; there would always be someone who understood you. This objectively based, sociologically based claim to the universal implies an imperialism of the universal. And I believe that the particularly vicious character of French imperialism lay in its imperialism of the universal. This imperialism has been transferred today from France to the United States;[19] American democracy has taken up the baton from French democracy, with all the clear conscience this implies.

We should also study the same imperialism of the universal on the part of the Communist regimes from 1917 to I don't know when (people differ as to when it ended), the imperialism of the universal could equally be found in Communist messages coming from the 'land of the revolution' . . .

All this is to say that in what is apparently the most favourable case of cultural imperialism and the nationalist use of culture, that is, the case of universal imperialisms, it is clear that culture is never pure, that it always has dimensions not only of domination but also of nationalism. Culture is an instrument of legitimization and domination. Weber said of religion that it gives the dominant a theodicy of their own privileges. I prefer to speak of 'sociodicy': it offers a legitimation of the social order such as it is. But that is not all. Culture succeeds religion, with quite similar functions. It gives the dominant the sense of being justified in their domination, not only on the level of a national society but also on that of global society, so that the dominant or colonizers, for example, can see themselves in all good conscience as bearers of the universal. I take a position that seems to be merely critical, but it is actually more complicated than this. Things would be very easy if the imperialism of the universal did not contain at least a little bit of what it says and believes itself to be.

The process I shall describe, that is, the process of unification by which the state is constituted, is not without ambiguity. There are regions, local rights, local customs, local languages, and a process of concentration and unification leads to a single state, with a single language and law. The process of unification is also a process of concentration. There were mercenary armies, there is now a [national] army. This process leads to unity, but it also leads to the monopoly of those who benefit from the process, those who produce the state and are in a position to dominate the profits that the state provides. There is a monopolization of everything that the state produces in the process of producing itself, a monopolization of the universal, of reason. The process of concentration I have described is like a sheet with a recto and a verso side. The more you move towards universal unity, the more you delocalize and de-particularize (in Kabylia, each village had different measures), the more you move towards a unified state with a standard metre, more universal. People can understand one another, they can cross frontiers and communicate. Simultaneously, on the other side, there is national – and nationalist – concentration; the advance towards universalism is at the same time an advance towards the monopolization of the universal. At the level of relations between states you find the same problems that you find within the state.

If there is something of the universal in history, this is because people have an interest in the universal, which means that the universal is genetically corrupt, though this does not therefore mean it is not universal. You could take by way of example today what is most universal in culture, in human achievement, that is, mathematical culture, and show how the social uses of mathematics can make possible and justify technological triumphalism. This would show how the formalism, formalization and pure logic with which we spontaneously associate the idea of universality are bound up, still after the model of recto and verso, with effects of domination and manipulation – a perfect domination, being the domination of reason, and an implacable domination, as there is nothing to oppose reason with except reason itself, or a still more reasonable reason.

Corrigan and Sayer, who triggered this *topos* I had not envisaged, oppose the tendency of Marxism to reduce forms of domination to the most brutal aspects of domination, to military force. With the extreme example of mathematics, I am introducing the idea that there are forms of domination that are perfectly gentle, associated with the highest accomplishments of humanity. These forms of domination, which a certain philosophical tradition calls symbolic, are so fundamental that I find myself wondering whether a social order could function, even in its economic foundations, without the existence of these forms of domination. In other words, the old model of infrastructure and superstructure – a model that has done a lot of harm in social science – must be rejected, or, if you insist on keeping it, it must at least be turned upside down. Do we not have to start from symbolic forms if we want to explain an economic miracle? Doesn't the foundation of things that seem to us the most fundamental, the most real, the most determinant 'in the last analysis', as Marxists say, lie in mental structures, symbolic forms, these pure, logical, mathematical forms?

[. . .] After having worked a lot on the state, re-reading today my article 'On symbolic power' makes me see the extent to which I was myself a victim of state thought. I was not aware that I was writing an article on the state; I thought I was writing an article on symbolic power. I see this now as evidence of the extraordinary power of the state and state thought.

Lecture of 7 February 1991

Theoretical foundations for an analysis of state power – Symbolic power: relations of force and relations of meaning – The state as producer of principles of classification – Belief effect and cognitive structures – The coherence effect of state symbolic systems – The school timetable as a state construction – The producers of *doxa*

Theoretical foundations for an analysis of state power

As I announced in the last lecture, I will now tackle the second group of problems raised by Corrigan and Sayer's book, that is, the theoretical foundations of their analysis of the constitution of the English state. Before undertaking this analysis, and perhaps the better to give you a sense of the issues involved in the arguments I am going to put forward, I would like to read you a little-known passage from an article by David Hume. 'Of the first principles of government' (*Essays and Treatises on Several Subjects*, published in 1758):

> Nothing appears more surprising to those, who consider human affairs with a philosophical eye, than the easiness with which the many are governed by the few; and the implicit submission, with which men resign their own sentiments and passions to those of their rulers. When we enquire by what means this wonder is effected, we shall find, that, as Force is always on the side of the governed, the governors have nothing to support them but opinion. It is therefore, on opinion only that government is founded; and this maxim extends to the most despotic and most military governments, as well as to the most free and more popular.[1]

I see this text as extremely important. Hume is surprised by the ease with which the few who govern do so, a fact that is very often overlooked because we are in a vaguely critical tradition, just as the ease with which social systems reproduce themselves is overlooked.

When I first studied sociology, the word most frequently uttered by sociologists was 'mutation'.[2] 'Mutation' was discovered everywhere: technological mutation, mutation in the media, etc., whereas the least analytical effort demonstrates how powerful the mechanisms of reproduction are. In the same way, people are often struck by the most outwardly striking aspect: rebellions, conspiracies, insurrections, revolutions, whereas what is staggering and amazing is the opposite: the fact that order is so frequently observed. The problem is rather when it is not observed. How is it that the social order is so easily upheld, despite the fact that, as Hume says, the governors are so comparatively few in number? It is surprise of this kind that is the starting-point of observations of the kind I am going to offer today. It seems to me that no real understanding of the fundamental relations of force in the social order is possible without introducing the symbolic dimension of these relations. If relations of force were simply physical ones, military or even economic, it is likely that they would be infinitely more fragile and very easy to overthrow. Basically, this is the starting-point of much of my reflection. Throughout my work, I have sought to reintroduce this paradox of symbolic force, symbolic power, the power that is exercised in such an invisible way that people are unaware of its very existence, and those subject to it are the first among these, since the very exercise of this power depends on this lack of awareness. This is the typical case of invisible power. What I shall try to present rapidly today are the theoretical foundations for an analysis that restores symbolic power to its proper place.

Symbolic power: relations of force and relations of meaning

My article 'On symbolic power', published in 1977, sought to construct the instruments of thought that are indispensable for conceiving this strange effectiveness based on opinion, though one could equally well say based on belief. How is it that the dominated obey? The problem of belief and the problem of obedience are in fact one and the same. How is it that people submit, and as Hume says, that they submit so easily? To answer this difficult question, you have to go beyond the traditional oppositions between intellectual traditions that are considered profoundly incompatible, and that no one before me has tried to reconcile or combine – I don't say this just to be original. My work is not inspired by a scholastic intention of blending traditions and overcoming oppositions; it is rather in the course of pursuing this work that I have gradually elaborated concepts – symbolic power, symbolic capital, symbolic violence – that go beyond these oppositions between different traditions, which I have shown, for ex post pedagogic reasons, have to be reconciled in order to conceive 'symbolic power'.

(This is important, since I believe that people often have a very scholastic view of theoretical thinking, especially in France: they act as if there was a theoretical parthenogenesis, one theory generating another, and so on. In actual fact, this is not how work is done at all; it is not necessarily by reading theoretical books that you produce theory. That said, it is clear that a certain theoretical culture is needed so as to be able to produce theories.)

As the first point in this approach, I believe that you have to start from the fact that relations of force are relations of communication, that is, that there is no antagonism between a physicalist view of the social world and a semiological or symbolic view. You have to reject the choice between the two types of model that the whole tradition of social thought has always swung between, models of a physicalist type and models of a cybernetic type such as were the fashion for a while: this alternative is completely mistaken and mutilates reality. The most violent relations of force – as Hume says – are at the same time symbolic relations.

Relations of force are inseparable from relations of meaning and communication, the dominated are also people who know and acknowledge. (Hegel touched on this problem with his famous dialectic of master and slave, but as often happens, this kind of exploratory analysis, which opens a path at a certain moment, blocks the road and prevents it being thought through. That is why the tradition of theoretical commentary often has more of a sterilizing effect than a fertile one.) The dominated know and acknowledge: the act of obedience presupposes an act of knowledge, which is at the same time an act of acknowledgement. This acknowledgement clearly includes 'knowledge', meaning that the person who submits, who obeys, who bends to an order or a discipline, performs a cognitive action. (I am putting these things in a number of different ways. Today there is a lot of talk about cognitive sciences; I said 'cognitive' to produce a trigger effect and let you see that sociology is in fact a cognitive science, something that is completely ignored by people who write about these sciences, and not by chance.) Acts of submission and obedience are cognitive acts, and as such they bring into play cognitive structures, categories of perception, patterns of perception, principles of vision and division, a whole series of things that the neo-Kantian tradition emphasizes. I would count Durkheim in this neo-Kantian tradition; he never hid the fact that he was a neo-Kantian, and even one of the most consistent neo-Kantians there has been. To understand acts of obedience, therefore, you have to conceive social agents not as particles in a physical space (which they may also be), but as particles who think their superiors or subordinates with mental and cognitive structures. Hence the question: does the fact that the state manages to impose itself so easily – I am again using the reference to Hume – have to do with its being able to impose the cognitive structures by which it is thought? In other words, I believe that in order to understand this almost magical power that the state holds, you have to examine cognitive structures and the contribution of the state to their production.

(I deliberately use the word 'magical', in the technical sense of the term. An order is a magical act. You act on someone at a distance; you say to someone 'get up' and he really does get up, without you exercising the least physical force. If you are an English lord reading your newspaper – this example is taken from Austin, an English pragmatist – you say: 'John, don't you find it rather cold in here?', and John goes and closes the window.[3] A statement of fact that is not even expressed as an order can have a physical effect. The question is to know under what conditions such a sentence can have this effect. Does the force of the sentence lie in the sentence itself, in its syntax, its form? Or does it rather lie in the conditions of its exercise? You have to ask who utters it, who hears it, in what categories of reception the person who hears it has received the message.)

The state as producer of principles of classification

The state, as I see it, must be conceived as a producer of principles of classification, that is, of structuring structures that are applicable to all the things of the world, and in particular to social things. Here you are typically in the neo-Kantian tradition. I refer you to Ernst Cassirer, who generalized the Kantian notion of form with the notion of 'symbolic form', which includes not only the forms that are constitutive of the scientific order, but also those of language, myth and art.[4] For anyone still trapped in the sorry dichotomies perpetuated by the educational system, I remind you that Cassirer, in a little note to one of his last books, *The Myth of the State*, published in the United States, wrote literally: 'When I say "symbolic form", I am saying nothing more than what Durkheim says when he speaks of "primitive forms of classification".'[5] I believe this will startle 'pure' philosophers, but for any well-ordered mind it is self-evident. The fact that he said it gives it a small preliminary value.

These symbolic forms are the principles of construction of social reality. Social agents are not simply particles moved by physical forces, they are also knowing agents who are bearers of cognitive structures. What Durkheim contributes in relation to Cassirer is the idea that these forms of classification are not transcendental, universal forms, as in the old Kantian tradition, but historically constituted forms associated with historical conditions of production, and thus arbitrary in the Saussurean sense of the term, that is, conventional, not necessary, acquired in connection with a given historical context. Putting things in a more rigorous fashion, these forms of classification are social forms, which are socially established and arbitrary or conventional – relative, that is, to the structures of the group in question. If you follow Durkheim a bit further, you are led to examine the social genesis of these cognitive structures. You can no longer say that such structures are a priori, without a genesis. In another aspect of his work (conducted with Mauss), Durkheim stressed that logic itself has a genealogy, and that the principles of classification observed in primitive societies have a relationship with the actual structures of the social order in which mental structures are established. Durkheim's hypothesis, in other words, which is a very strong one, both risky and very powerful, is that there is a genetic relationship between mental structures, that is, the principles on the basis of which we construct social and physical reality, and social structures, so that oppositions between groups are translated into logical oppositions.

I have just recalled the broad lines of this tradition, and I would relate what I have just said to the state. If you follow this tradition, you can say that we have forms of thinking produced by the incorporation of social forms, and that the state exists as an institution. (The word 'institution' is a particularly vague word in sociological diction, and I shall try to give it a certain rigour by saying that institutions always exist in two forms: in reality – civil status, the civil code, a bureaucratic form – and in people's minds. An institution only works when there is a correspondence between objective structures and subjective structures.) The state has the ability to impose in a universal fashion, on the scale of a certain territorial foundation, principles of vision and division, symbolic forms, principles of classification, what I often call a *nomos* – taking up the etymology proposed by Benveniste, in which *nomos* comes from *nemo*, 'share', 'divide', 'partition', by a kind of *diakrisis*, as the Greeks said, meaning 'original division'.[6]

Belief effect and cognitive structures

The most paradoxical effect of the state is the belief effect, the effect of generalized submission to the state, the fact that the majority of people, for example, stop at a traffic light, which is surprising. (I would like to communicate to you my surprise at the fact that there is so much order – perhaps it is my anarchistic temperament that makes me think this ... I think it anyway – and an order obtained without any cost at all. We are struck by outwardly striking displays of disorder, which make us forget the tremendous number of everyday actions that make the world liveable, predictable, so that one can anticipate what people will do, barring accidents. Examples are easy enough to give.)

The state, therefore, is this institution that has the extraordinary power of producing a socially ordered world without necessarily giving orders, without exerting a constant coercion – there isn't a policeman behind every driver, as people often say. This kind of quasi-magical effect deserves explanation. All other effects – the military coercion that Elias discusses, economic coercion by way of taxation [explored by Tilly] – are in my view secondary in relation to this. I believe that the initial accumulation, contrary to what is maintained by a certain materialist tradition (materialist in the impoverished sense of the term), is an accumulation of symbolic capital: the whole of my work is intended to produce a materialist theory of the symbolic, which is traditionally opposed to the material. Impoverished materialist traditions that do not leave space for the symbolic have a hard time accounting for this kind of generalized obedience without appealing to coercion, and moreover they cannot understand the phenomenon of initial accumulation. It is no accident that Marxism finds the question of initial accumulation of state capital so awkward, as I believe the primary form of accumulation takes place on the symbolic level. There are people who get themselves obeyed, respected, because they are literate, religious, holy, healthy, handsome . . . in other words, for many reasons that materialism, in the ordinary sense, does not know what to do with. Which does not mean, I repeat, that there cannot be a materialist analysis of the most evanescent things . . .

In order to understand this kind of miracle of the symbolic effect, the fact that the government governs, it is necessary therefore to adopt this sociologized neo-Kantian tradition, and say – here I shall follow Durkheim, even if he did not have the state in mind when he wrote this – that the state inculcates similar cognitive structures in all the agents subject to its jurisdiction. The state – and here I do quote Durkheim – is the foundation of both 'logical conformity' and 'moral conformity'. Social agents, if correctly socialized, have logical structures in common that, if not identical, are at least similar, rather like Leibnizean monads who do not necessarily need to communicate or collaborate to be in harmony with one another. Social subjects are in a sense Leibnizean monads.

(I may appear to you in the role of Pangloss here,[7] but I believe I have to run the risk of saying things like this so that you will understand surprising things while being well aware that they need correction. It is always necessary, as a sociologist – and I can cite Chairman Mao here – to 'bend the stick the other way'. Most foolish criticism made of sociological works that seek to do what I am trying to do consists in unbending the stick. Common sense holds naively to propositions that are not even put forward as such, to non-thetic theses, and to shatter these non-proposed propositions, you have to make stronger counter-propositions in the other direction, exaggerating a bit. When everyone is talking about the 'mutation' of the social system, you have to say: 'It's reproducing itself . . .' The break must be hyperbolic, to use Descartes's term, since people always put too much store by appearances, and appearances are always for appearance only. You have to overdo it in the direction of a break, despite knowing very well that things are not so simple. That is one of the factors of misunderstanding. Some people make a bit of celebrity for themselves by unbending the stick and saying: 'But that's a bit exaggerated!' To give an example, in order to explain inequalities in school, it is not enough to take into account the economic factors that leave a large part of the variation unexplained, you also have to take into account cultural factors, cultural capital . . . And someone will come along and say: 'Look at this, they've left out economic capital!' When I bring in Leibniz in connection with relationships to the state, I know that this is dangerous, but it hardly weighs in the balance against the unconscious resistance to what I am in the process of saying. You can never be too excessive in struggling against *doxa* . . .)

By inculcating common cognitive structures (largely by way of the school system), structures that are tacitly evaluative (you can't say 'white and black' without tacitly saying that white is better than black), by producing and reproducing them, having them deeply recognized and incorporated, the state makes an essential contribution to the reproduction of the symbolic order that has a determining effect on the social order and its reproduction. To impose identical cognitive and evaluative structures means establishing a consensus about the meaning of the world. The world of common sense that phenomenologists speak about is a world that people agree on without realizing it, agreeing without any contract, without even knowing that they have asserted anything about the world. The state is the principal producer of instruments of construction of social reality. In societies that are undifferentiated or little differentiated, that do not have a state, what takes the place of all the operations that the state carries out are rites of institution – which are wrongly called rites of passage.[8] A rite of institution is a rite that institutes a definitive difference between those who have undergone the rite and those who have not undergone it. In our societies, the state organizes a host of rites of institution, such as examinations. The whole operation of the school system may be viewed as an immense rite of institution, even if it can naturally not be reduced to this; it does also transmit skills. But the representation that we have of the school system as site of distribution of competence, and of certificates that ratify competence, is so strong that a certain audacity is needed to recall that this is also a site of consecration, a site where differences are instituted between the consecrated and the non-consecrated – in the philosophical sense, and that of constitutional law – establishing durable, definitive, indelible divisions that are often insurmountable since they are inscribed in individual bodies that are constantly reminded of them by the social world (shyness, for example, which is very unevenly distributed between social classes and the two sexes, is not something that can easily be shrugged off).

In our societies it is the state that organizes the major rites of institution, akin to the dubbing of nobles in feudal society. Our modern societies are also full of dubbing rites; the awarding of university degrees, the ceremonies of consecrating a building, a church . . . Reflection is needed on what exactly is being consecrated. I shall leave that exercise to you. By way of these major rites of institution that contribute to reproducing social divisions, that impose and inculcate the principles of vision and social division by which these divisions are organized, the state constructs and imposes on agents categories of perception that, being incorporated in the form of universal mental structures at the level of a nation-state, harmonize and orchestrate agents. The state is endowed with an instrument of constitution of conditions for internal peace, a form of collective, universal 'taken-for-granted' on the national level. Here I am standing in the neo-Kantian and Durkheimian tradition, which I see as the indispensable foundation for the existence of a symbolic order, and by the same token of a social order. One example I can give is that of the calendar. When several cities federate, the first act of public agents, priests, is to establish common calendars, to harmonize the calendars of men, women, slaves and people of the different cities, so that as a result people will agree on the principles of division of time. The calendar is the very symbol of the constitution of a social order that is simultaneously a temporal and a cognitive order, since in order for internal experiences of time to agree, they have to be adjusted to a public time. The constitution of a state coincides with the constitution of common temporal references, categories of construction of fundamental oppositions (day and night, opening and closing hours for offices, days off and working days, annual holidays, etc.). I shall go on to show this in relation to the use of the school timetable, and you will see how these constitutive oppositions of the objective order also structure minds, which find such arbitrary orders natural.

This leads me to the question of the function of this order. If you remain with the neo-Kantian and Durkheimian perspective, that is, that of social integration, you [realize that] the state is an instrument of social integration, an integration based not only on affective solidarity, but also on the integration of mental structures as cognitive and evaluative structures. To think state domination, in fact, something that the Marxist tradition stresses, to think it not necessarily correctly, but to think it at all, you have to introduce the Durkheimian tradition, since Marxism does not have the theoretical means to think state domination, or indeed any species of domination. Paradoxically – and here I am bending the stick – Marxism is unable to think what it never stops talking about. To understand this kind of immediate submission that is stronger than any explicit submission, to understand this submission without an act of submission, this act of allegiance without an act of allegiance, this belief without an act of faith, to understand everything that makes up the foundation of the social order, you have to emerge from the instrumentalist logic in which the Marxist tradition thinks ideology, ideology being perceived as the product of the universalization of the particular interest of the dominant that is imposed on the dominated. (You could also invoke the notion of false consciousness, but what is superfluous in 'false consciousness' is precisely 'consciousness'. There is nothing sadder than Marxist discussion of these problems, as you are stuck within a philosophy of consciousness, of the relationship of submission as a relationship of alienation based on something like a failure of political *cogito*.)

The coherence effect of state symbolic systems

I said, therefore, that the Marxist tradition does not have the means to fully understand the effects of the ideology that it constantly evokes. To go further, drawing on the sociologized neo-Kantian tradition, you have to introduce the structuralist tradition (it would take too long to show here in what way the neo-Kantian tradition is opposed to the structuralist

tradition). But in order to understand what lies at the heart of the opposition between these two traditions, I shall take by way of example Cassirer's
Philosophy of Symbolic Forms. When he talks of mythology, Cassirer
emphasizes the mythopoïetic function, the fact that the human agent
is creative, generative, producing mythical representations by applying
mental functions, symbolic forms [that are structuring].[9] Structuralism,
on the other hand, is not interested at all in the active dimension of mythical production, it doesn't concern itself with the creation of myth; when
it speaks of myth, what interests it is not the *modus operandi* but the
opus operatum. It postulates – this was Saussure's contribution – that in
language, a myth or a rite there is meaning, logic, coherence. The question is to reveal this coherence, remove it and replace what Kant called
the 'rhapsody of phenomena' with a series of logically – we should say
socio-logically – interconnected features, without forgetting that the logic
inherent to symbolic systems is not the logic of logic.

I see the structuralist tradition as completely indispensable in order to
go beyond the generative understanding proposed by the neo-Kantians
and perceive one of the very important properties of symbolic systems,
that is, their coherence [as structured structures]. I said that Marxists
lacked the means to explain the actual effect of ideologies, and so the
structuralist dimension has to be added to the Durkheimian aspect. One
of the strengths of ideologies, especially those of a rational kind – such as
rational law – derives from the symbolic effectiveness of coherence. This
coherence may be either of a rational or a super-rational type – law, for
example, is a product of the historical action of rational agents of rationalization. To remember that symbolic systems are not simply cognitive
forms but also coherent structures is to acquire the means for understanding one of the most hidden aspects of symbolic effectiveness, one of the
hardest to grasp, in particular that of the symbolic order of the state: the
effect of coherence, of quasi-systematicness, of apparent systematicness.
One of the principles of the symbolic effectiveness of everything the state
produces and codifies – educational system, highway code, language code,
grammar, etc. – lies in these kinds of coherences or apparent coherences,
rationalities or simili-rationalities. Symbolic systems exert a structuring
power because they are structured, and a power of symbolic imposition,
extortion of belief, because they are not constituted by chance.

On this basis it is possible to trace ramifications in all directions.
Ethnomethodology, for example, which is rather fashionable in Paris
today, fifteen years behind the United States, like the neo-Kantian tradition
in which it stands without knowing this (it is the heir of phenomenology
and follows in the constructivist tradition), locates the act of knowledge
at the individual level; people speak of the 'social construction of reality' –
the title of Peter L. Berger and Thomas Luckmann's celebrated book.[10]
It is said that social agents construct social reality, which is a tremendous
step forward. But having said this, who constructs the constructors? Who
gives the constructors the instruments of construction? You can see the

difficulty of theoretical work here. If you are in a tradition that raises the question of the state, you generally do not read ethnomethodologists, you're involved in the macro, in global problems. But in order to raise questions of the state in an adequate way, you have to bring ethnomethodologists together with those who raise global questions – Wallerstein, for example.[11] And to have this communication, you need to reach a very deep level of reflection, which could be called philosophical. And you then see that the ethnomethodologists have never posed the question of whether there is a state construction of the principles of construction that agents apply to the social world. This is readily explicable, given the genesis of their thought. Just as phenomenologists have never raised the question of the conditions of doxic experience of the world, so ethnomethodologists never ask how it is that agents apply categories to the world that make it appear as proceeding from itself, omitting to raise the problem of the genesis of these categories. (It is important for a young philosopher to know which things lose their meaning when seen from the heights of philosophy.) The question of the conditions of constitution of these principles of constitution is thus not raised. And on this basis you could define the limits of even those ethnomethodological works that are the most interesting from the standpoint of the question I am in the process of raising. This does not prevent me from reading ethnomethodologists and finding great things in what they are doing. For example, the work of Cicourel on administrative regulations, on what an administrative form is,[12] is very exciting in that it de-trivializes the trivial. But to my mind this work comes to a sudden halt, unable to raise the question I have raised here . . .

The school timetable as a state construction

It is impossible to understand the existence of a symbolic order and a social order, and the domination effects exerted by the imposition of this symbolic order, without recourse to both the neo-Kantian and the structuralist tradition, so as to account for the fact that the cognitive structures we apply to the social world, and that are adjusted to it, are both constructive and coherent, their historical coherence being bound up with a state tradition.

I would like, by way of suggestion, to discuss the analysis of the effects of the school timetable by the psychologist Aniko Husti.[13] Starting from her own experience, an experience both scientific and practical, she was struck by how arbitrary the school timetable and the division of the day into lessons was. How does it come about that, no matter what the discipline or the educational level, from primary school up to university, you have the same division? Secondly, why is this division so unanimously accepted? When you put this question to teachers and pupils, you discover that they find it absolutely natural, and that the very idea of doing anything different seems inconceivable to them. But how can all the constraints and frustrations that the timetable generates be overlooked? Psychologists speak of the 'Zeigarnik effect',[14] to denote the frustration people feel when an activity they want to continue is interrupted. The school timetable is bound to produce Zeigarnik effects constantly. Pupils are in the middle of doing something, getting excited and thinking for themselves, and suddenly they have to stop and move on to something else; they move from philosophy to geography, for example. Another quite bizarre effect that is overlooked is that the constraints associated with the division into one-hour lessons prevent a whole series of activities that are either too short or too long, so that these disappear from the timetable without people even realizing that they are deprived of them. There is also a whole series of justificatory discourses. It is said, for example, that an hour is the maximum possible attention span for children, a theory based on a crude psychology.

The school order also has political foundations. The power of the principal is exercised by manipulation of the teachers' time. Older teachers may have what is called a good timetable; young teachers are given timetables that are fragmented and dispersed, which no one wants. Teachers have a lot of interests involved, for example they have lessons prepared in advance for one-hour periods. You discover a lot of things, attachment to a routine that is strong precisely because the strength of this adherence derives from the fact that it is unchallenged. If what Aniko Husti calls a 'movable timetable' is established – experiments have been made (naturally with the agreement of the teachers, who are not the easiest to convert) – you discover that teachers are forced to negotiate among themselves to get continuous slots of two or three hours, that this makes certain communications necessary. You discover that the famous limit of one hour is completely arbitrary. Husti interviewed children who said after three hours of maths: 'I wasn't able to finish it . . .' Tasks are organized differently; the teacher speaks for twenty minutes, gets things under way, gives an exercise, a presentation; the whole structure of pedagogy changes, and once the shackles have been removed you discover a new freedom. Teachers discover the freedom this gives them in relation to the principal – no matter how progressive they may be, teachers are always against any change . . . They discover this freedom vis-à-vis the principal, they are released from the shackles of the lecture form, this monologue discourse so hard to keep going.

That is an example of the 'taken-for-granted' whose origin lies completely in a state regulation; you can describe its historical genesis. When you give three senior teachers slots of three hours simultaneously (maths, French, history), pupils can choose to attend whichever one of these lessons they prefer, depending on the sense they have of their particular strengths and weaknesses. This organizational imagination, this little symbolic revolution, is absolutely exceptional, whereas, as Aniko Husti quite rightly suggests, all the reforms that seek to change the content of lessons, but do not start by changing these time structures, are condemned to failure. In other words, there is a kind of unconscious that is one of the most powerful factors of inertia. You see that when I cited Hume at the start of this lecture, this was not mere speculation. The school system, which is constantly questioned, constantly examined, is fundamentally protected from such challenge, largely by both teachers and pupils alike. Having known no other school system than the one they are in, they reproduce its essential features without knowing it, what they themselves have been subjected to without knowing. And this particularly involves all those deprivations they would discover if they saw just three minutes of a foreign school system. There is nothing more extraordinary than when deprivations are reproduced quite contentedly. The same holds for teachers, but also for the working class and many other categories.

The producers of *doxa*

You see now how the introduction of the neo-Kantian and Durkheimian way of thinking into the analysis of domination makes it possible to understand something that is quite fundamental: that the *nomos*, the principle of vision and division of the world, imposes itself in a very powerful manner, far beyond anything that a contract would involve. Everything I am saying here is the absolute antithesis of all contract theories. Durkheim said, which was already quite right, that 'in a contract not everything is contractual',[15] that is, that what is essential is often outside the contract. But we need to go further. The best contracts are those that are not signed, that are not even perceived as such. The social order rests on a *nomos* that is ratified by the unconscious in such a way that it is essentially the incorporated coercion that does the work. In relation to Marx, it was Weber who put the Humean question: how is it that the dominant dominate? He invoked recognition of legitimacy, a notion that he had established sociologically. In a perspective such as I am now elaborating, recognition of legitimacy is an unknowing act of knowledge, an act of doxic submission to the social order.

Knowledge, logic and theory are always contrasted with practice. There are acts of knowledge that are not cognitive in the sense that is generally understood. This is the case, for example, with the feel for a game. A football player carries out cognitive acts at each moment, but these are not acts of knowledge in the sense that the theory of knowledge generally understands them. They are acts of corporeal knowledge, infra-conscious, infra-linguistic, and it is this kind of act of knowledge that we have to start from in order to understand the acknowledgement of the social order, the state order. It is the agreement between these incorporated cognitive structures that have become completely unconscious – such as timetables, for examples – and the objective structures, that is the real foundation of the consensus about the meaning of the world, of the belief and opinion, the *doxa* that Hume talks about.

That said, we should not forget that this *doxa* is an orthodoxy. This

UNIVERSITY OF WINCHESTER
LIBRARY

is why the genesis of the state is important. What is today a *doxa* – the timetable, the highway code, etc. – was often the product of a struggle; it was established at the end of a struggle between dominant and dominated, with opponents – this was the case with taxation, for example, which I shall go on to discuss. There is nothing that is constitutive of the state as it is taken for granted today that was not obtained without drama; everything was conquered. The strength of historical evolution, however, is to dismiss the defeated lateral possibilities, not to the realm of the forgotten, but to the unconscious. Analysis of the historical genesis of the state, as constitutive principle of these categories that are universally prevalent in its social base, has the virtue of making it possible to understand both the doxic adhesion to the state and the fact that this *doxa* is an orthodoxy, that it represents a particular standpoint, the standpoint of the dominant, the standpoint of those who dominate by dominating the state, perhaps without having this as their goal, and contribute to the construction of the state in order to dominate it.

This leads us to another branch of the theoretical tradition, that of Weber. Weber made a decisive contribution to the problem of legitimacy. But *doxa* is not the acknowledgement of legitimacy, it is a proto-legitimacy in itself. On the other hand, Weber emphasized that all symbolic systems – he did not put it in these terms, as he was not concerned with symbolic systems in their internal logic, like the structuralists, but with symbolic agents, essentially religious agents – must be related to [the position of] their producers, that is, to what I call the religious field – which he did not name in this way, thus marking the limits of his analysis.[16] He has the credit of having established religious, legal and cultural agents (writers) as indispensable for understanding religion, law and literature. If you can always find texts in the Marxist tradition [that point in the same direction], such as Engels saying that in order to understand law you must not overlook the body of lawyers,[17] the fact remains that this tradition has always obscured, passed over in silence, the existence of specific agents of production and specific spheres of production, spheres and agents that must be kept in mind and whose autonomous logic of operation must be understood in order to understand symbolic phenomena. To repeat this in an even more simple way, one of Weber's contributions was to recall that if you want to understand religion, it is not enough to study symbolic forms of the religious type, the immanent structure of the *opus operatum*, religion or mythology. You must also ask who the myth-makers are, how they are influenced, what interests they have, what is their space of competition, how they struggle among themselves, and what the weapons are with which the prophet excommunicates, and the priest canonizes, the good prophet and excommunicates the others. In order to understand symbolic systems, you have to understand the systems of agents struggling over these symbolic systems.

The same holds for the state. In order to understand the state, you have to see that it has a symbolic function. To understand this symbolic dimension of the state effect, you have to understand the logic of operation of this world of state agents who created state discourse – legists, jurists – and understand what generic interests they had in relation to others, as well as what specific interests they had as a function of their position in the space of their struggles – the *noblesse de robe*, for example, in relation to the *noblesse d'épée*.[18]

To be quite complete, to explain the effects of rationality, you would also have to understand why these people had a certain interest in giving a universal form to the particular expression of their interests. Why the jurists and legists created a theory of public service, public order, of the state as irreducible to the dynasty, the republic as transcending the social agents who embody it at a certain time, even if these include the king, etc. What interest did they have in doing all this, and what was the logic of their functioning, their recruitment, the fact that they had privileges, a capital – Roman law – etc.? Understanding all this, you can understand how, producing an 'ideology' (a word that does not mean very much) to justify their position, they constructed the state, state thinking, the mode of public thinking, and this mode of public thinking that corresponded to their particular mode of thinking, that was congruent with their particular interests until a certain point in time, having a particular strength precisely because it was public, republican, with a universal appearance.[19]

Lecture of 14 February 1991

Sociology, an esoteric science with an exoteric air – Professionals and lay people – The state structures the social order – *Doxa*, orthodoxy, heterodoxy – Transmutation of private into public: the appearance of the modern state in Europe

Sociology, an esoteric science with an exoteric air

I want to mention very briefly – something I do from time to time when I feel the subjective need – the problem of teaching sociology orally, both as a general problem and in the particular form facing me here. I bring up this question because I believe it can facilitate communication. The analysis I am going to propose to you is not a gratuitous meta-discourse; I believe it can have practical effects on the way that you listen, and help you understand certain difficulties I experience in saying what I am trying to say . . .

I have often stressed that sociology comes up against a particular problem. More than any other science, it raises questions that concern everyone, as is said, and on which everyone feels entitled to have information and even make a judgement. Like all sciences tend to be, it is quite esoteric and anchored to its own problematics, to its findings built up over time, but it is an esoteric science with an exoteric air. This makes all kinds of double games possible. For example, people who call themselves sociologists can give themselves esoteric airs despite being exoteric, which means that researchers who really are esoteric even when they give themselves exoteric airs (as you are obliged to do in teaching) can be taken for people who, being spontaneously exoteric, give themselves esoteric airs so as to look scientific. This is a major problem that the sociologist has to reckon with. Journalists very readily allow the least sociologist among sociologists a jargon that, in many cases, has no other function than to display a distance and a symbolic capital, while they reject the recourse [to concepts] that is indispensable for scientific progress when these are demanded by the concern to build up results.

This problem particularly arose in my last lecture, in which I tried, perhaps in a rather monstrous way, to bring together theoretical traditions that have never been related to one another, and that no one, as far as I know, has attempted to bring together, for reasons that are social ones. By combining traditions that are sociologically incompatible, and showing what each of these traditions contributes, I did something very esoteric. When I said that ethnomethodology failed to raise the question as to who constructed the constructors, this proposition was for some of you, I believe, quite devoid of meaning, whereas it could give rise to hours of scientific discussion, particularly with ethnomethodologists. Why do I insist on saying this? Not in order to recreate the differences I am trying to overcome, at the cost of efforts that are sometimes laborious, but rather to try and break down, especially among those whom I call, after Pascal, the semi-wise, those resistances that may deprive them of a full understanding of what I am trying to offer.

(In a teaching situation such as this, the difficulty that all teachers at the Collège de France feel bears on the fact that their listeners are extremely diverse. The logic of the school system does not just structure time but also ages; it instils in us age classes, and, through age classes, categories of memory. Maurice Halbwachs's magnificent book *On Collective Memory* shows that our memory is largely structured by our school career: 'That was the time when I was in the third form under So-and-so . . .' The school system not only structures our temporality but also our memory, as well as the audience in the normal case. Someone who addresses a school audience knows whom he is dealing with; even if there is diversity within the class, this diversity is not so extreme as in the case of an audience that can without offence be called *omnibus*. An *omnibus* public, but one evidently self-selected as a function of principles of selection that are similarly observed with visits to museums or art galleries . . . Even in this case, in the presence of a specialized discourse, you are obliged to take note of a diversity in terms of the specific competence that can be applied in the reception of a discourse with scientific claims.

I feel this diversity very strongly, and part of the speaking work I am trying to do here – this is why I am not reading my lecture, despite the fact that it is written out – bears on the fact that I think I can see signs in the hall . . . The particularity of oral discourse in relation to written discourse is that you are facing an audience. I refer here to an important model that introduced a revolution in the understanding of the Homeric poems, the idea that the oral poets were addressing an audience. They used patterns of improvisation – you never improvise with nothing – and they also improvised in the presence of the particular censorship represented by the presence of an audience that was before their eyes. The recent publications of the Hellenist Jean Bollack on the pre-Socratic poets,[1] those of other people on the poetries of traditional societies, my own dialogue with the great Kabyle writer Mouloud Mammeri,[2] have shown how, in those societies where the mode of communication of cultural works is oral, poets as creators have an art of playing with the plurality of audiences; they are able to hold discourses that are at the same time esoteric and exoteric.

Thus there was a sub-space of Berber poets, a kind of training school. People learned to create verses in the forge . . . I am not saying that there was a field of Berber poets, but there were poetry competitions, examinations of a kind. These poets, who were semi-professionals, who devoted a large part of their time to inventing poetry, were able to speak simultaneously to their peers, to a few initiated listeners, and at the same time to the general public who could hear what they said. I will give an example here taken from the work of Jean Bollack. Empedocles played on the word *phos*, which normally means 'light' in Greek, for the general run of Greek speakers, but that in certain very particular cases can mean 'mortal'. He gave his verses double meanings in this way. The pre-Socratic poets used very refined procedures that consisted in giving what Mallarmé called 'a purer sense to the words of the tribe', taking up sayings, proverbs, ready-made phrases from common language, and making tiny alterations that might [be contained] simply in intonations – which means that reading them today it is hard indeed to perceive these unless you know that they exist. Hellenists do not raise these kinds of questions. These poets managed to speak to their peers, above the heads of the ordinary listener, by using a kind of polysemic language, almost polyphonic – like musical chords, whether simple or more unusual.

This is a bit the way in which I shall try to speak. Naturally, poetry lends itself to this better than does scientific discourse. The work I am trying to do is often subjectively very disappointing, since it demands a very great effort and I constantly have the sense of my words being lost, at least for those who have least in the way of prior familiarity with sociology, and for whom I have not been able to find the right example that would make them understand everything right away. Likewise for those who think I am always repeating the same thing, and should have said it a thousand times more quickly . . . I wanted to justify this feeling of disappointment, to myself as well as you, by trying to make you understand the effort I am making. I try to say things each time I think of them, and I cannot avoid thinking of them, since when you are completely swallowed up by a problematic, you no longer sense its arbitrary character, you say things that may seem quite extraordinary as if they were self-evident, to people who are not prepared for them . . .)

Professionals and lay people

I shall quickly mention the reception effects that this polysemic language can produce. I have eliminated the worst of these, I am not masochistic . . . First of all on lay people. '*Profane*', the word says it well. It comes from religious language and denotes someone who does not belong to the field, who is not initiated, who has not learned the specific history of the field, that is, the history of a problematic, who does not know that Durkheim was opposed to Tarde and Spencer, etc., who does not have the historical assumptions that are operative in the world of professionals and mean that such people find a problematic interesting despite its having no interest for non-professionals. One of the major effects of a scientific field is to define what things are interesting at a certain point in time, what needs to be investigated and discovered. The lay person wonders: why does the speaker ascribe such importance to the problem of the state? If a lay person does so, it is for example because it is talked about in the papers, or because a legal reform is under way. And clearly many semi-sociologists, those responsible for most of the fictitious esoteric effects, are precisely those who only find problems interesting when everyone else does so. For example, I was recently talking with a woman in charge of the Vaulx-en-Velin project,[3] who told me she had seen politicians and sociologists descend on the community, interested because of the coverage it had received in the media, so it was interesting to discuss it further in the media. The same thing [happened] with May 68. There were books on May 68 almost as soon as it happened. I spent ten years working on May 68, when it was no longer topical and could no longer produce the profits of immediate interest.[4] If I say to you: 'So-and-so isn't a sociologist', you will say: 'That's an arbitrary decision, an authoritarian act of a censor looking for distinction.' But I am giving you very important criteria here. A professional sociologist is someone who finds interesting the problems that the scientific field establishes as interesting at a certain point, and that sometimes coincide with those that everyone finds interesting, but not necessarily so.

What is true for problematic is also true for method. The professional is someone who raises certain problems bound up with a cumulative history, and seeks to resolve them with certain methods that are themselves produced by this cumulative history. Those lay people who judge the work of professionals – that happens all the time in the papers, the worst of them being the semi-wise, who are doubly 'profane' – hasten to judge professionals with lay criteria, so as to legitimize themselves as pseudo-professionals despite their really being lay. What do lay people look for in a scientific work, especially in the human sciences? In psychology, the issues are far less vital. The other sciences have a better chance, since their results do not impinge on most citizens, at least in the short term – what happens in the laboratories of the Collège de France hardly excites crowds, except by accident. The sociologist, however, is constantly subject to an instant verdict, as what he is talking about is spontaneously seen by most people as important. The majority of lay people, including journalists, are not even aware of their lay status in this regard; the best of them are those aware of their limitations. What lay people look at is the results. They reduce scientific work to propositions, positions taken up, which can be discussed, which are the object of opinion just like colours or tastes, which anyone can judge with the ordinary tools of ordinary discourse. You take a position on a scientific work like you take a position on the Gulf War, as a function of your position on the political spectrum, whereas what counts are problematics and methods; in the extreme case, the result is a secondary matter. The most interesting thing from the standpoint of scientific discussion is the manner it was obtained: how did the researcher proceed in order to obtain this? How did he conduct his investigation?

To take an example in the social science field, but far removed from politics, we have the debate that recently took place around the work of Georges Dumézil. This debate was a misjudged initiative of the Italian historian Carlo Ginzburg, who took up the baton from a very great historian, Arnaldo Momigliano. The issue was the relationship between Dumézil's work and Nazi or fascist symbols.[5] Accusations made by Dumézil's opponents are periodically repeated, without reference to the conditions in which his work was produced, or to the responses he provided. What is in question is his trilogy on Indo-European myth.[6] The root of this mistake, and the injustice of this kind of accusation, is to act as if Dumézil, in writing *Mitra-Varuna*,[7] was situated in the political space, as if he was taking up a position on those questions that people took positions on at the time of Daladier, Chamberlain and Ribbentrop. In fact, he was situated in the relatively autonomous thread of a relatively autonomous field. The people he had in mind were Sylvain Lévi, Émile Benveniste, specialists who raised questions about the origin and unity of languages in strictly scientific terms, in a strictly scientific logic, etc. What scientists could be criticized for is that, speaking of this kind of problem, they did not realize that others were thinking about it in a different way; that is a common error of scientists enclosed in their field. In the esoteric problematic of a field, the error lies in forgetting that naive people can interpret it differently. Having this concern makes life very difficult. You have to put quote marks and brackets everywhere, and then people criticize you for being unreadable . . .

Every scientist makes the mistake of living in an ivory tower – the autonomous logic of a field that develops its own problems in an autothetic manner – and by the same token, when he does encounter the problems of his time, he encounters them by chance. There is an inherent injustice in this. Here I would criticize both Ginzburg and Momigliano, despite their being great scientists, for blocking a specific problematic with a view, among other things, to obtaining symbolic profits in the scientific field. That is a way of discrediting an opponent . . . Momigliano must have struggled with Dumézil for ten years without ever making a dent in him; but he only needed to say: 'Beware, Dumézil is a bit of a Nazi', in order for his work to be challenged. What do you do when you read a scientist as if he was not situated in the specific history of an accumulation of questions, theses, methods? You read Dumézil like you would read a television philosopher, Régis Debray for example, and all those who have responded in the last few weeks on the question of the Gulf War, like people who talk about democracy, about all the questions people talk about in the media, but who talk about them in the way they are talked about in the media, that is, without making the [epistemological] break, without instituting a whole series of ruptures. If I have preceded a presentation that will go on to make positive statements with several years of what I call 'negative sociology', a rupture with pre-notions, it is not simply for pleasure. It would be much easier to give the results right away . . .

Lay people are also in danger of trusting. If my work is successful, they are bound to find it all very natural, and sometimes they wonder why I raise problems in such an emotional way that they find very simple once I have formulated them. They too readily ascribe to me a certain number of theses that are not constituted as theses. If I manage to find good examples, the right equivalent, something that acts as a trigger in everyone – I took the school timetable rather than another example, as I assume that a large proportion of the audience here are former teachers or former pupils – if I find the right trigger, they will say: 'What he was saying there wasn't so abstract, it wasn't just speculation – Kant, Durkheim, Cassirer – it touched on quite immediate things', and they will be convinced. But does that mean that they have gained the knowledge I am trying to offer? I would say no. To say yes would be demagogy, as they do not have a mastery of the generative principles of such problems, despite my trying to give them elements of this. Which does not mean that this knowledge is without interest.

The danger here, paradoxically, is that [things are seen as] self-evident. Having said that I was going to denounce this effect, I produce another similar one, an effect of naturalness that may also be accepted in turn as a kind of *doxa*. For the semi-wise who know a bit of sociology (I am sorry for expressing myself in these terms, but after all, you sometimes do have to speak sharply), who have read some sociology, whether written by myself or others, more likely by me if they are here, they can have the feeling that it's already been said, it's familiar . . . Now when I came into the room last week, I did not completely know what I was going to say. And I don't know where anyone could have read it – which is in no way to defend my originality.

This sense of being already known and familiar, which I am not denigrating but simply spelling out, is a protection against the effort of thought that has to be made in every science, and specially in sociology, to be equal to what has already been thought. If sociologists were equal to the findings of all earlier sociologists, they would be superb; but very few sociologists are. Mithridatism by means of half-knowledge has dreadful effects in terms of protecting people from confronting knowledge that is explained to them, that takes risks.

The semi-wise also have a similar feeling of naturalness. I only strengthen this illusion by deliberately refusing to seek professorial distinction. If I gave you *doxa*, you would think of discipline, and believe I was debating with Foucault. I don't like playing this little game, because if you want to play it fully, you need a great deal of time to be fair to the people you have differences with, those in relation to whom you view yourself. I would

have to give lectures and make clear that, when I say *doxa*, I am locating
myself in relation to a certain theoretical tradition, and when I speak of
legitimacy, this is not in Habermas's sense. That is something I don't like
to do in the peremptory form of authoritarian assertion of my distinction.
And I don't have the means to do so, except occasionally, for Elias, in a
completely didactic way. If I gave a thousand hours of lectures each year –
God forbid! – I could get into the esoteric . . .

Then there are the genuinely wise. I will flatter them, and I hope they
will all recognize themselves . . . The wise, who have read the article that I
based myself on to get started, will have seen that I repeated all the points
I had gone through, but more in the form of a spiral than horizontally. I
can use a very pretentious metaphor that Proust used to characterize his
way of writing books. There are people like cars, who spend their energy
horizontally, and others like planes, who spend their energy vertically.
With my discourse on this text, I am going over this ground again, but
from a higher standpoint that I was completely unaware of when I was
writing it. I said at the beginning that when I wrote 'On symbolic power'
I did not know that I was speaking of the state. The fact of knowing that
I was speaking of the state without knowing this enables me to say things
both on the state and on what I had learned that were not contained in
the article. Clearly, if I had not written this article I could not speak of the
state as I am doing today. The wise ones will not just have the pleasure of
seeing concepts developed in a rather more satisfactory way, but also and
above all of finding patterns of thought, hypotheses for research. Those
people involved in the same kind of research as I am doing will go away
from here, not with ready-made ideas, but with patterns of thinking, programmes for research and action. (Forgive me for what is both a defence
and an illustration of what I am doing, a kind of self-praising apologia,
but I need to say this because I felt more than uneasy after the last lecture.)

The state structures the social order

Very quickly, for the wise who are familiar with the tools I have been
using, one of the connections I established in preparing the last lecture,
and that I had not established previously, is the connection between the
state and the rite of institution, a notion I developed some years ago in
reaction to Van Gennep's notion of the rite of passage.[8] This notion is
located typically in the field, therefore, and not in a search for distinction.
Van Gennep, in the guise of constructing a scientific concept, which has
been universally adopted, sanctioned an idea of common sense: you pass
from youth to old age . . . Certain concepts owe their success precisely to
the fact that they have not made the [epistemological] break. To make the
concept scientifically valid, I replaced it by rite of institution. I took as my
example circumcision, showing that what is important in the rite of institution is that it establishes a difference, not between before and after the rite,

but between those who have undergone it and those who have not. My definition of the rite of institution was constructed by thinking about those rites specific to traditional societies.

Since then, working on education, I have gradually discovered that the school system is perhaps an immense rite of institution, and that the stages of the school career could ultimately be viewed as steps in a process of initiation, in which the initiate, as in legends or initiation myths, is consecrated in stages to reach a final consecration, obtaining at the end the symbol of his election that is the academic qualification. On the one hand, you have the rites of institution, the school system that performs the rites of consecration; on the other, the state that makes the school system function. I tell myself: the state, by organizing the school system and all the rites of institution that are performed through it, establishes very important rites of institution that not only structure social hierarchies – *agrégé/ non-agrégé, énarque/non-énarque*[9] – that is, what you can read in sociology of education textbooks, but also the mental structures by which these social structures and social hierarchies are perceived. The school system not only establishes people in an objective hierarchy, with objective divisions in the world of labour, a legitimate division of labour, it establishes at the same time, in minds that have undergone its action, principles of vision and division in conformity with these objective divisions. The state contributes both to producing hierarchies and to producing principles of hierarchization in conformity with these hierarchies. Among these principles are the 'social frameworks of memory', systems of values, the hierarchy of disciplines and genres.

The state, accordingly, is not simply an instance that legitimizes an established order by a kind of 'propaganda' action. The state is not simply an instance that says: this is how the social order is, and it's fine that way. It is not simply the universalization of the particular interest of the dominant, which manages to impose itself on the dominated (the orthodox Marxist definition). It is an instance that constitutes the social world according to certain structures. You need to bear in mind the multiple sense of the word 'constitution'. The oppositions that the state produces are not a superstructure. That is another word that should be swept out of the language, along with the architectonic metaphor of superstructure and infrastructure, society like a house, with a cellar, an attic, etc. (To give this discussion a more noble name, it's psychoanalysis. What I am doing in the guise of a joke, Bachelard would have called psychoanalysis of the scientific mind.)[10] The state is not simply a producer of legitimization discourses. When you think of 'legitimacy', you think of 'discourses of legitimization'. It is not a propaganda discourse by which the state and those who govern through it justify their existence as dominant, it is far more than this.

The state structures the social order itself – timetables, budget periods, calendars, our whole life is structured by the state – and, by the same token, so is our thought. State thought of this kind is not a meta-discourse about the world, it is constitutive of the social world, inscribed in the social world. This is why the image of the superstructure, of ideologies as things that float above, is completely damaging, and something I have spent my life struggling against. State thinking constitutes school life, the timetable, in the sense of being part of it. The state is partly constitutive; it also constitutes state thought and makes it what it is. That holds for everything that the state produces. *Nomos*, with its opposite, anomie, is one of the words I have played with in order to create connections for those people with a Durkheimian culture. You can play on 'constitution' in the same way, in the sense of constitutional law and that of 'constitution' in the philosophers' sense.

Doxa, orthodoxy, heterodoxy

These constitutive acts of the state, in so far as they contribute to constituting both the objective truth and the perceiving subjects (I am summing up now what I said in the last lecture), contribute to producing an experience of the social world as self-evident, what I call the doxic experience of the social world, applying a corrected version of the phenomenological tradition. The social world presents itself in the form of a *doxa*, a kind of belief that is not even perceived as belief. The social world is a historical artefact, a product of history whose genesis is forgotten by virtue of an amnesia of genesis that touches all social creations. The state is not recognized as historical, but recognized with an absolute recognition that is the recognition of misrecognition. There is no more absolute recognition than the recognition of *doxa*, since it is not even perceived as recognition. *Doxa* is answering 'yes' to a question I have not asked.

Doxic adhesion is the most absolute adhesion that a social order can obtain, since it is situated beyond even the constitution of the possibility of doing otherwise; that is what separates *doxa* from orthodoxy. Orthodoxy appears from the moment that there is an alternative. As soon as the heterodox appear, the orthodox are obliged to appear as such; the *doxa* is obliged to make itself explicit as orthodoxy when it is challenged by a heresy. The dominant are generally silent, they do not have a philosophy, a discourse. They only begin to have one when they are rankled, when people say to them: 'Why are you like you are?' They are obliged then to establish as orthodoxy, as an explicitly conservative discourse, what had previously been maintained below the level of discourse in the mode of 'taken-for-granted'. Here I bring into play concepts that I have often used: misrecognition, recognition, *doxa*. I can give an example here to show the strength of *doxa*. You must certainly have the impression that the school system is being constantly questioned. This is indicated even by the titles of books on the subject ('the school question'). I believe however that the functioning of the school is basically doxic: basic things are not questioned. The strength of the school system is that, being able to produce the incorporation of the structures according to which it is organized, it removes from challenge the very basis of its functioning, which is at a lower level than the defence of corporate interests – such interests being often [bound up with] the defence of the 'taken-for-granted', that is, the defence of mental structures that make it possible to perceive the world as self-evident. That is why school wars become wars of religion, wars of life and death . . .

At the end [of the previous lecture] I mentioned Max Weber and the question: whom does the state benefit? That is how people generally begin, and [the reason] why right away nothing is understood. If you put questions in this way, you are doing what is called 'criticism'. One of the dramas of sociology is that it is often confused with criticism. Anyone who likes to do so can denounce corruption, misappropriation, etc. Sociology is often read in the way that people read *Le Canard enchaîné*, even if this is a good read and offers the sociologist much information. Sociology often faces questions that common sense has raised first of all, but it puts them quite differently. For example, who uses the state? Do people who serve the state serve themselves by serving the state? In other words, doesn't public order bring private benefits? Are there people who have a particular interest in public order, who have a monopoly of public order?

You find the Weberian question here, one that Weber does not ask about the state (you see how one can use an author against himself). This is the main criticism I make of Weber, by asking a Weberian question about the state that Weber did not ask: that of knowing who benefits from the state. He speaks about rationalization. I have read Weber even between the lines, what Davidson calls the 'principle of charity',[11] it would be better to call it the 'principle of justice', [which consists in] ascribing to an author the best possible arguments in favour of his thesis. I have applied this principle of charity to Max Weber (see the final chapter of *The State Nobility*). I even read Weber's parentheses. Weber was a great thinker, he has parentheses that can destroy everything he says in the main text. Weber touched on this problem, but without making it the guiding principle of his work.

Transmutation of private into public: the appearance of the modern state in Europe

That was supposed to be a brief introduction, and I went quickly into the bargain . . . I shall now begin the positive construction of a reply to the question of the genesis of the state, which I shall try to sketch on the basis of what I have been able to gain from my historical reading. This is neither false modesty nor academic caution, it is the reality. Given the problematic I have taken on, I would need a historical culture disproportionate to the strength of a single man. And so I shall constantly fail to match up to what I want to prove. This is an invitation for help. If you have observations, criticisms, references, I shall take them up with enthusiasm. I shall try to construct, not a description of the genesis of the state (that would need fifteen years of lectures), not even a sketchy research into the explanatory factors for the appearance of the state, but a simplified model of the logic that this followed, in my own view and that of most writers – because you end up with relatively commonplace things on which everyone is in agreement. I shall propose a model of the logic by which the state seems to me to have been constituted (I shall try to construct this in a rather more systematic way), that is, the process of concentration of different kinds of capital, this process being accompanied by a process of transmutation. I have already made the essential point.

The state is the product of the gradual accumulation of different kinds of capital – economic, physical force, symbolic, cultural or informational. This accumulation, which was carried out with the birth of the dynastic state – whose specific properties have to be characterized – was accompanied by a transmutation. Accumulation is not simply addition. Changes take place that are bound up, for example, with the fact that the same instance combines different kinds of capital that are normally not combined by the same categories of people. You thus have a model of the accumulation of different kinds of capital, of their concentration. In a second phase – it would be better to do everything at the same time – a model of qualitative transmutation of these different kinds of capital, associated with their concentration. The second part could be: how are private capitals transformed into public capitals? How is something constituted as a public capital, if such a thing exists? Those are the broad lines of my approach.

One more preliminary, the question of the specific factors that may explain why the West was a particular case as far as the birth of the state is concerned. There is a whole literature on this question; philosophers and even certain sociologists have raised the question of the specificity of European history: Husserl, Valéry, Heidegger ... Recently, Jacques Derrida produced a kind of synthetic re-evaluation of this whole tradition (one in which I do not situate myself).[12] Even Max Weber raised this question, which is a question of a certain era – that of the inter-war years – in the famous introduction to *The Protestant Ethic* in which he presents all human civilizations as sketches for European civilization, in the way that the Babylonians had sketched calculus, for example.[13] All these views strike me as dangerous and Eurocentric. Despite everything, the question I am formulating might itself appear just as Eurocentric to many specialists. A researcher such as Jacques Gernet[14] would reject some of the differences I am going to raise, but by introducing them explicitly, I lay myself open to scientific criticism. He would [probably] reject the difference between the earlier empires and the states that appeared in the West. But in terms of scientific debate, what interests me here is the specificity of the Western state. This is a very complex debate on which there is an immense literature. The merit of Charles Tilly is to have tried to remove the construction of a model of state genesis from the eternal couple formed by the French and English cases, extending it to the European level. Others would say that Tilly remains Eurocentric despite his efforts, as the majority of states across the world were not generated after the model of the Western states ... This debate is often overloaded with ideology, since the first beginning is a priority, and priority is a privilege. Thus there are political issues beneath debates that should be purely scientific.

I shall draw here on a historian of the Middle Ages whom I see as giving a clear formulation with which I am sufficiently in agreement: Joseph R. Strayer, *On the Medieval Origins of the Modern State*.[15] This is a book that must be read. He provides weapons for criticizing what I am telling you, in so far as he proposes a theory of the genesis of the state that is fairly different, despite coinciding in part with what I shall suggest to you. Strayer insists that the Western states, the French and the English above all, owe nothing to previous [political forms]. It is uncontestable that states existed before the appearance of the Western states, in the form of the Greek polis, the Han empire in China or the Roman empire. But according to him, these cannot be seen as antecedents or precursors [of the Western type of state], because the men who founded the European state were completely unaware (an argument of fact) of the Asiatic model, had a very poor familiarity with the Roman empire, and only knew the Greek polis through Aristotle. And above all, which is a stronger argument, the European states that appeared after 1100 AD were radically different from earlier models and distinct from empires with a loose degree of cohesion.

The question of the specificity of the trajectory of the Western states has greatly concerned me, in so far as, depending on the way it is answered, one can either have recourse to comparison at the level of [world] history, or limit this exercise to that of Europe. This naturally has a major effect on the bibliography, and on the manner of treating documents. It is not a trivial question but a genuine preliminary one: in what way were the European states distinct from the empires – Russian, Chinese, Roman? These empires, says Strayer, enjoyed a military strength that gave them a very extensive power of control, but they did not really involve their inhabitants (or only involved a very small number) in the political game or in economic activity that went beyond immediate local interests. These empires – I think many people would agree on this point – appear as a superstructure – you can use that word here – that allowed social units with a local base to remain relatively independent. Kabylia, for example, was under Turkish domination for centuries without the local structures, based on the clan or the village, being even slightly affected by the exercise of a central power. You can pay tribute, you can be subject to military operations of repression, which are usually temporary and intermittent, while continuing to preserve your structures unaffected, for example the autonomous village and its customs. You have a kind of verification of this *a contrario* when the collapse of these empires – this was true for the

Turkish empire – neither aroused great resistance nor changed much at all, as far as we can tell, in the social life of the lower-level units.

Historians often have a normative attitude. For them, this structure of extensive control implies a considerable waste of human resources. Empires have a relatively reduced power of mobilization, and this has a very low yield. In parallel with this, they arouse only a very moderate loyalty towards the state; they mobilize little either objectively or subjectively. In contrast with empires, city-states are small political units that integrate their citizens very strongly, that have them participate very closely in political life and in all community activities. With the establishment of public rituals, for example, rich citizens contribute to cultural expenditures, which are the largest part of the state budget. In contemporary societies, the culture economy is a completely artificial one that would not survive the disappearance of the state. All those institutions – the TNP [Théâtre National Populaire], museums, etc. – that offer culture make a loss, they can only exist thanks to a body capable of raising resources and redistributing them; no rich patron could maintain a provincial symphony orchestra . . . It's a case of alchemy, the state transforms taxation into culture. Here we can see very well that the logic of the state has a relative autonomy. If you held a referendum to find out whether the funding of France Culture [radio channel] should be maintained, and the effect of cultural legitimacy produced by the state was not exerted, in other words if people replied on the basis of their actual use of France Culture, the funding would be cut off immediately. With the ritual, people contribute to this expenditure that is a loss economically – there are still symbolic profits – that is cultural expenditure . . .

For Strayer, in these city-states, loyalty towards the state is very strong and takes forms that resemble modern nationalism. That is what he says. For my part, I believe this is a priori impossible. Even the word patriotism is not appropriate. The Greek citizen's love for his city had nothing in common with modern patriotism, which is the product of a work whose agents, as we know, did not exist at that time (the school system). These city-states had capacities that empires did not, but they could not grow beyond a certain threshold, integrate new territories and diverse populations, or ensure the participation of large populations in political life. They applied a *numerus clausus* because they only worked on a small scale. Faced with the test of growth, the city-state [either] became the kernel of an empire, [or] it was annexed and underwent all the contradictions of this. That was also the case with the Italian cities annexed to the Austro-Hungarian empire, which had kept their small dimensions and, being militarily weak, were condemned to be annexed.

Strayer writes that the European states after 1100 combined the capabilities and virtues of both models; they had power, extent and extension, as well as broad participation and the sense of a common identity. With this he raises a very important issue. It is a very constructive definition. Strayer calls 'state' those instances that succeeded in resolving the problem of the integration of large populations at the cost of a specific work, work that was lacking in the small cities, by means of the deployment of specific instances of mobilization. What we need to retain from this distinction is that the question that needs to be tackled is that of the relationship between state and territory, state and population, the state and a control that is not just external and military, but is also control of belief, opinion (we find Hume here), what I previously discussed in relation to the accumulation of symbolic capital.

I have then defined my field of enquiry. My model holds good for those prototypical states seen as essentially different from both empires and city-states. In the next lecture I shall sum up for you the article by the English historian Victor Kiernan, 'State and nation in Western Europe',[16] in which he proposes a synthesis aiming to describe the factors that explain historically what is different about Europe as far as states are concerned.

Lecture of 21 February 1991

Logic of the genesis and emergence of the state: symbolic capital – The stages of the process of concentration of capital – The dynastic state – The state as a power over powers – Concentration and dispossession of species of capital: the example of physical force capital – Constitution of a central economic capital and construction of an autonomous economic space

Logic of the genesis and emergence of the state: symbolic capital

Kiernan's article is interesting because it seeks to list a series of factors that may explain the particularity or singularity of the modern states in the West: the existence of a particularly strong feudal society that put up such resistance to the king that he was obliged to establish an administration; then the existence of a more well-defined property law than that of the Ottoman tradition, owing to the existence of a strong law in general; a further factor was the existence of a number of fairly equal states with regular armies, and thus the necessity of rivalry with other states by war, as distinct from Rome or China, which Kiernan sees as having suffered from the absence of any equivalent rival; the existence of the church as a centralized body, disciplined and monopolistic, that provided a model. This is an important factor on which all historians agree: other theorists of the state, such as Michael Mann, [have demonstrated] the importance of the church, not as a constituted body but as an assembly of believers, [Mann] seeing the Christian message as an important ideological factor in establishing the notion of citizen.[1] Finally, another factor also on Kiernan's list, the town as a totally or partly autonomous political entity involved in a complex dialectic with the state. We could also add other factors; I have simply listed these to give you an idea of this kind of reflection – there is a wide literature of this kind that tries to define the set of singular factors that brought about the singularity of the Western state. The existence of Roman law should be included in these, something that many French historians emphasize.

I simply want to point out to you a path that I am not going to follow here. My aim is not to make a contribution to the construction of systems of factors to explain the birth of the state, but rather to try to construct a kind of model of the logic of its genesis. What I shall try to present, therefore, is a kind of model that is partly original inasmuch as it brings things together but does very little original with them, given that the things brought together have been said by several authors. By successively analysing one by one – this goes against the specific logic of the state, but I am obliged for the purpose of analysis to successively examine the birth of taxation, law, etc. – the dimensions by which the concentration of the particular type of capital that lies at the origin of the state was effected, I want to show both the logic of genesis and the logic of emergence – this is an important word – of a reality that is irreducible to the sum of the elements that constitute it. The metaphor of crystallization is often used in speaking of this process, or, more rigorously, the notion of emergence, which is useful because it says that, by way of a continuous accumulation, transmutations can come about, changes of 'order' to use a Pascalian expression: it is possible to pass from one logic to another. I am going to point out to you very quickly the overall pattern, the broad lines I am going to follow, a kind of anticipatory plan so that you will not get lost in the details of the analysis I shall go on to offer. What I want to show, to analyse, to grasp, is the logic of the initial accumulation of different kinds of capital, which undergo a transmutation by the process of combination. I shall tacitly bring in here the notion of different species of capital, which I explained at length in previous lectures, such as economic capital, cultural capital (or in its more general form, informational capital), social capital and finally symbolic capital.

I want to say a few words on symbolic capital, which is the most complex notion here and the most necessary one for understanding what I am going to say.[2] By symbolic capital I understand the form of capital that is born from the relationship between any particular kind of capital and those agents socialized in such a way as to be familiar with and acknowledge this species of capital. Symbolic capital, as the term suggests, is located in the order of cognition and recognition. For the sake of understanding, I shall take a simple example that I have explained at length in previous years: physical force as analysed by Pascal. Force acts directly, by physical constraint, but also through the representation that those subject to it have of this force; the most brutal and violent force obtains a form of recognition that goes beyond mere submission to its physical effect. Even in the most extreme case, with a species of capital that is closest to the logic of the physical world, there is no physical effect in the human world that is not accompanied by a symbolic effect. The strange logic of human actions means that brute force is never only brute force: it exerts a form of seduction, persuasion, which bears on the fact that it manages to obtain a certain form of recognition.

The same analysis can be applied to economic capital. Wealth never acts simply as wealth; there is a variable form of recognition extended to wealth, depending on societies and moments, which means that the most raw economic power also exerts a symbolic effect granted to wealth by recognition. Social capital and cultural capital already imply the symbolic. The propensity of cultural capital to function as symbolic capital is so strong that the scientific analysis that has established cultural capital as such is particularly difficult, since cultural capital is identified with a gift of nature; the person with the cultural capital of eloquence, intelligence, knowledge is spontaneously perceived as holding a legitimate authority. This is why administrations of a technocratic kind have a different kind of authority than purely military ones, inasmuch as their authority rests on a species of capital that is spontaneously recognized as legitimate. Rulers who have an authority bound up with knowledge or culture are recognized as worthy of exercising their power in the name of a competence that seems to be founded on nature, virtue or merit. Social capital, as a relational capital, is spontaneously predisposed to function as symbolic capital. Symbolic capital is the capital that any holder of capital holds as an extra.

I shall dwell here on certain forms of symbolic capital that are almost completely pure, such as nobility. In the etymology of the word noble, *nobilis* means known and recognized, or notable. The political field is the field par excellence for the exercise of symbolic capital; it is a place where to exist, to be, is to be perceived. A man of politics is in large part a man known and recognized; it is no accident that political men should be particularly vulnerable to scandal, scandal being the generator of discredit and discredit being the opposite of the accumulation of symbolic capital. Garfinkel wrote a very fine article on ['ceremonies of degradation', among them] the rituals of military degradation – how Captain Dreyfus had his epaulettes cut off – these being the opposite of rites of consecration; they consist in removing the signs of recognition from the person who holds titles deserving recognition, and reducing him to the rank of a mere anonymous citizen deprived of symbolic capital.[3] If I don't just say 'prestige', it is because that word does not say it all. I mention this as evidence of the trouble I had in constructing it. I know how difficult and complicated it is. What I have told you here in a few sentences seemed unthinkable to me for a long time. I tell you this as a guarantee that I did not invent it just for pleasure . . .

The stages of the process of concentration of capital

I shall now try to demonstrate the logic of this initial accumulation of capital. The state is constructed by initially concentrating around the king – later on it's a bit more complicated – different species of capital and each one of these. There is a double process here, firstly of massive concentration of each of these species – physical power, economic power, etc. – and then of concentration of the different species in the same hands – concentration and meta-concentration – which generates this quite amazing reality that is the state. This process of concentration, in fact, can also be described as a process of autonomization of a particular space, a particular game, a particular field in which a particular game is played. The object of my analysis is to describe the process of autonomization of a bureaucratic field within which a raison d'état operates, this being understood in both the objective and the subjective sense, that is, a particular logic that is not that of morality, religion, politics, etc. I shall trace four stages that correspond to both a logical and a chronological order, since the genesis of the state passes through stages that broadly correspond to an order of historical succession, but I don't think I could be satisfied with just repeating a chronology.

The first stage is the process of concentration and the process of emergence that accompanies it. I shall analyse the different dimensions of the state capital that is accumulated by showing that, in order to understand the genesis of the state, priority has to be given to symbolic capital. This reverses the materialist view, in the restricted sense of this term. The function of the notion of symbolic capital is to make possible a materialist theory of the symbolic. If you are determined to pin a label on what I am trying to do, you could say that this is an expanded materialism. Certain people will say, I know, that because I put symbolic capital before economic capital, reversing the old opposition between infrastructure and superstructure, I am therefore an idealist, a spiritualist, or what you like. This is mistaken, since I reject this dichotomy. I am going to describe the process of concentration analytically, dimension by dimension, well aware that it is impossible to remain within one dimension alone. Thus, analysing the genesis of taxation, of fiscality, for example, I shall be led to show that this cannot take place without a simultaneous accumulation of symbolic capital, even in the work of tax-raising. So I shall describe this process of concentration of each species of capital, and at the same time inquire into the meaning of this concentration. I shall bring into play the opposition between universalization and monopolization: a process of concentration may be described as a process of universalization – a movement from the local to the national, from the particular to the universal – and at the same time as a process of monopolization. But the two must be kept distinct.

The second phase is that of the logic of the dynastic state. I shall try, following a number of historians who insist that it is not possible to speak of a state before the seventeenth century, to characterize the patrimonial state in which state property is personal property. First of all I shall describe the specificity of this dynastic state, its specific logic, using concepts that I have developed for another purpose, that is, the idea of reproduction strategies.[4] I shall try to show that the politics of a dynastic state, as seen in wars of succession, is located in the logic of family wars around a patrimony. It is possible therefore to move logically from models built to understand household politics among the peasantry or in big noble families to a model applicable on the scale of the state. Dynastic politics is largely a politics organized according to a system of interdependent reproduction strategies. The second point then is to examine the specific contradictions of the dynastic state. Inasmuch as it rests on reproduction strategies with a family basis, the dynastic state contains contradictions that lead to an advance beyond dynastic policy. This is a problem raised by historians. Andrew Lewis, for example, asks how it is possible to emerge from the dynastic state, to move from the state identified with the property of the king to the state separate from the person of the king.[5] I believe that dynastic logic contains contradictions, particularly the relationship between the king and his brothers, which can be seen on the level of elementary household units and force an emergence from the purely patrimonial model.

In the third stage, which can be called 'from the king's house to raison d'état',[6] I shall try to show what the process of concentration and transformation consists of. This is very hard, as we do not have detailed observations of the transition processes that are interesting for sociologists because they show the conflicts between the two principles. Many social conflicts are conflicts between the bearers of an old model of reproduction and those of a new model. But the essential aspects of these conflicts remain tacit, below the conscious awareness of agents, and in order to grasp what would be pertinent and indispensable for constructing a model, we would need very detailed observations. One of the key issues in this process of transition is the transition from a mode of reproduction with a family basis, the mode of succession that the dynastic state has brought to perfection, to a more bureaucratic mode of reproduction that is more complicated, in which the school system plays a determining part.[7] The family mode of reproduction continues to have its effects both through the school model and alongside it. Those people who have a connection with the bureaucratic state, with powers independent of the king, also have a connection with the school mode of reproduction, and by the same token are increasingly intolerant of the mode of reproduction with a family and hereditary basis. That is by and large everything I have to say. I am wrong in doing this, because I'm taking away the suspense, but at the same time it is important for you to know where I am taking you, otherwise you will think I am getting lost in historical details that I am not totally certain of and that other people teach far better than I do.

There is a fourth phase which I shall do no more than mention, which is the transition from the bureaucratic state to the welfare state, and raises the problem of relationships between the state and social space, social classes, the transition from struggles for state construction to struggles for the appropriation of this quite particular capital that is associated with the existence of the state. There is a process of autonomization with a specifically bureaucratic logic; that is the whole direction of this process, but we are not in a Hegelian logic, simply linear and cumulative. The bureaucratic field, like all fields, sees advances and retreats; it is possible to regress towards a patrimonial state by way of a form of presidency of the republic of a royal type, with all the characteristics of a patrimonial state. With the coming to power of François Mitterrand in 1981, I cut out [newspaper] articles which said: 'Monsieur So-and-so, a personal friend of the president, has been appointed president of the Banque de France', this friendship being the most ostensible sign of the legitimacy of the person appointed and of his appointment. That is an example to show that we are not in a linear logic such as is suggested by the Weberian concept of rationalization.

This remark is not made lightly, but to prevent you from thinking that there is an increasingly formal, increasingly fair, increasingly bureaucratic and increasingly universal process at work. The question I am raising here is very central: we can ask whether the bureaucratic model, with its logic of delegation and particularly of control, does not imply almost inevitably – this is something I hate saying as a sociologist – but almost inevitably, as a very strong propensity, the threat of misappropriation of authority and power, and particularly of every form of corruption. Does the corruption that is customarily associated with the primitive stage of the state, with states of the personal type, disappear as structures of the bureaucratic type develop, or is it not inscribed in the very logic of bureaucratic delegation? Interesting models of this have been developed by contemporary economists. Jean-Jacques Laffont, for example, proposes an econometric model of corruption,[8] in which raison d'état necessarily fails to impose itself completely, even in the sphere of the state. In my preparatory work for this course I elaborated at length the problem of disinterestedness,[9] the legal sanctions that the state has at its disposal to punish those who transgress the command of disinterestedness. If the state really is as I have said, that is, a process of concentration and accumulation, it is understandable why it should be so hard to think, because there are so many things to be brought together. This means that I constantly feel like the child Plato speaks of, who wants to catch three apples with two hands . . .

The dynastic state

I shall now begin at the beginning, that is, with the dynastic state. Why speak of a dynastic state? Some historians, particularly vigilant and cautious not to commit anachronisms (historians often speak of the past with ideas of the present that they do not pass through the sieve of sociological criticism), have said that it is anachronistic to speak of a state for earlier periods. I refer for example to the book by Richard J. Bonney, *The European Dynastic States (1494–1660)*, and his article in the CNRS collective work on *La Genèse de l'État moderne*.[10] Bonney emphasizes the fact that by applying the concept of nation-state in the modern sense of the term to elementary forms of state, we risk losing sight of the specific character of the dynastic state:

During the greater part of the period before 1660 [and in some respects well beyond this], the majority of European monarchies were

not nation-states as we now conceive these, with the rather chance
exception of France. The majority of monarchies were composite col-
lections of territories [the typical example being the Habsburgs who
ruled Austria and Spain], states essentially unified in the person of the
prince.

That is one of the characteristics of dynastic states. The major bond, both
objective and subjective, is by way of love of the prince, the elementary
principle of patriotism. He remarks – I liked this a lot – that many wars at
this stage were wars of succession. And he stresses the fact that, unless a
clear distinction is made between the dynastic state and the nation-state,
it is impossible to grasp the specificity of either the dynastic state or the
modern one. A few years ago I happened to write a controversial paper
on modern sport.[11] People working on sport, a dominated object in the
space of the human sciences, felt they were obliged – I give their reasons
before saying what they did, but for me the two are inseparable – in order
to ennoble both themselves and their discipline, to offer a genealogy of
modern sports, for example to look for the ancestor of football in *soule*,
the ancestor of hockey in a twelfth-century mallet game, etc. I showed that
this was a historical error, as there was a break in the nineteenth century:
modern sports are the result of a reinvention or a new invention in a new
context – the development of the English boarding schools. The same kind
of work has to be done in order to conceive both the dynastic state and
the modern state. You have to know that in a certain sense the modern
state is no more the continuation of the dynastic state than football is the
continuation of *soule*.

I will draw on another author, Joachim Stieber, who goes so far as to
reject the name 'state' for what Bonney is still prepared to call the dynastic
state.[12] According to Stieber, there was no such thing as the state before
the seventeenth century. He stresses the limited power of the Holy Roman
emperor as a monarch chosen by an election that required papal consent.
The whole German history of the fifteenth century was marked by the
factional politics of princes, characterized by patrimonial strategies geared
towards the prosperity of families and their patrimony. It was only in
seventeenth-century France and England that the major distinctive features of the emerging modern state appear: a political entity separate from
the person of the prince and from political entities existing within the territorial limits of the nation, including the feudal nobility and the church.
For Stieber, an essential property of the modern state is the existence of
a bureaucracy separate from the king and other powers, the feudal lords
and the church. On the other hand, he shows that European politics in the
years 1330 to 1650 was marked by a proprietary point of view. The princes
had this proprietary view: they treated their government and their posses-
sions as a kind of personal property; by the same token, they managed politics the way people manage a patrimony. According to him, the term state
is therefore anachronistic if applied before the seventeenth century. I agree

with these two historians, but they are clearly a minority in their profession . . .

The state as a power over powers

In order to analyse the specific logic of the dynastic state as a concentration of the different species of capital, I will now turn to describing this process of concentration.[13] The different forms of accumulation of military, economic and symbolic capital are interdependent and form a whole, and it is this totalization that makes for the specificity of the state. The accumulation of different kinds of capital by the same central power generates a kind of meta-capital, that is, a capital with the particular property of exercising power over capital. This may seem speculative and abstract, but it is important. Among other possible definitions, one could say that the state is *meta*, that it is a power above powers. Analysing the accumulation of different forms of capital is a way of acquiring the means for understanding why the state is associated with the possession of a capital that has power over other kinds of capital. I refer here to an analysis by the economist François Perroux,[14] according to whom, when you speak of capital, you have to distinguish two states of capital: the holder of cultural capital who has for example a degree in geography, and the holder of a capital giving power over this capital – for example, a publisher of geography books. The latter has a meta-capital that decides whether the holder of a simple capital can publish or not.

This distinction between possession of capital and possession of a capital that gives power over this capital is operative in every domain. The state, inasmuch as it combines different species of capital in large quantity, is endowed with a meta-capital that enables it to exercise a power over all capital. This definition, which may appear abstract, becomes very concrete if it is related to the notion of field of power, the place where holders of capital confront one another, among other things over the rate of exchange between different species of capital. I shall give some examples and you will understand right away: the struggle for the revalorization of university degrees or the struggle over a reform of the École Nationale d'Administration, etc. In short, you have a large number of struggles, on which *Le Monde* – specifically addressed to those in the field of power – is full of interesting news for the holders of capital, which may be read as acts in the constant struggle waged between holders of capital to define rates of exchange, relations of domination between the different species of capital, and by the same token, between the different holders of these species of capital. The state, then, as holder of a meta-capital, is a field within which agents struggle to possess a capital that gives power over the other fields. Suppose it were decreed that the retirement age for members of the Conseil d'État would be changed from seventy to sixty-five. That would be a state measure of tremendous importance from the standpoint of the struggle for capital – a reform that would certainly be hard to get passed, since it brings a lot of things into play, in particular the balance of forces between generations. When people dance attendance on or telephone the prime minister, it is most often to talk about promotion and the preservation of a particular species of capital that might be threatened by one of these cross-field measures of redistribution . . .

Another example is that of the equivalence [of qualifications]. Laurent Fabius said that graduates from the École Normale Supérieure would be considered equivalent to those from the École Nationale d'Administration.[15] That is a tremendous measure in terms of the logic of the field of power, as it affects the rate of exchange between different species of capital. It's as if it was said that the dollar would be worth three francs instead of five. In this case, the stock of *normaliens* rises from three to five . . . The state can take cross-field measures of this kind because it has gradually established itself as a kind of meta-field of a field where a capital is produced, preserved and reproduced that gives power over the other species of capital. This is where I establish the link, the relationship, between the field of power and the state. One of the unifying principles of the field of power is that those people who belong to it struggle for power over the state, for this capital that gives power over the preservation and reproduction of the different species of capital. This was the 'meta-heading' intended to give you a lead into what I am in the process of doing . . .

Concentration and dispossession of species of capital: the example of physical force capital

I shall now come back to the substance of things, that is, to describing the different dimensions of accumulation. I start with military power. To know how the state was established, certain historians, who did not wait for me, have listed a number of factors that explain accumulation, and I shall give these here. But it is very rare for them to have combined them clearly [as I shall do] with a theory of the forms of capital. I do not say this to stress the originality of [my analysis], but rather so that you will not have an impression of déjà vu [. . .]. There is a kind of minimal definition of the genesis of the state [as having emerged with] military power and taxation. It is actually far more complicated than this. The process of concentration of this physical force capital subsequently becomes what we call the armed forces. This process was at the same time a process of separation, a monopoly established on the basis of a dispossession. This is again the same ambiguity that I already stated: concentration = universalization + monopolization. To establish a public force means removing the use of force from those who do not belong to the state. In the same way, establishing a cultural capital with a basis in formal education means dismissing those who do not have this capital as ignorant and barbaric; establishing a capital of the religious type means relegating non-clerics to the status of laity. It is very important [to emphasize this] because one of these aspects is often forgotten – this is particularly the case with the models of Weber and Elias. The process of concentration – Elias was correct in this respect – implies a process of separation, dispossession. See Elias's discussion of [the long-term] regression of violence. (I am a strong defender of Elias's ideas, but I begin to be somewhat vexed by the fact that he enjoys a kind of sacralization today . . . I like him less for what he actually contributed than for what he left out along the way.)

The process of concentration of public physical force was accompanied by a demobilization of day-to-day violence. Elias wrote some very fine texts on the birth of modern sport, in connection with this process by which the state removes from individual agents the right to deploy physical violence.[16] A whole part of Elias is contained in Weber's phrase that the state has the monopoly of legitimate violence. Those who are not the state, or mandated by the state, may not deploy violence, hit people, defend themselves . . . Physical violence may only be applied by a specialized grouping, specially mandated for this end, clearly identified within society by a uniform, and thus a symbolic grouping, centralized and disciplined. The notion of discipline, on which Weber wrote some magnificent pages,[17] is key. It is impossible to concentrate physical force without at the same time controlling it, otherwise there is a misappropriation of physical violence, and the misappropriation of physical violence is to physical violence what the misappropriation of capital is in the economic dimension, the equivalent of extortion. Physical violence may be concentrated in a body formed for this purpose, clearly identified in the name of society by a symbolic uniform, specialized and disciplined, that is, capable of obeying like a single man a central order that is not in itself the generator of any order.

The set of institutions mandated to guarantee order, that is, the forces of police and judiciary, are thus gradually separated from the everyday social world. This process is not without regressions. The concentration of physical force in the initial phase of the dynastic state is effected first of all against the feudal order. The first to be threatened by the construction of the monopoly of physical violence are the feudalists, the nobles, whose specific capital rested on the right and duty of exercising physical force. The statutory monopoly of the *noblesse d'épée* over the war-making function is threatened by the constitution of a capital of physical force, a professional army, especially when this is made up of mercenaries who may, in strictly technical terms, be superior to the nobles on what is the terrain of nobility par excellence. An analysis could be made of the masters of arms, commoners who may be the masters of the statutory masters of arms. Hence the questions that gave rise to casuistic debate in the seventeenth century: isn't a commoner who is highly skilled in the use of arms more noble than a noble who does not know how to use arms? You will find this in Elias. All this is the consequence of the concentration of physical capital.

This concentration of physical capital is accomplished in a double context. What is difficult, in constructing a model here, is to hold several dimensions together; some [researchers] see one dimension very well but not the others. Scientific debates are often the product of a mono-ideic, unilateral perspective; often you need only bring two or three things together in order to clear up a hundred debates. For some people, the development of the professional army is bound up with war, as is taxation; but there is also internal war, civil war, the raising of taxes as a kind of civil war. The state is thus established in relation to a double context. On the one hand, to other states whether actual or potential, that is, competing princes – there is accordingly a need to concentrate the capital of physical force in order to wage war for land and territories. On the other hand, in relation to an internal context, to counter-powers, that is, competing princes or dominated classes that resist the raising of taxes or of soldiers. These two factors favour the creation of powerful armies within which specifically military forces are gradually distinguished from specifically police forces intended to maintain internal order. This distinction between army and police, very clear today, has an extremely slow genealogy, the two forces having for a long time been combined.

To be surprised at this process that strikes us as self-evident, comparison should be made with so-called non-state societies, in which there are customs, 'law', but [no specialized] force in the service of the correct decision. In these societies, the exercise of physical violence is thus left to the responsibility of the family, in the form of vengeance. The absence of a *meta* instance (meta-household, meta-clan) leads to interminable cycles of vengeance, each person being caught up in the logic of challenge and response – as I have described for the case of Kabylia.[18] Every offended party inevitably becomes an offender in turn, for fear of losing his symbolic capital, and so the cycle of violence continues indefinitely, since there is no instance able to stop it, or if there is one, it does not have the necessary [concentration of] physical force capital [. . .]. These societies raise very clearly problems that our own societies have obscured, in particular moral problems bound up with the exercise of physical violence as we see this today before our eyes [in Yugoslavia]. Are there meta-national powers, powers that can intervene at the international level to impose an international law?

I refer you on this subject, in Aeschylus' tragedy *Orestia*, to what the chorus says about Orestes: How is it that we are obliged to resort to crime in order to punish crime? How can we escape from this cycle? Is not the act of Orestes, no matter how correct it might appear to us, a crime just as much as the crime it is intended to punish? Is not punishment itself a crime, the same as the crime that it punishes? These are questions that recognition of the legitimacy of the state makes us completely forget, except when debates are launched on the death penalty that are a bit wooly and pataphysical. That is an example of the doxic adhesion that we extend to the state, and that reflection on the original situation in pre-state times allows us to revive. Naturally, it is clear right away that the accumulation of physical [force] capital does not take place without accumulation of symbolic capital, inasmuch as the accumulation of physical [force] capital rests on a work of mobilization (it is not accidental that this word should have crossed from the army into politics), thus of construction of adherence, acknowledgement, legitimacy. To make the accumulation of physical [force] capital the prime mover in the construction of the state displays a mono-causal logic that is quite naive. There is no accumulation of physical [force] capital, then, without simultaneous or prior accumulation of symbolic capital.

Constitution of a central economic capital and construction of an autonomous economic space

The second factor is taxation, which is often associated with physical force capital so as to bring in money. The construction of the state as meta-field, as a power of construction of all fields, [involves] the construction of each of these fields. I am saying things that will strike you as highly speculative, but this is not just juggling with words. In my work of developing the notion of field, I focused on the process that Durkheim, Weber and Marx described, that is, how societies, as they advance over time, differentiate into separate and autonomous spheres – that is one of the very few tendential laws on which I believe everyone can agree. For Durkheim, 'primitive' societies mixed everything together: religion, science, economics, ritual, politics; you have actions that are 'multifunctional', or what Althusser would call 'overdetermined' (multifunctional is better). As societies [evolve], these orders separate, societies establish spheres that each have their own *nomos*, their specific law-like character. For example, the economy as economy, that is, the tautology 'business is business', or 'there's no room in business for sentiment'. An order of economic exchange is distinguished that is not the domestic order, something that many societies do not get round to doing.

The constitution of the state is connected with this process of differentiation, and here again that is something I did not understand until quite recently, which is why I emphasize it. The state is established as the meta-field instance while itself contributing to the constitution of fields. In the economic field, for example, taxation is bound up with the construction of a central economic capital, a treasury that is to some extent central and gives the holder of this treasury a power; he has the right to coin money, the right to set exchange rates, the right to take economic decisions, etc. The constitution of this central economic power gives the state the power to contribute to the construction of an autonomous economic space, the construction of the nation as a unified economic space. Polanyi (whom I admire greatly), in *The Great Transformation*, shows how the market did not come into being by itself, *motu proprio*, but was the product of an effort, in particular on the part of the state, often guided by mercantilist theories. The state deliberately contributed to structuring this space that appears to us as something given, whereas it is an institution. The genesis of a fiscal power and an economic power with a fiscal basis goes hand in hand with the unification of economic space and the creation of a national market.

The levying of tax by the dynastic state has a quite particular characteristic that historians have noted. It is very clearly distinct from all earlier forms in that the levy it makes is directly applied to all subjects, and not, like the feudal levy, to a certain number of subjects bound to the prince by a personal relationship. We move, in other words, from a mode of taxation of the feudal type, in which only dependents pay, this naturally meaning that they make their own dependents pay in turn, to something more universal and impersonal. Forerunners of this state taxation can be found. (In literature, being avant-garde means always pressing forward; among historians, it means going further back into the past. With historians, this infinite regression into the past is the homologue of the temptation of the avant-garde among artists. It is an effect of the field; those inside the field are tempted to say that something already exists. In fact there is never a first beginning.)

The development of taxation is bound up with the expenses of war. There is a connection between these two forms that I have arbitrarily separated. Levies that are made in the logic of gift and counter-gift give way to bureaucratic levies. I draw here on a book by Gerald Harris that analyses the appearance of elementary forms of taxation in the English case.[19] Harris emphasizes that feudal levies were collected as *dona*, 'freely accepted despoliations'. This is something to bear in mind in connection with tax fraud today . . . We are again here in the order of faith, obedience, submission, good will, thus of symbolic capital and legitimacy. The exchange of gifts differs from quid pro quo in that it is a quid pro quo that is not perceived as such. I give you something and you repay me when you can; if you repay me right away, that's quid pro quo, that means that you reject [my gift; otherwise] you leave an interval, you invite me over in two weeks' time . . . There is a whole social work involved in transforming economic exchange into symbolic exchange as a denied economic exchange. In the feudal system, exchanges between the prince and his supporters were understood in the logic of gift, economic exchanges that were not admitted as such. That is the form taken by an economic levy in the case where the relationship between the person who levies and the person levied is a personal relationship of dependence that implies a personal recognition.[20]

This precapitalist logic of levy is replaced by a logic of taxation with a capitalist appearance. Levies become compulsory, regular, at fixed dates. In the Kabyle economy, the worst you can do is set a due date; you leave things vague, and if there are real limits these are not spelled out. It is women who, not having any honour, that is, any concern for symbolic capital, can allow themselves to say: 'You will repay me on such-and-such a date' and not lose face. In contemporary domestic units, the economic division of labour is also conducted on this model when the man says to his wife: 'You should ask the price . . .' Taxation is collected 'with no limit in time other than what the king assigns from time to time', the rules of the game are defined by a central instance, taxation being directly or indirectly applied to all social groups. The development of this rational and formal taxation is accompanied by the birth of a fiscal administration and a series of constructions that presuppose writing: the accumulation of economic capital is inseparable from the accumulation of cultural capital, the existence of scribes, records, investigations. Investigation is a capital invention. If there had not been state investigations designed for tax-raising, there would be no work for historians today. The raising of taxes presupposes accounting, verification, archives, arbitration, the adjudication of differences, techniques for assessing property, thus investigation.

The birth of taxation goes hand in hand with an accumulation of capital held by the professionals in bureaucratic management and the accumulation of an immense informational capital. This is the connection between the state and statistics; the state involves a rational knowledge of the social world. Here you have relationships of circular causality – A causes B causes A – between the construction of an army and the construction of taxation, the construction of taxation and the accumulation of informational capital. This relationship of interdependence is particularly visible with the systematic raising of taxes on a territorial scale, which is bound up with the existence of an army capable of imposing this, the recovery of taxes being a kind of legitimate civil war. For Yves-Marie Bercé, 'taxation is necessarily bound up with the force that founds it and makes it possible',[21] even if, to the extent that the doxic relationship to the state is established, the use of physical force becomes necessary only in extreme situations. The institutionalization of taxation is the culmination of a kind of internal war waged by agents of the state against the resistance of subjects. Historians very rightly inquire as to the moment when the feeling appeared of belonging to a state, which is not necessarily what is called patriotism, the feeling of being subjects of the state. The experience of belonging to a defined [territorial] unit is very strongly connected with the experience of taxation. You discover that you are a subject by discovering you are subject to tax. There was an extraordinary invention of legal and police measures designed to make bad payers pay up, such as bodily constraint and responsibility *in solidum*.

One final point to show the interdependence between all these factors and particularly between the accumulation of economic capital and the accumulation of symbolic capital. The exercise of the physical violence needed to levy taxes is only completely possible to the extent that physical violence is disguised as symbolic violence. Not only does the bureaucracy build up archives, it also invents a discourse of legitimization: taxes are necessary to be able to make war; war affects us all, we have to defend ourselves against the foreign enemy. There is then the transition from taxes raised in time of war to taxes permanently raised for national defence, a transition from the discontinuous to the continuous, which presupposes a very major work of symbolic construction. The construction of the state is largely a mental invention. Even in the exercise of tax-raising, the use of symbolic force is very important.

Like all scientists, historians only see certain objects or themes as important inasmuch as they have been constituted as important by a historian who seems important to them. In the inter-war years, Schramm established the theme of the symbolism of royal power.[22] Ever since, there have been countless works on royal entrances, ritual, coronation, that is, the whole central symbolism: this is the self-reinforcement effect of subjects defined as important by the fact that bureaucratic routine is a major factor of scientific inertia. Other phenomena that are just as important were suddenly forgotten. One historian [Yves-Marie Bercé] emphasizes the fact, which may appear secondary, that in order to raise taxes, livery and special clothing had to be given to those who were mandated for this by the king.[23] Some would inevitably raise taxes on their own account. (The same problem arises in relation to charity.)

Elias's metaphor that the state is simply a legitimate racket is more than a metaphor. A body of agents had to be created, charged with collection and able to conduct this without misappropriating it to their own benefit. The agents and the methods of collection had to be readily identified with the person, the dignity of the power, whether it was that of the city or the lord or the sovereign. The bailiffs had to wear his livery, be authorized by his emblems, notify people of his commands in his name.[24] They had to be perceived as mandatories having *plena potentia agendi*, and this delegation was expressed not only in a signed order, but also by a livery that made manifest the dignity and, by the same token, the legitimacy of their function. This delegation, which was not without problems – any mandatory might misappropriate for himself the profits he drew from the power delegated to him – implied a control over the mandatories; thus controllers of these tax-raisers were necessary. In order for the mandatories to exercise their office without having on each occasion to resort to physical force, their symbolic authority had to be recognized. Tacit reference was made to the idea that the levying of taxes was legitimate; the authority of the person who mandates those exercising this extortion of funds must be legitimate, even when the extortion in question appears unjust.

One of the principles of the genesis of the idea of the state as an instance transcending the agents who embody it may be bound up with the fact that the justice of the king could be opposed to the injustice of these agents: 'It is impossible that the king should want this'; [in our own day] it's a 'letter to the President of the Republic', that is, the idea of an instance superior and irreducible to its empirical manifestations in the day-to-day world. A fine historical study could be made of indignation against unjust agents, bad mandatories of the king, an indignation that implies this irreducibility of the king. We can see here the connection with the genesis of a law transcending particular rights by way of procedures of appeal, the king being the last instance of appeal – an idea found again in Kafka. This last instance may be bound up with the primary experience of the medieval peasant who discovered the state in the form of these people who came and asked him for money in the name of some other body . . . The transcendence [of the state] can be understood on this basis.

Lecture of 7 March 1991

Reply to questions: conformity and consensus – Concentration processes of the kinds of capital: resistances – The unification of the juridical market – The constitution of an interest in the universal – The state viewpoint and totalization: informational capital – Concentration of cultural capital and national construction – 'Natural nobility' and state nobility

Reply to questions: conformity and consensus

I shall try to reply to a question for which I thank the author, but which upsets me because it makes me realize the lack of understanding that [my analyses] may receive . . . I am going to read part of it and try to respond just a little: 'You stressed that Marxism sees the state as oppression and that you see it as consensus . . . [That is not what I was trying to say.] Don't you realize that Marxism is far more complex? You need only look at Gramsci. Isn't the fundamental thing in Marxism to see the society as the assumed foundation of the state? Do you view the state as the foundation of civil society?' This question shows the strength of problematics imposed by habit, which resist the most methodical challenge. I have often had the feeling of marking time, going too slowly, despite saying that, in relation to conveying what I wanted to convey, one can never be too slow, since it is a question of uprooting conventional ways of thinking. A question like this makes me think I am still going too fast. And I would like to remind you of what I said at length, drawing on Marx, Durkheim, Weber and others: I tried to show how, in order to understand the modern state, it was necessary to supersede the opposition between these three great traditions and their extensions in contemporary science, to conceive the state as an organizational instrument able to found a logical and a moral conformity, and by the same token a consensus, but in a very special sense of the term. I stressed that this logical and moral integration that the state produces was the very condition for the domination that the state is able to exercise in the service of those who may appropriate the state. There is not an alternative between the two, they are linked in a complex and effective fashion. The misfortune of complex ideas is that they are hard to articulate and very easy to disarticulate . . .

The present lecture is the last but one of this year. Clearly, I am lagging behind in relation to my programme – just as every year – for reasons that bear on the gap between what I have in mind and the conditions of transmission. I am led each time to make digressions in order to develop preliminaries, and because of this I make slower progress than I would like. Last time I gave a kind of anticipatory plan of what I am going to tell you, and I believe it is important for you to keep this in mind so as to lessen the disappointment of this premature interruption, and so that you can go back to it in order to have an idea of what I wanted to do and what I shall do in another year.

Concentration processes of the species of capital: resistances

I shall try today, therefore, to finish the description of the concentration process that I sketched out last time, so as to keep the final session for describing the properties of the dynastic state at least in their broad lines. I mentioned two dimensions of this concentration process: (1) the concentration of physical power, military and police; (2) the concentration of economic capital by the monopoly of taxation. I have shown how, in my view, these processes of concentration of physical or economic force had as their precondition a concentration of symbolic capital. For me, symbolic capital is the foundation. To justify this proposition I pointed out that the invention of taxation in the modern sense was accompanied by a considerable work of justifying and legitimizing taxation. By drawing on passages from contemporary historians, I indicated that the imposition of taxation was the culmination of a kind of civil war; I mentioned the analogy made by Elias between taxation and racketeering. You have to bear in mind that taxation is a legitimate racket, that is, one not understood as such, and so recognized as legitimate. At its origins, however, this ambiguity of taxation is recalled very clearly by the fact that people ask why their money should be taken away, and they are not sure that those who levy this money are well-founded in doing so, [and] that the money levied does not end up in the pockets of the people who levy it.

Corrigan and Sayer highlight the often forgotten idea that the construction of the state came up against tremendous resistance, which is not even dead today. There are still forms of peasant rebellion. In a similar way today, the establishment of a transnational European state arouses resistance of various kinds, including resistance to taxation. To combat such resistance, politicians have to carry out a double work. First of all, a work of justification: we see the elaboration, essentially from the pens of jurists who are among the inventors of the state, of a discourse justifying the projects of 'official despoliation' that the king's agents have to conduct. The second work consists in setting up tax-levying organs that are both technically effective, able to keep accounts – which presupposes writing – but also able to impose themselves as legitimate. I mentioned on this subject the importance of liveries here, of a basic state symbolism, of the state agent as functionary, a person who is a legitimate mandatory or delegate, with the right to say that he has *plena potentia agendi* in the name of the state, the full power to act in the name of the state. People are not minded to take his word for this, and so he has to present qualifications: the uniform or livery is the emblem that, like the noble's coat of arms, attests to the legitimacy of the functionary. 'Those simply required to contribute were able to recognize the livery of the guards and the banners of the sentries. They could distinguish the tax farmers' guards, detested and despised financial agents, from the royal horsemen, the archers of the constabulary, the provostship and the life-guards, reputedly immune from attack because of their coat in the royal colour.'[1]

That is an example of symbolic force contributing to physical force; the symbolism of the royal power associates this power with a rite, the rite as such constituting a force of execration. 'From the tax farms agreed in good and proper form with the royal treasury down to the lowest sub-farmer charged with the local levy, a whole cascade of leases and sub-farms was interposed, constantly giving rise to the suspicion of an alienation of taxation and a usurpation of authority.'[2] The state, that mysterious entity, is embodied in a series of hierarchically ordered individuals, each being the mandatory of the other, so that the state is always the end term of an infinite regression; this is the Kafkaesque expression of the state as last instance that is pursued from one appeal to the next.[3] We find the same model still more clearly in relation to law. This cascade of delegation always gives rise to two suspicions: the suspicion that the mandatories are not real mandatories, and that if they are so, they do not pass on the product of their exactions to their principals. I refer you to two books here, *La Psychologie sociale de l'impôt*[4] and *Psychologie des finances et de l'impôt*.[5]

There is a tremendous body of work on corruption, one of the most important problems from the standpoint of understanding the genesis of the state. I will shortly be referring to a very fine article by a French Sinologist on corruption in the Chinese empire, China being a kind of enlarged image of what could be seen in the West at the origins of the state.[6] It is possible to ask whether corruption is an inevitable feature, inherent to any process of delegation, or whether it is a function of habitus, of dispositions and control systems. The lower administration really was very corrupt, and the rebellion against taxation focused completely on this. I can also give you an approximate translation of an article by Hilton:[7] 'There was a whole network of petty officials, sub-collectors of taxes, sheriff's officers, bailiffs; these officials, as is generally seen in societies, were correctly organized and correctly paid, but they were corrupt, and were known to be corrupt, both by their victims and by the monarchy's more senior officials.' They were doubly stigmatized, and by the same token, this generally known and recognized corruption could be one of the principles of the disassociation between the real state and the theoretical state, the state embodied in officials and the state that transcended the officials and was embodied by the king.

My hypothesis is that people could conceive the idea of the state as irreducible to those who embodied it, transcending these in the form of the king, so long as the king could be the embodiment of that last instance to which it was possible to resort. This reference to a transcendent state, present already in law, was a step on the path of construction of an impersonal and pure state entity, leading to the modern idea of the state as abstract entity, irreducible to those who embody it. Observers also emphasize the fact that in a general sense recognition of the legitimacy of taxation, or acceptance of submission to taxation, develop in correlation with the emergence of a form of nationalism, of chauvinism. Hilton points out that it was by way of the development of the feeling that taxes were necessary for the defence of the territory that the idea of patriotism gradually developed, this idea of patriotism being the main justifying element for the raising of taxes.

The unification of the juridical market

What I now want to explain very quickly is the process of unification of the juridical market. In the beginning, around the twelfth century in Europe, one can see the coexistence of several mutually exclusive bodies of law: ecclesiastical jurisdictions, 'courts of Christianity', secular jurisdictions – with the king's justice in the strict sense one among these; seigniorial jurisdictions; the justices of communes or towns; the justices of corporations; the justices of commerce. I refer you here to two authors, Adhémar Esmein and Marc Bloch. [Esmein was the author of an] *Histoire de la procédure criminelle en France, et spécialement de la procedure inquisitoire, depuis le XIIe siècle jusqu'à nos jours.*[8] This book, which makes no theoretical claim, is extremely interesting because it enables us to see how, by the establishing of appeal procedures, jurisdictions other than those of the king, seigniorial ones in particular, were dispossessed of the power of judgement. Seigniorial justice, like seigniorial military power, was originally a personal justice: the lord had a right of justice over his vassals, but only over them, that is, over all those who lived on his lands, including noble vassals, free men and serfs, each of these being subject to different rules. The king had jurisdiction only over the royal domain. As a kind of great lord, he only decided cases between his immediate vassals, and between the inhabitants of his own fiefdoms. The competence of the royal jurisdiction grew as the domain itself grew. To cite Marc Bloch, our second author here: 'Royal justice began to insinuate itself into the whole of society. [The penetration of royal justice] was relatively belated; we can say by and large that it scarcely began before the twelfth century; it was slow; above all, it took place without an overall plan, without legislative texts, and, if I can say so, haphazardly.'[9]

I already quoted this text last year, so as to suggest to you the philosophy of history that I am applying in my analysis of the state, that kind of apparently haphazard construction process whose product none the less has a certain necessity. Marc Bloch's formula is highly interesting. It is the idea that the genesis has a logic that is not that of logic, despite leading to products that do have a logic. A trans-seigniorial judicial apparatus is established step by step, with the appearance of provosts, bailiffs, parliaments, etc. I will not go into detail here, but try to give you the general law of this process, which is clear enough in relation to law but is a very general process and at the same time a process of differentiation, the juridical field being constituted as such, in a separate and autonomous sphere, obeying its own laws that are irreducible to those of the spheres with which it coexists. And you have on the other hand, without this being contradictory, a process of concentration: the formation of the royal monopoly of judicial power in relation to that of the lords. The two processes, seemingly antagonistic, are in fact mutually reinforcing. It is by way of the unification of the legal market that the concentration is accomplished.[10]

Concentration should not be imagined as simply a process of capital accumulation, a game of marbles in which they all end up in the king's possession. Concentration means the establishment of a single game. Where there were several games – seigniorial justice, town justice – there is now a single game, with the result that all players are summoned to locate themselves in this space of play, and occupy a certain position within it. Clearly it is possible for this field to be dominated: the monopolistic concentration of juridical power is a function of the fact that the parliament, and through it the king, tends to dominate the juridical field. But in order for this capacity of domination to be exercised, the juridical field has to be unified and constituted as such.

Having formulated the principle, I shall rapidly go over the main lines of the process by which this concentration was effected. I refer you to the recently published book on the birth of the state edited by Jacques Revel and André Burguière; the chapter on the Middle Ages was written by Jacques Le Goff.[11] Royal justice gradually concentrated the criminal cases that had previously been dealt with by the lord or the church. Faustin Hélie's book *Traité de l'instruction criminelle* shows how royal jurisdictions gradually extended their competence:[12] 'royal cases' where the rights of the monarchy were infringed were reserved for royal bailiffs, such as, for example, the crimes of lèse-majesté, counterfeiting, which meant appropriating a property [monopolized by the] king, and forging the royal seal (*sigillum authenticum*), which was the material embodiment of royalty, the equivalent of today's company sign, the symbolic embodiment of a collective entity, a corporation, an entity that existed only on paper. Appropriating the symbolic power of the king was the exemplary case of a crime against what was sacred. The royal jurisdiction appropriated all the royal cases, and bit by bit it also appropriated seigniorial or ecclesiastical cases, by way of the theory of appeal that jurists developed. This is a fine example of an interest in the universal: jurists were involved in the unification of the juridical market because it was their market; they had an interest in disinterestedness, in universalization.

The constitution of an interest in the universal

In order to understand the appearance of universal or formally universal institutions, or ones that make formal reference to respect for the universal, such as the state, justice or science, we can assume that there is an interest in the universal, that there are people who have the advancement of the universal as their particular interest. Jurists, as producers of legal treatises and sellers of juridical services, clearly had an interest in the unification of the law; by virtue of this they were functionaries or devoted soldiers of the universal. They develop the theory of appeal, insisting that feudal courts are not sovereign; they were so, but no longer are. It is accepted that any judgement rendered by a lord justiciary can be referred to the king by the party affected if this judgement is contrary to the customs of the country, a procedure known as 'supplication'. If appeal is already a formal procedure, supplication still remains a feudal act. I want to describe this hybrid phase in which words like supplication, which sound feudal, already function in a universal, impersonal mode. The supplication procedure is gradually transformed into an appeal that submits all the jurisdictions of the kingdom to the king; bit by bit, the spontaneous judges and jurors of feudal courts disappear in favour of professional jurists, officers of justice. Appeal follows the rule of the territory, a transition from personal relations with a feudal lord to territorial relations, territory of course being hierarchically ordered; appeal is from the lower lord to the higher, from the count to the duke and finally to the king. It is impossible to skip these stages. A unified and hierarchically ordered space is established, which is only traversed in a particular direction. The monarchy draws support from the specific interests of the jurists, who create at the same time all kinds of legitimizing theories by which the king represents the common interest and owes security and justice to all; jurists develop legitimizing theories by which the king restricts the competence of feudal jurisdictions and subordinates them to him. The process is the same with ecclesiastical jurisdictions; state law, for example, tends to circumscribe the right of asylum that belongs to the church, and gradually limits these rights until they are reduced to nothing.

The judiciary develops in parallel with the establishment of the juridical field. The interest of the notion of field is that very often descriptions of the genesis of a field are limited to describing the genesis of a body. The difference however is considerable. Though there cannot be a field without a body, or a religious field without a priestly body along with its prophets, a field cannot be reduced to a body.[13] A text of Engels is often brought up to justify the existence of a theory of the relative autonomy of law in the Marxist tradition; he notes in this text that bodies of jurists appear.[14] The existence of a juridical body, however, is not enough to constitute a juridical field. That said, to the extent that the juridical field establishes itself as a unified space within which matters can only be dealt with legally (fields are always defined tautologically), in conformity with the dominant definition of law, that is, the state definition of law, a body of people is constituted who have an interest in the existence of this field and who owe their legitimate existence to the existence of this field.

This judicial body is organized in a hierarchy: provosts, bailiffs, seneschals. They become sedentary, the competence they are guaranteed by the state being inseparable from their territory of operation. This is the modern definition of the functionary, the person who has an institutionally guaranteed competence, valid within the limits of a certain territory. Beyond that territory it is invalid and can no longer be exercised. They cease to be their own mandatory and become lieutenants of the *plena potentia agendi*, mandatories who perform a function and stand in for a higher authority, irrevocable officers of justice.

In parallel with the constitution of this body, we see a codification and formalization of procedures: unification is accompanied by standardization, homogenization, as we have seen with weights and measures, the extreme case being the creation of a universal standard. Universal juridical standards and formal juridical procedures are created that are very similar to algebraic operations. The law must be valid for all 'x' over a territorial set, with specifications that are themselves formally defined. We have a process of concentration and codification which seems to have come to an end historically with the decree of 1670 that ratified the progressive conquests of the jurists: (1) the competence of the place of the offence becomes the rule (link between competence and sphere of operation); (2) the precedence of royal judges over seigniorial ones; (3) the listing of royal cases; (4) the abolition of ecclesiastical and communal privileges, with appeal judges always being royal. The competence that the royal power delegates to lieutenants in a certain sphere takes the place of personal and direct dependence. This process leading from the personal to the impersonal is characteristic of every process of concentration.

The state viewpoint and totalization: informational capital

A further dimension of this process is the concentration of a capital that can be called cultural, though a better term would be informational, which renders its full generality, cultural capital being only a dimension of informational capital. This concentration goes hand in hand with the unification of the cultural market: the university degree, for example, as a qualification that is valid in all markets. Right from the start (this is attested to in every tradition – ancient Rome, China), the appearance of a state instance is accompanied by an effort on the part of the public powers to measure, count, assess, investigate. The birth of the state is inseparable from an immense accumulation of informational capital. The secret services, for example, an essential dimension of modern states, develop along with the state itself. The public powers conduct investigations into the condition of the resources to be 'appraised'. Georges Duby points out that in 1194 there was the 'sergeants' appraisal', a valuation made by sergeants: 'It listed the number of carts and armed men to be supplied by eighty-three towns and royal abbeys when the king summoned the feudal host.' The connection between the accumulation of informational capital and that of military capital is very clear here. Another example given by Duby is that in 1221 we see the first beginnings of a budget, with a division between receipts and expenses: the state not only concentrates information, but processes it and redistributes it (it is a scarce resource), this redistribution being differential.[15]

The work of concentration is a work of unification, a theoretical one in this case. I much like to cite a phrase of Virginia Woolf on general ideas: 'General ideas are generals' ideas.'[16] This fine phrase reminds theorists of what they are. If theory has such a seductive power over young thinkers, it is because they dream of being generals ... Analysis of the scientific mind is part of the socioanalysis of the specific impulses by which we may be inspired. It is important to know that a certain global view, total, from above, encompassing, theoretical – the Greek *theorein* means to contemplate, to see, to see from above, to accede to a viewpoint – is bound up with the state. Many things appear along with the state that we tend to see as self-evident: geographical maps, for example. As a young ethnologist just setting out, it took theoretical work on my part to deconstruct the idea of a plan. I drew plans of houses, villages;[17] I was not aware that I was acting like a general. The fact of conceiving this act as a general's act enabled me to free myself from [what this implied], from what that very particular construction prevented me from seeing, that is, that people do not move around according to map-like plans but according to what phenomenologists call itineraries; they [evolve in] a hodological space, a space of routes. As scientists, when we draw up genealogies we are acting like a general; the accumulation of symbolic capital by the state is accompanied by an effort to draw up genealogies; officials are appointed with responsibility for drawing up noble genealogies. Genealogy is an elementary anthropological act, and there is no anthropologist who does not draw up genealogies, but the anthropologist is unaware that he is doing exactly what the king does ... The majority of declarations, the plan, the map, genealogy, are acts performed from a higher, elevated standpoint, from a hilltop. *Actes de la Recherche* published a very fine article by the art historian Svetlana Alpers proposing a theory of Dutch painting as inspired by cartography; this painting adopted a cartographic point of view.[18]

The state is a theoretical unifier, a theorist. It carries out a unification of theory; it takes a central and superior viewpoint, that of totalization. It is not by chance that the state's instrument par excellence is statistics. Statistics make it possible to totalize information from individuals and obtain from this, by totalization, information that none of the individuals who provided the basic information have. Statistics is precisely a transcendent technique that makes it possible to effect a totalization (everything I am saying about the state holds good also for statistics), but it is not easy to have the means to 'raise' information. In former times, tax collectors needed to have a livery; today, if you are going to conduct a study of consumption, you need to show your credentials; people resist the extraction of information. The state has to have the means for doing this, it says that it's compulsory and you have to respond. Then it must have the means for recording this information, processing it (computers, accountants), thinking it and drawing out statistical regularities, relationships that transcend the individuals and which they are unaware of (individuals don't control these relationships). The state takes control by a totalization of the social world that the social agents do not possess. Another typical state operation is synthesis; the higher you rise in the administrative hierarchy, the greater your powers of synthesis.

The state involves objectivation and all the techniques of objectivation. It deals with social facts as things, with men as things – it is Durkheimian *avant la lettre*. That is why Durkheim's theory of the state was the internalized state. As a state functionary who did not see himself as a state functionary, he was in the state like a fish in water; he had an objectivist theory of the social world, which is the implicit perception that the state has of its subjects. The state is the unitary, overhead viewpoint on a space that is unified theoretically and homogenized by the act of construction. Basically, this is Cartesian space. If you wanted to do sociology of knowledge here, you might say that there is a link between the birth of a philosophy of space of the Cartesian type and the birth of the state; I am being careful not to propose this as a hypothesis, but now that I've said it, you can make what you will of it . . .

The viewpoint of the state is the viewpoint of writing, which is the instrument of objectivation and combination par excellence, and makes possible a transcendence of time. I refer you here to Jack Goody and his book *The Domestication of the Savage Mind*.[19] In the limiting case, an ethnologist can separate himself fundamentally from his informants because he writes, and can thus totalize what these informants do not totalize because they do not have the means of doing so. You have an idea, but if you are unable to write, one idea supplants another and they get lost; that's what happens without writing. Societies without writing certainly develop skills that we have lost; that said, however, totalization is particularly hard without writing. The superiority of the investigator over the investigated is a function of the fact that the investigator knows what he is looking for (at least he is supposed to know), whereas the person investigated does not know. Moreover, the investigator has the means for totalizing everything that the person investigated tells him at different moments. By this totalization, he acquires a synthetic and synoptic apprehension that is often the whole of his understanding.

(Thomas Bernhard has a fearful sentence about the state: 'Man today is only a state man.'[20] I can give the example here of the idea of a national sample. It took the age I've reached and my work on the state for me to realize that a national sample presupposes the idea of the state. People say: 'The sample is representative and national', but why not take a sample from Beauce or Picardy? Something extraordinary is thus implicit in the fact of taking a national sample. Apropos statistical theories, I always say that the most serious theoretical mistakes arise from the fact that attention, reflection, is drawn to a secondary point, as in symbolic traps or a conjuror's tricks, with the result that what is essential is hidden. The major epistemological mistakes are of this type. Someone says to you: 'What is important is the level of representation, representativeness; the error has to be calculated, the quality of the sample [controlled].' They forget to say: 'Beware, what is important is the box that you draw from . . .' You can take a magnificent sample, following all the rules, but perhaps there are only black balls in your box, or you've selected Picardy when you should have selected France. Accepting a national sample means accepting the imposition of a fundamental definition of the object.)

Concentration of cultural capital and national construction

Writing, therefore, is the state instrument par excellence, the instrument of totalization: the first written signs were associated with the keeping of records, accounting records in particular. It is therefore the specific instrument of cognitive accumulation, making possible codification, that is, the cognitive unification that makes possible a centralization and monopolization to the benefit of those who hold the code. The codification established by grammar is also a work of unification inseparable from a work of monopolization.

The link between the concentration of capital and the birth of the state needs to be developed. I suggested this theme in relation to Japan and England; I shall now take it up in more general terms. The construction of the state is inseparable from the construction of a national cultural capital that is at the same time a national symbolic capital. Any state construction, for example, is accompanied by the construction of a pantheon of great men. The pantheon is a state act par excellence. It is the monument of selected great men, which indicates both those men who merit admiration (as is also the case with state funerals), and subliminally also the principles by which those great men have been selected. Since these principles are hidden in the products selected, they impose themselves all the more subtly.

In terms of culture, the state is to private patrons what royal justice is to seigniorial justice. The state acquires a monopoly of cultural action, and by the same token dispossesses private individuals of the power to spend their money on cultural projects. If the lack of private patrons is deplored – [I welcome it], such patronage being a dreadful form of domination over the cultural world – or the difficulty of developing private patronage in the French case, this is precisely because the process of monopolization of the exercise of culture has been particularly concentrated here, and in a particularly precocious way. I shall make a simple historical remark that I noted to help you understand. It was in the same year [1661] as Louis XIV established his personal power that he arrested Nicolas Fouquet, the last of the great patrons. He immediately took into his service all the artists who had been protégés of Fouquet, [the painter Charles] Le Brun, [the gardener André] Le Nôtre, etc. We should not forget that this is a strange monopoly, a monopoly of expenditure of this kind. One of the characteristics of the economics of culture is that it is not economic in the narrow sense of the term. But economic expenditure comes back on the symbolic level, otherwise there would be no cultural expenditure at all . . . So if there is cultural practice without a public, as is the case with most highbrow practices, this is only because there are grants written off by the state. Paradoxically, the state takes on a monopoly of these expenses, which may seem contradictory if you do not see that the concentration of these expenditures is inseparable from the concentration of the profits of cultural logic and the symbolic returns by which such expenditure is repaid, all societies rewarding symbolically acts performed in violation of the law of economic interest. The state therefore concentrates culture, and the idea of the unification of mental structures should be borne in mind here, the fact that the state appropriates mental structures, producing a unified cultural habitus whose genesis it controls, as well as its structure by the same token.

'Natural nobility' and state nobility

It was by way of the concentration of juridical capital that I introduced the concentration of symbolic capital, given that law may be viewed as a dimension of symbolic capital. I shall rapidly describe the process of concentration of honours, and the basic line I shall follow is that honour gives way to honours – [the honour in question is] hereditary honour, that of the noble, for example, or of the Spanish gentlemen mentioned by Kiernan, who are 'nobles by nature', by contrast with those ennobled by the state. The concentration process of symbolic capital effected by the state, and leading to the power of nomination, the power to award decorations, educational certificates, titles of educational or bureaucratic nobility – the Légion d'Honneur, for example – can be seen very well in the evolution of the treatment of nobility effected by the state in the transition from the seigniorial model to that which is wrongly called absolutist and should rather be called centralist, that of Louis XIV.

Little by little, the state becomes the central bank of symbolic capital, and then the only nobility is a state one. [In our own day,] it is the ENA that appoints nobles, choosing at most 5 to 6 per cent of its graduates [from the nobility]. Nowadays there is no instance of consecration that is not connected with the state in one way or another. A major difficulty of the intellectual or scientific field, then, is to establish a legitimacy independent from the state. At all times, and recently in particular when the left was in government, the state bends its efforts to intervene and impose its jurisdiction on specific juridical instances in order to award prizes in painting, photography, etc. When it comes to matters of artistic judgment, ministers of culture are very 'intrusive', as it would be called in the English-speaking world; they always tend to challenge the claim of intellectuals to say who is intellectual, [and that] of artists to say who is an artist, etc. It is this process that I want to describe.

The old nobility was a 'nobility by nature', as the Aragon gentlemen said, that is, a nobility based on heredity and public recognition. A noble was someone that the nobles recognized as noble, because he was the son, grandson or great-grandson of a noble, etc. – thus going back a long time. This is the feudal, personal form of consecration. Once the central state power is established, it breaks into this autonomous management of nobility to establish state nobles: between 1285 and 1290, Philippe le Bel began to ennoble commoners. At this time, no one was bothered, as notables did not have a great need of royal patents in order to enter the nobility, they could enter it de facto by marriage, while the ennobled, especially in southern France, did not derive any great profit from their titles unless they managed to obtain the recognition of other nobles. In other words, the logic of the relatively autonomous field of the nobility was still strong enough to restrain state action (the analogy with the intellectual field of today is always there in my analysis).

I refer you here to a book by Arlette Jouanna, *Le Devoir de révolte. La noblesse française et la gestation de l'État moderne (1559–1561)*,[21] which has been a great inspiration to me. This is a book that, beneath its monographic appearance, raises general questions – the definition of a fine scientific work in my view – and studies a particular case in such a way as to magnificently raise very general questions. She analyses the progressive concentration of the power to create nobles in the hands of the king. This process tends to replace statutory honour, which was inherited but had to be defended, by honours attributed by the state. There was a specific work of maintenance of this capital: prowess, challenge, response; and it was not by chance that the challenge was the major test of honour, and that responding as a point of honour to an attack on one's honour was the major imperative imposed on the noble, [as in] all societies based on honour. [Subsequently,] honours were attributed by the state, and positions increasingly viewed as rewards that implied nobility. The logic of honour was replaced by that of the *cursus honorum*; there is a *cursus honorum* of nobility just as there is a bureaucratic one. Then nobility became bureaucratized by the imposition of the royal monopoly of enno-bling, that is, the distribution of symbolic capital guaranteed by the state. Here again, Elias both saw this and did not see it. The 'curialization' of the nobility is patently obvious, whereas what is far more subtle is the mechanism by which nobles were controlled.[22] Why were they made to go to court? Why were they ruined if they didn't go? Why does a minister of culture invite intellectuals to his court, and why are those who do not go in danger? The analogy is perfect . . .

The submission of the nobility to the royal power is both a bureauc-ratization and a clericalization, that is, the nobles come to be appointed, nominated, as against self-designated. An indication of this is how under Louis XIV, just as the state initiated surveys and censuses, it conducted censuses of the nobility. Colbert, who originated all state actions at this time, created the Académie; he appointed writers, he appointed nobles. A decree of 1666 stipulated 'the establishment of a catalogue containing the names, surnames, dwellings and arms of true gentlemen'; intendants were given responsibility for sifting through the nobility. The state set itself up as judge of the quality of nobles, which was a problem for the nobles. (Just as for the intellectuals of today, who are always struggling to know who is truly an intellectual and are divided among themselves. If the state inter-venes, it only has to play one lot off against the other and say: 'I will say who is truly an intellectual.' One of the only ways of mobilizing intellectu-als may well be to tell them: 'Look out, the state will intervene.' Unhappily, however, they are not clear-headed enough. The nobles understood all this more quickly than the intellectuals do.) And so the intendants sifted the titles of nobility, established genealogies, judges for conflicting claims, etc. Analysis is needed here of the arrival of the *noblesse de robe*, which is most interesting because it is a transition between the old, feudal nobility and the modern nobility, that of the *grandes écoles*. This is a nobility appointed by the state, and on the state basis of educational qualifications.

There is thus a gradual transition (the process I am describing here takes place over centuries) from a diffuse symbolic capital, based on col-lective, mutual recognition, to an objectified symbolic capital that is codi-fied, delegated, guaranteed by the state, that is, bureaucratized. There are arms, coats of arms, hierarchies, titles with quartering, genealogies. This process can be seen in something that scarcely anyone, to my knowledge, has considered: the famous sumptuary laws that governed the external signs of symbolic wealth, the outward quality of building facades or cloth-ing. To my mind, these sumptuary laws can be understood as one of the state's interventions in the domain of the symbolic. The state defines who has the right to wear what, and defines the system of differences. In our society, games of distinction obey the law of the market. Each person acts for himself, whereas in former times these were managed and established by the state, which said: 'You have the right to three ropes of ermine and not four; if you wear four, that's a usurpation of livery.' I refer you here to Michèle Fogel's article 'Modèle d'État et modèle social de dépenses.

Les lois somptuaires en France de 1545 à 1560',[23] in which she shows how the state managed differences between nobles and commoners, and more precisely between the different degrees of nobility. The desire of members of the Parlement de Paris, and all the officials behind them, to have their share in state consumption, the demands of the nobility, at the États Généraux of 1559 among other occasions, but also the action of the high nobility against the petty nobility at this time of crisis for the aristocracy, were all signs of state intervention. The state governed the use of different cloths, and of gold, silver and silk trimmings; in this way, it defended the nobility against the usurpations of commoners, but at the same time it extended and reinforced the hierarchy within the nobility itself. This was a way of controlling the exhibition of a symbolic capital that existed only by exhibition; controlling the exhibition of symbolic capital thus amounts to controlling symbolic capital itself.

I shall end with a very fine text from [the legal historian Frederic William] Maitland's *Constitutional History of England*. This kind of constitutional history is one of the most boring reads imaginable, but it contains some quite extraordinary passages, for example how the power of appointing and dismissing the high officers of state was established. [Maitland] writes: 'the king has a very general power of appointing not only those whom we speak of as collectively forming the ministry, but all or almost all of those who hold public offices of first-rate importance.' Blackstone had called the king 'the fountain of honours, of office and of privilege.'[24] In other words, he was the unique source of all symbolic power. '[T]he making of knights and baronets, the invention of new orders of knighthood, the conferring of ceremonial precedence, is no very great matter.' But the power to name peers is very important. 'But look at the whole legal structure of society, and we shall generally find that the holders of important public offices are appointed by the king and very commonly hold their posts merely during his pleasure.'[25] [Maitland] describes what has been called 'absolutism', the power of making and unmaking positions and the occupants of these positions, which is state power. He describes in a very detailed manner the very subtle processes of delegation, particularly the delegation of signature, by which this power of delegation is concentrated and composed: the king signs, the chancellor countersigns, the person who countersigns ratifies that the signature is that of the king, and by the same token he also controls the king; if the king has signed something foolish, it is he who is responsible. Then the vice-chancellor countersigns the act signed by the chancellor. There is in this way a cascading chain of delegation, increasingly anonymous in appearance. The symbolic power is concentrated, and at the same time it spreads and penetrates the whole of society (the metaphor of the fountain, of ripples). Tyranny supervenes when this central power ends up losing control of itself.

Lecture of 14 March 1991

Digression: an overthrow in the intellectual field – The double face of the state: domination and integration – *Jus loci* and *jus sanguinis* – Unification of the market in symbolic goods – Analogy between the religious field and the cultural field

Digression: an overthrow in the intellectual field

Exceptionally here, I shall speak of yesterday's television programme about intellectuals, as this is a socially important phenomenon, even if intellectually worthless.[1] My general rule is never to speak of these semi-intellectual productions. And I remember disapproving of Gilles Deleuze when he wrote a pamphlet against the 'new philosophers', believing that he did them too much honour.[2] That said, I believe that this little event, which will naturally become a big media event, deserves a few words. I think that this kind of discourse, written very likely by Alain Decaux[3] and pronounced in the tone of Frédéric Mitterrand, is important because it represents one of the strategies by which the autonomy of the intellectual field is increasingly threatened, an autonomy that is not necessarily just that of intellectuals, since there are always, in an autonomous intellectual field, those intellectuals who are more autonomous than others, and others who are more heteronomous than others.

The autonomy of the intellectual field is a historical conquest that was extremely long and hard.[4] For a while now this autonomy has been threatened in a fairly systematic way, by a convergence of actions [arising] from the political field and from journalistic and media actions, with the intervention of those 'media intellectuals' who are servants of this heteronomy. Certain weeklies – *Le Nouvel Observateur*, *L'Événement du Jeudi* – have begun to appoint individuals they consider as meriting the title of intellectuals. This is a usurpation of power, since it is up to intellectuals themselves to say who is an intellectual, even if they dispute among themselves, just as it is up to mathematicians to say who is a mathematician.[5] There are a series of forcible interventions of which yesterday's event was an extreme case: it is a typical kind of coup d'état. In former times my predecessors here protested against Napoleon III,[6] they had an opponent of their own calibre. Unfortunately, I am obliged to protest against opponents who are infinitely more derisory, but the danger is the same if not worse. It is the same danger, but worse because it has a less dangerous air.

These interventions are coups d'état. I have often referred to Pascal's theory of tyranny.[7] For Pascal, tyranny consists in one order imposing its own norm on a different order. Military order imposes its force on the intellectual order, the order of grace on the order of charity, etc. A field experiences tyranny when it is the object of constraints that are not its own – autonomy being, in the Kantian definition, obedience to laws that one has oneself prescribed, and heteronomy submission to external constraints that obey other principles, such as media visibility, publicity, and behind all of this, money, success, audience figures, etc. These constraints are being imposed with increasing strength on the intellectual field, and very profoundly threaten a certain type of intellectual production and work and a certain type of intellectual. It is for this reason that I permit myself to make use of this platform to warn against this danger. It is a specific kind of coup d'état in the sense that a force external to the logic of the intellectual field is being used to effect an overthrow. When it was Pinochet, people understood right away, but when the overthrow has an intellectual appearance it is less visible, and because of this many people may be deceived, by the effects of *allodoxia*. The misfortune of these intellectuals is that, as in a famous story, they are familiar with the tune of intellectual life, but they don't know the words . . .

The intellectual – Zola being the paradigm of this – is someone who, on the basis of a specific authority acquired in struggles within the intellectual, artistic or literary field, according to the inherent values of these relatively autonomous spheres, intervenes in the political field on the basis of an authority, a work, a competence, a virtue or an ethic.[8] This is not the case with the people I am talking about here, as they have very little work to their credit, very little authority, competence, morality or virtue . . . This coup d'état is dangerous, firstly because it affects the representation that young researchers may have of intellectual work. It is possible to devote twenty years to your work without appearing in the media, whereas there are ever more people who publish something simply so as to get on television the following season. It threatens a certain specific authority that intellectuals have acquired by struggle, and which is very useful. It is a historical conquest that is threatened, and this threatens the possibility of there being intellectuals who conform to the definition I have just formulated, one that particularly authorizes them to speak in the name of a work, and values associated with this work, and to intervene in political life. These interventions, which are useful ones, are threatened. That is why this problem is also very important politically.

The double face of the state: domination and integration

I shall now come to a partial conclusion of these lectures, so that you will have an initial idea of the totalization I am heading towards. We have often seen, particularly in writings critical of my own work – Dutch, British, German – an opposition between two theories of the functions of the educational system in the modern social world: on the one hand, one that recognizes the function of the system in terms of domination, the maintenance of social and symbolic order; and on the other, one that stresses the functions of integration and unification, closely associating the birth of mass education, [beginning with] compulsory primary education, with the development of the state. We see an opposition here between domination and unification/integration. I would like to show that this opposition is not one between two theories, but rather something inherited from the reality of the social world, and inherent to the very functioning of the state. The state is a reality with a double face. We may say that the development of the modern state can be described as a progress towards a higher degree of universalization (de-localization, de-particularization, etc.), and in the same movement, as a progress towards monopolization, the concentration of power, thus towards the establishment of the conditions of a central domination. In other words, the two processes are [both linked] and contrary. To a certain degree, one could say that integration – which must be understood in Durkheim's sense, but also the sense of those who spoke of the integration of Algeria, which includes the idea of consensus – is the condition for domination. This is basically the key thesis that I want to develop. The unification of the cultural market is the condition for cultural domination: for example, it is the unification of the linguistic market that creates dialect, bad accents, dominated languages.[9]

This thesis marks a radical break with Weber and his process of rationalization, also with Elias and his process of civilization. I can go some of the way with these two authors, who are the most important as far as the state is concerned, but they miss one aspect of the universalization process, concealing – or concealing from themselves – the fact that this unification is at the same time a monopolization. The second process, which I shall describe in another year, is the transition from the personal state to the impersonal (or partly impersonal) state, from the dynastic state embodied by the king to the state that I call semi-bureaucratic, to the extent that there remain in the bureaucratic state as we know it – this is another break with Weber – traces of the dynastic state. That is why I called my last book *The State Nobility*: there remain in bureaucratic societies transmission mechanisms of economic and cultural inheritance by the mediation of the family which have a certain resemblance to the mechanisms that were the condition for the reproduction of the dynastic state.

Having presented my thesis so that things will be clear, I shall now make the case for it. In what way can the unification process be described as a process of universalization? The construction of differentiated and relatively autonomous fields (economic field, cultural field) is accompanied by a unification of the corresponding spaces (economic market, cultural market) and the construction of a unified space. The construction of the state itself, as the holder of a meta-capital that enables it to partly dominate the functioning of the different fields, is accompanied by the construction of a unified social space. When I wrote in my article on 'Social space and the genesis of "classes"'[10] of a global social space (in opposition to fields) as a space of spaces, a field of fields, I was in fact referring to the national social space that is constructed at the same time as the state is constructed, that the state constructs as it constructs itself.

The genesis of the dynastic state on the basis of feudal principalities may be described as the transformation of fiefs with a personal basis into a province with a local basis, of direct powers between the lord and his dependants with a personal basis into an indirect power on a territorial basis, often exercised by the mediation of delegates. The establishment of the dynastic state is accompanied by a transformation of the divisions that previously existed: where there were provinces alongside one another, entities that existed in and for themselves, these provinces become parts of the national state; where there were autonomous rulers, there are delegated rulers who hold their power from the central state. A double process is under way: a process of establishing a unified and homogeneous space, such that all points of the space may be located in relation to one another and to the centre, on the basis of which the space is established. This kind of centralization reaches its limit in the French case (though it is also true for the English or the American state). This unification of space, the development of which is accompanied by the birth of a central power, implies the unification and uniformization of both the geographical and the social space. This unification has a negative characteristic, it implies a work of de-particularization. People speak of regional and linguistic particularisms; what is specific to centralization is that the dominant modes of expression are de-particularized, and non-official cultures made into more or less accomplished forms of the dominant definition of culture. The particularisms associated with localization in social or geographical space are abolished, with the result that, from autonomous elements that can be thought in and for themselves, they become constituent elements of a part that can be referred to a central norm.

Jus loci and *jus sanguinis*

By saying that the genesis of the state is accompanied by the establishment of a unified territory, it is not made fully clear what is encompassed in the idea of territory and in the fact that the establishment of groups no longer has personal relations as its principle, what could be called *jus sanguinis*, the personal tie between chief and subjects, but *jus loci*, the law of place, belonging to the same territory. In the end, cousins are replaced by neighbours. This is an extraordinary change. In Kabylia [under colonial domination], there was a conflict at the local level between two principles of unification, that of clan and that of territory. The French administration, which was centralist, territorialist and localist, had imposed the village unit. The village that I worked on, however, was composed of two clans with an agnatic basis: all members saw themselves as descendants of the same ancestor, as cousins – the terms of address used were terms of kinship, and they had genealogies in common that were more or less mythical. At the same time, the village unit combined two moieties in a unit with a territorial basis, and there was thus a kind of floating between the two structures. I had a good deal of trouble understanding this because, transposing the local structure into my unconscious, I was unclear about this territorial unit – the village – which, at the end of the day, did not exist. Alongside the family, the clan and the tribe, the village unit was an artefact that ended up existing as a consequence of the existence of bureaucratic structures – there was a town hall . . . In many societies, you still have this seesaw between two forms of belonging, belonging to a lineage group and belonging to a place. The state thus establishes a unified space, and makes geographical proximity predominate in relation to social, genealogical proximity.

(Social segregation arises when social principles of distribution by income and culture coincide with local principles of division. An article on Fifth Avenue in New York, very intelligent but at the same time naive, describes a unit with a local basis that is the apex of all possible fields and their intersection.[11] Sociologists are very often trapped because units with a local basis, sanctioned by administrative boundaries and with an objective and subjective existence – censuses are conducted in such a way that a street exists, because the postal system sorts by streets – obstruct the view of the genuine principles of construction of reality, which have either a genealogical basis, as in precapitalist society, or a social one, structured in fields. I offer this little parenthesis to show you that what I have just been saying was not a general *topos*, abstract and basically rather commonplace. These commonplace things hide important theoretical issues.)

The transition from the fief to the province is accompanied by a total change in the mechanisms of domination. The provincial government – this is true of the great empires of antiquity, of the Chinese empire – has no genuine autonomy in relation to the centre except when empires break up, and in this case a province may revert to being an autonomous fief. In certain cases, the former province of an empire may continue to enjoy the myth of central legitimacy in order to arbitrate struggles between provincial leaders. The provincial government has no genuine autonomy in relation to the centre whose directives it executes. By the same token, local officials – that is one of the big changes, as large empires are formed – do not have to be locally based, but are recruited outside the territorial foundation of their power. That was the case with China; in France this rule is still applied to bishops.

This is a very significant index of bureaucratization, the aim of which is to counteract in advance temptations of nepotism, particularism, as well as the temptation to draw on locally based genealogical resources to challenge the central power – in short, to transform the province which is simply part of a whole back into an autonomous fiefdom that exists in and for itself. Either rulers are appointed from another locality, or populations de-localized, a frequent practice in the ancient world: the aim of these massive deportations was to break the genealogical bond in favour of the territorial relationship. This all leads to consideration of the opposition between *jus sanguinis* and *jus loci*, which is a very important opposition and one still alive today, particularly in current discussions – greatly fogged up by the media intellectuals I was speaking about earlier on – about immigration, the Islamic veil and secularism. There is always a question of this duality of the principle by which identity is constituted: *jus sanguinis*, the fact of being a descendant of someone who was a member of the nation, as in the German model, or *jus loci*, the fact of being born on the territory, as in France. Concerning the first aspect of the process of statization, universalization, I would say that in one sense *jus loci* is more progressive, more universal than *jus sanguinis* to the extent that it offers more abstract and formal criteria of belonging, less freighted with the ideology of blood and soil . . . Expressed in this way, this is completely at the level of what I criticized earlier on; but if you bear in mind everything I said elsewhere, and that I cannot return to now without making an enormous bubble that would destroy the logic of my argument, you can put substance behind what I am saying in a rather peremptory way.

Unification of the market in symbolic goods

As it constructs itself, therefore, the state unifies and universalizes. This double process could be traced for each of its spaces, in particular for the economic space, with the creation of a unified market. Polanyi emphasizes the fact that state policy – mercantilism, for example – was indispensable for counteracting the tendency of markets to a local particularism. He co-authored a very fine book on markets embedded in kinship or social relations.[12] In this he described societies in which market relations are not yet established as universal, independent of the contracting agents, being still subordinated to the social imperatives that govern their operation. The market such as we know it, which economists accept as universally given, as nature, is in fact an artefact largely constructed by the state. One of the contributions that sociology can make to economics, without claiming to correct it or challenge it, is to recall that a notion treated by economists as natural is in fact a historical and social construction that can be more or less complete.

The same holds also for the cultural market. I shall dwell on this a bit more, as it is here that you can see the opposition I mentioned earlier on between the aspect of monopolization and the aspect of universalization.

Much emphasis has been placed on the existence of a kind of historical link, apparent everywhere, between the construction of a national society and that of a system of education based on the idea of universal educability, which was a progressive conquest of the Reformation (everyone has the right to read and write) and the Enlightenment. This idea of the universal educability of the individual goes hand in hand with an egalitarianism of decision that consists in treating individuals as equal in rights and duties from the cultural point of view. It goes along with the attribution of the educational function to the state. For citizens to be worthy of the name, the state has to give everyone those elements of education that will enable them to perform the rights [and duties] of citizens in an enlightened manner. And the great reformers of the nineteenth century, such as Jules Simon, stressed the link between minimal political capacity and education.

(This connection has been completely forgotten, so much so that when I recalled a few years ago that the capacity to formulate conscious and controlled opinions was closely connected with the level of schooling, and that consequently many opinion surveys carried out an act of force by omitting non-respondents and acting as if all social subjects were equal in the face of the questioning, I triggered a crisis and a great amazement simply because there is a kind of amnesia about the genesis:[13] people have forgotten what the object of debate was in the late nineteenth century, and the possible functions of perpetuating social order that were allocated to the school system. What was a conscious stake of struggle at the moment the institution was established was very quickly forgotten – sometimes the sociologist only reawakens and organizes the return of the repressed.)

There is thus a connection between the unification of the national state and compulsory education, a connection established via the idea of universal educability related to the idea of the duties of the enlightened citizen, with the state having to fill the gap that may exist between education and talent. The objection is then made that the school is not an institution of domination but of integration, as its function is to give everyone the instruments of citizenship, of being an economic agent, the capacity indispensable for [minimal participation in] different fields. In fact – this is the second aspect – I would say that the school effectively is an instrument of integration, but it is this integration that makes submission possible.

To sum up, then: the state is an instrument of unification that contributes to the social processes in question (culture, economy) gaining a higher degree of abstraction and universalization. In all cases, it contributes to prising them away from the particularity of the local and establishing them at a national level. Many of today's debates – on nationality, on the integration of immigrants, etc. – bear on these problems in a confused way. This ambiguity inherent to the state means that it is impossible to take a simplistic position on the problem of nationalism, since nationalisms, like the nation, always have two faces – both regressive and liberating. This political conclusion makes it very hard to evaluate national movements: they have our sympathy if they are liberatory but they can also lead to unhappiness. I had a discussion with Eric Hobsbawm, who cannot be suspected of conservatism, in which he told me that one could no longer support nationalisms. He said this naively, as one might when talking in a café. The unease that certain nationalisms arouse may be based on this ambiguity that I am in the process of describing.

The first face [of the state], therefore, is that of universalizing integration; the second face is that of alienating integration as a condition of domination, subjugation, dispossession. And the two faces are inseparable. The unification of the market – cultural, economic, symbolic – has a reverse side, a counterpart. This involves the dispossession that is inscribed in the imposition, on the unified market, of the recognized domination of a mode of production or a product. This is immediately understandable on the economic level. I will give an example to show you how this statement that may strike you as speculative has very concrete applications. In one of my first projects I studied the phenomenon of bachelorhood in Béarn; this has since become a fashionable journalistic subject, but at the time it was unknown in more central places. I noted that the peasants of a certain generation, even relatively large proprietors, were no longer able to marry, a fact lamented by the old women who were responsible in the division of labour for marrying off their sons. The little country dance that I already mentioned struck me as an embodiment, a material realization, of the matrimonial market. [Whatever] economists [say], the [actual] market on Place Maubert has something in common with the [abstract] market that they are talking about. I saw this dance as an embodiment of the matrimonial market. There were young women dancing with young men of a more urban appearance, often office-workers or soldiers from the parachute regiment's nearby barracks; and on the edges, peasants (recognizable by their demeanour and their clothing) who watched without dancing. I analysed [in this] little market the appearance of a new kind of product: men able to dance, to speak to girls, dressed for the town, who took away from the peasants their 'traditional object'.

This dance was an embodiment of the unification of a market for symbolic goods on which women circulated. Still today, in many milieus, women are circulating objects, preferably moving upward: as a woman, you marry someone older and with a higher social position. This market was the manifestation of the unification of a market with a local basis that had until then been fenced off by a kind of protectionism. There were local matrimonial sites that I studied by way of genealogies: each agent had a set of potential partners, their 'promised' – a magnificent word – that is, individuals to whom they had been promised, and who had been promised to them according to statistical laws helped by social norms and the work of 'matchmakers' [who were] their mothers. This market of the 'promised', on which male peasants had a value (their bodily *hexis*, their way of speaking), was a protected market. 'He's a fine peasant' meant that he had good land, no matter how he walked, how he was dressed, how he spoke . . . This protected market was then swallowed up, with the school system and the new means of communication, in a larger market. Just as handmade pots are supplanted by enamel basins, so the unification of the market in symbolic matrimonial goods has cast out to the sidelines, to the edge of the dance, those who had nothing to offer but a prewar bodily *hexis*, a peasant *hexis*. It is not by chance that 'peasant' has become a motorists' term of abuse. Peasants have become 'peasant oafs' . . .

That is a very concrete example of the link between unification and domination. In order for peasants to become 'peasants', in other words for them to lose out on the markets where they used to have a privileged value, their market had to be annexed to the national market, a whole work of unification had to be performed, largely by the school but also by the media. Subjugation and dispossession are not opposed to integration, this is their very condition. This rather complicated mode of thought is difficult because we are so accustomed to seeing integration as the opposite of exclusion; it is hard to understand that in order to be excluded, just as in order to be dominated, you have to be integrated. If you take the example of the Algérie Française campaign, why did those most unfavourable to integration become champions of Algerian integration at a certain point in time? Because dominating the Arabs necessitated integrating them and making them into 'wogs', a racially despised dominated group. Nothing is simple in the social world, and I am not complicating matters for the sake of it – I often even regret, after a lecture, that I simplified terribly in relation to what I should have said.

I took the example of the matrimonial market, but it would also be possible in the same way to take the unification of the linguistic market.[14] Pronunciations perceived as 'wrong' are the product of the unification of this market. In a Derridean play on words, we can say that there is a connection between capital and the capital, and that the capital, by producing itself as the site of concentration of all the species of capital – the extreme being Faubourg Saint-Honoré – produces the provinces. The provincial is stigmatized a priori: he is backward, ignorant, speaks with an accent, etc. The production of the state implies the production of the provinces as a lesser existence, as the deprivation of [everything done in the] capital. By the same token, the provincial [is endowed with] an inferior symbolic capital: to accede to the species of capital [that he lacks], he has to make an effort that seems like aping.

The ape metaphor is very pertinent. There is a very fine text in the *Tales of Hoffmann* that I often cite: a German chancellor had the idea of educating an ape; the ape dances the minuet, converses with ladies, but he can't prevent himself from leaping up when someone cracks a nut . . . Here we have the founding parameter of racism: the provincial knows what he is and tries not to be it, and this is precisely how he is seen to be provincial. The concentration of capital produces the capital, and the provincial then finds himself defined by the lack of all the monopolies associated with residence in the capital. The integration of those dispossessed of capital is the condition for a form of dispossession and a form of subjugation.

Analogy between the religious field and the cultural field

I shall rapidly mention the constitution of religious capital, as I believe this is the paradigm of all forms of dispossession. It is no accident that the [French] word for non-clerics is *'profanes'*. It is clear in this case that it is the constitution of the church that generates the profane. That is already implicit in Weber, but strangely he never saw that aspect, for reasons that were personal (though he saw so many other things that it is impossible to criticize him, as so many things I am able to notice are thanks to him. I don't want to act clever on his shoulders . . .). When Weber describes the construction of the body of clerics, he sees very well that this is accompanied by the religious dispossession of the laity; in other words, it is the cleric who establishes the layman. It is impossible, as Weber put it, to become a 'religious virtuoso' without constituting other people as profane and hopeless in religion. The opposition between religion and magic that Durkheim mentions, without noticing what I am saying here, is the opposition of masculine and feminine, dominant and dominated. For example, when there was the *aggiornamento* [of Catholic liturgy] in the 1960s, [priests] did not abolish rituals such as lighting candles or taking water from the magic spring at Lourdes, but they transfigured them by asking the common laity who were constituted as profane to spiritualize them. The analogy with culture is self-evident.[15] I wanted to write a paper comparing popular painting and popular religion; there is exactly the same opposition, cultivated/uncultured, clerical/lay, expressed exactly in the same terms, and it was not accidental that the *aggiornamento* was accompanied by a clean-up of churches in conformity with the aesthetic canons of the clergy. The institution of the church, of legitimate religion, with a work of codification, purification and rationalization on the part of the clergy, multiplies the distance between the laity and the clergy – the clergy holding the monopoly of the reading of sacred texts. (Marxologists do the same: Althusserianism was largely the restoration of a clerical monopoly over the reading of [Marx's] texts, which moreover no one reads any more if they are not Marxologists.)

All of this about the religious field should be transferred to the cultural monopoly that the school [arrogates to itself]. The school is to the cultural field what the church is to the religious field, and so everything I have said can easily be transferred. The state's school institution is the holder of the monopoly of legitimate education, that is, the transmission of legitimate culture, or rather the constitution of culture as legitimate by the transmission of this corpus in legitimate modes (the classics are the canonical authors of culture), with the legitimate sanction of the acquisition of this corpus by examination. The school, which is the most advanced form of monopoly in the cultural domain, also has a reverse side of dispossession: the school system produces the uncultured, the culturally dispossessed. This is something that people working in the educational system do not like to hear, myself first among them, but that's how it is. You have to

explain why it is like that. Because of unequal access to a system theoretically charged with universally inculcating a culture that claims to be
universal, the universalization of cultural demands – what one is entitled
to demand in terms of culture – is not accompanied by the universalization of access of the means to satisfy these universal demands. There is a
gap between the universal distribution of cultural demands and the very
particular distribution of the means to satisfy these demands. It is this
gap that makes integration, in the case of the school, inseparable from
domination.

Let me just mention again a simplification that caricatures my analysis
of the school system in an uncomprehending fashion. There are hierarchies
of cultural legitimacy, [. . .] an objective social order that means someone
who cites Dalida in their exam gets zero marks and someone who cites
Bach gets 18: that is not something I have to take a position on. People
confuse a statement that Weber called a 'statement referring to values'
with a 'value judgement'.[16] In reality there are values, which the sociologist refers to and records: not to be aware of and recognize a hierarchy
of values would make reality absurd. Confusing reference to values with
value judgements, the latter are attributed to the sociologist, though all
he is doing is refer to values [that exist in reality]. The people who do this
are those particularly caught up in struggles for legitimacy: they are often
the 'poor whites' of culture – that's how I call them, rather nastily, since
I also have to defend myself against those who go overboard in cultural
orthodoxy and have the greatest difficulty in tolerating the objectivation of
cultural hierarchies. Avant-garde artists, for their part, tolerate sociological objectivation very well, often making use of it for artistic coups – to the
displeasure of sociologists . . .

The process of constitution of the universal is accompanied by a process
of monopolization of the universal and, by the same token, a process of
dispossession of the universal which can correctly be described as a kind
of mutilation. If the sociology of culture has a critical dimension, if it may
seem very violent, this is because it brings to light, for people who see
themselves as humanists, the fact that part of humanity are dispossessed
of their humanity in the name of culture. If it is true that culture is universal, it is not normal that everyone does not have access to the universal,
that the conditions of access to the universal are not universalized. Instead
of saying: 'Bourdieu says that Aznavour is as good as Bartok', they should
say: 'Bourdieu says that culture with a universal claim, universally recognized as universal in the limits of a definite universe, is distributed in such
a way that only a part of those legitimately entitled to it in the name of
an ethical norm (egalitarianism) actually have access to this universal; a
very large part of humanity are dispossessed of the most universal conquests of humanity.' That is a fact, and it is normal to point it out. If I
was taking a normative position, I would say: 'Be consistent and don't
say that Bourdieu wants to relativize everything, that the integral calculus
is no better than the multiplication table; say that Bourdieu maintains

that if you want to take seriously the analyses that point out this kind of distribution, you have to work politically to universalize the conditions of access to the universal.' Even those problems recognized as political can be raised in a rational way, though that may do nothing to advance their solution . . .

What I wanted to say today is that historical analysis of the development of the state brings to light a fundamental ambiguity of this kind: both the negation of particularism, of regionalism (transcendence of everything in this that may be narrow, wretched, cramped), and, at the same time, the construction of monopolies by way of unification. Neither Weber nor Elias raises the question of state monopoly, which must be raised because it [is raised in] reality itself. If the state has the monopoly of legitimate violence, who has the monopoly of this monopoly? If it is true that the process of statization is a process of universalization, concentration goes hand in hand with monopolization by a certain category, those whom I call the state nobility. Those who are in a position to appropriate for themselves in a privileged manner the monopolies associated with the existence of the state have, if not a monopoly, at least a power of pre-emption over the state monopoly.

The state produces a dominant nationalism, the nationalism of those with an interest in the state. It may be discreet and polite not to assert this in too outrageous a manner. The state produces among those who are victims of the second face of the process, those who are dispossessed by the construction of the nation-state, induced and reactive nationalisms: among those who had a language and now only have a stigmatized accent (such as the Occitans). Many nations have been built upon the inversion of a stigma. These induced and reactive nationalisms inspire ambiguous feelings in me. They are clearly completely legitimate, to the extent that they seek to convert stigmas into emblems. For example, you might think that the Basque waiter who serves you a beer in Saint-Jean-de-Luz speaks French well for a Basque, or think that he speaks French with a disgusting accent . . . That's a considerable difference. But what to do about it? Do you have to be Basque? The ambiguity of two nationalisms is inherent in the process of construction of the state.

Is this process, which we are obliged to note as inevitable – it is associated with all known examples of the state – really universal? Could we not imagine, being entitled to a controlled utopia based on the study of realized cases, paths towards the universal that were not accompanied by a monopolization? This question was put by eighteenth-century philosophers in a manner that was both refined and naive. I shall end by offering you a very fine text of Spinoza, by way of thanks, as Lacan would say, for attending in both senses of the term:

> A dominion then, whose well-being depends on any man's good faith, and whose affairs cannot be properly administered, unless those who are engaged in them will act honestly, will be very unstable. On the

contrary, to insure its permanence, its public affairs should be so ordered, that those who administer them, whether guided by reason or passion, cannot be led to act treacherously or basely. Nor does it matter to the security of a dominion, in what spirit men are led to rightly administer its affairs. For liberality of spirit, or courage, is a private virtue [*virtus*]; but the virtue of a state is its security.[17]

Year 1991–1992

Lecture of 3 October 1991

A model of the transformations of the dynastic state – The notion of reproduction strategies – The notion of a system of reproduction strategies – The dynastic state in the light of reproduction strategies – The 'king's house' – Juridical logic and practical logic of the dynastic state – Objectives of the next lecture

A model of the transformations of the dynastic state

Having described [in the last two years] the concentration process of different species of capital that accompanies the birth of the state, I would like now to try to trace the transformation, effected over centuries, of the personal power concentrated in the person of the king into the diffuse and differentiated powers subsequently associated with the idea of the state. The process I am going to describe today could be called, to give you an overall pattern, 'From the king's house to raison d'état'.[1] How does the transition take place from power concentrated in an individual, even if signs of differentiation, of a division in the work of domination, are apparent right from the start, to a power that is divided and shared between different persons with relations of competition between them, conflictual relations within what I call a 'field of power'?[2]

I shall try to construct a model. As I have said several times, I do not have any ambition to compete here with historians, and as I always say without false modesty, I am aware of being unable to draw on the historical culture that would be needed to completely validate the model I propose. I want to construct both a model of the logic of the dynastic state, the state identified with the person of the king and the royal lineage, and a model of the process by which this state is transformed. I want both to describe the logic of the dynastic state and the contradictions that are inherent in its functioning, contradictions which, as I see it, bring about the supersession of the dynastic state in favour of impersonal forms of state.

In order to construct the model of the dynastic state, I shall draw on work that I carried out a long time back on the peasants of Béarn. If I permit myself to do this, it is because this work has since served as a basis for historical studies, and I believe that a certain number of historians, in particular Andrew Lewis whom I shall refer to here, have drawn on anthropological work of the kind I conducted in order to understand the logic of functioning of the royal family. Also – how can I say this without being arrogant? – my work on kinship in Béarn[3] marked a certain break with the tradition that was dominant at the time I conducted it, this being the structuralist tradition. My work aimed to show that far from being, as people thought, the product of conscious rules or unconscious models, matrimonial exchanges were the product of strategies guided by the 'interests' of a house. Since this work, Lévi-Strauss and others have spoken of 'house systems',[4] to refer to the type of kinship relation that can be observed in such places as south-west France. These house socie-ties are societies in which the family father is called *capmaysouè*, 'head of the house'. The king is a *capmaysouè*, a point that I shall return to, a head of the house, and heads of houses are in a sense the agents of an instance that transcends them and is called the house. In Béarn, for example, a person is known by his forename followed by the name of the house. People say 'Jean of So-and-so's place.'[5] In a certain sense, the subject of individual actions, matrimonial actions, is the house, which has interests that transcend those of individuals, and must be perpetuated both in its material inheritance – lands, etc., which must particularly be kept from division – [and in its] symbolic inheritance [which] is still more impor-tant: the name must remain free of any stain, it must avoid degradation, derogation, etc.

It is not by chance that it was American sociologists and historians who transferred onto royalty a model developed for the lowest strata of French societies. This was undoubtedly because there were unconscious resistances on the part of [French] historians – though they were all in love with ethnology, ethnology was all the rage with them – to apply models developed for the most backward regions of rural France in order to understand the summits of the state. There were other obsta-cles as well, and I believe that in the face of these problems, historians often swing between two poles . . . I was going to say two errors: that of assimilating former societies by an unconscious anachronism, or on the contrary relegating them to an absolute exoticism. In fact, it is only necessary to see that a very general model can account for phenomena that are seemingly very different, following the logic [that] the same cause produces the same effects. When you have a lineage that has a material and a symbolic inheritance – an inheritance which in one case is called 'crown', and in another case 'house' – that has to be perpetuated through time, you observe practices with very similar logics; and the social agents, whether they are kings of France or small proprietors of 15 hectares, will exhibit behaviours that are relatively intelligible according to the same principles.

The notion of reproduction strategies

On the basis of this model, I developed the idea of a system of reproduction strategies, which I would like to explain a bit, as it is indispensable for understanding the use I shall go on to make of the model. I tried to give a methodical formulation in *The State Nobility*,[6] where I very rapidly explain what I understand by a system of reproduction strategies, stressing on the one hand the idea of 'system' and on the other hand what precisely should be understood by 'strategies'. To start with 'system': I believe that in order to understand the conduct of royal or non-royal houses, and more generally of all social agents, certain practices that social science has studied separately have to be seen as constituting a whole, practices that are generally [assigned] to different social sciences: demography for fertility strategies, law for strategies of succession, the science of education for educational strategies, economics for economic strategies, and so on. With the notion of habitus, which is a generative principle of systematic behaviours, I try to account for the fact that, in order to understand a certain number of fundamental human behaviours that are oriented towards the preservation or elevation of the position in social space occupied by a family or an individual, you have to take into account a certain number of strategies that are seemingly unrelated, strategies without a palpable connection [between them].

I shall give a list of these strategies.[7] First of all they involve fertility: family planning strategies, for example,[8] which may be practised by way of matrimonial strategies – here you can immediately see the link between the different strategies. It is very well known how in many societies one of the ways of controlling births is to delay the age of marriage. Fertility strategies may be practised either directly or indirectly. Their function, in the logic of reproduction, is to reduce the dangers of property division; thus there is a clear relationship between the practice of limiting births and succession strategies. Then there are succession strategies in the strict sense, which are often governed by customs or laws of succession. In the peasant families of south-west France, for example, just as in royal families, the right of primogeniture, the right of the first-born, reserves succession to the eldest to the disadvantage of the younger, and solutions have to be found to provide for the latter. In Gascony, younger sons were the victims of a succession law that condemned them to be what the Béarn peasants called 'unpaid domestics', without a wage, or else 'émigrés'. Succession strategies may dictate fertility strategies, as the two are interdependent. Then there are educational strategies, in a very broad sense of the term: in relation to kingship, the education of the dauphin must be borne in mind. In his book *Royal Succession in Capetian France*, Andrew Lewis lays great emphasis on the mode of succession as a function of succession strategies, on the privileges granted to the heir and the compensations that must necessarily be made to the younger sons: apanages, etc. But as there is no explicit idea here of a succession strategy system – and I believe this is precisely why the effort of modelling is worthwhile – he does not take educational strategies into account at all.

Now, in order for a system such as the one I am going to describe, and that Lewis dissects, to function, agents have to be prepared to make it function, they have to be appropriately disposed. Paradoxically, heirs are not always spontaneously disposed to inherit – something that will not surprise those who have been listening to me for a long time, but for those among you who are newcomers, you will be surprised to hear that one of the problems for societies with inheritance is to produce heirs disposed to let themselves be inherited by this inheritance. A few years back I wrote a long commentary on Flaubert's *Sentimental Education*,[9] in which the principal hero, Frédéric, is precisely an heir who does not want to inherit, and who because of this constantly swings between breaking with his inheritance – he wants to become an artist – and accepting it. This is a paradox that people tend to forget, since you spontaneously think, in a naively critical view of the social order, that heirs are only too happy to inherit. But that is not true at all, there are unwilling heirs at all levels of the social scale: sons of miners, for example, who don't want to go down the mine, though far fewer than you might believe, precisely because the system of reproduction functions; and there are also sons of kings who have no desire to inherit or who behave in such a way that they do not really inherit the inheritance, that is, they are not what they should be to qualify for inheriting.

The role of educational strategies is thus absolutely capital, as a real work of inculcation is needed to produce a king who wants to inherit and is qualified to do so. It is very clear, when you think of the education of girls in societies in which the capital of honour is very important, how fundamental a strategy the education of girls is in the system of reproduction strategies: it is by way of girls that dishonour comes, or excessive fertility, etc. In these societies, the obsessional gaze directed at the virtue of girls is easy to understand as an element of the reproduction system. I spoke of educational strategies, but I could easily expand at length on the relationships between the different strategies that I list for purposes of analysis, even though they are all interdependent. Those strategies that I call *prophylactic* become very important in certain societies, such as our own: they are strategies aiming to ensure the perpetuation of the lineage in a good biological condition, as it were. Medical strategies, for example, with health expenditure, are also important: these are strategies by which labour-power and reproduction power are reproduced.

I come now to the more obvious strategies that one thinks of right away: economic strategies in the strict sense, such as strategies of investment, saving, etc., which are an element of the system. To the extent that the inheritance consists of land, a material patrimony, economic strategies to perpetuate the house require strategies of hoarding, investment, accumulation, etc. There are also strategies for the investment and accumulation of social capital, that is, strategies aiming to maintain relationships already established. In societies such as the Kabyle, for example, a very large part of the work that agents perform is a work of maintaining relationships with kinfolk in the very broad sense, whether kinship established by alliance or kinship established by succession; this work, which consists in visits, exchange of gifts and presents, etc. is extremely important inasmuch as it is in this way that the family's symbolic capital is perpetuated. Having a large family, for example, means being able to have a funeral procession of three hundred people, including two hundred men firing guns. [In these societies], processions and all group exhibitions are rather like demonstrations in our societies: exhibitions of symbolic capital, that is, a social capital built up by years and years of cultivation, exchanges, polite gestures, etc., which can be displayed when the need arises, for example when it is a question of manifesting the solemnity of a marriage or making a marriage arrangement.

The accumulation of succession capital is thus very important, and matrimonial succession strategies are only possible on the basis of methodical strategies of cultivating social capital, strategies that are clever, continuous, etc., and often attributed to women. [. . .] I wrote a paper on masculine domination[10] in which I developed a number of things, but I had not yet considered [. . .] one dimension of the division of labour between the sexes that is still very strong in our own societies: that which consists in ascribing to women the work of maintaining social relations, while men [concentrate on] succession strategies. These strategies of maintaining the social capital are ascribed by the division between the sexes primarily to women in the majority of societies; I dare not say all, because there is always the possibility of an exception. For example, there are some very amusing American articles that studied the stereotype according to which women spend their time on the phone – that's a stereotype in all modern societies. By studying telephone bills, they observed that the stereotype did indeed correspond to a certain reality, that women do spend a lot more time on the phone. But as good scientists, they were not satisfied with recording the same silly facts that can be found in the spontaneous magazine sociology we are deluged with every day. They tried to understand why this was the case, and discovered that in the majority of families, and all the more strongly as you go lower in the social hierarchy, the maintenance of family relations is ascribed to women, including relations with the husband's family. The wife sends greetings cards, rings up on birthdays and holidays, etc. We see then how the idea of a social investment strategy is important to give a status to all this invisible work. Women's work is always invisible . . . The Kabyles always say: 'Woman is like the fly in the whey, she busies herself and no one sees what she does.' The work of maintaining social relations is not only invisible, it is taboo: 'She spends her time on the phone, what on earth is she doing, etc.' [. . .]

I will come back now to matrimonial strategies in the strict sense, which are clearly a key element. I do not need to dwell on the fact that in many societies they are the main locus of [the house's] investment; it is by marriage that material patrimony can be increased, and especially symbolic capital – allies can be gained, etc. Matrimonial strategies are therefore the object of constant investment, of extraordinary attention, refinement and virtuosity well beyond the capacity of most ethnologists – that's why they have created mathematical models, it was far simpler . . .

Then I have a final category that I call strategies of sociodicy. To explain very rapidly, this is a word I made up following Leibniz's term theodicy.[11] Theodicy is the justification of God, and sociodicy is the justification of society. This notion indicates strategies whose function is to justify the fact that things are as they are. What is vaguely put under the notion of ideology, which is so vague and muddy that I prefer to avoid it and replace it by sociodicy – it's rather barbarous, but more precise. Strategies of sociodicy denote the whole work that a group does [in this respect], from the family up to the state. [People forget this,] but there is a whole work intended to justify that the family is the way it is, a symbolic order of the family that is constantly maintained by a discourse and a mythology. There are official foundation myths such as marriage, etc., but also family legends, family albums – a very fine work could be done on the family album, the family vault . . .

To recapitulate, fertility strategies, succession strategies, educational strategies, prophylactic strategies, economic strategies, social investment strategies, matrimonial strategies, sociodicy strategies. This is a big list, but I believe it is important. If you want to have more details on the relationships between these different strategies, I can refer you to [part IV of] *The State Nobility*.[12]

The notion of a system of reproduction strategies

[We come] now to the notion of a system. A system means that these different strategies share the same objective intention. Seen from outside, by an observer, they appear to be the product of a systematic intention, and there is an affinity of style, something in common . . . I often use an analogy that I borrowed from Merleau-Ponty:[13] you recognize someone's writing whether he writes in ink, with a fountain pen, with a metal nib, with a pencil, in an exercise book, on a blackboard, etc. There is a stylistic unity, a kind of physiognomy, by which you recognize handwriting. I think that the products of a habitus are of the same type, they have an affinity of style, or as Wittgenstein says, a 'family resemblance'.[14] It is no accident that Wittgenstein's metaphor here refers to the family.

All the strategies I have just mentioned, when they are carried out by a family, have a family resemblance inasmuch as they are inspired by the same apparent intention. Why is this? Because at the root of them are the same generative habitus and the same constraints, or the same objective ends. Whether we look at the Béarn peasants or the royal family, the object is to perpetuate the house or the crown, that is, a reality that transcends individuals and is irreducible to them, individuals being simply its temporary embodiment, which has precisely to be perpetuated beyond these individuals. The word strategy often gives rise to misunderstandings, as it is very strongly associated with a finalist philosophy of action, the idea that adopting a strategy means defining explicit ends in relation to which present action is organized. This is not at all the meaning I give to the word; I believe that strategies refer to sequences of action that are ordered in relation to an end without having the objectively sought end as their origin, without the objectively sought end being explicitly posited as the end of the action.

This is a very important question, and not at all a mere detail. [. . .] Andrew Lewis correctly criticizes those historians who [adopt] a false philosophy of action: we are spontaneously intentionalist, especially when other people are involved, and above all, of course, when the royal family is involved, who seem to have had no other end than to increase the kingdom, so that it reaches the state in which they have handed it down to us. [Lewis emphasizes] – I am saying this in a crude and vivid way, he puts it in a far more elevated fashion – that the construction of France should not be seen as a project that was carried forward by successive kings. The example of apanage is something I have added myself, but there are historians who argue over the institution of apanages – compensations that are given to the younger son who has been disinherited in favour of the elder. There are historians who condemn apanages and say: 'That was stupid, it led to the dismembering of the royal state, it's a shame, France would be bigger if it had not been necessary to give the duke of Burgundy a bit of it.' The finalist philosophy of action, in other words, which is the spontaneous tendency of understanding human action, can be reinforced by unconscious investments, naive interests. This naivety is immediately swept away if you bear in mind that there can be strategy without the [explicit] existence of ends. The subject of strategies is not a consciousness that explicitly posits its ends, nor an unconscious mechanism, but a feel for the game – that is the metaphor I always use: a feel for the game, a practical sense [guided by] a habitus, by dispositions to play not by rules, but by the implicit regularities of a game in which one has been immersed since early childhood.

For example, I read this morning the account of a scene in which François I convened a *lit de justice*:[15] the chancellor told him, in the name of the Parlement, certain things that displeased him, and suddenly, against all expectation, he stood up and left. No precise details are given, but I would have liked to know whether someone said to him: 'Sire, you have to leave', if he got up because he thought that his royal dignity was being infringed and he could not listen to this, because if he stayed he would give legitimacy to a contention that would tend to increase the power of the Parlement in relation to his own, etc. Historians do not even ask such questions, and perhaps they are right . . . but it is certain that there was a reason, because later on [the king] met with his counsellor and came up with a strategy to confront the Parlement and give a retrospective meaning to what may well have been a sudden impulse – an impulse that is a gesture of habitus, such are often inscribed in strategies – [. . .] an unreasoning anger, perhaps also the strategy of someone who no longer has a strategy. Anger is often the strategy of the poor, of people unable to respond on the level of words . . . I can't say any more on this, but [you see] how actions, whether those of François I or of a peasant negotiating the marriage of his son, may have every appearance of being what they would be if they were calculated, yet be the product not of calculation but of what is better called mood, a sense of dignity, etc.

Strategies and systems of strategies, these are the two main notions that I think I have explained. There remains that of reproduction, [which refers to] systems of strategies geared to the perpetuation of the position of the social entity in question in social space.

The dynastic state in the light of reproduction strategies

Having set up the instrument of analysis, I can now move quickly on to describing the dynastic state, which is a state in which reproduction strategies are the essential part of what this power does. Wars of succession, for example, are located in a succession strategy: [they are bound up with] fertility and – like all great rituals of symbolic exhibition – with the reproduction of symbolic capital. Having set up the model, I think it is possible to explain in a systematic and economical way the whole behaviour of the governing powers at a certain moment, at a certain state in the development of the state.

To return to Andrew Lewis's book *Royal Succession in Capetian France*: I shall give you a simple summary of this and then take his argument further. He criticizes the teleological view based on what Bergson calls the 'retrospective illusion', which consists in endowing France with a project that was borne forward by successive kings. His thesis is that royal family and succession to the throne are inextricably linked and indissociable; in other words, it is the mode of succession, what I call the mode of reproduction, that defines the kingdom. The truth of the whole political mechanism lies in the logic of succession.

Royalty is a hereditary *honor*,[16] and the state is reducible to the royal family. To cite Lewis: 'In the absence of ethnic or territorial unity, nationalism meant allegiance to the king and crown, exaltation of the royal line was susceptible of conflation with praise of the French people.'[17] The dynastic model was thus established in a kind of consecration of the royal family, and this consecration had a number of consequences. In order for the royal family to perpetuate itself, in a constant or expanded form, hereditary transmission in the agnatic line was necessary, that is, transmission through the male, by primogeniture, the right of the eldest and priority given to the transmission of the patrimony over any other imperative. According to Lewis, this model was invented bit by bit in the royal family, and gradually generalized to other feudal lords inasmuch as it offered a convenient solution to a common problem, that of perpetuating the patrimony while avoiding division as far as possible. Among the Béarn peasants this was an obsession, division had to be avoided at all costs. One of the ways [of doing so] was to have a single child, or a boy for inheritance and a girl for exchange – that was the ideal . . .

If it had been possible to control fertility, everyone would have wanted a boy first of all and then a girl, the boy to inherit and bring in an heiress, then a younger girl to maintain relations with another family by marrying an heir. But the hazards of fertility mean that there can be, for example, men who have six daughters, which is a catastrophe from the standpoint of the strategies and sense of the dynastic game, especially if one is set on having an heir at any cost; a very good player may manage to get by, he can make a lot of allies, but it's a very poor move. And there are families who pay the cost of bad fertility strategies for four or five generations, acts of love or chance that give a father six daughters. It is clear that in many cases succession strategies exist to catch those who fail in fertility strategies. Recently I read an article by a Japanese demographer who was inspired by this model, and studied with very refined statistical methods the connection between fertility strategies and succession strategies in Japan[18] – and it works well. It is impossible to understand these purely demographic questions without bringing them into relation with other strategies.

The right of primogeniture is an obvious way of protecting inheritance against fragmentation, but the younger sons also have to be compensated: apanages were intended to ensure harmony between brothers against the threat of division. Here again, further development is needed. There were other solutions: going into the army or the church in the case of noble families, emigration for peasant families, or again the solution, an extreme result of upbringing, by which the younger son, or especially the younger daughter, remained in the family and served as an unpaid domestic, loving the children of her brother as her own, etc. There are some very fine texts on this subject, and I think there is far more to develop on phenomena of domination within the domestic unit. I said just now that there is a sociodicy internal to the family – a younger son who stays at home and works for his brother is one of the most extraordinary successes of this ideology – all this expressed in the form of love, love of family, of the children, of the brother's children, the sense of solidarity, etc. The apanage, in the case of royal families, was likewise a compensation intended to limit conflicts within the domestic unit. And this problem of relations between brothers is a very thorny issue in many societies. Arab societies have a system of equal division balanced by joint possession, the relationship between brothers is one of the sensitive points of the social structure, to the point that marriage with a parallel cousin [a paternal one, that is, the daughter of the father's brother], which is a kind of exception in the universe of possible matrimonial exchanges, seems to me one of the means to perpetuate cohesion between brothers beyond the causes for conflict bound up with the potentialities of division, etc.

Apanages thus constituted a solution . . . As against those historians who deplore apanages, with their theological view of the expansion of the greatest possible France, Lewis shows how apanages were quite indispensable for perpetuating the unity of the royal family. I shall return to this, as it is one of the contradictions that all nascent states have to overcome: the contradiction arising from conflict between brothers, legitimate heirs according to dynastic logic, and on the other hand, contradictions between legitimate heirs and the holders of technical power, whom the main heir often supports against his brothers. Here you have the grand vizier, if you like. The grand vizier – perhaps Iznogoud[19] comes to mind, but that's not a good example . . . think rather of Bajazet,[20] that's a bit better – is someone who has a lifetime power that will die with him, who is already very powerful, to whom power can be delegated as he is unable to hand it down, and [to whom it is delegated] to prevent those from having it who, if they did, would indeed transmit it. I shall return to this very shortly. Contradictions within the dynasty are thus extremely important, and the principle of the dynamic that leads to the supersession of the dynasty.

I return now to the book [by Lewis] and the family strategies of the Capetians: the principal *honor* and the patrimonial lands went to the eldest son who is established as heir; the younger sons are then endowed with territories, apanages that are acquired territories (not counted in the patrimony). The Greeks had two words to express this: what is held as hereditary property, and what is acquired in the lifetime of the head of the family. The new acquisitions were given in the form of apanage. Lewis's book is indeed important, but from the standpoint of the system of succession strategies it stops rather short, as the only strategies he deals with are those of succession: he writes as if the centre of all actions of perpetuating a patrimony was strategies of this kind, whereas there are all the others, as I am going to explain. Having thus told you about Lewis's book, which you can look at yourselves if you want, I shall try to develop on the basis of this inspiration a rather more complex model of the dynastic state.

The 'king's house'

One of the characteristics of the dynastic state is that the political business is not separated from the domestic unit. This distinction was made by Max Weber in relation to the birth of capitalism: he emphasized that this was accompanied by a separation between business and house, a separation often expressed in a difference in space. It is a characteristic of the dynastic state that political business and domestic business are not separated, hence the expression 'the king's house', and this continued to a quite advanced stage. Marc Bloch, for example, in his book *Seigneurie française et manoir anglais*, says that the medieval *seigneurie* was based 'on a fusion between the economic group and the group of sovereignty'; just as Georges Duby, speaking of medieval property, says that 'Power is encompassed in the domestic sphere.'[21] The term *'enserré'* that he uses here is similar to Karl Polanyi's notion of 'embedded', meaning that in precapitalist societies the economy is immersed in kinship relationships, in the domestic world. In this model, in other words, paternal power is both the centre of the whole power structure and the model by which all power is understood. In traditional Kabylia, for example, politics was not constituted as such, so that using the word 'politics' is anachronistic in so far as any possible relationship, through to the level of the confederation as a whole, which was a kind of assemblage of tribes, was conceived on the model of kinship relations, relations between father and son or between brothers. The family model here was the principle of construction for any possible social reality.

Here again – I refer to Duby – power rests on personal and affective relationships that are socially instituted: that is a quite classical theme in the Durkheimian tradition. Marcel Mauss wrote a very famous article on laughter and tears,[22] [in which he showed that] affective relations are socially structured. Duby takes the example of three notions: fidelity, love and credence – three virtues, we could say, three dispositions that lie at the foundation of the original state order as he describes it. He shows that these three notions are both socially constructed and socially maintained. Credence, for example, must be maintained by largesse, generosity. It has been said a hundred times that aristocratic generosity is economic calculation in the symbolic domain.

The state is thus merged with the king's house. To cite Duby again: 'The king is still the head of a lineage.' Duby uses this expression in relation to Philip the Fair: he was the head of a lineage, surrounded by his close relatives. The family was divided into chambers, which were specialized services accompanying the king in his movements. Power clearly tended to be treated as a patrimony that was hereditary in terms of domestic logic, and the dominant principle of legitimation was genealogy. Genealogy is the ideology of a domestic-type unit. The most characteristic features of the model we can construct of this type of functioning all follow from this unit of power in terms of a house: the head of the house is socially mandated to perform what could be called a 'house politics' – politics being the word that must be put in quotation marks. Matrimonial strategies, which were central to this, have the function of increasing the patrimony of a lineage in both material and symbolic form.

It is possible then to explain the mystery of the transcendence of the crown in relation to its holder, over which so much ink has been spilled. There is Kantorowicz's very famous text on *The King's Two Bodies*. I admire this book very much and have cited it dozens of times, as he puts his finger on something very important. In fact I tend increasingly to believe that the mystery of the king's two bodies is simply the mystery of the transcendence of the house in relation to those who inhabit it – the house as *domus*, a building, endures beyond its inhabitants. Anyone who

wants to work on the sociology of household consumption has to deal
with this. When people buy a house,[23] it's not the same as buying a car,
even if psychoanalysts see the latter as involving a lot of baggage. A house
is freighted with a tremendous historical unconscious, largely because
the house is a dwelling, something that has to last, that guarantees the
endurance of the family and that can only endure if the family endures;
you have the family album, the family vault, etc. The head of the house is
in some way the temporary embodiment of this transcendent unit that is
the house, and his actions can be understood on the basis of this principle.
That goes without saying for matrimonial strategies, which in the case of
royal families are often motivated by territorial annexation. I took the
example, given my limited historical knowledge, of the Habsburg dynasty,
but I could have taken a hundred others. The Habsburgs are a very fine
example: they increased their patrimony without any war at all, by a series
of judicious marriages. Maximilian I acquired Franche-Comté and the
Netherlands by his marriage with Mary of Burgundy, daughter of Charles
the Bold. His son Philip the Handsome – who wanted a symbolic capital
as well – married Joan the Mad, queen of Castile, and that created the
great empire of Charles V, etc. Unfortunately, after Charles V the logic of
division set in again, and succession logic undid what matrimonial strategy had done: after Charles V the division between Philip II and Charles's
brother Ferdinand I, etc. Peasant histories are also full of similar stories
of division . . .

A very important part of matrimonial strategies bears on strategies of
reproduction, and the same holds for succession strategies [. . .]. I refer
you here to a book I have cited several times, *Genèse de l'État moderne*,
in which there is an article by Richard Bonney[24] that gives a long list of
wars of succession, the root of these being conflicts associated with the
interpretation of succession law, war being a way of continuing succession
strategies by other means. In many cases, war was a succession strategy
deploying violence. A very large part of dynastic strategies can be understood in this way, as likewise can strategies of reproduction. [. . .] I have
anticipated myself in giving you the model, you can apply it yourselves. It
is clear that a considerable part of the educational policies of royalty and
nobility, for example, can only be understood in the logic of the system of
strategies of reproduction.

Legal logic and practical logic of the dynastic state

The dynastic state has a practical logic, and is constituted step by step with
successive inventions that historians can date. The solution of apanages is
discovered, it is fine-tuned, Salic law is established. In parallel with this,
the case of Béarn peasants is of great interest for our analysis, as it allows
us to see dynastic strategies uncontaminated by the work of lawyers that
I shall come on to mention. These are dynastic strategies in the practical

state, even conducted against the work of lawyers, in the way that these Béarn peasants succeeded in perpetuating their strategy through to the twentieth century against the civil code which forbade primogeniture; they managed to get round the legal logic.

The dynastic strategies of royal houses were theorized and rationalized by legislators – here I believe an important distinction has to be made, after reading many historical works that put strategies in a practical state in the same bag with the explicit legal rules governing succession customs, and I believe it is in the transition from a practical logic to an explicit ideology that we can see the difference between a dynastic state and an absolutist state. (Those who know this must think I am being extremely bold here, and those who don't know [won't see] the interest. I am somewhat embarrassed, but there is a big debate over absolutism. For me, absolutism, at least what is known as absolutism, is perhaps the fact of having transformed, with the aid of Roman law which lends itself to this, a practical logic of the dynastic type into a legal logic with birthright, etc.)

Jurists are very involved in this work [of rationalization], they are committed to it because, in the elementary forms of division of the work of domination, they are among the first agents outside the royal family. Jurists therefore have every interest in legitimizing and being legitimized, acquiring autonomy by virtue of the power of legitimization that they have. They make use of the power that they have of legitimizing the monarchy to legitimize themselves as able, for example, to make remonstrations to the king: 'It is in the name of how I justify you that I am justified to say that you are not justified in doing this . . .' But the juridical work is partly a work that accompanies the exercise of power: Roman law makes it possible to legalize, as it were, the dynastic principle, and express it in a state language – when I say 'state' here I mean what is already universalized in a state language, that of Roman law, which lends itself to this by the notion of blood and birthright, for example. Already with the Capetians, you see the appearance of the first signs of this work of legal rationalization of lineage practice, the royal family beginning to be established as an entity legally guaranteed by the state. That is when 'princes of the fleur de lys', 'princes of the blood royal', were first invented, the fifteenth-century 'princes of the blood'. The metaphor of the royal blood, based on principles of Roman law, became central as a justificatory ideology, and paradoxically this justificatory ideology became increasingly indispensable – [a point] I shall develop next time. One of the contradictions of dynastic logic is that it has to coexist and fit together with a non-dynastic logic. Jurists do not reproduce themselves by heredity, at least not officially, but there is heredity of the kind we still have today, through the school system. Despite all kinds of phenomena such as the purchase of offices, etc., there was the coexistence of two modes of reproduction: the one that was founded on birthright, and the mode of reproduction of royal functionaries, particularly jurists, which was of a different kind. This conflict, which jurists help to resolve even though they raise it by their own existence, seems to me to be one of the factors – there are others as well – in the change and development from a dynastic state to a state that I do not at the moment have an appropriate word for, but is more 'depersonalized'.

Objectives of the next lecture

I shall attempt next time to describe these contradictions more precisely, and give a kind of phenomenology of them . . . This is both very hard and rather bold, but after all, I have already given a kind of phenomenology of a process that we find very difficult to conceive, because all our categories of thinking are its product. What is a delegation of signature, for example? Or the appending of a seal? What is a 'keeper of the seals'?[25] Why is there both a king and a keeper of the seals? I shall try to analyse this kind of gradual division of the work of domination . . . Unfortunately, historians are not very attentive to this, except legal historians who have the merit of being more so – I am thinking of Maitland, whom I make much use of.[26] These historians discovered the role of symbolism, for example, in the exercise of power (I often say that history, beneath its triumphant airs, is a science much dominated by the other social sciences). There have been canonical articles that have served as a basis for a great deal of work, but I believe that unfortunately they are not of intellectual interest for constructing what I believe should be constructed, that is, the kind of everyday work of the state bureaucracy, the high state bureaucracy. The king signs, the keeper of the seals countersigns: what does this counter-signing mean, who is in charge?

Finally, I want to describe this kind of genesis, this creation of a chain of signatures guaranteeing signatures, this chain of agents who are both controllers and controlled, responsible and not responsible. What I shall be saying is risky, but perhaps it can serve as a programme for one or other of you who wants to go and look at the documents, as I think there is [material] worth looking at . . . I shall thus say some uncertain things, continuing what I have said today.

Lecture of 10 October 1991

The 'house' model against historical finalism – The stakes of historical research on the state – The contradictions of the dynastic state – A tripartite structure

The 'house' model against historical finalism

I want now to take up my argument where I left it, and try to show you why I see it as interesting and important to demonstrate the functioning of the royal institution as a house.

The 'house' model is important in two respects. It makes it possible, first of all, to pose in a clear fashion the question of the genesis of the political from the domestic, and secondly, to account for dynastic strategies in the political domain. There are two problems that I want to raise. The first was brought up by Andrew Lewis's book that I cited to you last time, a problem that may appear naive, but that shows a certain necessity provided it is reformulated: who or what is the subject of the process of concentration of the different species of capital that I described to you last year? Is the subject of this process naively the king, as certain historians suggest, or is there a subject that transcends the person of the king? I will refer you to a book here: Cheruel's *Histoire de l'administration monarchique en France*.[1] This is an immense work, and very useful for the information it provides. But it very naively adopts the position I mentioned, placing the will of the king, the Capetians and their successors to build up the royal domain at the origin of the process of state construction, and does not go beyond the explanation that France was made by the monarch's intentions. And even in a more recent work on France conducted by a collective of historians,[2] you can see in an implicit state this constant idea that there is a kind of subject that made France. We can then ask quite simply whether questions as naive as that, which underlie historical research, should not be challenged in order to bring out a number of problems that they hide.

In this particular case, I believe that to understand the process of concentration you have to introduce two major factors. The first is what you could call 'house thought', as people spoke of 'Mao Zedong thought': the way of thinking in terms of the house is, I believe, an explanatory principle for a whole set of seemingly disparate strategies – as I said last time in relation to the system of reproduction strategies. And there is nothing natural about this way of thinking, it is a historical way of thinking that developed in certain traditions more than others. For example, I have recently been reading a book on a Japanese house, a book that has just been published in the Terre Humaine series.[3] This describes wonderfully well the whole history of a Japanese family, whose principles of operation are completely of the type that I analysed in my last lecture – thinking in terms of the house, the house being a reality that transcends those who occupy it, at the same time a building, a patrimony, the whole of the lineage, etc. This kind of entity transcending individuals can be the subject of a number of actions that continue over a long period of time: one of the characteristics of the house, which is so self-evident that I forgot to mention it, is that the house is durable: the main characteristic of the house is its claim to perpetuate itself in being, its claim to endure. And a large part of the actions it [demands] on the part of those who inhabit it is precisely [that they should act] beyond their temporal interests, beyond their own existence.

This kind of transcendent entity – and the type of thought that it inculcates in those who belong to it – seems therefore to be the real subject of the concentration process, rather than the royal will. But in order to understand how this will transcending the king was able to accomplish itself in history, I believe it is necessary to raise the question of the particular assets that the king has at his disposal. Strangely enough – perhaps as an effect of my ignorance – I have never seen this question put clearly. [Historians say] always: 'the king of France, that is, the person who became king of France', prevailed over the other feudal lords; economic assets are investigated, etc., but I think that the question of knowing in what way the fact of being the king could be an asset in the struggle against the feudal lords who had the particularity of not being the king is not clearly put. In other words, the explanatory principle I am proposing – which may seem derisory since it is purely symbolic – one of the explanatory principles for the success of the king is simply that he was the king, that is, that he occupied that particular place in the game that is the place of the king – which is the name I shall give to this subject: the king's place. I shall explain [this point] a bit more, as it is less obvious than it appears.

I said just now that no one, in my belief, has put this question clearly. If there is one exception, it is Norbert Elias, and I shall quote you a passage where he does so. But the reply that he gives is to my mind purely tautological; as I am not absolutely sure of what I am saying here, where a very great thinker is involved, I shall read you the text and you can judge for yourselves. Elias calls this the 'law of monopoly':

> If, in a major social unit, a large number of the smaller social units which, through their interdependence, constitute the larger one, are

of roughly equal social power and are thus able to compete freely – unhampered by the pre-existing monopolies – for the means to social power, that is, primarily the means of subsistence and production, the probability is high that some will be victorious and others vanquished, and that gradually, as a result fewer and fewer will control more and more opportunities, and more and more units will be eliminated from the competition, becoming directly or indirectly dependent on an ever-decreasing number.[4]

So what he is saying is: where there are several people struggling, there is one who wins, and power is concentrated. Why is it concentrated? Because it is concentrated . . . You can read it again: 'there is a high probability that some will emerge victorious in this combat and others will be defeated, and that the opportunities will end up falling into the hands of a small number, while the others are eliminated or fall under the rule of the former.' This is the iron law of oligarchy . . .[5] I do not think that Elias's solution is very satisfactory, but he does have the considerable merit of raising the question, and perhaps without him, I would never have done so.

You have therefore a kind of feudal field, a set of social agents in competition, having fairly similar assets in terms of resources, military capital, economic capital, etc., to list once again the species of capital that I have presented. But there is one point in which they are inferior: under the heading of symbolic capital, they precisely lack [the one property that distinguishes them from others], that singularizes them, that is, the power to call themselves king. I will cite Duby here, in the preface he wrote for Lewis's book: 'The king holds a power that is semi-liturgical in nature, and that places the sovereign apart from his rivals, the other potentates.'[6] The 'power of a semi-liturgical nature' is certainly important, the king had a power by divine right, but others too were always anointed, sacred and consecrated. That said, I believe that if it is agreed that there was a liturgical specificity, the reason this had its effect is that it was specially applied to someone who was singled out and whose particularity was marked by the fact that he received a particular anointing. What I see as important, therefore, and what Duby indicates, is the fact that the sovereign is apart from others.

I apologize for not explaining at the start that besides what I call the 'king's place' there are other arguments. The king clearly has other assets that have been emphasized by historians. He combines sovereignty – in the logic of Roman law, a sovereignty that canon lawyers granted him – with suzerainty. He can thus play a kind of double game. He can play the monarch in terms of feudal logic, that is, demand feudal submission, and also claim the particularity he is given within the feudal logic by the fact of being different from the others. He can thus make use of the very logic of the feudal game to change the feudal game, which is a familiar paradox: you have to make use of a game to change its rules. So he can make use of the feudal logic transformed into dynastic logic, as

I pointed out in the last lecture, in order to accumulate patrimony and increase his difference. But as well as these arguments that are generally used, I add the fact that he managed to achieve an initial accumulation of symbolic capital bound up with the effect of his distinction: the king is thus a feudal chief who has this particular property of being able, with a reasonable chance of success, to see his claim to be king socially recognized. In other words, to use Weberian vocabulary, the king is the person able to claim, with a prospect of being believed, that he is king – and symbolic capital, if you remember, is a capital based on belief. He can thus say that he is king with the prospect of having this accepted. I shall refer here to a recent discovery by economists who, in order to describe a phenomenon such as that which I have just described, speak of 'speculative bubbles': these are situations in which a social agent is justified in doing what he does because he knows that other social agents grant him that he is what he claims to be and has the right to do what he does; it's a kind of game with mirrors. The logic of the symbolic is always of this type.

As these arguments are rather complicated, I shall present them slowly by reading my text. The king is justified in believing himself king because others believe he is king – that is rational, there is a rationality in the economy of the symbolic. In other words, a small difference is enough to create a maximum gap inasmuch as this little gap differentiates him from everyone else. And this symbolic difference, to the extent that it is known and recognized, becomes a real difference inasmuch as each of the feudal lords must reckon with the fact that the other feudal lords reckon with the fact that the king is king. I'll repeat this sentence, as it's a summary: each of the feudal lords, everyone other than the king, is defined simply by privation, by the fact of not being the king; each of the feudal lords must reckon with the fact that he is not king and that the others reckon with the fact that the king is king.

(I believe this is a very general model and, if you reflect on it, you can apply it to many spheres that function by the symbolic, such as the intellectual field for example. Why was Jean-Paul Sartre the dominant intellectual in the intellectual field in the 1950s? Because others had to reckon with the fact that others reckoned with the fact that Sartre was the dominant intellectual. So these are very complicated processes, and it is hard to understand how they come into being ... I often use a paradigm to describe struggles among intellectuals. I shall present it here because it's quite funny: it's an experiment of [Köhler], a psychologist who worked a lot on the intelligence of apes. [Köhler] explained how one day he had the idea of suspending a banana out of the apes' reach. At a certain moment [one of the cleverest apes pushed another] under the banana, climbed up on him and caught the banana; and suddenly all the apes were there, with one paw in the air trying to climb up on the others, but no one wanted to be underneath, as they'd all understood that you had to be on top ... [7] This strikes me as a metaphor for intellectual struggles . . . If you bear this metaphor in mind when you attend these intellectual debates, it will give you a great deal of satisfaction as well as freedom, as you will not be tempted to raise your paw, you'll be much more controlled. This is what the intellectual field is like. Each person says that he would like to reckon with the fact that others reckon with the fact of his being first. These processes, which are endless circles, end up coming to a kind of halt. There are phenomena of initial accumulation, people who accumulate and accumulate, and from that point on they no longer need to raise their paw: everyone understands that they've accumulated . . .)

I think this is a very general model; and it is no accident that the paradigm of the king is so powerful in people's unconscious. Everyone knows the astonishing role that the paradigm of the king plays, to the extent that the king is the person who succeeds in imposing on the others the representation he has of himself. People all dream that other people will think the same of them as they do of themselves [. . .]. Now the king is the person who, as Weber again said, is able to believe that he is king with a good chance of success; he's a madman who takes himself for king, but with the approval of others. There's a kind of circularity . . . *Homo homini lupus, homo homini deus*[8] . . . The king is the person with divine power to impose his own representation. Here you could reflect on the role of art, or more precisely on the relations between art and power. Characteristic of the king is that he can have equestrian statues, that is, impose objective representations of himself that impose his view of himself and a dominant viewpoint – on horseback, etc. He constructs and he imposes his own construction as universal: he is in a position to universalize his particular view of himself, which is a tremendous privilege, very similar to divine privilege: he is his own perception. I will not develop this paradigm any further, it is hard to do so in the form of improvisation, but it would certainly be possible to develop a whole symbolism that was more or less deduced from this model – the Sun King, etc. A whole analysis of the king should be developed, as the place where the infinity of judgements that people have of one another comes to a halt: the place where truth about oneself, subjective truth and objective truth coincide. The king is this kind of last instance, last appeal: the person who is always above the above, beyond the beyond.

So as to show you that this model is not simply speculative, but corresponds to a certain reality, one of my audience here has kindly provided me with a bibliography on the subject of royalty in India; and in one of the books cited, I found a very precise application of this model of the king's place.[9] In this book, which I am not able to summarize because I do not have a sufficient grasp of it, [Muzaffar Alam] describes the decline of the Mughal empire. I assume [that he] goes against the traditional Indian historiography that generally presents the decline of this empire as a process of political fragmentation associated with economic decline. For [Muzaffar Alam] this pessimistic view conceals the process of an emergence of a new order, a new structuring, and this new structuring, if I understand correctly, is seen as based on the permanence of the king's place, in the sense that the local chiefs who struggle against one another, and draw a certain advantage from the weakening or demise of the imperial authority to strengthen their own authority and local autonomy, continue in fact to perpetuate a reference to – I translate here – 'what is at least the appearance of an imperial centre'. In other words, what remains of the empire is the idea that there is an empire and that the empire has a centre. From this fact, the occupant of the central position is placed in a superior position. In order to legitimize themselves, to legitimize a conquest or an abuse of power, the feudal lords are obliged to make some kind of reference to the centre, which remains the site of legitimation:

> In the conditions of unlimited military and political adventurism that accompanied and followed the decline of the imperial power, none of the adventurers was strong enough to win the allegiance of the others and replace the imperial power. All struggled separately [this is the idea of the metaphor of the apes raising their paws] to make their fortune and mutually threaten each other's position and success. Only a few of them could still establish their rule over others, when they sought validation or institutional legitimation of their seizures; and for this they needed a centre to legitimize their gains.

This is an illustration. If the king did not exist, he would have to be invented.

It seems to me that this is what this story shows. When rival powers confront one another, the fact that among these powers one emerges that can assert itself as pre-eminent, as different, is enough to establish it as an obligatory reference. And this kind of effect is an important element in accounting for the process of concentration that I was explaining to you. I said that there is a relationship between capital and the capital; I could also have said that there is a relationship between centre and concentration. But this is not a hypothesis that I invented: the concentration process results partly from the fact that there is a centre. This has the appearance of a tautology, but I think it is not the same as Elias has it: the fact of being the centre gives an advantage in the struggle for concentration – being the centre in the sense that I explained, that is, the recognized centre, rather than simply central in the geographical sense. But if it does turn out that someone is central geographically as well, I believe this gives further advantages. That then is the first question I wanted to raise, and I believe that considered in house terms, combined with the model of the king's place and the traditional explanations of historians that I rapidly mentioned (suzerainty, sovereignty, etc.), it is possible to understand why centralization took place in favour of the king even without any centralized will on his part.

The issues in historical research on the state

I want now to raise a second set of problems, which is more central from the standpoint of the logic [of the model]. Why is it interesting to study the genesis of the state, as I have been doing for several years, and what is the issue at stake in this historical research? The issue is to contribute to explaining the genesis of the state, that is, the genesis of the political as a specific logic. To say that the royal house, until a late date in the history of both France and England, had domestic strategies as its politics, means describing as political things that are not political, that are not yet established as political. To say that a war of succession is the succession strategy of a house is saying that war is not established as politics; and saying that matrimonial strategies are inspired by the concern to perpetuate a house amounts to saying that the break between the person and royal family and the state apparatus has not been made, etc. It is important to press the hypothesis of functioning as a house to the limit, to try and see what it cannot explain. [In the example of] Louis XIV, [this means] taking everything he did (in foreign policy, internal policy, etc.) and seeing everything that the model of functioning as a house allows us to explain, the residue being, as I see it, the first manifestation of the properly political – what I will not be able to explain is what I shall call 'properly political'. To present things in a different way, I told you last time that the argument I was proposing could be called 'From the king's house to raison d'état' . . .

There is a book I shall speak to you about by Étienne Thuau on raison d'état,[10] on the genesis of discourse of a 'raison d'état' type as a discourse of legitimization that brings in the state principle as justification of the king's actions; the appearance of this discourse is based on a break with house logic. I shall come back to this book, which shows how the notion of raison d'état appears among jurists who base themselves on the one hand on Tacitus, on a tradition of pessimistic history, and on the other hand on Machiavelli, to try and give justifications for state policy that are not purely personal, but either state or ethical. To the extent, for example, that house logic is an ethical logic, a morality (to put things in crude and simple terms, 90 per cent of what we count as morality, as I see it, is house thought), to invent a political logic it was necessary to break with house logic and say: 'In this case it is not enough to obey, the king cannot be satisfied with obeying his feelings; he might well have wanted to pardon de Thou,[11] for example, but he had to execute him.' Raison d'état is stronger than house reason, stronger than sentiment, pity, charity, feudal love, etc. It is therefore this process that I want to describe, in the context of the extremely long transition period that began in the twelfth century.

In my last lecture, I quoted to you texts in which historians show how, from the twelfth century on, you could see the appearance of a legal type of thinking that began to escape from the traditional logic of the house, even if only by rationalizing this. Part of this legal discourse consisted in dressing up house thought in Roman law. But giving reasons for obeying house thought already meant breaking with house thought. Merleau-Ponty has a very fine phrase about Socrates: Socrates was annoying because he gave reasons for obeying, and if you give reasons for obeying, that means it is possible to disobey.[12] To give reasons for house thought already means positioning oneself at a point from which house thought has to be justified. And the fact of justifying it already means opening the door to the possibility of heresy or transgression. That is the difference between *doxa* and orthodoxy. Basically, house thought in the Béarn style is what I call doxic thought, as the contrary is unthinkable; the assertions of *doxa* are assertions that have no contrary; this is how things are, it's tradition, there's nothing to say about it, 'lost in the mists of time', as the keepers of Béarn customs say – things were like that even before human memory. Traditionalism begins when tradition can no longer be taken for granted. As soon as people say that there is tradition or that tradition must be respected, this means that tradition is no longer taken for granted; as soon as people start speaking of honour, it means that honour is finished; as soon as people speak of ethics, it means that the *ethos* no longer holds – *ethos* is part of what is 'taken for granted' . . .

This work, in which jurists play a key role by making *doxa* into orthodoxy, reminds us that law is an orthodoxy. It's a *doxa* that people say is right, a right that people say is right, a 'must-be' that does not assert itself simply by the fact of being, in the mode of 'what is done', but a 'what is done' that asserts itself in the mode of 'what must be done'. The transition from *doxa* to orthodoxy, in which jurists are fundamentally involved, culminates in the construction of something completely different, that is, raison d'état. There is a very fine book by Pierre Vidal-Naquet entitled *La Raison d'État*,[13] written during the Algerian war, in which he asks the question whether the state is justified in some cases in invoking its own reason, deemed to be above morality, to transgress morality, practise torture, etc. Raison d'état is this kind of reason that goes beyond moral reason – that is the whole problem – that is, beyond house reason. That's it.

What I am going to study, not in detail because that would obviously need many hours of analysis, is the origin of this very long transition that leads from 'house reason' to raison d'état. This process of transformation comes up against tremendous difficulties. You get the impression that the specific logic of the state never completely frees itself from the logic of the house . . . And it is still not finished. When people speak about corruption, nepotism, favouritism, you see the problem that there is with public reason. When I entitled my book *The State Nobility*, it was to say that the state can be appropriated by people who use the state as people use an inheritance, and who have the state as their inheritance. There is always a temptation of regression from raison d'état to 'house reason'. The great transgressions of public morality are almost always bound up with reproduction strategies: it's for my son, my uncle, my cousin. And 'house reason' is always there in the dark background of raison d'état. That is what I wanted to analyse (even though a detailed historical analysis of the process goes beyond my competence; there are professors here who teach it). I will try to raise the question of this process, which is not self-evident, and even if I seem to you to be treading water and going slowly, I believe I am still going too fast. We are so accustomed to all this that we are not sufficiently surprised at the difficulty involved in this transition. From time to time, people say about African states: 'Oh, those new states are terrible, they haven't emerged from the household, there's no raison d'état', and that is called 'corruption' . . .

This extraordinary difficulty of establishing a specific state logic [relates to the] process of autonomization of a new type of field, as there is autonomization of the literary field, the scientific field, etc. Each time, a new little game is set up, within which extraordinary rules begin to function – by 'extraordinary' here [I mean] *extra-ordinary* in Weber's sense: rules that are not those of the ordinary world. In the ordinary world you have to be kind to your parents, supportive of children, etc. As opposed to this [. . . it is a well-known fact that] 'the government doesn't give presents': whereas in relations between a father and son, for example, a good father should give presents, and reciprocally – which is a transgression in the public order. What is involved here is the invention of a field in which the rules of the game are at odds with the rules of the game of the ordinary social world. In the public world you don't give presents; in the public world you don't have a father, a brother or a mother – in theory . . . In the public world (as in the New Testament), you repudiate the domestic or ethnic ties through which all the forms of dependence and corruption [manifest themselves]. You become a kind of public subject, whose definition is to serve the reality transcending local, particular, domestic interests that is the state.

It is this then that I will try to describe. What are the factors [. . .] that worked to promote this transition from domestic reason to raison d'état? The first is the fact that the very logic of the house has something that brings it into an affinity with the logic of the state. And in order to understand the famous paradox of the king's two bodies analysed by Kantorowicz, you need only make use of house logic: there is the house and there is the king. In other words, to the extent that the house is a kind of body – in the sense of what the scholastics called *corpus corporatum*, a corporation – belonging to a house means acquiring the logic of the 'thought of the house', devotion to the house, to an entity that transcends its agents. To a certain extent, during the entire process of transition – from the king's house to the state – the ambiguity of the house undoubtedly favoured, even in the king's own mind, slippages from devotion to the royal house, to the dynasty, which is at the same time the crown, the state, etc. In other words, the very ambiguity of the notion of the house as a reality transcending the individual has to be taken into account in order to understand this transition to the constitution of a transcendent entity. I have in mind the famous phrase of Louis XIV, which is certainly apocryphal: '*L'État, c'est moi.*' That amounts to saying: 'the state is my house'.

UNIVERSITY OF WINCHESTER
LIBRARY

This thinking in terms of house is [subsequently] objectified, canonized, codified by juridical discourse. I shall proceed more quickly, but I think that this factor is decisive. I read to you [in a previous lecture] a text of d'Aguesseau,[14] a great magistrate, one of those characters I shall be speaking to you about later on, one of the great inventors of the state – these are people who made the state because they had an interest in making the state – and what struck me particularly in d'Aguesseau's text, at the very moment I was reading it (though I did not understand this myself), was the fact that he moved seamlessly from a modern logic – he spoke of the republic, the *res publica*, the public, etc. – to forms that I felt were premodern, giving the notion of the state meanings that I found archaic. In fact, the transition between the two logics was present even in his own mind.

The contradictions of the dynastic state

Today I simply want to insist on what can be called the specific contradictions of the dynastic state [. . .]. To put things simply, [. . .] the house logic contains contradictions that lead to a superseding of dynastic thinking.

[. . .] Because Roland Mousnier, given his philosophy of French history, his political positions, etc. was attentive to things that the more Jacobin, more 'French Revolution' historians did not see, he was able to note in French institutions, down to a very late period, the survivals of models of action that are typically patrimonial, typically domestic.[15] For example, he laid great emphasis on the relationship between protector and creature – we understand this immediately, as it still exists: to be someone's creature means to [owe] one's social existence, one's bureaucratic career, to another person. This relationship between protector and creature is an example of the tendency of house thought to become generalized and annex politics. Dynastic thought does not just prevail as a principle of behaviour aiming to perpetuate the royal lineage and its patrimony; it becomes the general mode of thinking that is applied to everything: every human relationship tends to be conceived according to the domestic model, as a relationship of brotherhood, for example, or of father and son, etc. The protector/ creature relationship is an example of an annexationism in which house thought becomes the principle of all political thought. There are no social relationships that cannot be subsumed under these domestic categories. This is still visible today, even with movements that are seemingly most free from any dynastic thought, such as trade union movements, etc., [and their use of the] concepts of brotherhood or sisterhood: these domestic notions are invasive, and by the same token they prevent the constitution of properly political notions (such as that of citizen . . .).

I shall quote here a most interesting text [by Richard J. Bonney] on the relationship between patron and client that is consubstantial with the dynastic state at a very advanced state: 'It is the system of patronage and clientele that constituted the driving force behind the facade of the official system of administration, which is certainly easier to describe.' In other words, there is the appearance of a modern bureaucracy. 'This is because patronage relations, by their very nature, escape the historian.' They are not handed down in the texts, whereas bureaucracy is intimately connected with writing, law, etc. 'The importance of a minister, however, or of an intendant of finances or a royal councillor, depended less on his title than on his influence – or on that of his patron. This influence derived largely from the individual in question, but more still from patronage.'[16] Patronage is also capital here, a capital constituted around a personal name. Family logics underlie the bureaucratic structure, and in fact – the point I want to make – they contribute, by the contradictions they generate, to promoting the process of bureaucratization.

I shall explain very quickly two major contradictions of the dynastic state. The first of these is that the king expropriates private powers for the benefit of a private power. Hence the necessity of universalizing this particular case. One of the functions of the legists and jurists who act as ideologists for the king is to universalize this particular case and say: 'This particular case, this private, is not a private like the rest, this private is public.' And in this way, by this kind of pious hypocrisy – the notion of 'pious hypocrisy', as I have said at least a hundred times here, is extremely important for understanding the social world:[17] one could say, like the theorists of ideology, that jurists mystify to the extent that you have to mystify yourself in order to mystify, the hypocrisy here is pious – they contribute to developing a discourse that is the very negation of what they legitimize, that is, that if it is necessary to de-privatize the private in order to legitimize it, this is because the non-private is better than the private. That is the ambiguity of these ideological discourses: the public is invented in the effort to resolve the contradiction in the private property of dispossessed private properties.

The second contradiction, which is the most important, is that the king and the royal family perpetuate a mode of reproduction of the domestic type, a mode of reproduction with a family basis (the inheritance is handed down from father to son, etc.), in a world in which a different mode of reproduction is in the process of being established: the mode of reproduction of officials, which takes place via the education system. Very early on, from the twelfth century, the first state clerks were graduates who could appeal to their competence against the dynastic type of authority. This meant the establishment at the heart of the state of an opposition which is analogous to a classic opposition in business history, as formulated by Berle and Means:[18] the theory of the separation between owners and managers. Berle and Means developed the idea of a transition from the age of business owners to the age of managers, with businesses being the site of a struggle between owners and officials or technicians. At the heart of the state structure there is an opposition of a similar kind, which should of course not be reified. You have therefore, on the one hand, the heirs whose power rests on the dynastic principle, on blood, on nature, on transmission essentially through blood, and on the other hand you have the managers, that is, those who, in order to found their authority, have to appeal to other principles of authority, which are merit and competence.

I found in my notes something that Bernard Guenée said in *L'Occident aux XIVe et XVe siècles*: until the end of the fourteenth century, officials boasted of their loyalty, you were still in the logic of personal dependence, political relationships being conceived after the model of household relationships; but from then on, they began to boast of their competence[19] – competence being a principle of autonomous authority, basically with its own logic. From a certain point in time, in fact right from the start, the holders of a dynastic power, in order to triumph over their dynastic rivals, were obliged to obtain the services of the holders of military, technical, bureaucratic competence, etc.: they were obliged, therefore, in order to defend the dynastic principle, to draw support from people whose existence relied on a non-dynastic principle. Paradoxically, I was saying just now that the logic of parties (in which you can see a survival of house logic in a political state) led the king to make use of public resources to buy the leaders of parties; in other words, the royal treasury was used to make gifts. This means that bureaucratic logic is both inevitable – something that the dynasty cannot do without – and at the same time is antagonistic to the dynasty in its very principle.

D'Aguesseau's text is quite astonishing, if you have a good memory: he sketches out a kind of theology, an ideology of the clerk whose power is not that of blood but rather of competence. And in this text, he slips seamlessly [from one principle to the other]. *Noblesse de robe* can at the same time be a [genuine] nobility; you are caught up in extraordinary contradictions, which as I see it are constitutive of the division in the work of domination.

A tripartite structure

I will now give you in a few words a diagram that I found very illuminating, and that I can explain very easily. You will see then a structure with the king, the king's brothers, and all the dynastic rivals, that is, the other feudal lords, etc.

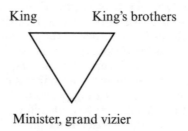

King   King's brothers

Minister, grand vizier

Here [you have the king's brothers, whose] principle of legitimation is the family, the logic of blood and nature, the mode of reproduction being the mode of household reproduction. There you have the king's minister, whom you could say is a delegate, a mandatory whose principle of legitimation is often schooling as the guarantee of competence. On one hand, competence, merit, what is acquired, and on the other hand, nature. In the end you have a kind of triangle, a tripartite division in Dumézil's style,[20] which you always find in the great empires. The king needs these people [the ministers] as a basis for his power vis-à-vis [his brothers, but they] can turn against the king both the competence that the king demands of them for his own service, and the legitimacy that this competence assures them.

There are then all kinds of solutions that I shall very quickly describe. Very often, for example, [ministers of a dynastic state] are vowed to celibacy, the extreme case being eunuchs, who are prevented from reproducing. These people, like the vizier, have power, but a lifetime power that is non-reproducible. Others are partly or totally excluded from power, but they are able to reproduce. In other words, you have the powerless reproducible and the powerful non-reproducible. And you can see very well why the problem of succession is important, why it is important to think in terms of reproduction. On the one hand you have heirs, and on the other hand what I call 'oblates', individuals who have been given to the church, generally from a poor background, whom their families offered to the church in early childhood. Oblates are individuals who owe everything to the king, who can obtain great devotion from them. This is, I believe, an 'iron law' of all organizations. Political parties, in particular Communist parties, offered great careers for oblates. It is a law of apparatuses that they do not promote people who have capital outside of the apparatus; that holds both for the church and for parties. Churches love oblates because oblates, owing everything to the church, are totally devoted to it. And bishops, for example, are often oblates from whom the church can take everything away.

This triadic structure, I believe, has a very powerful explanatory value. It makes it possible to understand, for example, why in many ancient empires you have bureaucracies made up of pariahs. The bureaucrats are very often pariahs, that is, excluded from political reproduction. They are eunuchs, or priests vowed to celibacy – 'reproduction forbidden' – foreigners with no kinship connection to local people – for example [in] the praetorian guards of palaces, or the financial services of empires, where Jews were often in this situation – [they are] slaves who are the property of the state and whose goods and position can revert to the state at any time.[21] You can give thousands of examples, but [the interest of a structure is that it] makes it possible to avoid having to display its cultural history and the limitations of that culture . . . I could take an example from ancient Egypt, or Assyria, [where] the officials known as *wadu* were both slaves and officials: the same word is used for both.[22] Or again with the Persians of the Achaemenid empire, where the high officials were often Greek. In the Ottoman empire, as shown by Mantran's very fine book, a radical solution to this problem was found from the fifteenth century on: the king's brothers were 'disappeared' [. . .] on his accession.[23] The arbitrary aspect of household transmission is removed, as the king no longer has a competitor under this relationship, and all that remains is the problem of the grand vizier, [the ministers], which he handles in his own way [. . .]. This is resolved by employing foreigners as officials, for the most part renegade but Islamized Christians who fill the posts of high dignitaries.

[. . .] There is therefore a basic law as regards the work of domination. And if you return to the history of royalty in France, you see very quickly that the important positions are held by what were called *homines novi*, new men, oblates who owe everything to the state and who have a disturbing specialized competence. [. . .] You see that the state is built up against nature, that the state is *antiphysis*: no reproduction, no biological heredity and no transmission, not even of land, whereas the king and his family are on the side of blood, land and nature.

The first measure that lies at the origin of the modern state is thus the rejection of any possibility of succession and any possibility of a lasting appropriation – that is, beyond an individual life – of the means of production, in particular, land, which always has the status of means of production, but also the status of a guarantee of social status. In the Ottoman empire, for example, high officials were granted the revenue of land, but never property in land. Another measure is hereditary offices; here you are in the order of the lifetime occupant, with two [opposing] temporalities: [that of the heir and that of the] official. For example, a study of officials that I organized[24] [included the questions:] 'Do you know your predecessor?' and 'Can you influence the nomination of your successor?' This is one of the big breaks: thinking in terms of predecessor and successor is, at least officially, excluded from bureaucratic thinking. By the same token, an official has a very special relationship to his position: an amputated relationship in terms of succession and from the standpoint of structure of perception, of the future, etc. Max Weber, in his sociology of religion, also tried, for each of the major positions in social space, [to note] the type of religiosity that was preferred[25] – there are traders' religions, etc. I believe that in order to understand the philosophy of history or the religious philosophy of officials, you need to bear in mind the constitutive structure of the actual temporality of their position. [. . .]

The role of specialized minorities needs further development. Gellner's book on the state shows the role of pariah groups in the constitution of the bureaucratic state – I believe this is the only interesting idea in that book. For example, he stresses at length the fact that in the case of the Jews, 'they displayed that reliability which is the presupposed anticipation of single-stranded modern relations' and 'their previous training and orientation often make them perform much more successfully than their rivals', yet 'they had to make themselves politically and militarily impotent, so as to be allowed to handle tools that could be, in the wrong hands, so very powerful and dangerous'.[26] The case of mercenaries is simply a particular application of this general model. Next time, I shall try to go further in [the analysis of] this transition process.

Lecture of 24 October 1991

Recapitulation of the logic of the course – Family reproduction and state reproduction – Digression on the history of political thought – The historical role of jurists in the process of state construction – Differentiation of power and structural corruption: an economic model

Recapitulation of the logic of the course

I shall rapidly repeat the logic of my argument. First of all, I tried to reveal the specific logic of the dynastic state, and show in what way this state owed a certain number of its characteristics to the fact that it was organized according to a fundamental principle, that is, the existence of reproduction strategies with a lineage basis. Then I went on to analyse the principle of the dynamic leading from the dynastic state to the more impersonal state such as we are familiar with. Finally, in the last lecture, I described what we could call the specific contradiction of the dynastic state, that is, the fact that it is the site of structural tensions between two categories of agents, and in fact between two modes of reproduction: one group of agents – the royal family – that reproduces itself through a transmission principle with a biological basis, and another group that is reproduced by mediations, the main one of which is clearly the educational system. And I think that the contradiction between these two categories of agents is one of the fundamental motors in the history of the state, making it possible to understand how the transition took place from power of a personal type, directly transmissible by heredity, to a power that is more impersonal and, we might say, partially transmissible by heredity. That is the path that I followed.

Today, I want first of all to dwell on what it is that makes for the contradiction between these two modes of reproduction, because it is only possible to understand things that are apparently very distant on condition that the principle of this opposition is fully grasped. Without claiming to overturn existing knowledge, I believe that it may well be far easier to understand the French Revolution if this is seen as the triumph of the mode of impersonal reproduction over that of personal reproduction. In the end – I tell you this so that you will immediately have the general intent of my argument – the categories with the greatest interest [in the Revolution] were those categories that could only perpetuate their [positions of] power through the educational system, cultural capital, etc.; they had an interest in promoting a more universal definition of the state than did those social categories whose power and transmission depended simply on heredity. The conflict between these two principles, if you keep it in mind, makes it possible to understand a lot of things. For example, next time I shall speak to you about a very fine book by an American historian on the king's *lit de justice*[1] – a very solemn ceremony in which the king presided over the Parlement and exercised his power as legislator in an extreme situation. She gives a history of this ceremony, and you can see here in a remarkable fashion the stages and steps in this struggle between power with a dynastic base and power with a non-genealogical base, a base of competence, [in particular] juridical competence. Her final chapter describes the last period in the reign of Louis XV. She contrasts the court ceremonial established under Louis XIV, where you see the king mounted on a kind of raised throne and surrounded by the entire royal family, and his subjects facing him, with the situation of the *lit de justice*, where the king is indeed in the same raised position, but surrounded by people whose authority has a juridical base. She contrasts these two opposing images, which are a kind of perceptible materialization of the opposition [between two modes of reproduction]. That is to give you something of the perspective I intend to adopt.

Family reproduction and state reproduction

The hypothesis I have in mind is that one of the main driving forces in the changes that led up to the modern state is this antagonism between the two different principles of reproduction: one being the family, if you like, and the other being [cultural or educational competence]. These two principles continue to operate, and today the state is still riven by the same tension between heirs and newcomers. The education system, which in the phase I am studying here appeared as an independent principle of reproduction opposed to the dynastic principle, has also become, by the logic of its operation, a quasi-dynastic principle of reproduction, serving as the foundation of a state nobility, which is a kind of synthesis of the two principles of reproduction I discussed. You thus have a combination of two modes of reproduction, which are the basis of two principles of fidelity or loyalty of groups united by two very different kinds of ties. Clearly, the assumption behind everything I am saying about modes of reproduction is that power is animated by a kind of *conatus*, as Spinoza called it, a tendency to perpetuate itself, a tendency to persist in its being. (When you do sociology, this is a postulate that you are obliged to explicitly accept in order to understand how the social world works. It is not at all like some kind of metaphysical principle, you are simply obliged to assume that people who hold power or capital act, whether they are aware of it or not, in such a way as to perpetuate or increase their power and their capital.) This *conatus*, which is the constant movement by which the social body is sustained, leads the different bodies that hold capital to confront one another and apply the powers that they hold in struggles designed to maintain or increase these powers.

There you have the broad lines of my argument. I shall now specify in more detail the characteristics of these two modes of reproduction. The period of transition was very long; you can follow it back to its origin, as right from the early Middle Ages the newcomers who held a lifetime power, and were often scholars, clerics, later on secular jurists, etc., were in confrontation with the dynastic heirs. [That transition period] stretches from the twelfth century through to the French Revolution. It is interesting because, to the extent that the field of power differentiates, you can observe the existence of a contradictory and ambiguous mode of reproduction. This contradiction arises from the fact that the non-lineage mode of reproduction is in itself, simply by its intrinsic logic, a critique of the hereditary mode of reproduction. These are two modes of reproduction that are intrinsically hostile: the bureaucratic mode of reproduction, to the extent that it is bound up with the education system, undermines by its very existence the foundations of the lineage mode of reproduction; it undermines its very legitimacy. The development of education, and the rise in the number of officials whose authority is based on competence, leads even without any ideological elaboration to a challenge to heredity based on ties of blood. And you can say that in a certain sense the state nobility – the nobility of competence embodied in the *noblesse de robe* – expels the old nobility.

Things are in fact less simple, because, as historians have shown, the *noblesse de sang* remained the legitimate nobility and the *noblesse de robe* were themselves divided. Françoise Autrand's book[2] on the history of the *noblesse de robe* in the fourteenth and fifteenth centuries is very stimulating: you see how the *noblesse de robe* were divided in a sense between their collective interests as a body and their private interests, the collective interests leading them to assert their difference in relation to the *noblesse de sang* while their private interests led them to merge together with the *noblesse de sang* by marriage. Historians would therefore be right to challenge my construction, I believe, and say: 'That is too simple a schema. You are contrasting two modes of reproduction, but in fact these were very mixed; 40 per cent of what were called *noblesse de robe* were in fact *nobles d'épée*[3] who had studied, etc.' In fact, to the extent that reproduction through the education system imposed itself, a section of the nobles by blood converted themselves and their capital as *nobles de sang* into a capital of *noblesse de robe* by obtaining educational qualifications. Things are indeed far more complicated. But this does not mean that the model is not true, rather that the social agents who held one or the other kind of nobility capital would play their particular and collective interests as best they could in order to maximize the profits associated with possession of the kind of nobility capital that they held.

The two forms, as I emphasized last time, are incompatible. [With] the king's house and all the dignitaries who held inherited, innate noble property, you are on the side of nature, of natural gift, of what is naturally transmissible, and the professional ideology of this category is a kind of naturalist ideology. Given that any ideology aims to naturalize a privilege, nobility still provides the model for all ideologies. [. . .] The officials, on the other hand, have an acquired capital, they are on the side of the life interest, the temporary, merit, even if they appeal to natural gift – the notion of being gifted is very important. Charisma lies on the side of the [old] nobility, and if transmission through blood gives legitimacy, this is because extraordinary and charismatic properties are transmitted through blood – the capacity to cure scrofula, for example, is one form among others.[4]

You thus have, on the one hand, a charismatic ideology of transmission by blood, in particular an ideology of innate gift, and on the other an ideology that will also become charismatic – as everyone knows, the ideology of the education system is typically charismatic, based on the idea of being gifted, a gift of nature that owes nothing to acquisition. At this time, however, the opposition was far more clear: the innate on the one hand, the acquired on the other; the side of blood and the side of merit, especially law. It was not by chance that the bearers of the universalist claim were jurists who owed their authority to the law and placed their juridical competence in the service of the universalization of their particular interests as possessors of a particular juridical capital. Jurists clearly played a fundamental role in the construction of the state, as they were both judge and party. They could legitimize the monarch – the theories of absolutism that justified dynastic transmission in the most radical way were produced by jurists. Which did not rule out that jurists, as they increasingly functioned as a field, were also divided, and that other jurists placed their juridical competence in the service of defence of the other possible foundation of authority, that is, authority with a constitutional basis. And they were the first, in these constant struggles against the monarchy, to try to press the necessity for the king and nobility to find another foundation for their legitimacy than mere hereditary transmission.

(That is the scene as I see it, and agents with their interests and groups are clearly associated with these two conflicting hostile principles. Very often, [. . .] you have a whole series of texts by jurists proposing either justifications of the monarchist state, or critiques more or less inspired by Rousseau. Historians who produce books on this subject tend to treat the texts in and for themselves, without relating them to their producers. According to the principle that I recall again here, I believe that in order to understand any text whatsoever, you always have to know that you have, on the one hand, a space of texts, and [on the other,] a space of producers of texts, and that you are obliged to relate the structure of the space of texts to the structure of the space of producers of texts in order to understand why texts are as they are. In order to understand why such-and-such a provincial jurist put forward Rousseauist theses in a pamphlet against the monarchy, it is important to know that he was a minor advocate from a major family, that his cousin held a very important position in the city of Bordeaux whereas he himself belonged to a branch of the family that had gone down in the world, etc. It is important to know all this, the position he occupies in the juridical field, the authority he holds, whether he is from Paris or the provinces, a chancellor of the Paris Parlement or a little advocate with no work in the south-west, etc. So you have to relate the space of texts and the space of producers of texts.)

To the extent that power becomes differentiated, therefore, you have a whole set of protagonists: those bound up with law and life interest, and those bound up with blood and heredity. These two [sets of] protagonists differentiate, and the confrontation is between agents involved in competitive struggles both within each camp and between the two camps. These very complex struggles generate innovative practices, inventions. In the courts of justice, for example, the Parlement people, by a combination of cunning and struggle, [enforced the wearing of a] red gown, which may seem ridiculous to us but was a very important conquest, as they succeeded in sitting in court in a red gown rather than a black one, a symbolic conquest that put them on the same level as this or that dynastic descendant. You [thus have] all kinds of struggles that are both practical and symbolic, these symbolic struggles being above all, naturally enough, the work of those on the side of life interest, of law, of discourse; they have both the capacity to obtain changes in practices (in precedence, in hierarchies, in ceremonials, etc.), and on the other hand [the capacity to wage] symbolic struggles and [produce] theories. And some of the political theories that are studied in the institutes of political science directly issued from struggles through which the different groups engaged in the division of labour of domination sought to advance their pawns.

Digression on the history of political thought

I believe that the whole history of political thought needs to be reworked (unfortunately I have neither the time nor the competence for this). It is in fact being reworked, and there is some very fine work I shall draw on that is halfway towards this. I shall explain myself in a few words, as it is important for you to understand the context of what I am telling you. There is a traditional history of political ideas, [illustrated] by Chevallier's book,[5] for example, which contains a chapter on each author (Plato, Bodin, etc.), without the reader knowing why these authors are singled out – a problem with all authors of histories of philosophy.

Fortunately, we are starting to have studies in the sociology of philosophy and the sociology of literature that are not satisfied with accepting an existing corpus and doing a sociology of the people in that corpus, but are rather doing the sociology of the corpus itself: why is this corpus what it is? How is it that in France, Kant is inevitable and Descartes still more so, whereas in the Anglo-Saxon tradition Hume and Locke have a far greater place? In other words, [reflection is needed] on the constitution of the 'table of honours'. The same work needs doing for political philosophy. You discover that, alongside Bodin, there were more than a dozen individuals who also produced theories of the state, theories of government, but who fell into oblivion. If you go further and study, as Sarah Hanley has, the public positions taken by the chancellor or the Parlement, or by the secretary whose transcriptions we have, you see that these people were also producers of theories of the state, of government and authority. You discover that the great figures whom the history of political philosophy has retained stood out on the basis of a world that was under construction. This type of reflection [makes it possible to] discover that political philosophy is generated in political action, in political work, and that it forms part of the object itself. One historian, for example, who was a court official and one of the first to write a history of the *lit de justice*, carried out a strategic coup. He reconstructed a kind of fiction of the history of *lits de justice* that to a certain extent became real, since one of the kings read his work and took him seriously, and the next *lit de justice* was constructed according to the model that this author had developed.[6]

In other words, the theoretical constructions of political philosophers are part of the construction of the reality that these historians themselves study. They are not simply a backing-up discourse. This is why the notion of ideology is very dangerous, suggesting that there is first an infrastructure and then a discourse. That is not true: the discourse forms part of the reality, and in this particular case the masters of discourse, that is, the jurists, have the tremendous asset that they can get what they say believed. They have an authority, they have the capacity first of all to speak, and to speak with authority; and having this capacity, they can get people to believe that what conforms to their interests is true. By making those who have the power to bring the true into existence, that is, the powerful, believe that something is true, they can make what they say real. Today's opinion polls are a bit like that . . . You will reflect, I'm going very quickly, but there are cases when discourse is a power that more or less verifies itself. This whole excursus is important for changing our ways of thinking. I often repeat that Marxism is 'impassable',[7] but only on condition that it is passed. Marxism has filled our heads with false problems, impassable oppositions or impossible subtle distinctions. The distinction between ideology and reality is one of those dramatic divisions that prevent us from understanding processes of the kind I am going to describe, which are precisely constant transitions from discourse to the reality of ritual.

I wanted to mention the fact that the state was the product of thousands of infinitesimal little actions. In history books, for example, you can see scenes of the meeting of the Paris Parlement: there is a crowd of people, and the king up above. Each of these individuals has a very strong existence; before entering the solemn session, he said to his neighbour: 'We have the right to make remonstrance!' Then they sent a delegation to the king, who dismissed it but none the less made a concession: 'Among these five remonstrances, I shall only accept one', about poverty for example. It's no bad thing to be obliged to remind the king, who is by definition the protector of the poor, that he has not concerned himself with the poor . . . The four other [remonstrances] are forgotten, etc. All these negotiations, these thousands of little actions that are left as unfinished business, must be integrated into theoretical models if these are to be sociologically valid.

In order to really explain the genesis of the state, we would need a day-by-day account of all these acts, these little actions, these pressure groups that are formed, these ruses by which a little variant is introduced into a ritual, the theoretical discourses I am studying being just one manifestation of these. Unfortunately, I cannot follow this work through, but I can give you the principle of it . . . I think that Bodin's speeches have to be put on the same level as the formula that some chancellor or other said to his neighbour before entering the royal presence; they are strokes, strategies. [The object is not] to discredit grand theories, disqualify them, but I believe we are obliged to bend the stick the other way. We have such a habit of respecting Machiavelli more than gossip that I am obliged to accentuate the other side.

The historical role of jurists in the process of state construction

To come back now to my theme. We thus have opposing principles of reproduction, social agents whose interests are more or less bound up with one or another principle of reproduction. These agents are themselves caught up in extremely complex games – the juridical game, the dynastic game, etc. – in which the collective interests of *nobles de robe* or *nobles d'épée* are spelled out, opposed and fragment; and these people are all operating within extremely complex little games, with their assets and their instruments. As I see it, jurists are the driving force of the universal, of universalization. They have the law on their side, that is, discourse with a universal claim; their particular capacity, which is their professional capacity, is to reason, to give reasons, produce reasons, thus to bring things from the order of fact – 'that's how it is', 'that's not possible', 'that's intolerable', etc. – to the order of reason, in two ways: by appealing to universal juridical principles – there is no state without a constitution, for example – and by recourse to history. Jurists were the first historians of constitutional law, the first to try and find precedents, to rummage through the archives. [It is interesting to note] how those people most involved in the battles to know whether members of the Parlement could wear red, those most involved in these micro-struggles, did unprecedented work as historians. They went and searched the archives to know whether, in the first *lit de justice* in the thirteenth century, the king entered preceded by someone or not, whether he placed the peers in the front rank, etc. This historical work was part of the construction of the state. What I simply mean is that these people, by their characteristics, their position, in order to advance their own interests, were obliged to advance the universal. This was their property, they couldn't be content with saying: 'That's how it is.' Even when they served the king and absolutism, they gave reasons for what could be asserted arbitrarily, they were the people who gave reasons, a fortiori when they wanted to advance their own interests.

That is then the pattern and the very principle of my way of reading documents, reading historians, but for reasons that I don't understand these things are not said. I am giving you the results of my research, of my work, of what I have read, and I have tried here to give you the philosophy of history that orients my reading, if there is one. I could say this in a more didactic way: the oppositions between structure and history, between individual agent and collective agent, individual rationality and collective rationality, all these oppositions filling our heads do not have any sense . . . I believe there is no action so trivial that it does not have its meaning in a complex system of action. That is the meaning of this excursus.

We thus have two conflicting modes of reproduction. And the king, as I showed in my diagram last time, is a third party: he is in some way above this opposition between those with life interest and the heirs. He can even use their antagonism to rule – to divide and rule. This means that he can use the competence of the people with life interest to discredit the authority of his brothers or cousins; and conversely, he can put those with life interest in their place by reminding them of their inferior rank in terms of blood. To understand fully the exercise of royal action, we have to know, as I showed last year, that the first phase of state construction was a process of accumulation of different species of capital in the hands of the king. In other words, there was a person who came to hold the power to manage this capital, which basically means the power to redistribute it. This has been said a hundred times, particularly by anthropologists who studied the genesis of the state. In African societies, for example, the first form of accumulation of legitimate power appears in association with redistribution. We still have to analyse what this 'redistribution' means. Historians have laid much emphasis, in the case of the French and English monarchies, on material redistribution, on the fact that the king, to the extent that the state is constituted, is in a position to distribute the products of taxation in ways that he determines. The money accumulated by taxation is distributed to specific categories of subjects: in the form of pay for soldiers, salaries for officials, for the holders of offices, administrators, people in the judiciary, etc.

Historians have emphasized the fact that the genesis of the state is indissociable from the genesis of a group of people who are involved with the state and whose existence is bound up with the state. We need to develop this point to understand the behaviour of agents, to understand why certain individuals today vote in this direction or that in relation to what could be called, for example, their 'religious convictions'. How do you explain the link between religious conviction and the adoption of certain political positions? Very often you can see a direct and simple connection: being a Catholic means voting for the right. That was true perhaps at a certain period, but the relationship is actually far more complex. To understand why a certain religious affiliation leads to a certain political position, you have to understand what is involved in being bound up with the existence of the church. You have to ask, for example, who are the people whose lives would be changed if the church disappeared. Think of the candle-sellers, who may not be Catholic . . . I won't go on.

The same thing holds for the state. Who has an interest in the public services? If you did a questionnaire on everyday social behaviour, with questions about who makes their dog mess in the gutter and who doesn't, who throws away plastic objects and who doesn't, you could investigate the principles that differentiate people in this way, and that is no simple thing. Personally, I tend to investigate things of the type I implied with the candle-seller: which people are bound up with the public order? Are they paid by the state? Did they go to state school? That is where you have to look. It is this kind of thing that you have to put under the notion of 'interest'. People divide in an apparently random way. The hypothesis that the sociologist makes is that beneath this haphazard appearance there is necessity. People are not crazy, they don't do just anything, they have 'interests'. I don't mean just interests à la Bentham, not simply material or economic interests, but very complex interests of belonging: '*inter esse*' means to belong, to 'be in'. Who 'is in' when we talk about the public? Who feels shattered when a public TV channel is abolished? This is very likely not completely independent of the status of state employee. Historians are right to [link] the state with wages, pay, etc. But behind all this there is the appearance of a body of people, more or less numerous, who have a connection with the state. Studying the material aspect of state construction thus already means studying something else. The fact of receiving a salary means a form of belonging, of dependence, which cannot be understood as servility. People say: 'Civil servants simply obey', but in fact this is not servility, there are deep interests that are beneath the threshold of consciousness, and only become apparent at critical moments. The candle-seller would only discover his interests if the church really did disappear. In other words, there are forms of affiliation, of belonging, of connection, that we have to establish. And behind salary there is a form of dependence, a tie that could be called moral.

I can refer you here to the article by Denis Crouzet, 'La crise de l'aristocratie en France au XVIe siècle'[8] to show you the difference from what I have just told you. In this article Crouzet adopts the most vulgar materialist view. He presents the struggles around the central power as struggles of influence in which the issue at stake was occupation of leading positions, that is, positions suited to obtaining financial advantage. He says very directly that, if this struggle was so intense, it was because in order to perpetuate their style of life, that is, their status, the nobles needed money. On the basis of these struggles around redistribution it is thus possible to understand what happens. He gives the examples of the rallying of Nevers to Henri II, the rallying of the duc de Guise to Henri IV against 12 million livres for paying his debts, etc. These are cases where it is very clear that the power of the state was exercised essentially by way of the redistribution of resources. That said, and this is the point I wanted to stress, dependence on state power goes well beyond material dependence . . . That is the first point.

The second point is that the state, by redistributing material resources, produces a symbolic effect. This is something extremely simple, which can be seen very well in precapitalist societies, where primitive forms of accumulation are based precisely on redistribution. We know today that things that appear as waste – the act of giving away blankets or yams – are in fact a kind of accumulation. The symbolic alchemy consists precisely in redistribution: I receive money and, by giving it back, I transfigure it into the creative donation of recognition – the word 'recognition' can be taken in both senses, meaning both gratitude and the recognition of legitimacy. The logic of centralization leads therefore, by way of redistribution, to a new form of accumulation: an accumulation of symbolic capital, of legitimacy. This alchemical work of redistribution is very clearly seen in what is the royal privilege par excellence, that is, the power of appointment.

In the first analyses I presented here,[9] I laid great emphasis on the need to be surprised by such commonplace things as 'he was appointed professor'. Nomination is precisely one of those acts that presupposes the concentration of a symbolic capital and the capacity to distribute it in specific ways. There is a sentence in [William Blackstone][10] that says: 'The king is the fountain of honours.' This image of the king as source of all benefits, especially symbolic ones, that is, what can be called benefits of identity, [happens when the king decides who is] noble and [who is] not noble, [who is] chancellor and [who is not] chancellor. This is an almost magical power. The material redistribution that historians rightly describe is complemented in this way by social effects of allegiance – which I began to mention just now – and recognition. In other words, redistribution is the producer of legitimacy.[11] That said, the process is highly ambiguous. It is a process of accumulation in which capital attracts capital inasmuch as, even when he redistributes, the king carries on accumulating. Even redistribution is a form of accumulation par excellence, by the transmutation of economic capital into symbolic capital. But this kind of accumulation is accomplished to the benefit of an individual: it is a kind of 'patrimonialism' in the Weberian sense, a public good. The king makes use of public resources accumulated by the state in the form of taxes, privileges, property titles, and makes use of it for himself.

Differentiation of power and structural corruption: an economic model

The process of state construction – this is a point I shall develop next time – is accompanied by a differentiation in the ruling body. By the logic of delegation, the king is led to devolve part of the power he holds onto others, who may be either members of his lineage or persons of competence (jurists, clerics, etc.). This leads to the creation of chains of dependence, and at each link in the chain there is a new possibility of misappropriation. In other words, what the king does for himself, each of his mandatories can do likewise. Just as the king may divert [the process] to his profit by a gift of the symbolic capital that he draws from redistribution, so the intendant of Nancy can make use of the authority he has received from the king to accumulate power and prestige, in particular by injustice, possibly even turning this against the king. We must therefore imagine the process of state development as a process of fissiparity. There is one individual, and then [the ruling power] breaks in two, divides; there are ever more agents who hold parcels of power, who are interconnected and often hierarchically ranked as a result of processes of delegation. Next week I shall analyse the process of delegation of signature which is one of the most interesting of these from a historical point of view – each person signing, counter-signing, being counter-signed, etc. This process of delegation is thus accompanied by a kind of multiplication of the ruling power, giving rise to the potentiality of diversion of power at each of its articulations. Corruption, therefore, which has been the subject of much writing, particularly in relation to the great empires, China, etc., is in a sense [inscribed] in the very structure. The potentiality of corruption is simply what the king does, but reproduced at a lower level; it is diversion, to personal benefit, of the profits procured by an authority of which the person concerned is the depositary, and which he has received by delegation.

It is possible to conceive the model in a simple way [so as to explain] the potentiality of misappropriation, that is, of direct extraction. An all-powerful king, really absolute, should be able to control the whole process of concentration and the whole process of redistribution. He should be able to prevent anything accumulating that does not go through him, and in that case, there would be no erosion of power. All economic capital, for example, would be transmuted into symbolic capital paid into the king's account. In actual fact, there are leaks in the circuit. At each of the links in the extremely complex network that constitutes the state, the individuals who occupy positions can make a direct extraction, that is, obtain direct profits that do not go back to the king, and they can also make a symbolic misappropriation of these extractions by directly redistributing them themselves at the level of a province, etc. One problem that arises then in all empires and in all [political] systems is that of the relationship between the provincial leader and his province. Still today, for example, the church does not allow a bishop to be appointed to the diocese from which he originates, or even to the neighbouring dioceses. That is a rule found in many regimes or empires. Much importance is placed on this break, since it is assumed that the existence of a direct connection can lead to direct extraction and direct redistribution, that is, to a short-circuit. And this short-circuit is corruption.

State concentration, which gives the king a power over all other agents who have a share in domination, has its limits. Precisely inasmuch as the king has need of auxiliaries in order to concentrate capital, he finds himself in a logic of compromise. I shall say a few words on this problem of intermediaries, which has been very well studied by economists on the basis of models, two economists in particular whose names I shall give you – I cannot give the references, for the simple reason that these are texts I have received that have not yet been published: Jean-Jacques Laffont, who is professor of economics at Toulouse and at the École des Hautes Études [en Sciences Sociales], who has written an article on 'Hidden gaming in hierarchies',[12] and Jean Tirole, who analyses the logic of favouritism[13] which I tried to describe as best I could. I am going to present their model to you in a few words, and next time I shall come back to the historical reality. Economists, as opposed to ethnographers who describe without a great deal of analysis, have the virtue of analysing, but too often they make models without understanding the reality. I believe that the construction of realistic historical models presupposes a mind for modelling that is able to bend itself to the complexity of historical facts, with the evident danger of disappointing both the pure modellers and the unyielding historiographers.

The model of these authors is very interesting, because they start out from what is called 'contract theory'; I shall not go into detail because that would lead me into an infinite regression. They distinguish three levels in every interaction, corresponding to three categories of agents. There is what they call the 'principal', for example the entrepreneur who has capital and is looking for labour, at the other end there are individual workers, and between the two there is the supervisor, the foreman, the intermediary. Their model is extremely interesting, because they show that the principal, such as the king in our particular case, has for example either to bring in money (collect taxes) or obtain obedience (raise soldiers). He cannot see to the supervision himself, that would be too time-consuming. He is thus obliged to turn to foremen, intendants, mandatories. The mandatory is then in a very strong position – contract theory always thinks in terms of information – because there is a whole part of the information that the principal cannot have without him. [Let us imagine] there are three workers, two of whom do nothing while a third works and the king wants to reward him. If the king wants to know which one he needs knowledge, but only the supervisor can say who is working and who is not; [the supervisor] thus has information that [the king] doesn't. But the supervisor has the possibility of not giving this information, but instead allying with the workers and saying to them: 'If you pay me, I won't say who is working and who isn't.'

The intermediary can thus draw profit from possessing the scarce resource of information. Whereas the principal sees only the result of the workers' work, the overall figure, the supervisor for his part knows who has indeed worked, and whether the result depends on chance or something else. As a result, the supervisor is in a very strong position, contrary to appearances. You might think that he is wedged between two sides, but in reality he is in a strategic position since he can either threaten the workers with telling the truth or hide it from the principal. And if the king wants to counteract the tendencies to profit inherent in the position of supervisor, he has to invent stronger incentives than the profits that the foreman can draw from the double game he plays with the two other parties. He has to establish systems of reward to [keep the attachment of] the intermediaries. But this requires him to make concessions. What the economists' model does not say is that, at a certain level of concession, the intermediaries can [take on the role of] principal. To get the intermediary to do what he has to do, for example control [or] exercise justice, the principal has to reckon with the potentiality of dissidence based on the capacity to use the strategic possibilities provided by a position of uncertainty, of intermediacy; and in order to counteract this potential dissidence, he has to make concessions that may lead to his own power of delegation being challenged. If you think of the case of the king [of France] and the Parlement, the latter was exactly in this position, [. . .] with agents pulling both ways: 'We are like the English Parliament, we represent the people', or 'We are on the side of the king.'

This model is certainly too simple. It needs to be made more complex, but [it shows] the contradiction that I want to try and develop, because it is here, as I see it, that you have the dynamic [of the emergence of the state], including the French Revolution, and perhaps even beyond. The whole process of evolution of the state is inscribed in this contradiction. Corruption is structural, all the more so as even those with life interest have families and they dream of founding a dynasty, either by marriage with the hereditary nobility, or by making their office venal and transmitting it. Those with life interest have reproduction interests that lead them to exploit the potentialities that their structural position in the network of delegation offers them; that is why corruption is inherent. How can state incentives be found that are capable of counteracting this propensity to corruption? By establishing controls within the networks? But potential corrupters and corrupted [control one another]. The centralist logic that economists describe is very dangerous, and the king is caught in this contradiction: he cannot concede without generating a power capable of destroying him. You can see for example a process of advance and retreat – the history of relations with the Parlement is very amusing in this respect. The king cedes a bit too much in order to obtain loyalty and allegiance in difficult circumstances, when he is weak, when he is young, in a situation of regency. The relationship evidently fluctuates, its structures varying according to the particular strength of the king: his age, his authority, his victories, etc.

I am a bit unhappy, as I wanted to try to model the historical reality without mutilating it too much, that is, by giving the history at the same time, and that is very complicated . . . but I shall try to do better next time.

Lecture of 7 November 1991

Preamble: the pitfalls of communication in social science – The example of institutionalized corruption in China: (1) the ambiguous power of sub-bureaucrats – The example of institutionalized corruption in China: (2) the 'pure' – The example of institutionalized corruption in China: (3) double game and double 'I' – The genesis of the bureaucratic space and the invention of the public

Preamble: the pitfalls of communication in social science

[Before I begin, I want to try and reply to two questions], the first of these on social space, and the second on a remark I made in passing about Marxism, on the relationship between ideology and infrastructure.

A preamble first of all. These questions make me realize once again that I am dealing with an audience at 'different speeds', and that is one of the reasons that make the task of teaching in this institution particularly hard ... You have alongside one another people who have followed my lecture courses from the beginning, that is, for almost ten years, who [. . .] understand the presuppositions behind what I say, and others who have just 'landed', which is not a criticism but a fact that I have to reckon with. There are also people with very different levels of background in sociology, who may believe that things I say in a peremptory fashion are impromptu theses, whereas they are actually based on work, analyses, etc. I said the other week, on the subject of problems of communication between the social sciences and the social world, [that] the hardest things to communicate are problematics. Listeners to a sociologist speaking on television, when this happens, interpret the statements they hear in terms of an often implicit problematic which is almost always political; so they reduce analyses to theses, that is, to attacks or defences. I believe this is less the case here, but very likely there is still a bit of it.

I say all this to explain why – I am not alone – all my colleagues in this institution find the experience of teaching here extremely hard, even though the majority of them have taught for a long time in different institutions. I think that one of the reasons for this extreme difficulty comes from the fact that it is impossible to constantly introduce all the assumptions that are necessarily involved in a talk, in the way that is possible in writing, for example. Because of this, you are constantly led to return back, to parentheses, etc. You are inevitably dissatisfied in all kinds of ways, you can never say as quickly or as well as you would like the things you set out to say, and even then still without saying as completely and necessarily what needs to be said for what you set out to say to be fully intelligible. That is a very painful feeling. I say this because it is a way both to help you and to help myself convey things, and also because [. . .] it does me good . . .

These two questions made me reflect on this, because they clearly bear on very fundamental things: the relationship between field and space. I devoted a course of a year or two, I believe, to the notion of field,[1] with the hope of also publishing it along the way. (That is another contradiction of these institutions. You build up things that you do not have time to publish, because you already have to prepare a course for the following year.) I developed [this point] at length, and it is impossible for me in a few sentences to go over even the foundations of the idea of field. Here I will take the bureaucratic field as given, particularly as concerns the relationship between field and space: these are two terms that I use alternately, and that are equivalent in certain cases and not so in others. I am therefore going to do something that I should not. [I am on the point of publishing,] together with one of my students who is in the United States, a book that arose from these questions.[2] I went to the University of Chicago, and the American students, who have a very different background from French students and are far more technical, far more pestering, far more rigorous, welcomed me with a hundred and twenty questions that came from a very serious collective reading they had made of my work, if not the whole of it then at least everything that was available in English, and I replied orally to these hundred and twenty questions. That took me a great deal of time, they had to be transcribed, reworked, etc., and this will soon be published here by Éditions du Seuil under the title *Réponses*.

If I allow myself to refer to this, it's not to advertise my books, rather a way of giving you convenient instruments, as those questions are naturally tackled there. I try in this book to reply to these objections [there are many of them], because these students did a great deal of work, hunting out all the critical reviews of my books in every language, etc. They made a kind of totalization, and it was terrifying for me to receive all these objections raised to me in every country. It is likely that your objections are contained in this list. On the other hand, I took the occasion to give some clarifications, both quite dense and very simple, I believe, on the notions of field, habitus, capital, the relations between the different kinds of capital, etc. If I have to start afresh each year in order to be sure I convey everything clearly, I would rather refer to this book.

As for the second question put to me, on the problem of Marxism, that is more complicated, because [. . .] in general [I only mention this in passing] I don't finish my statements, but say: 'Look where I'm pointing . . .' I imply that I've said too much on the subject, as I know that I have said too much given the conditions of reception and the conditions of transmission. If I [said] completely what I [wanted to] say, I would need a whole year of lectures. At the same time, it seems important for me to make very quick little signs in passing, as I believe it is one of the virtues of oral teaching that it enables things to be said very quickly that in writing you are forced to develop *in extenso*.

So I said in passing: 'Look, Marxism, which gives the appearance of speaking of these problems, is in reality an obstacle to the construction of these problems.' That was too little. The proof is that I am asked: 'But hasn't Marxism tackled the problem you mention of relations between the infrastructure and the superstructure, between social reality and so-called ideological relations, etc., for example relations between law, philosophy and art, three instances that Marx always mentions in a ritual way when he speaks of ideology?' Of course, it has tackled these problems, and I'm asked: 'Haven't they been settled, isn't the notion of dialectic . . .?' Here again, I will say things in a rather peremptory and abrupt way: I don't think so. I think that the word dialectic is a theoretical fig-leaf, and often what Spinoza called an asylum of ignorance, that a problem is not resolved simply by giving it a name – even if there is a good deal of merit in naming, of course. That is something that I wanted to say the other day very quickly in passing, and I got bogged down in the analysis of details, which was a practical way of responding to this problem that the Marxist tradition does not resolve.

I come back then to another problem that is also constantly raised. I shall speak to you next week about a book called *The Lit de Justice of the Kings of France* – I mentioned it the other day. If I had read this book five years ago I would not have understood any of it, or I would have said: 'These are anecdotal stories on the relationship between the king and the Paris Parlement.' Out of scholarly virtue I would have read it to the end, whereas today I think I could talk about it at great length. Will what I am going to tell you about it convey to you what I intend? That is a real problem. I am not going to play the great initiate who finds it hard to convey his knowledge to the [profane], but it is true that the problem is very difficult, that it would take a lot of time, and it is not certain that the audience that you make up would have the patience needed to understand it. In a research seminar it is possible to go more slowly, you can take the time to go back over this or that page . . . I am often obliged to ask you to take my word for things. I find it painful to tell you that something is important, for example, or ask you to take my word, when I would rather be able to take the time on each occasion to give you the reasons.

So there we are. I have not answered either of the two questions, but I have tried to explain why I was unable to, which should not discourage you from asking me questions, as it may be that I can reply . . .

The example of institutionalized corruption in China, 1: the ambiguous power of sub-bureaucrats

I will come back now to what I was saying last time. To recapitulate: I stressed that the process of concentration I described last year was the foundation for a very complex process of redistribution, and I suggested very simply that the concentration of resources in the hands of one person, embodied by the king, made possible a process of redistribution that was entirely controlled by one person. This ideal was realized – at least, according to anthropological studies – in many archaic societies, for example with systems of potlatch. You have societies in which redistribution can be virtually controlled by a single person, who can then receive the totality of the symbolic profits obtained by the transmutation of resources into symbolic capital as a result of redistribution. But I showed that, to the extent that political systems differentiate, redistribution is no longer controlled by one person. There are something like leaks in the redistribution circuits, each of these leaks representing a small site of transformation of economic capital into symbolic capital, or of juridical capital or bureaucratic capital into symbolic capital, siphoned off along the way by the holder of a delegated authority. This series of leaks is, I believe, one of the things that people deplore when they speak of bureaucracy.

These leaks in the circuit of redistribution are particularly marked in certain systems, and [on this subject] I would like rapidly to summarize for you an article that strikes me as exemplary on bureaucracy and corruption in China. There is an immense historical literature on corruption in practically all political systems, but I find this one very interesting, perhaps because the Chinese case is exemplary, but perhaps also because this Sinologist is exemplary. (That is a very important question when you read such studies. You tend to ascribe the singularity of a description to the singularity of the country studied, but it may also be due to the singularity of the analyst. This may be a more lucid and clever analyst, who sees things better and so dismantles the mechanisms better, and who is therefore particularly interesting, because you can then go back and examine realities that have been poorly seen and poorly expressed, you can examine them more completely on the basis of a different and more lucid point of view.) The article in question is by Pierre-Étienne Will, who has just been appointed to the Collège de France.[3]

This article illustrates the model of structural corruption made by the economists that I described to you last time, the model in which the person carrying out orders can make use of their intermediary position to draw profit from both directions. One of the key themes of the article is the conflict that we have just examined between family interests and state interests. How is it possible to reconcile the imperatives of service to the state with the imperatives of service to the family? Will shows how a whole series of Chinese theorists, inspired by Confucius but against him, tried to construct the idea of a loyalty to the state irreducible to loyalty to the family. The Confucian tradition presented a problem for the inventors of a public order, in so far as it prescribed loyalty to the family, in particular filial loyalty, making this the very model of every kind of loyalty, as well as itself the prime loyalty. The theorists had therefore to reckon with an authority that presented an obstacle to their project; a whole series of thinkers whom [Will] calls 'legalists', a whole series of men of state, in the warring states of the fourth century BCE, tried to counteract this appeal to filial piety, seeing it as an instrument for justifying corruption. They tried to invent a discourse that gave priority to obedience to the emperor over obedience to family duties. In general, they naturally proposed a solution of compromise between the two, which was translated into regulatory norms, for example in what is called the 'law of avoidance' – the law that I mentioned last time, which forbade appointing an official to his place of origin, in order to avoid corruption.

Strangely enough, however, it turned out that this law designed to avoid corruption actually promoted it, inasmuch as you are far better placed to exploit people when they are not your relatives – one among the countless ruses of house reason. In imperial China you had officials who were relatively poorly paid, with only a small number at the top, those who had passed through the system of mandarin competitions, and then a large number of petty officials who lived on what they could glean on the ground. In describing this structure, Will speaks of 'institutionalized corruption', in the sense that everyone knew that minor officials could not live without these illicit extractions.

I shall mention later on an article on the English bureaucracy that tends to show – something I didn't know, which my friend Eric Hobsbawm pointed out to me – how in the English bureaucracy, up to the middle of the nineteenth century, it was accepted that high officials should draw their resources – private resources – from the district to which they were appointed.[4] The system of public bureaucracy, in which officials are paid a salary, is thus an extremely recent invention, and relatively circumscribed. Although the English tradition established public appointment by the state far earlier than in France, it was only much later that it established remuneration of officials by the state, in place of direct extraction.

[To return to] China, you have a system of direct extraction, a 'flow of illicit funds that irrigates the whole system from bottom to top'. This kind of legal extortion of funds is designed to pay the personal and professional expenses of officials, and also the salaries of the sub-bureaucrats whom these officials have to maintain in order to carry out their tasks. To describe this institutionalized corruption, [Will] speaks of 'regular irregularities'. Then, after describing the overall logic of the system, he comes to what he calls a description of the structure of the bureaucracy. He shows that the central officials are completely cut off from their regional roots by the implementation of the law of avoidance. Then there are the private collaborators of these officials, who are partly maintained by the officials and in a sense trained to loyalty towards their masters; and finally – this is the essential thing – a 'sub-bureaucracy' as he calls it, who are raised in the provincial society, who are part of provincial society, who are stable in their positions, since this stability enables them to establish networks, and who are bound neither by loyalty to the state nor by loyalty to a master, as private collaborators are. These sub-officials or sub-bureaucrats thus have the object of extracting as much money as possible in the least possible time. The problem that then arises is how to do this. This is where the economists' model comes in: they can do it because they are in a position of apparent inferiority in relation to the central officials who are supposed to control and direct them, but actually in a position of superiority, since their duration in their positions gives them not only the networks I have mentioned, but also a familiarity with the terrain that enables them to block orders coming from above and information coming from below. And this kind of 'gatekeeper' position enables them to intercept whatever suits them, to let through only what they see as suitable, and so puts them in a position of permanent blackmail in relation to the central rulers.

This model, which appears very remote, has a wide application to French society today. I refer you to issue 81–2 of *Actes de la Recherche en Sciences Sociales* [1990], which I have already mentioned a number of times, and which deals with housing policy and the economic problems of house-building, the sale of houses, all the problems to do with construction permits, etc. You find here quite analogous problems, and I refer you to the last [article] that I wrote in this issue, entitled 'Droit et passe-droit', in which I try to show, according to the same logic, that people always forget that the person holding a right can draw profit either from exercising this right in an ultra-correct fashion, or on the contrary from suspending it and granting exceptions.

But to come back to China again. The lower official thus has a structural position, a position of intermediary, that is I believe very general. That is why the economists' model is extremely stimulating, despite being a bit rigid. The model can express the structural profits associated with the fact of being between the two – like the petty bourgeoisie between the big bourgeoisie and the popular classes, etc. There are structural inconveniences in being between the two; there are structural properties, people who are 'neither . . . nor' or 'both . . . and', who have many properties that are not bound up with their conditions of work, wages, etc., but are bound up with the fact of their being [in a] middle position . . . I often speak of social topology. Here we have a typical case, where you see that there is a topological aspect to sociological analysis, people who are neither one thing nor the other, [who are] neutral – *neuter* in Latin – between the two, who are 'neither . . . nor'. They have common properties, and you can use this model analytically in order to understand heaps of things about the position of intermediaries.[5]

To return yet again to China: the power of these intermediaries comes, on the one hand, from the fact that they can sell to their superiors a vital element of information that they hold. You will remember that the model

essentially said: the principal does not know who is working and who is
doing nothing; the intermediary can either tell him or avoid telling him.
The intermediaries can therefore divert a share of power by controlling
the information that they hold, and on the other hand, they can exercise
a power by blocking access to the master, the principal. This is the typical
case of what in English are called 'access fees': I pay to get an interview,
etc. Mutatis mutandis, secretaries are often in this intermediary position.
(This is for sociologists and for those who don't know it. It is common
practice that, in order to get an interview, it is better to approach the secretary, better to get round the secretary than the boss, because she can find
a gap in the schedule, she can present things in such a way [that her boss]
will either say: 'Yes, that's very good, ok', or else send [you] packing. That
is an example of the use of a structural intermediary position. Access fees
may be in money, but they can be in smiles, all kinds of things . . .)

The example of institutionalized corruption in China, 2: the 'pure'

To sum up: intermediaries are in a position to control the circulation of
information from bottom to top and from top to bottom, as well as the
circulation of advantages associated with information (this needs development with concrete analyses). One of the interesting contributions of
Pierre-Étienne Will's article on China is indicated in passing, perhaps
even in a note: the danger constituted by the 'pure' in a system such as
this. Oddly enough, moral indignation is not randomly distributed in the
social space [. . .]. The 'pure' are often amazed at not being rewarded, and
even being punished . . . These are things that you gradually discover with
age. You learn that there is no immanent justice in this world . . . It is not
only that virtue is not rewarded, but you have to think yourself lucky if
you are not punished when you do good – I think that's a good formulation! In the present education system, for example, people who do what
the system officially says that it does prevent the wheels from running
smoothly and are often sanctioned. Sociology, which should understand
everything, must understand that. This is an interesting case, because you
have a phenomenon of structural corruption. Will speaks of 'institutionalized corruption', that is, structural corruption that is officially accepted by
the institution. For my part, I call it 'structural corruption', a corruption
that is inevitable but that is not necessarily inscribed in the institution, not
necessarily recognized.

(In the French institution, you know that today, in the atmosphere of
neoliberalism, the cult of the market, etc., it is good form in the higher
reaches of the state bureaucracy to denounce [. . .] 'trade-union rigidities',
for example the rigidities of workers attached to 'historic gains' – that
makes them really petty-bourgeois, real morons [. . .]. But we should
remember that the same people who say this get extremely high bonuses,
the exact amount of which is very hard to establish. I have tried to do

so; you do find out, because each person criticizes the bonuses of others, but it is still very hard. In any case, you never find it on paper, and if you publish it, you are told: 'But no, that's not true, you're naive, it's not like that . . .' Here again there is institutionalized corruption, state privilege. And this institutionalized corruption is the work of those who denounce the corruption of intermediaries. I am not saying this by accident, because the model I am describing here would support the kind of thing that de Closets[6] and others have said – I cite him here because he is a social fact, he is one of those people who take an atmospheric theme that is part of the social climate – in executive conferences where people talk for example about how to get workers to work better, and this theme is orchestrated with the full power of the media and becomes a real social force that you are obliged to reckon with. It would be completely naive to discount de Closets on the pretext that his book is bad. This model can clearly be used to justify a technocratic view against small bosses such as trade union bosses, but it could also target small bosses such as middle-ranking executives of telephone companies who are not sufficiently instilled with the 'spirit of the firm', as people say today – hence the difficulty of communicating the results of social science. You have to believe that the people at the top, the principals, have the means for siphoning off profits of a different kind and a different order of magnitude than the little intermediaries at the bottom who manage to get a bit for themselves . . .

To come back then to the 'pure'. There was a famous mandarin called Li Zhi, whom we published a portrait of in *Actes de la Recherche*, and who was a kind of anti-mandarin:[7] a mandarin who attacked, in absolutely extraordinary books – one of them was called *A Book to Burn*, a magnificent title – mandarin corruption, the structure of mandarin reproduction (the ENA is a completely mandarin institution . . .). This kind of individual is quite intolerable for [the system]. These 'pure' tend to be found rather in the upper spheres: there are social conditions of access to purity – Aristotle said that virtue demanded a certain well-being . . .[8] The 'pure' also exist among the subaltern, but they tend to be perceived as naive and are not very effective – they are silenced. The next issue of *Actes de la Recherche* will publish, as I said, the interview that I conducted with a woman responsible for urban policy projects who is in charge of tackling poverty in the most wretched districts of France, and who explains – it's more complicated than this – that the more successful she is, the more she is punished; the more she does what she is told to do, the more she is punished . . . I'm summarizing accurately, I think – the title is 'An impossible mission'.[9] Another case that has not been published, but will be, is that of a judge who was transferred just as he had done what he had been asked to do – he was in charge of the reintegration of prisoners, etc.[10] Those are things that happen here, so that you don't think they just happen in China. In any case, I have taken China as an example.

The 'pure' – and this is what Will says – thus destroy the balance associated with functional corruption, because uncompromising integrity has a revelatory effect, that of denouncing the full truth of the structure, and it works as a criticism for everyone else. That is what the 'pure' are criticized for, being a living criticism: [. . .] for saying [tacitly] to the others that they are dreadful. The 'pure' are the ones who give the game away, who betray, and particularly betray their own peer group. In recent history, you have all kinds of people who experience misadventures because they simply do what it is said that other people do, but which other people actually do not. By this simple fact, they show in an exemplary way what the others are not doing. [When they are] outside critics, it is possible to say: 'That's resentment, bad faith, a lack of information, etc.' But when it is done in the same situation by someone who is mandated to do what he does, this has an effect of exemplary prophecy and rupture that is quite remarkable. What is interesting is that these pure ones, in discourse and ideology, are the object of some very special treatment: they are [right away] suspected, and people say: 'It's not possible for someone pure to be pure.'

(A sociologist, by profession, has the same type of reaction, and always wonders what lies behind this purity. Even if he is pleasantly surprised that the 'pure' exist, he is obliged by his very trade – something that others don't understand; they think that the sociologist is being unpleasant, suspicious, that he is inspired by resentment – to suppose that there are always reasons for what people do, and so he is obliged to ask himself: 'Why is this person pure?' 'What is particular about him that makes him particularly "pure"?' This is what spontaneous sociology does. If scientific sociology is difficult, this is because it is obliged to do what each person in everyday life does for his opponents [. . .]; we are all very good sociologists in relation to our opponents, because we have an interest in seeing what they do not see in themselves, or what they hide.)

The 'pure' are therefore suspected, combatted, defamed, and at the same time admired, because it is impossible not to recognize that they pay homage, even if hypocritically, to the virtues that everyone officially celebrates . . .

The example of institutionalized corruption in China, 3: double game and double 'I'

Another remark. This situation of institutional corruption places officials in a situation of constant ambiguity; Will speaks of 'permanent schizophrenia' and 'institutionalized hypocrisy'. I think this is something fundamental, perhaps a universal characteristic of bureaucrats. On bureaucracy, I wrote an article on delegation which is applicable to trade union delegates, political [representatives], mandatories, etc.[11] I tried to show, drawing from different arguments and documents, that there is a kind of structural hypocrisy of the delegate, who can always speak two languages: he can speak in his own name, or in the name of the institution in whose name he speaks. This is a kind of double game and double 'I'. Robespierre said: 'I am the people', which is the form of mandarin imposture par excellence. Nietzsche, who was very furious at clerical imposture – this type of imposture is typical of clerics in general, not just clerics of the church, but also intellectuals – [wrote that] clerical imposture consisted in usurping a legitimate personality in order to be able to accomplish the interests of the real personality.[12] And this kind of permanent prosopopeia – 'I am France', 'I am the Republic', 'I am the state', '*L'État, c'est moi*' '[I am] the public services' – is constitutive of the position of the mandatory, the delegate, and it is also typical of officials who are always officials of the public, and thus of the universal. This kind of schizophrenia was indicated [. . .] a year or two ago in an article by an American, Gordon,[13] which explained how American lawyers, who are no choirboys, used a kind of double discourse. Alongside their extremely realist practice, they had a whole ideological construction about the professional ideal, professional ethics, etc. [The author] used the very term 'schizophrenia'. I do not think that [either Gordon or Will] read the other's work, but the fact that they hit on the same image shows that they did indeed grasp something important, in very different contexts.

This is to say that bureaucracy is the object of a double image that contributes to its schizophrenia. It is seen at the same time as both rational and transparent, and as corrupt; all the examples that Will gives show these two images. Officials likewise have a duplicated image of themselves, the pure being those who, to put it simply, burst open the contradictions [hidden by] the permanent double game with the others, and above all with oneself – the double game being Sartrean bad faith: the act of lying to yourself, of telling yourself you are acting for the universal while appropriating the universal for your own particular interests. Here again, I remind you of a theme that I tackled last year: this private appropriation of the universal, which people tend to view as an abuse of power, [. . .] is despite everything something that advances the universal. This is a theme that I always come back to, because a transgression that [assumes the] mask of the universal is better than a transgression pure and simple. I would not have said this a few years ago. Transgression that is disguised in the name of the universal makes a certain contribution to advancing the universal, [to the extent that] it is possible to use the universal against it to criticize it . . . I am summing up here in a few short sentences analyses that I did at length in the past.[14] My introduction was useful because it allows me to say this, otherwise I would have omitted it.

I believe I have given you the essentials of this article. [Will] gives very good examples of the ways of preserving rights and dispensations in this logic. I have a certain right; for example in a French municipality I am the person who gives out building permits. There are invariants, [if you think of] China: I can transmit the request or not transmit it; I can transmit it quickly or slowly; and I can naturally siphon off a profit, ask for a contribution . . . Transactions between notables and bureaucrats, for example, are one of the major transactions on which the functioning of the public services rests. [Take the case] of a member of a departmental council who goes to see the person in charge of building permits: how does it happen that the person in charge of building permits grants one straight away when it's a departmental councillor? Because there are long-standing exchanges between them, they meet up at receptions; or again, in exchange for protection in case X, the other side gives protection in case Y; in exchange for a dispensation, etc.

Another example. One of the major dimensions in all this is time. People always speak about 'bureaucratic inertia'; these are words [which have Molière's] 'dormitive virtues' and don't explain anything. The logic I am trying to apply, that of right and dispensation, consists in making use of the spectrum of all possible behaviours between rigour and laxity. This is how it is. There is a rule and I can play and get profit from being either ultra-rigorous or ultra-lax, the whole spectrum of strategies available to anyone who holds a right; even someone in a ticket office has a bit of this power. You must not forget that, when this is the only power you have, it is very tempting to use it. This power of controlling entries and exits is a power over time, which is often retranslated into time – a long time back I gave a lecture on Kafka[15] [on the subject of this] play with the structure of time – an action on the temporal structure that is inherent to power – I gave a whole year's course on 'time and power', on the fact that in many cases power gave a power over other people's time . . . There is a very fine Chinese example that helps us understand the invariants of bureaucracy, the reports on which promotion or dismissal depend, etc. These provide an occasion to capitalize influence, to accumulate symbolic capital, because on this occasion, by exercising a control, it is possible to accumulate capital either by indulgence or by severity.

This would need more detailed examination, but I have the impression that you would think I was stretching things out, when in fact the work begins where I stop, in the precise analysis of situations and cases. Evidently – I say this in passing because there is a kind of return to the mode of phenomenology under cover of ethnomethodology – it is apparent that these fine analyses are at the same time analyses of structure, and that it is not in the end just a matter of finely describing interactions, but describing them as interactions under structural constraint.[16] Ethnomethodology often abstracts from structural constraints. Cicourel,[17] for example, who is one of the ethnomethodologists that I always single out, as he does at least have the intuition that there are structures, gives very fine analyses of what is involved in filling in a bureaucratic form: what filling in a form means when 'bureaucracy' means 'forms', what a form means, what filling it in means, whom it is addressed to, what is expected of the person who fills in a form, what you have to know about what a form is in order even to have the idea that it has to be filled in, etc. That said, even the finest phenomenological analysis of the experience of filling in a form still doesn't reveal the truth of the form, because the whole history of bureaucracy is needed, of the state, of structures, and also of models such as the one I am presenting to you, in order to discover what power and the experience of power are. In particular, doing a phenomenology of bureaucratic temporality can be very fashionable, but it doesn't get you anywhere if you've not made this kind of detour by way of China . . .

The genesis of the bureaucratic space and the invention of the public

I am now going to outline another theme. I have tried to show how, applying the idea of concentrated power and of the people who are in a position to redistribute it, this redistribution could itself be the occasion for the accumulation of subsidiary powers. I was clearly rather premature in describing and constructing the genesis of this bureaucratic space within which all the effects of unauthorized siphoning off take place. And this is what I want to try and do now. I shall develop three successive points [. . .].

First of all, the question of the extension of circuits of interdependence. To start with, you have the king and the subjects – this is just a sketch, it never actually exists just like this, since right from the start power is already a bit differentiated, [. . .] but we make the hypothesis that there is a principal [agent] and regular agents . . . You then have to see how this initial core becomes differentiated, and how chains of dependence are created. Where there was one person, there will be a series of agents who are both accomplices and opponents – accomplices in the use of power, and opponents in the competition to monopolize power and the competition for the legitimate use of power, or the monopoly of a particular form of power which claims to be the only legitimate one – you have the conflict between the Parlement and the king, etc. [You have to study] how networks extend and how the problem of relations between those with power is raised as this differentiation takes place – with palace wars, etc.

Secondly, I shall try and analyse how, alongside this process of differentiation, a collective work is conducted (I've already given the [outlines] of this in relation to the Chinese legalists who sought to reconcile Confucius with bureaucratic logic), the work of constitution [of the] public. How a work of invention of public logic in opposition to private logic was conducted. This was certainly one of the most difficult human inventions, since it was necessary to invent something that contradicted both singular interests, egoistic in the naive sense of the term, [and] interests bound up with membership of the primary group, that is, the family, etc.

Thirdly, having described how networks extend, and how the public was invented, I shall try to show what was the logic of the conflicts between agents with different positions in the networks that constitute the structure of power.

Very rapidly, today I shall simply indicate the theme; you could describe one part of the process of state constitution as a process of 'de-familization', to coin a convenient neologism. The point is to emerge from the logic of the familial, the domestic, and move towards a different logic whose shape is still ill-defined. You can put these things differently. You will know Malraux's famous book on art, *La Monnaie de l'absolu.*[18] [By calling art the 'currency of the absolute'] he means that art has become a substitute for religion – this is a very commonplace idea, which had been said a hundred times before him, like most of Malraux's ideas in aesthetics; it was a kind of scholarly common sense that Malraux orchestrated with a certain talent. You could say [therefore], to make a kind of pun – but puns are useful, they have always been used by the wise to transmit their knowledge, as they're like very thick sweets, you can suck them for a long time and find lots of good things – that the state, then, is the small change of absolutism; there is the king, who is the [big] coin, and a heap of smaller ones . . . I think this is a useful metaphor, as it sums up very well the intent of what I am going to say.

What I am going to say is extremely trivial in the literature on the state, but I am not sure that it is so for all of you listening to me. People always speak of the process of 'de-feudalization' – I discussed this problem last year, [but I emphasized then] the fact that the birth of the state is accompanied by a rupture of the 'natural ties' of kinship – clearly, ties of kinship are social ties – and the replacement of a mode of reproduction based on blood by a mode of reproduction mediated by institutions, the chief among them being the educational institution. On three essential points, therefore, the state is opposed to the family. First of all, it replaces primary family allegiance by formal allegiance, and condemns nepotism. Secondly, it replaces direct, family succession by reproduction based on the school system. Thirdly, it replaces the self-appointment of rulers or minor rulers, or their designation by local instances, by a central nomination; it concentrates the power of nomination.

What I want to show very quickly is that these three processes are real and observable. I want to explain what they consist in, but also show in what way they are incomplete: the family and the family way of thinking is always with us, in the very logic of functioning of the social world. We can take the example of the school, as it is the best known. The nineteenth-century illusion was to believe that education was a matter of merit and natural gift – [a word that] was already a bit suspect, so 'merit' was the general term used – and that the school accordingly cut the umbilical cord with family reproduction. And we know from the work of sociologists that by way of the school social heredity and the transmission of patrimony between generations takes place with certain losses, but [these are] basically negligible statistically – even if they are dramatic enough at the level of individual experience, they are not in the end dramatic in statistical terms.

I mention [this] very quickly as it is the simplest point in what I am going to say, and I will be able to proceed more quickly next time. I draw here on the book by Corrigan and Sayer that I discussed last year:[19] they show how, in England, the break between simple reproduction on the basis of the family and reproduction mediated by the state took place very early on; they show, for example, how appointment to local positions – sheriff, royal officials, etc. – was taken over by the state as far back as the thirteenth or fourteenth century. The public office was very early on distinguished from the fief, and the holder of such a position became very early on a royal appointee, no longer a hereditary figure who was more or less identified with his own fief. In other words, the crown resisted all the processes that tend to fragment power and establish local governors [who come from] the local universe. It is a key problem, to show you that general models are important. All the present discussions about decentralization have to do with this problem. Is what is gained in relation to power in terms of proximity to the base not lost in terms of the universality of power? It is ambiguous, these processes are never simple, they often have a double face: isn't it in many cases a regression back to less universal forms of management of power?

Another process cited by Corrigan and Sayer is the transition from the central level to the local level. The sheriff, I believe, is the significant character in this analysis: he is appointed rather than being self-designated or designated by heredity. At the central level, Corrigan and Sayer locate the generalized transition from the household to democratic forms of government around the 1530s; they emphasize that the aristocracy demilitarized. The same thing happened in France. You can see how, from the twelfth and thirteenth centuries, the central unit, which was the *curia regis* [the king's court, the royal council], divided; and you see the gradual birth of an administration with the Grand Conseil, the councils of government, councils of justice, etc. The same historians emphasize the parallel process that accompanies this differentiation in terms of the birth of a common law, a juridical space, a constitutional right, that mean that all authority relations are mediated by reference to the universal; they can no longer be exercised in a simple and direct manner.

That is more or less what I wanted to say; next time I shall try to describe rather more precisely the process of division of authority.

Lecture of 14 November 1991

Construction of the republic and construction of the nation – The constitution of the public in the light of an English treatise on constitutional law – The use of royal seals: the chain of warrants

Construction of the republic and construction of the nation

[I shall now continue] the discussion I began last time, so that you do not lose the general line. The objective I am slowly pursuing by way of these analyses, in as much detail as possible, is the question of the genesis of a public power: how was a de-privatized, de-feudalized, de-personalized power established? In this way, I am trying to reveal two processes that are both historically intertwined and relatively independent: firstly, the process of establishment of a public reality, as contained in the word 'republic'; and secondly, the process of establishing a national reality. You could say that everything I have been saying for years is one long commentary on the expression 'République française' . . . How were these two realities established? On the one hand, they are realities symbolized by the initials 'RF' (and I shall come back to the importance of such things), by a flag, by the symbol of Marianne, etc., and by individuals – the president of the French republic. This set of realities is the product of an extremely complex historical work.

To start with, I shall focus on the establishment of the republic. Then – and I shall proceed quickly, as this makes it easier both to understand and convey – I shall try to show how the idea of the nation is constructed, how the nation is produced and reproduced, and through it, nationalism. One of the political or philosophical questions that is raised by relating these two processes is the question of the necessity of the link between them: could you have the republic without having the nation? Is it possible to win on two tables, as it were? Could you have the benefits of universalization that the state brings without having the losses, the costs of particularization, nationalization and nationalism that are historically inseparable from the construction of a *res publica* and a state?

To locate ourselves explicitly on the normative terrain, you could describe the transition from feudalism to absolutism as the access to a higher degree of universalization, a progress in [the domain] of the universal. But this progress is accompanied by the construction of a nation both in objective social structures and in human minds. As I have said several times, the construction of the public is almost inevitably accompanied, at all events in historically attested examples, by a private appropriation of the public. There are proprietors – those whom I call the present-day state nobility – who effect an appropriation, a patrimonialization of the public. I believe that this is where the two processes are joined – I offer this as a hypothesis, and will return to it later on. One may ask whether it is not the private appropriation of the public that effects the diversion into nationalism of what is potentially universal or universalist in the state. Are the bearers of nationalism not frequently those who have a private interest in the appropriation of the public? I shall speak about this in relation to an important book entitled *Imagined Communities*.[1]

It has been shown how nationalist movements very often originate with small holders of cultural capital: authors of dictionaries and grammars. This is important, because these small holders of cultural capital are also the people who write on nations and nationalisms, and it is not by chance that they always exempt themselves from their historical descriptions, and that people eventually forget that there are particular interests in forms of construction with a universal claim. This is the question I wanted to raise, in order for you to see where I am heading; not that where I am heading is determined by this – that would give you a wrong impression of my analysis. For the moment, I will study the extremely difficult genesis, which would require hours of detailed analysis, of those realities that we call public, and which have become partly self-evident, taken for granted – if you wrote a dissertation on 'the French republic', I don't know what you would come up with, but certainly not what I am in the process of explaining. In fact, I want to show you that there are two processes involved, and I shall start by studying the first of these, keeping the second for later.

The constitution of the public in the light of an English treatise on constitutional law

I shall now embark on a fairly detailed description. Last week it was the history of China, this week it will be that of English constitutional law. (You will say that there are no limits to the sociologist's hubris . . .) I say this so that you realize how delicate a path this is. I know very well that there are specialists who've spent whole lifetimes on this subject . . . I risk saying imprudent things, but I believe that the analysis I derive from the texts I am basing myself on is well-founded – apart from errors of detail that I may commit, among other things because, for example, the sources on which I have drawn are not perhaps the latest state of research.

UNIVERSITY OF WINCHESTER
LIBRARY

(A parenthesis here. It often happens, at least in fields that I've studied well, where I feel relatively on top of things, that earlier writers offer things that more recent research has hidden or obscured. [These earlier writers] brought up problems that are today seen as resolved; I believe this is the case here, but I am not completely sure.) I shall try to show how a bureaucratic field, an administrative field, was gradually established, how this power, which was concentrated in the hands of the king, was gradually divided, and how an initial network of interdependence was established, on the basis of which there gradually developed a complex bureaucracy of agents tied by complex interconnections, in the two senses of control and delegation. I shall describe – in the next lecture – the broad lines of this process, that is, the establishment of autonomous fields: you can describe the process by which the church is separated from the state, or the state from the church, the process by which lawyers [become independent], etc.

Today I shall read you – slowly, and commenting on it – from a treatise on English constitutional law, which is terribly boring, but from which I have taken two passages that I see as important. To give you the reference first of all: the author, whom I have already spoken of, is F. W. Maitland.[2] This is a reissue of a canonical treatise, a course of lectures on constitutional history that Maitland gave. I shall begin by describing the process of differentiation of the two types of rulers: the dynastic rulers [of] the king's house and the bureaucratic rulers. Maitland describes this in detail, and I shall go slowly as I believe it is important to avoid sticking with crude oppositions. You will remember that I contrasted two modes of reproduction: those people who reproduce by way of blood, and those who reproduce through bureaucratic mediation. Maitland [seeks to] describe the genesis of those whom he calls the 'great officers of state'. There have always been such official figures. And it would be interesting, he says, to take each of these great officers one by one, but I haven't the time. Previously, in earliest times, the principal officials were officials of the king's house: there was the steward, the butler, the chamberlain, the marshal, etc. The activity of these people gradually extended beyond the king's house, it spread out over the whole of the kingdom. And the greatest men in the kingdom were proud to hold offices that originally could have been called domestic ones – 'domestic' often connoting 'servile'. [Maitland] also gives a whole series of examples from the German empire: the Count Palatine of the Rhine was 'steward', the Duke of Saxony was 'marshal', the King of Bohemia was 'cup-bearer' and the Margrave of Brandenburg was 'chamberlain' . . . In other words, the greatest could perform servile functions, and [Maitland] emphasizes the fact that all these functions were hereditary. The position of 'high steward' was hereditary in the House of Leicester, that of 'constable' was held by another family, and so on. Functions [were] thus assigned to a lineage.

And this is where it gets very interesting: 'But in England . . . we may state as a general rule that an office which becomes hereditary becomes politically unimportant,' [writes Maitland].[3] In other words, the lineage mode of reproduction gradually gives way to another; [these attributions] become unimportant, [they] become a 'show' office, one of exhibition and ceremony. In other words, these functions are relegated to the realm of symbolism. This is extremely important, because [the people who hold them] are not paid, they are on the side of symbolism, the side of ceremonial artistry – [Maitland] gives examples of this. Today, aristocrats are often diplomats or TV presenters, they are on the side of 'show', and this is not by chance. They are on the side of ceremonies, of ceremonial, [the work] of maintaining the symbolic capital of royalty by exhibition. To say that they are on the side of the symbolic does not mean that they have become unimportant – that is an error on the part of the author, a naive utilitarian prejudice that leads people to believe that symbolism means nothing. If there is a symbolic franc,[4] people say 'It's symbolic', they think it doesn't cost anything and therefore it's not worth anything. In actual fact, symbolism both costs and pays. The fact that people are paid in symbolism, in 'funny money' if you like, does not mean that they are therefore unimportant, on the contrary . . . I laid great emphasis on the particularity of the English royalty, and compared this also with Japan, both societies in which management of the symbolic is an important dimension of management of the collective patrimony and of the state. They gradually become, therefore, exhibition personalities in ceremonies, some of them being ascribed ad hoc functions, particularly in coronation ceremonies or pompous spectacles and exhibitions. Maitland gives an example: when a 'peer' is chosen by his peers, he has to be a personage of great dignity drawn from this category of holders of hereditary symbolic capital.

What is interesting is that these high offices are purely honorary. Here again, 'honorary', 'purely honorary', does not mean unimportant, [it means] that they no longer fulfil the technical aspect of the function and thus that the function must be duplicated; all these people are duplicated by others who do the real work. Instead of holding to a stupidly utilitarian view that would say: 'It's absurd, a waste of money, some people being paid to do what these others are supposed to do', you see that something is happening that is completely functional at a more complicated level. [Maitland] gives examples of this: besides the high chamberlain who does nothing and receives nothing, there is a 'lord high chamberlain' who does have duties in the royal household and receives a salary. He also gives other examples.

You thus have on the one hand the gratuitous, the symbolic, the pure, the disinterested, the noble – in fact these are all words that mean 'noble' – and on the other hand the domestic, but in the pejorative sense of the term, people who receive a wage, who are mercenary – it is hard to find the right word here – who actually fulfil technical functions. Having given this description, Maitland continues: alongside these officials who hold functions there gradually appears another group of office-holders, whose offices are not hereditary. They particularly include the *capitalis justitiarius Angliae* or justiciar.[5] He was the first official who was appointed

and not hereditary. Similarly, the two most ancient high officers whose
name and title are always preceded by 'Lord' – the Lord Chancellor and
the Lord High Treasurer – were the first two chief officers. Maitland gives
other examples: under the Tudors, you see the gradual appearance of
people who duplicate the honorific personages or who are positioned in
between them: the appearance of men of confidence, confidential clerks
interposed between the king and his chancellor. For example, there was
the Lord Keeper of the Privy Seal, the king's guardian of his private seal.
There is the king, there is the chancellor, and between the two there is
someone who keeps the king's seal. Then as time goes on, between the
king and this keeper of his seal we find another personage, who is called
the 'king's secretary'. In 1601 – I know this is a long time, I began in the
twelfth century – the latter becomes 'our principal secretary of estate'.
The same process happens on the side of the chancery, secretaries of state
appear according to the same process. You thus have a process in which
there are two points, A and B; then between the two you put a third point,
dividing in half; later in quarters, eighths, and so on. You thus have a
series of discontinuous points that become increasingly continuous by the
intervention of intermediate personages, who are explicitly commissioned
and mandated to perform functions that the initial official holders of the
function were themselves supposed to fulfil.

I will leave this here, even if it deserves to be read in detail. What is
important is that these commissioned servants are legally warranted and
legally sanctioned. They are subject to common law, which is not the
case with the others; they are subject to common law and they have legal
powers. In other words, progress in the direction of bureaucratization is
accompanied by progress in the direction of legalization: each act of 'com-
missioning' is accompanied by more explicit rules governing how those
commissioned are commissioned. By the same token, the function or post
is legally established, a description of the post being made – 'He will do
this, and only this, but he will be obliged to do this and do it completely
. . .' So there is elaboration and explanation.

Naturally, so long as you remain in dynastic logic, vagueness is the rule.
The nobility cannot stand bureaucratic strictness, [they prefer] vagueness,
indeterminacy, the symbolic (in our society the symbolic survives among
intellectuals, everything I have said here is applicable to the intellectual
field). Definition, delimitation, the juridical, are incompatible with the
specific logic of the nobility. The law imposed on the commissioned is thus
also imposed on the commissioner: the king himself is gradually enveloped
in law by the legalization of the relationships that unite him to those who
are charged with exercising the royal power by delegation. Suppose that
the queen wants to give someone a certain sum of money; money has to
be obtained from the royal treasury, and sorted out with the chancellor of
the exchequer. How to proceed? First of all, the money must be explicitly
obtained and warranted; so there is a warrant of this kind, the king's word
starts to be no longer sufficient. Someone has to warrant that the money

has been obtained according to the rules. And since the warrant given by this person is not sufficient by itself, it has to be warranted by a seal: this is the great seal or privy seal. The king's verbal order is no longer enough: to give a poor man 100 francs, someone has to warrant, and the person who warrants must be himself warranted by a seal. The seal must itself be countersigned by the secretary of the seal. So there must be the great seal, but also the little seal that warrants the great seal . . . Bit by bit, [in order to conduct] this operation – to obtain money from the royal treasury –

> A mass of laws grew up about this matter; for some purposes the great seal was indispensable, for others the privy seal would do, for others again the signet kept by the secretary: in a few cases the king's oral command would be enough – thus undoubtedly he could dissolve parliament by word of mouth. This doctrine of the seals practically compelled the king to have ministers entrusted with the seals who could be called in question for the use that they made of them. We must not think, even nowadays of 'the seals of office' as mere ceremonial symbols like the crown and the sceptre; they are real instruments of government.[6]

[We can refer here to] one of the earliest lectures I gave on this problem, around Kantorowicz's theory concerning the genesis of modern bureaucratic bodies on the model of the ecclesiastical bodies.[7] Kantorowicz emphasized the fact that these bodies were historically connected with what he called the *sigillum authenticum*, that is, the authentic seal capable of authenticating; an act becomes a state act when it bears the seal. And the seal, finally, *sigillum*, is also the '*sigle*';[8] the seal or the initials 'RF', for example, is a kind of magical imprint that condenses the whole state reality, transforming a private order, which [could otherwise] be just the brainwave of a mad king – this is important, historians have paid great attention to this, the king may be mad or weak, or manipulated by women (the Chinese were much obsessed with the problem of what to do with an irresponsible monarch). The legal order to pay only becomes legal, official, an act of state, if a seal is placed on it. How does the seal obtain this magic power? The same thing is true for a university degree: if it doesn't have a signature, the degree is not valid and may be challenged, etc. From where then does the *sigillum* obtain its authority?

This is a problem analogous to the one that Mauss raises about magic – if you've not read his 'Essay on magic', this is absolutely compulsory reading.[9] In this essay, Mauss asks what it is that gives what the magician does its magic, how he is recognized as a magician, and is thereby effective essentially because he is recognized as a magician. Is it the instruments he uses, is it the seal, is it the magic wand, is it other magicians? He raises a whole series of questions, and ends up saying that the magical effectiveness of the magician is the whole world within which he operates – the other magicians, the magic instruments, and the believers who grant the magician his power and thereby contribute to his existence ... The same is true with the act of state: how does the seal, *sigillum authenticum*, come to have this magic power to transform someone into a professor, for example, by the act of appointment? It is precisely this extremely complex network that is embodied in the *sigillum*, of which the seal comes to be the manifestation.

[I have presented] one aspect of the mechanism, but it is far more complicated than this. There are initially these two opposing categories; I placed a good deal of emphasis on the opposition between the king's house and the officials, showing that there were two antagonistic, competing, conflicting principles of domination, and that the king could play one lot off against the other, etc. I believe this is an invariant that is found in all embryonic state systems. Today I shall try to show how these two powers gradually differentiate, one falling on the symbolic side, the other on the technical side. But what Maitland does not say is that division does not imply absolute separation; it would be naive to describe this process as the withering away of dynastic power in favour of bureaucratic power. At least in the English case, the two powers continue to function in a complementary antagonism. And I believe that in our own society, the president of the republic, to come back to him, is someone in whom the two lines are combined, being simultaneously technical and symbolic.

The use of royal seals: the chain of warrants

I come now to the second dimension of the process that Maitland describes. I can give the page references for those of you who would like to look this up; that would be a good idea as I can only give a brief overview: what I already discussed is on pp. 390–5. What I shall explain to you now refers to a section entitled 'The doctrine of royal seals', on pp. 202–3 of the same book. This deals with relations between the king and his council, but these are the same problems that will recur with relations between the king and the parliament ... What powers can the king exercise over the councils, and what powers can the councils exercise over the king? [Maitland] raises a general question: originally, the only powers that a council could exercise were the powers of the king, it was purely and simply a mandatary, and ultimately – I shall come on to this right away – the struggle between the king and the parliaments in England and France bore precisely on this point. Does this mean that the parliaments were only the arm of the king, the expression of the king's will, or did they have a relative autonomy in relation to the king? Could they turn against him this authority that the king himself had delegated? Originally, the parliament only had the power delegated to it by the king, and the powers that any council could exercise were purely and simply powers of the king. In fact, Maitland says, this theoretical principle finds its extreme case in the practice concerning the royal seals; he goes on to describe how the use of the royal seals gradually placed a limit on the power of the king – this is a further differentiation that I want to describe.

First of all, the genesis of the chain of responsibilities that I mentioned in the previous lecture. From the time of the Norman kings down to our own day, the royal will was expressed by acts, charters, letters patent, sealed letters, etc., all these being acts sealed with the royal seal. The great seal of the king was entrusted to the chancellor, who was the head of the secretariat. He was the secretary of state for all departments. From the end of the Middle Ages through to the Tudors, the chancellor was the king's first minister. What symbolized his pre-eminent role was precisely his possession of the royal seal. Bit by bit, you have the appearance of other seals alongside the royal great seal. The chancellor had so many various activities to perform, particularly in the legal field (he also had to act as judge, etc.), he was so much caught up in the everyday bureaucratic routine, that for matters that concerned the king directly you have the appearance of a private seal that I mentioned above: under this 'privy seal' the king gave directives to the chancellor, directives concerning the use of the great seal. This is already the interposition of an intermediate point. By the same token, this private seal was entrusted to the care of an official, a functionary: the keeper of the privy seal. Then in the course of time, [this keeper himself required a secretary] who was called 'secretary of state'. You end up with the final state, the routine that is then established – you could draw a diagram of this, the succession of acts, the great chain.

(A little parenthesis here [about] a very famous book by Lovejoy on the history of ideas, called *The Great Chain of Being*.[10] This is a very fine book that shows how in very different works – from Plato and Plotinus through to Shakespeare, in other words, all kinds of authors – you find the same view that can be called 'emanatist', according to which at the top there is God, Heaven, all creatures being merely degraded forms of this supreme and perfect form. There is clearly an analogy with the king, which is interesting because the model I am in the process of describing is perhaps a mental structure. This famous great chain of being, which is so recurrent in the texts, could have both metaphysical and political foundations, as often happens. In other words, the great chain of being is perhaps a political ontology. What I am describing here is the great chain of being whose summit is the king; then, from one (de)gradation to the next, you end up with the petty executant. I believe that this metaphor is there in the unconscious of everyone in bureaucratic societies. We all have in our unconscious this view of relations between model and execution. For example – this may strike you as far-fetched, but I am just using the liberties associated with my function – I believe that if linguistic theory, structuralist theory, etc. was so readily accepted, it was because it is entirely based on the opposition between model and execution, language and speech – speech being simply the execution of language – perhaps because we have a bureaucratic unconscious that leads us to accept the philosophy of the great chain of being. This theory/practice model recurs in many domains, and the exploration of bureaucratic structures, as I have said dozens of times, is an exploration of our unconscious . . . Close of parenthesis.)

In the final state, therefore, you have something along these lines: a regular routine is established, documents are signed. First of all there is the king's word, but to be serious, an order is written, signed in the hand of the king and countersigned by the king's secretary, who is the keeper of the king's seal. This is the secretary of state. That is the first level – signed by the king, countersigned. Then the text is signed by the keeper of the private seal and the act in question becomes an instruction for the chancellor, who in his turn places on it the great seal of the kingdom; at that moment, it becomes properly authorized. I come back to Maitland's text because, in these acts of delegation, something very important happens: power is divided – this is the bad pun that I made last time: the small change of absolutism. Power fragments, that is clear, but there's more to it. We come back to the problem of the mad king that always preoccupied the canon lawyers: the person who countersigns controls, and the king is himself controlled by the person who countersigns. If the king should do something foolish, the person who countersigns takes responsibility for the folly and becomes guilty of not having informed the king of his mistake. The practice of countersignature thus generates a certain ministerial responsibility over royal acts. This is extraordinary, since in one sense the person responsible postulates the possible irresponsibility of the king. This is not just a matter of a division of royal authority; there is the construction of a delegated authority, and this delegated authority returns against the person who delegates it. No act is valid unless it is countersigned, and at every level the person who countersigns assures by his countersignature that he is engaging himself in the royal will. [. . .] The person who is commissioned is committed, the person who commits is committed: 'he gets his hands dirty', to put it trivially. When people say that bureaucracy dodges responsibilities, we begin to understand: the bureaucrat who countersigns controls and commits himself, and so exposes himself. I refer again to Maitland: the ministers themselves have an interest in the perpetuation of this routine; they are happy to countersign, but also to be countersigned because they are covered in this way by the person who countersigns, because they are afraid of being challenged for acts of the king. Towards their superiors, they are afraid of not having proof of the fact that these are royal acts, and towards their inferiors, of being finally responsible. In other words, they want to be guaranteed in relation to both above and below.

I don't dare [to go on], because you no doubt think I am treading water, whereas it seems to me that I am going very quickly . . . Basically, I am trying to give a kind of historical phenomenology of bureaucratic acts. If you were doing an analysis of emotion, it would seem quite normal to be going slowly, but people are not accustomed to doing this with political and legal things, which are terribly complicated and which, like lived experiences of this or that, are hidden by their very commonplaceness, by being self-evident. I believe that this kind of exercise was important to restore the surprise we should have when faced with a doctor signing a certificate. What is restored by this analysis is the fact that, if it works, this is because everyone has an interest in it; [. . .] what is lost in terms of power is gained in security, in the guarantee of power.

I shall continue very quickly. So we have the chancellor and all the ministers, all the delegates – *ministerium* means mandatory. This is another theme of Kantorowicz: *mysterium, ministerium*. He shows how for the canon lawyers this is the same word; he plays on the words: 'the mystery of ministry'.[11] That is basically what I am describing here: ministry as the exercise by a person of a power that is not his own, that is the mystery of the official – the mystery of the official is precisely delegation. What the official loses in power, he gains in security in the exercise of power, and in guarantees against subsequent challenges to his power; so he has an interest in it. The chancellor is afraid and hesitates to attach the great seal if he does not have a document with the private seal that he can present as guarantee. This other word 'guarantee', or 'warrant' in English, is very important; [he needs a] guarantee of the fact that the validity of the act he is going to countersign is guaranteed. He guarantees something guaranteed, something guaranteed by the state. And I guarantee all the more willingly if what I guarantee is guaranteed. When you take a degree, you are asked to present your previous qualification. I think that you see the foundations here of what is described as the critique of bureaucracy – as always, ordinary criticism touches on important matters, but it touches on them in such a way as to obscure them. People say 'bureaucrats cover themselves', 'bureaucrats dodge responsibilities', etc. That is the basic criticism of bureaucratic operation, which is uninteresting because it [forgets] that [if] it's like that, [this is] not by chance, it fulfils tremendous functions, and you need only place yourself in the logic of the process as a whole to understand that there is no other way of doing things.

The chancellor is thus afraid of affixing the great seal if there is not a document adorned with the little seal, the private seal, which he can produce as guarantee. The guardian of the private seal is concerned to have the king's signature guaranteed by the king's secretary. For the king, this is an interesting arrangement; on the whole, it satisfies everyone. That is very important, and by and large what the social mechanism is: everyone, often including the dominated, finds something in it. (This doesn't mean that you have to fall into functionalism, don't make me say things I am not saying, but as there are those of you who will think this, I am obliged to say so.) For the king it is also a good deal, a useful arrangement: his officers have the duty of remembering the king's interests; they have an interest in combining the interest of the king, you [could also say] of public service, with the interest of the state; they have an interest in knowing where things stand with the king's affairs. And to the extent that the king's affairs become multiple and complex, the division of labour becomes necessary, because in order to be always informed of the king's affairs, several people are needed, and several who mutually guarantee one another; and so you have a chain. (If you think of an analogy with science, everyone knows that scientists each work increasingly on a tiny point in an enormous space. A great theorist of science stresses the fact that the world of science is based on an immense chain of delegation:[12] 'I don't know how to judge this, but I judge the person who does judge, I trust him'; there are a series of guarantors in a chain.) Ultimately, bureaucracy is a field of this same type: a field in which it is evident that no one can guarantee everything and be guaranteed about everything.

I come back yet again to the dodging of responsibility, the fact of covering oneself that is inherent to the logic whose genesis I have described. This is inherent to the process; from the moment that you cease to have a single charismatic leader, who can decide everything on the basis of his charisma, that is, his exceptional gift in the face of exceptional situations, etc., you are led into a process of this kind, with, naturally, at each point in the network, mandatories who have to take advantage of all the guarantees that the system produces. But what gets forgotten is the fact that these guarantees are also conditions of operation. To go on, as the king's affairs become what is called necessary, so the division of labour becomes necessary. What I am describing is the genesis of a universe, the genesis of a division of labour of domination. There must therefore be someone here holding an office at the head of each department to make sure that the king is not deceived or badly informed. And the danger that the king's interests are neglected is reduced to the extent that the process of managing the king's affairs is differentiated and divided. We then have the problem of variations; what is described here is a structure, but this structure undergoes variations according to the relative weight of the individuals occupying positions. When you have a weak king, the whole structure shifts in the direction of dispossession; or there may also be unequal forces, agents occupying different positions in the chain. But what is important in the whole ensemble, contrary to the perception of historians who see the ends of the chain without seeing the chain and its logic as a whole, is this overall network of individuals who are all in a relationship of controller and controlled in relation to the others. The king is in an apparently exceptional position, but he becomes ever less so, becoming in the end a position like the others, as the chain increasingly differentiates and, while the king controls more and more people, he is also controlled by more and more people.

That is by and large the process that I wanted to describe. What general lesson can be drawn from it? I believe that, from the standpoint of the problem that I raised at the start of the year, the description of this process is important in order to see how a kind of depersonalization of power takes place. The king still remains 'the fountain of honours, offices and privileges', according to Blackstone's formulation – the metaphor of emanation is very important – he still remains the source of everything that happens. That said, however, the exercise of power is possible only at the price of a kind of withering away, in a sense, of absolute power: and this withering away is precisely the birth of the state, of the public. It is true that the first link in the chain appears to command all the others, but in actual fact this simple, linear, transitive view (A commands B, [who] commands C, etc.) is completely simplistic, given that at each stage delegation is accompanied by a concession of controls. In the end, one may ask whether the first link, the governor, is not just as much governed – this is what men of politics often say when you talk to them. It is clear that in complex societies the first link is often in the position of *Jean-Christophe*:[13] a novel that no one reads any more, in which one of the main characters gives orders to the clouds, telling them to go in the direction in which they are going – 'Go west!' (Those who govern are often in this position, and there is nothing surprising in that. What is disturbing is that those who govern believe that they do command the clouds, and succeed in making the governed believe this as well, with the complicity of people who are part of the network made up today of journalists, for example, who worry over sound bites, who have people believe that these sound bites have an active effect, and, ignoring the mechanisms of the kind I am describing, that is, the patterns of networks and causes in which those who govern are also caught up, overlook almost all the real causalities: [journalists] then deflect [attention, and privilege] a personalist view of power and forms of challenge to power, which are wrongly applied when they are applied to individuals.)

I ask your forgiveness for having been a bit slow and treading water. [I wondered]: 'Is it possible to convey this in a lecture?' I was very hesitant, I wanted to move on to things that are easier to convey and more general, but I think that basically this is the gist of what I have to say. I didn't want just to communicate a rather simple idea of the transition from a power monopolized by a single man to a power exercised by a network, a complex division of controlled controllers, but also to show what it meant to do an anthropology of what the public is, the state. Next time, I shall try to describe things in a broader fashion, which anyway I find easier. This process, which I described a very small piece of, is simply the history of the seals of the king of England, and it must be understood that the state of which we are the culmination is the product of thousands of little inventions of this type – and that is still a very simplified history. These thousands of little inventions constantly oppose people in conflicts of interest, which are first of all developed in practice, and then theorized, or which are sometimes theorized first when there start to be jurists, constitutionalists, and then transformed into practices by people who have an interest in them. It may happen that the king uses great jurists to express his decision in a legal fashion: there is a kind of exchange between theory and practice, in particular. The famous book [by Sarah Hanley] that I already spoke to you about, *The Lit de Justice*, and which I will speak about again in greater detail, shows the existence, for example, of exchanges between the technical exercise of power and the ritual of power – of which people may say: 'This is purely symbolic, without importance.' [And finally, I shall tackle] the legal legitimization of power, that is, its symbolic legitimation.

I shall try to show in what respect jurists, who played an enormous role through to the French Revolution, and even in this, are a pivotal cog inasmuch as they are at the same time those who regulate practices of delegation and those who develop the constitutional theory able to serve as a basis for these practices, very often by effecting a simple transmutation into the order of discourse of things that were invented in practice, with the particular interests of jurists who are neither the chancellor nor the keeper of the seals. They are third parties, and the jurist is the person who is in the [position of] third party; they are referees, which does not mean that they do not have their own interests as referees: there was a point when the referee wanted to join the game, and perhaps the French Revolution was a bit like that . . .

Lecture of 21 November 1991

Reply to a question on the public/private opposition – The transmutation of private into public: a non-linear process – The genesis of the meta-field of power: differentiation and dissociation of dynastic and bureaucratic authorities – A research programme on the French Revolution – Dynastic principle versus juridical principle as seen through the *lit de justice* – Methodological digression: the kitchen of political theories – Juridical struggles as symbolic struggles for power – The three contradictions of jurists

Reply to a question on the public/private opposition

[The start of this lecture was not recorded. Pierre Bourdieu is replying to a question on the pertinence of the public/private opposition.]

This is a complex question. I can refer you to work I did a few years ago on French employers,[1] in which, by statistical analysis among other instruments, we brought out one of the major oppositions in the world of employers: the opposition between distance and proximity in relation to the public. And one of the major dimensions by which the employers' space was organized turned out to be precisely the opposition between public and private. To reply very summarily to the question put to me, you can say that what is called private is largely inhabited by the public, and this is particularly true of the firm. You could even say more: at the end of the day there is no private. I have discussed at considerable length what is known as the theory of professions,[2] a theory developed in the United States, with a whole series of soft concepts as is common in English-language sociology. I showed that this notion of profession introduced a fundamental error by contrasting professions to the state, whereas the very existence of professions depends on the state, among other things because the professions are protected by various forms of *numerus clausus*, particularly that established by the diploma as a right of entry guaranteed by the state. It is no accident that professionals should be demonstrating against the state: [. . .] even the most naive observers have seen something very odd in the unanimous gathering of such different people. I believe therefore that the notion of profession, in the same way as the notion of employers, refers to bodies that are divided according to their distance from the public, and I believe there are no sectors of business that are not highly dependent on the state.

All the talk about economic freedom is highly naive, and the interest in studying the state is precisely to show the extent to which differentiated societies are penetrated through and through by state logic. This interpenetration clearly has consequences, and the ambiguity that there is in objective structures also exists in people's minds and in ideological strategies. It is one of the principles of the strategies of the dominant to take everything and pay nothing, as common sense puts it. The paradox of many current political strategies, such as those that appeal to the free market, is that these aim to ensure the dominant the profits of the free market, the profits of freedom, and the profits of state dependence . . . (This is a bit sharp and a bit simple, but I shall try to argue it in a more developed fashion some other time.)

([. . .] It is clearly impossible to speak about the state without getting responses that bear very directly on topical political questions. I often leave it to you to make this connection yourselves, but perhaps I am wrong, because you either may not do it or may do it differently from how I would. At the same time, I believe that my work, partly moreover because the 'public space' – a detestable concept that has reached us from Germany[3] – is encroached on by ideologists who talk a great deal, wrongly and at cross-purposes, about democracy, politics, the state, etc. My work is designed to place myself at a quite different level, precisely so as to try and question everything that is supposed to be already known, all the questions that are supposed to have been resolved by those who speak wrongly and at cross-purposes about the state, the public, the private, more state, less state, etc. This is a kind of deliberate asceticism that is in no way a flight from politics; it is a way of speaking about politics more seriously, or at least quite differently. I may perhaps come back to this later on, [. . .] it is a problem of professional ethics: can one use an academic chair as a tribune? I am not sure about this, I don't know. There are limits that I impose on myself, perhaps wrongly, but I tell you that I am aware of these limits and I invite you to ask yourselves what political implications the analyses I am doing may have.)

The transmutation of private into public: a non-linear process

To return now to my theme. As I have said from the start of this course, I am trying to analyse a process that took place over a long period of time, the process of transmutation of the private into the public; my object is a long historical period stretching from the twelfth to the eighteenth century, in the course of which an imperceptible alchemy was effected, of which I have given you a few examples. By way of analogy, I will refer you (those who know it will understand right away, and for those who don't, this is a way of prompting them to read this book) to the very fine book by Cassirer entitled *The Individual and the Cosmos in Renaissance Philosophy*,[4] a magnificent history of Renaissance thought. Cassirer describes here the new dawn, the inaugural period of modern thought, a time when the distinction was still unclear between astronomy and astrology, chemistry and alchemy, when it is hard to say whether Marsilio Ficino or Pico della Mirandola – to give a couple of names of this time – were the first great modern scientists or the last great rhetorical scholastics. And I believe that you have a situation of the same type with regard to the state, a situation in which there are advances and retreats, when you have ambiguous political structures that may be read in two ways like ambiguous gestalts: either as feudal survivals or as premises of modern forms. This ambiguous period is very fascinating, because it is in this historical work of refining, as it were – at least this is my hypothesis, otherwise I would not be interested in it – that you are perhaps best able to understand logics that [subsequently] become obscure and hard to access, precisely because they become commonplace.

There is thus a process, and it is not a linear process – that is very important. And I am going to speak to you today about two books, one on the *lit de justice*, the other on pre-revolutionary ideologies, in both of which you have evidence of the fact that there was not a continuous process of refining, de-feudalizing, invention, a continuous process leading, as I seem to be saying, from the private to the public. You have advances and retreats, for example the history I am going to tell you about the *lit de justice* shows that there was a kind of advance towards a constitutional theory in the sixteenth century, the elaboration of a certain number of public things, *res publica*, republics, followed then by a retreat with the rise of what is called absolutism.

The first idea is that this is not a linear process. Secondly, contrary to what historians of ideas would have people believe, I have already said – but I believe it is worth repeating – that if in the logic of the artistic or philosophical avant-garde you must always be one step beyond, be ahead of the avant-garde, in the logic of history it is rather the reverse: you must always discover a source of the source of the source. To take one example: who wrote the first novel? Was it [Rousseau with] *La Nouvelle Héloïse*, [Rabelais with] *Pantagruel*, or the *Satyricon* [attributed to Petronius]? And so you go further back, and you always find a predecessor of the predecessor of the predecessor. I believe that this search for a precedent is one of the biases of historical research, which leads to mistakes. People are led, as I see it, to place the first appearance of a phenomenon much too far back, because it is good to be seen by your colleagues as having discovered something still older – these are field effects that are scientific effects. And this is why I emphasized that, in the last analysis, these questions

308   *Year 1991–1992*

of first beginnings are meaningless. It is always said about [Ferdinand de] Saussure that he freed linguistics from the question of the origin of languages. I believe that almost always, or at least in all the fields I am familiar with, the question of the first beginning is meaningless: it is a historicist point of honour that has no real interest. And if you say, as I have just rapidly done, that the interesting thing is these great long transitions with advances and retreats, this makes the problem disappear of itself; it becomes clear that there is no great interest in knowing whether So-and-so borrowed from Such-and-such.

It follows from what I have been saying that you can place the first appearance of modern thought too early. When you look at historical works, you see that the notion of public had great difficulty in getting started, that it was very hard to understand. [As you can see with] Maitland, for example, whom I cited last week, the distinction between the king's public capacity and his private capacity was very long in the making. Likewise the distinction between the national income of the crown and the private income of the king. These are distinctions that were both made and not made, that could be made in certain areas of thought but not in others; they could be made in the mind of the high chancellor but not in the mind of the king. So there are always regressions.

In the same way, Maitland has on pp. 226–7 a very fine analysis of the notion of treason, which is a completely central question: when there is treason, who is being betrayed? Is it the king or the nation? You see, here too, that there is a kind of confusion. For a long time, treason essentially meant treason to the king; in dynastic logic it was a kind of personal offence against the king, which the king could absolve by saying that he did not consider himself offended. And it was only gradually, here again, that treason came to be constituted as treason against something abstract. In the Dreyfus affair, for example, it was clear that treason related to the state; at the time of the Manifesto of the 121 on the Algerian war,[5] the traitor was someone who attacked the idea of the state. It was therefore a very long process. And this dissociation between the house and the *curia* – what in the English tradition is called the cabinet – the hereditary house and the non-hereditary house – was made very slowly, with setbacks.

Here we touch on a point that I see as crucial. The whole history I am telling you today, drawing on these two books, is perhaps dominated by a contradiction bound up with inheritance, which I have already mentioned several times. Office-holders face an extraordinary contradiction in so far as their ideology, their view of the world, their interests, lead them to be on the side of law, and of transmission controlled by law, whereas their interests as a body with a claim to nobility, a claim to transmit offices in a venal way [. . .], make them lean to the side of heredity. How can they be critical of the dynastic hereditary model with respect to the king while they are in the process of establishing themselves as a *noblesse de robe* and obtaining a diverted kind of inherited privilege? You could buy a place on the Conseil d'État and then transmit it by inheritance. So we are dealing here with a primitive form of transmission of cultural patrimony. Being on the side of cultural capital, the side of education against the holders of noble titles, against the *noblesse d'épée* who stand on the side of nature, of blood, the office-holders find themselves in a contradiction when they start wanting to become hereditary, when they want offices to be a kind of function transmissible by the law of blood and nature. The ambiguities in their strategy towards the king are bound up with this contradiction: 'When it comes down to it, the dynastic principle does have its good side . . .' They never put it quite like that, you never read that, but it is clear that their ambivalence is not unrelated to the fact that they have a hidden interest in this model.

The genesis of the meta-field of power: differentiation and dissociation of dynastic and bureaucratic authorities

I am now going to take up what I said in the last lecture. I am not sure that I have made clear the central idea of my argument. I believe I did state it, but it was stated more by the facts I presented than expressly revealed – so I am going to repeat it. I described two processes to you. First of all, the process of differentiation: by analysing the delegation of seals, the process of division of signature, I described the constitution of a differentiated space of rule, a process of extension of chains of authority, and in this way I sought to describe the genesis of something like a public, that is, a form of power in which each holder of power is both controller and controlled. I tried therefore to describe the genesis of a structure, which is a relative protection against arbitrariness, by virtue of the fact that power is divided between interconnected individuals united by relations of mutual control. The executor is clearly controlled by the person who delegates to him, but at the same time he is protected. This is the logic of dodging responsibilities, but the executor also controls the person who delegates, he protects him and guarantees him. I emphasized the fact that the minister had to protect the king against error, and by guaranteeing the king he controlled and supervised him at the same time. By the same token, he could warn the king against attacks on public interests. This is what we shall see in the relations between the king and the Parlement that I shall go on to analyse. The Parlement played on this structural ambiguity of the mandatory that I have just described. The mandatory can always make use of his mandate against the person who grants it to him. The mandatory can turn back against the king the authority he has received from the king. That is the first process. And it leads to a law that I demonstrated by a specific example: I suggested that a modern ruler ultimately does not rule very much, inasmuch as – I can state the law here – the more the network [extends], the more that state power grows, the more people's dependence on a network of transmission belts of power grows with it. In other words, one of the consequences of this differentiation of powers is that paradoxically the ruler is increasingly ruled by those whom he rules – which gives us the paradoxes of the impotence of power, even power that is apparently most absolute.

This first process of differentiation is bound up with a second process, and I have myself had a great deal of difficulty seeing the link between the two, even though it seems to me absolutely central. This is the dissociation of dynastic authority – that is, the king's house, the king's brothers, the heirs – from the bureaucratic authority embodied by the king's ministers. In the case of France, as we shall see from the history of the *lit de justice*, it seems to me that this process of dissociation was partially blocked at a certain point in time. This process, which was very advanced in the sixteenth century, was basically blocked under Louis XIII and clearly so under Louis XIV, with the return of the princes of the blood and the dynastic principle based on nature as against the legal principle that was beginning to establish itself. Whereas in England, as I see it – subject to verification – the dissociation of symbolic power from bureaucratic power that Maitland explains was effected in a far more continuous manner. Moreover, it is still going on, since even today a royal power confined to the symbolic coexists with a government power confined to the technical. This difference strikes me as important [for] explaining [the difference between the French and English political regimes], in the logic of E. P. Thompson's famous article on the peculiarities of the English – identity being always a difference . . .

I want to tackle today something that results from the interpenetration of these two processes. Where there were two individuals, the king and the chancellor, you gradually see the appearance of seven, eight, nine or ten. You thus have a process of Leibnizian fragmentation, [a process] of differentiation. To understand this in its full implications, you have to see how each point – each link, I prefer to say – each link is in fact the apex of a field: the differentiation process that I described in connection with the seals actually involves individuals who are themselves positioned in fields. The general thesis on the genesis of the modern state, which I shall now illustrate as precisely as possible with historical facts, could be presented as follows: you have the progressive constitution of a differentiated space, an ensemble of fields – juridical field, administrative field, intellectual field, political field in the strict sense, which appeared only after the Revolution – and each of these fields is the site of [specific] struggles. This is where we find one of the mistakes, I believe, committed by historians who speak, for example, of juridical culture: what exactly does 'juridical culture' mean? There are jurists who struggle over law, there is a space of jurists who have different juridical strategies, and therefore a differentiated space of juridical texts. In the same way there is an intellectual field, a differentiated field of arguments about the general will, etc. You thus have a set of fields that are themselves differentiated and in mutual competition. Another example is the bureaucratic field. In the second book I am going to speak to you about, Keith Baker[6] gives a long analysis of a writer who expressed the revolt of the juridical field against the bureaucratic sub-field that was in the process of constitution; there was a kind of critique of bureaucracy and technocracy that arose from the parliamentary region.

These fields are thus in competition with one another, and it was by and large in this competition that the state was invented, a kind of 'meta-field' power that was embodied by the king so long as there was a king, but which subsequently became the state. Each of these fields seeks to act on the meta-field, to triumph both over other fields and within its own field. This is abstract, but you will see very concretely, when I tell you the historical sequence, [that the model] works very well. What is constituted is thus a differentiated space of power, which I call the field of power. Basically, I didn't know I was doing this, but I discovered it by doing: I wanted to describe the genesis of the state, and in reality I believe I described the genesis of the field of power, that is, a differentiated space within which the holders of different powers struggle for their power to be the legitimate one. One of the issues at stake in struggles within the field of power is power over the state as meta-power able to act on the different fields.[7]

I already said this last year. I could give examples. There is one very simple one, which is the retirement age. A change in the retirement age affects every field: obtaining a universal reduction in the retirement age, for example, is one of the ways of regulating the struggles within each camp: 'Make room for the young!', 'War on the gerontocracy!' Other examples would be quotas for various ethnic or sexual groups, etc. This is a general law that immediately has specific effects in each of the fields. As a consequence, struggles with a universal appearance, that is, cross-field struggles, have to be understood on the basis of the stakes that they represent within the logic of each field.

A research programme on the French Revolution

That then is the general line and, if I had nine lives, it is something I would certainly like to do: I believe that it would be possible to do a sociology of the state and the field of power on the eve of the French Revolution, and – this is the summit of hubris – that this would be the true discourse to give on the French Revolution. It is completely feasible – it would simply take a lot of time; you would need to study the world of individuals who are each located in a sub-field, who each have particular properties – you would have to know whether they were Jansenist, Gallican, if they had studied at a Jesuit college or elsewhere, if they had read Rousseau, if they had a position in the Parlement or elsewhere. You would need to have all their pertinent properties, just as in any ordinary study, and then relate these properties to the statements they made, which historians of ideas study as if they fell from the sky, as if they constituted a culture. (Some historians act as if it was a culture they were studying, which means strictly nothing, or still worse, like some of them who pride themselves on their philosophy – philosophy is a curse in France – as if it was political philosophy. When historians start doing philosophy, it's really the last straw. Consider François Furet's *Dictionnaire critique de la Révolution française*.[8] Furet and some others are in the process of inventing a history without history, in which the history of political strategies is reduced to the history of ideas. My little programme is thus a very serious one; unfortunately I do not have the energy to carry it out, otherwise I believe it would sweep away a certain number of discourses that regularly appear in *Le Nouvel Observateur*.)

. There is a space of agents who were engaged in the French Revolution, who have their individual names. Marat holds a very low position in the intellectual field; he settled accounts with Condorcet by cutting off his head[9] (just as today, many intellectuals fond of polemics would happily guillotine some of their rivals if they had the opportunity). The Revolution was an opportunity to settle accounts by physical violence that would usually be settled by symbolic violence. We thus have the intellectual field, the religious field, the administrative or bureaucratic field and the juridical-parliamentary field. Each of these fields has its own logic, and agents must be located in these spaces and the positions they may have formulated (on the Parlement, on constitutional law, on the general will, etc.) must be related to their position in these spaces and to the properties attached to individuals that make it possible to define their position in these spaces. I believe this would also greatly aid the historical genealogy of what are called 'republican' ideas, which were the product of struggles between agents occupying different positions in different spaces, with a view to defining in conformity with their interests those entities that were Parlement, king, law, nature, culture, heredity, etc. This is a very hard question; I only have a single research programme to propose, but those of you with a sufficient knowledge of research will see that this is a very major programme, and if one or other of you, or a group of you, are prepared to, I would be ready to collaborate or contribute whatever I can – I think this would be a very useful task.

I now come on to work that tends in this direction. If I have been able to tell you what I have done, if I have found the courage to tell you this, it is because there is work that tends in this direction, done – unfortunately, or fortunately – by American historians. (If I say 'unfortunately', this is not out of nationalism. As I have said several times, the further I proceed in my life, whether working on Manet, on Flaubert, on the French Revolution, etc., the more I read only English . . . This says a lot of things about the state of French research.) The books I am going to talk to you about are by Sarah Hanley[10] and Keith Baker.[11] These two books, especially the first of them, are in my view masterpieces of historical work, with the little reservation I made that the principal agents are not fully enough characterized in terms of their social properties. Even though [Sarah Hanley] breaks with the study of politics and moves towards the study of political agents and their actions, she does not follow this through to give all the pertinent information for analysing the social conditions of possibility of the discourses and practices that these people invented – they invent new practices, new ways of treating the king or treating problems of succession, and one would like to know better on what basis this is, what kind of interest. She gives several elements, far more than usual, but not quite enough.

Dynastic principle versus legal principle as seen through the *lit de justice*

Why do I see these two books as important? Because they offer, the first of them especially, a kind of historical chronicle of the extraordinary relations between the king and the Parlement. I deliberately say 'extraordinary relations', and can show you the definition given in Marion's *Dictionnaire des institutions de la France*:[12] 'The powers of the companies of justice being a delegation from the sovereign, they ceased when the king came himself to perform his royal duty in rendering justice.' The king delegated judicial powers to the companies of justice, that is, the Parlement; these powers ceased when the king came himself: he annulled this delegation by coming in person to the place where this delegation was exercised. The *lit de justice* was the act of the king to go and annul, as it were, his delegation. As a consequence, and this is very important, there is no possible definition of such an institution as the *lit de justice*. If you read it, you will see that the particular interest of this book is to show how people have struggled for six hundred years over what the *lit de justice* was, to try and impose a definition conforming to their interests. [Marion's] definition is itself rather favourable to the king, [though he was in fact] a modern historian and believed his approach was simply positivist. The parliamentarians said: 'Not at all! When the king comes, on the contrary, it's the time for us to exercise the legislative power with him, we will make remonstrance to him, we will fulfil the function of control which the delegation gives us.' To continue however with Marion: 'The powers of the companies of justice being a delegation from the sovereign, they ceased when the king came himself to perform his royal duty in rendering justice. Hence the custom of the kings to come to their Parlement to have their edicts registered with authority . . .' The formula was: 'Here is the king' – which is very surprising, completely the king's point of view . . . As the king understood that delegation ceased when he attended, he went there to exercise an act of authority, that is, to oblige the Parlement to submit to him. 'Hence the custom of the kings to attend their Parlements so as to have authoritatively registered there the edicts, declarations, etc. that these were resisting, came to be called *lits de justice*.'[13]

Sarah Hanley's book goes quite contrary to this definition, despite its being useful. She gives a history of all the conflicts around the *lits de justice*, of which there must have been around fifty from the sixteenth century onwards. The first of them was under François I in 1527, and there

was subsequently a whole series. Each time what was at stake was whether
the mandatory or the delegate would be the winner. And each had gains to
make. The problem of the parliamentarians, for example, was to harvest
the extraordinary symbolic profits that the arrival of the king represented,
the fact of being seated alongside him, in red robes, etc., and without
having the extraordinary costs that the violence inscribed in the definition
I have just read represented, when the king took back with one hand what
he had given with the other. How then to have the profit of being seated
alongside the king without losing the legislative power that the status of
the Parlement implied? I will not of course go into detail here about the
different *lits de justice*. If you turn to the book, you will see various cases.
Perhaps I am a bit reductionist, which is again my bias as a sociologist,
but it seems to me that when you have the model of relations between the
king and the Parlement, you can practically deduce the successive forms
that the different *lits de justice* take. What was at stake in these encounters
between the king and the Parlement was a struggle between two powers
within the field of power that was in the process of being constituted, a
struggle in which the balance of forces varied according to different variables. For example, you see right away that *lits de justice* were held already
when the king [Louis XIV] was only four years old . . . It is clearly of key
importance to know who carried the king; a few words were stammered
to him and his reply was interpreted. In this case the royal power was
particularly weak, even if there was a regent . . .

Another very interesting case is the starting point of revolutionary processes. In 1715, the king [Louis XV] was too young to govern and the duc
d'Orléans was recognized as legitimate regent. As he did not himself have a
very great legitimacy he made a tremendous concession to the Parlement:
'You recognize me and . . .' Of course it didn't happen just like that; what
is very exciting in this book are all the mediations, negotiations, etc. –
everything was settled before the collective, public and ritual display. [The
duc d'Orléans] took the position: '[You recognize me] and I will grant you
the right of remonstrance', something that the absolutist period had abolished – under Louis XIV there were no remonstrance and the *lit de justice*
had become a great Versailles ceremony, a great spectacle, headed no
longer by the high chancellor but the master of ceremonies. The Parlement
thus saw itself granted the right of remonstrance in exchange for recognizing the legitimacy of the regent, and above all, what was granted on top of
the right of remonstrance was the Parlement's main claim that it should
finally have its word to say in the appointment of the king.

The history is rather monotonous once the stake in this symbolic struggle has been grasped, this being one of the problems that arise with all
state powers. Max Weber, who theorized things in their generality, shows
for example that charismatic power is the most exposed power in a period
of succession: the charismatic leader can only perpetuate himself by the
destruction of his own charisma – what Weber called the 'routinization
of charisma'.[14] The charismatic leader is extraordinary, his charisma is

born out of a crisis, he is himself the foundation of his own legitimacy; the charismatic leader is the person who has shown himself extraordinary in an extraordinary period. How then to transform this charisma, this kind of extraordinary property, into something ordinary? How to transmit it to someone ordinary? This can be a son, a dauphin, etc. Weber made a theory out of the ways of settling the problem of succession – you cannot construct a theory of political regimes without constructing a differential theory of the ways in which a regime can ensure its own perpetuation. Even a traditional regime, such as hereditary monarchy, has to settle this problem. And in the sixteenth century, thanks to crises – François I had problems with the [Holy Roman] Empire, he had suffered military defeats, he had been faced with cases of treason – the Parlement, mandated by the king to exercise control over public law, constitutional law, everything concerning the state, found itself in a strong position, it was able to say: it is law that decides, and the transmission [of power] is guaranteed by law.

The stake in the struggle is as follows. In periods when the king is strong and the Parlement weakened, for example, coronation is the ratification of a legal act; the dynastic principle is victorious over the legal principle, the king is king because he is the son of a king, and he is king not by *nomos*, 'by law', as the Greeks said, but by nature; he is king by heredity. Sarah Hanley shows very well the change in vocabulary; there is a small and imperceptible change in vocabulary, but one that changes everything, and clearly in these cases the struggle is over words, over seemingly nothing, but in reality to replace one word by another. In the sixteenth century people would have said 'The kingdom is never unoccupied'; in the seventeenth century the saying was: 'The king never dies.' There is thus a transition from the kingdom to the king, from the public thing, *res publica*, to the dynastic private thing. In parallel with this, the whole lexicon in which transmission is expressed moves from a logic with legal connotations to one with natural connotations, with a whole accompanying symbolism – the metaphor of the phoenix that is reborn from its ashes, or the metaphor of the sun that is eternally reborn. 'The king is dead, long live the king!': this whole symbolism is a kind of orchestration of the dynastic principle based on nature.

I have given you the principle, now it needs [development]. I don't know if this is pertinent as it will take me hours, but I shall try and do it very quickly. You are dealing with the history of a balance of forces between two powers – its ups and downs, its vicissitudes – one of these is the royal power based on the dynastic principle, as I described it to you earlier on, with the principle of lineage, inheritance by blood, family, the king's brothers, etc.; the other is a legal principle in which every act must be guaranteed by law, in particular the inaugural act of the reign which is the coronation or nomination. This period may be very brief. With the death of Henri IV in 1610, for example, the king's party was severely criticized for having crowned his successor [Louis XIII] while Henri IV was still there in effigy. This period of interregnum is a dangerous period of discontinuity, in which the two powers particularly face one another: the upholders of law who particularly desire to be present at such moments, while the king's party carries out acts of force, according to Marion's definition, to try to avoid the encroachment of legal competence on dynastic competence.

In the period that Sarah Hanley calls legal, she says that there was a process that led from a legal monarchy to an authoritarian dynastic monarchy. I believe this is a minor mistake. As I showed, the monarchy was conceived in terms of dynastic logic from the start, and it was by way of transactions with the lawyers that the dynastic principle was led to make concessions to the legal principle – particularly in the sixteenth century with the return to the dynastic principle, but asserted no longer as a way of being, as with the Capetians, but as an 'ideology', the dynastic principle becoming a justifying ideology of the royal power. Clearly, you could [construct the sequence]: dynastic principle 1, legal principle, dynastic principle 2; I would agree with this, and you could then reserve the name of absolutism for dynastic principle 2, that is, the moment when the dynastic ideology was used to justify a mode of transmission. In the end these distinctions are unimportant, but I nevertheless found them awkward and hard to follow.

Methodological digression: the kitchen of political theories

One of Sarah Hanley's exciting contributions, as I see it, is that instead [of being satisfied] with doing what many historians do – for example those known as the Cambridge school, people like Skinner[15] who have done a lot of study of political theories, particularly from the sixteenth century – she also studies the [great] political [rituals], particularly the king's *lits* [*de justice*] and the 'royal sessions', that is, sessions when the king comes to the Parlement, [showing that these] have two functions. The first of these is to display, as in all ceremonies, a social structure, a hierarchy. (When I was working on the employers, I described a grand burial in the de Wendel family, which was reported in *Paris-Match*: you see how the funeral procession is the projection in space of a social structure.[16] In so-called 'archaic' societies, for example among the Kabyles, matrimonial processions were displays of symbolic capital: relatives were invited, rifles fired, your symbolic capital was displayed – and this is also what many theorists do, 'processional theories' are often the occasion to display symbolic capital . . .) These grand ceremonies like the *lit de justice* thus had the function of displaying capital and distributing it differentially; they were a projection of the social space in the form of protocol, with people in black, red, etc. This was all defined by way of interminable struggles, with seats being higher or lower, cushions or no cushions, on the right or the left – it was all done in such a way as to express a social hierarchy in a systematic fashion. Sarah Hanley shows that these rituals were very important, as they were an occasion for the parties present, that is, the king's party and the parliamentary party, to confront one another with the view of obtaining little points of precedence. Their weapon in these confrontations was discourse, so they produced discourses. Rhetorical strategies intended to justify profits in terms of protocol, that is, symbolic profits, were strategies in the invention of constitutional law, constitutional theory, the production of political discourse.

The interest of this book, even though this is something the author does not do explicitly, is that it shows the soil in which all the political treatises that are studied at Sciences-Po or elsewhere were born. Bodin and company were brought up on these chancellor's discourses, which they even often pronounced themselves; they might be charged with giving the opening speech at some ceremony or other. This is very important because you may think I am dealing with things that are irrelevant. Fritz K. Ringer's book on the German mandarins[17] has a similar merit to that of Sarah Hanley. Setting out to study the German mandarins between 1890 and 1933, he not only took official texts – such as Heidegger's writings, etc. – but also the texts of these characters that could be called trivial: speeches at prize-givings, inaugural speeches, at the Academy, etc., that is, the everyday ideology of these people. He showed that the questions we have all imbibed with the mother's milk of philosophy ('explain and understand', 'quality and quantity', etc.) were topics of ordinary academic discourse, things discussed between professors, part and parcel of educational rituals. There is of course a kind of 'celebrating' view: philosophers don't see Heidegger's rectorial speech as real Heidegger. But unfortunately it is, and it seems to me that this is in no way for the sake of demeaning Heidegger, for the pleasure of going into the kitchen – although Heidegger himself always liked to quote Heraclitus' saying: Heraclitus was in his kitchen one day, some visitors arrived, and in embarrassment said to him: 'Master, we have surprised you in your kitchen . . .', and he replied: 'No, not at all, there are gods here too.' Heidegger loved to quote this anecdote, but in actual fact he didn't like it at all if anyone went into his kitchen, any more than any other philosopher does. I believe this is the image people have of sociology, that it demeans, [it takes the] standpoint of suspicion, all these stupid things about sociology that you can hear.

There is a very fine book that was published four or five years ago in French, a collection of texts on the university by major German philosophers.[18] I don't say this to be mean, I believe that academics universalize their view of the university. Very often they tell you: 'Things are going badly, the barbarians are at the gates', and what they actually mean is that there are a lot of students . . . So it is very important on the contrary to place official discourses that are recognized as such, discourses that are canonized by academic awards, etc. within the whole of [discourse] production, while knowing very well that each discourse owes a certain number of its properties to the circumstances in which it was pronounced, and that a prize-giving speech cannot be treated in the same way as a *Tractatus philosophicus*, that is very clear . . . But what Sarah Hanley does is extremely important, as she shows how these pure discourses on Bodin's *Republic*, etc. are discourses of individuals who were engaged in their time, who had some contribution to make to the republic, who had interests – not in the utilitarian sense of interests, but a stake . . .

Juridical struggles as symbolic struggles for power

To return to my theme. On the occasion of these meetings, in these gatherings, the parliamentarians, the chancellor, the keeper of the seals, the first president of the Parlement, all these people confronted one another in great speeches which clearly had functions of legitimization, of immediate political strategy in the field of power and in the juridical sub-field of the royal power. When you read texts of this kind, you cannot help knowing, unless you deliberately want to blind yourself to it, that [the defence of the public order in Latin by this or that chancellor] has something to do with the fact [that the author] was on the side of the public, that this was a way of criticizing the king's claim to limit the competence of the Parlement, a way of criticizing the king, who wanted to limit the transmission of offices that the parliamentarians had themselves also begun to practise. In other words, it is impossible not to see that this claim to universality has something to do with the particular interests of parliamentarians occupying this or that position in the parliamentary space. This is the principal merit of Sarah Hanley's book.

I shall now try very quickly, in a few sentences, to give you the broad lines of the history of the *lits de justice*, that is, of the balance of forces between the two confronting powers. [. . .]

Jurists struggled for opposite ends with the same weapons, bringing into play for example a small number of formulas that came either from canon law, or from Roman law, or from the mixture of canon law and Roman law that developed between the twelfth and the sixteenth century. As with struggles in many archaic societies, the winner is the person who manages to turn a canonical formula to his advantage. In fact, the logic of symbolic struggles consists in having the last word, particularly on a word of the tribe, that is, a very important word before which everyone is obliged to bow. There are very fine examples, in Greek thought, of words that pervade the whole history of thought from Homer through to Aristotle, which all successive thinkers laboured because appropriating such a constitutive word of thought for oneself means winning a victory. What is very interesting is that these people are involved in a game, and this contributes to the confusion I mentioned. It is a very confused transition – as with the transition from alchemy to chemistry – to the extent that there are very small changes that are often intelligible only to people who are within this world, something that moreover is another property of fields. Within a field, people fight to the death over things that are imperceptible to those who find themselves in the next room. The nobles of blood, for example – who were present even though the author does not name them,

introducing them at the end as the winners with the return of absolutism –
I imagine that all these debates in Latin would not upset them, they were
not cultivated [enough] to know whether you had to say: 'The king is dead,
long live the king!'

So there are these little struggles on the basis of a common capital,
a common culture. I think this is the right word. In order to fight with
someone you must have many things in common, which is another property of fields. To fight here, you have to have Latin in common, recognition of the value of Latin, lots of things. In other words, for there to be a
struggle in a field there has to be agreement on the areas of disagreement,
on the legitimate weapons that are legitimately employed in the struggle,
even on the criteria of victory, which means that you can apparently speak
of a culture. But all these instruments that make for consensus only make
consensus for dissension. The infinitesimal differences effected over the
course of time were victories: [. . .] the public was the product of these little
semantic slippages, these infinitesimal inventions that may pass almost
unnoticed even by those who invent them. The people who invent them
are so taken by the symbolic profits victory brings them that they do not
know that they are in the process of sawing off the branch on which they
are sitting. Very often, the dominant can contribute to shaking the foundations of their domination because, caught up by the logic of the game,
you could say by the logic of struggles in a field, they can forget that they
have gone a bit too far and that what they say may be taken up by a commoner who is not in the field, who has neither noble capital nor scholarly
capital. This blindness or illusion is what I call the *illusio*,[19] the blindness
bound up with investment in a field, which is one explanatory principle for
the decay of elites. That is another major problem of history and you may
be aware that only Pareto posed it clearly: what leads to the perishing of
what he calls an 'elite'? Pareto said it was because [its members] became
demoralized.[20] I believe on the contrary that very often one of the mechanisms by which elites commit suicide relates to a field mechanism of this
kind – which seems incredible because normally [people think in terms of
demoralization]. The passion of internal struggles – as in the Trotskyist
sects – means that the wood is hidden by the trees, and the smallest difference with the enemy nearest at hand, that is, the friend, leads to forgetting
this basic logical principle. [As in] the Kabyle proverb: 'My brother is my
enemy, but the enemy of my brother is my enemy . . .'

I will continue with this line for a moment. The dynastic thesis was
shaken by legal criticism throughout the sixteenth century, by the claim
of the parliamentary jurists to be on an equal footing with the king, to
share the legislative work with him and not just the judicial work. The
absolute royal power reasserted the identity of both the function and
its holder, whereas the work of the jurists consisted in effecting this dissociation, a characteristic of modern bureaucracy according to Weber,
in which the functionary is no more than his function: the functionary
is independent of his function, he is interchangeable. The weakening of

the dynastic thesis led, from the start of the seventeenth century, [to a paradoxical reactivation of other principles]. In the sixteenth century you had the canonical principle: *dignitas non moritur*. *Dignitas*, the position, does not die; the king dies, but the *dignitas* does not die. To say *dignitas non moritur* meant that there is the king, and even the king's two bodies – that is the famous theory, there is the dignity of the king that is eternal and there is the biological king who is mortal. This distinction would be swept away by the return of the dynastic principle functioning as ideology, and the function would once again be confounded with its holder: 'The kingdom is never vacant', 'The royal authority never dies'. In the sixteenth century the formulations become: 'The king never dies' or 'The dead seizes the living',[21] which is the jurists' formula. And by the same token, the monarchical order is legitimized by the juridical order: the idea of the Parlement being a relatively autonomous instance, able to make use of the power that the king has delegated to it in order to control the king, or even to counteract him in the name of a public order that in a certain sense transcends the king, and of which the parliamentarians are the depositaries, even against the king – that vision disappeared, and jurists were reduced to the status of a legitimizing and consecrating instance of the monarchy.

The three contradictions of jurists

That said, and I am going to stop here – but I wanted to get to this point all the same, so that my argument had a certain coherence – jurists found themselves in a very uncomfortable situation, a kind of permanent 'double bind' to which a number of factors contributed. First of all, as jurists, they were clearly on the side of law against nature – by definition. They were as a minimum on the side of law as an instrument of legitimization of what is. The least that a jurist can say is: 'It's fine like this, but it's still better if I say that it has to be like this.' That is the minimum that a jurist can do, otherwise he abolishes himself as a jurist; if it is the sword that says what is right, that's the end of the jurist. The jurist as such is thus on the side of a duplication of what is, by an expression of 'what must be' that he has the monopoly of; this is the minimal function of legitimization. He cannot purely and simply adhere to the dynastic formula of natural transmission from father to son. But as the possessor of privileges, as the possessor of his office, he continually works to acquire the right to transmit his office by heredity. As holders of a cultural capital that opposed them to the nobles, jurists were on the side of merit, the side of the acquired as against the innate, innate gift, etc.; nevertheless, they began to see their acquisitions as something in a way innate that has to be transmitted, and so they were already in a contradiction. They could not justify the royal power without de facto limiting it, since it is already a limitation to say that it needs to be justified. A fortiori, however, from the moment that they began to argue, to give reasons for obeying the king, they tied the king by the reasons that they gave for obeying the king. That is then the first point.

The second point is that they were on the side of the king, but they also had a noble nature – the inheritance of offices. The third point – this is the contradiction of jurists that I have just mentioned – they were holders of a technical competence, a competence implying a 'territory', thus implying limits and a conflict over limits; and all the major struggles within the field of power are struggles of competence. The word 'competence' is very important, it is a juridical concept and at the same time a technical one. Competence is the right to exercise a technical competence in a certain 'territory'. The struggles of competence in which jurists confront the king are also technical struggles, but they have a symbolic dimension inasmuch as it is impossible to legitimize the king or limit his competence without asserting one's difference in relation to the king – a difference that demands recognition from the king. That begins already in the Middle Ages. There are works on the jurists at Bologna [showing how these] were always in this quite paradoxical position; they were obliged to seize from the king a power that they wanted the king to recognize, that is, to seize from the royal power a power of control, a power that becomes legitimate only when recognized. They were thus in a position of 'double bind' that is clearly seen in their relationship to the symbolic gratifications that the king gave them. For them, in fact, the *lit de justice* was a living contradiction. One problem, for example, is whether the king would go to them or they go to the king. Does the king come to the Parlement or do they go to the palace? To go to the palace is highly honorific, when they have to negotiate, to legitimize, to justify. And all these contradictions in which they are caught up are generators of theories – I believe that contradictions lie at the root of the most wonderful legal inventions.

The final point is that they were always tempted to abandon competence in terms of control for symbolic recognition. And as I see it, you have to keep these three contradictions in mind in order to understand the vicissitudes of the parliamentarians. The kings could play on these contradictions, which were more or less strong according to the strength of the king – I refer to what I previously called problems of transition in the infancy or regency of the king. And the kings could play on these contradictions in order to reduce the Parlement; so it is an extremely complex game. I shall come back to this next time, and go on to the second book which [deals with the] preludes to the French Revolution, the moment of the great crisis around Maupeou which is always narrated, which bore on the transmission of offices and thus on the jurists' dynastic problem.[22] The problem of transmission of offices was the following: did the dynastic principle also apply to offices? Maupeou became this frightful character who tried to establish a non-dynastic principle for those jurists who were critical of the dynastic power, which triggered a revolt of the *noblesse de robe* – as well as a whole series of writings that were very close to what led to the French Revolution . . .

Lecture of 28 November 1991

History as a stake in struggles – The juridical field: a historical approach – Functions and functionaries – The state as *fictio juris* – Juridical capital as linguistic capital and mastery of practice – Jurists face the church: a corporation acquires autonomy – Reformation, Jansenism and juridism – The public: a reality without precedent that keeps coming into being

History as a stake in of struggles

[In the last session I analysed] the quite strange history of relations between the king and the Parlement in connection with the institution known as the king's *lit* [*de justice*]. I tried to show how this institution was the stake in a constant struggle between two social figures confronting one another, a confrontation that bore on the very meaning of the institution. I believe this is a very general principle of social things. Social entities, institutions, are ongoing issues of struggle between agents who are themselves involved in these institutions, struggles over meaning, usage, etc. In the particular case of the king's *lit* [*de justice*], this institution was the stake in a struggle for power that bore both on details of practice, details of protocol and ceremonial, and on the very history of the institution. The interest of this historical retrospective is that it leads the historian to discover that the object of history is a stake in historical struggle, something that few historians fully understand. They often believe that relating a history means relating something that is a historical reality, whereas in reality historical realities, like all social realities, are realities in which the reality that the researcher is studying is in question. They are constructed entities, whose construction is conflictual. The two historians [I am drawing on here], Sarah Hanley whom I have already spoken about and Keith Baker whom I shall speak about today, place great emphasis – because they cannot fail to see it – on the fact that the individuals engaged in this struggle over institutions constantly used history as a weapon for understanding their institution, but also for imposing their construction of the institution and, by way of this, their power over the institution.

Louis Adrien Le Paige, for example, whom I shall speak about today, was a kind of bailiff, a profession with a relationship to history, who resurrected a history of the Parlement institution that was half real and half mythical. History is thus, in history itself, an instrument and a stake in struggle, and I think this is an important lesson that has to be kept in mind when working on historical material. The two parties in this struggle – the king's party and the Parlement party – made use of history, and in particular the history of law, the history of legal precedents, to try and impose their view of the institution – the king's party seeing Parlement as a purely judicial institution confined to the functions of recording the king's decisions, and the Parlement party seeing the king's *lit* [*de justice*] as an institution that offered parliamentarians the opportunity to exercise the right of remonstrance and thus assert their status as co-legislators, that is, with a legislative power and not simply a judicial one. The jurists were divided – I pointed this out last time, but I am particularly emphasizing it today: they began in the sixteenth century to constitute a field, that is, a space within which people struggle even about what the collective monopoly is that people who are in this space have. In other words, a juridical space is a site where it is always necessary to know who legitimately belongs to the space and what you have to be to participate in this space, etc. From the sixteenth century you see this dispersion, and one of the criticisms I shall make of these works – which otherwise I find quite remarkable, otherwise I would not speak about them – is that they tend too much to forget this space or to describe it in too partial and simple a fashion. If the jurists were in a difficult position in this struggle – and this is something very important, I believe, being also a very general social phenomenon – if they were both divided among themselves and also divided individually, if each one of them was divided, this was because their position was structurally ambiguous.

In order to make you understand this twofold division I could take the example of university teachers. A few years ago I conducted a study of the transformations of the university in the context of the movement of May 68,[1] and I was very struck to see, for example, how these teachers responded on a different basis according to the questions asked – this is something that everyone knows, but which you have to perceive clearly in order to see its importance. They could respond as parents, and in this context they were very critical of the teaching; they could respond as teachers, and then they were very indulgent; they could also respond as citizens and [take] a third position. In other words, this kind of division of the self, which is frequently observed and leads to contradictions in the positions taken, particularly on questions of politics, corresponds to the fact that the agents in question often occupy contradictory positions in a field, or belong to a field that is itself run through by contradiction. [In the present case], a teacher is both a user of the educational system as a parent, and an agent of the educational system as a teacher. The jurists were in exactly the same position, as I showed in the last lecture. One of the contradictions of the jurists resulted from the fact that, as holders of an office that they wished to be able to transmit to their successors, they were on the side of the dynastic principle; while as jurists and holders of a cultural power founded on institution and convention, they were on the side of law. So they could be divided against themselves. And these internal divisions were combined with divisions bound up with different positions in the juridical space, which was itself divided. So it goes.

I did not give you the end of Sarah Hanley's book. She emphasizes that the reform introduced by Maupeou in the late eighteenth century, which I mentioned, and which precisely touched a sensitive spot – a state reform that touched jurists precisely where it hurt, that is, the problem of their own reproduction – was a very clumsy reform. There could be no better way of putting jurists' backs up . . . (You can see something similar if you think of teachers today. It is very easy to put all teachers' backs up, which is why a number of reforms of the educational system are never carried out . . .) Maupeou's reform thus touched on the jurists' sensitive point, and swung them in their ambiguity onto the side of the juridical pole in opposition to the dynastic pole. As a consequence, the traditional opposition that set them against the king was reinforced and doubled.

The juridical field: a historical approach

I omitted to tell you that in the absolutist phase, under Louis XIII and Louis XIV, the king's party was to a degree swelled by the party of writers. This is extremely important for understanding the history of the literary field. You undoubtedly know Alain Viala's book *Naissance de l'écrivain*, in which he shows how it was in the seventeenth century that the writer appeared as a recognized profession.[2] Contrary however to what Viala sometimes suggests, the literary field was not established in the seventeenth century, inasmuch as artists paid for their recognition as a profession, as writers, by renouncing the autonomy that is the condition for functioning as a field. Writers, in other words, in order to be genuinely recognized as such, with the profits that flowed from it, that is, pensions, offices and honours, had to make concessions that were very major in terms of autonomy. And these writers – Racine among others, this is forgotten by literary history – were on the side of the king's party, they contributed to the royal hagiography, often as hagiographers themselves – history was once again here an instrument of struggle between two parties.

I turn now to the book by Baker that I mentioned to you last time, *Inventing the French Revolution*. Baker brings interesting additional information to the previous book, showing for example the major role played by a certain Louis Adrien Le Paige, who is mentioned in Hanley's book, where she says that her concern was to challenge the mythology that developed in the early eighteenth century, particularly from the pen of this Le Paige, a mythology according to which the royal *lit de justice* was a very ancient institution going back to the Middle Ages. This mythology was a kind of professional ideology of the parliamentarians, who as a basis for their authority gave themselves an ancient genealogy and said that they had always existed as a legislative body independent of the king – the Parlement seeing itself as a synthesis of itself and the États Généraux. This mythology of Le Paige, which Hanley seeks to challenge in her book, was constructed on the eve of the French Revolution; and Baker's book describes this political culture that was invented in the period 1750–80, with a number of principal agents, including Le Paige, who was the spokesperson or the ideologist of the Parlement. The merit of Baker's book, as I see it, is to sketch an analysis of the juridical space as a field. In speaking of juridical culture in general, he distinguishes [several categories of jurists] in a manner that to my mind is somewhat arbitrary and rather superficial. It is more of a classification: he read these authors in the Bibliothèque Nationale and he has to organize them; he places them in three categories, which is already better than putting them all together. He tries to show how the different ideologists who sought to construct a constitutional philosophy, all those philosophers, historians or jurists, fall into three main positions that correspond to three positions in the space of the field of power. So he distinguishes three types of discourse – this is on pp. 25–7 of his book.

The book's central idea is as follows. In this pre-revolutionary period (1750–60) there was a disaggregation of the traditionally undivided attributes of monarchical authority. This authority rested on three principles, reason, justice and will, and these three principles began to disassociate from one another in connection with the appearance of three interest groups. One the one hand, the Parlement, with a juridical discourse that emphasized justice; on the other hand, what could [be called] the 'people', but actually were the lower legal clerks,[3] whose political discourse emphasized the general will (these were the Rousseauists); and finally, an administrative discourse that emphasized reason. [Baker] illustrates these three discourses by analysing those writings that he sees as most representative of each of these forms of discourse. Like [the author of the] previous book, he discovers a struggle over the past. He shows this particularly with respect to Louis Adrien Le Paige, a Jansenist who tried for the first time to reconstruct an overall history of the Parlement. He was the keeper of the archives, and used his status to present on the political stage a kind of imaginary history of the Parlement and forge a kind of ideal representation of its function, to give it a historical foundation. I shall try and read to you rapidly the major themes of his presentation. Baker describes Le Paige as the representative theorist of the claims of the parliamentarians, who becomes their ideologist.[4] For Baker, he was far more important in his time than was Montesquieu, even though Montesquieu had put forward an ideology that was known and familiar to the parliamentarians, for example d'Aguesseau, whom I have cited here and who constantly referred to Montesquieu. Le Paige, for his part, insisted on the identity between the

modern Parlement de Paris and the deliberative and judicial assemblies of
the Franks. So he dates the Parlement back to the origins of the monarchy
and insists on the dual function of the royal court, of the Parlement. The
Parlement, for him, was both a royal court with the *lit de justice* and a
national assembly like the États Généraux, an assembly that existed therefore to limit the royal power; not simply to register but also to remonstrate,
to criticize. In this context the reference to the English Parliament, which
was on the side of the remonstrance model, was highly important, which
is why in the eighteenth century there was so much reference to it in these
milieus. Le Paige therefore represented the parliamentary position. Later
on, still in the same book, Baker rapidly analyses three authors – there
are far more, but I have singled out these three because they are the most
representative of the positions characterized by Baker. The first of these
is Malesherbes, the second is Turgot and the third is Guillaume-Joseph
Saige. I shall rapidly tell you what he says about them (which doesn't dispense you from reading the book, but you may spare yourselves doing so).

Malesherbes wrote a book called *Les Remontrances de la cour des aides*,
having himself been the first president of this court.[5] He gives a juridical
discourse of the same kind as that of Le Paige, but in a synchronic logic.
Whereas Le Paige sought to base the specificity of the Parlement in
history, Malesherbes focused on the present condition and developed at
length the capacities and functions of control and limitation that fell to
the Parlement. For Baker, Malesherbes represents the judicial pole in the
tripartite division he sketched out at the start, while Turgot represents the
bureaucratic pole; the latter, in his *Mémoires des municipalités*,[6] developed
a justificatory discourse of bureaucratic absolutism. Baker is to some
extent the victim of his own taxonomy, as he himself recognizes, because
the discourse was more complex than is suggested by the limited category
in which Turgot is classified. Turgot's arguments were complicated and
mainly administrative, but there is also a whole dimension that is also
found with the parliamentarians ... In the end, however, Baker sees
Turgot as representative of the administrative discourse.

The third category is discourse on the side of will. Baker finds this
in Guillaume-Joseph Saige, who wrote a book entitled *Catéchisme du
citoyen*,[7] a representative of what he calls political discourse, which emphasizes intention – the will of the citizen, the popular will, the general will, to
use Rousseau's term. Saige is the only one whom Baker characterizes sociologically; he came from a great parliamentary family in Bordeaux, but
his was the failed branch of this great family – which is why I spoke just
now of a kind of legal *lumpenproletariat*, the legal lower clerks. His cousin
and rival was mayor of Bordeaux, holding very important positions, pro-
prietor of a glass manufacture, etc., while his was the dead branch of the
family, so he was led to make himself the spokesman of collective wills,
the popular will, etc., in the transhistorical alliance between what Max
Weber calls the 'proletaroid intelligentsia' and the popular classes. [Saige]
thus developed a critique of the bureaucracy, even of parliamentarism, a

critique developed very strongly in the pamphlet literature that flourished particularly after Maupeou's reforms. [Baker] has collected a whole series of critiques of bureaucracy, particularly that of Mercier[8] on specifically bureaucratic despotism. At the cost of a historical misunderstanding, Baker reads Max Weber in these pamphlets, but I believe that, through the very quotations he offers, this critique of bureaucracy has nothing in common with that developed by Weber. I shall end my account of this book here, its interest being the way it advances towards an analysis of the world of the 'berobed' in terms of field, that is, of a differentiated space.

You find this again in a book by Donald R. Kelley called *The Beginning of Ideology*,[9] which contains quite an interesting history of the legal profession from the Middle Ages to the sixteenth century, but [also] elements for analysing the juridical world in terms of a field – he even gives a principle of coding, you see very clearly how you have to code these jurists in order to make a fine-grained statistical analysis of them. This author tends to privilege a particular fraction of jurists, seeing them as bastions of absolutism, the king's party; that is, he sees the jurists' contribution to the construction of the authoritarian state, something that is indeed a reality, but that represents only a fraction of the juridical field.

Having given you this reference and having said that the majority of authors concur in seeing the juridical world as a whole, ultimately as a body, I would like to emphasize the fact that, from the sixteenth century on, the juridical body is a field. The juridical world is a field that may exercise body effects – this is a distinction I developed at length in a previous year's course.[10] [. . .] It is impossible to understand the political effects that jurists have exercised historically without seeing that these are very closely bound up with the fact that they functioned as a field very early on. In particular, it is impossible to understand the history of the French Revolution or the Reformation without relating it to the jurists. And here I shall give you another reference: William Farr Church, *Constitutional Thought in Sixteenth-Century France*,[11] a book on the history of constitutional ideas that gives a great amount of information about the juridical field as it already functioned in the sixteenth century. Church analyses in this book the thought of a series of authors: Claude de Seyssel, Charles Dumoulin, Jean Bodin, Guy Coquille – who is very interesting, as a provincial with contradictory positions, from Toulouse – Guillaume Budé and a few others. He not only gives information on the content of their thought, but also on the social positions of these authors, in both the social space – their origins, etc. – and the juridical space, bringing in for example the hierarchy of the universities in which law was taught. It is possible then to relate the positions taken up on the constitutional problem to the respective positions in juridical and social space, and see how there is an intelligible link between the positions occupied in the juridical sub-space and the social space, and the positions taken on constitutional problems. Church emphasizes for example – this is evident enough but it should still be spelled out, some things are self-evident but when spelled out change completely the way that one conceives things – that the jurists with an absolutist discourse were almost all connected with the royal power, the central power. Whereas Kelley, whom I cited to you just now, said that the jurists were absolutists, Church shows that there was a propensity [to adopt absolutist positions].

By and large, you could construct a scale and establish an index of proximity to the royal power that would correspond to an index of proximity to absolutist positions. This is certainly a bit simplistic, social spaces are never one-dimensional, they always have several dimensions, but it is likely that this would be the prime dimension, the main explanatory factor, and you would go on to find secondary factors to study. For example, [Church] emphasizes the fact that the absolutist discourse of those people who were close to the central power always tended to establish a clear distinction between king and subjects, rulers and ruled, and abolish any reference to the intermediate powers in a constitutionalist logic – intermediary powers such as the États Généraux, the Parlements, etc. The Parlement members were themselves ambiguous, Parlement was a sub-field within the field, and among the parliamentarians, according to the position they occupied in the Parlement, there were people who leant more to the side of the king or more [towards the other powers]. There we are, I don't know if you can imagine these spaces and sub-spaces, but you have to conceive them in a space of several dimensions:[12] things move in relation to one another and people occupy positions in these things that move, and the positions that they take towards the things that move where they are and towards other things that move around them depend on the position that they occupy in each of these spaces. (I need only take an analogy with the university field for you to understand this right away.) So much for the first point in what I wanted to tell you today.

Functions and functionaries

In this long transition I am describing to you, this passage from absolutism to a [form of] juridism, the different agents were thus ambiguous and divided within themselves. I would like to quote you here a text that I already mentioned last week, but that I did not have to hand as I couldn't find it. This is a very fine text by Denis Richet, a great historian of the period I am in the process of studying, and I refer you to his book *La France moderne. L'esprit des institutions*. This is a quite fundamental text that should be re-read at the present time when so much is said wrongly about the French Revolution and its origins. [Richet] stresses how, in the course of the process of autonomization of a bureaucratic space, agents are bound by adherences: there is a kind of adherence of the person to the function ... To proceed quickly. Max Weber emphasized that the ideal and ultimate imposition of bureaucratic logic – what he calls the 'ideal type' – is when the functionary is completely disassociated from his function, when the person no longer brings anything to the function or borrows anything from the function; for example, he doesn't borrow the function's charisma, he doesn't make use of the function to exercise personal effects – this is a kind of pure state, an ultimate state. In the period I am studying – I have repeatedly emphasized this, showing the convergence with Cassirer – you are in a kind of uncertain state in which agents are precisely mixed with their function: they are invested in their function and their function invests them.

I shall read you a passage from Denis Richet's book:

> What we call 'public function' went so closely together with its holder that it is impossible to trace the history of any council or any position without writing that of the individuals that presided over it or occupied it. The person concerned either gave an office that had previously been secondary an exceptional importance, or, on the contrary, let a function that had previously been capital by virtue of its former holder slip to a secondary place. The man created the function to an extent that is today inconceivable.[13]

There is also an article, published in an obscure periodical, in which he analyses the dynasty of great agents, surrounded by a whole clientele, who acted as owners of their functions.[14] This is very important for understanding one of the things I shall elucidate now, that is, the specific logic of functioning of the state nobility that was in the process of being constituted at this time and that still exists today. And if I insist at such length on this idea of transition, it is because the transition is not finished, we are still in the process of transition that I have tried to describe, at the end of which you would have this pure functionary totally disassociated from his function and not drawing any personal advantage from this function.

The state as *fictio juris*

I come now to the main thing that I want to say today, which is a kind of balance sheet of the contribution that this strange body known as the *noblesse de robe* made to the genesis of the modern state. This is a way of summing up what I have done up to this point: I am going to give a kind of *longue durée* history, in great strides, of the rise of the body of legal clerks, the rise of the 'berobed', and thus also the rise of cultural capital in opposition to noble capital as a particular form of symbolic capital. Basically, the main body independent of the royal power, apart from the business bourgeoisie that was still very thin on the ground and moreover was itself often connected with the *noblesse de robe* – the only power or only counter-power, as it were, that was relatively established, was bound up with the 'berobed'. Describing the rise of the 'berobed' thus means describing the progressive constitution of a new power and a new foundation of power – a power based on law, education, merit, competence, and capable of opposing the powers founded on birth, on nature, etc. I am going to proceed by leaps and bounds, I have to go back to the twelfth century and I will repeat things that I said in past years.

Medieval historians have shown the extent to which the clerks were from the start instruments of the rationalization of power: it was they who introduced rigour, writing, recording, all the operations identified with bureaucracy – bureaucracy is the bureau, and the bureau is writing, accounts, the written word. As early as the twelfth century, the clerks had the monopoly of a category of resources that was extremely effective in the struggles within a field of power in its nascent state – that is, law. We should give a very rapid analysis of law from the standpoint of these struggles within the field of power, this competition in the exercise of domination: law is very powerful because it provides a kind of reserve of techniques of thought and techniques of action. The holders of juridical capital are holders of a social resource essentially composed of words and concepts – but words and concepts are instruments for the construction of reality and particularly of social reality. For example, as Kantorowicz has very well shown, jurists, in particular canon lawyers, borrowed from canon law, religious law or Roman law, such a notion as *corporatio*. The notion of *corporatio* underlies our notion of a body and the whole theory of the social body, the relationship between the social body and the spokesperson, which is extremely modern; I believe the discourse of canon lawyers was one of the most powerful discourses. I have already analysed the role of the seal, *sigillum authenticum*. When you read historians such as Kantorowicz, you don't know whether to read them as historians of ancient institutions or as thinkers, sociologists or specialists in political science who themselves offer instruments for thinking the social world of today. The canon lawyers were the inventors of a capital of words and concepts that jurists had at their disposal: very often, when it is a question of inventing the social, having the word already means making the thing.[15]

To sum up the general line of what I am going to tell you today, the state, as has often been said, is a *fictio juris*. This is true, but it is a jurists' fiction, using *fictio* in the strong sense of the term, that is, from *fingere* ['construct', 'make']: it is an artefact, a construction, a conception, an invention. Today therefore I want to describe the extraordinary contribution that jurists have collectively made to the work of state construction, in particular thanks to the resource composed of capital in words. In the case of the social world, there is a famous theory of language known either as the Sapir-Whorf or Humboldt-Cassirer hypothesis,[16] depending on whether your language is English or German. According to this, words are not just descriptive of reality but themselves construct reality. This hypothesis, which is highly debatable as far as the [physical] world is concerned, is very true for the social world. That is why struggles over words, struggles about words, are so important. Having the last word means having power over the legitimate representation of reality; in certain cases, imposing a representation means imposing reality when a reality has to be made. If you name something that had previously been unnameable, you make it public, publishable; the fact of being able to say 'homosexuals' instead of saying 'queers' is already making it possible to speak about something – in the field of sexuality this is clear. The fact of making the unnameable nameable means acquiring the possibility of making it exist, having it known and recognized, legitimizing it. In many cases, the power of words and the power over words are political powers; in the last analysis, political power is largely power by way of words, inasmuch as words are the instruments of construction of reality. And to the extent that politics is a struggle about principles of the vision and division of the social world, the fact of imposing a new language about the social world means, to a large extent, changing reality. I am repeating very well-worn themes, which I have gone over many times, but they underlie what I am saying here.

Juridical capital as linguistic capital and practical control

Jurists thus have a capital of words, a capital of concepts, and they can contribute in this way to the construction of reality.[17] I also repeat this theme, in the wake of a number of writings of an ethnomethodological type, but distinguishing myself very strongly from conceptions that remain individualistic and subjectivist. The work of construction of social reality is a collective work, but not everyone contributes to it to the same degree. There are people who have more weight than others in the symbolic struggles for the power to construct social reality. What I am studying here is a case in which jurists (as a differentiated body, etc.), by virtue of having the specific capital that they hold, exercise in the field of struggles for the construction of social reality a disproportionate influence in relation to other ordinary agents. This capital of words and concepts is also a capital of solutions and precedents for difficult situations of experience. This is very clearly seen in so-called archaic societies, in which the poet, who was the spontaneous, unestablished jurist, without a body of doctrine or a police – that is a big difference – was the person who had the last word when no one knew any more what to say; it was he whom people went to consult in case of distress, when the group no longer knew what to think, particularly in cases when it was necessary to transgress a rule in order to find a way forward. In the Kabyle saying, the poet is the person who says: 'There is always a door.' Every rule has a door. This is the person capable of uttering the transgression of the rule in the language of the rule, which is also one of the major rules of jurists. To be able to do this you have to know the rule especially well, and moreover, be mandated as a holder of the rule, thus being the only one with legitimacy to transgress it.

This capital of solutions in difficult situations is a capital of experiences in every sense of the term 'experience': validated experiences, stand-ardized [*homologuées*] experiences, giving the word the strong sense of *homologein* that means 'the same thing' [in Greek]. These are experiences that have received a social standardization, that is, on which there is social agreement: 'We all agree in saying that', or else, 'Everyone thinks that', or again *Satis constat* ['It's a well-established fact', 'It is certain that . . .']. And, what is perhaps most important, it is a capital of organi-zational techniques – what is nowadays required of communication or organization advisers, etc. To a large extent, ever since the twelfth century this function fell on jurists who could draw on an immense treasury – Roman law, etc. – of techniques, systems of standardized and socially validated procedures for solving problems. This is very commonplace, but generally people do not conceive law in this way. Jurists offer social formulas – some of you have perhaps attended secular funerals, there is a kind of disarray when no one in the group knows what to do, then someone invents and says: 'We'll place a flower', and everyone follows this, very happy that someone has found a solution. An institutional solu-tion is both nothing and very much: 'There is a priest for this', he'll say a few things, he no doubt fulfils other functions as well, but he fulfils [in particular] an organizational function, he provides prepared, tested, codi-fied solutions that are universally accepted, and no one will say: 'That's some mad priest!' The jurists plays, I believe, the same role, making it possible to eliminate improvisation, with all its attendant risks of conflict in critical situations.

I come back to the Kabyle example of marriages between families very distant in space. These are very prestigious marriages. The further away you marry, the more prestigious it is, but at the same time very risky, as people do not know one another . . . In situations of this kind, codification and protocol become absolutely vital, since they make it possible to avoid any occasion of friction, in particular when the meeting of groups involves a kind of challenge as to who has greater honour, more men, more guns, more ululation, etc. So there is a danger of people trying to outbid one another. Clerks are people who can offer a particular set of assets in this competitive situation, a capital that we can call organizational capital with a legal basis. (Perhaps I have laboured this point too long, but I am always torn between saying things as if they were self-evident, that is, as I see them, and saying them in such a way that they are also self-evident to you, which forces me into developments I did not envisage, so that I always fall behind in what I want to say.)

Jurists face the church: a corporation acquires autonomy

To return then to my main theme. From the Middle Ages on, jurists were in this position of *juris peritus*, the person who is an expert in law and who, by this fact, is able to offer solutions not only to past problems, for which there are precedents, but also to unexpected problems, problems without a precedent. To rapidly continue this history of jurists in big strides, [you need to see that] jurists had their own institution very early on, the Parlement. In the fourteenth century they received a kind of permanent delegation from the king to look after the law. Often they were ennobled. Very often, very quickly, they acquired the right to choose their successors – this is the worm that finds its way into the fruit, the nature that finds its way into the world of law, of counter-nature. They were the bearers of a rational habitus – on this point I cannot do better than follow Duby. They were involved with the Reformation and with Jansenism. Duby lays great emphasis on the constitutive virtues of prudence on the part of the body [of jurists], which we still find today when we do a sociology of magistrates: 'They have to practise a control of affective impulses, they have to act lucidly, in the light of intelligence, they have to have a sense of proportion. They are men of experience.'[18] Duby emphasizes courtesy as a kind of invention of the clerks: courtesy, courtly love, etc. [are defined] in opposition to impulses, in opposition to the wildness of the *juvenes*, a kind of knights errant, poorly civilized.[19] Here, in passing, we can compare Duby with Elias and say that they are both correct, the former saying that courtesy contributes to the state while the latter says that it is the genesis of the state that makes for courtesy. You see right away that this is a false problem, that one makes for the other and vice versa. You can call this 'dialectical', which does not mean anything; in reality, it is a process of struggle within fields . . .

The clerks were partly bound up with the church, this was the case of the canon lawyers (I am putting things in a rather peremptory and crude way, but I think I can back them up by argument). At the scale I am working on, I am forced to say very general things, but I believe these are also useful, since sometimes, I don't know why, historians do not say them. Jurists essentially made use of the church, of resources provided largely by the church, to set the state against the church. This is a way of summing up a very varied body of work, such as that of Kantorowicz for example, and here we really need a history of the emancipation of the clerks, of the rise of the clerks to power, a history of the differentiation of the legal field – and later of the intellectual field – in relation to the religious field. The problems of secularism, of relations between the state and the private, remain central down to the nineteenth century, because this is simply the extension of an age-old struggle on the part of the clerks with the state against the church. We would need to go into detail here, but it is possible to show, making use of Kantorowicz in particular – even if there are many other works – that the oldest states were constructed after the model of the pontifical state, and that in a certain sense the state was constructed on the model of the church but against it; it's like a part of the church turned back against the church. I spoke just now about the split in the ego in relation to professors or jurists. Among the divisions that there are in any clerk, it is not accidental that, since Kant, philosophers have been unwilling to marry. We should reflect on this kind of self-imposed celibacy. There is in every clerk, still today, someone who is a man of the church divided against the church. (Here again I am saying things that are peremptory and abrupt, but this is simply to trigger in you feelings that may generate reflection, it is not light-hearted joking, and certainly not a profession of faith.)

We can say then that the church provided the initial model, not only by way of Roman law and canon law, but also in terms of organizational structures. There are for example all kinds of writings on the birth of the Assembly model. For us this is self-evident, but the Assembly was an extremely difficult invention and it is in the direction of the church, and later the reformed church, that historians today look for the first forms of this very strange thing: people are gathered in a room, they discuss among themselves and then they vote – this is quite amazing, it's not self-evident at all; should they vote unanimously, or by majority? All these things were invented in part by people who drew on a treasure of experiences that were almost always religious, despite breaking [with the church].

To return to Kantorowicz: the essential thing that these clerks who broke with the church drew from the church was the idea of a body and a mystic body, the idea of the *corporatio* as a totality irreducible to the sum of its members, which could only be expressed by a person. Hobbes, on the contrary, was a scholastic thinker who drew on scholastic models. On scholasticism I shall be very peremptory, but I can give you references . . .[20] This description of the process of conflictual confrontation in the interpenetration between church and state needs further extension, and I believe it is still continuing today, still present in every man of state, in state ideas, in each of the men of state that we are, because we ourselves have the state in our heads, in the words of Thomas Bernhard.[21]

To be a bit more complete on this process of gradual separation, we need to recall very rapidly the role of major religious ruptures in the construction of the state. I have prepared what I am going to say, but I shall refer you to a book that is viewed as a classic of what is known as the Cambridge School: Quentin Skinner, *The Foundations of Modern Political Thought*. In this immense history, this immense genealogy of modern political thought that stretches from twelfth-century Italy with its small autonomous republics down to the French Revolution, Skinner gives a major place, in two chapters, to the invention in the Renaissance of what he calls 'civic humanism', the invention of a kind of secularized political theory in which the constitution takes the place of royal arbitrariness. On this point I refer you also to a very important book by the Hellenist Louis Gernet: *Les Grecs sans miracle*, an old book that was republished in 1983,[22] in which he lays great stress on the Greek invention of the idea of the constitution, an idea that would return by way of Roman law. He shows how the notion of constitution can only be conceived in terms of a break with the idea of divine decree, the idea of divine law. This is the precise moment when the political asserts itself as distinct from the religious, the religious being essentially, in its origin, a matter of the *conscience*; the mutual independence of these two functions grows, and they grow in the direction of freedom . . . In other words, he stresses the idea of a break between transcendence and the immanence bound up with the idea of personal freedom, the personal exercise of freedom. This Greek discovery returned in the Renaissance by way of this civic humanism . . . This is an enormous book that is impossible for me to sum up here, but I am happy to have cited it so as to encourage you to read it.

So it is in this context that the idea of the autonomy of politics was invented, that is, of a specific political order. Here again it was jurists, by their struggles within the juridical field, who formed a kind of practical metaphor of what would become the political field, that is, the relatively autonomous world within which struggle about the social world is conducted only with political weapons. Clearly, the theorist of the autonomy of politics, historically, was no doubt Machiavelli, who for the first time put forward the idea that politics has principles that are neither those of morality nor those of religion. What is called 'Machiavellianism' – which is quite ridiculous, as Machiavelli's theory has nothing to do with Machiavellianism – refers to a key idea, that there is a political logic that is indifferent to ethical ends, a logic of government and of the realities governed. Machiavelli did not arise out of nothing, he arose in a space, in a field of humanist thought. In Skinner's book there is also a chapter devoted to [. . .] Lutheranism, on the links between the Reformation and the development of constitutionalist thought, with the appearance of theories that radically challenged any transcendental principle of government, any principle of government based on reference to a transcendent authority. And finally there is a very important chapter on Calvinism, and the invention of what we might already call the right to resistance. This was a problem that arose for the Calvinists subject to religious persecution and repression: how to justify the right to resist the temporal power, and in the name of what?

Reformation, Jansenism and juridism

What is most important in all this? First of all, that you should read this book; then other things that I shall tell you from the standpoint of my demonstration – if we can speak of a demonstration. Keep in mind the idea that this political invention involved the major intervention of jurists, and here I shall refer to some other works. I am not saying that you can completely identify the Reformation or critical religious movements such as Jansenism with the jurists, but at all events there is an enormous intersection: the rise of the clerks and the parallel rise of a thought about politics are two connected phenomena. I shall give you another reference here (I have never given you so many as I have today), a book edited by Catherine Maire, *Jansénisme et révolution*,[23] which contains the proceedings of a conference held around the same time as other conferences on the Revolution – this one was really interesting.

In this collective volume there is an article by Dale Van Kley, entitled 'Du parti janséniste au parti patriote'.[24] You will have noted how Le Paige, the ideologist of the Parlement whom I spoke to you about just now, was a Jansenist. This book explicitly says, on the basis of historical work, that there was a continuity between the Jansenist party, made up of magistrates, advocates and lower clerks in the 1750s – studied also by Baker, whom I mentioned earlier – and the patriotism that appeared on the eve of the French Revolution in resistance to Maupeou's reforms. Dale Van Kley uses the expression 'party', and here again I believe that sociological concepts are important ('party' in the historical sense rather than anything like the modern one).[25] He emphasizes the proliferation of pamphlets, which Baker also alludes to, and he analyses 500 patriotic pamphlets that all appealed to the notion of public opinion, one of the inventions of this period. He tries to characterize Jansenism as a 'party'. To proceed quickly, this is rather as if you tried to characterize *gauchisme*, and as I see it Jansenism was a form of *gauchisme*, that is, a position that has only a relational meaning; it is impossible to understand Jansenism except in relation to a space – these are ideas that are not in [Van Kley's article] – and so you find in them a bit of everything, but not just anything. . . A bit of everything but not just anything, that is a good definition of a movement like *gauchisme*, an ideological combination . . . First of all, you find a bit of everything in the people who gather around this movement and in its ideological content. I remember how in 1968 people said [that the movement was due to] the influence of Marcuse; well clearly, 90 per cent of them hadn't read Marcuse, they reinvented him spontaneously. *Gauchisme* was a collection of postures, of very vague terms – 'repression', 'repressive', 'anti-repressive', etc. – a collection of slogan-concepts, that is, concepts that functioned in a logic of mystical participation far more than in the logic of logical thought. I tried to characterize the propensity to support *gauchisme* in 1968 in *Homo Academicus*: why did sociologists in every country tend to support *gauchisme*? You have to take [into account] the position of sociology in the space of disciplines . . .

The question of the Jansenists is in no way an unnecessary detour. It's to try and get out of substantialism and false problems, because on this point historians can get stuck for generations, saying: 'But no, the Jansenists weren't really that . . .', and they will never agree either on the ideological content of the movement or on its social composition. In characterizing Jansenism it is possible to say, quite honestly, 'Well, there was Gallicanism', that is, [that the Jansenists] were more on the Gallican side than on the papist side; 'there was constitutionalism', that is, they were more on the Parlement side than on the side of the king; and then there was Jansenism in the specifically religious sense, in varying doses . . . Modern techniques of analysing [multiple] correspondences are very useful in studying both these ideological spaces, which are fluid and vague, yet not at all indeterminate, as well as the corresponding groups. In the same article [by Dale Van Kley] you again find Le Paige, the spokesman of the Parlement, who was a kind of Marcuse of the Jansenist movement. It is with him that you find the greatest density of this collection of diverse elements that are found more or less everywhere to a lesser degree. You thus have affinities between the juridical world, the parliamentarians and Jansenism, as you had in an earlier epoch with the Reformation. I shall now explain right away what I want to end up with.

The public: a reality without precedent that keeps coming into being

This long and slow rise of the clerks is still not finished. In this logic, you can say that the French Revolution was in no way a complete break; it was rather a major step in the rise of the clerks, an important movement in full continuity – which does not mean that the French Revolution did not exist, that would be stupid. When I criticized Furet, this was not because he said that the French Revolution did not exist – he doesn't say quite that, but nearly. I criticized his method, I said that this was not the way to understand [an event of this kind]; you have to constitute the spaces in which [phenomena] are produced . . . everything that I am trying to do at an accelerated pace today. So it is not a question of saying that the French Revolution did or didn't take place, but rather of understanding processes, and I can refer you for the rest of my argument, which I shall not give today, to the final chapter of *The State Nobility*, in which I tried to give a constructed, accelerated account of this process that led to the constitution, within the field of power, of a category of social agents whose specific power in the struggles within the field of power rested on possession of cultural capital, and more particularly of that particular form of cultural capital that is juridical capital, which is not simply a capital of theories – this is what I would have liked to explain in relation to Skinner, but I have already mentioned it several times in passing, in previous lectures. The great interest of the book on the *lit de justice* is to have shown that there is a kind of permanent to and fro between practical innovations – in questions of protocol, in relations between the king and the Parlement – and the theoretical innovations designed to legitimize these little practical conquests, red cushion and red robe, etc. There is thus an immense work of construction of public practices that is inseparable from the work of construction of a discourse of public service, a discourse designed both to describe and to construct, according to the Sapir-Whorf theory, this reality without a precedent that is the public, and that has still not completed its coming into existence.

One final thing. [. . .] Skinner is important for analysing the relationship between the clerks and religion, but he is important on condition that you read him in the way that I say: he relates a series of theories that are not just political theories which you can debate about in the way that philosophers do. They are political theories that have contributed to constructing the political world in which we speak about these theories, and in which we take a position on the basis of positions that were created by these theories. If there are still people today who say that Machiavelli is interesting – I shall not give names – this is because there are public positions, thus people who are connected with these positions but who also have freedoms that derive from these positions, and because of this may still take a position on problems that these people created. But they did not just create problems, they created positions on the basis of which it is possible to pose these problems. And this means that the analysis is very difficult. Remember that I spent a whole year, no doubt very disappointing for my listeners, saying: you can't approach the state like this, because the state is in our thinking, you have to [instil] a radical doubt about the state . . . I believe you are beginning to understand something of why this is; this whole history is the history of our thinking of this history.

Lecture of 5 December 1991

Programme for a social history of political ideas and the state – Interest in disinterestedness – Jurists and the universal – The (false) problem of the French Revolution – The state and the nation – The state as 'civil religion' – Nationality and citizenship: contrast between the French and German models – Struggles between interest and struggles between unconscious forms in political debate

Programme for a social history of political ideas and the state

Today I want briefly to go over what I tried to present last time, and give you a kind of bird's-eye description of the process of construction of the nation subsequent to the revolutionary period. I have traced the steady rise of the clerks, that is, of cultural capital as a condition of access to power and as an instrument of reproduction of power. Basically, what is gradually established is a social space of the type we are familiar with today, with a structure that rests on two great principles: the economic principle and the cultural principle. In other words, the rise of the clerks is the assertion of cultural capital as an instrument of differentiation and reproduction. I mentioned last time the internal struggles among the clerks, and suggested that an important part of legal productions, and of cultural productions more broadly, could and should be understood in relation to the space of the producers of these representations. I indicated the process by which the juridical field was constituted, with the differentiation of a space of positions to which there corresponded a space of positions taken up. I sought also to show how a bureaucratic space began to be constituted on the basis of the juridical field. I rapidly mentioned the intersections between the religious field, the bureaucratic field and the juridical field itself. And finally, I indicated in passing how in order to understand this process of construction of representations, of which the state is an element, you had to take into account the nascent literary field, which at least in the absolutist period and certainly thereafter contributed to this construction, in the form of the *philosophes*, for example.

I suggested that in order to understand this process of invention of which the state is the culmination, and of which the invention of theories of the state forms part – this is rather a [research] programme than a statement of fact – you had to or should carry out a very fine-grained analysis of the different properties of the producers, and relate these to the properties of the products. I also indicated how those theories of the state that are taught in the logic of the history of ideas and that certain historians today undertake to study in and for themselves, without relating them to the social conditions of their production, are in fact doubly linked to social reality. There is no sense in studying ideas as if they floated in a kind of intellectual heaven, with no reference to the agents who produce them or, above all, to the conditions in which these agents produce them, that is, in particular to the relations of competition in which they stand towards one another. These ideas are thus linked materially to the social, and they also have quite a determining effect in contributing to the construction of the social realities we are familiar with. Today [we see a] return of the most 'primitive' forms of history of ideas, that is, a kind of idealist history of ideas, like the religious history of religion, for example. In this methodological regression, the relationship between ideas and institutions may well be retained, but what is forgotten is that these ideas have themselves arisen from struggles within institutions, and that it is only if they are seen to be both the product of social conditions and producers of social realities, constructors of social reality, that they can be fully understood.

In other words, the history of philosophy as practised by a sociologist is different from the history of political philosophy as commonly practised. [Take] the case of a ridiculous treatise that has been recently published in France, by François Châtelet, Olivier Duhamel and Évelyne Pisier, who is currently in an important job:[1] this is unthinkable from my point of view, writing as if political ideas were the product of a kind of theoretical parthenogenesis, as if theoretical ideas were born out of theoretical ideas and had baby theoretical ideas . . . There is in fact a social history of political philosophy, and of philosophy more generally, that is not practised in this way; there is a history of philosophy of the kind I recommend, but it is only in its early stages.[2] It is the same thing with law; philosophy and law are two disciplines that have kept a monopoly of their own history and that, by doing so, produce an internal history, a history without agents. The [social] history of political philosophy is a history that takes into account the space within which political ideas are produced, with everything I have mentioned: on the one hand, struggles between king and parliament, struggles among parliamentarians, struggles between the different sectors of the juridical-bureaucratic field, while on the other hand, the history of political philosophy is reintegrated into history in general. One of the things wrong with history as practised [nowadays] is that it has accepted the division into disciplines and has allowed the history of science, the history of technology, the history of law to be amputated. And the celebrated Annales school, which claims to reintegrate [these dimensions], actually does not do so at all. It accepts the same division de facto, with the history of science being a separate specialism – as well as containing far more epistemology, that is, pretentious reflection on the practice of science, than genuine history of science.

What I am saying here is programmatic, but it is a relatively important programme, involving the history of philosophy, the history of law and the history of the sciences by studying ideas as social constructions, which can have an autonomy in relation to the social conditions of which they are the product – I do not deny this – but which need none the less to be related to historical conditions, and not at all, as historians of ideas say, in the form of influence: they intervene in a far more powerful fashion. This is why the concession I made to the history of ideas was a sham concession – I do not actually concede very much – since ideas intervene as instruments in the actual construction of reality. They have a material function. Everything I have said throughout these lectures rests on the idea that ideas do things, that ideas make reality, and that the view [of the world], the standpoint, the *nomos*, all those things I have mentioned a hundred times, are constructors of reality, to the point that the purest and most abstract battles, which may be waged within relatively autonomous fields such as the religious field, the juridical field, etc. always have a relationship in the last resort with reality, in both their origin and their effects, which are extremely powerful. And I believe it is impossible to give a history of the state if the state as we see it is directly related to the economic conditions in which it functions, following a certain rudimentary Marxist tradition.

All this, therefore, is to say that what I sketched out, what I gave the programme of, is still to be done and implies a different form of history. [. . .] I have said this a hundred times: historians are the least reflexive of scholars and only to a very limited extent apply to themselves the historical science they may acquire. A further interest of a history of this kind [would be to produce a] reflexive history, a history of our own thinking. What I call habitus is a kind of 'historical transcendental': our 'categories of perception', as Kant called them, are historically constructed, and it is clear that producing a history of the genesis of state structures means producing a history of our thinking, thus a genuine philosophy of our own instruments of thinking, of our own thinking. In other words, I believe, it means actually realizing one of the indisputable programmes of the philosophical tradition . . . What I regret is being unable to present this programme to you. Perhaps it will be done, but it is clearly an immense work. It is far easier to write about a priori categories than to try to analyse the historical genesis of those categories that have all the appearances of the a priori by virtue of their genesis having being forgotten, this being one of the effects of every apprenticeship. A successful apprenticeship is an apprenticeship that gets forgotten. So there you have the philosophy, if you like, of what I have done on the subject of the genesis of the state, and that is the first conclusion of my analyses.

Interest in disinterestedness

The second conclusion is that those theories of the state that contribute to
the construction of the state, and thus to the reality of the state as we know
it, are the product of social agents located in social space.[3] As I have pointed
out several times in previous lectures, the jurists, the 'berobed', were people
with a connection to the state, and in order to make their interests prevail
they had to make the state prevail: they had an interest in the public and in
the universal. This idea that certain social categories have an interest in the
universal is a materialism that does not subtract anything from the universal. I believe it is a form of idealistic naivety to want above all for pure things
to be the product of pure acts. When you are a sociologist, you learn that the
purest things may have their origin in impulses that are quite impure. The
example par excellence is science, where it is evident that scientists, who are
always discussed in terms of a dichotomy – either glorified or put down – are
people just like anyone else, who have joined a game that is not easy to join,
that is increasingly hard to join; even within this game, they are obliged to
play by rules that are rules of disinterestedness, objectivity, neutrality, etc.[4]
In other words, in order to express their impulses – what Kant calls the
'pathological ego' – they have to sublimate these. A scientific field, a juridical field or a religious field is a place of sublimation, with censorship: 'Let no
one who is not a geometer enter here.'[5] [. . .] I have shown this with respect
to Heidegger:[6] he had Nazi things to say, but he could only express them in
such a way that they did not seem like that; besides, he believed they were
not Nazi and he laid the blame on Kant . . .

The logic of pure worlds, of these pure games, is a kind of alchemy
which makes the pure out of the impure, the disinterested out of the self-
interested, because there are people who have an interest in disinterestedness: a scholar is someone with an interest in disinterestedness. We may
even believe, from the standpoint of the researcher who is always seeking
a reason, that the most disinterested actions, humanitarian actions, all
those things that are celebrated, are always subject to the question: what
was his interest in doing this? Why did he do it? I mentioned a few years
ago the problem of the *salos* [the fool], a very strange character studied by
my friend Gilbert Dagron,[7] a character who, in tenth-century Byzantium,
acted against all the moral norms in a kind of moral challenge to ethical
pharisaism. From the fear of gaining the profits of respectability, honour
and virtue – the typical pharisaic profits that many intellectuals appropriate every day – he put himself in an impossible situation, he did frightful
things, he behaved like a pig, etc. This is the kind of paradox of purity in
impurity that raises the question very concretely: is he doing good? What
good does he derive from the act of doing good? Is there perhaps a perverted way of asserting one's integrity, purity, nobility and dignity, for
example, in a certain ostentatious rigorousness?

These are questions that are historical and sociological. This does not
necessarily lead to cynicism; it leads you to say that an angelic spirit is

not necessarily the root of the most generous actions. There is a kind of realism that social science teaches ... I find it far more reassuring that people do good things because they are forced to – far more reassuring. Kant, moreover, said that perhaps no moral act had ever been performed; he saw very well that if the only forces on which we can count to produce moral actions have to be drawn from within ourselves, we do not get very far. What underlies the analyses I have given is a kind of realistic philosophy of the ideal, a philosophy that is perhaps the only way of defending an ideal in a realist fashion, and in no way cynicism: for the ideal to come about, conditions must be met, many people must have an interest in the ideal. This implies certain consequences [in terms of] political strategies, for example if you want to end corruption in political parties ... I will not develop this, it is just so that you can understand the philosophy that underlies my analyses.[8]

Jurists and the universal

These jurists thus brought about an advance in the universal: they invented a certain number of social forms and representations that were explicitly constituted as universal. I have tried to show that they had different interests in the universal, and [this being so], they constituted a world, the juridical world, in which it was necessary to invoke the universal in order to win out. You had to be able to show that the arguments and statements you had advanced were more readily universalizable than those of others – [this meets the] Kantian criteria – that is, that they were less dependent on private interests: 'If I say this, it is good for everyone and not just for myself.' Clearly, the person saying this is immediately subject to the Marxist criticism: 'Isn't your discourse ideological?' 'Aren't you just universalizing your particular interest?' Professionals of the universal are virtuosi in the art of universalizing their particular interests. They produce simultaneously the universal and the strategies of universalization, that is, the art of imitating the universal and having their particular interests pass as universal ... This is the problem, you are no longer in those [entrenched positions]. The social world [. . .] is a world in which it is very hard to think in a Manichean fashion, and that is why very few people are good sociologists. Sociology demands a way of thinking that is uncommon in ordinary life, that is not spontaneous ...

These jurists thus had an interest in the public. For example, everyone has noted how they began to struggle to have their precedence recognized, that is, their cultural capital, well before the Revolution of 1789. They associated this precedence, which was also a privilege, with the idea of public service, the idea of civic virtue. Finally, by struggling to overthrow the hierarchy of orders, to put the *noblesse de robe* above the traditional nobility, they promoted ideas associated with juridical competence, the idea of universalism: they were the people who had a private interest in the public interest. This question can be posed in very general terms . . . Clearly, I am only going to raise the question, but I believe it is sometimes useful to raise a question even if you are unable to give a complete answer to it; I raise this about a particular case, but I believe that the question of interest in the public should be raised in its full generality. How is this interest in the public distributed in a differentiated society? Do the rich have a greater interest in the public than the poor, for example, or is it the other way round? Is there a significant statistical relationship between interest in the general interest and position in social space? There are some mystical answers to this question: the proletariat as a universal class is one response – the most deprived, the most destitute, being dispossessed of everything, have an interest in the universal. As always with Marx, this is almost true . . . I say 'almost true' because [it has been, if not refuted, at least nuanced by] a certain number of economists who have done a lot of work on public interests, on what is the public interest, on the specificity of public goods and the specific logic of the consumption of public goods.

(One of these economists, James Buchanan, in an article about clubs that I found most exciting, about the interest in functioning as a club, wrote: 'the optimal club size, for any quantity of good, will tend to become smaller as the real income of an individual is increased.'[9] In other words, the higher income you have, the more interest you have in clubs being limited: 'Goods that exhibit some "publicness" at low income levels will, therefore, tend to become "private" as income levels advance.'[10] [Buchanan] takes cooperatives as an example, and shows that they are used more by people with a low income than by those with a high income, other things being equal. In other words, what was public tends to become private: people only go public when they cannot do otherwise . . . There is another earlier article by Samuelson on the theory of public goods, in the periodical *Economics and Statistics* for 1954.[11] This article contains the beginnings of an answer to the question I raised in its most general form. You could say that individualism – which is spoken about a great deal today – tends to increase as income increases, and conversely that solidarity tends to increase as income declines, as poverty rises. This is simply a hypothesis: associations of the poor are forced associations between people more disposed than others to association, who have more in the way of associative habitus because they were subject in their forma- tive period and beyond to the necessity to associate in order to survive. You may think therefore that recourse to association tends to disappear as soon as people are able to shed it, that is, to the extent that they have the means to do without it – which does not mean that there is a linear progression: there are associations of poor, but there are also associations of rich. [. . .] Associations of rich people, which are elective associations, such as clubs, are independent, they are associations of people who double their capital by associating with other people who have capital – so they are not determined by necessity. In the work I conducted for *Distinction*, I was able to observe the extent to which the construction of clubs, these undertakings for creating social and symbolic capital that is collectively controlled, was undertaken in a quasi-rational fashion. You had to have sponsors, a whole work of selection, election of members[12] – a different logic [from that of common associations] . . . This is simply a parenthesis so that you bear this problem in mind. I shall return now to the French Revolution.)

The (false) problem of the French Revolution

The French Revolution . . . I am very hesitant in speaking in these terms. I do not want to settle the French Revolution in a quarter of an hour (which is more or less the time I have to devote to it), but I just want to say that, in the logic of what I have done up till now, we can raise a certain number of questions about the French Revolution to which I can respond, I believe, in a quarter of an hour . . . One of these questions is precisely to know in what way the *longue durée* process that I mentioned was expressed in the French Revolution. And how can we situate the Revolution in this process? I have already said that I believe the French Revolution is situated in this *longue durée*. It certainly marked a watershed, but in no way a rupture: it was a stage in the process of the assertion, the rise, of the clerks, the 'berobed', and it basically marked the victory of the clerks. In other words, it was more of a culmination of a process of *longue durée* that began in the twelfth century than an absolute beginning . . . Let us at least say, as much of a culmination as a beginning. The *noblesse de robe* that had developed a new vision of the state long before the Revolution, that had created a whole world of ideas – like the idea of the Republic – would become the dominant category, the state nobility, making the unified territorial state and nation. In other words, its victory was the victory of the modern state, the national state, the nation-state. This state nobility would thus both produce the new institution and appropriate the quasi-monopoly of the specific profits associated with this institution.

Last week I mentioned Denis Richet, who wrote about fiscal capitalism in the eighteenth century: he showed how the state, as it developed, generated a new kind of capital, a specific state capital, both material and symbolic, functioning as a meta-capital, a kind of power over other kinds of capital; this is a capital that gives power over other kinds of capital, including economic capital. By the same token, this public capital, this capital of general interest or public power, is both an instrument of social struggle and a stake in social struggles of the first magnitude. The 'post-revolutionary' state – here again, if I could, I would put quotation marks around all the words I am saying – was the site of a struggle, both instrument and stake in a permanent struggle to appropriate the specific profits it produces, that is, in particular for the redistribution of the meta-capital that it concentrates. This has often been said about economic capital and the redistribution of economic profits in the form of wages, etc., but

[we should also analyse the] redistribution of symbolic capital in the form
of credit, confidence, authority, etc.

All the debates about the French Revolution as a bourgeois revolution
are false debates. I believe that the problems Marx raised about the state,
the French Revolution, the revolution of 1848, are catastrophic problems
that have been imposed on all those who have reflected on the state in all
countries. You find the Japanese asking themselves whether they really
had a French Revolution; the English say, 'We certainly didn't have one,
it's not possible.' In every country people said: 'But if we didn't have a
French Revolution, then we're not modern . . .' The Marxist problematic
was imposed on the Marxist world and beyond as an absolute problematic, and every revolution is measured by the yardstick of the French
Revolution, with a kind of ethnocentrism that is absolutely unbelievable.
What I mean is that I believe we can get rid of these problems, at all events
I am convinced of this, so I am telling you, though that doesn't mean there
are not other questions besides those I am trying to raise. But I believe that
these Marxist dicta have obscured the question I want to raise, which is to
know whether the founders of the modern state did not place themselves
in a position of ensuring themselves a monopoly, whether they did not
monopolize the monopoly that they were in the process of constituting.

Max Weber said that the state was the monopoly of legitimate violence.
And I correct him and say it is the monopoly of legitimate physical and
symbolic violence. Struggles over the state are struggles for the monopoly
of this monopoly, and I believe that the founders of the modern state put
themselves in a well-placed position in the struggle for this monopoly –
as witness the permanence over time of what I call the state nobility. I
published *The State Nobility* in 1989 to show that the French Revolution
essentially did not change anything . . . The monopolization of juridical
capital and state capital, by the condition of access to state capital that
cultural capital provides, enabled the perpetuation of a dominant group
whose power rests largely on cultural capital – hence the importance of
all analyses that show the relation between distribution of cultural capital
and position in social space. All analyses of the school are in fact analyses of the state and the reproduction of the state. I shall not develop this
theme, I have done so in the past, but it is a way of concluding to some
extent the earlier analyses.

The state and the nation

Having said this, the 'berobed' with a direct interest in the construction of
the state did none the less advance the state towards universality. If you
recall the contrast I made, the juridical principle displaced the dynastic
principle in the most brutal and decisive manner, they guillotined them
. . . Much has been written about the death of the king: the king's physical
death was perhaps the indispensable symbolic break for asserting the irre-

versible imposition of a principle of the juridical type against a principle of the dynastic type. [Jurists], by their self-interested struggle, produced – this has been said countless times – the nation-state, the unified state against the regions and provinces, but also against class divisions. They did a work of unification that was both trans-regional and 'trans-class', if I can put it like that, 'trans-social'. What I want to describe here very rapidly are the three most decisive contributions: the appearance of the notion of state and nation in the modern sense of the term – I shall explain what this means; then the birth of a 'public sphere' – if I say 'public sphere', you can see the verbal automatisms, I hate this expression and it just slipped out – [the appearance] of a specific political field, a legitimate political field; and finally, the genesis of the notion of citizen in contrast to that of subject. (This is certainly the most difficult lecture for me to give, as I constantly touch on trivial things that everyone has said countless times and you get the impression of déjà vu, already seen and already spoken at each word, whereas I am trying to say something quite different, without being certain of it . . . I let you know my feelings so that you understand my hesitations.)

[Jurists] made the nation-state. This is quickly said: they made a state that they charged with making the nation. I believe that [this point is] quite original; I shall go on to make the comparison with the German situation. The German model is very interesting because it is a romantic model (whereas the French model is very eighteenth century): there was first of all the language, the nation, Herder,[13] and then there is the state, and the state expresses the nation. The French revolutionaries did not do that at all: they made the universal state, and this state would go on to make the nation through the school, the army, etc. There is a phrase of Tallien's that could be used as a motto: 'The only foreigners in France are bad citizens.'[14] That is a very good formula, a typically French legal-political formula. A citizen is anyone who meets the definition of the good citizen, that is, anyone who is universal; everyone has human rights, and so everyone is a citizen. This juridical-political and universalist view clearly conforms both to the competence of the jurists and to their own interest, it is a jurist's thinking . . . but the analogy needs to be made explicit. I have mentioned several times a book by Benedict Anderson entitled *Imagined Communities*, an important book that describes communities or nations as imaginary entities created by the collective work of a number of agents, who include writers, linguists, grammarians. In other words, nations are largely the construction of intellectuals who – this is what I would add – have an interest in the nation. Intellectuals are involved with everything that bears on cultural capital; and cultural capital is all the more national the more it is tied to the national language, and all the less national if it is more independent of the national language – jurists and teachers of French are more national than mathematicians and physicists.

Intellectuals are thus bound to the national cultural capital to different degrees depending on their specialism, and they accordingly have, far more than is generally believed, national and nationalist interests. [. . .]

For example, the Ukrainian nationalism about which much is being said today is a business of grammarians. These are often minor intellectuals whom Max Weber would call 'proletaroid intellectuals', with little recognition from the central bodies of the empire or nation, and who, so as to give value to their little specific capital that they want to become national – the capital of grammarians, authors of dictionaries, folklorists, etc. – constitute, as something that has to exist, a social entity in full conformity with their interests and justifying their existence ... National quarrels always have something of the quarrels of grammarians about them, that is good to know ... I am quite amazed, since I have read this book, to discover this phenomenon on all sides; it is far more true than I would ever have believed.

Imagined communities are the product of a work of construction. You need only take this theme and combine it with another I have gone over many times, earlier in the year, to have a more or less correct theory of the nation. I laid great emphasis on the idea of *nomos*, on principles of vision and division [of the social world], the idea that the state rests on a certain number of presuppositions concerning the manner of constructing social reality. The state is in a position to universalize, within its territorial limits, these categories of perception. According to this logic, a nation is the set of people who have the same categories of state perception and who, having undergone the same imposition and inculcation by the state, that is, by the school, have [common] principles of vision and division on a certain number of closely related fundamental problems. The notion of 'national character', which was very fashionable in the nineteenth century, thus actually appears simply as the ratification of national stereotypes and prejudices; it should be completely swept out of the theoretical space – it's a scarcely sublimated form of racism. Having said this, it does indicate something that indisputably does exist: the product, in people's minds, of the work of inculcating common categories of perception and appreciation, which is carried out by countless influences, including the action of the school, educational textbooks, and particular history textbooks. I spoke just now of the great constructors of the nation; [in France] the state made the nation, it made it by the school. For example, the Third Republic was the republic of Lavisse,[15] of history textbooks, etc.

The state as 'civil religion'

The state is thus the centre of what is called a 'civil religion'.[16] An American sociologist, Robert Bellah,[17] has spoken of this in relation to the ceremonials which American life is so full of – these religious rituals, ethical-political-civil rituals [. . .]. There is a work of production of a civil disposition by civil religion, ceremonies, anniversaries, celebrations and naturally history, which plays a determining role.

I would like here to summarize very rapidly a very important book by a major specialist in Nazism, George Mosse. Mosse was one of those German émigrés who spent the rest of their life asking how Nazism could have happened, and he made contributions of the first order to understanding the Nazi mass movements. In [*The Crisis of German Ideology*] he examined the intellectual origins of the Third Reich, with an analysis of what he calls the 'nationalization of the masses' – that is, how masses are constituted into a nation.[18] He makes an argument that at first sight is somewhat paradoxical but that I find quite convincing, that Nazism was simply an extreme case of the democracies from the point of view of this work of civil religion, since it pushed to the extreme the work of inculcation of homogeneous collective representations that is also at work in democratic societies. He accordingly emphasizes how, since the Napoleonic era, bourgeois national ideals gave birth to a public imaginary, and how the First World War saw the appearance of a new political order based on national self-representation mediated by the 'liturgy of a civil religion'.[19] In other words, in simpler language: nations put on a display of themselves; they make themselves exist by objectivizing themselves through the display they give of themselves to themselves; they make themselves exist in and by a civil liturgy, the liturgy of civil religion. It is at the level of this liturgy of power that the specificity of Nazism appears; [Mosse] shows how this liturgy of power has an affinity with the irrationalism of a mass politics that aims at the practical assertion of a kind of Rousseauian general will. Basically, according to him, Nazism is the heir of Rousseau (this is very paradoxical, he does not put it in these terms. I'm sorry, I should never speak like this, but it is very hard to say and would need a great deal of time . . .)

Mosse means that this mythical general will, which only exists on paper and which has presented a problem for all Rousseau's commentators, can be made palpable, in some sense, by great collective exhibitions of unanimity. [The general will is thereby] exhibited in collective emotion. Emotion is precisely both the cause and the effect of the exhibition: it is the product of the exhibition that presupposes a collective work of construction. Affective emotional unity is often the characteristic of small sects and groups, but this social construction of an emotional unity can be produced on the scale of a whole people, and not only that of little groups. Nazism carried this work to its ultimate extreme. We may say that it carried to the extreme tendencies that are also present in a certain type of democratic ceremonial. The nation is an imaginary embodiment of the people, a national self-representation, and this self-representation rests on the exhibition of what this people has in common: language, history, landscape, etc. And finally, Mosse says, the fascist state is a display-state that aestheticizes politics and politicizes aesthetics by a kind of civil religion that seeks to be timeless by using preindustrial symbols, eternal symbols. Mosse's text is itself rather extreme, as he describes the culmination of a process that begins with the French Revolution, but he has the merit of showing how a certain kind of collective construction of the nation contains extreme potentialities that people tend to locate in a different space . . .

The first point, then, is that by making the state, [jurists] made, not the nation, but the social conditions for the production of the nation. Here we have to bring in (but I have already said this) the whole work of construction and consolidation of the nation in which the republican historians of the nineteenth century, Augustin Thierry, Jules Michelet, Ernest Lavisse, played a very important role. We also have to take into account the role of the school and the army . . . The second point I shall skip here – I shall come back to parliament and the construction of a legitimate politics – to tackle right away the third point, the problem of the citizen, so that my argument today has a certain unity; I shall go back to this again next time.

Nationality and citizenship: contrast between the French and German models

You know how much discussion there is today about citizenship and immigration; people ask precisely who has the right to the status of citizen . . . Very rapidly – here again I shall be superficial and programmatic, but I at least want to leave you with the problem in mind, so that next time I can go further – the phrase 'territorialization of rules' has been used about the construction of the modern state. What is understood by this is that, starting from a somewhat utopian construction of a juridical state – not a 'state of law' as is said today, but a juridical state – starting from this legal representation of a purely juridical state, the task is posed of realizing the juridical space, the embodiment of law in a certain sense, in a definite territory. And this construction went together with the invention of the notion of citizen – the citizen being this juridical entity that exists in a relationship of law and duty with the state. Basically, the citizen is someone who is in juridical relations with the state, who has duties towards the state and has the right to demand an account from the state. The rise of the welfare state, for example, is often described as a kind of new discontinuity [with the rights of the citizen], whereas to my mind it is completely continuous with this . . . Here again, it is Marx, with the opposition between human rights and citizen's rights, who introduced the idea of discontinuity into our minds. The idea of the welfare state is in fact already contained in the notion of citizen; the welfare state is a state that gives the citizen what he has the right to, that is, not just the rights of the citizen, but human rights, the right to work, the right to health care, the right to security, etc. The citizen is thus defined by rights, and here we find the juridical inspiration of the French Revolution: nationality, in the French sense of the terms, is not a synonym for citizenship. It may be defined in ethno-cultural terms, by the possession of a language, a cultural tradition, the possession of a history, etc. Not everything that is in the German romantic tradition of nationality is citizenship. The citizen is defined in a purely juridical way, whereas the nation as ethno-cultural attribute, which can be juridically defined, is different from citizenship as this is defined by the [French] constitution. I quoted the expression of Tallien that is very typical of this definition: ultimately, the citizen is the person who is recognized as such by the constitution, and there is nothing else to say about him, he does not need to have particular properties bound up with blood, for example (*jus sanguinis*).

This abstract citizenship must be brought about by political work. Linguistic unity, for example, is not the condition of state unity but its product ... I am rather embarrassed here because I'm always thinking about the contrast between France and Germany, which I have not yet explained to you [clearly]. In the case of France, the state made the nation, that is, all the citizens of nation X had to speak language X; so they had to be put in a position to learn it. In the German model, it was the nation that expressed itself in the state, and suddenly all German speakers were citizens of Germany. All those who have the same ethnic, linguistic, cultural properties are citizens of Germany – which explains a lot of things in terms of the problems of reunification.[20] [In the French model,] political unity was the premise: this is a juridical-territorial unit, a territory established as such by a legal decree, the area on which a certain constitution is valid, and the citizen is the person who belongs to this area. People may speak a regional language or have different cultural traditions, different customs, but it is up to the state to create this unity, for example, by the work of inculcating a common language. Finally, the political philosophy that the French revolutionaries put forward was a universalist and thus assimilationist philosophy: universalist in that it saw itself as universal, so that assimilation was the highest thing it could offer people. It treated them as people, and thus granted them what everyone is granted, that is, access to the dignity of citizen, meaning French citizen; subsequently, so that the conditions for exercising this right of citizen were fulfilled, the citizens had to be given real means, whether cultural (a unified language) or economic.

The German path was a very different one – I shall describe it rapidly, in terms of a rough philosophy of history. If the English model emerged from the jurists of the sixteenth century, and the French model from the cosmopolitan *philosophes* of the eighteenth century, you can say that the German model emerged from the romantic thinkers of the nineteenth century, as corrected by the Prussian reformers – this is quite simplistic, but useful for getting your bearings. The French model is the model of the Enlightenment: cosmopolitanism, rationalism, an abstract and formal universalism; here Marx was right, it is the philosophy of assimilation conceived as universalization, that is, as the identification of each person – an assimilation that is a priori, and if possible a posteriori – with the universal citizen who is the French citizen. The German path was bound up with the nineteenth century, with romanticism; it had to bring in everything about the theme of the nation, the obscure, the profound, *Kultur* versus *Zivilisation*, etc. The nation, in this perspective, is a historically rooted individuality united by a *Volksgeist*, a common spirit of the people that distinguishes it from other nations and is expressed in a language, a custom, a culture, and in the state. The state can naturally ratify all this legally, but it is more an expression, a product, than it is a producer. This is putting the contrast in extreme terms, but I shall end with this point and go back to say a few words on the problem of immigrants.

You could reframe the whole problem [of relations between nation and citizenship] on the basis of this contrast. In practice, French and Germans treat immigrants in more or less the same manner, that is, just as badly, but in law they treat them very differently; and in order to understand this difference, I believe that bringing in the state philosophy of the two traditions is not without its uses. The universalistic, cosmopolitan, eighteenth-century view, that of France, led to *jus soli* [law of the soil]: the state was a territory, that is, the area of a certain law. It was thus a community with a territorial base. To become a citizen, all that was needed was to be born on this soil; this is an automatic naturalization, in an assimilationist logic in which the state has to make the nation, by a work of integration, etc. In the German case, the state goes back to the romantic philosophy of the nineteenth century, to the spirit of a people, etc., a conception that can be called ethno-cultural or ethno-linguistico-cultural, and that leads to *jus sanguinis* [law of blood]. [Citizenship here] is bound up with heredity, blood, a transmission that is 'natural' as well as historical. You thus have communities with a linguistic and cultural basis: German speakers are called to become Germans, and foreigners born in Germany are not Germans: there is no automatic integration or assimilation. In concrete terms, starting from these two philosophies of the state, you thus have two very different immigration policies: even if actual treatment is very similar – the Turks are treated more or less like the Algerians – in law there is a big difference.

Struggles between interests and struggles between unconscious forms in political debate

What complicates this whole debate is that in both cases the intellectuals who speak about all these things have vested interests, concealed interests invested in all these things: there are the interests of poets, musicians, lawyers or philosophers. It is important to connect what I said at the start [of this lecture] with what I am saying now to understand the extent to which, on problems such as these, it is illuminating to apply a sociology that relates positions taken with social positions. As soon as you hear someone talking to you about these problems, always ask: what interest does he have in telling me this? As people said after 1968: where is he speaking from? In the very precise sense: are these the words of a professor of mathematics or of a professor of law? Are they the words of a first-generation intellectual or a third-generation one? When I say 'interest' I always explain that I do not mean interest in the sense of the utilitarians, it's not a direct material interest; the interests involved here are far more complicated, of the kind that I mentioned last time when I said to you that having an interest means being connected with. For example, the fact of being a civil servant or the son of a civil servant means being predisposed, even without knowing it, to be on the side of the public – like a kind of unconscious.

In order to connect what I said at the start with what I am ending with now, these extremely confused and murky debates in which people invest their ultimate values, things become clear (they would be far more clear if I had developed [this theme further], but I made a firm decision to end next week, so I am forced to give you an abbreviated view of things that I could well have developed at greater length) [if you bear] in mind that you have to bring together the whole social history of the problematic in relation to which we are taking a position. You have to understand that there is an English history of the state, a French one, an American one, a German one, and that there are logics that are common to these histories, otherwise there could be no possible theory of the genesis of the state (relative to the role of jurists, etc.). That said, there are different philosophies, especially for the period that begins with the French Revolution. The first point is that these philosophies diverge. The second point is that we take a position on the problems that arise in this way, that is, that arise historically, as a function of the positions that we occupy in relation to these problems, in the space in which they are produced and the space in which they are debated. The extreme confusion and violence of discussion of these problems results from the fact that they are struggles at the level of the unconscious: people do not know what they are saying when they speak about these problems. I have tried [to do something] very difficult, because throughout I have censored associations that I would like to express to dissolve misunderstandings and destroy simplifications, as you can never be too careful with problems such as these. Unfortunately, the logic of political debate has nothing in common with the logic of scientific debate. And we are far from the time when it will be possible to do what is necessary for politicians to have an interest in virtue . . .

Lecture of 12 December 1991

The construction of political space: the parliamentary game – Digression: television in the new political game – From the paper state to the real state – Domesticating the dominated: the dialectic of discipline and philanthropy – The theoretical dimension of state construction – Questions for a conclusion

The construction of political space: the parliamentary game

This final lesson will not be the easiest, since I shall try to extend the historical analyses I have conducted through to the present, and try to reveal, if not all the conclusions, at least a few out of the various analyses I have presented up to now.

Last time I emphasized the simultaneous birth, on the one hand, of the juridical state, the state as juridically governed territory, by way of a process that one author called the 'territorialization of rule', and, on the other hand, the birth of the citizen as an individual of a completely new kind, in connection with the notion of subject. But in order for the analysis to be complete, we have to bring in a further highly important process that took place at the same time in the case of France: the birth of a political space that is socially and juridically constituted, that is, the parliament, in the English sense of the term, the Chambre des Députés, etc. Still in this broad perspective of historical comparison, I find it very interesting that certain dimensions of the modern state that in other countries, such as England for example, appeared both in a more organic, that is, slower and more continuous, fashion, and by the same token over a much longer timeframe, appeared simultaneously in France with the French Revolution. I believe that the singularity of the French Revolution – which is a fact, despite everything – and the extraordinary symbolic effect it has exercised and continues to exercise, could consist in the fact that these different processes were accomplished simultaneously. In particular, what I see as the two conditions for the production of the citizen, that is, the constitution of a state as a juridically governed territory and the constitution of a site of regulated exercise of the rights associated with belonging to the state, that is, parliament, appear simultaneously. I shall develop this second point very rapidly. Alongside the appearance of a juridical space as a set of citizens bound by rights and duties towards the state and towards one another, you have to take into account the appearance of parliament as site of an organized consensus, or rather, the site of a regulated dissension.

Some authors have emphasized that parliament, in particular the English Parliament, is a historical invention that, if you reflect on it, has nothing self-evident about it. It is a site where struggles between groups, interest groups, classes if you like, are waged according to rules of the game, meaning that all conflicts outside these struggles have something semi-criminal about them. Marx saw this 'parliamentarization' of political life as analogous to the theatre, with parliament and parliamentarianism a kind of collective delusion that citizens allow themselves to be caught up in, a shadow play that obscures the real struggles taking place elsewhere.[1] I believe this was a systematic error on Marx's part. I have said repeatedly here that it's basically always the same: the Marxist critique is not wrong, but it goes wrong once it fails to integrate into its theory what this theory is constructed against.[2] There would be no need to say that parliament was a shadow play if people did not believe it was something else. There would not even be any merit in saying so. In a certain sense, Marx reduces his own merits by forgetting that what he asserted his theory against survives this theory: parliament may be this site of regulated debates, in a certain sense somewhat mystified and mystifying, a mystification that is one of the conditions for the functioning of regimes, and particularly the conditions for the perpetuation of those regimes called democratic. So parliament is indeed this site of regulated consensus, or dissension within certain limits, which may rule out both objects of dissension and perhaps above all ways of expressing dissension. People who lack the right way of expressing dissension are excluded from legitimate political life.

Digression: television in the new political game

To proceed very quickly, you can transpose [this analysis] to television, which has become, unfortunately, one of the substitutes for parliament. This is putting the matter rather lightly, but for those who need convincing that it is more complicated, I invite them to read the book by Patrick Champagne entitled *Faire l'opinion*,[3] where he shows that the contemporary political space extends to things that we do not usually take into account in a description of the political sphere: that is, polling companies, television, political broadcasts on television, etc., which are [all now major] elements of the actual political space. If we analyse very rapidly the logic of televised debates, as has been done on several occasions in *Actes de la Recherche en Sciences Sociales*,[4] it is immediately apparent that these debates fit completely the definition I have just given of parliament: they are regulated debates, regulated [in such a way] that in order to join them you have to have certain properties, you have to be legitimate, you have to be a spokesperson – which is already a tremendous limitation. From time to time, what is called 'civil society' is brought in, that is, non-political personalities who enjoy wide approval on the part of the population, but this is the exception that confirms the rule and actually strengthens it. You really to have to be the archbishop of Paris, the president of a political party or the general secretary of a movement, which is a limitation. Then again, the classical conditions also include access to a certain language, a certain way of speaking . . . We need only reflect on the incidents created in the few cases when angry citizens, for example, have invaded television studios; the transmission is immediately switched off.

[This analogy between parliament and television] shows that these seemingly formal definitions I have put forward are by no means anodyne. One of the virtues of genetic analysis, and I shall put this more completely below, is that it removes the appearance of commonplaceness, and these definitions strike us as anodyne precisely because we have internalized their presuppositions to such an extent that they seem to us self-evident. I simply wanted to give you an idea of how far the parliamentary definition of parliament is arbitrary, and how far, in a certain sense, a whole part of the game is already played as soon as the game is defined in its particular way – this is by no means anti-parliamentarianism, of course not. To make you aware of this, we would need a full development of those things on which I am simply giving you indications, in the hope that you will develop them for yourselves.

From the paper state to the real state

Parliament is accordingly the institution, the juridically constituted and juridically controlled space, within which conflicts are regulated, and one can say that official politics is what can be discussed in parliament. Clearly, this tacit definition tends to get forgotten as such: every definition is a delimitation, and people end up forgetting everything that is ruled out by this definition, everything ruled out by the fact of the limits inherent to this definition, that is, all those conflicts that are in a way criminalized by the fact of not conforming to the norms, as I can say at the risk of a little exaggeration. This is a problem that troubled the working-class movement in the nineteenth century: should we join the parliamentary game or remain outside? These discussions, moreover, deserve a historical analysis designed to remove their appearance of commonplaceness, as I have tried to do here: do we join the game or not? Do we resort to strikes and demonstrations, or to the mediation of parliamentarians?[5] These debates have been forgotten, but their outcome remains in our unconscious and in our institutions.

These two institutions that were invented simultaneously in the case of France, that is, the state as juridical space and parliament, are in a sense the foundation of citizenship. To have the citizen in the modern sense of the term, you need to have these two things that are in no way automatic. The citizen is the person with the right to join the political game as this has already been defined, and who has in a sense the duty to participate in it – the obligation to vote, for example, is no more than a logical conclusion of the definition of the citizen. The new institution that was the French Republic, which saw itself as universal – I have already emphasized the ambiguity of this – was actually defined as national, even if, in the case of France and the French Revolution, the constitution of the nation was accompanied by the feeling of universality. As I have already said, it is impossible to understand the specific logic of French colonialism and decolonization, which took particularly striking forms, if you do not understand that France, by the particularity of its history, the particularity of the Revolution, has always viewed itself as the bearer of the universal. With the result that even its imperialism saw itself as an 'imperialism of the universal'. And I believe that still today, for example, French intellectuals have an arrogance that the majority of other nations find intolerable, because for better or worse they view themselves as bearers of the universal. The total intellectual, à la Sartre, is also an embodiment of this.[6] We are speaking here not just of politicians, of a Gaullist illusion, but rather of an element of the national unconscious in which intellectuals who feel entitled to give lessons [to the rest of] the world also participate. This deserves further reflection with respect to Europe, but I shall not say any more on it now . . .

This French Republic is a juridical institution based on a constitution. One of the major problems then is to make the law a reality – this was the work of several generations that followed the French Revolution. How to make the French Republic become what it claims to be, how to make real this obligation, these duties of the citizen? We could offer a simple formula, in fact, to sum up what I am going to say: what to do so that the 'people', in the sense of the popular class, should be part of the 'French people'? The word 'people', as everyone knows, has two main meanings.

(I have a tendency to emphasize continuities, first of all because I believe this is correct, and also because I believe that one of the facile effects that intellectuals obtain for themselves is to introduce breaks: it is always trendy to proclaim that 'it's over' – Marxism is over, the welfare state is over, you either have the 'return of' or the 'end of'. This is a basic prophetic strategy that leads to a lot of mistakes. Sociologists, especially French ones, have always proclaimed new classes, new ruptures, mutations, etc. My job is to show how difficult and rare these ruptures and mutations are . . . This is a kind of professional bias, which is perhaps strengthened by the experience I have had of all these discoverers of the unprecedented.)[7]

One problem, then, is to make the republic of law a reality. This required a work of constructing the nation. It was not enough to construct the state on paper – because the state of the jurists, the state of the French

Revolution, was a paper state; you have to make the real state. To proceed very quickly – I jump straight from the French Revolution to 1935, but I shall come back to the intervening period – the welfare state is completely continuous with this, all it does is fulfil on one essential point, that is, the economic conditions of access to the rights of the citizen, what was implicit already in the Declaration of the Rights of Man. Marx made the distinction between civil rights and human rights, or if you like between formal equality and real equality, saying that the French Revolution gave civil rights but not human rights. One problem is to act so that human rights follow from civic rights, and for this, the 'people' have in a sense to be brought into the game. The whole dialectic, which should not be described in Machiavellian terms or naive terms of a 'plot', does not consist in saying 'We'll give the people just enough to bring them in'. No one thinks in that way . . . The problem is what to do so that the people come into the game and are caught in the game, caught in the political illusion – but to be caught in the political game you have to have a minimum chance in the game.

This is a fundamental law of the theory of fields: if you do not have a minimum chance in the game, you don't play. You need to have a minimum chance in the game in order to want to play. If you are playing marbles with your son, you have to let him win from time to time, or else he'll say to you: 'I'm not playing with you any more, you always win . . .' We can say that in a certain sense the whole nineteenth century is a kind of work around this boundary: how to give them enough so that they'll stop bothering us? Enough so that they participate but not too much, so that they'll leave us in peace. This is again a very general law: the 'modest' categories always present this problem – besides, the word 'modest' is interesting. In the nineteenth century, to give another example, how could primary school teachers be given enough instruction to be *instituteurs*, but not enough to claim to be *professeurs*? This was one of the problems of managing the *instituteur*, which still presents itself today. How to give people enough so that they invest in the game? This is a very general model, [which can be transposed for example to] the celebrated 'participation' in companies. How to give enough so that [the wage-earners] participate, psychologically invest, commit themselves, believe in it, do what is needed, devote themselves to it?

Domesticating the dominated: the dialectic of discipline and philanthropy

The welfare state is the product of [this dilemma]. Clearly, no one posed the problem in these terms. At Sciences-Po, for example, this is what was taught a few years ago, but they went on to [other subjects] and it's no longer spoken about. There is thus the problem of knowing how to manage social affairs. It all [seems] contradictory, you can always say something and the opposite without contradicting yourself: you are going to make the state with the people, but also against the people. For example, you work to 'domesticate the dominated' – these are not my own words, but those of Max Weber. (Specialists in Max Weber, who was the great weapon against Marx, never read him well enough, even though Weber called himself a Marxist, something that bothers Marxists and Weberians alike.) Max Weber spoke of 'domesticating the dominated': part of the work of the state is oriented towards these dangerous classes who have to be tamed, made to join the game. At the same time, you can say it was a question of helping the dominated, relieving them from the intolerable state of misery that they were in. Philanthropists thus played a key role in the invention of the modern state, especially the welfare state, being here what the lawyers of the Middle Ages were for the revolutionary state as I described this to you: the philanthropists were people who muddled these two things, in all good faith . . . The theories of Norbert Elias and Michel Foucault rather annoy me because they only keep the disciplinary aspect of the state. But the state would not work at all if it were solely domestication: it is also assistance, philanthropy, etc.

Building the nation, building the state, building the nation starting from the state, means promoting the 'integration' of the dominated. Integration – this is again one of those words that has been used a great deal in different political contexts, and has come up again today, but it means two different things. It is a movement towards the centre, participation in the *illusio* (joining the game), and at the same time, integration as opposed to secession, to the act of leaving the state. One thing that people forget, which comes up for example when movements against the state take a national form, is that one of the alternatives in these struggles is the alternative between integration/assimilation and secession, and secession can take the form of a break. We have an example of the dissolution of a state before our eyes:[8] my whole work has been to show how a state is constituted, but we could also, almost as well, have done the work starting from the dissolution of the state. Genesis and involution, as some biologists have said, have the same virtues of removing the appearance of commonplaceness: the dissolution of a state makes it possible to see everything that is implicit and taken for granted in the functioning of a state, such as frontiers and everything that is unitary. The dissolution of a state makes it possible to see how the construction of national unity is achieved against secessionist tendencies, which may be regional, but may also [arise] from [social] classes. There can be secessions of a civil war type, but there can also be de facto secession, for example when the Chicago ghetto is in a state of secession: the police no longer go there, there is a state within the state, a non-state within the state;[9] there are forms of crime that are forms of secession . . .

To return to the central point. Making the state, making the nation, means in a sense managing two sets of relatively independent phenomena. First of all, managing the consequences of the interdependences between dominant and dominated – I shall refer here very rapidly to the work of a Dutch anthropologist, sociologist and historian, Abram de Swaan, who studied the role that major epidemics have played in the birth of the state.[10] I am summarizing here, as this is a complex book that would take at least a good hour to present, but I shall give you the outline. Epidemics, like nuclear accidents – this is an interesting analogy – do not have class frontiers. Nuclear accidents cross frontiers, and perhaps it is these that will give rise to a universal state, since everyone has a universal interest here – in any case, all rulers of all states have both sufficient awareness and sufficient interest – in limiting the spread of dangers, and we may expect from this the same as we owe partly to epidemics. It is to epidemics, for example, that we owe the sewage network. (I am schematizing, and apologize for doing so, this seems like rather simplistic slogans.) The sewage network, which is a typical state invention, is an organized collective response to the fact that the dangerous classes are dangerous in an objective sense: they are carriers of microbes, diseases, etc.

In the politics that followed from the enlightened self-interest of nineteenth-century philanthropists there was always something of this: the dangerous classes, the dominated classes, are objectively dangerous because they are carriers of poverty, contagion, contamination, etc. I believe that these things are still present in the collective unconscious. You can see this when people start speaking of 'mental AIDS';[11] when the far right manipulates the metaphor of disease, it reawakens vestiges of all these things that remain, I believe, very deeply embedded in the collective unconscious. The dominated classes are objectively dangerous, and enlightened self-interest leads to what is called the 'collectivization of risk'; it is a question of responding by collective measures to dangers that strike universally. You can say therefore that one of the driving forces of philanthropy, and by the same token of the welfare state – and this has always been one dimension of the role of philanthropists, who were interested in health policy or in the politics of maintaining the economic and symbolic order – [consisted in] domesticating the dominated, teaching them to calculate, to save. A major role of the school in the nineteenth century was to minimize the dangerousness – as we would say today – of the dominated. One way of minimizing this dangerousness was precisely to take into account all those cases where the interests of the dominant and those of the dominated were interdependent, as with cholera for example.

The second dimension is that the dominated are also dangerous because they mobilize, they protest, they riot because of hunger, they threaten not only public health but also collective security and public order. By the same token, there are interests in order that are clearly greater, the higher you go in the social hierarchy, but are never zero: Albert Hirschman has shown that there is always a choice between 'exit' and 'voice'[12] – an alternative that is rather obvious but useful all the same. The dominated have the choice between exiting, being excluded, dissenting, seceding or protesting, which is a way of being in the system. This alternative, however, forgets that there are costs of secession for the dominated associated with the loss of the profits of order; and the profits of order, I repeat, are never zero. The dominated, in a certain sense, force the dominant to make concessions, and these concessions are largely associated with the threat of secession, and bear on what are known as social advantages and the social state.

(Nineteenth-century philanthropists, who were generally either on the left of the right, or the right of the left, were highly ambiguous individuals, and thus extremely interesting. Protestant employers, for example, played this role in some contexts, Jewish bourgeois in others, etc. They were often dominated-dominant, with the characteristics of dominants but with secondary properties that placed them on the side of the dominated – this is often the case with intellectuals, who are dominated-dominant. These philanthropists – whom I shall mention very rapidly, but this really is history in big strides – produced a discourse integrating both properties: that is, the interdependence of the dominant and the dominated, which makes concessions necessary to the dominated in the logic of enlightened self-interest. If you consider the problem of immigration today, you will see how what I am saying seems to me very applicable, in a very direct manner: 'In any case they are here, you have to live with it, so you have to give them the minimum so that they don't cause trouble.' You find the same interdependence of the dominant and the dominated and the same anticipation of danger, of potential violent outbreaks. Philanthropists are thus always in a discourse that is both descriptive and normative. Philanthropists are often scientistic; sociologists are spontaneous philanthropists . . . That's all I wanted to say on this, end of parenthesis.)

Philanthropists, as the avant-garde of the dominant and themselves dominated among the dominant, become prophets of unification; they are always prophets of the unification of all markets, and the cultural market in particular. [In this perspective], access to culture has to be provided for the great majority, because access to national codes, the national language for example, is perceived as a condition for access to exercising civic rights; elementary education is viewed as a condition for access to the exercise of these rights. Philanthropists become prophets of two forms of redistribution: they want access to national codes to be redistributed, particularly access to the national language, to writing, etc.; and they want the minimal economic and social conditions for exercising civil rights to be made possible by access to national codes – so they demand political participation, participation in wealth for example by a guaranteed minimum wage. We may say that this is a highly complex and overdetermined work of integration into the central order, a work of the moralization of the dominated – philanthropists are very much moralists. It is a work of politicization – you could say of nationalization. It is a work that sets out to create a national habitus, which may imply adhesion, by way of civic religion, to national or even nationalist values – everything to do with this moralizing dimension needs further development, it still makes a return today from time to time, for example when people speak about over-indebted families. In the nineteenth century, however, it was an obsession of the philanthropists, and by way of them, of the educational system: how to give the dominated the elementary means to manage their household economy. In other words, how to bring the dominated to rational economic calculation, the rational management of time, by way of saving, by denouncing the desire to have more, to have everything right away: learn to moderate yourself, to save, to regulate births . . . all those things that are not unconnected and all have as their foundation an attitude towards time and a perspective on time.[13] All this needs further development, but I shall simply point it out. I would however like to emphasize a bit more, even though I have already implicitly given the essence of it in what I have just been saying, the ideal, conceptual and theoretical dimension of the construction of the modern state as welfare state.

The theoretical dimension of state construction

There are several reasons why I want to mention very quickly this important theoretical dimension. First of all, because I believe it is important for understanding what our modern states are; and also for understanding what is happening today, that is, perhaps the destruction of this hundred-year-old construction.[14] I should do some work on this equivalent to what I did on jurists. There are a number of texts that point in this direction, for example work by American lawyers, [inaudible passage]: this is a study of the development of indemnity law, compensation; it is a very fine study, in fact a study in political philosophy, on the genesis of a philosophy of the management of mistakes and miseries. Is misfortune a fault? – a typical nineteenth-century question that is making a comeback today. Is it attributable to individual freedom – people proclaim the return of the individual, of liberalism and liberty – or is it susceptible of collective treatment because bound up with collective causes? These are the questions raised by a whole series of theorists, philanthropists, philosophers, etc. I shall simply recall the context very superficially.

   One of these key questions, from the standpoint of the construction of the state in the nineteenth century, was the question of responsibility for accidents: who is to blame? And it was not accidental that French sociologists in the late nineteenth century had so much to say about responsibility: was responsibility a private or a public matter? Is responsibility incumbent on individuals, or is it up to public bodies to take responsibilities? Because, in the end, it is public authorities that are responsible for the real causes, concealed beneath the apparent responsibilities of agents. The second way of putting the question is, should the guilty party be blamed or understood? And didn't a certain type of liberal theories, which are making a comeback today, but which this whole philosophy of the welfare state was developed against, have the collective function of blaming the victims, saying: 'They're poor, but it's their own fault.'[15] On the question of AIDS, for example, the rampant, endemic, permanent temptation of common consciousness is very clear ... We need a social history of the moral revolution that took place, I believe, in the nineteenth century, taking indicators such as the juridical system in particular, which is clearly central. This is the old Durkheimian precept: when you want to study morality, look at the law.[16] You need to take the law and see how the movement took place from a logic of social blame to a logic of social cost – the notion of social costs has become completely commonplace, but it is an extraordinary invention. There is a text by Remi Lenoir published in *Actes de la Recherche en Sciences Sociales* on industrial accidents:[17] to simplify, is an industrial accident attributable to the worker, to the person who is its apparent subject, or rather to the structures that he finds himself in? In the nascent phase of capitalism, the victims of industrialization themselves bore the cost of its effects, in a logic that we could call the principle of blame, the principle of fault: the victim was responsible for his own mistake, for whatever happened to him. We could, following the law, see how this logic of fault and negligence was gradually replaced by a logic of public interest and collective risk; negligence is on the part of the individual, risk is an objective fact that can be measured in terms of probabilities, and particularly plays a very important role in insurance. The question, then, was whether accidents were a matter for the individual or for the collective ability to pay, that is, the social costs.

There are certainly those among you who are more familiar with this history than I am, but I believe that the history of law should be read again, no longer at the first level but at a second level, taking each event in the law as an indicator of something else and as the objectivized product of all the discussions in which the theoretical dimension [of the construction of the state] is highly important. What I meant is that philanthropists were to the welfare state what lawyers were to the pre-revolutionary state, that is, that [their views of the state] were not just theories, they were theories that made reality. What I have said about jurists is applicable also to philanthropists. The social sciences were clearly involved [in this process]. In the critical phase of this course on the state, I gave a preamble that lasted too long, in which I tried to show all the attachments that there were in us, all the confusions we could have about the state, and particularly all the unconscious aspects we could bring in as a consequence of the fact that sociology had itself participated in the birth of the state. I devoted four lectures, I believe, to a social history of relations between the state and the social sciences. The social sciences have played a key role, we can say that they were involved with the socialization of risk, with the social state, with the public, which is why they are detested in periods such as the one we are in now ... I shall quote a sociologist who was one of the founders of sociology but a liberal sociologist, Herbert Spencer, whom no one reads any more: 'The individual is an efficient creature.'[18] The individual is an efficient creature, normally master of his own destiny and thus responsible for his situation in life: this is the definition of the individual, the pure definition of a liberalism that dares not assert itself. Essayists today speak of the 'return of the individual'; essayists are always performative, that is, the opposite of philanthropists, and contemporary essayists are undoing what the philanthropists did. When they say 'return of the individual' this is both an observation and a prophecy; it is a way of saying: 'Let's return to the responsible individual!', a causally efficient creature, normally master of his own destiny and thus responsible for his own situation in life, that is, a creature who can be blamed when he is the victim, who can be attacked for the deficit in the social security system, etc.

On the one hand, the social sciences were built up against this philosophy of individualism, and there was a kind of common front of all social sciences including the biological ones. There is a very fine article that associates the development of thinking in terms of collective risk with the discovery of the microbe, with Pasteur.[19] The discovery of the microbe was on the side of the collectivization of risks; if there are microbes, then individuals are not responsible for their own diseases. At that time, the discovery of the microbe was an argument on the side of the socialization of risks and the dissolution of individual responsibilities into the social state – you could make an analogy with genetics today. I have just written a preface to a book by an American sociologist, Troy Duster,[20] a book that shows a [social] use of genetics for which geneticists are not responsible. Today genetic thinking is spreading ever more widely among the dominant strata [in the United States], and explanations in terms of genetic factors are invoked ever more frequently to explain poverty, educational failure, crime, etc.

The social sciences are connected with the dissolution of the individual in favour of the systems of relationships in which he is caught up. If you ask a sociologist, even a very bad one, to study a coach accident on the Paris–Avignon road, he will conclude straight away that it was not the fault of the driver – which is the simple and monocausal way of thinking – but rather because the road was slippery, people were returning from holiday, there was heavy traffic, because drivers are poorly paid and are therefore forced to drive too much and are tired, etc. He will substitute for an explanation in terms of direct responsibility, imputable to a free individual, a system of complex factors each of which has to be given its weight . . . The social sciences have played a very important role in the construction of the state of mind and philosophy that led to the welfare state. I say all this to show that the welfare state was not born suddenly after the great crisis [of 1929]: it had been prepared for a very long while, by the work of all these ideologists, all these jurists, all these philanthropists, etc. In the same way, you need to seek the origins of the ethical-philosophical transformation in the business world.

There is a famous and classic book by Burnham that describes something that was subsequently vulgarized and repeated by everyone: the transition from owners to managers, from the firm owned by a single individual, in which the boss was the owner, to the firm managed by a set of people.[21] At the level of company law, also at the level of the logic of company operation, there is a whole work that accompanies the process I mentioned just now, that is, the transition from systems that are apparently attributable to one individual to complex systems in which there is interpenetration of the public and the private, of decisions, deciders and decided, etc. All these changes are also found at the level of the state; this needs development, but I shall go on . . . Basically, what I wanted to say by way of this sketch of a research programme is that what is called the welfare state was prepared by a whole set of actual transformations of institutions that were themselves in a performative relationship of the kind I described in connection with relations between jurists and the state, with theoretical transformations, transformations in the mode of thinking.

In the end, it is impossible to understand the modern state without understanding this kind of cultural revolution – I don't think the word is exaggerated – something extraordinary, that goes against all the habits of thinking. When I mentioned, deliberately, the fault of the driver, it was to recall how this is how we think spontaneously. Ordinary thinking, even among sociologists when they get agitated, is monocausal, simplistic, [displaying] all the errors that scientific methodologies were constructed against. Ordinary agents commit these spontaneously, especially in a situation of crisis: faced with accident, catastrophe, etc., people look for the guilty parties. And it is true that one of the difficulties in the practice of history [as a discipline] is that historians always have to overcome the temptation of looking for the guilty party. Instead of investigating, for example, what the structure of relationships was under the Third Republic, or indeed under Pétain, they are often summoned by their unconscious and by the demand of the public to answer the question as to who is really guilty. Correct methodology demands that we remove this question – which does not mean that some people are not more responsible than others.

I mentioned the pre-revolutionary process that led from a private responsibility to a public responsibility, and I should develop what I simply indicated. This process is linked, by a relationship of circular rather than dialectical causality – it is clearer and more rigorous to put it like this – with the development of an insurance process. There is some very fine work on the origin of insurance, of thinking in terms of probabilities, risks, calculable risks, risks susceptible to being shared and adopted collectively.[22] We would need to analyse here the development of what can be called an 'insurance' mentality. Insurance can be either social – that is, insurance provided by the state – or individual – the state can make individual insurance compulsory. There is nothing anodyne about this collective philosophy, as I tried to show in my book on Heidegger,[23] who attacked the notion of social insurance – *soziale Fürsorge. Sorge* plays a fundamental role in Heidegger's theory of time, and is translated as 'foresight', 'anticipated concern', 'anticipation', etc. *Soziale Fürsorge*, which is involved in a concept such as collective insurance, is something that Heidegger's whole philosophy was constructed against. The whole Heideggerian discourse on authenticity, freedom, etc. is a kind of exaltation of the Spencerian individual who is master of his actions and does not delegate to anyone, particularly not to the state, the care of managing his future. The Heideggerian individual is the ideal individual of contemporary technocracy, the individual who faces with resolution risks to his security, everything that is guaranteed by the social security system, including death. This philosophy, which was a collective development, has become part of the unconscious, even in the case of people who oppose this philosophy today. Here again it would be interesting to see how the philosophy of the welfare state comes into the discourse of methodological individualists and ethnomethodologists – this being another face under which individualism makes its return.

Questions for a conclusion

I have five minutes to try and present a few conclusions. First of all, very quickly, why was it necessary to make such a long historical regression? Why was it necessary to practise this rather interminable yet very superficial genetic investigation? I am deeply convinced that we never finish freeing ourselves from the self-evidence of the social; and among the instruments for producing self-evidence, the feeling of self-evidence, the state is certainly the most powerful. I quoted you a magnificent saying by Thomas Bernhard, who writes in *Old Masters* that we all have the state in our heads. The long detour by way of genesis was designed therefore to allow some opportunities for escaping state thinking, an empirical way of practising radical doubt. This is to my mind the major function of history, to provide instruments for overthrowing the overly familiar and seemingly natural [. . .]. It is a characteristic of successful socialization that such socialization is forgotten, giving the illusion of innateness to what is actually acquired – what I call the amnesia of genesis. Against the amnesia of genesis, genetic thinking is the only weapon. We could have proceeded differently and taken the dissolution of states – we could take the Soviet Union today, but also everything that happened at the time of the separation between France and Algeria, a territory that was treated as part and parcel of the national territory. Everything that is natural, everything that is ruled out of discussion, suddenly comes into question: the question of frontiers, the question of knowing who is a citizen and who is not, the question of the conditions of citizenship. Wars of secession are a further example that could be considered in this logic; wars of secession are sociological wars, a kind of sociological experimentation that raises to consciousness and discourse the whole unthought that the regular order assumes to have been acquired and accepted. And if wars of secession are among the most violent of wars – think of Yugoslavia, for example – this is undoubtedly because they challenge mental structures.

There is always a symbolic dimension in revolutions. Symbolic revolutions include, for example, the great religious revolutions. May 68 was [perhaps] a false revolution, but it was perceived as a true revolution and is still producing effects, since it affected the mental structures of the whole academic body across the whole world. Symbolic revolutions unleash terrible violence because they attack the integrity of minds, they attack people in what is most essential for them, it's a question of life and death. Seemingly anodyne symbolic revolutions, such as that effected by Manet in painting (a revolution I am studying, and on which I shall perhaps one day publish), [can lead us to] ask why they give rise to such violence if it's simply a revolution in painting. In fact, I have undertaken to understand why an apparently symbolic revolution – in the sense of 'it's a symbolic franc', that is, 'it doesn't count' – why such a seemingly anodyne revolution was able to trigger verbal violence at least on the same scale as all of Marx's writings. Manet was as violently detested, abused, hated and stigmatized as was Marx. I believe that all these cases are revolutions that touch on mental structures, that is, on fundamental categories of perception, on principles of vision and division, on the *nomos*: these revolutions make you say that what is close is distant, what is up is down, what is male is female, etc. It is because these revolutions touch on mental integrity that they generate great violence. The interest of revolutions bound up with secession, that is, revolutions that attack national unity – as is the case with Yugoslavia[24] – is that they operate as experiments that bring to light the same things that appear from genetic analysis.

Having justified my use of the genetic method, I would like [to recall] the results of this as far as the state is concerned. I shall not repeat all the conclusions regarding the structure of the state today, as I believe I presented these along the way, for example in relation to the monopoly of symbolic violence. I simply want to recall what we can understand about the present functioning of the state on the basis of this historical reconstitution of its genesis.

First of all, about what we can call the bureaucratic field, that is, the space of agents and institutions that have this kind of meta-power, power over all powers: the bureaucratic field is a field that overshadows all fields, a field in which interventions are decreed that may be economic, such as subsidies, or may be juridical, such as the imposition of retirement regulations, etc. The bureaucratic field, as a field in which norms are produced for other fields, is itself a field of struggle, in which can be found traces of all previous struggles. I believe this is something highly important. Even at Sciences-Po, for example, they constantly make a distinction between finance ministries and spending ministries, a distinction that is a historical trace. The spending ministries are by and large the ministries of the welfare state, they arose from the process that I described in big strides today, the site where the traces of these conquests are deposited – in other words, they are the social ministries. And the agents engaged in this world are in struggle within the state, in which you find all the divisions of society. Struggles about the state, struggles to appropriate the meta-powers held by the state, also take place within the state – here I am trying to describe very complicated things in a very cavalier fashion. The greater part of political struggles involve agents outside the bureaucratic field, but having a relationship of homology with agents involved in the bureaucratic field and in the struggles within it.

I shall explain this again very quickly. The state is a space. Let us take an example that Remi Lenoir is currently studying[25] – I take this example because you all have it in your minds by way of crime novels. In crime novels you always see the police chief and the judge, two categories of state agent. If you give a description of the social space, they are fairly close. But they are none the less divided by a set of systematic differences: police chiefs come from a lower social origin, they are more provincial (often from the south-west), first generation; judges are more bourgeois, more Parisian, more Catholic. It is a bit left-right, but not completely so. There is a struggle among them and a little 'civil war' within the state – I could take the example of teaching, it's the same – in which the protagonists have state weapons, state instruments: one side prefers to use regulation, the other the regulatory use of time; one wants to go slowly, the other wants to hurry up, etc. All these struggles in the microcosm of the bureaucratic field are homologous, meaning that they have the same structure. To proceed quickly, there is a right-hand state and a left-hand state.[26] Take the order in which graduates of the ENA are ranked. If you are near the top you become inspector of finances, on the side of the right-hand state; if you are lower down, you will be in the social ministries, education, etc. The hierarchy of graduates reflects the social hierarchy, and so there is within the state a constant struggle between these two states, the right-hand state and the left-hand state. It is not a single front, but a whole series of sub-fields.

In the work I did on government policy on the question of housing, and which I have cited to you several times, I constructed a space of people who took part in commissions charged with drawing up new regulations to decide who gets state loans when they want to build. This is a highly important issue, as it particularly implies the choice between collective and individual habitat. In this space, there was exactly what I have just described to you. There were inspectors of finances who, at the start of the inquiry, were on the side of the state, and who were often, at the end of the study, in a private bank – which presented problems of coding for me; there were engineers from the [Corps des] Mines, engineers from the [Corps des] Ponts, etc., who in this case represented the left-hand state, as they were connected with the collective, with public housing, etc. If the law were changed, their own position in the state would be weakened. There were elected representatives, etc. All these people constituted a field, a field of play in which people get injured, insulted, come to blows, appeal to higher authorities, lobby, write to the president of the republic, etc. The space of the game is itself, in its structure, homologous with the social space, and the most disadvantaged interests, those connected with public housing, were championed by those people who were connected with the interests of the dominated, because they were in institutions that owed their existence to the struggles of the dominated or to the action of philanthropists who spoke for the dominated.

The left-hand state is always threatened, and particularly so at the present time, under a government of the left. I believe this needs development, and I could take up each of the points that I studied on the birth of the philosophy of the welfare state, in law, in the social sciences, in business and in the state; I could show, on each of these points, how the last twenty years have deconstructed everything that had been built up since the eighteenth century. There is a systematic work in which the ideologists who are read so much in the papers today play a considerable part, a whole work of deconstruction of a collective morality, a public morality, a philosophy of collective responsibility, etc. A number of sociologists are also involved in this, which is a paradox because, almost by definition, sociology is on the side of the collective. But there are people who embody the tour de force of doing a sociology in contradiction with the fundamental postulates of the discipline, a sociology that is on the side of the demolishers, as you can call them, of everything that is associated with the public, with public service, with this form of universalization by the public.

I shall end now – it really is the end this time, but I haven't managed to finish, as I still have much to say and I could have gone on talking a great deal longer. I recently read an article by Hellmut Brunner on the crisis of the ancient Egyptian state, entitled 'the religious response to corruption in Egypt'.[27] I shall just give you the essence of this article. Starting with the heresy of Amarna,[28] you have the appearance of a kind of dissolution of the spirit of public service, the idea of divine will associated with the idea of the state. The dissolution of the conviction that the state is just, that it expresses the divine, is accompanied by two phenomena that are apparently unconnected: on the one hand, the development of corruption, and on the other hand, the development of personal piety. Today, there is a lot of talk about the 'return of religion', and I have been able to establish myself how, in regions devastated by the crisis, such as around Longwy, where people have lost all hope of any political or trade union recourse,[29] you see forms of return to religion, which, according to this article on ancient Egypt, are one of the forms that express despair, not towards politics, as is said today, but towards the state. If you look at *Le Nouvel Observateur* or *Le Point* in the kiosks, with posters advertising the 'return of religion', the 'return of the individual', etc., doesn't all this doxic discourse [on these phenomena], which is not always wrong, owe part of its effectiveness to the fact that they are wrongly naming things that have an element of truth? Do not all these phenomena that are described to us in a prophetic mode have some connection with the dissolution of much of those things that were progressively built up? Isn't this a kind of despair about the state, a kind of despair that is expressed both in corruption, which touches those who, participating in the state, are supposed to manifest the spirit of public service in the highest degree, as well as in the attitudes of those who, not participating in the state, no longer have any temporal recourse and so retreat into the spiritual, into a form of reverie? Isn't the 'return of religion', in actual fact, an effect of the retreat of the state?

Appendices

Course summaries as published in the Annuaire of the Collège de France

1989–1990

In the lectures I devoted to the problem of the state, I first of all continued a preliminary critique of the representations of this institution, which as 'organized fiduciary endowed with automatic mechanisms and independent of individuals' (Valéry) has the strange property of also and above all existing by way of representations. I accordingly set out to analyse the notion of 'official' as the viewpoint of the *officium*, that is, of the institution invested with the monopoly of legitimate symbolic violence, or of the functionary, the title-holder of the *officium* who speaks and acts *ex officio*, as a legal person mandated to act in the name of an 'illusory community' (Marx). By drawing on my empirical analyses of the operation of the commissions that developed a new policy of housing support in the early 1970s, I sought to grasp the logic of the work of officialization, which consists in establishing a particular viewpoint as legitimate, that is, universal. This led me to analyse the most characteristic procedures of the rhetoric of the official that is incumbent on 'officials' and, to a certain extent, on all those who have to face a 'public' or a 'public opinion', embodiments of the 'generalized other' (G. H. Mead) that functions as a censor recalling universal values, that is, those officially professed by the group. Prosopopoeia is the form par excellence of the 'evocatory magic' by which an official agent presents the imaginary referent (the nation, the state, etc.) in whose name he speaks, and that he produces by speaking, but in the proper form. To become symbolically effective, it must be accompanied by a theatricalization of the consensual and consenting group, and by an interest in the general interest on the part of the person who claims to embody it, that is, their disinterestedness. Analysis of the conditions in which the border between the private and the public is crossed, the conditions of publication in the broadest sense of the term (conditions that the logic of scandal, as an assault on the official image of 'officials', reveals very clearly), leads to the principle of specifically political fetishism. Based on a reversal of causes and effects, this specific fetishism depends on perceiving the state, understood as the set of agents or institutions exercising sovereign authority over a set of people settled on a territory, as the legitimate expression of this human group.

Once these critical preliminaries are established, it is possible to proceed to the research programme that they open up, that is, a genetic sociology (or a social history) of the state institution, which should itself subsequently lead to an analysis of the specific structure of this institution. But on a terrain so intensively explored, it is impossible to tackle works of history directly without first of all examining the major works of comparative history or historical sociology that have been devoted to the sociogenesis of state formation. Without claiming to offer an exhaustive account of the work conducted in this direction, I gave a critical depiction of those authors whom I see as offering the most interesting solutions to the problem raised (that is, Shmuel Eisenstadt, Perry Anderson, Barrington Moore, Reinhard Bendix, Theda Skocpol). This had two intentions: to present general hypotheses able to orient the analysis of historical work, and to submit to criticism different ways of understanding and of applying the comparative method. This critical examination led to the methodological decision to restrict analysis to a study of the genesis of the state in England and France, two singular cases treated as particular cases in the universe of possible cases. This had a double objective: on the one hand, to disclose the logic of the genesis of a state logic or, in other words, the emergence of the specific social world that I call the bureaucratic field, and on the other hand, to establish how the 'concentrated and organized social force' (Marx) that we call the state was constituted, in other words how the different kinds of specifically bureaucratic resource are concentrated, these being at the same time instruments and issues at stake in struggles of which the bureaucratic field is the site and also the issue at stake (particularly in the political field).

1990–1991

Before presenting the model of the genesis of the state that I wished to propose, it seemed indispensable to me to analyse three previous attempts that I see as quite exemplary, even given their limitations: that of Norbert Elias who, following the line of Max Weber, describes very well the concentration of instruments of violence and tax collection in the hands of a single ruler and administration, and territorial extension by victorious competition with competing leaders, but who ignores the symbolic dimension of this concentration process; that of Charles Tilly who, while remaining very close to Weber and Elias on essential points, expects a kind of multivariant analysis to account both for the common features and the observed variations in the process of constitution of the state, that is, the concentration of physical capital and armed force bound up with the state bureaucracy, and the concentration of economic capital bound up with the town; and finally, that of Philip Corrigan and Derek Sayer, who have the merit of breaking with the economism of the two previous models and introducing the real 'cultural revolution' that they see as lying at the root of the modern state, that is, the construction of the series of legitimate and codified 'forms' that govern social life (national language, parliamentary forms, law courts, etc.).

In order to go beyond these partial models while integrating them, it is necessary to combine theoretical legacies that are traditionally held to be exclusive. One of the major effects of state action has certainly been the imposition of a common principle of vision and division (*nomos*), which founds both a logical and a moral conformity (in Durkheim's terms), and a consensus on the meaning and value of the world. The state is the principal producer of instruments of construction of the social reality: it is the state that organizes the great institutional rituals that contribute to producing the major social divisions and to inculcating the principles of division according to which these are perceived. This common code, this official ensemble of structured instruments of knowledge and communication (such as national language and culture), exists in affinity with the structures of the state, and thus in harmony with those who dominate it.

On the basis of these preliminary considerations, it was then possible to tackle the construction of a model of the genesis of the state as a process of concentration of different species of capital (physical, economic, cultural and symbolic), leading to the emergence of a kind of 'meta-capital' capable of exercising a power over the other species of capital, and of the state as a field in which struggles take place in which the stake is power, in particular the power that is embodied in law and in all kinds of regulation with a universal validity (on the scale of a territory). By way of the concentration of symbolic capital, of which the concentration of juridical capital is one aspect, tending for example to replace the statutory honour of the noble caste with honours awarded by the central power, the state gradually establishes itself as a central bank of symbolic capital invested with the power of 'nomination', as the 'fountain of honour, of office and of privilege' in the words of Blackstone (cited by Maitland).

The ambiguous character of the process from which the modern state emerged is revealed in this way, as well as that of this state itself: the process of concentration (and unification) is always both a process of universalization and a process of monopolization, integration being the condition for a particular form of domination, that which is accomplished in the monopolization of the state monopoly (with the state nobility).

1991–1992

Having described the process of concentration of capital (in its different forms), I aimed to construct a model of the genesis of the state, seeking first of all to understand the logic of the initial accumulation of symbolic capital, and in particular those assets inscribed in the fact of occupying the position of king, as *primus inter pares*. The dynastic state, organized around the royal family and its inheritance, as a house, is the site of a specific contradiction bound up with the coexistence of a personal power and a nascent bureaucracy, that is, two contradictory principles of domination (respectively embodied by the king's brothers and his ministers), and two modes of reproduction, through the family and through the school. It is the conflicts based on this contradiction that lead from the *king's house* to *raison d'état*, step by step ensuring the victory of the 'state' principle over the dynastic principle. Various institutions that tend to counteract the processes of natural reproduction of the nobility (of which entrusting bureaucratic power to foreign technicians, or to slaves, is the most extreme example) have the effect of breaking the ties of personal appropriation of state institutions and the profits they provide, making the state a kind of *antiphysis* (which is seen very well when we analyse the procedures gradually applied to counteract the tendency to corruption, which is inscribed in bureaucratic logic).

The invention of the new state logic is the product of a collective work of construction of a set of completely new social realities, that is, the institutions sharing the idea of the *public*. The body of agents such as jurists who are involved with state logic, more 'universal' (or universalist) in its principle than is dynastic logic, play a determining role in the construction of the *res publica* and the space (the bureaucratic field) within which bureaucratic institutions are invented (office, secretary, signature, seal, decree of appointment, certificate, attestation, registration, etc.). An analysis of the process leading to the long chain of agents charged with managing the royal seals makes it possible to demonstrate the logic of genesis of the division of the work of domination that leads to the transmutation of dynastic authority into bureaucratic authority based on limited delegation between agents who mutually guarantee and control one another.

The process, through which the power initially concentrated in the hands of a small number of individuals is differentiated and distributed among agents tied by the organic solidarity implicit in the division of the work of domination, leads to the constitution of a relatively autonomous bureaucratic field, which is the site of competitive struggles whose stake is the specifically bureaucratic power exercised over all other fields. These struggles, such as those we can observe around the king's *'lit [de justice]'*, may bear on details of bureaucratic practice (its ceremonial, for example) or on the history of institutions, and are one of the occasions in which the work of collective construction of 'public' institutions is performed. The gradual rise of the holders of the bureaucratic principle, the clerks whose authority is founded on cultural capital, to the detriment of the dynastic principle, underwent a decisive acceleration in the French case with the Revolution, when the universal principles of the new bureaucratic republic were asserted inseparably together with the privileged right of the holders of cultural capital to appropriate the universal. The state nobility asserted itself as such in the very act by which it made the territorial state and the unified nation, annexing to itself the public capital and the power of controlling this capital and redistributing its profits.

Again, it is also over a long timeframe that we can grasp the collective work of construction by which the state makes the nation, that is, the work of constructing and imposing common principles of vision and division, in which the army and especially the school play a determining role. (In parentheses, the social construction of reality that is involved here is not reducible to a mechanical aggregation of individual constructions, but is carried out in fields subject to the structural constraint of the prevailing balance of forces.) The construction of the nation as juridically governed territory goes hand in hand with the construction of the citizen, bound to the state (and to other citizens) by a set of rights and duties. But the bureaucratic field is always the site and stake of new struggles, and the work needed to ensure the participation of the citizen in public life – and particularly in official politics, as regulated dissension – has to be extended into a social policy that defines the welfare state, aiming to ensure everyone the minimum economic and cultural conditions (with initiation into national codes) for the exercise of the rights of the citizen, by assisting, economically and socially, and by disciplining. The building of the welfare state presupposes a genuine symbolic revolution, at the centre of which lies extension of public responsibility in place of private responsibility.

Knowing that the bureaucratic field bears within it the trace of all past conflicts, we understand better the struggles of which it is the site and the relations that these maintain, on the basis of homologies of position, with the struggles of which it is the object, and in which the issue at stake is the powers that it controls.

Position of the lectures on the state in Pierre Bourdieu's work

Among the lecture courses that Bourdieu delivered over the twenty years that he held the chair of sociology at the Collège de France, some have already been published with his own revisions and corrections, in particular his final course devoted to 'the science of science'.[1] The present volume is the first in a coming series that intends to publish not only his so far unpublished lectures at the Collège de France but also the many seminars he gave in the 1970s, first at the École Pratique des Hautes Études (EPHE) and subsequently at the École des Hautes Études en Sciences Sociales (EHESS). The present volume contains the complete lectures devoted to the state, which were given over three academic years (December 1989 to February 1990, January to March 1991, October to December 1991).

Nothing leads us to suppose that Bourdieu intended to make these into a book, and he did not undertake any preparation for publication in this sense. He did indeed publish a number of distinct texts devoted to the emergence of the juridical field,[2] to the functioning of the administrative field on the basis of a study of French housing policy,[3] and to the genesis and structure of the bureaucratic field.[4] To which must be added his occasional oral interventions (conferences, interviews).[5] In his article 'De la maison du roi à la raison d'État' (1977), he added at the head of the text a note about this article being as he saw it simply 'a lightly corrected transcription of a lecture at the Collège de France; as a provisional summary designed above all to serve as a research instrument, [this text] is a continuation of the analysis of the concentration process of the different kinds of capital that leads to the constitution of a bureaucratic field able to control the other fields'.[6]

It is somewhat unexpected, therefore, to find from Pierre Bourdieu a programme for a sociology of the state. Indeed, in the whole of his scientific publications this word does not make its appearance in his work until the early 1980s, with his inaugural lecture at the Collège de France.[7] Even when his research was focused, from the second half of the 1960s, on what is almost always associated with the state in France – the 'dominant ideology', 'political representation', the 'effectiveness of political action', the 'sciences of government' and, more generally, 'modes of domination'[8] or 'strategies of reproduction',[9] extending his work on the structure and function of the French educational system[10] – he used this word only in its most current senses such as 'welfare state' or 'nation-state', without subjecting it to the least critical analysis. Furthermore, the studies that he had given the impulse to from the late 1970s onwards, in the context of the Centre de Sociologie de l'Éducation et de la Culture, on the structure of the ruling classes, whether the employers (1978),[11] the church hierarchy (1982),[12] or the top civil service and the system of *grandes écoles*,[13] dealt with fractions of the upper classes that played a structuring and causal role in the 'field of power'.[14]

In 1982, the book *Ce que parler veut dire* gathered together a series of studies on the symbolic effectiveness of discourses of authority, in particular the article 'Description and prescription'.[15] But the state was never assimilated there to the political field, the operation of which Bourdieu studied in articles on opinion polls[16] and political representation.[17] This confusion, however, was maintained by the majority of jurists who studied the state in and for itself, and in an opposite sense by Marxist theorists who reduced the state to an instrument or 'apparatus' in the service of the ruling class, no matter what its particular history, and particularly the history of the agents that have produced it and the economic and social factors that determine its functions and structures.

It was only in 1984 that Bourdieu used the word 'state', in *Homo Academicus*, where this is defined in passing as 'holder of the monopoly of symbolic violence'.[18] He then fully adopted it, even for the title of his book *The State Nobility*, published in 1989 to celebrate 'differently' the bicentenary of the French Revolution, as well as in a series of texts analysing the 'science of the state',[19] 'state minds',[20] or 'state magic'[21] – somewhat enigmatic expressions if we do not know that subsequent to his work on the field of power Bourdieu used the term 'state' to designate the social institutions and agents that are at the same time, and inseparably, producers and products of the state.

In these formulas the notion of the state refers to what in France is consubstantially associated with the state and, more specifically, with the bureaucratic system, that is, the notions of 'public service', 'public good', 'public interest' and disinterestedness, the genealogy and mechanisms of which Bourdieu traced in his lectures at the Collège de France between 1986 and 1992.[22] Finally, the notion of the state is more frequently deployed in *The Weight of the World*, which was completed in 1990–1 and published in 1993, some extracts having been introduced and offered earlier in an issue of *Actes de la Recherche en Sciences Sociales* (an interview from this book is cited on two occasions in the lectures on the state).[23] In this book, which was an immediate success in publishing terms, increased in particular by the public stand he took in support of the strikers at the time of the movement of December 1995 against the proposed pension reforms, Bourdieu analysed the effects of neoliberal politics in terms that echo his lectures: 'demolition of the idea of public service', 'retreat and abdication of the state',[24] 'dismantling of the *res publica*' and devalorization of 'humble devotion to the collective interest'.[25]

We thus see the key position, often unnoticed by commentators, that the subject of the three years of this course occupied in Bourdieu's sociology. The steady focusing of his work on the state, however, owed less to the proliferation of his interventions in the political world[26] than to his work on the genesis and structures of the fields he successively studied in the perspective of a general theory of social space. In a 1988 interview he declared that the research he had conducted since *Distinction* (1979) on the literary, artistic, university, intellectual, employers', religious, juridical and bureaucratic fields resulted from the normal logic of his work, and particularly from 'seeking to understand the process of genesis of a field'.[27] This was also the case with the field of state institutions: the state is a field that occupies a position in the structure of fields such that it plays a large part in conditioning the functioning of the latter.

Moreover, the state may even appear as the field par excellence, even, in Bourdieu's expression, a 'meta-field', because 'the state is meta', a field of struggle in which the stake is the determination of the position that the different fields (economic, intellectual, artistic, etc.) should legitimately occupy in relation to one another. As a result, one could put forward the idea that the state is the almost necessary product of a double process: on the one hand, the differentiation of societies into relatively autonomous fields, and on the other hand, the emergence of a space that concentrates powers over the latter, and in which the struggles are between the fields themselves, between these new agents of history.

In his communication to the Association des Sociologues de Langue Française in October 1982,[28] Bourdieu made explicit the epistemological and sociological reasons why the state had to be analysed as the 'field of public institutions' and 'sector of the field of power'.[29] The bureaucratic field,

> like all fields, is the instituted result at a given moment of past and present struggles and confrontations between the contradictory interests of agents who are within or outside the field, but all finding, within the field of positions, supports and resources, particularly legal, for defending them according to the specific logic of the field [. . .]. The field of state institutions – and this is the foundation of the effect of real and ideological neutrality that it produces – tends to make an ever greater place for institutions that are the product of the transaction between classes and are partly situated above class interests, or at least appear to be so [. . .].

And, more precisely:

> Without being the functionary of the universal that Hegel made of it, the field of state institutions, by virtue of the very struggles of which

it is the site, can produce policies that are relatively autonomous in relation to what would be a policy narrowly and directly conforming to the interest of the dominant: because it offers a set of specific and institutionalized powers and resources, such as the power to raise taxes or the right to impose regulations (e.g. customs protection or credit regulation), or again the specifically economic power of ensuring financing, either direct (such as our subsidies) or indirect (such as the construction of road and rail networks).[30]

Here Bourdieu announces the programme he would follow from the second half of the 1980s, which would culminate in the three years of lectures explicitly devoted to the state. The problematic of the course rests on three previous studies that Bourdieu would constantly return to in order to explain the course's historical perspective. First of all, his research conducted in Kabylia, during which he developed the notion of symbolic capital, the key notion in his work; secondly, his early study of the matrimonial and succession strategies of Béarn peasants, which he refers to in connection with understanding the structures and functioning of the dynastic state; and finally, the studies of the higher civil service carried out under his supervision by members of the Centre de Sociologie Européenne, as well as those conducted by himself and his fellow-workers, particularly on the housing policy of the 1970s and 1980s (in particular, the production of individual houses).

In order to elaborate a genetic model of the state, Bourdieu draws on many works, into which the Bibliography here gives an insight: historians, but also authors that historians most often 'do not take seriously', yet who present 'the interest of raising questions that historians do not raise'.[31] He starts here from the definition that Max Weber gave of the state as the monopoly of legitimate physical force, but extends its action to the whole of symbolic activity, which he thus places at the root of the functioning and legitimacy of the institutions studied in his previous lectures, devoted to law and to the anthropological foundations of the notion of interest and public interest, 'which puts forward as its official law the obligation of disinterestedness'.[32]

Finally, the importance of the lectures on the state lies in the specifically sociological attention that Bourdieu gave to all forms of domination. In each of these fields the state is present, in both their origin and their functioning, and the general theory that he set out to make of the state required an analysis specifically devoted to it. The state can be reduced neither to an apparatus of power in the service of the dominant nor to a neutral site where conflicts are reabsorbed: it constitutes the form of collective belief that structures the whole of social life in highly differentiated societies. This shows the importance of this lecture course in Bourdieu's work – a course from which he wanted, as he said in one of his last interviews, 'something to remain'.[33]

Notes

Editors' note

1 See below, pp. 113, 124, 177, 280.
2 Pierre Bourdieu, 'Prologue', *Sociology in Question* (Thousand Oaks, CA: Sage Publications, 1993).
3 Pierre Bourdieu, 'Understanding', Pierre Bourdieu (ed.), *The Weight of the World* (Cambridge: Polity Press, 1999), p. 622.
4 See below, pp. 378–81.

Lecture of 18 January 1990

1 The theme of disinterestedness was tackled in the previous year's lecture course (1988–9): 'Is a disinterested act possible?', in *Practical Reason: On the Theory of Action* (Cambridge: Polity, 1998), pp. 75–91. See also Pierre Bourdieu, 'The interest of the sociologist', in *In Other Words: Essays towards a Reflexive Sociology* (Cambridge: Polity, 1990), pp. 87–93.
2 Pierre Bourdieu, 'On symbolic power', in *Language and Symbolic Power* (Cambridge: Polity, 1991), pp. 163–70. [The original article was first published in 1977.]
3 Max Weber, *Economy and Society* (Berkeley: University of California Press, 1978), vol. 1, p. 54, and *The Vocation Lectures* (Indianapolis: Hackett, 2004), p. 33. [In English editions of Weber, '*legimite Gewaltmonopol*' is usually translated as 'monopoly of the legitimate use of physical force'; but the '*violence légitime*' that Bourdieu takes from French translations of Weber has become established in English as 'legitimate violence', and is therefore followed here. – Translator.]
4 Émile Durkheim, *The Elementary Forms of the Religious Life* (Oxford: Oxford University Press, 2001), p. 19.
5 Antonio Gramsci, *Prison Notebooks* (3 vols, New York: Columbia University Press, 2010), notebooks 10, 11, 12 and 13.
6 Louis Althusser, 'Ideology and ideological state apparatuses', in *Lenin and Philosophy and Other Essays* (New York: Monthly Review Press, 1971).
7 Alain, *Le Citoyen contre les pouvoirs* (Paris: Sagittaire, 1926).
8 On this point, see Pierre Bourdieu, *Homo Academicus* (Cambridge: Polity, 1990), p. 175.

9 Bourdieu often referred in his seminars to this 'pessimistic functionalism', to denote a pessimistic teleological view of the social world. See on this notion the Chicago seminar of 1987, published in Pierre Bourdieu and Loïc Wacquant, *An Invitation to Reflexive Sociology* (Cambridge: Polity, 1992), p. 102: 'I am very much against the notion of apparatus, which for me is the Trojan horse of "pessimistic functionalism": an apparatus is an infernal machine, programmed to accomplish certain purposes no matter what, when or where. (This fantasy of the conspiracy, the idea that an evil will is responsible for everything that happens in the social world, haunts critical social thought.) The school system, the state, the church, political parties, or unions are not apparatuses but fields. In a field, agents and institutions constantly struggle, according to the regularities and the rules constitutive of this space of play [. . .]. Those who dominate in a given field are in a position to make it function to their advantage but they must always contend with the resistance, the claims, the contention, "political" or otherwise, of the dominated.'

10 Durkheim, *The Elementary Forms of the Religious Life*, pp. 25–46.

11 Maurice Halbwachs, *Les Cadres sociaux de la mémoire* (1925; Paris: Mouton, 1976); in English as *On Collective Memory* (trans. and ed. Lewis A. Coser), University of Chicago Press, 1992.

12 Pierre Janet held the chair in experimental and comparative psychology at the Collège de France from 1902 to 1934. Bourdieu is clearly alluding here to his book *L'Évolution de la mémoire et de la notion du temps* (Paris: Chahine, 1928).

13 [The term *'clerc'* plays a key role in Bourdieu's presentation of the development of the modern state. It has a broader sense than any single word current in English, including what could be rendered according to context as 'cleric', 'intellectual' or 'literatus'. As Bourdieu uses the term to indicate the continuity of the bureaucratic function from the Middle Ages down to the present, 'clerk' has seemed the most appropriate English option. – Translator.]

14 Lucien Febvre, *Le Problème de l'incroyance au XVIe siècle. La religion de Rabelais* (1947; Paris: Albin Michel, 1968).

15 Jürgen Habermas, *The Structural Transformation of the Public Sphere: An Inquiry into a Category of Bourgeois Polity* (1962; Cambridge: Polity, 1989). [The French edition of Habermas's book uses the term *'espace publique'*. – Translator.]

16 [Institut National de la Statistique et des Études Économiques, a French government body. – Translator.]

17 Philip Corrigan and Derek Sayer, *The Great Arch: English State Formation as Cultural Revolution* (Oxford: Blackwell, 1985), p. 3.

18 Bourdieu, *Language and Symbolic Power* ('The production and reproduction of legitimate language', pp. 43–65; 'Authorized language: the social conditions for the effectiveness of ritual discourse', pp. 107–16, 116–26 and 'Rites of institution', pp. 107–26).

19 Pierre Bourdieu, 'The categories of professional judgement', in *Homo Academicus* (Cambridge: Polity 1988), pp. 194–226.

20 Pierre Bourdieu, *Sociology in Question* (Thousand Oaks, CA: Sage, 1994), pp. 177–80 ('The racism of intelligence'), and *The State Nobility* (Cambridge: Polity, 1996), p. 151.

21 Karl Marx, 'The German Ideology', in Karl Marx and Frederick Engels, *Collected Works*, vol. 5 (London: Lawrence & Wishart, 1976), p. 36.

22 Weber, *Economy and Society*, vol. 1, ch. 3, sec. 2.
23 Marc Bloch, *Seigneurie française et manoir anglais* (1934; Paris: Armand Colin, 1960).
24 On the performative, see Bourdieu, 'Authorized language'.
25 See 'The house market', in Pierre Bourdieu, *The Social Structures of the Economy* (Cambridge: Polity, 2005).
26 The government commissioned a number of reports in the mid 1970s, in order to establish a new housing policy that found expression in the law of 3 January 1977; inspired by the commission chaired by Raymond Barre, this asserted the principle of reducing 'bricks and mortar' support in favour of support for individuals.
27 [HLM stands for *'habitation à loyer modéré'* (housing at moderate rent), the main form of social housing in France. – Translator.]
28 [The Corps des Mines, the leading body of state engineers attached to the ministry of industry. The Corps des Ponts et Chaussées is responsible for bridge and highway construction. – Translator.]
29 Marc Bloch, *The Historian's Craft* (1949; Manchester: Manchester University Press, 1967).
30 This passage refers to the factorial analysis in 'The state and the construction of the market', in *The Social Structures of the Economy*.
31 [Engineers are recruited to the Corps des Ponts et Chaussées after studying at the Polytechnique. – Translator.]
32 Joachim Hirsch, *Staatsapparat und Reproduktion des Kapitals* (Frankfurt am Main: Suhrkamp, 1974).
33 On the notion of a sociologically constructed individual, see Bourdieu, *Homo Academicus*, pp. 22–5.
34 Robert Lion (1934–), a senior civil servant, a socialist and an officer for voluntary organizations, directed the Caisse des Depôts from 1982 to 1992. In the early 2000s he was a regional councillor for Île-de-France, elected on the Europe Écologie list.
35 For a synthetic presentation of the social space that Bourdieu constructs in *Distinction: A Social Critique of the Judgement of Taste* (Cambridge, MA: Harvard University Press, 1984), see Pierre Bourdieu, 'The new capital', in *Practical Reason*, pp. 19–30.
36 Pierre Bourdieu, 'The field of local powers', in *The Social Structures of the Economy*. ['Droit et passe-droit' was the original title – Translator.]

Lecture of 25 January 1990

1 Erving Goffman, *The Presentation of Self in Everyday Life* (Edinburgh: University of Edinburgh Press, 1959), and *Behavior in Public Places: Notes on the Social Organization of Gatherings* (New York: Free Press, 1963).
2 E. P. Thompson, 'Patrician society, plebeian culture', *Journal of Social History*, 7.4 (1976), pp. 382–405.
3 Joseph Gusfield, *The Culture of Public Problems: Drinking-Driving and the Symbolic Order* (Chicago: University of Chicago Press, 1981).
4 Alfred Schütz, *Der sinnhafte Aufbau der sozialen Welt. Eine Einleitung in der verstehende Soziologie* (Vienna: Springer, 1932). This book had recently been published in French at the time of Bourdieu's course.

5 George Herbert Mead, *Mind, Self and Society* (Chicago: University of Chicago Press, 1934).

6 Bourdieu is drawing here on his fieldwork in Kabylia. See 'Kinship as will and representation', in *Outline of a Theory of Practice* (Cambridge: CUP, 1972).

7 Mouloud Mammeri and Pierre Bourdieu, 'Dialogue on oral poetry in Kabylia', in Pierre Bourdieu, *Algerian Sketches* (Cambridge: Polity, 2013).

8 On this notion, see Pierre Bourdieu, 'The scholastic point of view', in *Practical Reason*, pp. 127–40.

9 Gabriel Naudé, *Considérations politiques sur les coups d'État* (1667; Paris: Le Promeneur, 2004); Charles Loyseau, *Traité des ordres et simples dignités* (Châteaudun, 1610).

10 Bourdieu is referring here to the debates around law no. 89-462 of 6 July 1989 on landlord–tenant relations, the so-called *loi Mermaz*, which aimed to set a ceiling on rent increases following the departure of a tenant.

11 Ernst Kantorowicz, 'Mysteries of state: an absolutist concept and its late medieval origins', in Ernst Kantorowicz, *Selected Studies* (Locust Valley, NY: J. J. Augustin, 1965), pp. 381–98. [See also Kantorowicz's best-known work in English, *The King's Two Bodies: A Study in Medieval Political Theology* (Princeton: Princeton University Press, 1957). – Translator.]

12 For Bourdieu's further developments on this point, see 'Delegation and political fetishism', in *Language and Symbolic Power*, pp. 203–18 and 'The mystery of the ministry: From particles wills to the general will', in Loïc Wacquant (ed.), *Pierre Bourdieu and Democratic Politics* (Cambridge: Polity, 2005).

13 On this notion, see Benedict de Spinoza, 'A political treatise', ch. V, 4, in *The Chief Works of Benedict de Spinoza*, trans. R. H. M. Elwes (New York: Dover, 1951), vol. 1, p. 314, as well as Pierre Bourdieu, *The Logic of Practice* (Cambridge: Polity, 1990), p. 292 n. 1, where he refers to the work of Alexandre Matheron (*Individu et communauté chez Spinoza* [Paris: Minuit, 1969], p. 349): 'The term *obsequium* used by Spinoza to denote this "constant will", produced by the conditioning through which "the state fashions us for its use and which enables it to survive", could be reserved to denote the public testimonies of recognition that every group requires of its members.' [In English, including the translation referred to above, '*obsequium*' is generally rendered as 'obedience'. – Translator.]

14 Raymond Aron, *Peace and War: A Theory of International Relations* (Garden City, NY: Doubleday, 1966).

15 [The *Journal Officiel* is the official publication of the French government. – Translator.]

16 Maurice Halbwachs, *La Classe ouvrière et les niveaux de vie. Recherche sur la hiérarchie des besoins dans les sociétés contemporaines* (1912; Paris: Gordon & Breach, 1970), pp. i–xvii and 387–455.

17 Paul Valéry, *Cahiers* (1894–1914), vol. 2 (Paris: Gallimard, 1980), pp. 1558–9; in English as *Cahiers: Notebooks* (Peter Lang: New York, 2003).

18 Rodney H. Hilton, 'Resistance to taxation and to other state impositions in medieval England', in Jean-Philippe Genet and Michel Le Mené (eds), *Genèse de l'État moderne. Prelèvement et redistribution* (Paris: Éditions du CNRS, 1987), pp. 167–77.

19 Émile Durkheim, *Leçons de sociologie* (1922; Paris: PUF, 1990), pp. 79–141; in English as *Professional Ethics and Civil Morals* (New York: Routledge, 2003).

20 Bourdieu returns to Perry Anderson's work later on in the lecture course. He is doubtless referring here to the polemic in which Anderson was involved some

years previously with E. P. Thompson. See E. P. Thompson, *The Poverty of Theory and Other Essays* (New York: Monthly Review Press, 1978), and Perry Anderson's response, 'Socialism and pseudo-empiricism', *New Left Review*, I/35 (Jan.–Feb. 1966), pp. 2–42, and later *Arguments within English Marxism* (New York: Schocken Books, 1980).

21 Reinhard Bendix, *Max Weber: An Intellectual Portrait* (1960; Berkeley: University of California Press, 1977).

22 Norbert Elias, *The Civilizing Process* (Oxford: Blackwell, 2000).

23 See in particular Max Weber, *The Protestant Ethic and the Spirit of Capitalism* (New York: Scribner, 1958).

24 Theda Skocpol, *States and Social Revolutions: A Comparative Analysis of France, Russia, and China* (New York: Cambridge University Press, 1979).

25 See in particular Talcott Parsons, *Societies: Evolutionary and Comparative Perspectives* (Englewood Cliffs, NJ: Prentice Hall, 1966).

26 Gerald Holton, *The Scientific Imagination* (Cambridge: Cambridge University Press, 1978).

27 See Lecture of 8 February 1990, 'The problem of the three routes according to Barrington Moore'.

28 Émile Durkheim, *The Evolution of Educational Thought* (1938; London: Routledge, 2005).

29 Barrington Moore, *The Social Origins of Dictatorship and Democracy* (London: Penguin Books, 1974); Shmuel Eisenstadt, *The Political Systems of Empires* (New York: Free Press, 1963); Perry Anderson, *Passages from Antiquity to Feudalism* (London: New Left Books, 1974) and *Lineages of the Absolutist State* (London: New Left Books, 1974).

Lecture of 1 February 1990

1 Émile Benveniste, *Le Vocabulaire des institutions indo-européennes*, vol. 1: *Économie, parenté, société*; vol. 2: *Pouvoir, droit, religion* (Paris: Minuit, 1969).

2 John L. Austin, *How to Do Things with Words* (Oxford: Clarendon, 1962).

3 Bourdieu is referring here to Max Weber's texts published in 1920–1, *Gesammelte Aufsätze zur Religionssoziologie*. [Max Weber, *Sociology of Religion* (Boston: Beacon, 1993), pp. 46–59.]

4 Claude Lévi-Strauss, *Tristes tropiques* (London: Penguin, 1992), p. 408.

5 Jean Bollack, *Empédocle* (3 vols, Paris: Minuit, 1965–9).

6 Ernst Kantorowicz, 'The sovereignty of the artist', in Kantorowicz, *Selected Studies*, pp. 352–65.

7 Mammeri and Bourdieu, 'Dialogue on oral poetry in Kabylia'.

8 Henri-Francois d'Aguesseau, *Oeuvres*, vol. 1 (Paris, 1759), pp. 1–12, discussed by Pierre Bourdieu in *The State Nobility*, pp. 371 and 380–2.

9 This refers to the final moment of 'hyperbolic doubt' when Descartes imagines that a higher power could induce an error about the most apparently rational truths, such as those of mathematics.

10 Pierre Bourdieu, 'A paradoxical foundation of ethics', in *Practical Reason*, pp. 141–5.

11 Goffman, *The Presentation of Self in Everyday Life*.

12 Erving Goffman, 'The interaction order', *American Sociological Review*, 48 (1983), pp. 1–17; see also Erving Goffman, *Interaction Ritual: Essays on Face-to-Face Behavior* (New York: Anchor, 1967).

13 On this point, see Bourdieu, *The Logic of Practice*, pp. 101–1.

14 On this point, see Bourdieu, 'Is a disinterested act possible?'.

15 'Thus there is an asceticism inherent in all social life that is destined to survive all mythologies and dogmas; it is an integral part of all human culture. And fundamentally, that is the rationale and justification for the asceticism that religions have taught in every era.' Durkheim, *The Elementary Forms of Religious Life*, p. 235.

16 Pierre Bourdieu, 'Censorship and the imposition of form', in *Language and Symbolic Power*, pp. 137–60.

17 Mead, *Mind, Self and Society*.

18 On this point, see Alban Bensa and Pierre Bourdieu, 'Quand les Canaques prennent la parole', *Actes de la Recherche en Sciences Sociales*, 56 (1985), pp. 69–85.

19 See below in this lecture, in the section on 'Public opinion'.

20 [Freud's *Überich*, 'superego' in English, is rendered in French as *surmoi*. Bourdieu uses '*super ego*' here to stress the derivation. – Translator.]

21 A character in the eponymous comic strip. ['Walter Melon' in the English version. – Translator.]

22 See on this point Pierre Bourdieu, 'The force of law: toward a sociology of the juridical field', *Law and Anthropology* (2002), pp. 109–57; also *The State Nobility*, ch. 5.

23 Weber, *Sociology of Religion*, pp. 46–59.

24 Alain Bancaud, 'Une "constance mobile". La haute magistrature', *Actes de la Recherche en Sciences Sociales*, 76–7 (1989), pp. 30–48.

25 Weber, *Economy and Society*, vol. 1, ch. 3, sec. 5.

26 Pierre Bourdieu, *The Political Ontology of Martin Heidegger* (Cambridge: Polity, 1996). For a short presentation of this, see 'Censorship', in *Sociology in Question*, pp. 90–3.

27 Johan Huizinga, *Homo Ludens* (Boston: Beacon Press, 1955).

28 See on this point Pierre Bourdieu, 'Public opinion does not exist', in *Sociology in Question*, pp. 149–57; and the more extensive development in chapter 8 of *Distinction*, pp. 397–464.

29 The exact quotation is as follows: 'The vicar-general can smile at a statement against religion, the bishop can actually laugh, and the cardinal can add a word of his own.' Nicolas de Chamfort, *Maximes et pensées* (Paris, 1795).

30 Dominique Memmi, 'Savants et maîtres à penser. La fabrication d'une morale de la procréation artificielle', *Actes de la Recherche en Sciences Sociales*, 76–7 (1989), pp. 82–103.

31 J. D. Y. Peel, *Herbert Spencer: The Evolution of a Sociologist* (London: Heinemann, 1971), p. 70. William Alexander Mackinnon (1789–1870) had a long career as an MP.

32 Percy Ernst Schramm, *Der König von Frankreich. Das Wesen der Monarchie von 9 zum 16. Jahrhundert. Ein Kapitel aus der Geschichte des abendländischen Staates* (2 vols, Weimar: H. Böhlaud Nachf., 1939).

33 Thompson, 'Patrician society, plebeian culture'.

Lecture of 8 February 1990

1 Bourdieu, *Language and Symbolic Power*, p. 120.
2 Leo Spitzer, *Linguistics and Literary History: Essays in Stylistics* (New York: Russel & Russel, 1962).
3 See on this point Bourdieu, 'The production and reproduction of legitimate language'.
4 Bourdieu returned to this theme in *Pascalian Meditations* (Cambridge: Polity, 2000), pp. 229–30 and 237–8.
5 Bourdieu is referring here to the formula in the *Physics*, *'ananke stenai'* ['one really must stop'], where Aristotle asserts that the search for causes cannot be infinite; one has to stop at first causes that have no other reason than themselves, in particular one 'first motor' that drives the movement without itself receiving movement.
6 Halbwachs, *La Classe ouvrière et les niveaux de vie*.
7 An allusion to the work of George Weisz, who wrote on Durkheim, the Sorbonne, the emergence of medicine and the elite. See George Weisz, 'The medical elite in France in the early nineteenth century', *Minerva*, 25.1–2 (1987), pp. 15–70.
8 Georges Gurvitch, *La Vocation actuelle de la sociologie* (Paris: PUF, 1950), pp. 358ff.
9 Bourdieu, *The Political Ontology of Martin Heidegger*.
10 Bourdieu is alluding here to Barrington Moore. He develops this critique further in this lecture, in the section 'The problem of the three routes according to Barrington Moore'.
11 See in particular Raymond Aron, *Main Currents in Sociological Thought* (London: Weidenfeld & Nicolson, 1955).
12 See in particular part 8 of *Capital* vol. 1, on 'Primitive accumulation'.
13 Bourdieu is referring to Hegel's *Phenomenology of Spirit* (1807), trans. A. V. Miller (Oxford: Oxford University Press, 1977), particularly paragraphs 178–96 on lordship and bondage.
14 Karl Polanyi, *The Great Transformation* (1944; New York: Octagon, 1975).
15 Karl Polanyi et al. (eds), *Trade and Market in the Early Empires* (Glencoe, IL: Free Press, 1957).
16 Karl Wittfogel, *Oriental Despotism: A Comparative Study of Total Power* (New Haven: Yale University Press, 1957).
17 Rushton Coulborn, *Feudalism in History* (Princeton: Princeton University Press, 1956) (with contributions by Joseph R. Strayer, Williams F. Edgerton and Edwin O. Reischauer).
18 The reference is particularly to Talcott Parsons, 'The professions and social structure', *Social Forces*, 17.4 (1939), pp. 457–67, and by the same author, *The Structure of Social Action* (Glencoe, IL: Free Press, 1949). For Bourdieu's critique of the notion of profession, see Bourdieu and Wacquant, *An Invitation to Reflexive Sociology*, p. 243.
19 On the idea of the autonomy of the political field, see Bourdieu, 'Delegation and political fetishism', and *Propos sur le champ politique* (Lyon: PUL, 2000), esp. pp. 52–60.
20 Weber, *Economy and Society*, vol. 1, ch. 3, pp. 212ff.
21 Francisco Benet, 'Explosive markets: the Berber highlands', in Polanyi et al., *Trade and Markets in the Early Empires*.
22 Max Weber, 'Enquête sur la situation des ouvriers agricoles à l'est de l'Elbe.

Conclusions et perspectives', *Actes de la Recherche en Science Sociales*, 65 (1986), pp. 65–9.

23 See on this point Bourdieu and Wacquant, *Invitation to Reflexive Sociology*, pp. 248–52. For a sociological use of the notion of double bind, see Pierre Bourdieu and Gabrielle Balazs, 'Double binds', in Pierre Bourdieu et al., *The Weight of the World* (Cambridge: Polity, 1999), pp. 202–12.

24 Bourdieu is referring here to Thomas Kuhn, *The Structure of Scientific Revolutions* (Chicago: University of Chicago Press, 1962).

25 Alexander Gerschenkron, *Economic Backwardness in Historical Perspective: A Book of Essays* (Cambridge, MA: Belknap Press, 1962).

26 Bloch, *Seigneurie française et manoir anglais*, pp. 56–7 and 137–8.

27 Karl Marx and Frederick Engels, *Collected Works*, vol. 25 (London: Lawrence & Wishart, 1987): Frederick Engels, *Anti-Dühring* [1877], part 1, ch. 10 ('Morality and law. Equality').

28 [This quote is a paraphrase of the appropriate passage in Moore's text. – Translator.] On this point, see the comparison that Moore develops between Japan and Germany in *The Social Origins of Dictatorship and Democracy*, ch. 5, 'Asian fascism: Japan', pp. 228–313, and part 3, 'Theoretical implications and projections', pp. 413–508.

Lecture of 15 February 1990

1 Monique de Saint Martin, 'Les stratégies matrimoniales dans l'aristocratie. Notes provisoires', *Actes de la Recherche en Sciences Sociales*, 59 (1985), pp. 74–7, reprinted in *L'Espace de la noblesse* (Paris: Metaillé, 1993), pp. 217–43.

2 Bloch, *Seigneurie française et manoir anglais*.

3 Durkheim's position in the controversy, which has remained famous, and opposed him to the historian Charles Seignobos, is presented in 'Débat sur l'explication en histoire et en sociologie', *Bulletin de la Société Française de Philosophie*, 8 (1908), reprinted in Émile Durkheim, *Textes* (Paris: Minuit, 1975), vol. 1, pp. 199–217 and in English in *The Rules of Sociological Method* (Basingstoke: Palgrave Macmillan Higher Education, 2013), pp. 160–173.

4 Émile Durkheim and Marcel Mauss, *Primitive Classification* (Chicago: University of Chicago Press, 1967).

5 On this point, see Pierre Bourdieu, 'Irresistible analogy', Book II, ch. 3 of *The Logic of Practice*, esp. pp. 267–70, and also 'From rules to strategies', in *In Other Words*, pp. 59–74.

6 Norman W. Storer, 'The hard sciences and the soft', *Bulletin of the Medical Library Association*, 55 (1967).

7 Bourdieu, *Homo Academicus*, pp. 73–127; and 'Academic forms of classification', in *The State Nobility*, pp. 7–53.

8 Bourdieu, *The Logic of Practice*, esp. Book I, ch. 5 on 'The logic of practice', pp. 80–97, and the whole of Book II.

9 Françoise Autrand (ed.), *Prosopographie et genèse de l'État moderne* (Paris: École Normale Supérieure de Jeunes Filles, 1986); Jean-Philippe Genet and Bernard Vincent (eds), *État et Église dans la genèse de l'État moderne* (Madrid: Casa de Velázquez, 1986); Jean-Philippe Genet and Michel Le Mené, *Genèse de l'État moderne*; *Culture et idéologie dans la genèse de l'État moderne* (Rome: École Française de Rome, 1985).

10 See on this point 'Codification', in *In Other Words*, pp. 76–86.
11 Ernst Cassirer, 'Structuralism in modern linguistics', *Word*, 1.2 (1945). See also Pierre Bourdieu, 'Structuralism and theory of sociological knowledge', *Social Research*, 25.4 (1968), pp. 681–706.
12 See on this point Pierre Bourdieu, 'Men and machines', in Karin Knorr-Cetina and Aaron V. Cicourel (eds), *Advances in Social Theory and Methodology: Towards an Integration of Micro- and Macro-sociologies* (London: Routledge & Kegan Paul, 1981), pp. 304–17.
13 Bourdieu is referring here to the case of the hand-loom weavers as discussed by Weber in *The Protestant Ethic and the Spirit of Capitalism*, p. 312.
14 Bloch, *Seigneurie française et manoir anglais*, pp. 85–6.
15 Bourdieu developed this theme in his lectures at the Collège de France in 1988–9, and in 'Is a disinterested act possible?'.
16 [The journalist Bernard Pivot is a leading presenter of cultural programmes on television. – Translator.]
17 Joseph Richmond Levenson, *Confucian China and its Modern Fate: A Trilogy* (3 vols, Berkeley: University of California Press, 1958–65).
18 Bourdieu developed this connection between the various kinds of capital, and the capital city, in 'Site effects', in Bourdieu et al., *The Weight of the World*, pp. 123–80.
19 On legitimate language and the accompanying process of dispossession, see the first part of Bourdieu, *Language and Symbolic Power*, esp. pp. 43–65.
20 See the description of this 'initial scene' in the introduction to Pierre Bourdieu, *The Bachelors' Ball* (Cambridge: Polity, 2007).
21 Translated as 'Reproduction forbidden: the symbolic dimension of economic domination', in *The Bachelors' Ball*, pp. 165–90.

Lecture of 10 January 1991

1 Michel Crozier, *État modeste, État moderne* (Paris: Seuil, 1987).
2 Gaston Bachelard, *The Formation of the Scientific Mind* (Manchester: Clinamen Press, 2006).
3 Blaise Pascal, 'By space the universe encompasses and swallows me up like an atom; by thought I comprehend the world', in *Pensées*, para. 348.
4 Peter Evans et al. (eds), *Bringing the State Back In* (Cambridge: Cambridge University Press, 1985).
5 Atul Kohli, 'The state and development', *States and Social Structures Newsletter* (Social Science Research Council), 6 (1988), pp. 1–5.
6 See *Actes de la Recherche en Sciences Sociales*, 81–2 (1990).
7 [As *inspecteur des finances*, Jacques de Fouchier had been a senior civil servant before going on to found a series of banks soon after the Second World War. – Translator.]
8 Edward O. Laumann, *Bonds of Pluralism: The Form and Substance of Urban Social Networks* (New York: Wiley, 1973); Edward O. Laumann and Franz Urban Pappi, *Networks of Collective Action: A Perspective on Community Influence Systems* (New York: Academic Press, 1976); Edward O. Laumann and David Knoke, *The Organizational State* (Madison: University of Wisconsin Press, 1988). See Bourdieu and Wacquant, *Invitation to Reflexive Sociology*, p. 113.

9 See Lecture of 8 February 1990, note 23. Also Gregory Bateson et al., 'Towards a theory of schizophrenia', *Behavioral Science*, 1.4 (1956).

10 On the notion of genealogy, see Michel Foucault, 'Qu'est-ce que la critique? Critique et *Aufklärung*', lecture of 27 May 1978 to the Société Française de Philosophie, *Bulletin de la Société Française de Philosophie*, 84.2 (April–June 1990), pp. 35–63.

11 Bourdieu, 'Men and machines'.

12 [A '*topos*' in the academic context is a self-contained presentation of a subject – Translator.]

13 Bourdieu is referring here to the lecture on disinterestedness that he gave on 9 February 1989. The projected law that he mentions modified the practice of the legal professions by requiring a university degree.

14 [The Fédération Nationale des Syndicats d'Exploitants Agricoles, founded in 1946, is the main union of farmers of all kinds. – Translator.]

15 See the document 'Les rectifications de l'orthographie', published by the Conseil Supérieur de la Langue Française in the *Journal Officiel de la République Française, Documents Administratifs*, 100 (6 Dec. 1990). The polemic was in full swing at the time of this lecture; the Association pour la Sauvegarde de la Langue Française (ASLF), established in December 1990, particularly mobilized French Nobel Prize winners and members of the Académie des Sciences Morales et Politiques to intervene in the media against reform. It was probably one of its members who brought Bourdieu the following week a dossier with all the press clippings on this subject, particularly an article by Claude Lévi-Strauss, published in *Le Figaro* on 3 January 1991, entitled 'Tout reprendre à zéro'.

16 Bourdieu, *Distinction*, p. 189.

Lecture of 17 January 1991

1 Ernst Kantorowicz, '*Pro patria mori* in mediaeval political thought', in Kantorowicz, *Selected Studies*, pp. 138–50.

2 André Lalande, *Vocabulaire technique et critique de la philosophie* (1926; Paris: PUF, 2006), pp. 303–4.

3 Richard Bonney, 'Guerre, fiscalité et activité d'État en France, 1500–1600. Quelques remarques préliminaires sur les possibilités de recherche', in Genet and Le Mené, *Genèse de l'État moderne*, pp. 193–201.

4 Georges Duby, *Histoire de France*, vol. 1: *Le Moyen Age, de Hugues Capet à Jeanne d'Arc (987–1460)* (Paris: Hachette, 1987); in English as *France in the Middle Ages 987–1460: from Hugh Capet to Joan of Arc* (Oxford: Blackwell, 1991).

5 This idea is particularly suggested by Michel Serres in *Le Passage du Nord-Ouest* (Paris: Minuit, 1980).

6 Françoise Autrand, *Naissance d'un grand corps de l'État. Les gens du Parlement de Paris, 1345–1454* (Paris: Sorbonne, 1981).

7 Bourdieu is referring here to Weber's definition of the state as 'the form of human community that (successfully) lays claim to the monopoly of legitimate physical violence within a particular territory'. Weber, *The Vocation Lectures*, p. 33.

8 Elias, *The Civilizing Process*, esp. part 3, chs 2.III ('On the monopoly mechanism') and 2.VI ('The last stages of the free competitive struggle and establishment of the final monopoly of the victor').

9 Elias covers this point in *The Civilizing Process*, part 3, ch. 2.VIII, on 'The sociogenesis of the monopoly of taxation'. This question is taken up again by Charles Tilly in *Coercion, Capital and European States, AD 990–1990* (Oxford: Blackwell, 1990), ch. 3, entitled 'How war made states, and vice versa'. See also, by the same author, 'War making and state making as organized crime', in Evans et al., *Bringing the State Back In*, pp. 169–91.

10 Jacques Le Goff, 'L'État et les pouvoirs', in André Burguière and Jacques Revel (eds), *Histoire de la France*, vol. 2 (Paris: Seuil, 1989), p. 36.

11 Bourdieu translated this passage verbally during his lecture, from the German edition of Norbert Elias, *Über den Prozess der Zivilisation* [part 3, ch. 2.III in *The Civilizing Process*].

12 Norbert Elias, *The Court Society* (Oxford: Blackwell, 1963), p. 88. 'What Louis XIV, who marked both the culmination and the turning point of this development, attempted, was to organize his country as his personal property, as an enlargement of his household (p. 46).'

13 Elias, *The Civilizing Process*. See note 11 above.

14 Tilly, *Coercion, Capital and European States*, p. 26.

15 Bourdieu is referring here to Hilton, 'Resistance to taxation and to other state impositions in medieval England'.

16 Philip Corrigan and Derek Sayer, *The Great Arch: English State Formation as Cultural Revolution* (Oxford: Blackwell, 1985).

Lecture of 24 January 1991

1 Raymond Ruyer, *L'Utopie et les utopies* (Paris: PUF, 1950).

2 Henri Bergson, *The Creative Mind: An Introduction to Metaphysics* (Mineola, NY: Dover, 2010).

3 Corrigan and Sayer, *The Great Arch*, p. 2.

4 Corrigan and Sayer, *The Great Arch*, p. 3.

5 Bourdieu, 'On symbolic power', which the author explicitly refers to below.

6 [Here and in subsequent discussion, Bourdieu uses the English term 'welfare state'. – Translator.]

7 Durkheim, *The Elementary Forms of the Religious Life*, p. 19.

8 Corrigan and Sayer, *The Great Arch*, p. 191.

9 Corrigan and Sayer, *The Great Arch*, p. 192.

10 Bourdieu undoubtedly has in mind here the notion of 'proxemy' developed by Edward T. Hall, 'A system for the notation of proxemic behaviour', *American Anthropologist*, 65 (1963), pp. 1003–26.

11 Douglas Hay et al. (eds), *Albion's Fatal Tree* (London: Allen Lane, 1975), and E. P. Thompson, 'Modes de domination et révolution en Angleterre', *Actes de la Recherche en Sciences Sociales*, 2–3 (June 1976), pp. 133–51.

12 [The French '*État de droit*' follows the German '*Rechtsstaat*', roughly equivalent to the English 'constitutional state'. – Translator.]

13 The expression denoting both the Westminster Parliament and, more generally, the United Kingdom as recognized and celebrated model of the parliamentary political regime.

14 Corrigan and Sayer, *The Great Arch*, pp. 119–20.

15 Bourdieu, *The Logic of Practice*, pp. 162–99.

16 V. I. Lenin, 'The state: a lecture delivered at the Sverdlov university', 11

July 1919. At www.marxists.org/archive/lenin/works/1919/jul/11.htm (accessed June 2013).

17 Durkheim, *Leçons de sociologie*, pp. 79ff.
18 Corrigan and Sayer, *The Great Arch*, p. 188. [Bourdieu is paraphrasing here. – Translator.]
19 Corrigan and Sayer, *The Great Arch*, p. 202.
20 Corrigan and Sayer, *The Great Arch*, p. 188.
21 Hilton, 'Resistance to taxation and to other state impositions in medieval England'.
22 On this continuity between the 'berobed', lawyers and technocrats, see Bourdieu, *The State Nobility*, part IV, ch. 2, and part V.

Lecture of 31 January 1991

1 Bourdieu is very likely alluding to Thomas Kuhn, who showed in *The Structure of Scientific Revolutions* how the 'crisis' of a 'normal science' produces under certain social conditions a change of 'paradigm'.
2 Sam Whimster and Scott Lash (eds), *Max Weber, Rationality and Modernity* (London: Allen & Unwin, 1987). This collection contains Bourdieu's text on Max Weber's theory of religion: 'Legitimation and structured interests in Weber's sociology of religion', pp. 119–36.
3 For a critique of this theory, see Pierre Bourdieu, 'Structures sociales et structures de perception du monde social', *Actes de la Recherche en Sciences Sociales*, 1–2 (1975), pp. 18–20.
4 Friedrich Nietzsche, *Beyond Good and Evil* (New York: Vintage, 1966), p. 228.
5 Max Weber, 'Economy and law (The sociology of law)', in Weber, *Economy and Society*, vol. 2, ch. 8.
6 For a deeper discussion of the six meanings of the notion of rationality in Max Weber, see Rogers Brubaker, *The Limits of Rationality: An Essay on the Social and Moral Thought of Max Weber* (London: Allen & Unwin, 1984).
7 Émile Durkheim, *The Division of Labour in Society* (1893; New York: Free Press, 1964).
8 Michio Shibata and Tadami Chizuka, 'Marxist studies of the French Revolution in Japan', *Science and Society*, 54.3 (1990), pp. 366–74, and Germaine A. Hoston, 'Conceptualizing bourgeois revolution: the prewar Japanese left and the Meiji restoration', *Comparative Studies in Society and History*, 33.3 (1991), pp. 539–81.
9 On Bourdieu's use of this concept, see *The Political Ontology of Martin Heidegger*.
10 Arlette Jouanna, *Le Devoir de révolte. La noblesse française et la gestation de l'État moderne (1559–1661)* (Paris: Fayard, 1989).
11 The Ligue Catholique or Sainte-Union, born from the struggle against Protestantism during the wars of religion and led by the duc de Guise, developed into an insurrectionary movement, appealing to the États Généraux and the liberties of the provinces against the monarchy. Bourdieu referred on this subject to Robert Descimon, *Qui étaient les Seize? Mythes et réalités de la Ligue parisienne (1585–1594)* (Paris: Klincksieck, 1983).
12 Todai, in Tokyo, is Japan's most prestigious university, where most of the country's political elite are educated.

13 Joseph Needham, *The Grand Titration: Science and Society in East and West* (Toronto: University of Toronto Press, 1979).
14 See the explanation Bourdieu gives of May 1968 in *Homo Academicus* (esp. ch. 5: 'The critical moment'). This mechanism also plays a key role in his analysis of the conversion strategies of déclassé bourgeois that are analysed in *Distinction* (pp. 125–68), in the internal struggles within the ruling class involving 'deviant' members, described in *The State Nobility* (pp. 183–7), and in 'the invention of the life of the artist' in late nineteenth-century France as traced in *The Rules of Art: Genesis and Structure of the Literary Field* (Cambridge: Polity, 1996), pp. 54ff.
15 For an extension of this in the case of Second Empire France, see Bourdieu, *The Rules of Art*, pp. 48–56. For more detail on what follows from it, Pierre Bourdieu, 'How can free-floating intellectuals be set free?', in *Sociology in Question*, pp. 41–8.
16 Philippe Pons, *D'Edo à Tokyo. Mémoire et modernité* (Paris: Gallimard, 1988).
17 Herman Ooms, *Tokugawa Ideology: Early Constructs, 1570–1680* (Princeton: Princeton University Press, 1985).
18 Bourdieu is most likely referring here to René Sieffert, 'Le théâtre japonais', in Jean Jaquot (ed.), *Les Théâtres d'Asie* (Paris: Éditions du CNRS, 1968), pp. 133–61.
19 Pierre Bourdieu, 'Deux impérialismes de l'universel', in Christine Fauré and Tom Bishop (eds), *L'Amérique des Français* (Paris: François Bourrin, 1992), pp. 149–55.

Lecture of 7 February 1991

1 David Hume, 'Of the first principles of government', in *Essays and Treatises on Several Subjects*, vol. 1 (Edinburgh, 1777), pp. 33ff.
2 See Pierre Bourdieu and Jean-Claude Passeron, 'Sociologues des mythologies et mythologies des sociologues', *Les Temps Modernes*, 211 (1963), pp. 998–1021.
3 Austin, *How to Do Things with Words*.
4 Ernst Cassirer, *The Philosophy of Symbolic Forms* (4 vols, New Haven: Yale University Press, 1953–65).
5 Ernst Cassirer, *The Myth of the State* (New Haven: Yale University Press, 1961). [Cassirer's reference to Émile Durkheim and Marcel Mauss, *Primitive Classification*, does not appear in the English edition. – Translator.]
6 Benveniste, *Le Vocabulaire des institutions indo-européennes*, vol. 1: *Économie, parenté, société*, pp. 84ff.
7 In *Candide*, Voltaire parodies Leibniz in the character of Pangloss, this teacher of 'metaphysico-theologico-cosmolo-nigology', who claims, despite everything, that 'all is for the best in the best of worlds'.
8 Pierre Bourdieu, 'Rites of institution', pp. 117–26. Here Bourdieu explicitly criticizes Arnold Van Gennep, *Les Rites de passage* (Paris: Émile Nourry, 1909; reissued Paris: Picard, 1981). See Lecture of 14 February 1991, 'The state structures the social order'.
9 Ernst Cassirer, *The Philosophy of Symbolic Forms*, vol. 2: *Mythical Thought* (New Haven: Yale University Press, 1965).
10 Peter L. Berger and Thomas Luckmann, *The Social Construction of Reality: A Treatise in the Sociology of Knowledge* (New York: Anchor, 1967).

11 See for example Immanuel Wallerstein, *The Modern World-System*, vol. 1: *Capitalist Agriculture and the Origins of the European World-Economy in the Sixteenth Century* (Waltham, MA: Academic Press, 1974).

12 See among others Cicourel, *Cognitive Sociology*, and Cicourel's articles later collected for French publication by Pierre Bourdieu and Yves Winkin: Aaron Cicourel, *Le Raisonnement médical. Une approche socio-cognitive* (Paris: Seuil, 2002).

13 Aniko Husti, *Le Temps mobile* (Paris: Institut National de Recherche Pédagogique, 1985).

14 After the Russian psychologist Bluma Zeigarnik (1900–88) who showed the tension produced in children when tasks allotted them were not finished.

15 Durkheim, *The Division of Labour in Society*, p. 158.

16 For Bourdieu's notion of the religious field, see 'Legitimation and structured interests in Weber's sociology of religion'; 'Genesis and structure of the religious field', *Comparative Social Research* (Greenwich, CT), 13 (1991), pp. 1–44, and the two connected texts 'Sociologues de la croyance et croyances de sociologues' and 'La dissolution du religieux', in *Choses dites* (Paris: Minuit, 1987), pp. 106–11 and 117–23.

17 Frederick Engels, letter to Conrad Schmidt, 27 October 1890, in Karl Marx and Frederick Engels, *Collected Works*, vol. 49 (London: Lawrence & Wishart, 2001), pp. 57–64.

18 [The hereditary nobility in France were variously referred to as *noblesse de sang* (blood), *noblesse d'épée* (sword) or *noblesse de race* (descent). – Translator.]

19 Bourdieu, *The State Nobility*, pp. 382–9.

Lecture of 14 February 1991

1 Bollack, *Empédocle*.

2 Bourdieu, 'Dialogue on oral poetry in Kabylia'.

3 Six months before this time, following the death of a motorcyclist at a police roadblock, the Lyon suburb of Vaulx-en-Velin had experienced violent confrontations between young people and the police. Bourdieu had recently begun the investigation that would later be published as *The Weight of the World*, in which the interview he mentions here was published: 'An impossible mission', pp. 189–202.

4 Bourdieu, *Homo Academicus*, pp. 169ff.

5 Arnaldo Momigliano, 'Premesse per una discussione su Georges Dumézil', *Opus II* (1983); Carlo Ginzburg, 'Mythologie germanique et nazisme. Sur un livre ancien de Georges Dumézil', *Annales ESC*, 4 (1985), pp. 985–9.

6 Georges Dumézil, *Mythe et épopée*, vol. 1: *L'idéologie des trois fonctions dans les épopées des peuples indo-européennes* (Paris: Gallimard, 1968).

7 Georges Dumézil, *Mitra-Varuna. Essai sur deux représentations indo-européennes de la Souveraineté* (Paris: PUF, 1940).

8 Bourdieu, 'Rites of institution'.

9 [*Agrégé*: someone who has passed the higher examination for teachers; *énarque*: a student or ex-student of the École Nationale d'Administration. – Translator.]

10 Bachelard, *The Formation of the Scientific Mind*.

11 The 'principle of charity' was coined by the philosopher Neil L. Wilson, then

theorized by Willard Van Orman Quine, *Word and Object* (Harvard: MIT Press, 1960). It was particularly taken up by Donald Davidson, in *Inquiries into Truth and Interpretation* (Oxford: Clarendon Press, 1984).
12 Jacques Derrida, *The Other Heading: Reflections on Today's Europe* (Bloomington: University of Indiana Press, 1992).
13 Weber, *The Protestant Ethic and the Spirit of Capitalism.*
14 The French Sinologist Jacques Gernet was professor of Chinese social and intellectual history at the Collège de France from 1975 to 1992. In 1997 he published an article in *Actes de la Recherche en Sciences Sociales*, 118, under the title 'Le pouvoir d'État en Chine' (pp. 19–27), in fact a more general argument on the genesis of the modern state.
15 Joseph R. Strayer, *On the Medieval Origins of the Modern State* (Princeton: Princeton University Press, 2005).
16 Victor J. Kiernan, 'State and nation in Western Europe', *Past and Present*, 31 (July 1963), pp. 20–38.

Lecture of 21 February 1991

1 Michael Mann, 'The autonomous power of the state: its origins, mechanisms and results', *Archives Européennes de Sociologie*, 24 (1985), pp. 185–213. Also by the same author, *The Sources of Social Power* (2 vols, Cambridge: Cambridge University Press, 1986–93).
2 On the notion of symbolic capital, see among other sources, Pierre Bourdieu, *Outline of a Theory of Practice* (Cambridge: Cambridge University Press, 1977), pp. 171–82; *Practical Reason*, pp. 92–123; *Pascalian Meditations*, pp. 240ff.
3 Harold Garfinkel, 'Conditions of successful degradation ceremonies', *American Journal of Sociology*, 61.5 (1956), pp. 240–4.
4 See on this notion Pierre Bourdieu, 'Stratégies de reproduction et modes de domination', *Actes de la Recherche en Science Sociales*, 105 (1994), pp. 3–12.
5 Andrew W. Lewis, *Royal Succession in Capetian France* (Cambridge, MA: Harvard University Press, 1981).
6 Pierre Bourdieu used this expression later as the title of an article, 'De la maison du roi à la raison d'État. Une modèle de la genèse du champ bureaucratique', *Actes de la Recherche en Sciences Sociales*, 105 (1994), pp. 55–68. [English translation: 'Rethinking the state: genesis and structure of the bureaucratic field', in *Practical Reason*, pp. 35–74.]
7 This schema served as the basis of Bourdieu's analysis in 'Le patronat', *Actes de la Recherche en Sciences Sociales*, 20 (1978), pp. 3–82 (with Monique de Saint Martin), then in *The State Nobility*, part 4.
8 Jean-Jacques Laffont, 'Hidden gaming in hierarchies: facts and models', *Economic Record*, 64.187 (1988), pp. 295–306.
9 See Lecture of 18 January, note 1.
10 Richard J. Bonney, *The European Dynastic States (1494–1660)* (New York: Oxford University Press, 1991), and 'Guerre, fiscalité et activité d'État en France (1500–1660)', in Genet and Le Mené, *Genèse de l'État moderne.*
11 Bourdieu is referring here to 'How can one be a sportsman?', reprinted in *Sociology in Question*, pp. 117–31, and as 'Programme for a sociology of sport' in *In Other Words*, pp. 156–67.
12 Joachim W. Stieber, 'Pope Eugenius IV, the Council of Basel, and the secular

and ecclesiastical authorities in the Empire: the conflict over supreme authority and power in the Church', in Heiko A. Oberman (ed.), *Studies in the History of Christian Thought*, vol. 13 (Leyden: Brill, 1978).

13 Bourdieu, 'Rethinking the state: genesis and structure of the bureaucratic field'.

14 See among others, François Perroux, *Pouvoir et économie* (Paris: Dunos, 1973).

15 Laurent Fabius, who was prime minister from 1984 to 1986, was himself a *normalien*.

16 Norbert Elias, 'Sport and violence', *Actes de la Recherche en Sciences Sociales*, 6 (1976), pp. 2–21.

17 Max Weber, 'The meaning of discipline', in Hans H. Gerth and Charles Wright Mills (eds), *From Max Weber: Essays in Sociology* (New York: Oxford University Press, 1946).

18 Pierre Bourdieu, 'From the "rules" of honour to the sense of honour', in *Outline of a Theory of Practice*, pp. 10–15.

19 Gerald L. Harris, *King, Parliament and Public Finance in Medieval England to 1369* (Oxford: Clarendon Press, 1975).

20 Bourdieu, *Outline of a Theory of Practice*.

21 Yves-Marie Bercé, 'Pour une étude institutionelle et psychologique de l'impôt moderne', in Genet and Le Mené, *Genèse de l'État moderne*, p. 164.

22 Percy Ernst Schramm, *Kaiser, Rom und Renovatio. Studien und Texte zur Geschichte des römischen Erneuerungsgedankens vom Ende des karolingischen Reiches bis zum Investiturstreit* (2 vols, Berlin: Teubner, 1929).

23 Bercé, 'Pour une étude institutionnelle et psychologique de l'impôt moderne', p. 164.

24 Elias, *The Civilizing Process*, part 3, ch. 2, III, 'On the monopoly mechanism'.

Lecture of 7 March 1991

1 Bercé, 'Pour une étude institutionnelle', p. 164.

2 Bercé, 'Pour une étude institutionnelle', p. 164.

3 Pierre Bourdieu, 'La dernière instance', in *Le Siècle de Kafka* (Paris: Centre Georges-Pompidou, 1984), pp. 268–70.

4 Jean Dubergé, *La Psychologie sociale de l'impôt dans la France d'aujourd'hui* (Paris: PUF, 1961).

5 Günter Schmolders, *Psychologie des finances et de l'impôt* (Paris: PUF, 1973).

6 Pierre-Étienne Will, 'Bureaucratie officielle et bureaucratie réelle. Sur quelques dilemmes de l'administration impériale à l'époque des Qing', *Études Chinoises*, 8 (spring 1989), pp. 69–141. Pierre-Étienne Will subsequently edited, together with Olivier Christin and Pierre Bourdieu, issue 133 of *Actes de la Recherche en Sciences Sociales* on 'Science de l'État' (2000).

7 Hilton, 'Resistance to taxation and to other state impositions in medieval England', pp. 173–4.

8 Adhémar Esmein, *Histoire de la procédure criminelle en France, et spécialement de la procedure inquisitoire, depuis le XIIe siècle jusqu'à nos jours* (1882; Paris: Panthéon-Assas, 2010).

9 Bloch, *Seigneurie française et manoir anglais*, p. 85.

10 See Bourdieu, 'The force of law'.

11 Le Goff, 'L'État et les pouvoirs', p. 32.

12 Faustin Hélie, *Traité de l'instruction criminelle*, vol. 1 (Paris, 1866).
13 See Pierre Bourdieu, 'Effet de champ et effet de corps', *Actes de la Recherche en Sciences Sociales*, 59 (1985), p. 73.
14 Engels, letter to Conrad Schmidt, 27 October 1890.
15 Georges Duby, *Histoire de France*, vol. 1, pp. 283–4; in English as *France in the Middle Ages 987–1460: from Hugh Capet to Joan of Arc* (Oxford: Blackwell, 1991), p. 176.
16 See Pierre Bourdieu, *Masculine Domination* (Cambridge: Polity, 2002), pp. 54–80.
17 See what Bourdieu says of these studies in *Sketch for a Self-Analysis* (Cambridge: Polity, 2008), and for a practical application, 'The Kabyle house or the world reversed', in *Outline of a Theory of Practice*, pp. 271–83.
18 Svetlana Alpers, 'L'œil de l'histoire. L'effet cartographique dans la peinture hollandaise au XVIIe siècle', *Actes de la Recherche en Science Sociales*, 49 (1983), pp. 71–101.
19 Jack Goody, *The Domestication of the Savage Mind* (Cambridge: Cambridge University Press, 1977).
20 Thomas Bernhard, *Old Masters* (London: Penguin Books, 2010), p. 41. [The French translation that Bourdieu cites has: 'Nous sommes tous étatisés' ('We are all state-ized'). – Translator.]
21 Jouanna, *Le Devoir de révolte*, passim.
22 Elias, *The Court Society*.
23 Michèle Fogel, 'Modèle d'État et modèle social de dépenses. Les lois somptuaires en France de 1545 à 1560', in Genet and Le Mené, *Genèse de l'État moderne*, pp. 227–35.
24 Frederic William Maitland, *The Constitutional History of England* (1908; Cambridge: Cambridge University Press, 1948), p. 429. The lawyer Sir William Blackstone (1723–80) was a British MP. Maitland cited this formula from chapter 7 of Blackstone's *Commentaries on the Laws of England* (Oxford: Clarendon Press, 1765–9).
25 Maitland, *The Constitutional History of England*, p. 429.

Lecture of 14 March 1991

1 Bourdieu is referring to a programme shown on Antenne 2 on 13 March 1991, entitled 'The adventures of freedom'. This was conceived by Bernard-Henri Lévy, who brought up the subject of the Communist regimes established in Eastern Europe and asked: 'How could the intellectuals of that era accept all those crimes, those trials, that archipelago of suffering, that nightmare?'
2 Gilles Deleuze, 'Supplément à propos des nouveaux philosophes et d'un problème plus général', *Minuit*, supplement, 24 (May 1977), at www.acrimed.org/article2989.html (accessed June 2013).
3 [The writer and historian Alain Decaux, born 1925, served as minister for *Francophonie* in 1988–91. – Translator.]
4 See Bourdieu, *The Rules of Art*. This theme was first expressed in Pierre Bourdieu, 'Intellectual field and creative project', in Michael F. D. Young (ed.), *Knowledge and Control: New Directions in the Sociology of Education* (London: Collier-Macmillan, 1971), pp. 161–88. [Originally an article of 1966 in *Les Temps Modernes*. – Translator.]

5 Pierre Bourdieu, 'The hit parade of French intellectuals, or who is to judge the legitimacy of the judges ?' in *Homo Academicus*, pp. 256–70.

6 Bourdieu is referring to the dismissal from the Collège de France in 1852 of Jules Michelet, Edgar Quinet and Adam Mickiewicz, following the coup d'état by Louis Napoléon to whom they refused to swear allegiance.

7 An explanation of this is found in Bourdieu, *Pascalian Meditations*, pp. 103–4.

8 See on this point Pierre Bourdieu, 'For a corporatism of the universal', *Telos*, 81 (1989), pp. 99–110, reprinted in *The Rules of Art*, pp. 337–48.

9 See on this point Bourdieu, *Language and Symbolic Power*, part I.

10 Pierre Bourdieu, 'Social space and the genesis of "classes"', in *Language and Symbolic Power*, pp. 229–50.

11 Arthur Minton, 'A form of class epigraphy', *Social Forces*, 28 (1950), pp. 250–62.

12 Polanyi et al., *Trade and Market in the Early Empires*.

13 Bourdieu, 'Public opinion does not exist'.

14 Bourdieu, 'The production and reproduction of legitimate language'.

15 For an empirical development of this idea, see Pierre Bourdieu and Yvette Delsaut, 'Le couturier et sa griffe: contribution à une théorie de la magie', *Actes de la Recherche en Sciences Sociales*, 1.1 (1975), pp. 7–36.

16 Weber, *The Vocation Lectures*.

17 Spinoza, 'A political treatise', in *The Chief Works of Benedict de Spinoza*, vol. 2, ch. I, 6, pp. 289–90.

Lecture of 3 October 1991

1 Bourdieu, 'Rethinking the state'.

2 On this notion, see Pierre Bourdieu and Loïc Wacquant, 'From ruling to field of power', *Theory, Culture and Society*, 10.1 (Aug. 1993), pp. 19–44, as well as a text by Bourdieu recently published for the first time, 'Champ du pouvoir et division du travail de domination', *Actes de la Recherche en Science Sociales*, 190 (Dec. 2011).

3 Bourdieu, *The Bachelors' Ball*.

4 Claude Lévi-Strauss, 'L'ethnologie et l'histoire', *Annales ESC*, 6 (1983), pp. 1217–31.

5 ['*Jean de chez X.*' In Béarn and many other Occitan regions, farmhouses are often named 'chez Guillaume', 'chez Fernand', etc. – Translator.]

6 Bourdieu, *The State Nobility*, pp. 272–7.

7 This list is given systematic formulation in a text published in 1994: Bourdieu, 'Stratégies de reproduction et modes de domination'.

8 Pierre Bourdieu and Alain Darbel, 'La fin d'un malthusianisme?', in Darras, *Le Partage des bénéfices. Expansion et inégalités en France* (Paris: Minuit, 1966), pp. 135–54.

9 See on this point Pierre Bourdieu, 'The invention of the artist's life', in *Yale French Studies*, 73 (1987), pp. 75–103, and *The Rules of Art*, pp. 1–46.

10 Pierre Bourdieu, 'La domination masculine', *Actes de la Recherche en Sciences Sociales*, 84 (1990), pp. 2–31.

11 Gottfried Wilhelm Leibniz, *Theodicy: Essays on the Goodness of God, the Freedom of Man and the Origin of Evil* (London: Routledge, 1951).

12 Bourdieu, *The State Nobility*, pp. 272–7.

13 Maurice Merleau-Ponty, 'Indirect language and the voices of silence', in *Signs* (Evanston, IL: Northwestern University Press, 1964), pp. 39–83, esp. p. 78; see also part I, chs 3 and 6 of his *Phenomenology of Perception* (London: Routledge, 1964).

14 Ludwig Wittgenstein, *Philosophical Investigations* (Oxford: Blackwell, 1968), paras 66–7.

15 The reference is to Sarah Hanley, *The Lit de Justice of the Kings of France: Constitutional Ideology in Legend, Ritual, and Discourse* (Princeton: Princeton University Press, 1983).

16 [Bourdieu is using the Latin word here, which has also the sense of a hereditary office. – Translator.]

17 Lewis, *Royal Succession in Capetian France*, p. 121.

18 Kojima Hiroshi, 'A demographic evaluation of P. Bourdieu's "fertility strategy"', *Journal of Population Problems*, 45.4 (1990), pp. 52–8.

19 Iznogoud is the hero of an eponymous comic series created by René Goscinny and Jean Tabary, in which the vizier of the caliph of Baghdad, Haroun el-Poussah, is always trying to kill his sovereign and become 'caliph in place of the caliph'.

20 Racine's *Bajazet* (1672) was inspired by the murder in 1635 by the Ottoman sultan Murad IV (Amurat in the play) of his brothers and potential rivals Bayezid (Bajazet) and Orcan.

21 Georges Duby, *The Knight, the Lady, and the Priest: The Making of Modern Marriage in Medieval France* (New York: Pantheon, 1981).

22 Marcel Mauss, 'Salutations par le rire et les larmes', *Journal de Psychologie*, 21 (1922); also 'L'expression obligatoire des sentiments', *Journal de Psychologie*, 18 (1921), reprinted in Marcel Mauss, *Oeuvres* (Paris: Minuit, 1969), pp. 269–79.

23 See Bourdieu, 'The house market'.

24 Bonney, 'Guerre, fiscalité et activité d'État en France, 1500–1660'.

25 [The Garde des Sceaux is today an official title of the French minister of justice. – Translator.]

26 Maitland, *The Constitutional History of England*.

Lecture of 10 October 1991

1 Adolphe Cheruel, *Histoire de l'administration monarchique en France depuis l'avènement de Philippe Auguste jusqu'à la mort de Louis XIV* (1855; Geneva: Slatkine, 1974).

2 This work is presented in Jean-Philippe Genet (ed.), 'La genèse de l'État moderne. Enjeux et bilan d'un programme de recherche', *Actes de la Recherche en Sciences Sociales*, 118 (June 1997), pp. 3–18.

3 Laurence Caillet, *La Maison Yamazaki. La vie exemplaire d'une paysanne japonaise devenue chef d'une entreprise de haute coiffure* (Paris: Plon, 1991).

4 Elias, *The Civilizing Process*, part 3, ch. 2.III ('On the monopoly mechanism'), p. 269.

5 An allusion to Robert Michels's famous 'iron law of oligarchy' in *Political Parties: A Sociological Study of the Oligarchical Tendencies of Modern Democracy* (1911; New York: Free Press, 1968).

6 Georges Duby, preface to the French edition of *Royal Succession in Capetian*

France: A. W. Lewis, *Le Sang royal. La famille capétienne et l'État, France, Xe–XIVe siècles* (Paris: Gallimard, 1986).

7 Wolfgang Köhler, *The Mentality of Apes* (1925; London: Routledge, 1999).
8 Literally: 'Man is a wolf to man, man is a god to man', Bourdieu's addition to Hobbes's celebrated phrase. In his inaugural lecture at the Collège de France, Bourdieu had already proposed that 'it is also because man is a God unto man that man is a wolf unto man' (Pierre Bourdieu, 'A lecture on the lecture', in *In Other Words*, p. 196).
9 Muzaffar Alam, *The Crisis of Empire in Mughal North India: Awadh and the Punjab, 1707–1748* (Oxford: Oxford University Press, 1986), p. 17.
10 Étienne Thuau, *Raison d'État et pensée politique à l'époque de Richelieu* (1966; Paris: Albin Michel, 2000).
11 An allusion to the beheading of François-Auguste de Thou (c.1607–42), a state councillor under the reign of Louis XIII, executed for taking part in the Cinq-Mars conspiracy.
12 The quotation is from Maurice Merleau-Ponty, *In Praise of Philosophy* (Evanston: Illinois University Press, 1963), and is further developed by Bourdieu in 'A lecture on the lecture': 'He gives reasons for obeying the laws, but it is already too much to have reasons for obeying [. . .]. What they expect of him is just what he can't give: assent to the thing itself, without preamble' (p. 197).
13 Pierre Vidal-Naquet, *La Raison d'État* (1962; Paris: La Découverte, 2002).
14 See Lecture of 1 February 1990, 'The public and the official'.
15 Roland Mousnier, *Les Institutions de la France sous la monarchie absolue (1598–1789)* (2 vols, Paris: PUF, 1974 and 1980). Mousnier is generally viewed as a historian of the Catholic right. As a precursor of social history at the Sorbonne, he belonged neither to the Annales school nor to the Marxist current.
16 Bonney, 'Guerre, fiscalité et activité d'État en France, 1500–1600', p. 199.
17 Pierre Bourdieu, 'Les juristes, gardiens de l'hypocrisie collective', in François Chazel and Jacques Commaille (eds), *Normes juridiques et régulation sociale* (Paris: Librairie Générale de Droit et de Jurisprudence, 1991), pp. 95–9.
18 Adolf A. Berle and Gardiner C. Means, *The Modern Corporation and Private Property* (New York: Macmillan, 1932).
19 Bernard Guenée, *L'Occident aux XIVe et XVe siècles* (Paris: PUF, 1971), p. 230.
20 Dumézil, *Mythe et épopée*, vol. 1.
21 Bourdieu is referring here to Keith Hopkins, *Conquerors and Slaves* (Cambridge: Cambridge University Press, 1978).
22 Paul Garelli et al., *Le Proche-Orient asiatique*, vol. 1: *De ses origines aux invasions des peuples de la mer* (Paris: PUF, 1969).
23 Robert Mantran, *L'Empire ottoman, du XVe au XVIIe siècle. Administration, économie, société* (London: Variorum, 1984); also Robert Mantran (ed.), *Histoire de l'Empire ottoman* (Paris: Fayard, 1989), pp. 27 and 165–6.
24 See Alain Darbel and Dominique Schnapper, *Les Agents du système administratif* (The Hague: Mouton, 1969).
25 Weber, *Sociology of Religion*, ch. 1.
26 Ernest Gellner, *Nations and Nationalism* (Oxford: Blackwell, 1983), p. 101. [Gellner does not just refer here to the Jews, but equally to such groups as Greeks, Armenians and Parsees. – Translator.]

Lecture of 24 October 1991

1 Hanley, *The Lit de Justice of the Kings of France*.
2 Autrand, *Naissance d'un grand corps de l'État*.
3 [See Lecture of 7 February 1991, note 18. – Translator.]
4 An allusion to the power to cure this disease of tubercular origin, attributed to kings both in France and England from the Middle Ages on. See Marc Bloch, *The Royal Touch: Monarchy and Miracles in France and England* (1924; New York: Hippocrene, 1990).
5 Jean-Jacques Chevallier, *Histoire de la pensée politique* (3 vols, Paris: Payot, 1979–84).
6 See Hanley, *The Lit de Justice of the Kings of France*.
7 An allusion to Jean-Paul Sartre's dictum that 'Marxism is the impassable philosophical horizon of our time' (*Search for a Method* [New York: Vintage, 1968]).
8 Denis Crouzet, 'Recherches sur la crise de l'aristocratie en France au XVIe siècle: les dettes de la Maison de Nevers', *Histoire, Economie et Société*, 1 (1982), pp. 7–50.
9 See the developments that Bourdieu devotes to the theme of appointment in *Language and Symbolic Power*, esp. pp. 105–6.
10 See Blackstone in Lecture of 7 March 1991, '"Natural nobility" and state nobility'.
11 On this notion, see Pierre Bourdieu, 'Modes of domination', in *The Logic of Practice*, pp. 122–34.
12 Jean-Jacques Laffont, 'Hidden gaming in hierarchies: facts and models', *Economic Record*, 64.187 (1988), pp. 295–306, and 'Analysis of hidden gaming in a three-level hierarchy', *Journal of Law, Economics, and Organization*, 6.2 (1990), pp. 301–24.
13 This article is Jean Tirole and Jean-Jacques Laffont, 'Auction design and favoritism', *International Journal of Industrial Organization*, 9 (1991), pp. 9–42. In 1990, Jean Tirole and Jean-Jacques Laffont published an article entitled 'The politics of government decision making: regulatory institutions', *Journal of Law, Economics, and Organization*, 6.1 (1990), pp. 1–32, and in 1991 'The politics of government decision making: a theory of regulatory capture', *Quarterly Journal of Economics*, 106 (1991), pp. 1089–127. They subsequently co-authored a fundamental book on the new economics of regulation: *A Theory of Incentives in Procurement and Regulation* (Cambridge, MA: MIT Press, 1993).

Lecture of 7 November 1991

1 Bourdieu tackled the notion of field in all the courses he gave between 1982 and 1986, especially from 1982 to 1984.
2 Bourdieu and Wacquant, *An Invitation to Reflexive Sociology*.
3 Will, 'Bureaucratie officielle et bureaucratic réelle'.
4 Hilton, 'Resistance to taxation and to other state impositions in medieval England'.
5 On the position of intermediary, see Pierre Bourdieu, 'Condition de classe et position de classe', *Archives Européennes de Sociologie*, 7.2 (1966), pp. 201–23.

6 The journalist François de Closets enjoyed substantial sales in the 1980s with his books *Toujours plus!* (Paris: Grasset, 1982), which sold nearly 2 million copies, and *Tous ensemble. Pour en finir avec la syndicratie* (Paris: Seuil, 1985), which criticized the blockages of French society, with particular focus on the supposed corporatism of officials and trade unions.
7 Jean-François Billeter, 'Contribution à une sociologie historique du mandarinat', *Actes de la Recherche en Sciences Sociales*, 15 (1977), pp. 3–29.
8 Aristotle, *The Politics*, Book II, v.
9 See Lecture of 14 February 1991, note 3.
10 Remi Lenoir, 'A living reproach', in Bourdieu et al., *The Weight of the World*, pp. 239–44.
11 Pierre Bourdieu, 'Delegation and political fetishism', pp. 203–19.
12 Nietzsche, *Beyond Good and Evil*, ch. 3, 'The religious mood'.
13 Robert W. Gordon, '"The ideal and the actual in the law": fantasies and practices of New York City lawyers, 1870–1910', in Gerald W. Gawalt, *The New High Priests: Lawyers in Post-Civil War America* (Westport: Greenwood Press, 1984).
14 See Bourdieu, 'Is a disinterested act possible?'.
15 Bourdieu, 'La dernière instance'.
16 For an example of such an analysis conducted by the author at this point in time, see Pierre Bourdieu, Salah Bouhedja and Claire Givry, 'Un contrat sous contrainte', *Actes de la Recherche en Sciences Sociales*, 81 (1990), pp. 34–51, translated as 'A contract under duress', in *The Social Structures of the Economy*, pp. 148–84.
17 Cicourel, *Cognitive Sociology*.
18 André Malraux, *The Twilight of the Absolute* (New York: Pantheon, 1950). [The English title significantly changes the original meaning. – Translator.]
19 Corrigan and Sayer, *The Great Arch*.

Lecture of 14 November 1991

1 Benedict Anderson, *Imagined Communities: Reflections on the Origin and Spread of Nationalism* (London: Verso, 1983).
2 Maitland, *The Constitutional History of England*.
3 Maitland, *The Constitutional History of England*, p. 391.
4 [As when a court awards a symbolic sum for damages. – Translator.]
5 Maitland, *The Constitutional History of England*, p. 392. The *capitalis justitiarius* was the highest of the English king's judges, president of the King's Bench and guardian of the kingdom in his absence.
6 Maitland, *The Constitutional History of England*, p. 393.
7 Kantorowicz, *The King's Two Bodies*, pp. 193–206.
8 [The French *sigle*, from Latin *sigillum*, is today used mainly to mean an acronym. –Translator.]
9 Marcel Mauss, 'Esquisse d'une théorie générale de la magie', *L'Année Sociologique* (1902–3), reprinted in *Sociologie et Anthropologie* (Paris: PUF, 1950), pp. 1–141.
10 Arthur Oncken Lovejoy, *The Great Chain of Being: A Study of the History of an Idea* (Cambridge, MA: Harvard University Press, 1936).
11 The title of an article by Bourdieu subsequently published: 'Le mystère du ministère. Des volontés particulières à la "volonté générale"', *Actes de la*

Recherche en Sciences Sociales, 140 (2001), pp. 7–11. The same theme is tackled in *Language and Symbolic Power*.

12 Bourdieu presumably has in mind here Joseph Ben-David, *The Scientist's Role in Society: A Comparative Study* (Chicago: University of Chicago Press, 1971).

13 Romain Rolland, *Jean-Christophe* (17 vols, 1904–12; New York: Modern Library, 1938).

Lecture of 21 November 1991

1 Bourdieu and Saint Martin, 'Le patronat'.

2 See Lecture of 8 February 1990, note 18.

3 [An allusion to Habermas, *The Structural Transformation of the Public Sphere*. As noted earlier, the French edition of Habermas's book uses the term '*espace publique*', 'public space'. – Translator.]

4 Ernst Cassirer, *The Individual and the Cosmos in Renaissance Philosophy* (1927; Chicago: University of Chicago Press, 2010).

5 A petition signed by 121 French intellectuals and artists, published on 5 September 1960 to coincide with the trial of the 'Jeanson network', the 'suit-case carriers' accused of treason for their support of militants of the Algerian Front de Libération Nationale. Their position in support of conscientious objectors and their call for an end to the fighting led to a wave of censorship and the suspension of the academics who had signed the petition.

6 Keith M. Baker, *Inventing the French Revolution: Essays on French Political Culture in the Eighteenth Century* (Cambridge: Cambridge University Press, 1990).

7 See on this point chapter 4 of *The State Nobility*, and the recently published text by Pierre Bourdieu, 'Champ de pouvoir et division du travail de domination'.

8 François Furet and Mona Ouzouf (eds), *Dictionnaire critique de la Révolution française* (Paris: Flammarion, 1988).

9 Condorcet, who was condemned for treason by the Convention, actually died in prison in circumstances that have never been clarified. The hostility that Marat bore towards him because of the rejection of his work by the Académie des Sciences is well attested, but even assuming this was transferred on to the political terrain, Marat was already ill and no longer played any role in the Convention when the mathematician was disgraced, and his assassination was a year before the death of Condorcet.

10 Hanley, *The Lit de Justice of the Kings of France*.

11 Baker, *Inventing the French Revolution*.

12 Marcel Marion, *Dictionnaire des institutions de la France aux XVIIe et XVIIIe siècles* (1923; Paris: Picard, 1972).

13 Marion, *Dictionnaire des institutions*, pp. 336–7.

14 Weber, *Economy and Society*, vol. 1, ch. 3, sec. 5.

15 Quentin Skinner, *The Foundations of Modern Political Thought* (2 vols, Cambridge: Cambridge University Press, 1978).

16 Bourdieu and Saint Martin, 'Le patronat', p. 28.

17 Fritz K. Ringer, *The Decline of the German Mandarins: The German Academic Community (1890–1933)* (Cambridge, MA: Harvard University Press, 1969).

18 Luc Ferry et al. (eds), *Philosophes de l'Université. L'idéalisme allemand et*

la question de l'Université (texts from Schelling, Fichte, Schleiermacher, Humboldt and Hegel) (Paris: Payot, 1979).

19 See among others Bourdieu, *The Logic of Practice*, pp. 66–7.

20 Vilfredo Pareto, *The Mind and Society* (1916; 4 vols bound as 2, New York: Dover, 1963). The same problematic is also found in other works, particularly *Les Systèmes socialistes* of 1902. See also the selection of texts, Vilfredo Pareto, *The Rise and Fall of Elites: An Application of Theoretical Sociology* (New Brunswick, NJ: Transaction, 1991).

21 [The French legal phrase '*le mort saisit le vif*', still in use today, is the doctrine that the heir is considered as having succeeded to the deceased from the instant of the latter's death. –Translator.]

22 In the wake of the many conflicts in which the Paris Parlement was opposed to the higher courts, Louis XVI and René Nicolas de Maupeou, his chancellor and keeper of the seals, reformed the legal system in 1771, and particularly the sale of offices, this being a condition for the relative independence of the parliamentarians in relation to the royal power.

Lecture of 28 November 1991

1 See on this point Bourdieu's discussion in *Homo Academicus*, pp. 159ff.

2 Alain Viala, *Naissance de l'écrivain. Sociologie de la littérature à l'Age classique* (Paris: Minuit, 1985).

3 [See above, p. 383 n. 13.]

4 Louis Adrien Le Paige, *Lettres historiques sur les fonctions essentielles du Parlement, sur le droit des pairs et sur les lois fondamentales du royaume* (2 vols, Amsterdam (?), 1753–4). Cf. Hanley, *The Lit de Justice*, pp. 3–6.

5 Malesherbes, *Très humbles et très respectueuses remontrances, que présentent au roi, notre très honoré souverain et seigneur, les gens tenants sa Cour des Aides à Paris* (Paris, 1778). Under the ancien régime, the Cours des Aides dealt with lawsuits over questions of taxation.

6 Turgot, *Des administrations provinciales: mémoire présenté au Roi* (1788).

7 Guillaume-Joseph Saige, *Catéchisme du citoyen, ou Éléments du droit public français, par demandes & réponses* (1778 or 1775).

8 Louis-Sébastien Mercier, *Tableau de Paris* (12 vols, Amsterdam, 1783[1781?]– 8). In this famous testimony of the customs of the time, one of Mercier's targets was the 'automaton' or 'writing agent'.

9 Donald R. Kelley, *The Beginning of Ideology: Consciousness and Society in the French Reformation* (Cambridge: Cambridge University Press, 1981).

10 See Bourdieu, 'Effet de champ et effet de corps', p. 73; also 'The force of law'.

11 William Farr Church, *Constitutional Thought in Sixteenth-Century France: A Study in the Evolution of Ideas* (Cambridge, MA: Harvard University Press, 1941).

12 On the multidimensional character of the social space, see chapter 2 of *Distinction*, esp. pp. 114–24.

13 Denis Richet, *La France moderne. L'esprit des institutions* (Paris: Flammarion, 1973), pp. 79–80.

14 Denis Richet, 'Élite et noblesse. La fonction des grands serviteurs de l'État (fin XVIe–début XVIIe siècle)', *Acta Poloniae Historica*, 36 (1977), pp. 47–63.

15 Kantorowicz, *The King's Two Bodies*, pp. 193–231.

16 The 'Sapir-Whorf hypothesis', according to which mental representations derive from linguistic categories and are thus relative according to cultures, was named after the anthropologists Edward Sapir and Benjamin Lee Whorf. The linguist Wilhelm von Humboldt, and in his wake the philosopher Ernst Cassirer, are ascribed the comparable idea according to which each language contains a view of the world. On Bourdieu's use of these hypotheses, see 'On symbolic power'.

17 See Bourdieu, 'The force of law'.

18 Duby, *L'Histoire de France*, vol. 1, *Le Moyen Âge*, p. 288; available in English as *France in the Middle Ages 987–1460 from Hugh Capet to Joan of Arc* (Oxford: Blackwell, 1991), pp.180–1. [Bourdieu is paraphrasing this passage from Duby. – Translator.]

19 *Juvenes* were excluded from the allocation of fiefs.

20 See for example Bourdieu, 'Delegation and political fetishism'.

21 On this allusion to the criticism of the omnipresence of the state by the Austrian dramatist, see in particular Bernhard, *Old Masters*, p. 41.

22 Louis Gernet, *Les Grecs sans miracle* (Paris: Maspero, 1983). (This is actually a collection of texts taken from different periodicals and published between 1903 and 1960.)

23 Catherine Maire (ed.), *Jansénisme et révolution* (Paris: Chroniques de Port-Royal, Bibliothèque Mazarine, 1990).

24 Dale Van Kley, 'Du parti janséniste au parti patriote. L'ultime sécularisation d'une tradition religieuse à l'époque du chancelier Maupeou (1770–5)', in Maire, *Jansénisme et révolution*, pp. 115–30.

25 A party at that time could be a clan or a faction championing common interests, often with a family basis.

Lecture of 5 December 1991

1 François Châtelet, Olivier Duhamel and Évelyne Pisier, *Dictionnaire des oeuvres politiques* (Paris: PUF, 1986). Évelyne Pisier was subsequently appointed director of the book division of the ministry of culture.

2 See Pierre Bourdieu, 'Les sciences sociales et la philosophie', *Actes de la Recherche en Sciences Sociales*, 47–48 (1983), pp. 45–52.

3 For the whole of this section, see Bourdieu, 'Is a disinterested act possible?', as well as 'For a corporatism of the universal'.

4 Pierre Bourdieu, 'Le champ scientifique', *Actes de la Recherche en Sciences Sociales*, 3 (1976), pp. 88–104. Bourdieu would return to this point in his final lecture course at the Collège de France, in 2000–1, published as *Science of Science and Reflexivity* (Cambridge: Polity, 2004).

5 The motto said to have been displayed on the entrance gate of Plato's Academy.

6 Bourdieu, *The Political Ontology of Martin Heidegger*.

7 Gilbert Dagron, 'L'homme sans honneur, ou le saint scandaleux', *Annales HSS*, 4 (1990), pp. 929–39. In the Orthodox Church, the *salos* is the person 'mad in Christ', the ascetic who deliberately adopts the behaviour and language of the madman in order to reach an ascetic perfection.

8 See Bourdieu, 'A paradoxical foundation of ethics'.

9 James M. Buchanan, 'An economic theory of clubs' (1965), in Robert

E. Kuenne (ed.), *Readings in Social Welfare* (Hoboken, NJ: Wiley, 2000), pp. 73–85 (p. 85 n9). This US economist received the Nobel Prize for economics in 1986 for his work on 'public choice theory', which developed a critique of public intervention by relating this to state agents.

10 Buchanan, 'An economic theory of clubs'.

11 Paul Samuelson, 'The pure theory of public expenditure', *Review of Economics and Statistics*, 36.4 (1954), pp. 387–9.

12 Bourdieu, *Distinction*, p. 162.

13 The philosopher and poet Johann Gottfried von Herder, viewed as the inspirational figure of the romantic *Sturm und Drang* movement, was also the author of a definition of the nation based on common land and language.

14 The words of the journalist and parliamentarian Jean-Lambert Tallien are actually reported as: 'I will not say [. . .] that there are any foreigners in France except bad citizens.' (Session of the National Convention of 27 March 1795; the debates were published in *Le Moniteur Universel*, no. 190 [30 Mar. 1795].)

15 The textbooks of the historian Ernest Lavisse (1842–1922), including the famous 'Petit Lavisse' for the elementary level, trained generations of schoolchildren by inculcating into them the patriotic and citizen spirit celebrated by republicans.

16 'Of civil religion' is the title of chapter 8 of Book IV of Jean-Jacques Rousseau's *The Social Contract*.

17 Bourdieu is referring here to Robert N. Bellah, *The Broken Covenant: American Civil Religion in Time of Trial* (New York: Seabury Press, 1975).

18 George L. Mosse, *The Crisis of German Ideology: Intellectual Origins of the Third Reich* (New York: Grosse & Dunlap, 1964). See also George L. Mosse, *The Nationalization of the Masses: Political Symbolism and Mass Movements in Germany from the Napoleonic Wars through the Third Reich* (Ithaca, NY: Cornell University Press, 1975).

19 On this point, see Mosse, *The Crisis of German Ideology*, esp. the preface and ch. 2.

20 An allusion to the reunification of Germany proclaimed on 3 October 1990.

Lecture of 12 December 1991

1 Karl Marx, 'The Eighteenth Brumaire of Louis Bonaparte' (1852), in Karl Marx and Frederick Engels, *Collected Works*, vol. 11 (London: Lawrence & Wishart, 1979).

2 See Bourdieu, *In Other Words*, p. 36.

3 Patrick Champagne, *Faire l'opinion. Le nouveau jeu politique* (Paris: Minuit, 1990).

4 See in particular Pierre Bourdieu and Luc Boltanski, '"À armes égales". La parade d'objectivité et l'imposition de problématique', *Actes de la Recherche en Sciences Sociales*, 2–3 (1976), pp. 70–3; Patrick Champagne, 'L'Heure de vérité', *Actes de la Recherche en Sciences Sociales*, 71–2 (1988), pp. 98–101.

5 See Pierre Bourdieu, 'Strikes and political action', in *Sociology in Question*, pp. 168–76.

6 See Bourdieu, 'For a corporatism of the universal'.

7 Bourdieu and Passeron, 'Sociologues des mythologies et mythologies des sociologues'.

8 This lecture was given at the time of what were later called the 'Balkan wars', leading among other things to the dissolution of Yugoslavia: the war in Slovenia had taken place in June–July 1991, the war in Croatia began in August of that year, and the Bosnian war would begin in April 1992.

9 See on this subject *Actes de la Recherche en Sciences Sociales* 124 (1998): 'De l'État social à l'État pénal', and Loïc Wacquant's essay on 'America as social dystopia' in Bourdieu et al., *The Weight of the World*, pp. 130–9.

10 Abram de Swaan, *In Care of the State: Health Care, Education and Welfare in Europe and the USA in the Modern Era* (Cambridge: Polity, 1988).

11 At the time of the university and school student demonstrations against the planned Devaquet law, one measure of which was to increase university fees, the founder of *Le Figaro* magazine, Louis Pauwels, diagnosed a 'mental AIDS' on the part of the young demonstrators.

12 Albert O. Hirschman, *Exit, Voice and Loyalty: Responses to Decline in Firms, Organizations, and States* (Cambridge, MA: Harvard University Press, 1970).

13 Pierre Bourdieu, 'Traditional society's attitude towards time and economic behaviour', in *Algerian Sketches*; and *Algeria 1960* (Cambridge: Cambridge University Press, 1979).

14 This theme is found again later in an intervention by Pierre Bourdieu at the time of the social movement of 1995, 'Against the destruction of a civilization', in *Firing Back: Against the Tyranny of the Market* (London: Verso, 2003).

15 See William Ryan, *Blaming the Victim* (New York: Pantheon Books, 1971).

16 Émile Durkheim, 'Morale et science des mœurs', in *Textes*, vol. 2, pp. 255ff.

17 Remi Lenoir, 'La notion d'accident du travail. Un enjeu de luttes', *Actes de la Recherche en Sciences Sociales*, 32–3 (1980), pp. 77–88.

18 Bourdieu was presumably translating directly from the English here. On Spencer's position on the state, see for example *The Man Versus the State* (1884), and 'The right to ignore the state', in *Social Statics* (1851).

19 Bourdieu is probably referring here to the article by Gerald L. Geison, 'Les à-côtés de l'expérience', *Les Cahiers de Science & Vie*, special issue 'Pasteur. La tumultueuse naissance de la biologie moderne', 4 (Aug. 1991), pp. 69–79. A few years later, the same author published *The Private Science of Louis Pasteur* (Princeton: Princeton University Press, 1995), subsequently cited by Bourdieu in *Science of Science and Reflexivity*, p. 28.

20 Troy Duster, *Backdoor to Eugenics* (New York: Routledge, 1990); published in French as *Retour à l'eugénisme* (Paris: Kimé, 1992).

21 James Burnham, *The Managerial Revolution: What Is Happening in the World* (1941; New York: Greenwood Press, 1972).

22 See for example Éliane Alio, 'L'émergence des probabilités', *Actes de la Recherche en Sciences Sociales*, 54 (1984), pp. 77–81, and 'Un nouvel art de gouverner. Leibniz et la gestion savante de la société par les assurances', *Actes de la Recherche en Sciences Sociales*, 55 (1984), pp. 33–40.

23 Bourdieu, *The Political Ontology of Martin Heidegger*.

24 See note 8 above.

25 Lenoir, 'A living reproach'.

26 On this point, see Pierre Bourdieu, 'The abdication of the state', in *The Weight of the World*, pp. 181–8, 'The left hand and the right hand of the state', in *Acts of Resistance* (Cambridge: Polity, 1999), and 'The invisible hand of the powerful', in *Firing Back*, pp. 26–37.

27 Hellmut Brunner, 'Die religiöse Antwort auf die Korruption im Ägypten', in

Wolfgang Schuller (ed.), *Korruption im Altertum*, Constance conference, 9–10 Oct. 1979 (Munich: Oldenbourg, 1982), pp. 71–7.

28 Amarna was the new city inspired by the religious reform of Amenhotep IV/ Akhenaten, who in opposition to the clergy imposed the exclusive cult of the Sun god, displacing the rest of the Egyptian pantheon.

29 At the time that this lecture was given, Bourdieu had already begun his study of this badly affected iron and steel region. See Bourdieu et al., *The Weight of the World*.

Position of the lectures on the state in Pierre Bourdieu's work

1 *Science of Science and Reflexivity*.
2 'The "berobed" and the invention of the state'.
3 'The state and the construction of the market'.
4 'Rethinking the state'; 'Stratégies de reproduction et modes de domination'.
5 See for example Pierre Bourdieu, 'Social space and symbolic power' (lecture given at the University of San Diego in March 1986), in *In Other Words*, pp. 123–39; *Invitation to Reflexive Sociology*, pp. 18ff.; Pierre Bourdieu, 'L'État et la concentration en capital symbolique' (Paris, Jan. 1993), in Bruno Théret (ed.), *L'État, la finance et le social. Souveraineté nationale et construction européenne* (Paris: La Découverte, 1995), pp. 73–105; and especially Bourdieu's unpublished intervention 'Le sociologue devant l'État' at the Association des Sociologues de Langue Française in October 1982.
6 'De la maison du roi à la raison d'État', p. 55 n1.
7 'A lecture on the lecture'.
8 'Modes of domination'.
9 'Stratégies de reproduction et modes de domination'.
10 Pierre Bourdieu, 'La transmission de l'héritage culturel', in Darras, *Le Partage des bénéfices*, pp. 135–54, and 'Cultural reproduction and social reproduction', in Richard Brown (ed.), *Knowledge, Education and Cultural Theory* (London, 1973), pp. 71–112.
11 Bourdieu and Saint Martin, 'Le patronat'.
12 Pierre Bourdieu and Monique de Saint Martin, 'La sainte famille. L'épiscopat français dans le champ du pouvoir', *Actes de la Recherche en Sciences Sociales*, 44–5 (Nov. 1982), pp. 2–53.
13 Pierre Bourdieu, 'The field of the grandes écoles and its transformations', in *The State Nobility*, pp. 129–228.
14 Pierre Bourdieu, 'Champ du pouvoir, champ intellectuel et habitus de classe', *Scolies*, 1 (1971), pp. 7–26. In 1971, Bourdieu gave the following definition of this: 'The field of power is the objective structure of relations established between systems of agents and authorities that tend to maintain the established structure of relations between classes', *Séminaires EPHE* (for future publication).
15 Pierre Bourdieu, 'Description and prescription: the conditions of possibility and the limits of political effectiveness', in *Language and Symbolic Power*, pp. 127–36.
16 'Public opinion does not exist', and especially Pierre Bourdieu, 'Questions de politique', *Actes de la Recherche en Sciences Sociales*, 16 (Sept. 1977), pp. 55–89.

17 Pierre Bourdieu, 'Political representation: elements for a theory of the political field', in *Language and Symbolic Power*, pp. 171–202. 'Delegation and political fetishism'; and 'The mystery of the ministry'.

18 *Homo Academicus*, p. 27.

19 Pierre Bourdieu, Olivier Christin and Pierre-Étienne Will, 'Sur la science de l'État', *Actes de la Recherche en Sciences Sociales*, 133 (June 2000), pp. 3–9.

20 Pierre Bourdieu, 'Rethinking the state'.

21 'The mystery of the ministry'.

22 See Pierre Bourdieu, 'State power and power over the state', in *The State Nobility*, pp. 371–89, as well as the lectures Bourdieu devoted to the legal field, the bureaucratic field and the state at the Collège de France (1986–92, for future publication), as summed up in a number of articles: 'The force of law'; 'Is a disinterested act possible?'; 'Esprits d'État'; 'Rethinking the state'.

23 'La souffrance'.

24 *The Weight of the World*, pp. 181ff.

25 'The left hand and the right hand of the state'.

26 Pierre Bourdieu, *Political Interventions: Social science and political action* (London: Verso, 2008).

27 Pierre Bourdieu and Roger Chartier, *Le Sociologue et l'historien* (Marseille: Agone, 2010), p. 90.

28 'Le sociologue devant l'État'.

29 See, in particular, Pierre Bourdieu, 'Men and machines', in Karin Knorr-Cetina and Aron V. Cicourel (eds.), *Advances in Social Theory and Methodology: Towards an Integration of Micro- and Macro-Sociologies* (Boston and London: Routledge, 1981), p. 705. for an initial critical development of the notion of state.

30 'Le sociologue devant l'État'.

31 On the relationship that Bourdieu had with French historians in the late 1980s and early 1990s, see Pierre Bourdieu, 'Sur les rapports entre la sociologie et l'histoire en Allemagne et en France. Entretien avec Lutz Raphael', *Actes de la Recherche en Sciences Sociales*, 106–7 (Mar. 1995), pp. 108–22.

32 'Résumé des cours et travaux', in *Annuaire du Collège de France*, 1988–1989 (Paris, 1989), p. 431.

33 Pierre Bourdieu, 'Entretien sur l'esprit de la recherche, avec Yvette Delsaut', in Yvette Delsaut and Marie-Christine Rivière, *Bibliographie des travaux de Pierre Bourdieu* (Pantin: Le Temps des Cerises, 2002), p. 224.

Bibliography

This bibliography of documents used by Pierre Bourdieu during his lectures on the state was established on the basis of his personal archives. Available texts and references have been added to the texts cited during the lectures. For this translation, English-language texts and references have been given where possible.

1 Books and articles on the state, the field of power or the history of political thought

Actes de la Recherche en Sciences Sociales, special issue 'L'économie de la maison', 81–2 (1990) (with contributions from Rosine Christin, Salah Bouhedja, Claire Givry and Monique de Saint Martin).

Culture et Idéologie dans la Genèse de l'État Moderne, proceedings of the round table organized by CNRS and École Française de Rome, 15–17 Oct. 1984 (Rome: École Française de Rome, 1985) (with contributions from Daniel Arasse, Attilio Bartoli Angeli, Jean-Louis Biget, Jean-Claude Hervé and Yvon Thébert, Marie-Thérèse Bouquet-Boyer, Alain Boureau, Roger Chartier, Michael Clanchy, Janet Coleman, Claudio Finzi, Michèle Fogel, Wilhem Frijhoff, Carla Frova, Claude Gauvard, Antonia Grandsen, Martine Grinberg, Christian Jouhaud, Christiane Klapisch-Zuber, Jacques Krynen, Jean-Claude Mairevigueur, Christiane Marchello-Nizia, Cesare Mozzarelli, Claude Nicolet, Ezio Ornato, Michel Pastoureau, Armando Petrucci, Diego Quaglioni, Gérard Sabatier, Claude Tardits).

Daedalus, special issue 'The state', 108.4 (autumn 1979) (with contributions from Clark C. Abt, Hedley Bull, Harry Eckstein, James Fishkin, Richard Haas, Michael Howard, George Armstrong Kelly, Annie Krigel, John Logue, Douglas Rae).

Le Journal Officiel de la République Française. Cent ans au service des citoyens (1981).

Nuovi Argumenti, Italian-French supplement, 'La piazza et la città – La place et la ville', Institut Culturel Italien, Paris (Dec. 1985).

Revue Internationale des Sciences Sociales, special issue 'De l'État', 32.4 (1980) (with contributions from Nicos Poulantzas, Maurice Godelier, Shmuel N. Eisenstadt, Romila Thapar, Pierre Birnbaum, Aristide R. Zolberg, Guillermo

O'Donnell, Issa G. Shirji, Immanuel Wallerstein, Silviu Brucan, Zevin Zalmanovich).
La Revue Nouvelle, special issue 'Néo-libéralismes', 79.3 (Mar. 1984).

Abrams, Philip, 'Notes on the difficulty of studying the state', *Journal of Historical Sociology*, 1.1 (Mar. 1988), pp. 59–89.
Aguesseau, Henri François d', *Oeuvres*, Paris: Libraires Associés, 1759.
Alain, *Le Citoyen contre les pouvoirs*, Paris: Sagittaire, 1926.
Alam, Muzaffar, *The Crisis of Empire in Mughal North India: Awadh and the Punjab, 1707–1748*, Oxford: Oxford University Press, 1986.
Alphandéry, Claude, et al., *Pour nationaliser l'État. Réflexions d'un groupe d'études*, Paris: Seuil, 1968.
Althusser, Louis, 'Ideology and ideological state apparatuses', in *Lenin and Philosophy and Other Essays*, New York: Monthly Review Press, 1971.
Altwater, Elmar, 'Some problems of state interventionism: the particularization of the state in bourgeois society', in John Holloway and Sol Picciotto (eds), *State and Capital: A Marxist Debate*, London: Edward Arnold, 1978, pp. 40–3.
Alvesson, Mats, 'On focus in cultural studies of organizations', *Scandinavian Journal of Management Studies*, 2.2 (Nov. 1985), pp. 105–20.
Aminzade, Ronald, 'History, politics, and the state', review of Charles Bright and Susan Harding, *Statemaking and Social Movements: Essays in History and Theory*, Ann Arbor: University of Michigan Press, 1984, *Contemporary Sociology*, 15.5 (1986), pp. 695–7.
Anderson, Benedict, *Imagined Communities: Reflections on the Origin and Spread of Nationalism*, London: Verso, 1983.
Anderson, Perry, *Lineages of the Absolutist State*, London: New Left Books, 1974.
Anderson, Perry, *Passages from Antiquity to Feudalism*, London: New Left Books, 1974.
Anderson, Perry, *Arguments within English Marxism*, New York: Schocken Books, 1980.
Antoine, Michel, 'La monarchie française de François Ier à Louis XVI', in Emmanuel Le Roy Ladurie (ed.), *Les Monarchies* (conference proceedings, Paris, 8–10 Dec. 1981), Paris: PUF, 1986, pp. 185–208.
Apter, David E., 'Notes on the underground: left violence and the national state', *Daedalus*, special issue 'The state', 108.4 (autumn 1979), pp. 155–72.
Archambault, Paul, 'The analogy of the "body" in Renaissance political literature', in *Bibliothèque d'Humanisme et Renaissance. Travaux et documents*, vol. 19, Geneva: Droz, 1967, pp. 21–53.
Ardant, Gabriel, 'La codification permanente des lois. Règlements et circulaires', *Revue de Droit Public* (1951), pp. 35–70.
Ardant, Gabriel, *Technique de l'État. De la productivité au secteur public*, Paris: PUF, 1953.
Ardant, Gabriel, *Théorie sociologique de l'impôt*, 2 vols, Paris: SEVPEN, 1965.
Argyriades, Demetrios, 'Neutralité ou engagement politique. L'expérience de la fonction publique en Grande-Bretagne', *Bulletin de l'ITAP*, 38 (April–June 1978), pp. 277–308 (quoted in Dominique Chagnollaud, *L'Invention des hauts fonctionnaires*, Lille: ANRT, 1989, p. 494).
Aron, Raymond, *Peace and War: A Theory of International Relations*, Garden City, NY: Doubleday, 1966.
Arriaza, Armand, 'Mousnier and Barber: the theoretical underpinning of the

"society of orders" in early modern Europe', *Past and Present*, 89 (1980), pp. 39–57.

Auby, Jean-Marie and Roland Drago, *Traité de contentieux administratif*, 2 vols, Paris: Librairie Générale de Droit et de Jurisprudence, 1984.

Autrand, Françoise, *Naissance d'un grand corps de l'État. Les gens du Parlement de Paris, 1345–1454*, Paris: Sorbonne, Paris, 1981.

Autrand, Françoise, *Prosopographie et genèse de l'État moderne* (proceedings of the round table organized by CNRS and École Normale Supérieure de Jeunes Filles, Paris, 22–23 Oct. 1984), Paris: École Normale Supérieure de Jeunes Filles, 1986.

Aylmer, Gerald E., 'The peculiarities of the English state', *Journal of Historical Sociology*, 3.2 (June 1990), pp. 91–107.

Badie, Bertrand, *Le Développement politique*, 2nd edn, Paris: Economica, 1980.

Badie, Bertrand, 'Contrôle culturel et genèse de l'État', *Revue Française de Science Politique*, 31.2 (April 1981), pp. 325–42.

Badie, Bertrand, and Pierre Birnbaum, 'L'autonomie des institutions politico-administratives. Le rôle des cabinets des présidents de la République et des Premiers ministres sous la cinquième République', *Revue Française de Science Politique*, 26.2 (1976), pp. 286–322.

Badie, Bertrand, and Pierre Birnbaum, *Sociologie de l'État*, Paris: Grasset, 1979.

Baker, Keith M., *Inventing the French Revolution: Essays on French Political Culture in the Eighteenth Century*, Cambridge: Cambridge University Press, 1990.

Balazs, Étienne, 'Les aspects significatifs de la société chinoise', *Asiatische Studien*, 6 (1952), pp. 79–87.

Balazs, Étienne, *La Bureaucratie céleste. Recherches sur l'économie et la société de la Chine traditionnelle*, Paris: Gallimard, 1968.

Balibar, Étienne, 'Es gibt kein en Staat in Europa. Racisme et politique dans l'Europe d'aujourd'hui', contribution to the conference 'Migration und Rassismus in Europa', Hamburg, 27–30 Sept. 1990, mimeo.

Bancaud, Alain, 'Considérations sur une "pieuse hypocrisie". Les magistrats de la Cour de cassation et l'exégèse', mimeo, n.d.

Bancaud, Alain, 'Une "constance mobile". La haute magistrature', *Actes de la Recherche en Sciences Sociales*, 76–77 (Mar. 1989), pp. 30–48.

Barber, Bernard, 'Some problems in the sociology of the professions', *Daedalus*, 92 (1963), pp. 669–86.

Barret-Kriegel, Blandine, *L'État et les esclaves*, Paris: Calmann-Lévy, 1979.

Barret-Kriegel, Blandine, *Les Chemins de l'État*, Paris: Calmann-Lévy, 1986.

Bercé, Yves-Marie, 'Pour une étude institutionnelle et psychologique de l'impôt moderne', in Jean-Philippe Genet and Michel Le Mené (eds), *Genèse de l'État moderne* (conference proceedings, Fontevraud, 16–17 Nov. 1984), Paris: Éditions du CNRS, 1987.

Bergeron, Gérard, *Fonctionnement de l'État*, 2nd edn, Paris: Armand Colin, 1965.

Bernard, Yves, and Pierre-Yves Cossé, *L'État et la prévision macroéconomique*, Paris: Berger-Levrault, 1974.

Bien, David D., 'Les offices, les corps et le crédit d'État. L'utilisation des privilèges sous l'Ancien Régime', *Annales ESC*, 43.2 (Mar.–April 1988), pp. 379–404.

Billetter, Jean-François, 'Contribution à une sociologie historique du mandarinat', *Actes de la Recherche en Sciences Sociales*, 15 (June 1977), pp. 3–29.

Birnbaum, Pierre, *La Fin du politique*, Paris: Seuil, 1975.

Birnbaum, Pierre, 'La conception durkheimienne de l'État. L'apolitisme des fonctionnaires', *Revue Française de Sociologie*, 17.2 (1976), pp. 247–58.

Birnbaum, Pierre, and François Chazel, *Sociologie politique*, Paris: Armand Colin, 1971.

Bloch, Marc, *Seigneurie française et manoir anglais* [1934], Paris: Armand Colin, 1960.

Bloch, Marc, *Feudal Society*, 2 vols, London: Routledge & Kegan Paul, 1961.

Bloch, Marc, *The Royal Touch: Monarchy and Miracles in France and England* [1924], New York: Dorset Press, 1989.

Bloch-Lainé, François, and Pierre de Vogüé, *Le Trésor public et le mouvement général des fonds*, Paris: PUF, 1961.

Block, Fred, Richard A. Cloward, Barbara Ehrenreich and Frances Fox Piven, *The Mean Season: The Attack on the Welfare State*, New York: Pantheon, 1987.

Bluche, François, *Les Magistrats du Parlement de Paris au XVIIIe siècle, 1715–1771*, Paris: Belles Lettres, 1960.

Bonney, Richard J., 'Guerre, fiscalité et activité d'État en France, 1500–1600. Quelques remarques préliminaires sur les possibilités de recherche', in Jean-Philippe Genet and Michel Me Mené (eds), *Genèse de l'État moderne* (conference proceedings, Fontevraud, 16–17 Nov. 1984), Paris: Éditions du CNRS, 1987, pp. 193–201.

Bonney, Richard J., *The European Dynastic States (1494–1660)*, New York: Oxford University Press, 1991.

Bonney, Richard J., 'Rethinking nationhood: nation as institutionalised form, practical category, contingent event', contribution to the Sociological Research Association annual banquet, Miami, 14 Aug. 1993, mimeo.

Borgetto, Michel, 'Métaphore de la famille et idéologies', in *Le Droit non civil de la famille*, Paris: PUF, 1983, pp. 1–21.

Braibant, Guy, *Le Droit administratif français* (esp. 'fascicule 1, 1982–1983'), Paris: Presses de la Fondation Nationale des Sciences Politiques, 1988.

Brelot, Claude J., *La Noblesse réinventée. Nobles de Franche-Comté de 1814 à 1870*, Paris: Belles Lettres, 1992.

Brubaker, William Rogers, 'Immigration, citizenship, and nationhood in France and Germany: a comparative historical analysis', contribution to the conference 'Rethinking the theory of citizenship', American Sociological Association, 1990, mimeo.

Burawoy, Michael, 'Two methods in search of science: Skocpol versus Trotsky', mimeo, n.d.

Burdeau, Georges, *L'État*, Paris: Seuil, 1970.

Burdillat, Martine, 'La difficile démocratisation industrielle. L'expérience des conseils d'administration des filiales du secteur public', *Cahiers de Recherche du Groupement d'Intérêt Public 'Mutations Industrielles'*, 10 (15 Oct. 1987).

Burguière, André, and Jacques Revel (eds), *Histoire de la France*, vol. 2, Paris: Seuil, 1989.

Carneiro, Robert L., 'A theory of the origins of the state', *Science*, 169 (1970).

Carneiro, Robert L., 'The chiefdom: precursor of the state', in Grant D. Jones and Robert Kautz (eds), *The Transition to Statehood in the New World*, Cambridge: Cambridge University Press, 1981.

Carnoy, Martin, *The State and Political Theory*, Princeton: Princeton University Press, 1984.

Carré de Malberg, Raymond, *Contribution à la théorie générale de l'État* [1920–2], Paris: Éditions du CNRS, 1962.

Cassirer, Ernst, *The Myth of the State*, New Haven: Yale University Press, 1961.

Catach, Nina, 'La bataille de l'orthographe aux alentours de 1900', in Gérald Antoine and Robert Martin, *Histoire de la langue française, 1800–1914*, vol. 14, Paris: Éditions du CNRS, 1985.

Cazelles, Raymond, *Société politique, noblesse et couronne sous Jean le Bon et Charles V*, Geneva: Droz, 1982.

Chagnollaud, Dominique, *L'Invention des hauts fonctionnaires*, Lille: ANRT, 1989.

Chandler, Alfred Dupont, *Strategy and Structure*, Cambridge: MIT Press, 1962.

Chapus, René, *Droit administratif général*, Paris: Montchrestien, 1987.

Charle, Christophe, 'Les grands corps. Rouge, noir et or', mimeo, n.d.

Charle, Christophe, 'Review of Marie-Christine Kessler', *Les Grands Corps de l'État*, Paris: Presses de la Fondation Nationale des Sciences Politiques, 1986, *Annales ESC*, 42.5 (1987), pp. 1177–9.

Charle, Christophe, 'Où en est l'histoire sociale des élites et de la bourgeoisie? Essai de bilan critique de l'historiographie contemporaine', *Francia: Forschungen zur Westeuropäischen Geschichte*, 18.3 (1991), pp. 123–34.

Chartier, Jean-Luc, *De Colbert à l'Encyclopédie*, vol. 1: *Henri Daguesseau, conseiller d'État, 1635–1716*, Montpellier: Presses du Languedoc and Max Chaleil éditeur, 1988.

Chartier, Roger, and Jacques Revel, 'Université et société dans l'Europe moderne. Position des problèmes', *Revue d'Histoire Moderne et Contemporaine*, 25 (July–Sept. 1978), pp. 353–74.

Chaunu, Pierre, and Richard Gascon, 'L'État et la ville', in Fernand Braudel and Ernest Labrousse (eds), *Histoire économique et sociale de la France*, vol. 1: *De 1450 à 1660*, Paris: PUF, 1977.

Cheruel, Adolphe, *Histoire de l'administration monarchique en France depuis l'avènement de Philippe Auguste jusqu'à la mort de Louis XIV* [1855], Geneva: Slatkine, 1974.

Chevallier, Jean-Jacques, *Histoire de la pensée politique*, 3 vols, Paris: Payot, 1979–1984.

Chirot, Daniel, 'Ideology and legitimacy in Eastern Europe', *States and Social Structures Newsletter*, 4 (spring 1987), pp. 1–4.

Church, William Farr, *Constitutional Thought in Sixteenth-Century France: A Study in the Evolution of Ideas*, Cambridge: Harvard University Press, 1941.

Citron, Suzanne, 'Enseignement secondaire et idéologie élitiste entre 1880 et 1914', *Le Mouvement Social*, 96 (July–Sept. 1976), pp. 81–101.

Constant, Jean-Marie, 'Clans, partis nobiliaires et politiques au temps des Guerres', in Jean-Philippe Genet and Michel Le Mené (eds), *Genèse de l'État moderne* (conference proceedings, Fontevraud, 16–17 Nov. 1984), Paris: Éditions du CNRS, 1987, pp. 221–6.

Coronil, Fernando, and Julie Skurski, 'Reproducing dependency: auto policy and petrodollar circulation in Venezuela', *International Organization*, 36 (1982), pp. 61–94.

Corrigan, Philip, and Derek Sayer, *The Great Arch: English State Formation as Cultural Revolution*, Oxford: Blackwell, 1985.

Coulborn, Rushton (ed.), *Feudalism in History* (with contributions from Joseph R. Strayer, Williams F. Edgerton, Edwin O. Reischauer), Princeton: Princeton University Press, 1956.

Crouzet, Denis, 'Recherches sur la crise de l'aristocratie en France au XVIe siècle. Les dettes de la Maison de Nevers', *Histoire, Economie et Société*, 1 (1982), pp. 7–50.

Crozier, Michel, *État modeste, État moderne. Stratégie pour un autre changement* [1987], Paris: Seuil, 1991.

Crozier, Michel, Ehrard Friedberg, Catherine Grémion, Pierre Grémion, Jean-Claude Thoenig and Jean-Pierre Worms, *Où va l'administration française?*, Paris: Éditions d'Organisation, 1974.

Cunéo, Bernard, 'Le conseil d'administration et les rapports État/entreprise à Air France', *Cahiers de Recherche du Groupement d'Intérêt Public 'Mutations Industrielles'*, 9 (15 Sept. 1987).

Dale, Harold E., *The Higher Civil Service of Great Britain*, Oxford: Oxford University Press, 1941.

Darbel, Alain, and Dominique Schnapper, *Les Agents du système administratif*, The Hague: Mouton, 1969.

Day, C. Rod, 'The making of mechanical engineers in France: the École des Arts et Métiers, 1903–1914', *French Historical Studies*, 10.3 (spring 1978), pp. 439–60.

De Jasay, Anthony, *The State*, Oxford: Basil Blackwell, 1985.

Dessert, Daniel, and Jean-Louis Journet, 'Le lobby Colbert. Un royaume ou une affaire de famille?', *Annales ESC*, 30 (1975), pp. 1303–36.

de Swaan, Abram, 'In care of the state: state formation and the collectivization of wealth care: education and welfare in Europe and America during the Modern Era', proposed project (14 pages including a list of contents), followed by a preliminary translation: 'Introduction à une sociogenèse de l'État providence' (12 pages).

Dewald, Jonathan, *The Formation of a Provincial Nobility: The Magistrates of the Parlement of Rouen, 1499–1610*, Princeton: Princeton University Press, 1980.

Douglas, Mary, *How Institutions Think*, Syracuse: Syracuse University Press, 1986.

Dubergé, Jean, *La Psychologie sociale de l'impôt dans la France d'aujourd'hui*, Paris: PUF, 1961.

Duby, Georges, *France in the Middle Ages 987–1460: from Hugh Capet to Joan of Arc* (Oxford: Blackwell, 1991).

Duby, Georges, *The Knight, the Lady, and the Priest: The Making of Modern Marriage in Medieval France*, New York: Pantheon, 1981.

Duccini, Hélène, 'Un aspect de la propagande royale sous les Bourbons. Image et polémique', in *Culture et idéologie dans la genèse de l'État moderne* (proceedings of the round table organized by CNRS and École Française de Rome, 15–17 Oct. 1984), Rome: École Française de Rome, 1985, pp. 211–29.

Duccini, Hélène, *Histoire de France*, vol. 1: *Le Moyen Âge, de Hugues Capet à Jeanne d'Arc (987–1460)*, Paris: Hachette, 1987.

Dufour, Alfred, 'De l'École du droit naturel à l'école du droit historique. Étude critique pour le bicentenaire de la naissance de Savigny', *Archives de Philosophie du Droit*, 26 (1981).

Dufour, Alfred, 'La théorie des sources du droit dans l'École du droit historique', *Archives de Philosophie du Droit*, 27 (1981).

Duguit, Léon, *Traité de droit constitutionnel*, vol. 1, 3rd edn, Paris: De Boccard, 1927.

Dumézil, George, *Mitra-Varuna. Essai sur deux représentations indoeuropéennes de la souveraineté*, Paris: PUF, 1940.

Dumézil, George, *Mythe et épopée*, vol. 1: *L'Idéologie des trois fonctions dans les épopées des peuples indo-européens*, Paris, Gallimard, 1968.

Dupont-Ferrier, Gustave, *La Formation de l'État français et l'unité française* [1934], 3rd edn, Paris: Armand Colin, 1946.

Dupuy, François, and Jean-Claude Thoenig, *Sociologie de l'administration française*, Paris: Armand Colin, 1983.

Durkheim, Émile, *'The Rules of the Sociological Method'* (Basingstoke: Palgrave Macmillan Higher Education, 2013).

Durkheim, Émile, 'L'État', in *Textes*, vol. 3, Paris: Minuit, 1975, pp. 172–8.

Eckstein, Harry, *Division and Cohesion in Democracy: A Study of Norway*, Princeton: Princeton University Press, 1966.

Eckstein, Harry, 'On the "science" of the state', *Daedalus*, special issue 'The state', 108.4 (autumn 1979).

Eckstein, Harry, and David E. Apter, *Comparative Politics: A Reader*, New York: Free Press, 1963.

Eckstein, Harry, and Ted Robert Gurr, *Patterns of Authority: A Structural Basis for Political Inquiry*, New York: Wiley-Interscience, 1975.

Egret, Jean, 'L'Aristocratie parlementaire française à la fin de l'Ancien Régime', *Revue Historique*, 208 (1952), pp. 1–14.

Eisenstadt, Shmuel Noah, *The Political System of Empires*, New York: Free Press, 1963.

Elias, Norbert, *The Civilizing Process*, Oxford: Blackwell, 2000.

Elias, Norbert, *The Court Society*, Dublin: University of Dublin Press, 2006.

Elliot, John H., 'Concerto barroco', review of José Antonio Mapavall, *Culture of the Baroque: Analysis of a Historical Structure*, Minneapolis: University of Minnesota Press, 1986, *New York Review of Books*, 34.6 (9 April 1987).

Elster, Jon, 'Négation active et négation passive. Essai de sociologie ivanienne' (on Alexandre Zinoviev, *Les Hauteurs béantes*, Lausanne: L'Âge d'homme, 1977, and *L'Avenir radieux*, Lausanne: L'Âge d'homme, 1978), *Archives Européennes de Sociologie*, 21.2 (1980), pp. 329–49.

Engels, Friedrich, Letter to Conrad Schmidt, 27 October 1890, in Karl Marx and Frederick Engels, *Collected Works*, vol. 49, London: Lawrence & Wishart, 2001, pp. 57–64.

Esmein, Adhémar, *Histoire de la procédure criminelle en France et spécialement de la procédure inquisitoire, depuis le XIIe siècle jusqu'à nos jours*, Paris: Larose, 1882.

Evans, Peter B., *Embedded Autonomy: States and Industrial Transformation*, Princeton: Princeton University Press, 1995.

Evans, Peter B., Dietrich Rueschemeyer and Theda Skocpol (eds), *Bringing the State Back In*, Cambridge: Cambridge University Press, 1985.

Ferraresi, Franco, 'Los elites periferiche dello stato: il quadro comparativo. La burocrazia centrale', mimeo, n.d.

Finer, Samuel E., 'State and nation-building in Europe: the role of the military', in Charles Tilly (ed.), *The Formation of National States in Western Europe*, Princeton: Princeton University Press, 1975, pp. 84–163.

Finer, Samuel E., *Five Constitutions*, Brighton: Harvester, 1979.

Fogel, Michèle, 'Modèle d'État et modèle social de dépenses. Les lois somptuaires en France de 1545 à 1560', in Jean-Philippe Genet and Michel Le Mené (eds), *Genèse de l'État moderne* (conference proceedings, Fontevraud, 16–17 Nov. 1984), Paris, Éditions du CNRS, 1987, pp. 227–35.

Foucault, Michel, 'La gouvernementalité', *Actes. Les Cahiers d'Action Juridique*, special issue 'La gouvernementalité. Foucault hors les murs', 54 (summer 1986).

Fougeyrollas, Pierre, *La Nation. Essor et déclin des sociétés modernes*, Paris: Fayard, 1987.

Frankel, Boris, *Marxian Theories of the State: A Critique of Orthodoxy*, Melbourne: Arena, 1978.

Frêche, Georges, and Jean Sudreau, *Un chancelier gallican. Daguesseau, et un cardinal diplomate. François Joachim de Pierre de Bernis*, Paris: PUF, 1969.

Friedberg, Erhard, 'Generalized political exchange and interorganizational analysis', for workshop on 'Political exchange: between governance and ideology' organized by Bernd Marin and Alessandro Pizzorno, Abbaye Fiesolana, Florence, 15–18 Dec. 1986, mimeo.

Frijhoff, Wilhem, and Dominique Julia, 'L'Éducation des riches. Deux pensionnats, Belley et Grenoble', *Cahiers d'Histoire*, 21.1–2 (1976), pp. 105–31.

Frijhoff, Wilhem, and Dominique Julia, 'Les grands pensionnats de l'Ancien Régime à la Restauration', *Annales Historiques de la Révolution Française*, 243 (Jan.–Mar. 1981), pp. 153–98.

Furet, François, and Mona Ozouf (eds), *Dictionnaire critique de la Révolution française*, Paris: Flammarion, 1988.

Fussman, Gérard, 'Le concept d'empire dans l'Inde ancienne', in Maurice Duverger (ed.), *Le Concept d'Empire*, Paris: PUF, 1980, pp. 378–96.

Fussman, Gérard, 'Pouvoir central et régions dans l'Inde ancienne. Le problème de l'empire maurya', *Annales ESC*, 4 (July–Aug. 1982), pp. 621–47.

Garelli, Paul, Jean-Marie Durand, Hatice Gonnet and Catherine Breniquet, *Le Proche-Orient asiatique*, vol. 1: *Des origines aux invasions des peuples de la mer*, Paris: PUF, 1969.

Gaudemet, Paul-Marie, *Le Civil Service britannique*, Paris: Presses de la Fondation Nationale des Sciences Politiques, 1952.

Gellner, Ernest, *Nations and Nationalism* [1983], Oxford: Blackwell, 2006.

Genet, Jean-Philippe (ed.), *L'État moderne, genèse. Bilans et perspectives* (CNRS conference, 19–20 Sept. 1988), Paris: Éditions du CNRS, 1990.

Genet, Jean-Philippe, and Michel Le Mené (eds), *Genèse de l'État moderne. Prélèvement et redistribution* (conference proceedings, Fontevraud, 16–17 Nov. 1984), Paris: Éditions du CNRS, 1987.

Genet, Jean-Philippe, and Bernard Vincent (eds), *État et Église dans la genèse de l'État moderne* (proceedings of conference organized by CNRS and Casa de Velázquez, Madrid, 30 Nov.–1 Dec. 1984), Madrid: Casa de Velázquez, 1986.

Gernet, Jacques, 'Fondements et limites de l'État en Chine', mimeo, n.d.

Gernet, Jacques, 'Histoire sociale et intellectuelle de la Chine', mimeo, n.d.

Gernet, Jacques, 'L'Homme ou la paperasse. Aperçu sur les conceptions politiques de T'Ang Chen, 1630–1704', in Dieter Eikemeier and Herbert Franke (eds), *State and Law in East Asia*, Wiesbaden: Harrassowitz, 1981, pp. 112–25.

Gernet, Jacques, 'Clubs, cénacles et sociétés dans la Chine des XVIe et XVIIe siècles', lecture to the annual public session of 21 Nov. 1986, Paris: Académie des Inscriptions et Belles-Lettres, Institut de France, 1986.

Gordon, Robert W., '"The ideal and the actual in the law": fantasies and practices of New York City lawyers, 1870–1910', in Gerard W. Gawalt (ed.), *The New High Priests: Lawyers in Post–Civil War America*, Westport: Greenwood Press, 1984, pp. 51–74.

Goubert, Pierre, *L'Ancien Régime*, Paris: Armand Colin, 1963.

Gramsci, Antonio, *Prison Notebooks* (notebooks 10, 11, 12 and 13), 3 vols, New York: Columbia University Press, 2010.

Grawitz, Madeleine, and Jean Leca (eds), *Traité de science politique*, Paris: PUF, 1985.

Grémion, Pierre, *Le Pouvoir périphérique. Bureaucrates et notables dans le système politique français*, Paris: Seuil, 1976.

Griffin, Larry J., Joel A. Devine and Michael Walllace, 'Accumulation, legitimation and politics: neo-Marxist explanation of the growth of welfare expenditures in the United States since the Second World War', manuscript, n.d.

Guenée, Bernard, 'L'histoire de l'État en France à la fin du Moyen Âge vue par les historiens français depuis cent ans', *Revue historique*, 232 (1964), pp. 331–60.

Guenée, Bernard, *L'Occident aux XIVe et XVe siècles. Les États* [1971], 2nd edn, Paris: PUF, 1981.

Gusfield, Joseph R., *The Culture of Public Problems: Drinking-Driving and the Symbolic Order*, Chicago: University of Chicago Press, 1981.

Habermas, Jürgen, *Legitimation Crisis* [1973], Boston: Beacon Press, 1975.

Hall, John A., *Powers and Liberties: The Causes and Consequences of the Rise of the West*, Oxford: Basil Blackwell, 1985.

Hall, John A. (ed.), *States in History*, Oxford: Basil Blackwell, 1986.

Hamelin, Jacques, and André Damien, *Les Règles de la profession d'avocat*, Paris: Dalloz, 1987.

Hanley, Sarah, *The Lit de Justice of the Kings of France: Constitutional Ideology in Legend, Ritual and Discourse*, Princeton: Princeton University Press, 1983.

Hanley, Sarah, 'Engendering the state: family formation and state-building in early modern France', *French Historical Studies*, 16.1 (spring 1989), pp. 4–27.

Harris, Gerald L., *King, Parliament and Public Finance in Medieval England to 1369*, Oxford: Clarendon Press, 1975.

Harsanyi, John C., 'Measurement of social power in n-person reciprocal power situations', *Behavioral Science*, 7.1 (Jan. 1962), pp. 81–91.

Haskell, Francis, 'L'art et le langage de la politique', *Le Débat*, 44 (1987), pp. 106–17.

Haskell, Francis, *Past and Present in Art and Taste*, New Haven: Yale University Press, 1987.

Hay, Douglas, Peter Linebaugh and E. P. Thompson (eds), *Albion's Fatal Tree: Crime and Society in Eighteenth-Century England*, London: Allen Lane, 1975.

Hegel, Georg Wilhelm, *The Phenomenology of Spirit* [1807], trans. A. V. Miller, Oxford: Oxford University Press, 1977.

Held, David, et al. (eds), *States and Societies*, Oxford: Martin Robertson, 1983.

Hélie, Faustin, *Traité de l'instruction criminelle*, vol. 1, Paris, 1866.

Henry, Louis, 'Perspectives d'évolution du personnel d'un corps', *Population*, 2 (Mar.–April 1975), pp. 241–69.

Hilton, Rodney H., 'Resistance to taxation and to other state impositions in medieval England', in Jean-Philippe Genet and Michel Le Mené (eds), *Genèse de l'État moderne* (conference proceedings, Fontevraud, 16–17 Nov. 1984), Paris: Éditions du CNRS, 1987, pp. 169–77.

Hirsch, Joachim, *Staatsapparat und Reproduktion des Kapitals*, Frankfurt am Main: Suhrkamp, 1974.

Hirsch, Joachim, 'The state apparatus and social reproduction: elements of a theory of the bourgeois state', in John Holloway and Sol Picciotto (eds), *State and Capital: A Marxist Debate*, London: Edward Arnold, 1978, pp. 57–108.

Hirschman, Albert O., 'How Keynes was spread from America', *States and Social Structures Newsletter*, 10 (spring 1989), pp. 1–8.

Hopkins, Keith, *Conquerors and Slaves*, Cambridge: Cambridge University Press, 1978.

Hoston, Germaine A., 'Conceptualizing bourgeois revolution: the prewar Japanese left and the Meiji Restoration', *Comparative Studies in Society and History*, 33.3 (1991), pp. 539–81.

Hunt, Lynn, *Politics, Culture and Class in the French Revolution*, Berkeley: University of California Press, 1984.

Hunter, Floyd, *Community Power Structure: A Study of Decision Makers*, Chapel Hill: University of North Carolina Press, 1953.

Hurst, James W., *The Growth of American Law: The Law Makers*, Boston: Little Brown, 1950.

Jessop, Bob, 'Putting states in their place: state systems and state theory', presented at Historical Sociology Workshop, University of Chicago, Nov. 1988, mimeo.

Jobert, Bruno, and Pierre Muller, *L'État en action. Politiques publiques et corporatismes*, Paris: PUF, 1987.

Jobert, Bruno, and Bruno Théret, 'La conversion républicaine du néolibéralisme', in Bruno Jobert (ed.), *Le Tournant néo-libéral en Europe*, Paris: L'Harmattan, 1994, pp. 21–85.

Johnson, Terence J., *Professions and Power*, London: Macmillan, 1972.

Jouanna, Arlette, *Le Devoir de révolte. La noblesse française et la gestation de l'État moderne (1559–1661)*, Paris: Fayard, 1989.

Kantorowicz, Ernst H., *The King's Two Bodies: A Study in Mediaeval Political Theology*, Princeton: Princeton University Press, 1957.

Kantorowicz, Ernst H., 'Kingship under the impact of scientific jurisprudence', in *Selected Studies*, Locust Valley, NY: J. J. Augustin, 1965, pp. 151–66.

Kantorowicz, Ernst H., 'Mysteries of state: an absolutist concept and its late medieval origins', in *Selected Studies*, Locust Valley, NY: J. J. Augustin, 1965, pp. 381–98.

Kantorowicz, Ernst H., '*Pro patria mori* in medieval political thought', in *Selected Studies*, Locust Valley, NY: J. J. Augustin, 1965, pp. 138–50.

Kantorowicz, Ernst H., 'The sovereignty of the artist', in *Selected Studies*, Locust Valley, NY: J. J. Augustin, 1965, pp. 352–65.

Karpil, Lucien, 'Avocat. Une nouvelle profession?', *Revue Française de Sociologie*, 26 (1985), pp. 571–600.

Katznelson, Ira and Bruce Pietrykowski, 'Rebuilding the American state: evidence from the 1940s', *Studies in American Political Development*, 5 (autumn 1991), pp. 301–39.

Keane, John, *Public Life and Late Capitalism*, Cambridge: Cambridge University Press, 1984.

Kelley, Donald R., *The Beginning of Ideology: Consciousness and Society in the French Reformation*, Cambridge: Cambridge University Press, 1981.

Kelsall, Roger K., *Higher Civil Servants in Britain: From 1870 to the Present Day*, London: Routledge & Kegan Paul, 1955.

Kelsall, Roger K., 'Recruitment to the Higher Civil Service: how has the pattern changed?', in Philip Stanworth and Anthony Giddens (eds), *Elites and Power in British Society*, Cambridge: Cambridge University Press, 1974.

Keohane, Nannerl O., *Philosophy and the State in France: The Renaissance to the Enlightenment*, Princeton: Princeton University Press, 1980.

Kiernan, Victor J., 'State and nation in Western Europe', *Past and Present*, 31 (July 1963), pp. 20–38.

Kingsley, Donald J., *Representative Bureaucracy*, Yellow Springs: Antioch Press, 1944.

Kingsley, Donald J., Glenn O. Stahl and William E. Mosher, *Public Personnel Administration*, 5th edn, New York: Harper, 1962.

Kleiman, Ephraïm, 'Fear of confiscation and redistribution: notes towards a theory of revolution and repression', given to a seminar of the Institute for International Economic Studies, Stockholm, 1983.

Klein, Jacques-Sylvain, 'La procédure des fonds de concours ou l'art de tourner les règles budgétaires', *Revue Administrative* (Sept.–Oct. 1981), pp. 466–471.

Kohli, Atul, 'The state and development', *States and Social Structures Newsletter* (Social Science Research Council), 6 (1988), pp. 1–5.

Laffont, Jean-Jacques, 'Hidden gaming in hierarchies: facts and models', *Economic Record*, 64.187 (1988), pp. 295–306.

Laffont, Jean-Jacques, 'Analysis of hidden gaming in a three-level hierarchy', *Journal of Law, Economics, and Organization*, 6.2 (1990), pp. 301–24.

Laitin, David B., and Ian S. Lustick, 'Hegemony, institutionalization and the state', mimeo, n.d.

Laitin, David B., and Ian S. Lustick, 'Hegemony and the state', *States and Social Structures Newsletter* (Social Science Research Council), 9 (winter 1989), pp. 1–8.

Lattimore, Owen, 'Feudalism in history', review of Rushton Coulborn, *Feudalism in History*, Princeton: Princeton University Press, 1956, *Past and Present*, 12 (Nov. 1957), pp. 50–57.

Lattimore, Owen, *Studies in Frontier History, Collected Papers 1928–1958*, The Hague: Mouton, 1962.

Laumann, Edward O., *Bonds of Pluralism: The Form and Substance of Urban Social Networks*, New York: Wiley, 1973.

Laumann, Edward O., and David Knoke, *The Organizational State*, Madison: University of Wisconsin Press, 1988.

Laumann, Edward O., and Franz U. Pappi, *Networks of Collective Action: A Perspective on Community Influence Systems*, New York: Academic Press, 1976.

Leca, Jean, Jean Bouvier, Pierre Muller, Lucien Nizard, Yves Barrel, André Nicolai, Claude Hermann-Origet, René Leyral and Gabriele Gottelmann, 'Recherches sur l'État. Élaboration d'un bilan interdisciplinaire des travaux concernant l'État français d'aujourd'hui', report of Institut d'Etudes Politiques CERAT, Commissariat Général du Plan, CORDES, vol. 1, 1980.

Leff, Gordon, *History and Social Theory*, London: Merlin, 1969.

Legendre, Pierre, 'Histoire de la pensée administrative', in *Traité de science administrative*, Paris: Mouton, 1966.

Legendre, Pierre, 'La facture historique des systèmes. Notations pour une histoire comparative du droit administratif français', *Revue Internationale de Droit Comparé*, 23.1 (Jan.–Mar. 1971), pp. 5–47.

Le Goff, Jacques, 'L'État et les pouvoirs', in André Burguière and Jacques Revel (eds), *Histoire de la France*, vol. 2. Paris: Seuil, 1989.

Lenin, V. I., 'The state: a lecture delivered at the Sverdlov university', 11 July 1919, at www.marxists.org/archive/lenin/works/1919/jul/11.htm (accessed June 2013).

Lenoir, Remi, 'A living reproach', in Pierre Bourdieu (ed.), *The Weight of the World*, Cambridge: Polity, 1999, pp. 239–44.

Le Paige, Louis Adrien, *Lettres historiques sur les fonctions essentielles du Parlement, sur le droit des pairs et sur les lois fondamentales du royaume*, 2 vols, Amsterdam: Aux Dépens de la Compagnie, 1753–4.

Le Pors, Anicet, *L'État efficace*, Paris: Robert Laffont, 1985.

Levenson, Joseph Richmond, *Confucian China and its Modern Fate: A Trilogy*, 3 vols, Berkeley: University of California Press, 1958–65.

Lewis, Andrew W., *Royal Succession in Capetian France*, Cambridge: Harvard University Press, 1981.

Liebermann, Jethro K., *The Tyranny of Experts: How Professionals Are Closing the Open Society*, New York: Walker, 1970.

Lindblom, Charles E., *Politics and Markets*, New York: Basic Books, 1977.

Lindenberg, Siegwart, James S. Coleman and Stefan Nowak (eds), *Approaches to Social Theory*, New York: Russell Sage Foundation, 1986.

Lipietz, Alain, 'Crise de l'État-providence. Idéologies, réalités et enjeux pour la France des années 1980', contribution to the Congrès de la Société Québécoise de Science Politique 'Crise économique, transformations politiques et changements idéologiques', Trois-Rivières, May 1983, Document CEPREMAP, 8306, 1983.

Lowi, Theodore J., 'The reason of the welfare state: an inquiry into ethical foundations and constitutional remedies', mimeo, n.d.

Lowie, Robert H., *The Origin of the State*, New York: Harcourt, Brace, 1927.

Loyseau, Charles, *Traité des ordres et simples dignités*, Châteaudun, 1610.

Macpherson, Crawford B., 'Do we need a theory of the state?', *Archives Européennes de Sociologie*, 18.2 (1977), pp. 223–44.

Maire, Catherine (ed.), *Jansénisme et révolution. Actes du colloque de Versailles tenu au Palais des Congrès les 13 et 14 octobre 1989*, Paris: Chroniques de Port-Royal, Bibliothèque Mazarine, 1990.

Maitland, Frederic W., *English Law and the Renaissance*, Cambridge: Cambridge University Press, 1901.

Maitland, Frederic W., *Equity: The Forms of Action at Common Law*, Cambridge: Cambridge University Press, 1913.

Maitland, Frederic W., *The Constitutional History of England: A Course of Lectures Delivered* [1908], Cambridge: Cambridge University Press, 1948.

Manley, John, 'Neopluralism: a class analysis of pluralism I and pluralism II', *American Political Science Review*, 77 (1983), pp. 368–84.

Mann, Michael, 'States, ancient and modern', *Archives Européennes de Sociologie*, special issue on the state, 28.2 (1977), pp. 262–98.

Mann, Michael, 'The autonomous power of the state: its origins, mechanisms and results', *Archives Européennes de Sociologie*, 25.1 (1984), pp. 185–213.

Mann, Michael, *The Sources of Social Power*, vol. 1: *A History of Power from the Beginning to AD 1760*, Cambridge: Cambridge University Press, 1986.

Mantran, Robert, *L'Empire ottoman, du XVIe au XVIIIe siècle. Administration, économie, société*, London: Variorum, 1984.

Mantran, Robert (ed.), *Histoire de l'Empire ottoman*, Paris: Fayard, 1989.

Marion, Marcel (ed.), *Dictionnaire des institutions de la France aux XVIIe et XVIIIe siècles* [1923], Paris: Picard, 1972.

Marsch, Robert M., 'The venality of provincial office in China and in comparative perspective', *Comparative Studies in Society and History*, 4 (1962), pp. 464–6.

McClelland, Charles E., 'Structural change and social reproduction in German universities, 1870–1920', *History of Education*, 15.3 (1986), pp. 177–93.

Meisel, James H., *The Myth of the Ruling Class*, Ann Arbor: University of Michigan Press, 1962.

Memmi, Dominique, 'Savants et maîtres à penser. La fabrication d'une morale de la procréation artificielle', *Actes de la Recherche en Sciences Sociales*, 76–77 (Mar. 1989), pp. 82–103.

Mesnard, Pierre, *L'Essor de la philosophie politique au XVIe siècle*, Paris: Vrin, 1969.

Michels, Robert, *Political Parties: A Sociological Study of the Oligarchical Tendencies of Modern Democracy* [1911], New York: Simon & Schuster, 1997.

Miliband, Ralph, *The State in Capitalist Society: An Analysis of the Western System of Power* [1969], New York: Basic Books, 1978.

Miller, Benjamin, 'The colonial polo club: an examination of class processes in the suburban-rural fringe', in Leith Mullings (ed.), *Cities of the United States*, New York: Columbia University Press, 1987, pp. 198–218.

Miller, Delbert C., 'Power, complementarity, and the cutting edge of research', *Sociological Focus*, 1.4 (summer 1968), pp. 1–17.

Mills, Charles Wright, *The Power Elite*, New York: Oxford University Press, 1956.

Moore, Barrington, *The Social Origins of Dictatorship and Democracy*, London: Penguin, 1974.

Mosse, George L., *The Crisis of German Ideology: Intellectual Origins of the Third Reich*, New York: Grosset & Dunlap, 1964.

Mousnier, Roland, *La Vénalité des offices sous Henri IV et Louis XIII*, Rouen: Maugard, 1945.

Mousnier, Roland, 'Le trafic des offices à Venise', *Revue Historique de Droit Français et Étranger*, 30.4 (1952), pp. 552–65.

Mousnier, Roland, *La Plume, la faucille et le marteau. Institutions et société en France du Moyen Age à la Révolution*, Paris: PUF, 1970.

Mousnier, Roland, 'La fonction publique en France du début du XVIe siècle à la fin du XVIIIe siècle', *Revue Historique*, 530 (April–June 1979).

Mousnier, Roland, *Les Institutions de la France sous la monarchie absolue, 1598–1789*, vol. 1: *Société et État*, Paris: PUF, 1974; vol. 2: *Les Organes de l'État et la société*, Paris: PUF, 1980.

Müller, Wolfgang, and Christel Neusüss, 'The illusion of state socialism and the contradiction between wage labor and capital', *Telos*, 25 (autumn 1975), pp. 13–91.

Murray, Robin, 'The internationalization of capital and the national state', *New Left Review*, I/67 (1971), pp. 84–109.

Naudé, Gabriel, *Considérations politiques sur les coups d'État* [1667], Paris: Gallimard, 2004.

Nicolaï, André, 'Les efficacités de la planification', in Lucien Nizard and Pierre A. Bélanger (eds), *Planification et société*, Grenoble: Presses Universitaires de Grenoble, 1975, pp. 583–98.

Nordlinger, Eric A., *On the Autonomy of the Democratic State*, Cambridge: Harvard University Press, 1981.

Nozick, Robert, *Anarchy, State and Utopia*, Oxford: Basil Blackwell, 1974.

O'Connor, James, *The Corporations and the State*, New York: Harper & Row, 1974.

Offe, Claus, 'Laws of motion of reformist state policies: an excerpt from "Berufabildungs Reform: eine Fall Studie über Reform Politik"', manuscript, n.d.

Offe, Claus, 'Structural problems of the capitalist state: class rule and the political system: on the selectiveness of political institutions', in Claus von Beyme (ed.), *German Political Studies*, vol. 1, London: Sage, 1974, pp. 31–55.

Offe, Claus, *Disorganized Capitalism: Contemporary Transformations of Work and Politics*, Cambridge: Polity, 1985.

Offe, Claus, and John Keane (eds), *Contradictions of the Welfare State*, London: Hutchinson, 1984.

Olesen, Virginia, and Elvi W. Whittaker, 'Critical notes on sociological studies of professional socialization', in John A. Jackson (ed.), *Professions and Professionalization*, Cambridge: Cambridge University Press, 1970.

Ooms, Herman, *Tokugawa Ideology: Early Constructs, 1570–1680*, Princeton: Princeton University Press, 1985.

Orloff, Ann Shola, and Theda Skocpol, 'Why not equal protection? Explaining the politics of public social spending in Britain, 1900–1911, and the United States, 1880–1920', *American Sociological Review*, 49.6 (Dec. 1984), pp. 726–50.

Ory, Pascal (ed.), *Nouvelle histoire des idées politiques*, Paris: Hachette, 1987.

Pareto, Vilfredo, *The Mind and Society: A Treatise on General Sociology* [1916], 4 vols bound as 2, New York: Dover, 1963.

Pareto, Vilfredo, *Les Systèmes socialistes* [1902], vol. 5 of *Oeuvres complètes*, Geneva: Droz, 1965.

Pareto, Vilfredo, *The Rise and Fall of Elites: An Application of Theoretical Sociology* [1901], New Brunswick, NJ: Transaction, 1991.

Parsons, Talcott, *Societies: Evolutionary and Comparative Perspectives*, Englewood Cliffs, NJ: Prentice Hall, 1966.

Parsons, Talcott, *The Structure of Social Action* [1937], New York: Free Press, 1967.

Pascal, Blaise, *Pensées* [1670], London: Penguin, 1995.

Péan, Pierre, *Secret d'État. La France du secret, les secrets de la France*, Paris: Fayard, 1986.

Perez-Diaz, Victor, *Estado, burocracia y sociedad civil. Discusión crítica, desarrollos y alternativas a la teoría política de Karl Marx*, Madrid: Alfaguara, 1978; in English as *State, Bureaucracy and Civil Society: A Critical Discussion of the Political Theory of Karl Marx*, London: Macmillan, 1978.

Perez-Diaz, Victor, 'El proyecto moral de Marx cien años después', in Angel Rojo Luis and Victor Perez-Diaz (eds), *Marx, economía y moral*, Madrid: Alianza, 1984.

Perlin, Frank, 'State formation reconsidered', *Modern Asian Studies*, 19.3 (1985), pp. 415–80.

Perroux, François, *Pouvoir et économie*, Paris: Dunod, 1973.

Petot, Jean, *Histoire de l'Administration des Ponts et Chaussées (1599–1815)*, Paris: Marcel Rivière, 1958.

Peuchot, Éric, 'L'obligation de désintéressement des agents publics', Doctorat d'État thesis, Université de Paris-2, 1987.

Pirotte, Olivier, *Vivien de Goubert*, Paris: Librairie Générale de Droit et de Jurisprudence, 1972.

Pisier-Kouchner, Évelyne, 'Le Service public dans la théorie de l'État de Léon Duguit', *Revue Internationale de Droit Comparé*, 25.4 (1973), pp. 970–1.

Pocock, John Greville Agard, *The Machiavellian Moment: Florentine Political Thought and the Atlantic Republican Tradition*, Princeton: Princeton University Press, 1975.

Pollock, Sheldon, 'From discourse of ritual to discourse of power in Sanskrit culture', *Journal of Ritual Studies*, 4.2 (summer 1990), pp. 315–45.

Post, Gaines, *Studies in Medieval Legal Thought*, Princeton: Princeton University Press, 1964.

Poulantzas, Nicos, *Political Power and Social Classes*, London: New Left Books, 1973.

Przeworski, Adam, *Capitalism and Social Democracy*, Cambridge: Cambridge University Press, 1985.

Przeworski, Adam, 'Marxism and rational choice', *Politics and Society*, 14.4 (Dec. 1985), pp. 379–409.

Przeworski, Adam, and Michael Wallerstein, 'Corporatism, pluralism and market competition', manuscript, n.d.

Przeworski, Adam, and Michael Wallerstein, 'Structural dependence of the state on capital', manuscript, n.d.

Putnam, Robert D., *The Comparative Study of Political Elites*, Englewood Cliffs: Prentice Hall, 1976.

Quadagno, Jill, 'Theories of the Welfare State', *Annual Review of Sociology*, 13 (1987), pp. 109–28.

Rampelberg, Renée-Marie, *Aux origines du ministère de l'Intérieur, le ministère de la maison du Roi, 1783–1788*, Paris: Economica, 1974.

Rév, Istvan, 'The advantages of being atomized', presented at the Institute for Advanced Study, Princeton, Feb. 1986, mimeo.

Richet, Denis, *La France moderne. L'esprit des institutions*, Paris: Flammarion, 1973.

Richet, Denis, 'Élite et noblesse. La fonction des grands serviteurs de l'État (fin XVIe–début XVIIe siècle)', *Acta Poloniae Historica*, 36 (1977), pp. 47–63.

Riker, William H., 'Some ambiguities in the notion of power', *American Political Science Review*, 63.2 (June 1964), pp. 341–9.

Ringer, Fritz K., *The Decline of the German Mandarins: The German Academic Community (1890–1933)*, Cambridge: Harvard University Press, 1969.

Rolland, Patrice, 'L'enjeu du droit', in Michel Charzat (ed.), *Georges Sorel*, Paris: Éditions de l'Herne, 1986, pp. 28–44.

Rosanvallon, Pierre, *La Crise de l'État-providence*, Paris: Seuil, 1981.

Ross, George, 'Redefining political sociology', review of Peter B. Evans, Dietrich Rueschemeyer and Theda Skocpol (eds), *Bringing the State Back In*, Cambridge: Cambridge University Press, 1985, *Contemporary Sociology*, 15.6 (1986), pp. 813–15.

Rouquié, Alain, 'Changement politique et transformation des régimes', in Madeleine Grawitz and Jean Leca (eds), *Traité de science politique*, vol. 2, Paris: PUF, 1985, pp. 599–633.

Rousselet, Marcel, *Histoire de la magistrature française. Des origines à nos jours*, 2 vols, Paris: Plon, 1957.

Rubinstein, William D., 'Wealth, elites and the class structure of modern Britain', *Past and Present*, 76 (1977), pp. 99–126.

Runciman, W. Garry, 'Comparative history or narrative history', *Archives Européennes de Sociologie*, 21 (1980), pp. 162–78.

Rupp, Jan C. C., and Rob De Lange, 'Social order, cultural capital and citizenship: an essay concerning educational status and educational power versus comprehensiveness of elementary schools', *Sociological Review*, 37.4 (Nov. 1989), pp. 668–705.

Ryan, William, *Blaming the Victim*, New York: Pantheon, 1971.

Saige, Guillaume-Joseph, *Catéchisme du citoyen, ou Éléments du droit public français, par demandes & réponses*, n.p., 1775.

Saint Martin, Monique de, *L'Espace de la noblesse*, Paris: Métailié, 1993.

Salmon, J. H. M., 'Venality of office and popular sedition in seventeenth-century France: a review of a controversy', *Past and Present*, 37 (July 1967), pp. 21–43.

Samoyault, Jean-Pierre, *Les Bureaux du secrétariat d'État des Affaires étrangères sous Louis XV*, Paris: Pedone, 1971.

Sarfatti, Larson Magali, *The Rise of Professionalism: A Sociological Analysis*, Berkeley: University of California Press, 1977.

Schapiro, Meyer, Review of Joseph C. Sloane, *Between the Past and Present. Artists, Critics, and Traditions from 1848 to 1870*, Princeton: Princeton University Press, 1951, *Art Bulletin*, 36 (1954), pp. 163–5.

Schmitter, Philippe, 'Neo-corporatism and the state', Working Paper 106, European University Institute, Florence.

Schmolders, Günter, *Psychologie des finances et de l'impôt*, Paris: PUF, 1973.

Schramm, Percy Ernst, *Kaiser, Rom und Renovatio. Studien und Texte zur Geschichte des römischen Erneuerungsgedankens vom Ende des karolingischen Reiches bis zum Investiturstreit*, 2 vols, Berlin: Teubner, 1929.

Schramm, Percy Ernst, *Der König von Frankreich. Das Wesen der Monarchie von 9 zum 16. Jahrhundert. Ein Kapital aus Geschichter des abendlischen Staates*, 2 vols, Weimar: H. Böhlaud Nachf, 1939.

Seyssel, Claude de, *La Monarchie de France* [1519], ed. Jacques Poujol, Paris: Librairies d'Argences, 1960.

Shibata, Michio, and Tadami Chizuka, 'Marxist studies of the French Revolution in Japan', *Science and Society*, 54.3 (1990), pp. 366–74.

Shinn, Terry, 'Science, Tocqueville, and the state: the organization of knowledge in modern France', *Social Research*, 59.3 (autumn 1992), pp. 533–66.

Skinner, Quentin, *The Foundations of Modern Political Thought*, vol. 1: *The Renaissance*; vol. 2: *The Age of Reformation*, Cambridge: Cambridge University Press, 1978.

Skocpol, Theda, *States and Social Revolutions: A Comparative Analysis of France, Russia, and China*, Cambridge: Cambridge University Press, 1979.

Skocpol, Theda, 'Rentier state and shi'a Islam in the Iranian revolution', *Theory and Society*, 11 (1982), pp. 265–83.

Skocpol, Theda, 'Bringing the state back in: strategies of analysis in current research', 1984 version subsequently published in Peter B. Evans, Dietrich Rueschemeyer and Theda Skocpol (eds), *Bringing the State Back In*, Cambridge: Cambridge University Press, 1985.

Skocpol, Theda, 'Cultural idioms and political ideologies in the revolutionary reconstruction of state power: a rejoinder to Sewell', *Journal of Modern History*, 57.1 (Mar. 1985), pp. 86–96.

Skocpol, Theda, 'Social history and historical sociology: contrasts and complementarities', revised version of 'Historical sociology and social history: a dialogue', Annual Meeting of the Social Science History Association, Chicago, 23 Nov. 1985; also as 'Social history and historical sociology: contrasts and complementarities', *Social Science History*, 11.1 (spring 1987), pp. 17–30.

Skocpol, Theda, 'A society without a "state"? Political organization, social conflict, and welfare provision in the United States', *Journal of Public Policy*, 7.4 (Oct.– Dec. 1987), pp. 349–71.

Skocpol, Theda (ed.), *Vision and Method in Historical Sociology*, Cambridge: Cambridge University Press, 1984.

Skocpol, Theda, and Edwin Amenta, 'States and social policies', *Annual Review of Sociology*, 12 (1986), pp. 131–57.

Skocpol, Theda, and Margaret Weir, 'State structures and the possibilities for "Keynesian" responses to the Great Depression in Sweden, Britain, and the United States', Aug. 1984 version subsequently published in Peter B. Evans,

Dietrich Rueschemeyer and Theda Skocpol (eds), *Bringing the State Back In*, Cambridge: Cambridge University Press, 1985.

Social Science Research Council (New York), *States and Social Structures Newsletter* (2 issues: 'Hegemony and the state', winter 1989; 'The state and development', winter 1988).

Sorman, Guy, *L'État minimum*, Paris: Albin Michel, 1985.

Spinoza, Benedict de, 'A political treatise', in *The Chief Works of Benedict de Spinoza*, trans. R. H. M. Elwes, vol. 2, New York: Dover, 1951.

Stanworth, Philip, and Anthony Giddens (eds), *Elites and Power in British Society*, Cambridge: Cambridge University Press, 1974.

Stein, Burton, 'State formation and economy reconsidered', *Modern Asian Studies*, 19.3 (1985), pp. 387–413.

Steinmetz, George, 'The myth and the reality of an autonomous state: industrialists, Junkers, and social policy in Imperial Germany', *Comparative Social Research*, 12 (1990), pp. 239–93.

Stieber, Joachim W., 'Pope Eugenius IV, the Council of Basel, and the secular and ecclesiastical authorities in the Empire: the conflict over supreme authority and power in the Church', in Heiko A. Oberman (ed.), *Studies in the History of Christian Thought*, vol. 13, Leyden: Brill, 1978.

Stone, Deborah A., *The Disabled State*, Philadelphia: Temple University Press, 1984.

Stone, Lawrence, 'Theories of revolution', *World Politics*, 18.2 (Jan. 1966), pp. 159–76.

Strayer, Joseph R., 'The idea of feudalism', in Rushton Coulborn (ed.), *Feudalism in History*, Princeton: Princeton University Press, 1956, pp. 3–11.

Strayer, Joseph R., *On the Medieval Origins of the Modern State* [1970], Princeton: Princeton University Press, 2005.

Suleiman, Ezra N., *Les Élites en France. Grands corps et grandes écoles*, Paris: Seuil, 1978.

Suleiman, Ezra N., 'Hauts fonctionnaires. Le mythe de la neutralité', *Le Monde*, 27 Feb. 1986.

Supiot, Alain, 'La crise de l'esprit de service public', *Droit social*, 12 (Dec. 1989), pp. 777–83.

Sweezy, Paul M., *Marxian Socialism: Power Elite or Ruling Class*, pamphlet, New York: Monthly Review Press, 1956.

Tessier, Georges, *Diplomatique royale française*, Paris: Picard, 1962.

Théret, Bruno, 'L'État. Le souverain, la finance et le social', prepared for Franco-European seminar on interdisciplinary research and the future, 25 Mar. 1990, mimeo.

Théret, Bruno, 'Néolibéralisme, inégalités sociales et politiques fiscales de droite et de gauche dans la France des années 1980. Identité et différences, pratiques et doctrines', *Revue Française de Science Politique*, 41.3 (June 1991), pp. 342–81.

Théret, Bruno, 'Quel avenir pour l'État-providence dans un contexte d'intégration des marchés nationaux?', given to the international conference 'Amérique du Nord, Communauté européenne: intégration économique, intégration sociale?', Université du Québec à Montréal, 22–24 Oct. 1992.

Thoenig, Jean-Claude, *L'Ère des technocrates. Le cas des Ponts et Chaussées*, Paris: Éditions d'Organisation, 1973.

Thompson, Edward P., 'The peculiarities of the English', in Ralph Miliband and

John Saville (eds), *The Socialist Register*, London: Merlin, 1965, pp. 311–62; reprinted in Edward P. Thompson, *The Poverty of Theory and Other Essays*, New York: Monthly Review Press, 1978.

Thompson, Edward P., 'Modes de domination et révolution en Angleterre', *Actes de la Recherche en Sciences Sociales*, 2–3 (June 1976), pp. 133–51.

Thompson, Edward P., 'Patrician society, plebeian culture', *Journal of Social History*, 7.4 (1976), pp. 382–405.

Thuau, Étienne, *Raison d'État et pensée politique à l'époque de Richelieu*, Paris: Armand Colin, 1966 (new edn, Paris: Albin Michel, 2000).

Thuillier, Guy, *Bureaucratie et bureaucrates en France au XIXe siècle*, Geneva: Droz, 1980.

Tilly, Charles, 'Major forms of collective action in Western Europe 1500–1975', *Theory and Society*, 3 (1976), pp. 365–75.

Tilly, Charles, *From Mobilization to Revolution*, Cambridge: Harvard University Press, 1986.

Tilly, Charles, 'Cities and States in Europe, 1000–1800', *States and Social Structures Newsletter*, 7 (spring 1988), pp. 5–9.

Tilly, Charles, *Coercion, Capital and European States, AD 990–1990*, Oxford: Blackwell, 1990.

Tilly, Charles (ed.), *The Formation of National States in Western Europe*, Princeton: Princeton University Press, 1975 (with contributions by Gabriel Ardant, David H. Bayley, Rudolf Braun, Samuel E. Finer, Wolfram Fischer, Peter Lundgreen, Stein Rokkan and Charles Tilly).

Tirole, Jean, and Jean-Jacques Laffont, 'The politics of government decision making: regulatory institutions', *Journal of Law, Economics, and Organization*, 6.1 (1990), pp. 1–32.

Tirole, Jean, and Jean-Jacques Laffont, 'Auction design and favoritism', *International Journal of Industrial Organization*, 9 (1991), pp. 9–42.

Tirole, Jean, and Jean-Jacques Laffont, 'The politics of government decision making: a theory of regulatory capture', *Quarterly Journal of Economics*, 106 (1991), pp. 1089–127.

Turgot, Anne-Robert-Jacques, *Des administrations provinciales. Mémoire présenté au Roi*, 1788.

Useem, Michael, and Jerome Karabel, 'Pathways to top corporate management', *American Sociological Review*, 51.2 (1986), pp. 184–200.

Vaillant, Roger, *Éloge du Cardinal de Bernis*, Paris: Fasquelle, 1956.

Van Kley, Dale, 'Du Parti janséniste au parti patriote. L'ultime sécularisation d'une tradition religieuse à l'époque du chancelier Maupeou (1770–1775)', in Catherine Maire (ed.), *Jansénisme et révolution, Actes du colloque de Versailles tenu au Palais des congrès les 13 et 14 octobre 1989*, Paris: Chroniques de Port-Royal, Bibliothèque Mazarine, 1990, pp. 115–30.

Vidal-Nacquet, Pierre, *La Raison d'État*, Paris: Minuit, 1962 (new edn, Paris: La Découverte, 2002).

Wacquant, Loïc J. D., 'De l'État charitable à l'État pénal. Notes sur le traitement politique de la misère en Amérique', mimeo [1989].

Wallerstein, Immanuel, *The Modern World-System*, vol. 1: *Capitalist Agriculture and the Origins of the European World-Economy in the Sixteenth Century*, New York: Academic Press, 1974.

Walzer, Michael, *Interpretation and Social Criticism*, Cambridge: Harvard University Press, 1987.

Weber, Max, *The Methodology of the Social Sciences* [1922], New York: Free Press, 1969.
Weber, Max, *Economy and Society: An Outline of Interpretive Sociology* [1921], 2 vols, Berkeley: University of California Press, 1978.
Weber, Max, *Gesammelte Aufsätze zur Religionssoziologie* [1920–1], 3 vols, Tübingen: Mohr, 1978–1986.
Weber, Max, *General Economic History* [1927], New York: Dover, 2003.
Weber, Max, *The Vocation Lectures* [1919], Indianapolis: Hackett, 2004.
Wickham, Chris, 'Historical materialism, historical sociology', *New Left Review*, I/171 (Sept.–Oct. 1988), pp. 63–78.
Will, Pierre-Étienne, *Bureaucratie et famine en Chine au XVIIIe siècle*, Paris and The Hague: EHESS-Mouton, 1980.
Will, Pierre-Étienne, 'Bureaucratie officielle et bureaucratie réelle. Sur quelques dilemmes de l'administration impériale à l'époque des Qing', *Études Chinoises*, 8 (spring 1989), pp. 69–141.
Will, Pierre-Étienne, Review of Beatrice S. Bartlett, *Monarchs and Ministers: The Grand Council in Mid-Ch'ing China, 1723–1820*, Berkeley: University of California Press, 1991, *Harvard Journal of Asiatic Studies*, 54.1 (July 1994), pp. 313–37.
Williams, Mike, 'Industrial policy and the neutrality of the state', *Journal of Public Economics*, 19 (1982), pp. 73–96.
Wittfogel, Karl August, *Oriental Despotism: A Comparative Study of Total Power*, New Haven: Yale University Press, 1957.
Wittgenstein, Ludwig, *Philosophical Investigations*, Oxford: Blackwell, 1968.
Wittrock, Björn, Peter Wagner and Hellmut Wollmann, 'Social science and the modern state: knowledge, institutions, and societal transformations', original version, subsequently published in Peter Wagner, Carol H. Weiss, Björn Wittrock and Hellmut Wollmann (eds), *Social Sciences and Modern States: National Experiences and Theoretical Crossroads*, Cambridge: Cambridge University Press, 1991.
Woolley, John T., 'The politics of monetary policy in Western Europe', given to the annual conference of the American Political Science Association, Chicago, 1983.
Wright, Erik O., *Class, Crisis and the State*, London: Verso, 1979.
Zeitlin, Maurice, W. Lawrence Neuman and Richard E. Ratcliff, 'Class segments, agrarian property and political leadership in the capitalist class of Chile', *American Sociological Review*, 41 (1976), pp. 1006–29.
Zeldin, Theodore, *The Political System of Napoleon III*, London: Macmillan, 1958.
Zeller, Gaston, *Les Institutions de la France au XVIe siècle* [1948], Paris: PUF, 1987.
Zolberg, Aristide R., 'Interactions stratégiques et formation des États modernes en France et en Angleterre, *Revue Internationale des Sciences Sociales*, 32.4 (1980), pp. 737–67.
Zolberg, Aristide R., 'L'influence des facteurs "externes" sur l'ordre politique interne', in Madeleine Grawitz and Jean Leca (eds), *Traité de science politique*, Paris: PUF, 1985, pp. 567–98.

2 Books and articles not directly bearing on the state

Alpers, Svetlana, 'L'oeil de l'histoire. L'effet cartographique dans la peinture hollandaise au XVIIe siècle', *Actes de la Recherche en Sciences Sociales*, 49 (1983), pp. 71–101.

Anderson, Perry, 'Socialism and pseudo-empiricism', *New Left Review*, I/35 (Jan.–Feb. 1966), pp. 2–42.

Aron, Raymond, *Main Currents in Sociological Thought*, London: Weidenfeld & Nicolson, 1955.

Austin, John L., *How to Do Things with Words*, Oxford: Clarendon, 1962.

Bachelard, Gaston, *The Formation of the Scientific Mind*, Manchester: Clinamen Press, 2006.

Balazs, Étienne, 'Les aspects significatifs de la société chinoise', *Asiatische Studien*, 6 (1952), pp. 79–87.

Bateson, Gregory, et al., 'Towards a theory of schizophrenia', *Behavioral Science*, 1.4 (1956).

Ben-David, Joseph, *The Scientist's Role in Society: A Comparative Study*, Chicago: University of Chicago Press, 1971.

Bendix, Reinhard, *Max Weber: An Intellectual Portrait* [1960], Berkeley: University of California Press, 1977.

Benet, Francisco, 'Explosive markets: the Berber highlands', in Karl Polanyi, Conrad M. Arensberg and Harry W. Pearson (eds), *Trade and Market in the Early Empires*, Glencoe, IL: Free Press, 1957.

Benveniste, Émile, *Le Vocabulaire des institutions indo-européennes*, vol. 1: *Économie, parenté, société*; vol. 2: *Pouvoir, droit, religion*, Paris: Minuit, 1969.

Berger, Peter L., and Thomas Luckmann, *The Social Construction of Reality: A Treatise in the Sociology of Knowledge*, New York: Anchor, 1967.

Bergson, Henri, *The Creative Mind: An Introduction to Metaphysics*, Mineola, NY: Dover, 2010.

Berle, Adolf A., and Gardiner C. Means, *The Modern Corporation and Private Property*, New York: Macmillan, 1932.

Bernhard, Thomas, *Old Masters*, London: Penguin Books, 2010.

Bloch, Marc, The *Historian's Craft* [1949], Manchester: Manchester University Press, 1967.

Bollack, Jean, *Empédocle*, 3 vols, Paris: Minuit, 1965–9.

Brubaker, Rogers, *The Limits of Rationality: An Essay on the Social and Moral Thought of Max Weber*, London: Allen & Unwin, 1984.

Burnham, James, *The Managerial Revolution* [1941], Bloomington: Indiana University Press, 1960.

Caillet, Laurence, *La Maison Yamazaki. La vie exemplaire d'une paysanne japonaise devenue chef d'une entreprise de haute coiffure*, Paris: Plon, 1991.

Cassirer, Ernst, 'Structuralism in modern linguistics', *Word*, 1.2 (1945).

Cassirer, Ernst, *The Philosophy of Symbolic Forms*, 4 vols, New Haven: Yale University Press, 1953–65.

Cassirer, Ernst, *Individual and Cosmos in Renaissance Philosophy* [1927], Philadelphia: University of Pennsylvania Press, 1972.

Chamfort, Nicolas de, *Maximes et pensées*, Paris, 1795.

Champagne, Patrick, *Faire l'opinion. Le nouveau jeu politique*, Paris: Minuit, 1990.

Cicourel, Aaron, *Cognitive Sociology: Language and Meaning in Social Interaction*, New York: Free Press, 1974.

Davidson, Donald, *Inquiries into Truth and Interpretation*, Oxford: Clarendon Press, 1984.

Deleuze, Gilles, 'Supplément à propos des nouveaux philosophes et d'un problème plus général', *Minuit*, supplement, 24 (May 1977).

Derrida, Jacques, *The Other Heading: Reflections on Today's Europe*, Bloomington: University of Indiana Press, 1992.

Descimon, Robert, *Qui étaient les Seize? Mythes et réalités de la Ligue parisienne, 1585–1594*, Paris: Klincksieck, 1983.

Dumézil, Georges, 'Science et politique. Réponse à Carlo Ginzburg', *Annales ESC*, 5 (1985), pp. 985–9.

Durkheim, Émile, *Division of Labour in Society* [1893], New York: Free Press, 1964.

Durkheim, Émile, 'Débat sur l'explication en histoire et en sociologie', *Bulletin de la Société Française de Philosophie*, 8 (1908), reprinted in *Textes*, vol. 1, Paris: Minuit, 1975, pp. 199–217.

Durkheim, Émile, *Leçons de sociologie* [1922], Paris: PUF, 1990.

Durkheim, Émile, *The Elementary Forms of the Religious Life* [1912], Oxford: Oxford University Press, 2001.

Durkheim, Émile, *The Evolution of Educational Thought* [1938], London: Routledge, 2005.

Durkheim, Émile, and Marcel Mauss, *Primitive Classification*, Chicago: University of Chicago Press, 1967.

Elias, Norbert, 'Sport et violence', *Actes de la Recherche en Sciences Sociales*, 6.2 (Dec. 1976), pp. 2–21.

Febvre, Lucien, *Le Problème de l'incroyance au XVIe siècle. La religion de Rabelais* [1947], Paris: Albin Michel, 1968.

Ferry, Luc, Jean-Pierre Pesron and Alain Renaut (eds), *Philosophies de l'Université. L'idéalisme allemand et la question de l'Université* (texts from Schelling, Fichte, Schleiermacher, Humboldt, Hegel), Paris: Payot, 1979.

Feyerabend, Paul, *Realism, Rationalism and Scientific Method*, vol. 1 of *Philosophical Papers*, Cambridge: Cambridge University Press, 1985.

Foucault, Michel, 'Qu'est-ce que la critique? Critique et Aufklärung', conference at Société Française de Philosophie, 27 May 1978, *Bulletin de la Société Française de Philosophie*, 84.2 (April–June 1990), pp. 35–63.

Garfinkel, Harold, 'Conditions of successful degradation ceremonies', *American Journal of Sociology*, 61.5 (1956), pp. 240–4.

Gernet, Louis, *Les Grecs sans miracle*, Paris: Maspero, 1983.

Gerschenkron, Alexander, *Economic Backwardness in Historical Perspective: A Book of Essays*, Cambridge: Belknap Press, 1962.

Ginzburg, Carlo, 'Mythologie germanique et nazisme. Sur un livre ancien de Georges Dumézil', *Annales ESC*, 4 (1985), pp. 695–715.

Goffman, Erving, *The Presentation of Self in Everyday Life*, Edinburgh: University of Edinburgh, 1959.

Goffman, Erving, *Behavior in Public Places: Notes on the Social Organization of Gatherings*, New York: Free Press, 1963.

Goffman, Erving, *Interaction Ritual: Essays on Face-to-Face Behavior*, New York: Anchor Books, 1967.

Goffman, Erving, 'The interaction order', *American Sociological Review*, 48 (1983), pp. 1–17.

Goody, Jack, *The Domestication of the Savage Mind*, Cambridge: Cambridge University Press, 1977.

Gurvitch, Georges, *La Vocation actuelle de la sociologie*, Paris: PUF, 1950.

Habermas, Jürgen, *The Structural Transformation of the Public Sphere: An Inquiry into a Category of Bourgeois Polity* [1962], Cambridge: Polity, 1989.

Halbwachs, Maurice, *La Classe ouvrière et les niveaux de vie. Recherche sur la hiérarchie des besoins dans les sociétés industrielles contemporaines* [1912], Paris: Gordon & Breach, 1970.

Halbwachs, Maurice, *Les Cadres sociaux de la mémoire* [1925], Paris: Mouton, 1976.

Hiroshi, Kojima, 'A demographic evaluation of P. Bourdieu's "fertility strategy"', *Journal of Population Problems*, 45.4 (1990), pp. 52–8.

Holton, Gerald, *The Scientific Imagination*, Cambridge: Cambridge University Press, 1978.

Huizinga, Johan, *Homo Ludens*, Boston: Beacon Press, 1955.

Hume, David, 'Of the first principles of government', in *Essays and Treatises on Several Subjects*, vol. 1, Edinburgh, 1777, pp. 33ff.

Husti, Aniko, *Le Temps mobile*, Paris: Institut National de Recherche Pédagogique, 1985.

Janet, Pierre, *L'Évolution de la mémoire et de la notion du temps*, Paris: Chahine, 1928.

Köhler, Wolfgang, *The Mentality of Apes* [1917], New York: Vintage, 1959.

Kuhn, Thomas, *The Structure of Scientific Revolutions*, Chicago: University of Chicago Press, 1962.

Lalande, André, *Vocabulaire technique et critique de la philosophie* [1926], Paris: PUF, 2006.

Leibniz, Gottfried Wilhelm, *Theodicy: Essays on the Goodness of God, the Freedom of Man and the Origin of Evil*, London: Routledge, 1951.

Lévi-Strauss, Claude, 'L'ethnologie et l'histoire', *Annales ESC*, 38.6 (1983), pp. 1217–31.

Lévi-Strauss, Claude, *Tristes Tropiques*, London: Penguin, 1992.

Lovejoy, Arthur Oncken, *The Great Chain of Being: A Study of the History of an Idea*, Cambridge: Harvard University Press, 1936.

Malraux, André, *The Twilight of the Absolute*, vol. 3 of *The Psychology of Art*, New York: Pantheon, 1950.

Matheron, Alexandre, *Individu et communauté chez Spinoza*, Paris: Minuit, 1969.

Mauss, Marcel, 'Salutations par le rire et les larmes', *Journal de Psychologie*, 21 (1922).

Mauss, Marcel, 'Esquisse d'une théorie générale de la magie', *L'Année Sociologique* (1902–3), reprinted in *Sociologie et Anthropologie*, Paris: PUF, 1950, pp. 1–141.

Mauss, Marcel, *Essais de sociologie*, Paris: Minuit, 1969.

Mauss, Marcel, 'L'expression obligatoire des sentiments', *Journal de Psychologie*, 18 (1921), reprinted in *Oeuvres*, Paris: Minuit, 1969.

Mead, George H. H., *Mind, Self and Society*, Chicago: University of Chicago Press, 1934.

Mercier, Louis-Sébastien, *Tableau de Paris*, 12 vols, Amsterdam, 1781–8.

Merleau-Ponty, Maurice, *In Praise of Philosophy*, Evanston, IL: Northwestern University Press, 1963.

Merleau-Ponty, Maurice, *Phenomenology of Perception*, London: Routledge, 1964.

Merleau-Ponty, Maurice, *Signs*, Evanston, IL: Northwestern University Press, 1964.

Minton, Arthur, 'A form of class epigraphy', *Social Forces*, 28 (1950), pp. 250–62.

Momigliano, Arnaldo, 'Premesse per una discussione su Georges Dumézil', *Opus II*, 2 (1983), pp. 329–41.

Needham, Joseph, *The Grand Titration: Science and Society in East and West*, Toronto: University of Toronto Press, 1979.

Nietzsche, Friedrich, *Beyond Good and Evil*, New York: Vintage, 1966.

Parsons, Talcott, 'The professions and social structure', *Social Forces*, 17.4 (1939), pp. 457–67.

Parsons, Talcott, 'Professions', in David L. Sills (ed.), *International Encyclopedia of the Social Sciences*, vol. 12, New York: Macmillan and Free Press, 1968, pp. 536–47.

Peel, John David Yeadon, *Herbert Spencer: The Evolution of a Sociologist*, London: Heinemann, 1971.

Polanyi, Karl, *The Great Transformation: The Political and Economic Origins of Our Time* [1944], Boston: Beacon, 1957.

Polanyi, Karl, Conrad Arensberg and Harry W. Pearson (eds), *Trade and Market in the Early Empires*, London: Macmillan, 1957.

Pons, Philippe, *D'Edo à Tokyo. Mémoire et modernité*, Paris: Gallimard, 1988.

Quine, Willard Van Orman, *Word and Object*, Cambridge: MIT Press, 1960.

Rolland, Romain, *Jean-Christophe* [17 vols, 1904–12], New York: Modern Library, 1938.

Ruyer, Raymond, *L'Utopie et les Utopies*, Paris: PUF, 1950.

Saint-Simon, Louis de Rouvroy de, *Memoirs, 1715–1723: Fatal Weakness*, Warwick, NY: 1500 Books, 2007.

Sartre, Jean-Paul, 'The problem of method', introduction to *Critique of Dialectical Reason*, London: Verso, 2004.

Schütz, Alfred, *Der sinnhafte Aufbau der sozialen Welt. Eine Einleitung in der verstehende Soziologie*, Vienna: Springer, 1932.

Schütz, Alfred, *Le Chercheur et le quotidien. Phénoménologie des sciences sociales*, Paris: Klincksieck, 1987.

Sieffert, René, 'Le théâtre japonais', in Jean Jacquot (ed.), *Les Théâtres d'Asie*, Paris: Éditions du CNRS, 1968, pp. 133–61.

Spitzer, Leo, *Linguistics and Literary History: Essays in Stylistics*, New York: Russel & Russel, 1962.

Thompson, Edward P., *The Poverty of Theory and Other Essays*, New York: Monthly Review Press, 1978.

Valéry, Paul, *Notebooks* (volume 2), New York: Peter Lang, 2003.

Van Gennep, Arnold, *Les Rites de passage* [1909], Paris: Picard, 1981.

Viala, Alain, *Naissance de l'écrivain. Sociologie de la littérature à l'Âge classique*, Paris: Minuit, 1985.

Wacquant, Loïc, Review of Randall Collins, *Three Sociological Traditions*, Oxford: Oxford University Press, 1985, *Revue Française de Sociologie*, 28.2 (April–June 1987), pp. 334–8.

Weber, Max, 'The meaning of discipline', in Hans H. Gerth and Charles Wright Mills (eds), *From Max Weber: Essays in Sociology*, Oxford: Oxford University Press, 1946, pp. 253–64.

Whimster, Sam, and Scott Lash (eds), *Max Weber: Rationality and Modernity*, London: Allen & Unwin, 1987.

Index

UNIVERSITY OF WINCHESTER
LIBRARY

UNIVERSITY OF WINCHESTER
LIBRARY